A LABORATORY COURSE IN

DOS, WORDPERFECT 5.1, LOTUS 1-2-3, AND dBASE IV

ERNEST S. COLANTONIO

D. C. HEATH AND COMPANY
LEXINGTON, MASSACHUSETTS   TORONTO

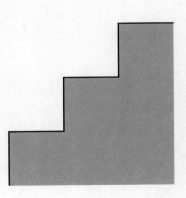

Address editorial correspondence to:
D. C. Heath
125 Spring Street
Lexington, MA 02173

Acquisitions Editor: John Carter Shanklin
Developmental Editor: Katherine T. Pinard
Production Editors: Kathleen A. Savage/Tina V. Beazer
Designer: Cornelia L. Boynton
Production Coordinator: Michael O'Dea
Composition and pre-press: Graphic Typesetting Service
Photo Researcher: Martha L. Shethar
Cover: John D. Kramer/ImageSet Design

Trademark Acknowledgments:
dBASE IV is a trademark of Ashton-Tate.
IBM-DOS and PC-DOS are trademarks of IBM Corporation.
MS-DOS is a registered trademark of Microsoft Corporation.
1-2-3 is a registered trademark of Lotus Development Corporation.
WordPerfect is a registered trademark of WordPerfect Corporation.

Published simultaneously in Canada.

Printed in the United States of America.

International Standard Book Number: 0–669–28195–6

10   9   8   7   6   5

PREFACE

The microcomputer has become standard equipment in most schools, offices, and businesses. A wealth of exceptional software is available to apply this versatile tool to a wide range of tasks. *A Laboratory Course in DOS, WordPerfect 5.1, Lotus 1-2-3, and dBASE IV* has been written for the novice end-user of microcomputers and application software.

Most end-users are not computer engineers; therefore, we discuss hardware only to help students understand how to use software. Most end-users are not computer programmers; we do not teach programming languages such as BASIC and Pascal. Most microcomputer users, however, do work with operating system, word processing, spreadsheet, and data base management software. This text teaches students how to use such software in their everyday lives. In particular, this text concentrates on DOS, WordPerfect 5.1, Lotus 1-2-3, and dBASE IV.

Text Content and Organization

A Laboratory Course in DOS, WordPerfect 5.1, Lotus 1-2-3, and dBASE IV has been carefully designed for use in any first course in microcomputer application software.

Computer Skills   The text is designed for use in courses with microcomputer laboratory facilities. Specifically, the text teaches DOS 3.3, 4.0, and 4.1; WordPerfect 5.1; Lotus 1-2-3 Releases 2.01, 2.2, and 3.1; and dBASE IV Version 1.1. We assume that students have access to these software packages and a computer that can run them.

Appendixes   The text's four appendixes provide additional material that may be of interest to students and instructors. Appendix A, Selecting a System, provides valuable tips for those individuals faced with the daunting task of purchasing hardware and software. Appendix B, Software Installation, briefly summarizes how to set up DOS, WordPerfect, Lotus 1-2-3, and dBASE IV on a computer. Appendix C presents comprehensive command summaries for DOS, WordPerfect 5.1, Lotus 1-2-3, and dBASE IV. Appendix D, Command Structure Outlines, includes command charts that help users navigate the menus of WordPerfect 5.1, Lotus 1-2-3 Version 2.2, and dBASE IV 1.1.

iii

▉   Text Learning Aids

A Laboratory Course in DOS, WordPerfect 5.1, Lotus 1-2-3 and dBASE IV combines a relaxed writing style with an outstanding array of pedagogical features to facilitate understanding and encourage reader enthusiasm.

Chapter Outline   Each chapter opens with *In This Chapter*, an outline of the chapter's headings.

Chapter Preview   Students learn more effectively if they are presented with clear learning objectives. Each chapter's *Preview* section introduces the material and provides learning objectives.

Computer Insights   Several *Insight* boxes throughout the text pose intriguing questions about microcomputers and then answer them with information obtained from computer experts.

Real World   Throughout the text, selections from magazines, newspapers and books are discussed in *Real World* boxes. This feature is designed to help the reader understand how microcomputers and application software are actually being used in today's world.

Readability   The text's engaging writing style ensures that concepts are explained clearly and simply. Editors, course instructors, and reviewers have carefully monitored the reading level to maintain accessibility for students.

Design and Illustrations   Students prefer a textbook that will hold their interest. We have created a design that is simple, but that effectively presents the material. High-resolution computer screen views are liberally inserted throughout each chapter to help illustrate major topics.

End-of-Chapter Materials   A carefully graded set of review materials is provided at the end of each chapter. First, the *Summary* briefly reviews the information that parallels the learning objectives stated in the chapter's *Preview*. Next, the *Key Terms* presents all of the chapter's boldfaced glossary terms. Twenty *Multiple Choice* and twenty *Fill-In* questions test students' understanding of the material. Ten *Short Problems* and ten *Long Problems* provide computer exercises that let students apply their new skills. After each section, several comprehensive exercises require hands-on treatment.

Glossary   A complete glossary includes clear definitions for all the boldfaced terms in the text.

Command Summaries   Appendix C contains comprehensive command summaries for DOS, WordPerfect 5.1, Lotus 1-2-3, and dBASE IV that serve as quick-reference guides to the software packages.

Keyboard Templates   Color-coded keyboard templates for DOS, WordPerfect 5.1, Lotus 1-2-3, and dBASE IV are included just inside the back cover of the book. Designed to be detached from the book and placed on top of the keyboard, these invaluable reminders list the important keyboard commands of each software product. The color-coding indicates at a glance whether the Shift, Control, or Alternate key should be pressed in conjunction with another key to execute a command.

Acknowledgments

Many people helped make *A Laboratory Course in DOS, WordPerfect 5.1, Lotus 1-2-3, and dBASE IV* possible. I would like to thank Robert Hendersen and Nancy Sampson of the University of Illinois Department of Psychology Instructional Computer Laboratory for the use of various microcomputer hardware and software. Paul W. Ross of Millersville University provided many helpful suggestions throughout the development of this project. In addition to her work as copyeditor, Ann Hall helped extensively with the *Insight* and *RealWorld* features.

I would like to thank all of my colleagues who reviewed the manuscript:

- Professor Harvey Blessing, Essex Community College
- Professor Walter Bremer, California Polytechnic University
- Professor Frank S. Butash, University of Hartford
- Dr. William J. Engelmeyer, Anne Arundel Community College
- Professor Clinton P. Fuelling, Ball State University
- Professor C. Brian Honess, University of South Carolina
- Professor Susan Karian, Denison University
- Professor Gladys Norman, Linn-Benton Community College
- Dr. J. Douglas Robertson, Bentley College
- Professor Jerry Sitek, Southern Illinois University at Edwardsville
- Professor Karen Watterson, Shoreline Community College

Thanks also to the Lotus Development Corporation, Ashton-Tate, and the WordPerfect Corporation for their support of students and faculty.

Finally, my special gratitude and appreciation go to all the people at D. C. Heath who worked long hours and sweated endless details to make this text the best that it could be, especially Kathleen Savage, Cia Boynton, and Mike O'Dea.

E. S. C.

About the Author

Ernest S. Colantonio brings combined teaching, technical, and writing skills to this textbook. He received his undergraduate degree in psychology and completed several semesters of graduate work in computer science at the University of Illinois at Urbana-Champaign. While in graduate school, he taught introductory courses in computer science for nontechnical majors. Since 1982, Mr. Colantonio has developed microcomputer software for various organizations, including the Illinois State Geological Survey, the University of Illinois Department of Psychology, the Office of Naval Research, Psychology Software Tools Corporation, and SubLOGIC Corporation. He is the author of several data processing and microcomputer textbooks. Currently, Mr. Colantonio spends most of his time writing new textbooks from his home north of Green Bay, Wisconsin. He also develops and teaches introductory computer courses for Lakeland College and Northeast Wisconsin Technical College.

CONTENTS

Advanced DOS   DOS99

Beginning WordPerfect   WP1

Intermediate WordPerfect WP**59**

Intermediate Lotus 1-2-3   L51

Advanced Lotus 1-2-3   L97

Beginning dBASE IV   dB1

THE MICROCOMPUTER SYSTEM

Preview

We begin this first chapter by introducing IBM and IBM-compatible microcomputers, their hardware components, and popular types of software. (By *IBM-compatible* we mean any computer that works like a comparable IBM model and can run the same software.) Then we discuss a few helpful hints for working with microcomputers.

After studying this chapter, you will understand

- what is meant by the term *microcomputer*.
- the basic operations performed by all computers.
- the four major hardware components of a typical microcomputer system.
- the major components inside a microcomputer's system unit.
- the three major types of microcomputer displays.
- how the various special-purpose keys on a microcomputer keyboard are used.
- the four most popular types of microcomputer printers.
- the three major categories of microcomputer software.
- how to turn on a microcomputer.
- how to operate a microcomputer printer.
- how to care for floppy disks.

What Is a Microcomputer?

Its very name tells us that a **microcomputer** is a small computer. A **computer** is an electronic device that performs calculations and processes data. Most people think of a microcomputer as being small enough to fit on top of a desk. Although some powerful models can serve several users simultaneously, most microcomputers are used by only one person at a time. For this reason, microcomputers are also often called **personal computers.**

Another characteristic of microcomputers is that their "brain" or **central processing unit (CPU)** consists of a single electronic device known as a **microprocessor.** This device, a marvel of miniature engineering, controls the microcomputer, performs its calculations, and processes data. A microprocessor is just one type of **integrated circuit chip,** which is a thin slice of semiconductor material, such as pure silicon crystal, impregnated with carefully selected impurities. These chips are commonly used in computers and many other modern electronic devices.

One way to define microcomputers is by what they do. They can be used to help accomplish many different tasks. At the lowest level, however, a microcomputer performs the same basic operations as all computers. This can be summed up as *input, processing,* and *output* (see Figure 1).

First, a **program** is needed to tell the computer what to do. This is a set of instructions that controls a computer's operation. The program lets you enter raw **data,** which can consist of numbers, text, pictures, and even sounds. These data entered into the computer are called **input.** The program instructs the computer to process the data by doing calculations, comparisons, and other manipulations. The final result is processed data or **information,** hopefully a more organized and useful form of the original input. This information produced by the computer is called **output.** Keep in mind that there is no magic here—a program is needed to tell the computer what to do and the output information is only as valid as the original input data.

Figure 1 What a Computer Does

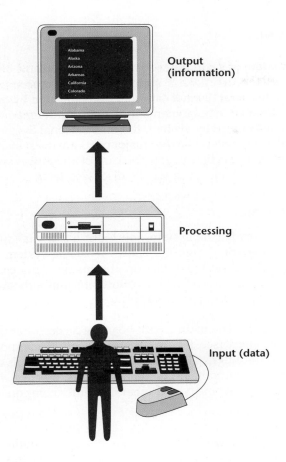

Output
(information)

Processing

Input (data)

Although microcomputers perform the same basic operations as larger computers, they differ in speed and capacity. Larger computers can generally process data faster than microcomputers. They can also internally store more data at a time than microcomputers. These factors make larger computers better for performing lots of extremely complex and time-consuming computations. Microcomputers are also less adept than larger computers at handling several different users or tasks at the same time. On the other hand, microcomputers are superbly adapted to help with many work-a-day tasks like typing papers, figuring taxes, maintaining mailing lists, sending messages, drawing charts, managing finances, and even playing games.

Finally, microcomputers generally fall within a given price range. This can be as little as $100 or as much as $15,000. Today the average price of a typical microcomputer used in business is around $2500. This is, however, a good deal less than the cost of much more powerful computers, which may run into many thousands or millions of dollars. Although microcomputers are by no means cheap, their prices have been generally dropping even as their capabilities have increased. For example, in late 1983 the list price of a basic IBM Personal Computer XT was $5675. The list price of its successor, a similarly-equipped IBM Personal System/2 Model 30, was only $2545 when first released in mid-1987. Even though the newer Model 30 costs less than half as much as the old XT, it still has more than twice the speed and storage capacity, along with many other improvements.

Hardware

The **hardware** of a computer system is the electronic and mechanical equipment that make it work. Like a stereo system, microcomputer hardware generally consists of several distinct components connected by cables. Although there are several possible arrangements and many different models, Figure 2 shows a typical microcomputer system, the IBM Personal System/2 Model 30 and an IBM Personal Pageprinter. The four major parts are the system unit, display, keyboard, and printer. In this figure, you also can see the power switch, a floppy disk drive, and a mouse, all of which will be discussed later.

System Unit

From the outside, the system unit looks like a shallow box about the size of a portable typewriter. Figure 3 shows what the system unit of an IBM Personal System/2 Model 50 looks like on the inside. This central component houses important elements such as the computer's motherboard, microprocessor, memory, disk drives, and power supply.

Motherboard   The main circuit board of a computer is called the **motherboard** or **system board** (see Figure 4). Among other components, the motherboard holds the computer's CPU, some memory, and much of its control circuitry. In addition, the motherboard contains the **bus,** a set of wires and connectors that link the CPU to memory and other computer components.

Figure 2 A Microcomputer System

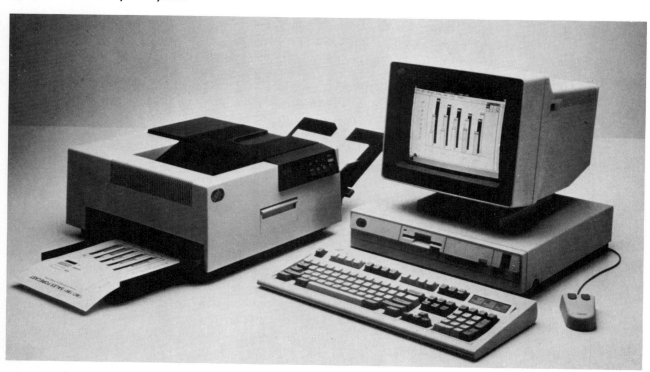

Figure 3 Inside the System Unit

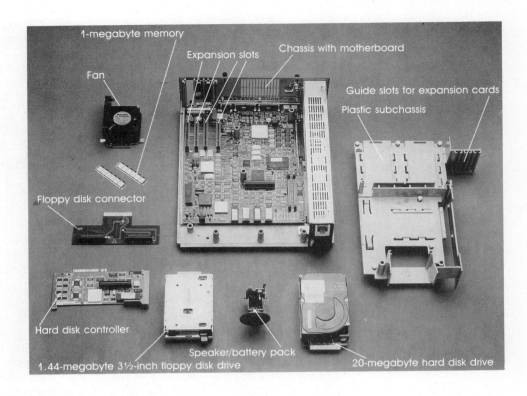

1-megabyte memory

Expansion slots

Chassis with motherboard

Fan

Guide slots for expansion cards

Plastic subchassis

Floppy disk connector

Hard disk controller

Speaker/battery pack

1.44-megabyte 3½-inch floppy disk drive

20-megabyte hard disk drive

In most microcomputers, the bus is accessible through a series of **expansion slots.** Each expansion slot is an internal connector that allows you to plug an additional circuit board into the motherboard. The IBM Personal System/2 Model 50, for example, has four expansion slots, which can be seen in Figure 4. Some computers come with eight or more expansion slots. A circuit board that plugs into an expansion slot is called an **expansion board, card,** or **adapter.** Such circuit boards make it possible to connect a wide variety of extra equipment to a computer, thus *expanding* its capability.

The motherboard or expansion boards also contain device controllers. A **device controller** is a set of chips or a circuit board that operates a piece of computer equipment such as a disk drive, display, keyboard, mouse, or printer. Recently, there has been a trend toward building device controllers onto microcomputer motherboards. The IBM Personal System/2 Model 50 shown in Figure 4, for example, has most of its device controllers on the motherboard.

Microprocessor   As we said, the microprocessor is a microcomputer's central processing unit (CPU). It consists of a single integrated circuit chip that is usually soldered or plugged into a socket on the motherboard (see Figure 4). IBM and IBM-compatible microcomputers use microprocessors from the Intel 8088 family, which includes the 8088, 8086, 80286, 80386, and 80486 chips. The 8088 is used in older IBM and IBM-compatibles such as the original IBM Personal Computer and PC/XT. The slightly more efficient 8086 chip is used in IBM's newer low-end models, such as the IBM Personal System/2 Models 25 and 30. The more capable 80286 chip is used in mid-range microcomputers, such as the original IBM Personal Computer AT and the newer IBM Personal System/2 Models 50 and 60.

**Figure 4 A Motherboard
or System Board**

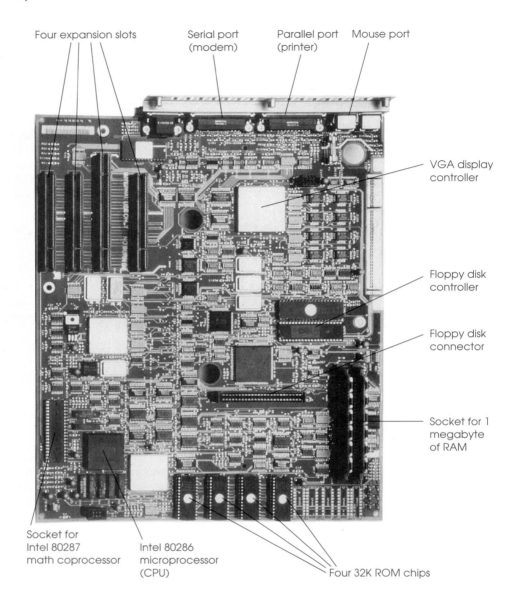

Four expansion slots

Serial port
(modem)

Parallel port
(printer)

Mouse port

VGA display
controller

Floppy disk
controller

Floppy disk
connector

Socket for 1
megabyte
of RAM

Socket for
Intel 80287
math coprocessor

Intel 80286
microprocessor
(CPU)

Four 32K ROM chips

The fast and powerful 80386 chip is used in high-end models, such as the IBM Personal System/2 Models 70 and 80. Finally, the faster and even more powerful 80486 is used in IBM's Power Platform upgrade for the Personal System/2 Model 70 and high-performance computers such as the Apricot VX FT Server and the Hewlett-Packard Vectra 486 PC.

Memory   **Memory** is a computer's internal storage, used to hold programs and data. Also called **primary storage,** memory is measured in bytes. A **byte** is the amount of storage needed to hold a single character, such as the letter *A*, or a number between 0 and 255. Since computers can store thousands, millions, or even billions of bytes, the terms kilobyte, megabyte, and gigabyte are often used. One **kilobyte (K)** is equal to 1024 bytes, one **megabyte (M)** is equal to 1,048,576 bytes, and one **gigabyte (G)** is equal to 1,073,741,824 bytes. In general, microcomputer memory is made up of two types of integrated circuit chips: RAM and ROM.

RAM, which stands for **Random Access Memory,** is temporary storage. Programs and data can be kept there while they are being used and then overwritten by other programs and data later. When the computer is turned off, RAM loses its contents. Most microcomputers can now have at least 640K of RAM on the motherboard. Many can have much more installed on expansion boards. For example, the IBM Personal System/2 Model 80 can be equipped with up to 16 megabytes of RAM.

ROM, which stands for **Read Only Memory,** is permanent storage. The contents of ROM chips, which are encoded at the factory, remain intact when the computer is turned off. The programs and data permanently stored in ROM can be read and used, but never erased, changed, or augmented. Many microcomputers use ROM to store programs and data that are used frequently but need never be changed, such as portions of the operating system. Most microcomputers contain at least one ROM chip as part of their primary storage. The IBM Personal System/2 Model 50, for example, uses four 32K ROM chips on the motherboard to store essential programs and data (see Figure 4).

Disk Drives   A **disk drive** is a piece of equipment that can read and write programs and data on magnetic disks. A **magnetic disk** is a semi-permanent storage medium that can be erased and rewritten over and over again. Most microcomputers can be equipped with two basic kinds of disk drives: floppy disk drives and hard disk drives.

A **floppy disk drive** works with **floppy disks** (also called **diskettes**), which are inexpensive, flexible magnetic disks encased in plastic (see Figure 5). Floppy disks can be inserted and removed from their disk drives. The IBM Personal System/2 Model 50, for example, comes standard with one floppy disk drive. This drive accepts a 3½-inch floppy disk which can hold up to 1.44 megabytes

Figure 5 Floppy Disks

Figure 6   Hard Disk Drive

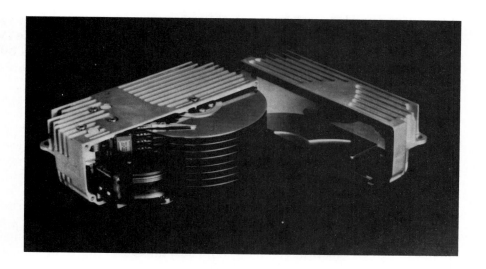

of programs and data. Although most newer microcomputers now come with 3½-inch floppy disk drives, many microcomputers still use 5¼-inch floppy disk drives. A typical 5¼-inch floppy disk holds 360K, but many drives can use 5¼-inch disks that hold 1.2 megabytes.

A **hard disk drive** uses one or more rigid, magnetic platters to hold programs and data (see Figure 6). Most hard disk drives have their magnetic disks permanently sealed inside. These disks spin much faster and have much greater capacity than floppy disks. Hard disk drives come in sizes ranging from 10 megabytes to several hundred megabytes. The most popular sizes are now 20, 30, and 40 megabytes. The IBM Personal System/2 Model 50, for example, comes standard with a 20-megabyte internal hard disk. On a microcomputer with a hard disk, programs are usually run from the hard disk. The floppy disk drive is generally relegated to copying software to or from the hard disk and making backup copies of important programs and data.

Display

A **display,** also called a **monitor,** is similar in many ways to an ordinary television screen. The display is used to present text and **graphics,** which are simply any kind of pictures, drawings, charts, or plots. Almost all computer monitors create text and graphics on the screen with tiny dots called **pixels** (short for picture elements). The number and size of these pixels determine a monitor's sharpness or **resolution.** There are three basic types of displays:

- **Monochrome Text** These monitors can display only letters, numbers, punctuation, and a limited set of other symbols in just one color, usually green on black, amber on black, white on black, or black on white.
- **Monochrome Graphics** In addition to text, these monitors can also display graphics on the screen. Only one color can be presented, but different shades of that color may be used.
- **Color Graphics** These monitors can display text and graphics in more than one color.

The capabilities of a particular display system are dependent on both the monitor itself and its device controller. The device controller for a display is called a **display adapter.** Several display adapters are available for IBM and IBM-compatible microcomputers:

- **Monochrome Display Adapter (MDA)** This is the controller used with early low-end IBM microcomputers. It can display only text on a monochrome screen, but it generates crisp, easy-to-read characters.
- **Color Graphics Adapter (CGA)** This is IBM's first microcomputer color graphics adapter. It can produce color graphics, but the quality is rather poor. In other words, its low resolution makes text and graphics look rather fuzzy. Furthermore, the CGA is limited to a maximum of only 16 different colors, of which only four can be on the screen at the same time.
- **Hercules Graphics Adapter** This adapter, made by Hercules Computer Technology, acts as a monochrome display adapter, but adds monochrome graphics capability.
- **Enhanced Graphics Adapter (EGA)** This color graphics adapter from IBM can do everything the CGA can do, yet is much better than the CGA. The resolution is significantly higher and the maximum number of different colors on the screen is 16 out of 64 possible choices.
- **Multi-Color Graphics Array (MCGA)** This is the display adapter built onto the motherboards of the IBM Personal System/2 Models 25 and 30. It can be used with either a monochrome graphics or color graphics monitor. Its maximum resolution is better than the EGA and can display a maximum of 256 different colors on the screen at once out of 262,144 possible choices.
- **Video Graphics Array (VGA)** This is the display adapter built onto the motherboards of the IBM Personal System/2 Models 50, 60, 70, and 80. It can also be purchased as a separate expansion board for other types of IBM and IBM-compatible computers. Slightly more advanced than the MCGA, the VGA can also do everything the EGA can do.

Keyboard

The keyboard is the primary device for entering text and telling the computer what to do. It is similar, in many respects, to a typewriter keyboard. Many microcomputers also have an auxiliary input device known as a **mouse.** This little box, which is slid across the table top, allows the user to manipulate objects on the display screen, draw pictures, and select actions to be performed by pressing one or more buttons.

Three basic keyboard designs are used on IBM and IBM-compatible microcomputers: the original IBM Personal Computer keyboard, the original IBM Personal Computer AT keyboard, and the new IBM Enhanced keyboard. Figure 7 shows all three of these keyboards. Besides the usual letters and punctuation marks found on any typewriter, a computer keyboard has other important keys:

- **Enter** (or **Return**) Analogous to the carriage return on a typewriter, this key is used to signal the end of an entry. Basically, it tells the computer to go ahead and process what was just typed.
- **Backspace** Like the Backspace key on a typewriter, this key is used to go back and type over a previously typed character.
- **Shift** Located at either side of the keyboard, one of the Shift keys is held down while pressing another key to produce a capital letter or the symbol shown on the top part of the key.

Figure 7   IBM Keyboard Designs
*(top) Original IBM PC Keyboard,
(center) "AT-Style" Keyboard, and
(bottom) IBM Enhanced Keyboard*

- **Caps Lock** This key is like the Caps Lock key on a typewriter, except that it works for only letter keys. When the Caps Lock key is pressed, capital letters will appear when you press letter keys. When Caps Lock is pressed again, small letters will appear when their keys are pressed.
- **Tab** Like the Tab key on a typewriter, this key is used to advance to the next tab stop.
- **Escape** The Escape key (abbreviated **Esc**) is often used to cancel a previously typed entry or to prematurely end a program.

- **Break** This key is much like the Escape key and is used by some programs in a similar fashion.
- **Control** Somewhat like a Shift key, the Control key (abbreviated **Ctrl**) is pressed in conjunction with other keys. It's used to control a program's actions by sending certain codes to the computer.
- **Alternate** Similar to the Control key, the Alternate key (abbreviated **Alt**) is also pressed in conjunction with other keys. It's used to give an alternate meaning to the keys pressed along with it.
- **Insert** This key (abbreviated **Ins**) is often used to insert a new entry between existing entries.
- **Delete** This key (abbreviated **Del**) is often used to erase an entry or a single character.
- **Function Keys** These are keys that are pressed to activate frequently used operations within a program. They are used differently by different programs. IBM-compatible keyboards have either 10 function keys along the left side or 12 function keys across the top. The function keys are labeled with an F followed by a number, like this: F1, F2, F3, and so on.
- **Cursor Movement Keys** Most programs use these keys to let you move the **cursor** (a little blinking underscore or box) around the screen. In a word processing program, for example, the cursor marks the place where text is inserted, deleted, or otherwise manipulated. The cursor movement keys include Up Arrow, Down Arrow, Left Arrow, Right Arrow, Home, End, Page Up, and Page Down.
- **Numeric Keypad** This is an array of keys at the right side of a keyboard that resembles the layout of a calculator's keys. It includes the ten digits and other symbols that facilitate the entry of numbers and formulas. On the IBM PC and AT keyboards, the numeric keypad is superimposed on the cursor movement keys.
- **Num Lock** This key is used to switch the function of the numeric keypad. In one state, the numeric keypad acts as number keys. In the other state, the numeric keypad acts as cursor movement keys. You press the Num Lock key to switch between these two states.
- **Print Screen** If you have a printer, this key is pressed to send a copy of the current screen to your printer. On some keyboards, it is abbreviated **PrtSc.**
- **Pause** This key is used to temporarily suspend the operation of the current program.
- **Scroll Lock** This key is used by few programs and it has no standard function. Some programs use it to switch the Cursor Movement keys into a state in which they can move (or scroll) the whole screen up, down, left, or right.

Printer

A **printer** is a device that produces permanent copies of text and graphics on paper. Although a printer is not absolutely necessary to run most programs, it is handy because microcomputers are commonly used to produce letters, reports, books, tables, figures, charts, graphs, diagrams, maps, and pictures. Paper output, or *hard copy*, is a convenient medium for distributing text and graphics to others. The four kinds of printers most frequently used with microcomputers are dot-matrix printers, daisy-wheel printers, ink-jet printers, and laser printers.

Dot-Matrix Printers   A **dot-matrix printer** is an output device that uses tiny dots to create text and graphics on paper (see Figure 8). Just as graphics monitors use pixels to construct characters and pictures on a screen, dot-matrix printers

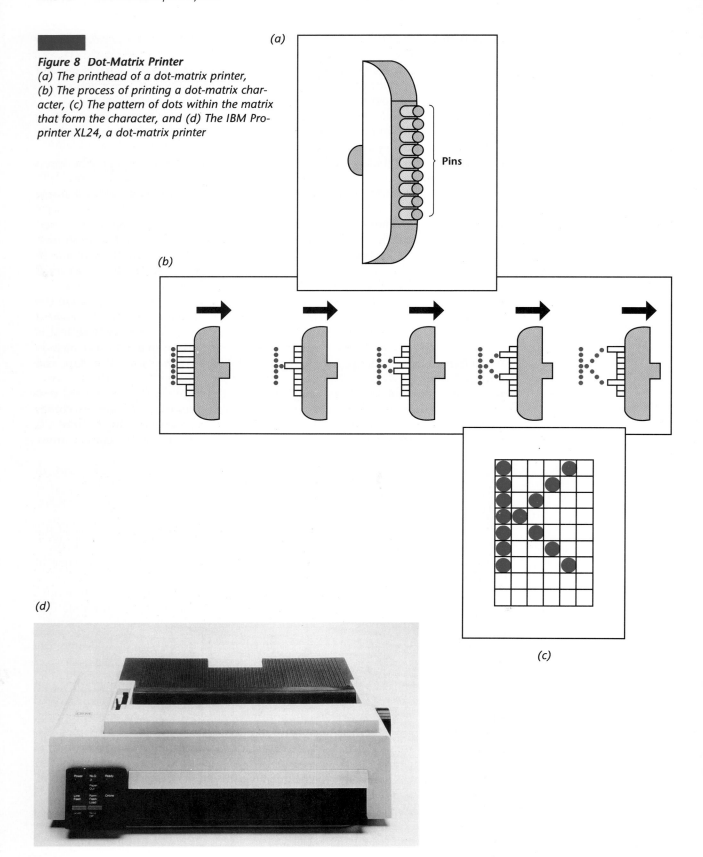

Figure 8   Dot-Matrix Printer
*(a) The printhead of a dot-matrix printer,
(b) The process of printing a dot-matrix character, (c) The pattern of dots within the matrix
that form the character, and (d) The IBM Pro-
printer XL24, a dot-matrix printer*

similarly use dots of ink on pages of paper. Inside the dot-matrix printer a **printhead** is moved across the paper from left to right, and sometimes also from right to left (see Figure 8). This printhead may contain anywhere from 7 to 27 pins arranged in a vertical column. While most dot-matrix printers use 9 pins, more expensive printers with 24 pins are also common. As the printhead moves horizontally, it constructs a character by repeatedly striking these pins against an inked ribbon and the paper. Electrical signals cause the appropriate pins to be thrust out at the proper moment to form the successive columns of dots that make up a character's image. Each column of the character is struck in turn against the ribbon and paper until the complete image has been formed. Dot-matrix printers are sometimes described as being impact printers because of the way the pins hit the ribbon and paper. This printing mechanism is most often used for text, but dot-matrix printers can usually produce graphics, too.

Dot-matrix printers are the most popular type of microcomputer printer. They are reasonably priced, fairly quick, and pretty reliable. Prices range between $150 and $3000, but the typical cost of a 9-pin dot-matrix printer is about $500. The speed of a dot-matrix printer depends upon what print mode it is using. The fastest mode is called **draft mode,** in which characters are formed by just a single pass of the printhead. Some expensive dot-matrix printers are able to achieve speeds of 400 characters per second in draft mode. Many dot-matrix printers also have a **near letter-quality (NLQ) mode.** In this mode, the printhead makes two or more passes over each character, slightly shifting its position each time. This tends to fill in the gaps between the dots and makes text appear more like it was produced by an electric typewriter. Using NLQ mode may slow some printers down to only 15 characters per second. Generating graphics with a dot-matrix printer can also be time-consuming. Depending upon how dark the images are, it may take several minutes per page to produce graphics on a dot-matrix printer.

Daisy-Wheel Printers   A **daisy-wheel printer** uses a circular printing mechanism called a **daisy wheel.** Solid, raised characters are embossed on the ends of little "arms" arranged in a circle like the spokes of a wheel or the petals of a daisy. As this daisy wheel spins, a tiny, stationary hammer strikes the back of the proper character when it passes (see Figure 9). This impact drives the character pattern, which is embossed in reverse, against an inked ribbon and the paper. Daisy-wheel printers are true **letter-quality** printers because they produce well-defined text just like electric typewriters. Their prices are comparable with that of dot-matrix printers. Unlike dot-matrix printers, however, daisy-wheel printers cannot produce graphics. They are also noisier and slower than dot-matrix printers. The typical daisy-wheel printer can only print about 10 characters per second, and even the most expensive models generally cannot do better than 100 characters per second. Daisy-wheel printers are still common, but they are being supplanted by 24-pin dot-matrix printers and laser printers.

Ink-Jet Printers   An **ink-jet printer** has a mechanism that squirts tiny, electrically-charged droplets of ink out of a nozzle and onto the paper (see Figure 10). No pins or hammers strike the paper, so ink-jet printers are classified as nonimpact printers. Ink-jet printers are fast, quiet, and can produce high-quality print, but they are slightly more expensive than dot-matrix printers. Some ink-jet printers require special paper to avoid smearing. On the other hand, many ink-jet printers can print in color, a capability most other types of printers lack.

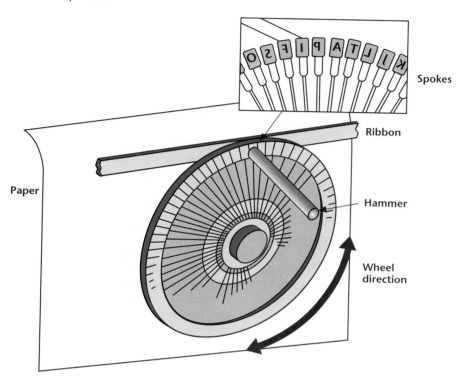

Figure 9 Daisy-Wheel Printer
*The Daisy-Wheel printing mechanism
and a daisy wheel*

Laser Printers   A **laser printer** is an output device that uses tightly focused beams of light to transfer images to paper (see Figure 11). A tiny laser emits pulsating pinpoint bursts of light that are reflected off a special spinning mirror. This mirror reflects light onto a rotating drum. Light striking the drum causes it to become charged with electricity. An inklike toner is attracted to the drum in these electrically charged spots. When the drum is rolled over a piece of paper, the toner is transferred to the paper and an image is permanently fixed through a combination of heat and pressure. This image transfer process is similar to that found in a plain-paper photocopy machine. The result is high-quality text and graphics that almost look as if they were typeset. Like ink-jet printers, laser printers are classified as nonimpact printers.

Laser printers represent the most advanced printing technology. Although the images they produce are made up of dots, these dots are much smaller and more densely packed than the dots created with a dot-matrix printer. The typical microcomputer laser printer is capable of printing at a resolution of 300 dots per inch, both horizontally and vertically. This means 90,000 dots per square inch. Besides printing high-quality images, laser printers are also fast and quiet. The

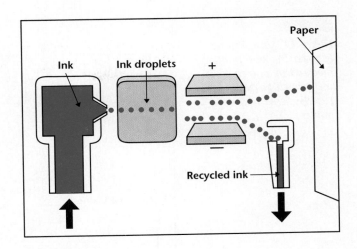

Figure 10 Ink-Jet Printer
(above) Ink jet printing, and (below)
the Hewlett-Packard PaintJet color
graphics printer

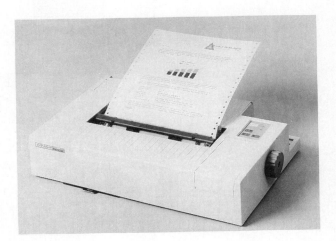

average speed of most laser printers is 8 pages per minute. This is equivalent to about 400 characters per second. Because laser printers don't use impact methods like dot-matrix and daisy-wheel printers, they are very quiet by comparison. The major disadvantage to laser printers is their cost. Prices generally start at around $1000. Despite the cost, more and more laser printers are being used with microcomputers every year. They are especially popular in office situations where the printer can be shared among several users.

Software

By itself, computer hardware is useless. Programs are needed to operate the hardware. As we mentioned earlier, a program is simply a sequence of instructions that tells a computer what to do. **Software** is a general term that refers to any single program or group of programs. In contrast to hardware, which is

Figure 11 Laser Printer
*(above) The laser printing
mechanism, and (below)
the Hewlett-Packard
LaserJet Series II laser
printer*

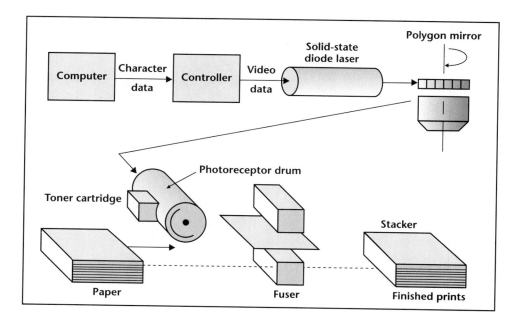

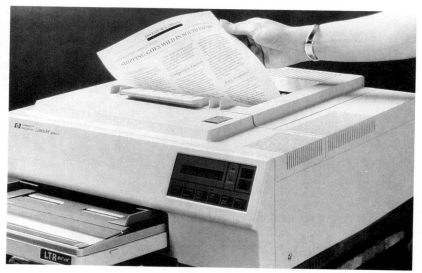

constructed from physical materials like metal and plastic, software is built from
knowledge, planning, and testing. A person who creates programs is called a
programmer. Programmers use their knowledge of how a computer works to
plan sets of instructions that accomplish useful tasks. These instructions are
entered into the computer and repeatedly tested and modified until they achieve
the desired results. Programs and data are generally kept on magnetic disks,
where they can be accessed and used over and over again. Note that the disks
themselves aren't the software, they are just the medium on which software is
stored.

As an analogy, think of a stereo system. The amplifier, compact disc player,
and speakers are the hardware. The amplifier is like the central processing unit
and memory, the compact disc player is like a disk drive, and the speakers are
like the display, except they present audio instead of video output. The music,

which is stored on compact discs, is like software, which is stored on floppy disks. Just as you can amass a huge music collection by buying more compact discs, you can build a bigger software library by purchasing additional programs on floppy disks. The stereo system is of little use without the compact discs and the compact discs are useless without the stereo system. Similarly, a computer system is useless without software and software is useless without a computer system on which to run it.

Just as there are different types of hardware, there are also different types of software. Basically, there are three major categories: system software, programming languages, and application software.

System Software

System software handles the many details of managing a computer system. A computer's **operating system** makes up most of its system software. This is the set of programs that controls a computer's hardware and manages the use of software. One small part of the operating system, for example, is a program that identifies which key you've pressed, determines the character that corresponds to that key, and forms that character on the display screen. Another example is a program that lets you erase the contents of a magnetic disk. Some system software is built into a computer's ROM chips, while other system software comes on magnetic disk and must be purchased separately.

Programming Languages

Computer programs are developed with programming languages. A **programming language** is simply a set of symbols and rules to direct the operations of a computer. There are many different programming languages in common use, each designed to develop certain types of programs. A few of the most popular programming languages are BASIC, Pascal, C, FORTRAN, COBOL, and Ada. Although it can be helpful to learn a programming language for some very specific applications, most people who use computers don't actually program them. They just use programs, such as operating systems and application software, that have been developed by professional programmers.

Application Software

Application software is the software that applies the computer to useful tasks such as helping you create documents, figure your taxes, maintain mailing lists, and draw charts. Also called **application packages** or simply **applications,** these programs are the real reason most people buy and use microcomputers. The three most widely used applications are word processing, spreadsheet, and data base management.

- **Word Processing** A **word processing package** is software that helps you prepare documents by letting you enter, store, modify, format, copy, and print text.
- **Spreadsheet** A **spreadsheet package** is software that lets you manipulate tables of columns and rows of numbers, text, and formulas. It is an extremely flexible tool that can be used to handle typical accounting chores, monitor investments, balance a checkbook, and work out a budget.
- **Data Base Management** A **data base** is an organized collection of one or more files of related data. A **file** is a mass of individual data items kept together on

a disk. A **data base management package** is software that lets you create, add to, delete from, update, rearrange, select from, print out, and otherwise administer data files such as mailing lists and inventories.

Besides these "big three" application packages, there are many other types of popular software, including the following:

- **Communications** Using an auxiliary device called a **modem,** a computer can transmit and receive programs and data over ordinary telephone lines. Communications software makes it possible for a computer to use a modem to call other computers and access on-line information services.
- **Graphics** Graphics packages let you use a computer to create all kinds of pictures including graphs, charts, maps, paintings, drawings, diagrams, blueprints, simulated slide shows, and animated presentations.
- **Desktop Publishing** Combining the results of word processing and graphics, desktop publishing or page layout software lets you use a computer and laser printer to produce near-typeset quality documents.
- **Integrated Software** Integrated software combines word processing, spreadsheet, data base management, communications, and graphics applications in a single package.
- **Windowing Environment** Working closely with the operating system, a windowing environment allows you to divide your screen into a number of different boxes, or *windows*, and run a separate program in each one.
- **DOS Shell** A DOS shell is a program that enhances PC-DOS or MS-DOS, the operating system used with IBM and IBM-compatible microcomputers. Basically, it is an easy-to-use front-end to DOS that helps you execute commands and manage disk files.
- **Utilities** There are a host of small, specific programs called utilities that add handy features and functions to a particular operating system or application package. These include disk and file utilities, printer utilities, keyboard utilities, and desk accessories such as calculators, calendars, and address books.
- **On-Line References** Software to help you check your spelling, find a synonym, or look up a word's definition are all examples of on-line references.
- **Statistics and Math** Many programs exist for performing statistical analyses and helping solve mathematical equations.
- **Project Management** A project management package is software that helps you formally plan and control complex undertakings, such as the construction of a building, the development of a new product, or the installation of a large computer system.
- **Accounting** Accounting software lets you use a computer to record, analyze, and report business transactions.
- **Personal Finance and Taxes** Many programs exist for helping you manage your money and prepare your federal and state income tax returns.
- **Education** There is a wide range of programs for teaching skills and concepts, from learning the alphabet to designing physics experiments.
- **Entertainment** An amazing variety of microcomputer software exists for playing games, simulating cars and planes, and playing music.
- **Hypertext** A hypertext package is software that lets you store and retrieve all kinds of information in a nonsequential manner. In other words, you can randomly jump from topic to related topic, accessing any kind of information the computer can store, including text, graphics, audio, and video.
- **Expert System** An expert system is a computer program that contains a collection of facts and a list of rules for making inferences about those facts. Such software can use these facts and rules in a particular field to advise, analyze, categorize, diagnose, explain, identify, interpret, and teach.

Helpful Hints for Using a Microcomputer

Now that we've covered the general topics, let's go over a few specific details that can help prepare you for using a microcomputer.

Turning on the Computer

Sometimes, just turning on the computer can be an adventure. It seems that some manufacturers are fond of "hiding" the **power switch.** This has the practical purpose of making it difficult to turn off the computer by accident while in the middle of some critical task. Not being able to find the power switch, however, can make you feel lost before you even begin.

On the new IBM Personal System/2 computers, the power switch is a big red toggle right up front on the system unit. No problem here. On other computers, if the switch isn't immediately obvious up front, then it is probably on the right side of the system unit toward the rear. This is the case in IBM PCs, XTs, and ATs. Some models from other companies have the power switch mounted somewhere on the back of the system unit or monitor.

Many color graphics displays have a separate power switch that must also be turned on, otherwise you will be looking at a permanently blank screen. The on/off switch is usually the top knob of three on the front of the monitor and is turned on by rotating it to the right. The other two knobs are the contrast and brightness controls, just like the ones on many television sets. If these three controls aren't right up front, they may be present as slightly protruding little disks located just under the bottom front edge of the monitor or on the back of the monitor.

Operating the Printer

Like the system unit and monitor, the printer also has a power switch that must be turned on. This power switch is frequently positioned at the rear on the left or right side. In addition, there are at least three other buttons on most printers. Usually stationed on the top or front of the printer, these three buttons may be labeled *On Line, Line Feed,* and *Form Feed.* The **On Line button** is very important and is usually paired with an indicator light. When the On Line light is on, the printer is connected to and controlled by the computer so that printing can occur. Make sure the On Line button is pressed so that the On Line light is on before attempting to print. The **Line Feed** and **Form Feed** buttons let you advance the paper in the printer, usually only when the printer is off line.

Caring for Floppy Disks

Although floppy disks are quite durable and can take quite a bit of punishment, here are a few guidelines you should follow in their handling:

- Don't touch the exposed surfaces on 5¼-inch disks. Don't open the metal shutter on 3½-inch disks.
- Don't bend or fold 5¼-inch floppies.
- Don't expose disks to extreme heat.

- Keep 5¼-inch disks in their sleeves when not in use.
- Don't write on 5¼-inch disks with pencils or hard point pens.
- Keep disks dry.
- Don't expose disks to strong magnetic fields (keep them away from magnets and powerful motors).
- Always try to keep at least one backup copy of all important disks.
- Carefully insert and remove disks from disk drives. Wait until the drive's red access light is off before changing disks.

Summary

- *What is meant by the term microcomputer.* A microcomputer has a microprocessor as its CPU, is small enough to fit on a desk, is used by one person at a time, and costs between $100 and $15,000.

- *The basic operations performed by all computers.* A computer program lets you enter input, processes data, and produces output.

- *The four major hardware components.* A typical microcomputer has a system unit, a keyboard and perhaps a mouse, a display, and a printer.

- *The major components inside the system unit.* The system unit contains the motherboard, microprocessor, memory, and disk drives.

- *The three major types of displays.* Monochrome text, monochrome graphics, and color graphics are the three basic types of displays.

- *How the various special-purpose keys are used.* Enter signals the end of an entry; Backspace and Delete erase characters; Alternate, Control, and Shift keys are pressed along with other keys; Escape and Break keys cancel or stop actions; Tab advances to the next tab stop; Insert adds a new entry; function keys perform common operations; cursor movement keys move the cursor; the numeric keypad resembles the keys on a calculator; Num Lock switches the function of the numeric keypad; Print Screen prints the screen; and Pause suspends the current program.

- *The four most popular types of printers.* Dot-matrix, daisy-wheel, ink-jet, and laser are the four most popular types of microcomputer printers.

- *The three major categories of software.* System software, programming languages, and application packages are the three major categories of microcomputer software.

- *How to turn on a microcomputer.* Flip the power switch located on the front, side, or rear.

- *How to operate a printer.* Flip the power switch and make sure the On Line indicator is lit.

- *How to care for floppy disks.* Don't touch exposed disk surfaces; don't expose disks to temperature extremes, dust, or water; don't bend, fold, or write on 5¼-inch disks; keep disks away from magnets; keep backup copies of important disks; and carefully insert and remove disks only when the drive's access light is off.

Key Terms

As an extra review of this chapter, try defining the following terms.

application package (application)
bus
byte
central processing unit (CPU)
computer
cursor
daisy wheel
daisy-wheel printer
data
data base
data base management package
device controller
disk drive
display (monitor)
display adapter
dot-matrix printer
draft mode
expansion board (card, adapter)
expansion slot
file
floppy disk (diskette)
floppy disk drive
Form Feed button
gigabyte (G)
graphics
hard disk drive
hardware
information
ink-jet printer
input
integrated circuit chip

kilobyte (K)
laser printer
letter-quality
Line Feed button
magnetic disk
megabyte (M)
memory
microcomputer (personal computer)
microprocessor
modem
motherboard (system board)
mouse
near letter-quality (NLQ) mode
On Line button
operating system
output
pixel
power switch
primary storage
printer
printhead
program
programmer
programming language
random access memory (RAM)
read only memory (ROM)
resolution
software
spreadsheet package
word processing package

Multiple Choice

Choose the best selection to complete each statement.

1. A microcomputer is a computer in which the central processing unit consists of
   (a) a RAM chip.
   (b) a ROM chip.
   (c) a microprocessor chip.
   (d) a device controller chip.
2. A set of instructions that controls a computer's operation is
   (a) a program.
   (b) data.
   (c) input.
   (d) output.
3. The main circuit board of a computer is called the
   (a) expansion board.
   (b) device controller.
   (c) bus.
   (d) motherboard or system board.

4. IBM and IBM-compatible microcomputers use microprocessors from the
    (a) Motorola 68000 family.   —(b) Intel 8088 family.
    (c) Zilog Z80 family.   (d) GTE G65SC816 family.

5. A byte is the amount of storage needed to hold a
    —(a) single character.   (b) single page.
    (c) single line.   (d) single file.

6. Which of the following does NOT describe random access memory (RAM)?
    (a) It is temporary storage.   (b) It loses its contents when the
                                            power is turned off.
    —(c) It is permanently encoded at   (d) It can be read and written over
        the factory.   again and again.

7. The two most popular floppy disk sizes are
    (a) 3½-inch and 8-inch.   (b) 5¼-inch and 8-inch.
    —(c) 3½-inch and 5¼-inch.   (d) 3-inch and 12-inch.

8. Which of the following types of display systems can present text and pictures
   on the screen, but only in a single color?
    (a) monochrome text display   —(b) monochrome graphics display
    (c) color graphics display   (d) monochrome display adapter

9. Which of the following microcomputer keyboard keys is used to tell the
   computer to go ahead and process what was just typed?
    —(a) Enter key   (b) Escape key
    (c) Control key   (d) Function key

10. The most advanced and expensive type of printer in the following group is
    the
    (a) dot-matrix printer.   (b) daisy-wheel printer.
    (c) ink-jet printer.   —(d) laser printer.

11. A set of programs that controls a computer's hardware and manages the use
    of software is called
    —(a) an operating system.   (b) a programming language.
    (c) an application package.   (d) a data base management
                                            package.

12. Which of the following types of software lets you manipulate tables of num-
    bers, text, and formulas?
    (a) word processing package   —(b) spreadsheet package
    (c) data base management   (d) operating system
        package

13. Which of the following types of software lets you use a modem to transmit
    and receive programs and data over ordinary telephone lines?
    —(a) communications package   (b) graphics package
    (c) desktop publishing package   (d) windowing package

14. Which of the following types of software lets you use a computer to record,
    analyze, and report business transactions?
    (a) graphics package   —(b) accounting package
    (c) DOS shell   (d) utilities

15. Small, specific programs that add handy features and functions to a particular operating system or application package are called
    (a) on-line references.
    (b) hypertext programs.
    (c) spreadsheets.
    —(d) utilities.
16. Which of the following types of software would be the best choice for maintaining a mailing list?
    (a) word processing package
    (b) spreadsheet package
    —(c) data base management package
    (d) accounting package
17. Which of the following types of programs would you use to help plan and control the construction of a new office building?
    (a) word processing package
    (b) spreadsheet package
    (c) integrated software package
    —(d) project management package
18. Which of the following types of software lets you store and retrieve all kinds of information in a nonsequential manner and then randomly jump from topic to related topic?
    (a) word processing package
    (b) spreadsheet package
    —(c) hypertext package
    (d) expert system
19. Which printer button determines whether the printer is connected to and controlled by the computer?
    (a) Power
    —(b) On Line
    (c) Line Feed
    (d) Form Feed
20. Which of the following should you NOT do to a floppy disk?
    (a) Keep it in its sleeve when not in use.
    (b) Keep it away from extreme heat.
    —(c) Keep it near a magnet when not in use.
    (d) Keep it dry.

Fill-In

1. An _____ microcomputer works like a comparable IBM model and can run the same software.
2. At the lowest level, the basic operations of all computers can be summed up as input, _____, and output.
3. The _____ of a computer system is the electronic and mechanical equipment that make it work.
4. A microcomputer's motherboard contains the _____, which is a set of wires and connectors that link the CPU to memory and other computer components.
5. _____ is temporary storage for programs and data, which can be used and then overwritten by other programs and data. _____, on the other hand, is permanent storage encoded at the factory with frequently used programs and data that need never be changed.
6. Most microcomputers can be equipped with two basic types of disk drives: floppy disk drives and _____.
7. The number and size of a monitor's _____ determine its sharpness, or resolution.

8. The _____ is the display adapter that comes built onto the motherboards of high-end IBM Personal System/2 microcomputers.

9. Many microcomputers have an auxiliary input device known as a _____, which is a little box with one or more buttons that is slid across the table top.

10. On an IBM keyboard, the _____ Movement keys include Up Arrow, Down Arrow, Left Arrow, Right Arrow, Home, End, Page Up and Page Down.

11. _____ printers are by far the most popular type of microcomputer printer.

12. _____ is a general term that refers to any single program or group of programs.

13. BASIC, Pascal, C, FORTRAN, COBOL, and Ada are all examples of popular programming _____.

14. _____ software is the software that applies the computer to useful tasks such as helping you create documents, prepare a budget, or maintain a mailing list.

15. _____ packages let you use a computer to create all kinds of graphs, charts, maps, paintings, drawings, diagrams, slide shows, and presentations.

16. Combining the results of word processing and graphics software, _____ software lets you use a computer and laser printer to produce near-typeset quality documents.

17. _____ software combines word processing, spreadsheet, data base management, communications, and graphics applications in a single package.

18. A _____ environment allows you to divide your screen into a number of different boxes and run a separate program in each one.

19. A _____ management package is software that helps you formally plan and control complex undertakings.

20. An _____ system is a computer program that contains a collection of facts and a list of rules for making inferences about those facts.

BEGINNING DOS

In This Chapter

Preview

According to *Business Week,* some 10 million IBM and IBM-compatible microcomputers were being used in businesses around the world by the middle of 1987. Joseph R. (Rod) Canion, president of Compaq Computer Corporation, figures that customers have spent $80 billion on IBM PCs, IBM-compatibles, and the hardware and software that work with them. IBM sold approximately 2.7 million microcomputers in 1988. Compaq, the leading "clone" manufacturer and number 2 business computer maker in the United States, sold around 500,000 that same year. The number 3 business computer manufacturer is Apple, which makes machines that are not IBM-compatible unless they are fitted with special equipment. Frederic E. Davis, editor-in-chief of *MacUser* magazine, estimates that IBM and IBM-compatibles outnumber Apple Macintoshes in the marketplace six to one. Clearly, IBM and IBM-compatibles are by far the most popular class of microcomputer. The overwhelming majority of these machines are running DOS.

After the original IBM Personal Computer was unveiled in 1981, DOS quickly became popular in offices, large corporations, and other businesses where IBM has traditionally wielded a great deal of influence. As soon as various hardware manufacturers started selling lower cost IBM-compatible computers, DOS also began popping up in small businesses, organizations, and institutions, as well as in schools, libraries, and homes. Because of this "hardware explosion," many software developers began to write application packages to run under DOS. This attracted even more users, who attracted still more software developers. At the same time, hardware manufacturers began to develop expansion boards and peripheral devices to be used with computers that run DOS. Today, a huge body of application software and a multitude of hardware devices are devoted to DOS microcomputers. Despite more advanced operating systems, such as OS/2 and XENIX, designed for high-end IBM and IBM-compatible machines, DOS is still the most popular microcomputer operating system in the world. In 1988 alone, IBM and Microsoft shipped 9.8 million copies of DOS, and approximately 75 percent of all microcomputers sold used DOS. This percentage is expected to increase until at least 1991.

After studying this chapter, you will know how to

- start up DOS with the computer turned off.
- start up DOS with the computer turned on.
- obtain a directory of the files on a disk.
- use the special DOS keys.
- change the default disk drive.
- obtain a disk and memory status report.
- clear the display screen.
- format a diskette.
- format a system diskette.
- copy files.
- copy an entire diskette.
- change file names.
- erase files.
- protect a diskette from accidental erasure.
- display on the screen and print text files.
- run an application package.

Insight

Will PC-DOS Be Replaced by Another Operating System?

Watch out, PC-DOS—there are a couple of hounds nipping at your heels.

PC-DOS (or MS-DOS) has been enjoying a fairly safe and secure life as a leader of the operating system pack since the microcomputer population explosion of the 1980s. But time is taking its toll, and the gray hairs are starting to show.

DOS was originally designed to be a single-user, single-tasking operating system, allowing only one program to be run at a time. Today, there are some clever applications packages that seem to let you do two things at once, such as print a file in the background while you're still working with the word processor. DOS doesn't handle this well.

When you want to perform more involved tasks, such as processing a large number of accounting transactions while still working on a spreadsheet, DOS is definitely inadequate. In large business, scientific, and engineering applications, these kinds of tasks are almost required today.

More elaborate *multitasking* operating systems can run several programs at the same time. Actually, they switch back and forth between tasks, giving each program a small slice of time. The switching is so fast that it's not apparent to the user.

People who use their IBM-compatible microcomputers for multitasking have two main choices in operating systems today—UNIX and

OS/2. UNIX is a very powerful and flexible operating system that was developed by Bell Laboratories and originally ran on minicomputers. OS/2 was developed jointly by Microsoft and IBM. It is a memory-hungry system that runs only on the more powerful IBM-compatible microcomputers that use the Intel 80286, 80386, and 80486 processors.

UNIX and OS/2 are being groomed as the operating system leaders of the next generation of powerful microcomputers. But it's unlikely that DOS will just slink off into the woods. DOS has a huge, installed base and many devoted users. For many simple computing needs, it will undoubtedly remain on top.

DOS Versions

DOS stands for **Disk Operating System.** It was originally written for IBM by Microsoft, which kept the right to sell DOS under its own name. Today, DOS is developed jointly by both IBM and Microsoft. When it is sold by IBM for IBM microcomputers, it is called PC-DOS or IBM DOS. When it is sold by Microsoft for IBM-compatibles, such as those made by Compaq, Tandy, or Zenith, it is called MS-DOS. Although a few minor differences exist between the system software sold by IBM and Microsoft, from the user's standpoint PC-DOS and MS-DOS are almost identical. So, they are often both referred to generically as DOS.

Computer technology advances quickly. To remain popular, an operating system must be continually upgraded to accommodate new computers and new capabilities for existing models. Several versions of DOS have been released by IBM and Microsoft. In each release, bugs have been worked out and improvements have been made to previous versions. The driving force behind each new version of DOS, however, has been new hardware capabilities, usually related to disk drives.

It is important to know which version of DOS you are using, because some hardware and software can only be used with more recent releases. Fortunately, each new DOS version is **upwardly compatible** with former versions. This means, at least in theory, that every official command that worked with previous versions should work with the new version. In most cases, this is so. However, there always seems to be at least one command that doesn't work quite the same in the new release. Nevertheless, for the most part you probably don't have to change the way you did things before unless you want to take advantage of the added capabilities of a new DOS version.

If you don't need these additional capabilities, you don't have to buy the latest version of DOS each time a new release is issued. As long as the version you have works well with your hardware and software, you can continue using it. Keep in mind that although a new DOS version may add certain capabilities, you must pay for the upgrade and that new DOS versions typically use more memory and more disk space. In many cases, upgrading is simply not worth it. Unless you're buying a new machine or adding a different disk drive, you may not need the latest DOS version.

DOS versions are identified by numbers such as 1.00, 3.30, and 4.01. The number to the left of the decimal point reflects a major classification; the numbers to the right represent more minor differences. The larger the number, the more recent the version. This table summarizes the major DOS versions that have been released so far, along with the primary reason for each upgrade:

Version	Date	Reason for Upgrade (New Capabilities)
1.00	8/81	5¼" 160K single-sided floppy disk drives
1.10	5/82	5¼" 320K double-sided floppy disk drives
2.00	3/83	5¼" 360K floppy, 10M hard disk drives
2.10	10/83	5¼" 360K half-height floppy drives
3.00	8/84	5¼" 1.2M floppy, bigger hard disk drives
3.10	3/85	Network disks and file sharing
3.20	12/85	3½" 720K floppy disk drives
3.30	3/87	3½" 1.44M floppy disk drives
4.00	7/88	Hard disks larger than 35M, DOS Shell
4.01	10/88	Corrected errors in version 4.00

Throughout the DOS chapters we will be using MS-DOS 4.01 for the examples. Most of what we cover, however, also applies to DOS 2.00 and newer versions. Versions 1.00 and 1.10 are now considered obsolete. If you are using a version of DOS other than 4.01, the screens you see on your computer may be slightly different than the ones shown in this book.

Getting Started

Although DOS is a powerful microcomputer operating system, you can easily learn its most commonly used features. DOS might be set up at your particular computer site in any of several different ways. You are most likely to use DOS in one of the following arrangements:

1. On a microcomputer with two floppy disk drives and DOS installed on one or more diskettes.

2. On a microcomputer with a hard disk drive and DOS installed on the hard disk.

3. On a microcomputer connected to a local area network with DOS installed on the network file server. Some DOS commands do not work over a network, as we will point out.

You may need additional direction from your instructor to run DOS at your computer installation. You should then be able to complete the following lessons. If DOS has not already been installed on your hard disk (with a path to the DOS subdirectory) or on floppy disks for you, see the Software Installation Appendix.

Lesson 1: Booting DOS

DOS stands for Disk Operating System. Although some low-level parts of the operating system programs are stored in ROM chips, the higher level programs of the operating system are kept on a floppy or hard disk. Like any program, the operating system must be loaded into the computer's memory before it can start working. The operating system, however, is what loads programs into memory and sets up the computer to execute them. If this is so, how does the operating system itself get started? Does it load itself? In a way, yes. Basically, a small program in ROM is automatically invoked every time the computer is turned on or reset. After loading itself into memory, this program then loads the rest of the operating system into memory and begins execution. In a sense, the computer pulls itself up by its own bootstraps. The process of initially loading and executing the operating system is often called **booting up.** In the particular case of IBM and IBM-compatibles, this is also called booting DOS, loading DOS, or simply starting DOS. At this point, your computer should be turned off.

Step 1: Insert the DOS Startup Disk

If your computer has a hard disk, skip this step and go directly to Step 2. If your computer is connected to a local area network, you may have to complete this step. If your computer does not have a hard disk and is not connected to a network, you must insert a diskette containing DOS before you can turn it on. In most cases, this diskette will be labeled "DOS Startup."

If your computer has two or more floppy disk drives, the A drive is the one on top or to the left. This is the floppy disk drive from which you boot DOS.

If drive A accepts 5¼-inch diskettes, grasp the DOS Startup disk by the label and remove it from the paper sleeve. Be careful not to touch the exposed parts around the oval slot and circular hole. Hold the disk with the label side up and the oval slot pointing toward the computer. Slide the diskette all the way into the drive slot, where it may click into place, and close the door or lever (see Figure 1).

If drive A accepts 3½-inch diskettes, grasp the DOS Startup disk with the label up and the metal shield pointing toward the computer. The arrow embossed or printed on the disk should point toward the computer. Slide the diskette all the way into the drive slot, where it will click and drop into place (see Figure 1).

Figure 1 Inserting and Removing Diskettes

3 ¹/₂ - inch diskette

5 ¹/₄ - inch diskette

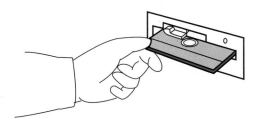

Insert diskette with arrow side up and arrow pointing to diskette drive. Press gently on diskette until it clicks and drops into place.

Remove by pressing eject button on lower right of diskette drive.

Insert diskette into drive until it clicks into place; label must be facing up with write-protect notch on left. Close drive door.

Remove by opening drive door and gently pulling out diskette.

Step 2: Turn On the Computer

If your display has its own power switch, turn it on first. Then turn on the computer. Older IBM microcomputers have a big red toggle switch on the right side of the system unit toward the rear; the newer Personal System/2 models have the switch right up in front (see Figure 2). Some IBM-compatibles have the power switch on the back side of the system unit. Flip the power switch. On many computers you will hear the cooling fan begin to hum.

Step 3: Watch the Display and Wait

After the power has been turned on, the computer completes some self-tests to ensure that it is working properly. One of these tests checks out all of the memory installed in the computer. This test could take several minutes, so don't be alarmed if nothing seems to be happening. After the power-on self-tests are complete, the computer will beep and check drive A to see if it contains the DOS Startup disk. If your computer has a hard disk and no diskette in drive A, it will boot up from the hard disk. Assuming the computer is in working order, the Startup diskette has been inserted correctly (if you need it), and DOS has been correctly installed on the Startup diskette or hard disk, you will see a message on the display screen. The exact contents of this message will depend on the type of computer and the way DOS was installed on the disk. If your computer does not have a built-in battery-maintained clock, DOS may ask you to enter the current date and time.

Step 4: Enter the Date and Time

If you don't see the following message on your screen, skip this step:

```
Current date is Tue 01-01-1980
Enter new date (mm-dd-yy):
```

Type today's date in the form of mm-dd-yy or mm/dd/yy. In other words, type in the month number, a dash or slash, the day of the month, another dash or slash, and the last two digits of the year.

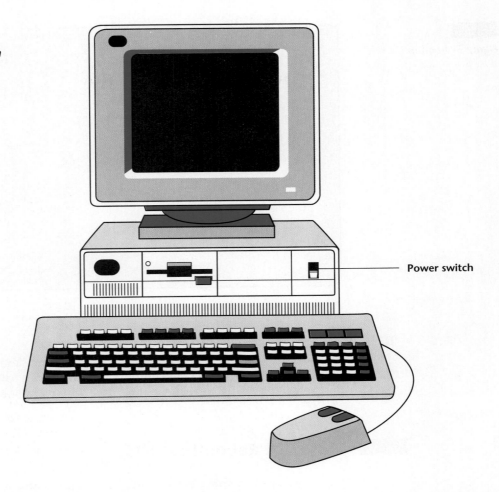

Figure 2 The Power Switch

Power switch

Press   **Enter**

Next, a message like this may appear:

```
Current time is 12:00:39.05a
Enter new time:
```

Type the hour, a colon, and the minute. If it is afternoon, add twelve to the hour as in the 24-hour clock format. For example, if it is 2 P.M., you would enter 14:00. You can also enter the second and hundredths of a second if you happen to carry a stop watch and feel so inclined. Just the hour and minute are sufficient, however.

Press   **Enter**

At this point, your screen may look like Figure 3. The C> on the last line is the **DOS prompt.** In this case, it indicates that disk drive C, the hard disk, is the default drive. The **default drive** is the disk drive that DOS assumes you want to use unless you specify otherwise. If you booted up from drive A, then drive A would be your default drive and the DOS prompt would be A>. The prompt tells you that DOS is waiting for a command.

Practice   Turn off the computer. Wait ten seconds. Turn it back on again. If it asks you to enter a new date, just press **Enter** without typing a date. If it asks you to enter

Figure 3 Booting Up

```
Current date is Tue 01-01-1980
Enter new date (mm-dd-yy): 7-10-89
Current time is 12:00:39.05a
Enter new time: 12:42


Microsoft(R) MS-DOS(R) Version 4.01
          (C)Copyright Microsoft Corp 1981-1988

C>_
```

a new time, just press **Enter** without typing a time. You don't have to enter a new date and time, but if your computer doesn't have a battery-maintained clock, it is best to enter the correct date and time when you boot up.

Lesson 2: Rebooting DOS

Occasionally, something goes wrong in a program and the computer may seem to be "stuck." Or after working with a program you may have to "reinitialize," or bring the computer back to the way it was when you first turned it on. You could, of course, just turn off the computer and boot it up as you learned in Lesson 1. There is another way to reboot the computer without shutting it off, however.

Step 1: Press Ctrl-Alt-Del

DOS has a special combination of keypresses that will reboot the computer without having to shut it off first. All you have to do is press the keys marked Control (or Ctrl), Alternate (or Alt), and Delete (or Del), and hold them down at the same time for a moment.

Press   **Ctrl-Alt-Del**

Step 2: Watch the Display and Wait

In most cases, the screen will go blank, the computer will beep, and the disk drive will spin and blink its red access light just as it did when you first turned it on. If all this doesn't happen, a serious program error has probably overwritten a crucial part of DOS in memory, and you will have to turn off the computer and boot it up as you did in Lesson 1. If all is well, DOS will again ask you to supply the date and time if your computer does not have a battery-maintained clock.

Step 3: Enter the Date and Time

If DOS asks you to enter a new date and time, do so as you did in Lesson 1. DOS will once again display its copyright message and the prompt, as shown in Figure 3.

Practice   Reboot your computer without turning it off. Enter the correct date and time if asked to do so.

Lesson 3: Listing a Disk File Directory

In most cases, you tell DOS what to do by entering commands or responding to prompts that ask you to supply more information. Some DOS commands are loaded into memory when the computer is booted up and kept there until the power is turned off. These **internal commands,** also called **resident routines,** are kept in memory because they are the most essential or most frequently used parts of the operating system. For example, one of the simplest and most commonly used DOS internal commands is DIR, which displays a file directory. After you boot up, internal commands are always available from any disk. The remaining DOS commands are called **external commands** or **transient routines,** because they are kept in disk storage and temporarily loaded into memory only when they are needed or specifically requested. CHKDSK, for example, is an external DOS command that displays information about a disk and the memory installed in your computer.

Programs, data, and text are kept on disks in files. Every file has a name, size, creation date, and creation time associated with it. The DIR command lets you see what files you have on a particular disk or in a particular subdirectory. A **subdirectory** is a group of files on a disk organized under a single name.

Step 1: Enter DIR

To execute the DIR command:

Type   **dir**
Press **Enter**

It doesn't matter whether you type DOS commands in lowercase letters, uppercase letters, or a combination of both. For example, DIR, dIr, and Dir are all equivalent.

DIR, which is short for DIRectory, displays information about the files on a disk or in a subdirectory. When the command is entered by itself, it will produce a directory listing on the screen of the default disk or current subdirectory. Figure 4 shows the screen after executing the DIR command. Your screen is probably different because your default disk most likely has different files on it.

Step 2: Examine the Directory Listing

Examine the screen in Figure 4. First it reveals the volume label of the disk. The volume label is just the name of the disk, which in this case is HARD DISK. Next is the volume serial number, which is just a code number assigned to the disk when it is formatted. DOS versions prior to 4.00 do not have volume serial numbers. Then DOS says that this is a directory of the disk in drive C, and it

Figure 4 Listing a Directory

```
C>dir

 Volume in drive C is HARD DISK
 Volume Serial Number is 3324-07CC
 Directory of   C:\

CONFIG   SYS       146 07-09-89    1:22p
AUTOEXEC BAT       145 07-09-89    1:22p
COMMAND  COM     37557 12-19-88   12:00a
DOS          <DIR>      07-09-89    1:23p
     4 File(s)   19701760 bytes free

C>_
```

lists the names, sizes, dates, and times of the files. Notice that the first three file names have two parts. We'll have more to say about this file name format shortly. The last file name in the list, DOS, is the name of a subdirectory. The <DIR> designation next to the name tells you that it is a subdirectory and not an ordinary file. This subdirectory, which we'll look at later, contains the files that make up most of DOS. It was created when DOS was installed on the hard disk.

Each file name, except for the DOS subdirectory, has a number to its immediate right. This is the size of that file in bytes. A byte, you'll recall, is basically equivalent to a single character. Finally, listed to the right of each file size is the date and then the time at which the file was created or last changed. The first file in the list, for example, is named CONFIG.SYS, occupies 146 bytes, and was created on July 9, 1989, at 1:22 P.M.

At the bottom of the listing, the DIR command tells you that four files are in this directory and there are 19,701,760 "bytes free." This means that 19,701,760 bytes of storage are still unused on the disk. Since it's important to know what files are on a disk and how much room is left, DIR is one of the most frequently used DOS commands.

Step 3: Examine Another Disk's Directory

The DIR command can also be used to list the directory of a disk in a drive other than the current default drive. You can do this by specifying the disk drive letter after DIR. For example, if your computer has a hard disk, you can examine the directory of a disk in floppy drive A. If you have a diskette with files on it, insert the diskette into drive A.

Type **dir a:**
Press **Enter**

The **a:** is the designation for the A disk drive. If you have a computer with two floppy drives, you can examine a disk in the second drive by entering DIR B:. Note that the hard disk is usually referred to as the C drive, regardless of whether a B floppy drive is installed.

Step 4: Examine the Contents of a Subdirectory

The DIR command can also be used to list the files in a subdirectory. All you
have to do is type the name of the subdirectory after the DIR. For example, if
your computer has a hard disk with a subdirectory named DOS, try the following
command:

Type   **dir dos**
Press   **Enter**

Figure 5 shows the result. Since 68 files are in this directory listing but only 25
lines can be shown on the screen, many of the names have moved up and
disappeared off the top of the screen. Figure 5, therefore, shows only the bottom
part of the listing. For the rest of this chapter, we will assume you have a computer with a hard disk that has a DOS subdirectory.

Step 5: Look For a Specific File

Frequently, you'd like to be able to check if a particular file is on a disk or in a
subdirectory without having to look at the entire directory listing. The DIR command can do this for you if you give it the name of the file you're looking for.
All you have to do is enter the name of the file after the DIR. If you want to look
in a subdirectory, type the subdirectory name, a backward slash (\), and then the
name of the file. DOS will either list an abbreviated directory with only that file
in it or tell you the file is not there. For example, if your computer has a DOS
subdirectory, execute this command:

Type   **dir dos\format.com**
Press   **Enter**

This command tells DOS to look in the DOS subdirectory for a file named FOR-
MAT.COM. Figure 6 shows the result. If your computer doesn't have a DOS
subdirectory, try this command instead:

Type   **dir format.com**
Press   **Enter**

*Figure 5 Looking at a
Subdirectory*

```
GRAPHICS COM     16693 10-06-88   12:00a
GRAPHICS PRO      9397 10-06-88   12:00a
HIMEM    SYS      6261 10-06-88   12:00a
MODE     COM     22960 10-06-88   12:00a
NLSFUNC  EXE      6878 10-06-88   12:00a
PRINTER  SYS     18914 10-06-88   12:00a
RECOVER  COM     10588 10-06-88   12:00a
4201     CPI      6404 10-06-88   12:00a
4208     CPI       720 10-06-88   12:00a
5202     CPI       370 10-06-88   12:00a
README   TXT     14148 10-12-88    9:13p
BACKUP   COM     36880 10-06-88   12:00a
EGA      CPI     49068 10-06-88   12:00a
LCD      CPI     10703 10-06-88   12:00a
RESTORE  COM     36946 10-06-88   12:00a
PCIBMDRV MOS       263 10-06-88   12:00a
SHELL    CLR      4406 10-06-88   12:00a
SHELL    HLP     66527 10-06-88   12:00a
SHELL    MEU      4588 10-06-88   12:00a
SHELLB   COM      3894 10-06-88   12:00a
SHELLC   EXE    153855 10-06-88   12:00a
DOSUTIL  MEU      6660 10-06-88   12:00a
       68 File(s)   19701760 bytes free

C>_
```

Figure 6   Looking for a Specific File

```
C>dir dos\format.com

 Volume in drive C is HARD DISK
 Volume Serial Number is 3324-07CC
 Directory of  C:\DOS

FORMAT   COM     22859 10-06-88  12:00a
        1 File(s)    19701760 bytes free

C>_
```

For the rest of this chapter, we will assume you have a DOS subdirectory on your default disk. If you do not, omit the dos or dos\ designations from the instructions given.

DOS File Names   This is a good time to digress a bit and discuss DOS file names in more detail. First of all, notice that each file in the directory you listed has a unique name. No two files in the same directory can have the same name because DOS wouldn't be able to tell them apart. Two files on different disks or in different subdirectories, however, can have the same name. A file name can consist of two parts: a primary filename and an optional extension. The first part, or **filename** as IBM calls it, can be from one to eight characters long. It can include any of the characters you see on the keyboard except for the following, which are considered invalid in filenames:

. " / \ [ ] : | < > + = ; ,

The second part, an optional short name, is called an **extension.** It is separated from the primary filename by a period and has from one to three characters in it. These characters also can be any of the keyboard characters except those we just listed. If a file's name does have an extension, you may have to use both parts when telling DOS to do something with that file. Extensions are most often used to classify files. For example, here are some of the more common file name extensions, along with the types of files they usually designate:

COM	DOS external command or an executable program
EXE	DOS external command or an executable program
BAT	Batch file
SYS	System setup file
ASM	Assembly language program
BAS	BASIC language program
PAS	Pascal language program
TXT	Text file
BAK	Backup copy of some other file
DOC	Document file of some word processing programs
WKS	Worksheet file of some spreadsheet programs
DBF	Data base file of some data base managers

Finally, a file name can be prefaced with the designation of its disk drive and subdirectory. For example, C:\DOS\FORMAT.COM is the full specification for the file FORMAT.COM on the hard disk C in the DOS subdirectory. Note that the colon must be used after the disk drive letter and the backslash must be used before and after the subdirectory name. If you don't enter part of the specification, such as the disk drive letter or subdirectory, DOS will assume you mean the default drive or current subdirectory.

Step 6: Look for a Specific Group of Files

Not only can the DIR command find a single file on a disk, it can also be used to list a group of files if their names have some characters in common. The DOS **global file name characters,** * and ?, can be included in a filename or extension to give you greater flexibility in designating DOS files. The * character can be used in a file specification to symbolize any character or group of characters. For example, *.SYS means "any file with an extension of SYS." The ? character is used to symbolize any single character. For example, MO?E.COM means "any file that has an extension of COM and a four-letter filename beginning with MO and ending with an E." Both global file name characters can be used together in the same specification, too. For example, ????.* means "any file with at most four characters in its first part." Try each of the following commands:

Type   **dir dos*.sys**
Press **Enter**
Type   **dir dos\mo?e.com**
Press **Enter**
Type   **dir dos\????.***
Press **Enter**

Figure 7 shows what you should see on your screen after entering the command DIR DOS*.SYS.

Figure 7 Looking for a Group of Files

```
C>dir dos\*.sys

   Volume in drive C is HARD DISK
   Volume Serial Number is 3324-07CC
   Directory of  C:\DOS

COUNTRY  SYS    12806 10-06-88  12:00a
DISPLAY  SYS    15692 10-06-88  12:00a
KEYBOARD SYS    23328 10-06-88  12:00a
EMM386   SYS    87776 10-06-88  12:00a
RAMDRIVE SYS     8235 10-06-88  12:00a
SMARTDRV SYS    10224 10-06-88  12:00a
XMA2EMS  SYS    29211 10-06-88  12:00a
ANSI     SYS     9105 10-06-88  12:00a
DRIVER   SYS     5241 10-06-88  12:00a
HIMEM    SYS     6261 10-06-88  12:00a
PRINTER  SYS    18914 10-06-88  12:00a
      11 File(s)   19701760 bytes free

C>_
```

Practice

1. List a directory of your default disk drive.

2. List a directory of the DOS subdirectory.

3. Try this command:

   Type   **dir *.***
   Press   **Enter**

   What does it do?

4. Try this command:

   Type   **dir dos*.exe**
   Press   **Enter**

   What does it do?

5. Create a listing of the DOS subdirectory that shows only those files that begin with the letter S.

6. Create a listing of the DOS subdirectory that shows only those files with primary filenames less than four characters long.

7. Notice that subdirectory names have no extensions. Try this command (follow the asterisk with a period):

   Type   **dir *.**
   Press   **Enter**

   What does it do?

Lesson 4: Using Special DOS Keys

Like most software, DOS assigns special meanings to certain keys and combinations of keypresses. You've already learned some of these. For example, you know that you must press the Enter key after typing in a command. This tells DOS to go ahead and process that command. The Backspace key can be used to correct typing errors on a line before the Enter key has been pressed. In Lesson 2 you learned that pressing the Control (Ctrl), Alternate (Alt), and Delete (Del) keys at the same time will reboot DOS without having to shut off the power and turn it back on. Let's explore some of the other keys DOS uses (see Figure 8).

Step 1: Press the Escape Key to Cancel a Line

As you've probably already discovered, it's pretty easy to make typing mistakes when using a keyboard. If the command you're typing is short and you haven't pressed the Enter key yet, the easiest way to fix a mistake is to backspace over it and retype it. If the command is long or if you really messed it up, you can cancel the entire line and start over. To do this, press the Escape (Esc) key. For example, type the following line at the DOS prompt (but don't press the Enter key):

   Type   **This line is really messed up!**

Suppose what you really meant to type in was DIR DOS, and you realized your mistake before you pressed the Enter key.

   Press   **Escape**

Figure 8 The Keyboard

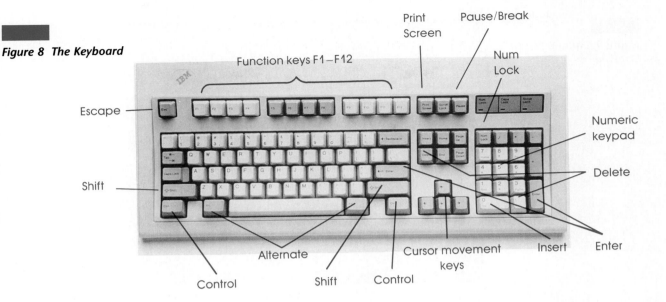

Pressing the Escape key cancels the current line. When you do this, DOS will display a / (slash) to signal that the line has been canceled, and it will skip down to the next line so you can start over. Now execute the following command to see the familiar DOS directory:

Type   **dir dos**
Press **Enter**

Step 2: Press Ctrl-Num Lock to Pause Screen Scrolling

As you watch the DOS directory scroll by on the screen, the first part of it disappears off the top. Sometimes, information scrolls by before you get a chance to read it all. It would be nice if you could temporarily stop the screen so that you wouldn't have to take speed-reading lessons to use the computer. Fortunately, DOS will pause for you if you hold down the Control key and press the Num Lock key. On the newer IBM Enhanced-style keyboards, you press the Pause key instead of Ctrl-Num Lock. In either case, this action will immediately pause any screen that is scrolling by. To resume scrolling, press any key (except a Shift, Lock, Ctrl, or Alt key). For example, execute the following commands:

Type   **dir dos**
Press **Enter**
Press **Ctrl-Num Lock** (or **Pause**)

Figure 9 shows what can happen. You can pause and resume scrolling as many times as you wish.

Step 3: Press Ctrl-Break to Cancel a Command

Suppose that you've entered DIR DOS or DIR by mistake and you don't want to wait for the whole directory to scroll by on the screen. Or perhaps you've seen enough and you just want to stop it. You can cancel a DOS command by pressing

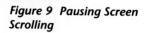

Figure 9 Pausing Screen Scrolling

```
C)dir dos

 Volume in drive C is HARD DISK
 Volume Serial Number is 3324-07CC
 Directory of  C:\DOS

 .            <DIR>       07-09-89   1:23p
 ..           <DIR>       07-09-89   1:23p
 DOSSHELL BAT          196 07-09-89   1:22p
 COMMAND  COM        37557 12-19-88  12:00a
 COUNTRY  SYS        12806 10-06-88  12:00a
 DISKCOPY COM        10396 10-06-88  12:00a
 DISPLAY  SYS        15692 10-06-88  12:00a
 FDISK    EXE        60935 12-19-88  12:00a
 FORMAT   COM        22859 10-06-88  12:00a
 KEYB     COM        14727 10-06-88  12:00a
 KEYBOARD SYS        23328 10-06-88  12:00a
 REPLACE  EXE        19415 10-06-88  12:00a
 SYS      COM        11456 10-06-88_
```

the Control and Break keys at the same time. This stops a command from finishing its job. In many cases, Ctrl-Break will also terminate programs other than just DOS commands. To see how this works, follow these directions:

Type   **dir dos**
Press   **Enter**
Press   **Ctrl-Break**

Pressing Ctrl-Break will terminate the directory command before it finishes. Figure 10 shows how this might appear on your screen. The ^C at the bottom stands for Ctrl-C, which means that the command has been canceled.

On IBM PC- and AT-style keyboards, the Break key is right next to the Num Lock key, and is also labeled Scroll Lock. On the newer IBM Enhanced-style keyboards, the Break key is the same as the Pause key. On all types of keyboards, you can also cancel a command by holding down the Control key and typing a C. Note that Ctrl-Break (or Ctrl-C) is different from the Escape key. Escape will cancel a line typed at the DOS prompt before the Enter key is pressed. Ctrl-Break cancels a command after the Enter key has been pressed and while the command is executing.

Step 4: Press Shift-PrtSc to Print the Screen

Frequently there is a sequence of commands or some information on the screen that you would like to save. If you have a printer connected to your computer, DOS can produce a hard copy of everything that is currently on the display screen. On IBM PC- and AT-style keyboards, you press one of the Shift keys along with the key marked PrtSc (Print Screen). On the newer IBM Enhanced-style keyboards, you simply press the key labeled Print Screen. If you have a printer, make sure it's turned on.

Press   **Shift-PrtSc** (or **Print Screen**)

You should get a copy of what's on your screen right now.

*Figure 10 Canceling a
Command*

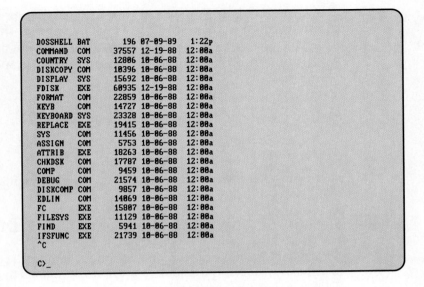

```
DOSSHELL BAT      196 07-09-89   1:22p
COMMAND  COM    37557 12-19-88  12:00a
COUNTRY  SYS    12806 10-06-88  12:00a
DISKCOPY COM    10396 10-06-88  12:00a
DISPLAY  SYS    15692 10-06-88  12:00a
FDISK    EXE    60935 12-19-88  12:00a
FORMAT   COM    22859 10-06-88  12:00a
KEYB     COM    14727 10-06-88  12:00a
KEYBOARD SYS    23328 10-06-88  12:00a
REPLACE  EXE    19415 10-06-88  12:00a
SYS      COM    11456 10-06-88  12:00a
ASSIGN   COM     5753 10-06-88  12:00a
ATTRIB   EXE    18263 10-06-88  12:00a
CHKDSK   COM    17787 10-06-88  12:00a
COMP     COM     9459 10-06-88  12:00a
DEBUG    COM    21574 10-06-88  12:00a
DISKCOMP COM     9857 10-06-88  12:00a
EDLIN    COM    14069 10-06-88  12:00a
FC       EXE    15807 10-06-88  12:00a
FILESYS  EXE    11129 10-06-88  12:00a
FIND     EXE     5941 10-06-88  12:00a
IFSFUNC  EXE    21739 10-06-88  12:00a
^C

C>_
```

Step 5: Press Ctrl-PrtSc to Echo to the Printer

The printout you got from the previous step contains only one screen of text. This output would not help much if you wanted a hard copy of the entire DOS directory, because the whole directory doesn't fit on the screen at once. Pressing Control and PrtSc (or Control and Print Screen on the Enhanced-style keyboards), however, will cause whatever you type and the computer's responses to be displayed both on the screen and sent to the printer. This echoing will continue until you press Ctrl-PrtSc again. So, you could, for example, get a hard copy of your entire computer session.

To get a hard copy of the DOS disk directory, follow these directions:

Press   **Ctrl-PrtSc**
Type   **dir**
Press   **Enter**

You should see the directory information being displayed on the screen a bit slower as it is also being sent to the printer. When it's finished and you see the DOS prompt, execute this command again to turn off printer echoing:

Press   **Ctrl-PrtSc**

Practice   1. Create a hard copy listing of this Practice session if you have a printer.

Press   **Ctrl-PrtSc** (or **Ctrl-Print Screen**)

2. Start typing a command, but don't press the Enter key:

Type   **dir a:**

Suppose you meant to type just **dir**, but made a mistake. Cancel the command:

Press   **Escape**

Now execute the command you meant to enter:

Type   **dir**
Press   **Enter**

3. Generate a directory listing of your DOS subdirectory or Startup disk. Pause and restart the screen scrolling at least twice before the command is finished.

4. Again, generate a directory listing of your DOS subdirectory or Startup disk. This time, however, cancel the command before it finishes by using Ctrl-Break or Ctrl-C.

5. Turn off printer echoing.

6. If you have a printer, make sure it is turned on.

> Type   **dir**
> Press **Enter**

Create a hard-copy listing of just the current contents of your screen.

Lesson 5: Changing the Default Disk Drive

IBM and IBM-compatible computers without hard disks boot up from the diskette in drive A, which is the default disk drive. Computers that have a hard disk with DOS installed on it boot up from drive C, which is considered the default drive. You will recall that the current default drive is indicated by the DOS prompt, for example, A> or C>. This means that whenever you enter a command that doesn't explicitly specify a particular disk drive, the current default drive is assumed. For example, when you enter DIR by itself, you get the directory of the current default drive. If your computer has more than one disk drive, like most IBM and IBM-compatible computers, you may occasionally want to change your default drive from A or C to another installed drive. This is a common procedure, sometimes called **switching drives.** Let's look at how and why you would change the default disk drive.

Step 1: Enter the Designation of the New Default Drive

If you have a computer with a hard disk and one floppy drive, put a disk with files on it into drive A. Then execute this command to change your default drive from C to A:

> Type   **a:**
> Press **Enter**

If you have a computer with two floppy disk drives, put a disk with files on it into drive B. Then execute this command to change your default drive to B:

> Type   **b:**
> Press **Enter**

DOS will respond with a prompt indicating the new default drive.

Step 2: Use the New Default Drive

Now when you execute a command, DOS will assume you are referring to the new default drive unless you specify otherwise. For example, try this command:

> Type   **dir**
> Press **Enter**

You will get a directory listing of the new default drive, A or B (see Figure 11). Although this might not seem terribly exciting at the moment, being able to

Figure 11 Changing the Default Disk Drive

```
A>dir

 Volume in drive A has no label
 Volume Serial Number is 0E1E-1BE0
 Directory of  A:\

COMMAND  COM     37557 12-19-88   12:00a
AUTOEXEC BAT        39 10-06-88   12:00a
CONFIG   SYS        96 10-06-88   12:00a
COUNTRY  SYS     12806 10-06-88   12:00a
DISKCOPY COM     10396 10-06-88   12:00a
DISPLAY  SYS     15692 10-06-88   12:00a
FDISK    EXE     60935 12-19-88   12:00a
FORMAT   COM     22859 10-06-88   12:00a
KEYB     COM     14727 10-06-88   12:00a
KEYBOARD SYS     23328 10-06-88   12:00a
REPLACE  EXE     19415 10-06-88   12:00a
SELECT   COM      3642 10-06-88   12:00a
SELECT   HLP     28695 10-06-88   12:00a
SELECT   PRT      1329 10-06-88   12:00a
SYS      COM     11456 10-06-88   12:00a
        15 File(s)       18432 bytes free

A>_
```

change the default drive enables you to make full use of all of your installed disk drives. As you become more proficient with DOS and application packages, you'll find yourself switching disk drives often. For example, on systems with two floppy drives, you may leave the DOS Startup disk in drive A and a disk containing a particular application package in drive B. Then, after booting up, you could switch to drive B to run your application program.

Step 3: Switch Back to the Original Default Disk Drive

If your computer has a hard disk, execute this command to switch back to it:

Type   **c:**
Press **Enter**

If your computer has no hard disk, execute this command to make A your default drive:

Type   **a:**
Press **Enter**

Practice

1. If your computer has a hard disk, put a diskette with files on it in drive A. If your computer has no hard disk, put a diskette with files on it in drive B. Change your default disk drive to A or B. Use the DIR command to generate a directory listing. Now switch back to your original drive.

2. Try switching to a disk drive that doesn't exist, such as Z. What happens?

3. Try switching to your current drive. For example, if C is your default drive, do this:

Type   **c:**
Press **Enter**

What happens?

Lesson 6: Checking Disk and Memory Status

You've already learned how one DOS command, DIR, can be used to list information about the files on a disk or in a subdirectory. Another DOS command, CHKDSK, can be used to display further information about a disk and the memory installed in your computer. CHKDSK is an external command, which means that it is kept in a separate file named CHKDSK.COM in the DOS subdirectory on a hard disk. External commands are available only when they are located on your default disk or in your current subdirectory, or when a path has been set up to the subdirectory that contains them. You will learn about paths in the next chapter. If DOS has been installed correctly on your hard disk, a path should already be set up to the DOS subdirectory so that the DOS external commands are always available. Note: the CHKDSK command does not operate when DOS is running on a local area network.

Step 1: Enter CHKDSK

To check the disk in your default drive, execute this command:

Type   **chkdsk**
Press **Enter**

Your screen should look like Figure 12, although the numbers probably will be different.

Step 2: Examine the Status Report

The CHKDSK status report supplies several useful items of information. First, it tells you that the total capacity of the hard disk is 21,204,992 bytes (a little more than 20 megabytes). This is roughly equivalent to about 6,575 pages of single-spaced typewritten text. **Hidden files** are special files used by DOS and some other programs. They're hidden because they do not appear in the disk directory so that you won't rename, change, or delete them. Next the CHKDSK command tells you how many subdirectories and ordinary user files are on the disk and how much space they occupy. It will also say whether any bytes on the disk are in "bad sectors," although there aren't any on the disk shown in Figure 12. Bad sectors occur when some of the disk is unusable due to manufacturing flaws—a fairly common occurrence with hard disks. The unusable areas are discovered when the disk is formatted and are marked so that DOS won't use them. The disk shown in Figure 12 has 19,701,760 bytes of empty space.

The CHKDSK command also reveals information about **allocation units,** which relate to how DOS assigns disk space to files. This is technical information that most users don't really need to know. Finally, CHKDSK reports that this particular computer has 655,360 bytes (or 640K) of RAM installed, of which 521,248 bytes are free to be used by application programs. The difference between these two figures, 134,112 bytes, is the amount of RAM taken up by the parts of DOS that remain in memory, such as the internal commands, and any memory-resident programs that have been loaded.

Practice

Like many DOS commands, CHKDSK can be used on a disk other than the default disk. Put a diskette with files on it into drive A. Then execute this command:

Type   **chkdsk a:**
Press **Enter**

Figure 12 The CHKDSK Report

```
C>chkdsk

Volume HARD DISK   created 01-01-1980 12:28a
Volume Serial Number is 3324-07CC

 21204992 bytes total disk space
    73728 bytes in 3 hidden files
     4096 bytes in 1 directories
  1425408 bytes in 69 user files
 19701760 bytes available on disk

     2048 bytes in each allocation unit
    10354 total allocation units on disk
     9620 available allocation units on disk

   655360 total bytes memory
   521248 bytes free

C>_
```

Lesson 7: Clearing the Screen

By now, you've probably accumulated quite a collection of commands and directory listings on your screen. Although this does no harm, it can be a bit distracting. Or, perhaps you want to type a sequence of commands and then do a print screen, and you would like to start off with a clean slate. It's easy to tell DOS to clear the screen with an internal command called CLS.

Step 1: Enter CLS

To clear the screen, execute the clear screen command:

> Type **cls**
> Press **Enter**

DOS will erase everything from the screen and start you off again with the system prompt on the first line in the upper left corner.

Practice Use the DIR command to generate a directory listing of your default disk drive. Now clear the screen.

Lesson 8: Formatting a Diskette

Every new disk must undergo an initial preparation known as formatting before it can be used to store programs and data files. Many manufacturers and retailers format the hard disks that are installed in the computers they sell. This initialization for diskettes, however, is not commonly done at the factory, so generally you must format each new floppy you're going to use with your own computer. You also can reformat a previously formatted disk to completely erase all the files that are stored on it. But you should be very careful whenever you format a previously used disk. Make sure that it doesn't hold any files that you want to save. Basically, DOS performs the following procedures when you format a disk:

- Checks the disk for bad or damaged spots that cannot reliably store data and marks these as unusable
- Completely erases any programs and data that might be on the disk
- Builds a directory to hold information about the files that eventually will be stored on the disk
- Marks off the empty space on the disk into equal-sized portions called **sectors**
- Creates a DOS startup disk if instructed to do so

The DOS FORMAT command, which is an external command, performs all of these functions. Note: the FORMAT command does not operate when running DOS on a local area network. This is a safety precaution to prevent users from reformatting shared hard disks.

Step 1: Get a Floppy Disk to Format

The most common and simplest use of the FORMAT command is to set up diskettes that will not be used to boot up the computer. Since the operating system is not installed on these diskettes, they can devote all of their space to holding programs and data files. For this lesson you'll need a new floppy disk or a previously used disk that can be completely erased. If you are going to format a diskette that's not new, double-check to make sure it doesn't have any programs or data files on it that you want to keep. Formatting a disk erases everything on it.

Step 2: Enter the FORMAT Command

To format a diskette in the A drive, execute the following command:

    Type   format a:
    Press   Enter

Step 3: Insert the Disk to Be Formatted

The FORMAT command will then tell you to insert the new diskette into drive A. Insert the disk as indicated, and then press the Enter key.

    Press   Enter

Step 4: Enter a Volume Label

The procedure takes about a minute for a 5¼-inch double-sided, double-density diskette, during which time DOS displays a percentage that shows how much it has formatted so far. When it is finished, the FORMAT command will prompt you to enter a volume label, or name, for the newly formatted disk. (Older versions of DOS don't automatically ask you to do this.) You can choose any name you like, but it must be no longer than eleven characters. If you don't want to enter a name, you can just press the Enter key. Name your disk like this:

    Type   my disk
    Press   Enter

Step 5: Examine the Screen

After you enter a volume label, FORMAT will tell you how much room is on the disk and whether it contains any bad sectors (see Figure 13). If the diskette has no bad sectors and DOS has not been installed on it, these two numbers will be the same: 362,496 bytes for a 5¼-inch double-sided, double-density diskette. The FORMAT command also displays information about the disk's allocation units and reports the volume serial number.

Step 6: Terminate the FORMAT Command

Finally, the FORMAT command asks you if you want to format another diskette. You can answer "no" like this:

Type   **n**
Press   **Enter**

You'll then get the DOS prompt back again, as shown in Figure 13.

Practice   Format another blank diskette or reformat the disk you have just formatted. This time, however, press **Enter** without typing a volume label.

Lesson 9: Formatting a System Diskette

The diskette you formatted in Lesson 8 can be used to store programs and data files. It cannot, however, be used to boot up the computer, because it doesn't have DOS installed on it. If you want to format a DOS startup diskette that can be used to boot up your computer from drive A, you must follow a slightly different procedure.

Figure 13 Formatting a Diskette

```
C>format a:
Insert new diskette for drive A:
and press ENTER when ready...

Format complete

Volume label (11 characters, ENTER for none)? my disk

    362496 bytes total disk space
    362496 bytes available on disk

    1024 bytes in each allocation unit
     354 allocation units available on disk

Volume Serial Number is 354B-8BD4

Format another (Y/N)?n
C>_
```

Step 1: Use the /S Parameter

A **parameter** is a specification that designates an alternate action for a command. Many DOS commands can be given one or more parameters to specify a slightly different way of performing their tasks. The FORMAT command, for example, can be instructed to install the operating system on the disk it's preparing. To do this, you add the /S parameter after the specification of the disk to be formatted. The /S tells FORMAT to put the DOS internal commands and the command processor on the disk being formatted. You can try this out by reformatting the disk you formatted in Lesson 8. To prepare a DOS startup disk, execute this command:

> Type   **format a: /s**
> Press   **Enter**

Step 2: Insert the Disk to Be Formatted

The FORMAT command will then tell you to insert the new diskette into drive A. Insert the disk you formatted in Lesson 8 into drive A and then press the Enter key.

> Press   **Enter**

Step 3: Enter a Volume Label

When the formatting procedure is complete, the FORMAT command will report that the system has been transferred to the disk. It will then prompt you to enter a volume label for the disk. Name your disk like this:

> Type   **startup**
> Press   **Enter**

Step 4: Examine the Screen

After you enter a volume label, FORMAT will tell you how much room is on the disk, whether the disk contains any bad sectors, and how much space is being used by DOS. Figure 14 shows a 5¼-inch double-sided, double-density diskette with MS-DOS 4.01 installed on it. The disk holds 362,496 bytes, DOS takes up 109,568 bytes, and 252,928 bytes of empty space are available. The FORMAT command also displays information about the disk's allocation units and reports the volume serial number.

Step 5: Terminate the FORMAT Command

Finally, the FORMAT command asks you if you want to format another diskette. You can answer "no" like this:

> Type   **n**
> Press   **Enter**

You'll then get the DOS prompt back again.

Step 6: Examine the Disk's Directory

Now, let's look at the directory of the disk you just formatted. Execute this command:

Figure 14 Formatting a System Diskette

```
C>format a:/s
Insert new diskette for drive A:
and press ENTER when ready...

Format complete
System transferred

Volume label (11 characters, ENTER for none)? startup

    362496 bytes total disk space
    109568 bytes used by system
    252928 bytes available on disk

      1024 bytes in each allocation unit
       247 allocation units available on disk

Volume Serial Number is 0308-07D1

Format another (Y/N)?n
C>_
```

> Type **dir a:**
> Press **Enter**

Your screen should look like Figure 15. Notice that only the file COM-MAND.COM is on the new system disk. It does not contain any of the external command files that are on the DOS disk. So, although you could boot up with this new disk and you could execute internal commands such as DIR, you could not use any external commands such as CHKDSK or FORMAT unless you copied their command files onto it.

Hard Disks   The FORMAT command also works for hard disks. Once a hard disk is initially formatted, however, it may seldom, if ever, be formatted again. Since computers with hard disks often have many important and sometimes irreplaceable files on them, you should be extremely cautious with them. Don't

Figure 15 Directory of the New System Diskette

```
C>dir a:

Volume in drive A is STARTUP
Volume Serial Number is 0308-07D1
Directory of  A:\

COMMAND  COM     37557 12-19-88  12:00a
        1 File(s)    252928 bytes free

C>_
```

attempt to format a hard disk unless you know exactly what you're doing and you're sure that all files on the hard disk have backup copies on other disks. As we said, many computers now come with their hard disks already formatted by the manufacturer or retailer.

Practice

1. Try booting up from your new system diskette. Make sure the newly formatted diskette is in drive A. If the drive has a door or lever, make sure it is closed.

   Press   **Ctrl-Alt-Del**

   Skip entering the date and time:

   Press   **Enter**
   Press   **Enter**

2. Use DIR to list a directory of your default disk, which should be the new system diskette in drive A. As you can see, internal commands like DIR always work after you boot up because they are kept in a hidden DOS file and automatically loaded into memory, where they remain.

3. Use CHKDSK to try to get a status report of your default disk. DOS will say "Bad command or file name." CHKDSK does not work on your new system disk because it is an external command, stored in its own file named CHKDSK.COM, and it has not been copied to the new disk. Similarly, FORMAT will not work from your new system disk either unless its file is copied to the disk first.

4. Remove the new system diskette from drive A. If your computer does not have a hard disk, put the original DOS Startup diskette back into drive A. Reboot your computer:

   Press   **Ctrl-Alt-Del**

   Enter the correct date and time if necessary.

Lesson 10: Copying Files

One of the reasons computers are so useful is that they make it simple to copy programs and data. Once information is entered into a computer, any number of copies usually can be made very easily and quickly. An important function of any operating system is duplicating files. DOS provides several methods of copying files. One of the most popular DOS commands is COPY, which reproduces one or more individual files.

Step 1: Copy a Single File (the Long Way)

Once a diskette has been formatted, it can be used to store program and data files. Let's use the COPY command to copy a single file from the DOS subdirectory onto your newly formatted diskette. First, we'll do it the longhand way, and then we'll show you a shortcut. To copy the file FORMAT.COM from the DOS subdirectory onto your formatted diskette, make sure the diskette is in drive A. Then execute this command:

Type   **copy c:\dos\format.com a:format.com**
Press   **Enter**

The first file specification after the COPY command is the **source,** or what you're copying from—the file FORMAT.COM on the hard disk C in the DOS subdirectory. The second file specification is the **target,** or what you're copying to—a file named FORMAT.COM on the diskette in drive A. The source and the target can have the same name because they are on separate disks. After you execute the COPY command, DOS will tell you that one file was copied. Now execute this command to see the contents of the diskette:

Type **dir a:**
Press **Enter**

You should see the file FORMAT.COM in the directory of the diskette in drive A, as shown in Figure 16.

Step 2: Copy a Single File (the Short Way)

In most cases, if you omit certain information from a command, DOS will make an assumption about what you mean. For example, if you don't supply a disk drive or subdirectory designation in front of a file name, DOS will assume that you mean the default drive and current directory. Similarly, if you don't specify a name for the target file, the COPY command will assume that it is to use the same name as the source. This assumption will work as long as the source and the target files are on different disks or in different subdirectories. Now try this shorter command to copy FORMAT.COM to the diskette:

Type **copy dos\format.com a:**
Press **Enter**

This command tells DOS to copy the file FORMAT.COM on the default disk in the DOS subdirectory to the diskette in drive A and give it the same name.

Note that you have just copied the FORMAT.COM in the DOS subdirectory to the FORMAT.COM that already existed on the diskette in drive A from the copy operation performed in Step 1. If you choose a name that already exists on the target, DOS will simply copy over it, destroying whatever was in that file

Figure 16 Copying a File

```
C>copy c:\dos\format.com a:format.com
          1 File(s) copied

C>dir a:

 Volume in drive A is STARTUP
 Volume Serial Number is 0300-07D1
 Directory of  A:\

COMMAND  COM     37557 12-19-88  12:00a
FORMAT   COM     22859 10-06-88  12:00a
          2 File(s)      229376 bytes free

C>_
```

before. Since you copied the same file, there's no problem here. As a rule, however, you should be very careful about the name you choose for a target file. If it already exists on the disk you're copying to, the original version will be overwritten. Make sure you no longer need any file on the target disk or subdirectory with the same name as a copy to be created.

Step 3: Copy a Group of Files

By using the global file name characters * and ? introduced in Lesson 3, you can copy several files at once with a single COPY command. For example, execute this command:

Type   **copy dos*.com a:**
Press   **Enter**

This command will try to copy every file in the DOS subdirectory with an extension of COM to the diskette in drive A. If you have only a 360K diskette in drive A, it will probably run out of room, as shown in Figure 17. Nevertheless, DOS will copy as many files as it can to the diskette.

Step 4: Copy a File to the Same Directory

You cannot have two files in the same directory with identical names. The COPY command simply will not allow you to duplicate a file in the same directory unless you provide a different name for the target file. So, the COPY command can reproduce a file on the same disk or in the same subdirectory, but the source and the target must have different names.

A common reason for duplicating a file in the same directory is for backup purposes. Let's say that you're going to change an existing file. If that file is especially important, you might want to keep a copy of the original version before you make any alterations. Then if some problem occurs, you will still have the original version intact. So, before you change a file, it might be a good idea to make a copy of it, but with a slightly different name. For example, suppose you

*Figure 17 Copying a
Group of Files*

```
C>copy dos\*.com a:
DOS\COMMAND.COM
DOS\DISKCOPY.COM
DOS\FORMAT.COM
DOS\KEYB.COM
DOS\SYS.COM
DOS\ASSIGN.COM
DOS\CHKDSK.COM
DOS\COMP.COM
DOS\DEBUG.COM
DOS\DISKCOMP.COM
DOS\EDLIN.COM
DOS\LABEL.COM
DOS\MORE.COM
DOS\TREE.COM
DOS\PRINT.COM
DOS\GRAFTABL.COM
DOS\GRAPHICS.COM
DOS\MODE.COM
DOS\RECOVER.COM
DOS\BACKUP.COM
Insufficient disk space
       19 File(s) copied

C>_
```

wanted to somehow change the file AUTOEXEC.BAT, but wanted to keep a copy of the original. You could make a backup copy of the original version on the same disk if you change its name slightly. For example, execute these commands:

Type   **copy autoexec.bat autoexec.bak**
Press **Enter**
Type   **dir**
Press **Enter**

The COPY command creates a copy of the AUTOEXEC.BAT file on the default disk and names it AUTOEXEC.BAK (the BAK is for backup), as shown in Figure 18. Now you could go ahead and safely make modifications to AUTOEXEC.BAT, because you've retained a copy of the original file in AUTOEXEC.BAK.

Practice

1. You can use the COPY command to duplicate every non-hidden file on a disk or in a subdirectory. For example, execute this command:

Type   **copy dos*.* a:**
Press **Enter**

You will probably quickly run out of room on the diskette in drive A, but this command would work if the target disk were large enough.

2. To see how the COPY command will not allow you to duplicate a file with the same name in the same directory, try this command:

Type   **copy autoexec.bak**
Press **Enter**

Because you omitted the target file name, DOS assumed you meant the same name as the source. Since two files in the same directory cannot have the same name, DOS aborts the command and displays the error message, "File cannot be copied onto itself."

Figure 18 Copying a File to the Same Directory

```
C>copy autoexec.bat autoexec.bak
        1 File(s) copied

C>dir

 Volume in drive C is HARD DISK
 Volume Serial Number is 3324-07CC
 Directory of  C:\

CONFIG   SYS      146 07-09-89   1:22p
AUTOEXEC BAK      256 01-01-80   5:52a
COMMAND  COM    37557 12-19-88  12:00a
DOS          <DIR>     07-09-89   1:23p
AUTOEXEC BAT      256 01-01-80   5:52a
        5 File(s)  19699712 bytes free

C>_
```

3. You should be careful with the COPY command. It is up to you to make sure you are copying the file you want and that the target name is correct. For example, execute this command (be sure you type *.bak* and not *.bat*):

Type **`copy command.com autoexec.bak`**
Press **Enter**

DOS will copy the file COMMAND.COM to the file AUTOEXEC.BAK, overwriting the previous contents of AUTOEXEC.BAK. It does not ask you if this is really what you want to do.

Lesson 11: Copying an Entire Diskette

DOS has a more specific copy command that lets you duplicate an entire diskette all at once. The DISKCOPY command formats the target diskette, if necessary, and copies all files, hidden or otherwise, exactly as they are on the original source diskette. DISKCOPY may be used to duplicate only floppy disks, not hard disks. Furthermore, DISKCOPY works only if the source and target are the same type of diskette. For instance, you cannot use the DISKCOPY command to duplicate the contents of a 5¼-inch diskette on a 3½-inch diskette. Fortunately, you can use DISKCOPY even if you have only one floppy drive. To see how the DISK-COPY command works, you can make an exact copy of the formatted system diskette you've been working with. You will need another diskette of the same type, either new and unformatted, or containing files you are sure you no longer need. Note: the DISKCOPY command does not operate when running DOS on a local area network.

Step 1: Execute the DISKCOPY Command

If your computer has two identical floppy disk drives, execute this command:

Type **`diskcopy a: b:`**
Press **Enter**

If your computer has only one floppy drive or two drives that are of different types, such as a 5¼-inch drive and a 3½-inch drive, execute this command instead:

Type **`diskcopy a: a:`**
Press **Enter**

Step 2: Follow the Directions

The DISKCOPY command will tell you which drive to put your source and target diskettes into and when to do so. Remember: the diskette you want to copy is the source, and the new diskette is the target. If your computer has only one floppy drive, you may have to swap the source and target diskettes in drive A several times, depending on how much memory is installed.

Step 3: Terminate the DISKCOPY Command

When it is finished, DISKCOPY will ask you if you want to copy another diskette. If the answer is no, do this:

Type **n**
Press **Enter**

If you have only one floppy drive, Figure 19 shows what you should see on your screen when DISKCOPY is finished.

DISKCOPY is a very useful command for making backup copies of important diskettes. In fact, the documentation that comes with many software packages suggests that you use the DISKCOPY command to duplicate all of your original diskettes as soon as you get them. Furthermore, you should put the originals away for safekeeping and only use your copies. Then, if you accidentally erase something or if a diskette you use daily becomes damaged or wears out, you will still have your original diskettes from which to make additional copies. These are good suggestions, and DISKCOPY will work fine as long as your software is not copy-protected.

Practice   Use DISKCOPY to duplicate some other diskette that you have.

Lesson 12: Changing File Names

When you create a file, either using a DOS command such as COPY or from within an application package such as a word processor, you assign it a name. This name need not be permanent, however. DOS lets you change file names very easily. There are several reasons why you might want to change an existing file name. Perhaps you've thought of a more appropriate name or maybe you would like to shorten the name. You may want to copy a file onto a disk that already contains another file with the same name. In this case, you could change the name of the file already on the disk so that its contents will not be overwritten by the file you want to copy. The RENAME command, which is an internal command, lets you change the name of one or more files.

Step 1: Rename a Single File

Changing a single file's name is quite easy. Just type RENAME (or its abbreviation, REN), followed by the file name you want to change and then the new

Figure 19 Copying an Entire Diskette

```
C>diskcopy a: a:

Insert SOURCE diskette in drive A:

Press any key to continue . . .

Copying 40 tracks
9 Sectors/Track, 2 Side(s)

Insert TARGET diskette in drive A:

Press any key to continue . . .

Volume Serial Number is 08E3-3224

Copy another diskette (Y/N)? n

C>
C>_
```

name that file is to have. For example, suppose you want to copy a new version of the file FORMAT.COM to the system diskette you created in Lesson 9, but you want to keep a copy of the original FORMAT.COM. You could rename the original FORMAT.BAK and then copy the new FORMAT.COM to your disk. Make sure your formatted system diskette is in drive A. Then execute these commands:

Type   **a:**
Press   **Enter**
Type   **rename format.com format.bak**
Press   **Enter**
Type   **dir format.***
Press   **Enter**

Your screen should look like Figure 20. The directory shows that you've successfully changed the name of FORMAT.COM to FORMAT.BAK.

Before you go on, change FORMAT.BAK back to FORMAT.COM to restore your disk to the way it was. This time, however, try using the abbreviated form of the RENAME command:

Type   **ren format.bak format.com**
Press   **Enter**

Step 2: Rename Several Files at Once

Using the global file name characters * and ?, you can rename several files at once. For example, with a single command you can rename each file on your system diskette with an extension of COM and give it an extension of BAK. Make sure the system diskette you formatted in Lesson 9 is in drive A and that drive A is your default drive. Then execute this command:

Type   **ren *.com *.bak**
Press   **Enter**

Figure 20 Renaming a File

```
C>a:

A>rename format.com format.bak

A>dir format.*

 Volume in drive A is STARTUP
 Volume Serial Number is 0308-07D1
 Directory of  A:\

FORMAT   BAK    22859 10-06-88  12:00a
        1 File(s)        2048 bytes free

A>_
```

Now execute this directory command to see what you've done:

Type   **dir *.bak**
Press **Enter**

Your screen should look something like Figure 21. There are now no files on your disk with COM extensions. They all have BAK extensions instead. Before you go on, change them all back to the way they were with this command:

Type   **ren *.bak *.com**
Press **Enter**

Practice   Change the name of the file AUTOEXEC.BAK, which you created in Lesson 10, to JUNK. Remember, this file is on your hard disk or DOS Startup disk.

Lesson 13: Erasing Files

Just as you accumulate old memos, notes, letters, clippings, and other scraps of paper on your desk, disks also can become cluttered with files that are no longer needed. Occasionally, you may have to clean up a disk and discard unnecessary files. Once you erase a file, however, it may be difficult or even impossible to retrieve its contents. In fact, DOS includes no utility for "unerasing" files, although such programs are sold by some independent software publishers. Before you erase any file, make sure you no longer need it. DOS makes it very easy to erase files, so you should be careful. Many instances of people losing files can be attributed to accidents or carelessness with the DOS ERASE command, also known as DEL. ERASE (or DEL) is an internal command.

Step 1: Erase a Single File

To erase a single file, just type ERASE or DEL (for delete) and follow it with the name of the file you want to erase. Make sure that the system diskette you

Figure 21 Renaming a Group of Files

```
    Volume Serial Number is 0308-07D1
    Directory of  A:\

COMMAND   BAK     37557 12-19-88   12:00a
FORMAT    BAK     22859 10-06-88   12:00a
DISKCOPY  BAK     10396 10-06-88   12:00a
KEYB      BAK     14727 10-06-88   12:00a
SYS       BAK     11456 10-06-88   12:00a
ASSIGN    BAK      5753 10-06-88   12:00a
CHKDSK    BAK     17787 10-06-88   12:00a
COMP      BAK      9459 10-06-88   12:00a
DEBUG     BAK     21574 10-06-88   12:00a
DISKCOMP  BAK      9857 10-06-88   12:00a
EDLIN     BAK     14069 10-06-88   12:00a
LABEL     BAK      4458 10-06-88   12:00a
MORE      BAK      2134 10-06-88   12:00a
TREE      BAK      6302 10-06-88   12:00a
PRINT     BAK     14131 10-06-88   12:00a
GRAFTABL  BAK     10239 10-06-88   12:00a
GRAPHICS  BAK     16693 10-06-88   12:00a
MODE      BAK     22960 10-06-88   12:00a
RECOVER   BAK     10588 10-06-88   12:00a
        19 File(s)      2048 bytes free

A>_
```

formatted in Lesson 9 is in drive A and that drive A is your default drive. Because you know this diskette holds only copies of DOS files that you have on the hard disk or on the original DOS Startup disk, you can safely erase files from it. Nevertheless, you should always be careful when erasing files. Data and programs are more frequently lost as the result of an accidentally or carelessly entered ERASE command than from any other cause. Suppose you want to erase the file FORMAT.COM from the diskette. Execute this command:

Type   **erase format.com**
Press   **Enter**

Now execute this directory command to see what you've done:

Type   **dir format.com**
Press   **Enter**

The file is now gone, so your screen should look like Figure 22.

Step 2: Erasing Several Files All at Once

By using the global file name characters * and ?, you can tell DOS to erase several files with a single ERASE command. In fact, you can even wipe out every file on a disk. Although this is often done to clear off a disk, it should be used with care. Make sure that the system diskette you formatted in Lesson 9 is in drive A and that drive A is your default drive. Then execute this command:

Type   **erase *.***
Press   **Enter**

Because this is a potentially disastrous command if entered by mistake, DOS will ask if you are sure you want to do this. If you answer yes, DOS will go ahead and erase everything. If you answer no, DOS will immediately cancel the ERASE command. You will get this chance to back out, however, only if you use the *.* designation. If you enter ERASE *.EXE, for example, DOS will not ask if you are sure and will immediately delete all files with an extension of EXE. So again, *be*

Figure 22 Erasing a File

```
A>erase format.com

A>dir format.com

 Volume in drive A is STARTUP
 Volume Serial Number is 8308-87D1
 Directory of  A:\

File not found

A>_
```

careful with the ERASE command! Answer yes and then list a directory to see what you have done:

Type **y**
Press **Enter**
Type **dir**
Press **Enter**

Your screen should look like Figure 23.

Practice Switch back to the hard disk or the DOS Startup disk you used to boot up the computer. Remember the AUTOEXEC.BAK file you created in Lesson 10 and that you renamed JUNK in the Practice section of Lesson 12? Erase it, but this time use DEL instead of ERASE. DEL and ERASE are two names for the same DOS command.

Lesson 14: Protecting Diskettes

In certain situations, commands such as FORMAT, COPY, DISKCOPY, RENAME, and ERASE won't work. Most diskettes have a feature that prevents them from being altered. This feature, called **write-protection,** is similar to the tabs on audio and video cassette tapes that you can remove to prevent accidentally recording over material you want to save.

Step 1: Write-Protect a 5¼-inch Diskette

Most 5¼-inch diskettes have a small rectangle cut out of one side, called the **write-protect notch** (see Figure 24(a)). This notch can be covered with a gummed tab or tape to write-protect the diskette. Files on a diskette protected in this manner can be read but not written or altered as long as the notch remains covered. Diskettes that are write-protected cannot be formatted, have files renamed

Figure 23 Erasing All the Files

```
A>erase *.*
All files in directory will be deleted!
Are you sure (Y/N)?y

A>dir

 Volume in drive A is STARTUP
 Volume Serial Number is 0308-07D1
 Directory of  A:\

File not found

A>_
```

Figure 24 *Write-Protecting Diskettes*

(a)

5 ¹/₄ - inch diskette

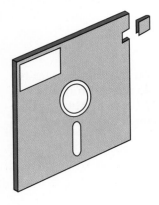

(b)

3 ¹/₂ - inch diskette

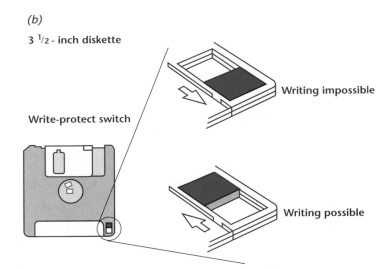

on them, have files copied onto them, or have files erased from them. If you attempt to do so, DOS simply issues a write-protect error message. Some 5¼-inch diskettes don't have a write-protect notch. These diskettes are permanently write-protected.

If you have a gummed tab or piece of tape, try write-protecting a 5¼-inch diskette. Then try copying a file to the diskette, or renaming or erasing a file already on the diskette.

Step 2: Write-Protect a 3½-inch Diskette

The smaller, 3½-inch diskettes also can be write-protected, but the mechanism is slightly different. These diskettes have a **write-protect switch** on the reverse side in the lower right corner (see Figure 24(b)). This switch is a tab that can be slid to open or close a little hole in the disk's plastic case. When the hole is open, the diskette is write-protected. When it is closed, files can be written and altered on the diskette.

If your computer uses 3½-inch diskettes, try write-protecting one. Then try copying a file to the diskette, or renaming or erasing a file already on the diskette.

Copy-Protection   With write-protection, you can safeguard programs and data that are stored on diskettes from accidental erasure. Some software developers use **copy-protection** to discourage you from duplicating their packages and illegally selling or giving away copies. Copy-protected diskettes are prepared in a manner that makes it difficult or impossible to copy them with ordinary DOS commands such as COPY and DISKCOPY. Since it is so easy to duplicate diskettes, some manufacturers feel that they must copy-protect their software to prevent widespread distribution to people who don't rightfully pay for it. Unfortunately, copy-protected software is often inconvenient for rightful owners to use or back up. Although manufacturers of most major application packages have since dropped copy-protection from their products, many game programs are still copy-protected.

If you try to use COPY or DISKCOPY on a diskette that is copy-protected, any one of several results might occur. The attempt could simply fail and cause an error message to be displayed. In other cases, the copy procedure might seem to successfully complete, but when you try to run the software it just won't work. Trying to duplicate copy-protected diskettes can be an effort in futility; to spare the user unnecessary frustration, manufacturers should clearly state whether their packages are copy-protected. The safest course is to follow the instructions for using and making backup copies of original diskettes.

Practice

Write-protect a new diskette or one containing files you don't need. Then try to format it.

Lesson 15: Displaying and Printing Text Files

So far, you've learned quite a bit about manipulating files with DOS. You haven't, however, looked inside one. The DOS TYPE command, which is an internal command, lets you display the contents of a file on the screen. The DOS PRINT command, which is an external command, lets you send the contents of a file to the printer. Although TYPE and PRINT will work with almost any file, unless it's a text file all you'll see is gibberish. A **text file** contains only ordinary letters, numbers, and punctuation marks. It is usually produced by a text editor or word processing program. AUTOEXEC.BAT and CONFIG.SYS, which we will explain further in the next chapter, are text files that tell DOS how to set up your computer when you boot up. Although these files are not absolutely necessary for booting up, they are created on most hard disks and DOS Startup diskettes when DOS is installed. If you don't have AUTOEXEC.BAT or CONFIG.SYS on your hard disk or DOS Startup disk, just read through this lesson.

Step 1: Execute the TYPE Command

Make sure the disk you booted up from is your default disk. Use the DIR command to see if AUTOEXEC.BAT and CONFIG.SYS are present on the disk. To examine the contents of the AUTOEXEC.BAT and CONFIG.SYS text files on your screen, execute these commands:

Type   **type autoexec.bat**
Press **Enter**
Type   **type config.sys**
Press **Enter**

DOS will display the contents of the files, as shown in Figure 25, although your screen will probably look somewhat different. The exact contents of the AUTO-EXEC.BAT and CONFIG.SYS files may vary quite a bit, depending on how DOS was installed and what options are being used. In the next two chapters, you will learn what all of the statements in these two files mean.

Step 2: Prepare the Printer

Many text files eventually wind up on paper, especially if they are produced by a word processing or text editing program. The DOS PRINT command lets you send a text file directly to the printer instead of displaying it on the screen.

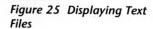

Figure 25 Displaying Text Files

```
C>type autoexec.bat
@ECHO OFF
SET COMSPEC=C:\DOS\COMMAND.COM
VERIFY OFF
PATH C:\DOS
APPEND /E
APPEND C:\DOS
C:\DOS\GRAPHICS
VER
PRINT /D:LPT1

C>type config.sys
BREAK=ON
BUFFERS=20
FILES=20
LASTDRIVE=E
SHELL=C:\DOS\COMMAND.COM /P /E:256
DEVICE=C:\DOS\ANSI.SYS
INSTALL=C:\DOS\FASTOPEN.EXE C:=(50,25)

C>_
```

Before you can print a file, your printer must be turned on. Make sure that the power is on and that the printer is on-line, that is, connected to your computer.

Step 3: Execute the PRINT Command

To use the PRINT command, type PRINT followed by the name of the file you want to print. Print the AUTOEXEC.BAT file by executing this command:

Type **print autoexec.bat**
Press **Enter**

DOS may ask you to supply the following (if it doesn't, don't worry):

Name of list device [PRN]:

This rather cryptic request allows you to tell DOS which printer to use if you have more than one connected to your computer. The expression [PRN] means that unless you tell it otherwise, DOS will send the output to the default printer, which has the device name PRN. If you have only one printer, then it is the default printer. All you have to do is press the Enter key.

Press **Enter**

DOS will ask you to supply the list device only the first time you use PRINT for any given computer session. After you do so, DOS will tell you the file is currently being printed.

To print the CONFIG.SYS file, execute this command:

Type **print config.sys**
Press **Enter**

DOS will tell you the file is currently being printed and will present the DOS prompt again (see Figure 26). From the printer you will get copies of the AUTOEXEC.BAT and CONFIG.SYS files, each on their own page.

Figure 26 Printing Text Files

```
C>print autoexec.bat

  C:\AUTOEXEC.BAT is currently being printed
C>print config.sys

  C:\CONFIG.SYS is currently being printed

C>_
```

Practice

1. You can use TYPE to display nontext files, although what you see on the screen won't make much sense. For example, execute this command and see what happens:

   Type   **type command.com**
   Press   **Enter**

2. Get a directory listing of your DOS subdirectory or Startup disk and examine it for any files with the extension BAT or TXT. If you are running MS-DOS 4.01, for example, the files DOSSHELL.BAT and README.TXT may be in your DOS subdirectory. Examine the contents of these files, or any others from the DOS subdirectory or Startup disk, with the TYPE command. You can preface the file name with the disk drive or subdirectory specification. For example, execute this command to view the README.TXT file from the DOS subdirectory:

   Type   **type dos\readme.txt**
   Press   **Enter**

3. Use the PRINT command to get a hard copy of the files you just examined.

Lesson 16: Running a Program

This lesson won't really teach you anything new, because you've been running programs throughout this chapter. Every time you used an external DOS command, you were running a program. Remember: files with an EXE or COM extension are stand-alone, executable programs that you can run.

Step 1: Switch to the Appropriate Disk

First, you must make sure a program you want to run is stored on a disk in one of your drives when you want to run the program. For example, to run an application program such as WordPerfect, Lotus 1-2-3, or dBASE IV, you must

Real World

Microsoft Branches Out

Microsoft Corp., one of the patriarchs of the software industry, believes there's strength in numbers.

The Redmond, Washington-based company could have sat back and watched profits roll in from its highly successful MS-DOS operating system software, but founder Bill Gates decided the company needed more than one star product.

After developing PC-DOS and OS/2 in conjunction with IBM, Microsoft moved into the UNIX field by buying a stake in The Santa Cruz Operation, Inc. and working to bring graphical applications to the UNIX environment.

Microsoft has been heavily involved in applications software for the Macintosh, as well. Gates saw

something in the Macintosh long before other software developers did. The result was that Microsoft became the number one software company for Macintosh products. It has three Macintosh best sellers: Excel, a spreadsheet package; Word, a word processor; and Works, an integrated software package.

Microsoft is also pushing its Windows operating environment, which has been described as a "halfway house for DOS users not ready to move to OS/2." Windows uses the experience that Microsoft's programmers gained from working with the Macintosh.

But the road has not been completely smooth for Microsoft. Apple sued Microsoft in 1988 over simi-

larities between Windows and the Macintosh operating system. The court case could drag on for years.

Delayed shipping is another bump in Gate's road. Both Microsoft Word 4.0 for the Macintosh and Microsoft Word 5.0 for DOS were not shipped when promised. The glitches haven't hurt Microsoft's profits, however. In 1988, they jumped almost 63 percent, to $151 million. Diversity apparently pays well.

Source: "New Conquests for the MS-DOS Master," *Datamation*, June 15, 1989, p. 131.

have it installed in a subdirectory on your hard disk or have it on a diskette in a floppy drive. If your computer is connected to a local area network, you could run the program if it's stored on your network's file server disk. DOS must be able to find a program before it can run it. You may have to change your default drive to the one containing the program to be run. An alternative is to preface the program name with the disk drive letter.

Step 2: Switch to the Appropriate Subdirectory

Some programs stored in a subdirectory may need to be run from inside that subdirectory. You will learn how to switch subdirectories in the next chapter. An alternative to switching subdirectories is to preface the program name you enter with the drive and subdirectory in which the program's file is stored.

Step 3: Type the Program Name and Press the Enter Key

As you now know, you invoke an external DOS command by entering its name along with any necessary file names and other information. In this sense, application programs such as WordPerfect, Lotus 1-2-3, and dBASE IV are the same as DOS external commands; all you have to do to run them is type the name of the EXE or COM file in which they're stored and press the Enter key. So, for example, to run WordPerfect from your default drive, you would execute this command (don't do it now):

Type   **wp**
Press   **Enter**

When you do this, DOS will load the WordPerfect program into primary memory and begin executing it.

Practice   Running an application package is just like running a DOS external command such as CHKDSK. You can run a program from a disk other than the one in your default drive. For example, copy the CHKDSK.COM file from your DOS subdirectory to a formatted diskette in drive A. With the hard disk as your default drive, execute this command:

Type   **a:chkdsk**
Press   **Enter**

Summary

- *Starting up DOS with the computer turned off.* Insert the DOS Startup diskette in drive A if the computer has no hard disk and then turn the computer on.

- *Starting up DOS with the computer turned on.* Press Ctrl-Alt-Del.

- *Obtaining a directory of the files on a disk.* Use the DIR command.

- *Using the special DOS keys.* Press Escape to cancel a line. Press Ctrl-Num Lock or Pause to interrupt screen scrolling. Press Ctrl-Break to cancel a command. Press Shift-PrtSc to print the screen. Press Ctrl-PrtSc to echo to the printer.

- *Changing the default disk drive.* Enter the new drive letter followed by a colon.

- *Obtaining a disk and memory status report.* Use the CHKDSK command.

- *Clearing the display screen.* Use the CLS command.

- *Formatting a diskette.* Use the FORMAT command.

- *Formatting a system diskette.* Use the FORMAT command with the /S parameter.

- *Copying files.* Use the COPY command.

- *Copying an entire diskette.* Use the DISKCOPY command.

- *Changing file names.* Use the RENAME (REN) command.

- *Erasing files.* Use the ERASE (DEL) command.

- *Protecting a diskette from accidental erasure.* Cover the notch with a gummed tab or piece of tape on a 5¼-inch disk. Slide open the write-protect switch on a 3½-inch diskette.

- *Displaying and printing text files.* Use the TYPE command to display text files on the screen and the PRINT command to send them to the printer.

- *Running an application package.* Switch to the proper disk drive and subdirectory, if necessary, and then enter the name of the program.

Key Terms

As an extra review of this chapter, try defining the following terms.

allocation unit

booting up

copy-protection

default drive

Disk Operating System (DOS)

DOS prompt

extension

external command (transient routine)

filename

global file name character

hidden file

internal command (resident routine)

parameter

sector

source

subdirectory

switching drives

target

text file

upwardly compatible

write-protect notch

write-protect switch

write-protection

Multiple Choice

Choose the best selection to complete each statement.

1. An operating system is a(n)
   - (a) hardware component of a mainframe computer system.
   - (b) application program that produces text files.
   - (c) set of programs that lets you use your computer's hardware and software resources.
   - (d) system of procedures for operating a computer.

2. Transient routines or external commands are
   - (a) kept in primary memory until the computer is shut off.
   - (b) kept on disk and loaded into memory only when needed.
   - (c) kept in ROM (read-only memory) chips.
   - (d) used once then deleted.

3. The driving force behind each new DOS release has usually been
   - (a) the addition of a new disk drive capability.
   - (b) an effort to improve the user interface.
   - (c) an attempt to eliminate all bugs.
   - (d) an effort by IBM and Microsoft to make more money.

4. Upwardly compatible means that
   - (a) you cannot take advantage of the new version's abilities.
   - (b) all old software versions must be upgraded.
   - (c) new hardware must be purchased to use the new version.
   - (d) operations that worked with former versions work with the new version.

5. A command is a(n)
   - (a) combination of hardware switch settings.
   - (b) operating system directive issued to a user.
   - (c) application package instruction.
   - (d) word or abbreviation that tells DOS to run a program.

6. To boot DOS with the power off

   (a) insert the DOS Startup disk (if necessary) and turn on the power.

   (b) hold down the Control, Alternate, and Delete keys at the same time.

   (c) turn the power on and issue the boot command.

   (d) turn the power on and kick the computer.

7. Pressing Ctrl-Alt-Del will

   (a) invoke a DOS transient routine.

   (b) delete a file.

   (c) reboot DOS without having to shut off the computer.

   (d) execute an application program.

8. The DOS directory command is

   (a) DIRECT.

   (b) LIST.

   (c) DIR.

   (d) CATALOG.

9. The two parts of a DOS file name are

   (a) a disk drive designation and a disk sector number.

   —(b) a primary filename and an optional extension.

   (c) a primary filename and a creation date.

   (d) a primary extension and the size in bytes.

10. Files with COM and EXE extensions usually designate

    —(a) external commands and executable program files.

    (b) command files and extension files.

    (c) configuration files and batch files.

    (d) BASIC and FORTRAN files.

11. Pressing Ctrl-Num Lock or Pause will

    (a) echo input and output to the printer.

    (b) print the screen.

    (c) cancel a command.

    —(d) temporarily halt screen scrolling.

12. To change the default disk drive

    (a) put a new disk in drive A.

    —(b) type the new disk drive designation and press Enter.

    (c) open up the computer and replace the faulty drive.

    (d) issue the DIR command.

13. To display a disk and memory status report, use

    (a) STATUS.

    (b) DIR.

    —(c) CHKDSK.

    (d) DISKCOPY.

14. Formatting a diskette does not do the following:

    (a) check the diskette for bad sectors.

    (b) wipe out all data on the diskette.

    (c) mark off the space into sectors.

    —(d) sort files in the directory.

15. To format a system diskette you must

    (a) reboot the system.

    —(b) use the /S parameter with the FORMAT command.

    (c) enter the COPY command.

    (d) purchase a master diskette from IBM.

16. Which command would you use to copy every file from disk drive A to B?

   (a) COPY A:*.* B: (b) DIR A: B:

   ⟶(c) COPY A: B: (d) REN

17. To make an exact copy of an entire diskette, use

   (a) COPY.   ⟵(b) DISKCOPY.

   (c) DIR.   (d) Ctrl-Alt-Del.

18. Entering the command DEL *.* will

   (a) reboot the system.   (b) copy all files to the disk in the
                                     default drive.

   (c) rename all files on the disk in   ⟵(d) erase all files from the disk in the
       the default drive.   default drive.

19. To display a text file on your screen, use the

   (a) PRINT command.   (b) DISKCOPY command.

   ⟵(c) TYPE command.   (d) Ctrl-Num Lock key.

20. To run a program you must

   ⟵(a) type its filename and press the   (b) reboot DOS.
       Enter key.

   (c) press Ctrl-Break.   (d) first make a backup copy.

Fill-In

1. A disk operating system has many utilities for dealing with the _____ that are stored on disks.

2. _____ is usually used with IBM computers while _____ is usually used with compatible computers such as those made by Compaq, Tandy, and Zenith.

3. Booting DOS refers to the process of loading the disk operating system into _____.

4. In some cases, when you first boot DOS it asks you to enter the _____ and the _____.

5. The _____ command can be used to list the names, sizes, and creation dates and times of all the files on a disk.

6. A file's primary filename can have from one to _____ characters in it.

7. File name extensions are often used to _____ files.

8. You can press the _____ key to cancel a command if you haven't pressed the Enter key yet.

9. You can press _____ to cancel a command before it finishes executing.

10. The DOS _____ indicates the current default disk drive.

11. The _____ command can tell you how much memory is installed in your computer.

12. A diskette must be _____ before it can be used to store program and data files.

13. The _____ command can be used to duplicate one or more files on the same or on different disks.

14. _____ file name characters can be used to refer to several files at the same time.

15. The DISKCOPY command will automatically _____ the target diskette if it's brand new.

16. The REN command can be used to _____ one or more file names.

17. To remove a file from a disk, you would enter _____ or _____ followed by the file's name.

18. The TYPE command lets you display _____ files on your screen.

19. You could use the _____ command to produce a hard copy of a text file.

20. To run a program, you must type its _____ and then press _____.

Short Problems

1. If you have access to a diskette other than DOS Startup, produce a directory listing of the files on it. If you have a printer, try using Ctrl-PrtSc to turn on printer echoing before you issue the directory command so that you can get a hard copy.

2. When you booted DOS, you may have been asked to supply the date and time. Two DOS commands, DATE and TIME, tell you the current date and time and let you change these settings. Try the DATE and TIME commands. If you don't want to change the date and time settings, just press the Enter key when asked for the new date or time. Notice how DOS automatically figures out and displays the day of the week.

3. Use the * global file name character to produce a directory listing of all the files in the DOS subdirectory or on the DOS Startup disk with an EXE extension.

4. Use the * global file name character to produce a directory listing of all the files in the DOS subdirectory or on the DOS Startup disk whose names begin with the letter K.

5. Use the ? global file name character to produce a directory listing of all the files in the DOS subdirectory or on the DOS Startup disk that have an *E* as the second letter of their primary filename.

6. DOS versions 3.0 and newer have a command that lets you supply or change a volume label without having to reformat a disk. If you have DOS 3.0 or newer try using the LABEL command on a diskette that you have formatted for a lesson in this chapter.

7. If you don't know what DOS version you have, enter **ver**. This command displays the number of the DOS version you are using.

8. Another way to find out the volume label of a disk is to use the VOL command. Enter **vol**. This command displays the volume label (if there is one) of the default disk.

9. It is possible to display a text file on your screen by using the COPY command instead of the TYPE command. In certain cases, DOS can refer to its peripheral devices as if they were files. There are several file names that have a special meaning to DOS. These are called DOS device names. For example, CON refers to the console, or the keyboard and screen. If your disk has a file named AUTOEXEC.BAT on it, execute this command:

    Type   **copy autoexec.bat con**
    Press   **Enter**

You should see the text of file AUTOEXEC.BAT displayed on your screen just as if you used the TYPE command.

10. Just as CON is a DOS device name that refers to the keyboard and screen, PRN is a DOS device name that refers to the printer. Try using the COPY command to get a printout of the AUTOEXEC.BAT file.

11. The DIR command has two optional parameters that can be useful when looking at disks with lots of files on them. The /P parameter will automatically pause the display when the screen is full and let you press a key to continue. The /W parameter will display the directory in a wide format across the screen, omitting the sizes and creation dates and times so that more file names will fit at once. Obtain a directory listing of the DOS subdirectory or DOS Startup disk using these options:

> Type   **dir /p**
> Press   **Enter**
> Type   **dir /w**
> Press   **Enter**

INTERMEDIATE DOS

In This Chapter

Preview

In the previous chapter you learned the basics of DOS, the operating system used on millions of IBM and IBM-compatible microcomputers. This chapter continues your exploration of DOS with slightly more advanced topics.

After studying this chapter, you will know how to

- use the DOS editing and function keys.
- set the BREAK option.
- work with subdirectories.
- use the PATH and APPEND commands.
- change the DOS prompt.
- back up and restore disks and files.
- recover files from damaged disks.
- use the prompt option when erasing files.
- append files and copy files to devices.
- set the VERIFY option.
- change file attributes.
- copy groups of files.
- update sets of files.
- transfer the DOS system files.
- compare files and disks.
- change volume labels.
- change the current date and time.
- display a memory report.
- reassign, join, and substitute drives.
- print multiple files.

Getting Started

You've already learned how to start DOS and use its most common features and commands. This chapter assumes you have completed all of the lessons and exercises in the Beginning DOS chapter. Furthermore, it assumes that you have a computer with a hard disk and DOS 3.30, 4.00, or 4.01 installed on it in a subdirectory named DOS. All of the screens in the following lessons were created with MS-DOS 4.01. To work the following lessons, boot up or reboot your computer if you have not already done so.

Lesson 1: Using the DOS Editing and Function Keys

As you learned in the previous chapter, DOS assigns special meanings to certain keys. By now you should know how to use Enter, Ctrl-Alt-Del, Escape, Ctrl-Num Lock (or Pause), Ctrl-Break, Shift-PrtSc (or Print Screen), and Ctrl-PrtSc. In addition, DOS has other key presses that can help you enter commands and save time. These are known as the DOS editing and function keys.

Step 1: Retrieve the Previous Command

Every time you enter a command, DOS saves what you have typed in a special area of memory. You can retrieve the previous command by pressing the F3 function key. For example, follow these instructions:

Type   **dir**
Press   **Enter**
Press   **F3**

When the directory command is finished, DOS will copy the previous command, which was DIR, to your screen at the cursor location, as if you had typed it again.

Press   **Enter**

DOS will execute the DIR command again. The F3 command is especially convenient for repeating the same command several times in a row, or for repeating an especially long command.

Step 2: Edit the Command Line

When you press F3, DOS only copies the previous command to the command line. You still have to press Enter to actually execute the command. You can, however, alter the command line if you like. For example:

Press   **F3**
Press   **Space Bar**
Type   **c:**
Press   **Enter**

This sequence of actions will retrieve the previous command, which was DIR, and add the disk drive specification C: onto the end. Once the previous command is retrieved, you can also use the Backspace or Left Arrow key to delete characters to the left of the cursor.

Step 3: Copy the Next Character from the Previous Command

Pressing F3 retrieves all of the previous command and presents it on your screen. You can also retrieve one character at a time from the previous command by pressing the F1 key. For example:

Press   **F1** (3 times)
Press   **Enter**

This sequence of commands will retrieve and then execute only the first three characters (DIR) of the previous command. The F1 key allows you to retrieve some of the previous command or make modifications to it.

Step 4: Retrieve Some of the Previous Command

Put a formatted diskette in drive A if it does not already contain one. Execute this command:

Type   **dir a:**
Press   **Enter**

Suppose you now want to examine disk drive C or B.

Press   **F2**
Type   **a**

This tells DOS to retrieve the previous command, but only up to the *a* character you've specified. So, now you can type a different end to the command:

Type   **c:**
Press   **Enter**

Step 5: Examine the Other Editing Keys

The editing and function keys we have discussed are probably the most frequently used. A few other keys, however, are available. The following table lists all of the DOS editing keys.

Key	Action
F1	Retypes one character at a time from the previous command.
F2	Retypes all characters up to the next character you type from the previous command.
F3	Retypes all of the previous command.
F4	Deletes all the characters from the previous command up to the next character you type.
F5	Saves the contents of your current command line as if it were the previous command.
F6	Inserts an end-of-file code (Ctrl-Z).
Delete	Skips over a character from the previous command.
Insert	Switches insert/overwrite mode in the command line.
Escape	Cancels the current line.

Practice

1. Try the F4 function key.

   Type   **garbage dir**
   Press   **Enter**

   Don't worry about the error message. To throw out the garbage, and execute the remaining DIR command, do this:

   Press   **F4**
   Type   **d**
   Press   **F3**
   Press   **Enter**

2. Try the F5 function key. Suppose you are typing a long command and realize you have made an error. You have not yet pressed the Enter key. For example, do this (but don't press Enter):

   Type   **ytpe autoexec.bat**
   Press   **F5**

   Pressing F5 will save what you have typed as if it were the previous command. Now, follow these instructions to correct your error, retrieve the rest of the command, and execute the correct TYPE command:

   Type   **ty**
   Press   **F3**
   Press   **Enter**

3. Try the Del editing key.

   Type   **xxdir**
   Press   **Enter**

Suppose you meant to type *dir.* To fix your mistake, do this:

Press **Del** (2 times)
Press **F3**
Press **Enter**

4. Try the Ins editing key.

Type **dir os**
Press **Enter**

Suppose you meant to type *dir dos.* To fix your mistake, follow these instructions:

Press **F1** (4 times)
Press **Ins**
Type **d**
Press **F3**
Press **Enter**

Lesson 2: Setting the BREAK Option

In the previous chapter you learned that you can press Ctrl-Break to cancel a program that is running. Normally, Ctrl-Break works only when DOS is checking the keyboard or sending characters to the screen or printer. You can also tell DOS to check whether Ctrl-Break has been pressed during disk reads and writes.

Step 1: Execute the BREAK Command

The BREAK command allows you to check or change the status of the BREAK option, which controls when Ctrl-Break will cancel a program. To see the current setting of the BREAK option, execute this command:

Type **break**
Press **Enter**

DOS will tell you whether BREAK is on or off.

Step 2: Change the BREAK Option

You can change the current setting of BREAK by entering the BREAK command followed by ON or OFF. For example, if BREAK is OFF, turn it on with this command:

Type **break on**
Press **Enter**

Now check what you have done:

Type **break**
Press **Enter**

Your screen should look like Figure 1.

Practice   Switch the BREAK option back to the way it was before you changed it.

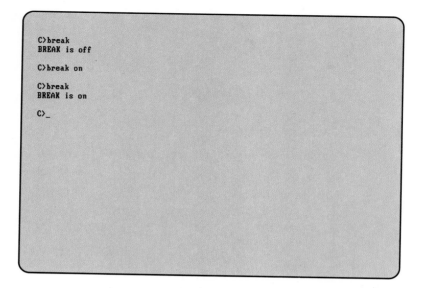

Figure 1 Setting the BREAK Option

```
C>break
BREAK is off

C>break on

C>break
BREAK is on

C>_
```

Lesson 3: Working with Subdirectories

As you can imagine, people who use microcomputers extensively often generate large numbers of files. Before hard disks became common, users stored their files in many different floppy disks. Organizing files meant physically organizing diskettes by keeping them well-labeled and storing them in subdivided boxes, racks, or cabinets. Once hard disks became common, however, operating systems had to devise a better method of organizing large numbers of files. Even a modest 20-megabyte hard disk can store thousands of different files. Looking for a particular file among hundreds or thousands of files is time consuming and tedious. Consequently, most microcomputer operating systems, including DOS, have evolved a **hierarchical** method of organizing files into groups. A hierarchical system allows you to cluster files into orders or ranks, each subordinate to the one above. These groups of files, called subdirectories, are like file folders that can be nested within one another. Disks can be organized into subdirectories, each of which can contain files and other subdirectories.

Subdirectories are an invaluable tool for organizing programs and data files on high-capacity storage devices. In addition, subdirectories make it easier for the operating system to locate a particular file, because large numbers of files are divided into smaller groups. Although subdirectories are most often, indeed almost always, found on hard disks, they are occasionally used on floppy disks, too. DOS includes commands that let you create, access, and remove subdirectories.

With DOS, every disk has a single main directory, known as the **root directory.** DOS automatically creates a root directory on every disk you format. This is the directory you are in when you first boot up DOS or when you first change your default drive. The root directory itself has no name, but it's represented by a backslash (\).

Step 1: Create a Subdirectory

The internal DOS command MD or MKDIR (short for "make directory") is used to create a new subdirectory. It is followed by the **path** of the new subdirectory. A path is an optional disk drive specifier followed by a list of subdirectory names, separated by backslashes. The rules for naming subdirectories are the same as the rules for naming files. The simplest path is a single backslash \, which represents the root directory of your current default drive. Let's create a new subdirectory on your hard disk. Execute this command:

> Type **md c:\myfiles**
> Press **Enter**

The command you just entered creates a subdirectory named MYFILES on the hard disk C. This subdirectory is one level below the root directory. To see the result, execute this command:

> Type **dir**
> Press **Enter**

You should see MYFILES followed by the <DIR> designation in the directory listing as shown in Figure 2.

Step 2: Change to the Subdirectory

Think of the subdirectory as a separate "sub-disk" on your disk. You use the change directory (CD or CHDIR) command, which is an internal command, to move into your new subdirectory. Execute these commands:

> Type **cd c:\myfiles**
> Press **Enter**
> Type **dir**
> Press **Enter**

Your screen should look like Figure 3, showing the directory listing inside the MYFILES subdirectory.

Figure 2 Using MD to Create the MYFILES Subdirectory

```
C>md c:\myfiles

C>dir

 Volume in drive C is HARD DISK
 Volume Serial Number is 3324-07CC
 Directory of  C:\

CONFIG   SYS      146 07-09-89   1:22p
MYFILES       <DIR>     07-12-89   2:10p
COMMAND  COM    37557 12-19-88  12:00a
DOS           <DIR>     07-09-89   1:23p
AUTOEXEC BAT      256 01-01-80   5:52a
        5 File(s)   19699712 bytes free

C>_
```

*Figure 3 Using DIR Inside
the MYFILES Subdirectory*

```
C>cd c:\myfiles

C>dir

 Volume in drive C is HARD DISK
 Volume Serial Number is 3324-07CC
 Directory of  C:\MYFILES

 .            <DIR>     07-12-89   2:10p
 ..           <DIR>     07-12-89   2:10p
        2 File(s)   19699712 bytes free

C>_
```

Step 3: Copy a File to the Subdirectory

Right now, the MYFILES subdirectory has no ordinary user files in it. You can, however, copy files into this subdirectory just as if it were a separate disk. For example, let's copy the AUTOEXEC.BAT file from the root directory into the MYFILES subdirectory. Execute this command:

> Type   **copy c:\autoexec.bat**
> Press **Enter**

This command copies the file AUTOEXEC.BAT from the root directory of the hard disk C into your current subdirectory, which happens to be MYFILES. Execute this command to see the contents of your subdirectory:

> Type   **dir**
> Press **Enter**

A copy of AUTOEXEC.BAT now also exists in the MYFILES subdirectory. It's important to realize that there are two separate copies of AUTOEXEC.BAT now on the disk: one in the root directory and one in the MYFILES subdirectory.

Step 4: Display the Directory Structure

A hard disk can hold a great many subdirectories and files. DIR will list the subdirectories and files of only one directory at a time; it cannot show the structure beneath that level. TREE, an external DOS command, can list all of the subdirectories on a disk. It can also list all of the files in each subdirectory. With DOS versions 4.00 and newer, TREE depicts the structure of the disk graphically. Older DOS versions simply list the paths and subdirectories. Execute this command to get a TREE listing of the root directory of your hard disk:

> Type   **tree c:**
> Press **Enter**

Figure 4 shows the result. You can also tell the TREE command to list all files in all directories by using the /F parameter. Execute this command to see how it works:

Type   **tree c: \ /f**
Press   **Enter**

Step 5: Remove the Subdirectory

Once you are in a subdirectory, you can almost think of it as a separate disk. You can run programs from within a subdirectory. Many DOS commands that deal with files will operate only on the files in your current subdirectory unless you specify otherwise. For example, you can delete every file in a subdirectory without affecting any of the files in the root directory or any other subdirectory. For example, make sure you are in the MYFILES subdirectory and then execute these commands:

Type   **erase *.***
Press   **Enter**
Type   **y**
Press   **Enter**
Type   **dir**
Press   **Enter**

DOS will erase every file in your current directory, the MYFILES subdirectory. The DIR command should reveal that this is true. Now change back to the root directory and check its contents by executing these commands:

Type   **cd c: **
Press   **Enter**
Type   **dir**
Press   **Enter**

As you can see, the AUTOEXEC.BAT file in the root directory is still intact.

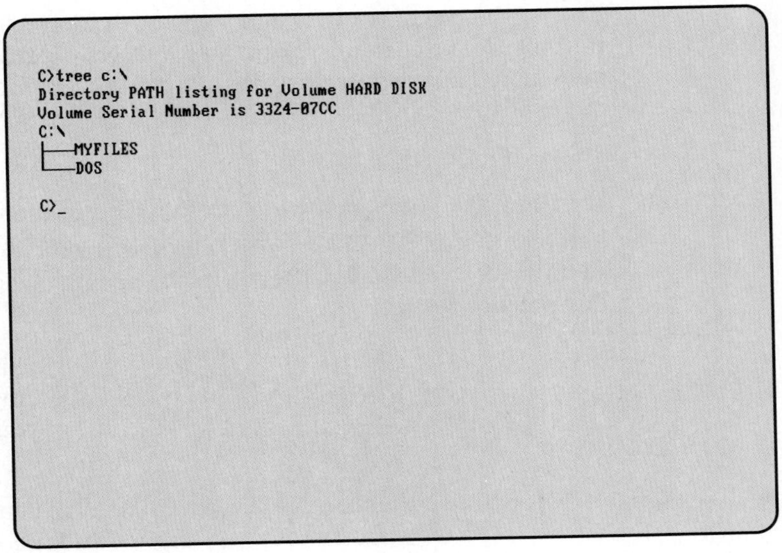

Figure 4 Using TREE to Display the Directory Structure

```
C>tree c:\
Directory PATH listing for Volume HARD DISK
Volume Serial Number is 3324-07CC
C:\
├──MYFILES
└──DOS

C>_
```

Just as you must occasionally delete unneeded files, sometimes you must remove subdirectories too. Suppose that you are finished with the MYFILES subdirectory and you want to remove it from your disk. To do this you must first erase any files inside the subdirectory and move out of the subdirectory. You have already done this. Now execute the remove directory command (RD or RMDIR) to remove the empty MYFILES subdirectory from your disk:

Type   **rd c:\myfiles**
Press   **Enter**
Type   **dir**
Press   **Enter**

You will see that the MYFILES subdirectory has indeed been removed, and your disk is the same as it was when you began this lesson. Like MD and CD, RD is an internal DOS command.

Practice

1. Create a new subdirectory on your disk and name it after yourself (eight characters or less). Change to your new subdirectory. Now create three additional subdirectories inside your new subdirectory and name them ONE, TWO, and THREE. Change to the ONE subdirectory and copy the AUTOEXEC.BAT file from the root, or some other file from the DOS subdirectory into the ONE subdirectory.

2. Use the DIR command to examine the contents of your ONE subdirectory. Notice the first two entries in the directory listing. The . (single period) is a special DOS designation that symbolizes your current directory. The .. (double period) symbolizes the directory above your current directory. For example:

Type   **dir .**
Press   **Enter**

See what happens. Now try this command:

Type   **dir ..**
Press   **Enter**

You will get a listing of the directory above ONE.

3. DOS pros often use the . and .. designations as shortcuts. The . is equivalent to *.*. Use it to erase all the files in your current subdirectory, which should be ONE. Now, change back to the subdirectory above ONE, the subdirectory you named after yourself:

Type   **cd ..**
Press   **Enter**

Try using the .. designation again to return to the root directory.

4. Remove the ONE, TWO, and THREE subdirectories and then remove the subdirectory you named after yourself, leaving your disk the way it was before this practice session.

Lesson 4: Using the PATH and APPEND Commands

In many ways, a subdirectory is like a separate disk. Unless you give DOS special instructions, you can access the files within a subdirectory only when you have switched to that subdirectory with the CD command. In order to fully realize the benefits of DOS subdirectories, you must also understand the PATH and APPEND commands.

Step 1: Execute the PATH Command

By default, you cannot gain access to the programs or data files in a subdirectory unless you are in that subdirectory. Alternatively, you can precede the name of every command or data file with its full path. For example, if you want to use the CHKDSK command (which is an external command kept in the file CHKDSK.COM), and you are not in the DOS subdirectory on the hard disk C, you could enter the command this way:

Type   **c:\dos\chkdsk**
Press   **Enter**

Typing the disk drive and path before every command, however, can be tiresome. Fortunately, the PATH command can eliminate the need to do this.

Use the PATH command to tell DOS which subdirectories to search through if it cannot find a program or batch file you request in your current directory. (You will learn about batch files later in this chapter.) For example, in most cases you want the commands in the DOS subdirectory to be accessible no matter which disk or directory you are using. Usually, DOS is installed so that a PATH command granting access to the DOS subdirectory is executed every time the computer is booted up. As you will learn later in this chapter, this is typically done by putting a PATH command in the AUTOEXEC.BAT file.

Execute the following command to see the current command search path that has been set up for you:

Type   **path**
Press   **Enter**

You can also use the PATH command to change the command search path. For example, suppose you want programs and batch files in the root directory and the DOS subdirectory to be accessible from any disk or directory. To set this up, execute the following PATH command:

Type   **path c:\; c:\dos**
Press   **Enter**

The PATH command is followed by a list of paths you want DOS to search whenever it cannot find the command you have entered. The paths are separated by semicolons. This PATH command has two search paths, c:\, the root directory of the hard disk C, and c:\dos, the DOS subdirectory beneath the root directory on the hard disk C. To see what you have done, execute this command again:

Type   **path**
Press   **Enter**

Your screen should look like Figure 5.

You need only enter the PATH command once, unless you want to change the list of subdirectories. Consequently, it is usually placed in the AUTO-EXEC.BAT file to be executed every time you boot up your computer.

Step 2: Execute the APPEND Command

The PATH command works only for files with extensions of BAT, COM, or EXE. In other words, PATH will allow DOS to find only programs and batch files in other directories. Users of DOS 3.3 and newer versions, however, can use the APPEND command, which can find other types of files.

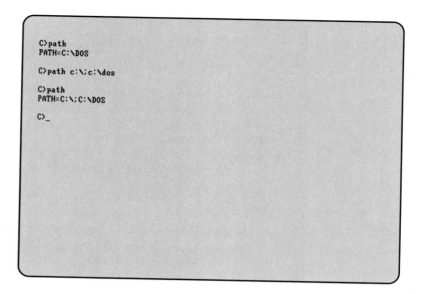

Figure 5 Using the PATH Command

```
C>path
PATH=C:\DOS

C>path c:\;c:\dos

C>path
PATH=C:\;C:\DOS

C>_
```

For example, create a subdirectory called LESSONS on your hard disk and change to it with these commands:

Type **md c:\lessons**
Press **Enter**
Type **cd c:\lessons**
Press **Enter**

Now, execute these commands to create a sample text file you can use:

Type **copy con sample.txt**
Press **Enter**
Type **This is a sample text file.**
Press **Enter**
Press **F6**
Press **Enter**

To see what you have created, execute this command:

Type **type sample.txt**
Press **Enter**

The text file you have just created should be presented on your screen. As you can see, it is accessible from within the LESSONS subdirectory. Now, move back to the root directory and try to type the file by executing these commands:

Type **cd c:**
Press **Enter**
Type **type sample.txt**
Press **Enter**

DOS should say "File not found," as shown in Figure 6, because you are at the root and the file SAMPLE.TXT is in the LESSONS subdirectory.

Now suppose that you want data files in the root directory, the DOS subdirectory, and the LESSONS subdirectory to be accessible from all other disks and directories. Like the PATH command, APPEND can be followed by a list of sub-

Figure 6 *SAMPLE.TXT Is Not Found in the Root Directory*

```
C>md c:\lessons

C>cd c:\lessons

C>copy con sample.txt
This is a sample text file.
^Z
        1 File(s) copied

C>type sample.txt
This is a sample text file.

C>cd c:\

C>type sample.txt
File not found - SAMPLE.TXT

C>_
```

directories separated by semicolons. Execute the following APPEND command:

Type   **append c:\;c:\dos;c:\lessons**
Press **Enter**

This command tells DOS the directories you want to search for files that have extensions other than BAT, COM, and EXE. Now try this command again:

Type   **type sample.txt**
Press **Enter**

The file should be displayed on your screen, as shown in Figure 7. DOS was able to find SAMPLE.TXT because the APPEND command you entered told it where to search.

Like PATH, the APPEND command is usually put in the AUTOEXEC.BAT file to set up the search paths for data files every time the computer is turned on.

Practice   1. You can also use the APPEND command to see the current search path for data files.

Type   **append**
Press **Enter**

If you enter this command without a list of subdirectories, DOS will display the search paths, if any, that have been established by the most recent APPEND command on your computer.

2. Use the TYPE command to examine the AUTOEXEC.BAT file in the root directory of your disk. Does it contain a PATH and APPEND statement?

Lesson 5: Changing the DOS Prompt

By default, the DOS prompt consists of the current drive letter followed by a > (greater than sign). For example, if hard disk C is your current drive, then the default DOS prompt is

C>

*Figure 7 APPEND Enables
DOS to Find SAMPLE.TXT*

```
C>md c:\lessons

C>cd c:\lessons

C>copy con sample.txt
This is a sample text file.
^Z
        1 File(s) copied

C>type sample.txt
This is a sample text file.

C>cd c:\

C>type sample.txt
File not found - SAMPLE.TXT

C>append c:\;c:\dos;c:\lessons

C>type sample.txt
This is a sample text file.

C>_
```

You can, however, change the appearance of the DOS prompt with the PROMPT command.

Step 1: Change the Prompt to a Text String

Suppose you want your DOS prompt to be Hello> instead of A> or C>. Execute this command:

Type **prompt Hello$g**
Press **Enter**

As soon as you enter this command, the DOS prompt will be changed to Hello>. The $g in the command is a special code that stands for the > (greater than sign).

Step 2: Change the Prompt to Show the Disk and Directory

You can probably think of any number of cute prompts such as Hello>. A more useful prompt would show your current disk drive and directory. This is especially handy if you frequently use subdirectories, because it's easy to forget your current path. To change your prompt to display your current path, execute this command:

Type **prompt pg**
Press **Enter**

If you are at the root directory of your hard disk, the prompt will immediately change to C:\>. Now change to your LESSONS subdirectory by executing this command:

Type **cd \lessons**
Press **Enter**

Your DOS prompt should now be C:\LESSONS>.

Step 3: Explore the Other Prompt Options

The PROMPT command allows several options besides $g and $p. The following table lists all of the special codes you can use with the PROMPT command. These codes can be combined and mixed with text to create an unlimited number of prompts.

Prompt Code	Action
$q	Presents the = (equal sign) character.
$$	Presents the $ (dollar sign) character.
$t	Presents the current time of day.
$d	Presents today's date.
$p	Presents the current path.
$v	Presents the version of DOS being used.
$n	Presents the current drive letter.
$g	Presents the > (greater than sign) character.
$l	Presents the < (less than sign) character.
$b	Presents the | (vertical bar) character.
$_	Starts a new line.
$e	Presents a left arrow symbol.
$h	Performs a Backspace.

Practice Try as many of the prompt options in the preceding table as you like. When you are finished experimenting, execute the following command to change the DOS prompt to the current disk drive and directory:

Type **prompt pg**
Press **Enter**

Lesson 6: Backing Up and Restoring Disks and Files

Floppy disks and hard disks, though quite reliable, are not infallible. Eventually, every disk or disk drive will fail. In addition, almost every computer user mistakenly erases important programs or data on occasion. It is essential, therefore, to keep backup copies of all files that may be difficult, if not impossible, to replace. DOS includes two external commands, BACKUP and RESTORE, that help you keep extra copies of your software and data files.

Step 1: Back Up the Entire Hard Disk

Although the DOS BACKUP command can be used to make extra copies of floppy disks on other floppy disks, it is most often used to back up all or part of a hard disk onto floppy disks. BACKUP is better than using the COPY command to back up a hard disk, because most hard disks contain too many files to fit on a single floppy disk. Unlike COPY, the BACKUP command will automatically use as many diskettes as needed to save the files from a hard disk. The BACKUP command will fill each diskette as much as possible, even if it means splitting a single file between two disks. Then, BACKUP will prompt you to insert additional floppy disks until it copies all of the files. Furthermore, the BACKUP command of DOS versions 3.3 or newer will even format the backup floppy disks if necessary.

Suppose you want to make a backup copy of your entire hard disk. Assume that you have never backed up your hard disk before. First, you would switch back to the root directory and use DIR or CHKDSK to estimate how many floppy disks you will need. For example, if your hard disk contains 10 megabytes of files, you would need 29 or 30 360K floppy disks. Don't do this on your computer (it might require too many diskettes and take too long), but here is the command you would enter:

backup c: a: /s

This command tells DOS to back up the C drive onto the floppy disks that you will put into drive A. The /S parameter tells DOS to back up all the subdirectories as well. If you are using DOS 4.00 or newer, the BACKUP command can automatically format new diskettes if necessary. If you are using DOS 3.3, you should tell the BACKUP command to format new diskettes (if yours are not already formatted) by including the /F parameter after the /S parameter. Finally, if you are using a DOS version previous to 3.3, you have to format all of your backup diskettes *before* you execute the BACKUP command.

The BACKUP command will then beep and present the message shown in Figure 8. It is up to you to make sure that the floppy disks you use for the backup do not contain any files you need. You would insert the first diskette into drive A, close the door, and press any key. DOS will then list the files as it copies them to the first diskette. When no more room is left on the diskette, DOS will beep and prompt you to enter the second diskette. This will continue until all the files are backed up. As DOS fills the diskettes, you should label them consecutively as backup disk 1, backup disk 2, and so on.

Step 2: Do an Incremental Backup

If you make it a practice of backing up your hard disk at regular intervals, say every day or week, there is no need to copy those files that have not changed. You do, however, want to make sure that you back up any new or modified files.

Figure 8 Using the BACKUP Command

```
C:\>backup c: a: /s

Insert backup diskette 01 in drive A:

WARNING! Files in the target drive
A:\ root directory will be erased
Press any key to continue . . .
```

This is known as an **incremental backup.** Fortunately, you can tell DOS to do an incremental backup with two additional parameters to the BACKUP command. The /M parameter tells the BACKUP command to copy only new or changed files. The /A parameter tells the BACKUP command to add the selected files to the existing backup diskettes and not erase their contents. So, this would be the command you enter to do an incremental backup (don't do it now):

backup c: a: /s/m/a

DOS would then tell you to insert the last backup diskette into drive A and press any key when you are ready. Any new or changed files would then be added to this diskette, and additional diskettes, if needed.

In addition to /S, /M, /A, and /F (for DOS 3.3), the BACKUP command also accepts the following parameters:

/D:*date*   Backs up only those files that were created or modified on or after the specified *date.*

/T:*time*   Backs up only those files that were created or modified at or after the specified *time.*

/L:*file*   Creates a backup log in the specified *file.*

Step 3: Restore the Backed Up Disk

Hopefully, you'll never have to use the backup diskettes of your hard disk. Suppose the worst has happened, however, and you must copy the files from your backup diskettes back onto your hard disk. This is done with the RESTORE command. First, you would make sure that you are at the root directory of the hard disk. Again, don't do this now, but the command to restore the entire hard disk would be:

restore a: /s

This command will restore the files from the backup diskettes in drive A to your current directory, which should be the root directory of the hard disk C. It will prompt you to insert the backup diskettes in the same order in which they were created. The /S parameter tells DOS to restore subdirectories as well.

Step 4: Back Up a Subdirectory

It is also possible to use the BACKUP command to save a copy of a single subdirectory. This is often done when the contents of a hard disk subdirectory will not fit on a single floppy disk. Although your LESSONS subdirectory is very small, let's create a backup of it to illustrate the procedure. Get a formatted floppy disk that is either empty or contains files that can be erased. Then execute this command:

Type   **backup c:\lessons a: /s**
Press **Enter**

Insert the floppy disk into drive A and press any key. DOS will back up the contents of the LESSONS subdirectory onto the diskette in drive A. Your screen should look like Figure 9.

*Figure 9 Backing Up the
LESSONS Subdirectory*

```
C:\>backup c:\lessons a: /s

Insert backup diskette 01 in drive A:

WARNING! Files in the target drive
A:\ root directory will be erased
Press any key to continue . . .

*** Backing up files to drive A: ***
Diskette Number: 01

\LESSONS\SAMPLE.TXT

C:\>_
```

Step 5: Restore a Subdirectory

Suppose that you accidentally erased the contents of the LESSONS subdirectory. Simulate this accident by executing this command:

Type   **erase c:\lessons*.***
Press   **Enter**
Type   **y**
Press   **Enter**

Now, execute the following command to restore the LESSONS subdirectory from the backup diskette:

Type   **restore a: c:\lessons*.* /s**
Press   **Enter**

DOS will ask you to insert backup diskette 1 in drive A and press any key when you are ready. After you do this and the RESTORE command is finished, your screen should look like Figure 10.

In addition to /S, which ensures the restoration of subdirectories, the RESTORE command also accepts the following parameters:

/P	Prompts you for permission to restore files.
/B:*date*	Restores only those files that were last modified on or before the specified *date*.
/A:*date*	Restores only those files that were last modified on or after the specified *date*.
/E:*time*	Restores only those files that were last modified at or earlier than the specified *time*.
/L:*time*	Restores only those files that were last modified at or later than the specified *time*.
/M:*file*	Restores only those files modified since the last BACKUP.
/N	Restores only those files that no longer exist on the target disk.

*Figure 10 Restoring the
LESSONS Subdirectory*

```
C:\>restore a: c:\lessons\*.* /s

Insert backup diskette 01 in drive A:
Press any key to continue . . .

*** Files were backed up 07-13-1989 ***

*** Restoring files from drive A: ***
Diskette: 01
\LESSONS\SAMPLE.TXT


C:\>_
```

Step 6: Back Up and Restore One or More Files

BACKUP and RESTORE can also be used for individual files and groups of files specified with the DOS global file name characters ? and *. Simply insert the file specification instead of just the drive letter or subdirectory of the disk to be backed up. For example, suppose you wanted to back up only those files with an extension of TXT on your hard disk. Make sure you are at the root directory of hard disk C and execute this command:

> Type **backup c:*.txt a: /s**
> Press **Enter**

Insert your floppy disk into drive A and press **Enter** again. All TXT files in all subdirectories on disk C will be backed up to drive A. To restore the files, enter this command:

> Type **restore a: c:*.txt /s**
> Press **Enter**

Practice

1. If you have several blank diskettes you can use, backup the DOS subdirectory from your hard disk onto them. If you have only one diskette available, back up only one file or a group of files (such as *.SYS) that will fit on a single diskette.
2. Use the DIR command to examine the backup diskette you have created.

Lesson 7: Recovering Files from Damaged Disks

Every hard disk and floppy disk will eventually wear out or become physically damaged or magnetically corrupted in some way. When one of these unfortunate events occurs, DOS may not be able to read the files stored in or around the bad spots. This is one reason why you should try to maintain up-to-date backup copies of all of your important files and disks. If you don't do this, however, and DOS cannot read one of your files or perhaps even an entire disk, the RECOVER command may be able to help. This external command should be used only as a last resort. RECOVER does not work when DOS is run from a local area network.

Step 1: Recover a Single File

Suppose you try to retrieve a file from a floppy disk in drive A and DOS reports that it cannot read that file. You may get one of the following messages from DOS:

```
Disk error reading drive A:
General failure reading drive A:
Read fault error reading drive A:
Sector not found error reading drive A:
Track 0 bad - disk unusable
Unrecoverable read error on drive A:
```

First, take out the disk, make sure it is inserted correctly, and close the disk drive door or lever again. Then try using the CHKDSK command on that disk. If the CHKDSK command reports that a sector on the disk is bad, RECOVER might be able to read all or part of the file by skipping over the bad spots. Suppose the file you are trying to read is SAMPLE.TXT. You would enter this command (don't do this now):

```
recover a:sample.txt
```

RECOVER would then try to read SAMPLE.TXT, part by part, ignoring the bad spots. Then it would try to rewrite the file without the bad spots, possibly allowing you to read at least some of the original SAMPLE.TXT.

Step 2: Recover an Entire Disk

If you cannot gain access to any files on a disk, then you can tell the RECOVER command to try and reconstruct the entire disk. Again, this should only be done as a last resort. Here is the command you would enter to recover all the files on the disk in drive A (don't do it now):

```
recover a:
```

Practice

1. Take a diskette with files on it that you don't need, such as the backup diskette you created in Lesson 6, and insert it into drive A. Suppose that it is a damaged disk. Execute the following command to try to get back readable information on the damaged disk:

   Type   **recover a:**
   Press **Enter**

   Press any key when the RECOVER command asks you to do so. When it is finished, RECOVER will report how many files it recovered.

2. RECOVER is to be used only as a last resort. When it recovers files, it changes their names to FILE0001.REC, FILE0002.REC, and so on. So, you have to examine and rename the recovered files to get them into usable form again. You don't need the files you recovered on the diskette in drive A, so reformat it:

Type   `format a:`
Press   **Enter**

Lesson 8: Using the Prompt Option When Erasing Files

You have already learned how to use the ERASE (or DEL) command to remove files from a disk. If you try to erase every file on a disk or in a subdirectory, DOS will ask you if you are sure this is what you want to do before it discards the files. The ERASE command, however, does not automatically ask this question when you erase several files at once with the global file name characters * or ?. Fortunately, an optional parameter is available that lets you have DOS prompt you before erasing each file. This option is also handy for selectively erasing some files from a group of many.

Step 1: Specify the /P Parameter

Copy some files from the DOS subdirectory into your LESSONS subdirectory so that you have some files you can erase safely. Execute the following commands:

Type   `cd c:\lessons`
Press   **Enter**
Type   `copy c:\dos\*.com`
Press   **Enter**

Use the DIR command to make sure that you are in the LESSONS subdirectory. Execute this command to erase the COM files from your LESSONS subdirectory with a prompt before erasing each file:

Type   `erase *.com /p`
Press   **Enter**
Type   `y`
Press   **Enter**

As Figure 11 shows, DOS will prompt you with "Delete (Y/N)?" before it actually deletes each file. For the remaining files, answer yes for some files and no for others. When the ERASE command has finished, execute this command to examine the LESSONS subdirectory:

Type   `dir`
Press   **Enter**

The files for which you answered no will still be present.

Step 2: Don't Specify the /P Parameter

To delete the remaining COM files from your LESSONS subdirectory, execute this command:

Type   `erase *.com`
Press   **Enter**

Practice   Make sure you are in your LESSONS subdirectory. Use the ERASE command with the /P parameter to tell DOS to delete every file in the subdirectory, but to prompt you first. Answer **n** for no to each prompt so that you don't erase any

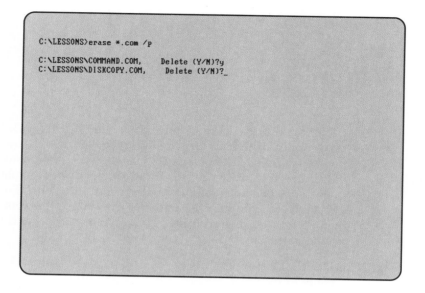

Figure 11 Using the /P Parameter When Erasing Files

```
C:\LESSONS>erase *.com /p

C:\LESSONS\COMMAND.COM,    Delete (Y/N)?y
C:\LESSONS\DISKCOPY.COM,   Delete (Y/N)?_
```

files. To be extra safe, you can make it a practice to always use the /P parameter with the ERASE or DEL command.

Lesson 9: Learning More About the COPY Command

COPY is a versatile command that can be used in several different ways. You have already learned how to use COPY to duplicate one or more files from one disk or subdirectory to another. By specifying different names for the source and the target files, you can also duplicate files in the same subdirectory.

Step 1: Copy from the Console to Create a Text File

The COPY command can create a new text file without using a word processing or text editing program. Actually, you already did this in Lesson 4, but let's go over it again.

DOS can refer to certain hardware devices as if they were files. These devices are given special file names called DOS device names. For example, CON refers to the console, or the keyboard and the screen. Similarly, PRN refers to the printer. You can use device names such as CON and PRN as if they were file names in commands such as COPY. Make sure you are in your LESSONS subdirectory and then execute this command:

Type   **copy con sample2.txt**
Press **Enter**

This command tells DOS to take every character you now type at the keyboard and copy it into a new file named SAMPLE2.TXT. Type the following text, pressing **Enter** at the end of each line:

```
A text file contains only letters, numbers,
punctuation marks, and other symbols that
appear on the keyboard.
```

An end-of-file mark is the Ctrl-Z character; it is the last character in a text file. When you are finished entering the text, you must insert an end-of-file mark into the file by doing this:

Press   **F6**
Press   **Enter**

To see what you have done, execute these commands:

Type   **dir**
Press   **Enter**
Type   **type sample2.txt**
Press   **Enter**

Your screen should look like Figure 12.

Step 2: Use COPY to Append Files

The COPY command is sometimes used to append or combine files. Suppose you wanted to create a new file named SAMPLE3.TXT that contained the contents of SAMPLE.TXT followed by the contents of SAMPLE2.TXT. Execute this command:

Type   **copy sample.txt+sample2.txt sample3.txt**
Press   **Enter**

Any number of source files can be combined by listing their names separated by plus signs. The last file name in the COPY command is the target file that will contain the combination of the source files. If you omit the name of a target file, DOS will combine the source files and copy them to the first source file listed. To see what you have done, enter these commands:

Type   **dir**
Press   **Enter**
Type   **type sample3.txt**
Press   **Enter**

Your screen should look like Figure 13.

Figure 12 Using COPY to Create a Text File

```
C:\LESSONS>copy con sample2.txt
A text file contains only letters, numbers,
punctuation marks, and other symbols that
appear on the keyboard.
^Z
        1 File(s) copied

C:\LESSONS>dir

 Volume in drive C is HARD DISK
 Volume Serial Number is 3324-07CC
 Directory of  C:\LESSONS

           <DIR>      07-15-89  11:06a
 .         <DIR>      07-15-89  11:06a
 ..
SAMPLE   TXT      29 07-15-89  11:06a
SAMPLE2  TXT     113 07-15-89  11:08a
        4 File(s)  19691520 bytes free

C:\LESSONS>type sample2.txt
A text file contains only letters, numbers,
punctuation marks, and other symbols that
appear on the keyboard.

C:\LESSONS>_
```

Figure 13 Using COPY to Append Files

```
C:\LESSONS>copy sample.txt+sample2.txt sample3.txt
SAMPLE.TXT
SAMPLE2.TXT
        1 File(s) copied

C:\LESSONS>dir

 Volume in drive C is HARD DISK
 Volume Serial Number is 3324-07CC
 Directory of  C:\LESSONS

.            <DIR>      07-15-89  11:06a
..           <DIR>      07-15-89  11:06a
SAMPLE   TXT         29 07-15-89  11:06a
SAMPLE2  TXT        113 07-15-89  11:08a
SAMPLE3  TXT        143 07-15-89  11:09a
        5 File(s)  19689472 bytes free

C:\LESSONS>type sample3.txt
This is a sample text file.
A text file contains only letters, numbers,
punctuation marks, and other symbols that
appear on the keyboard.

C:\LESSONS>_
```

Step 3: Use the /V Parameter

The COPY command has three optional parameters, /V, /B, and /A. The /V parameter tells DOS to verify that the copy has been made successfully with no errors. Each time data is written to the disk, a confirmation procedure will be performed to ensure that data can be read without error. The /V parameter is used only when making copies to disk files, not device names. Verifying a copy takes longer and is usually not necessary, but you may want to do it when copying especially important files, such as programs in which the scrambling of a single byte can cause a bug. For example, try this command:

Type   **copy c:\command.com command.bak /v**
Press **Enter**

You won't see any difference on the screen when the COPY command is used with the /V parameter, except that it works a little slower.

Step 4: Use the /B and /A Parameters

By default, the COPY command creates a target file that is the same type of file as the source. If you copy a text file, COPY produces a text file. Another term for text file is **ASCII file.** ASCII, which stands for American Standard Code for Information Interchange, is the most common scheme used to encode characters as numbers so that they can be manipulated by computers. A **binary file** is a file that contains programs or data that are not encoded as ASCII characters. Files with extensions of EXE and COM, for example, are binary files. If you copy a binary file, COPY normally produces a binary file.

The other two parameters of the COPY command, /B and /A, are used when the type of file you want to produce is different than the source. The /B parameter, when specified after a source file name, tells DOS to copy the entire file, including any end-of-file marks. When used with a target file name, the /B parameter tells DOS not to add an end-of-file mark to the end of the file. The /A parameter tells

DOS to treat the file as an ASCII file. If a source file name is followed by /A, only data up to and including the first end-of-file mark will be copied. If a target file name is followed by /A, an end-of-file mark will be added as the last character of the file.

In most cases, you don't have to use /B or /A. You can, however, use the /B command to view the entire contents of a binary file on your screen. First, try the following COPY command without the /B parameter:

> Type **copy command.bak con**
> Press **Enter**

Remember, COMMAND.BAK is a copy of COMMAND.COM, the DOS command processor, which is a binary file. When you copy it to the screen, the display will stop when the first end-of-file mark is encountered. Now, try this command to display the entire COMMAND.BAK binary file on your screen (the computer will beep quite a bit, so skip this command if you don't want to disturb others around you):

> Type **copy command.bak /b con**
> Press **Enter**

Don't be alarmed if your computer seems to be going crazy. All the strange characters and beeps occur because binary programming code is being displayed on the screen. Occasionally, you will see words or phrases that you can read, usually messages embedded in the command processor. It will take a couple of minutes for the entire COMMAND.BAK file to be copied to the screen, and Ctrl-Break won't stop it, so just be patient and wait.

Practice
1. Use the COPY command with the CON device name to display the contents of SAMPLE2.TXT on your screen.
2. Use the COPY command with the PRN device name to send SAMPLE2.TXT to your printer.
3. Use the COPY command with the /B parameter and CON device name to examine an EXE or COM file from the DOS subdirectory on your hard disk.

Lesson 10: Setting the VERIFY Option

In Lesson 9 you learned that the COPY command's optional /V ensures that files copied to the disk can be read without error. The VERIFY command lets you turn this option on or off whenever any files are copied to a disk, not just for a single COPY command like the /V parameter.

Step 1: Execute the VERIFY Command

To see the current setting of the VERIFY option, execute this command:

> Type **verify**
> Press **Enter**

The default setting of the VERIFY option is off.

Step 2: Change the VERIFY Option

You can change the current setting of the VERIFY option by following the command with ON or OFF. For example, execute these commands:

Type   **verify on**
Press **Enter**
Type   **verify**
Press **Enter**

Practice   Turn the VERIFY option off again.

Lesson 11: Changing File Attributes

A **file attribute** is a characteristic of a file. DOS has several attributes that can be associated with files. The two most commonly encountered by the average user are the read-only and the archive attributes.

When a file's **read-only attribute** is turned off, the default state, it can be read, written, modified, or deleted. If the file's read-only attribute is turned on, it cannot be changed in any way. The only way to modify or delete the file is to turn the read-only attribute back off again.

The **archive attribute** indicates whether a file has been changed since it was last saved with the BACKUP command. The archive attribute is turned on whenever a file is rewritten to disk (that is, changed in some way). When the BACKUP command saves a file, its archive attribute is turned off. This is how DOS can tell if a file has been changed since you last backed it up.

Step 1: Change the Read-only Attribute

Suppose the SAMPLE.TXT file was an extremely important file that you did not want to accidentally delete. One way to help ensure that it would not be deleted would be to turn on its read-only attribute. This can be done with the ATTRIB command.

Make sure you are in the LESSONS subdirectory, and then execute this command:

Type   **attrib +r sample.txt**
Press **Enter**

This command turns on the read-only attribute for the file SAMPLE.TXT. Now, this file cannot be changed or deleted. Try the following three commands:

Type   **type sample.txt**
Press **Enter**
Type   **erase sample.txt**
Press **Enter**
Type   **dir**
Press **Enter**

As you can see from Figure 14, you can read the file, but you cannot delete it after the read-only attribute has been turned on. DOS replies with "Access denied" when you try to delete a read-only file. Entering the DIR command confirms that the file SAMPLE.TXT has not been deleted.

*Figure 14 Using ATTRIB to
Set the Read-only Attribute*

```
C:\LESSONS>attrib +r sample.txt

C:\LESSONS>type sample.txt
This is a sample text file.

C:\LESSONS>erase sample.txt
Access denied

C:\LESSONS>dir

 Volume in drive C is HARD DISK
 Volume Serial Number is 3324-07CC
 Directory of  C:\LESSONS

 .            <DIR>      07-15-89  11:06a
 ..           <DIR>      07-15-89  11:06a
 SAMPLE   TXT        29 07-15-89  11:06a
 SAMPLE2  TXT       113 07-15-89  11:08a
 SAMPLE3  TXT       143 07-15-89  11:09a
 COMMAND  BAK     37557 12-19-88  12:00a
         6 File(s)   19650560 bytes free

C:\LESSONS>_
```

Step 2: Change the Archive Attribute

The ATTRIB command can also be used to change the archive attribute. You could, for example, turn off the archive attribute for a file, even though it has been changed, to prevent it from being saved by the next BACKUP command. Execute the following command:

Type   **attrib -a sample.txt**
Press **Enter**

This turns off the archive attribute for the SAMPLE.TXT file. Unless you change the file or the attribute again, it will not be saved by the next BACKUP command.

The ATTRIB command can also be used to view the current attributes of a file. Execute the following command:

Type   **attrib sample.txt**
Press **Enter**

As Figure 15 shows, if you omit the R and A switches between the ATTRIB and the file name, DOS will report which attributes are turned on for that file. Since the read-only attribute is turned on and the archive attribute is turned off, DOS replies with only R before the full file name C:\LESSONS\SAMPLE.TXT.

You can also set both attributes at once with a single ATTRIB command. Turn the read-only attribute back off and the archive attribute back on by executing this command:

Type   **attrib -r +a sample.txt**
Press **Enter**

Practice
1. Use the ATTRIB command to examine the file attributes of SAMPLE2.TXT.
2. Turn on the read-only attribute of SAMPLE2.TXT and then try to delete the file.
3. Turn off the read-only attribute of SAMPLE2.TXT.

Figure 15 Using ATTRIB to Display a File's Attributes

```
C:\LESSONS>attrib -a sample.txt

C:\LESSONS>attrib sample.txt
        R       C:\LESSONS\SAMPLE.TXT

C:\LESSONS>_
```

Lesson 12: Copying Groups of Files

In the previous chapter you learned that you can copy groups of files with the COPY command by using the global file name characters ? or * in your file specifications. Starting with version 3.2, however, DOS included XCOPY, a more sophisticated command for copying files. While the COPY command reads and then writes a single file at a time, XCOPY reads as many files as it can into memory first and then writes them. This makes XCOPY faster than COPY in some cases. In addition, XCOPY accepts more optional parameters, making it more flexible than COPY. On the other hand, unlike COPY, XCOPY is an external command. This means that XCOPY must be accessible on your disk if you want to use it.

Step 1: Copy a Group of Files with XCOPY

To see how XCOPY works, make sure you are in the LESSONS subdirectory on your hard disk and put a formatted diskette in drive A. Then execute this command:

Type   **xcopy *.* a:**
Press   **Enter**

Your screen should look like Figure 16. XCOPY read all of the files in the LESSONS subdirectory into memory first, and then copied them to the diskette in drive A.

Step 2: Copy Subdirectories

Unlike the COPY command, XCOPY can be instructed to copy files from all the subdirectories in the source disk or directory. In the process, it will create new subdirectories on the target disk if necessary. For example, change to the root directory of your hard disk and try the following XCOPY command:

Type   **cd **
Press   **Enter**
Type   **xcopy sample.* a: /s**
Press   **Enter**

Figure 16 Using XCOPY to
Duplicate a Group of Files

```
C:\LESSONS>xcopy *.* a:
Reading source file(s)...
SAMPLE.TXT
SAMPLE2.TXT
SAMPLE3.TXT
COMMAND.BAK
        4 File(s) copied

C:\LESSONS>_
```

XCOPY will look for all files with a primary filename of SAMPLE no matter what subdirectory they might be in. It will create corresponding subdirectories on the floppy disk in drive A and copy the files into the appropriate subdirectories. Execute the following two commands to see what you have done to your floppy disk:

Type   **dir a:**
Press   **Enter**
Type   **dir a:\lessons**
Press   **Enter**

Your screen should look like Figure 17.

Figure 17 Using XCOPY to
Duplicate a Subdirectory

```
C:\>dir a:

 Volume in drive A has no label
 Volume Serial Number is 1A3F-12C9
 Directory of  A:\

SAMPLE   TXT       29 07-15-89  11:06a
SAMPLE2  TXT      113 07-15-89  11:08a
SAMPLE3  TXT      143 07-15-89  11:09a
COMMAND  BAK    37557 12-19-88  12:00a
LESSONS      <DIR>     07-15-89  11:39a
        5 File(s)    319488 bytes free

C:\>dir a:\lessons

 Volume in drive A has no label
 Volume Serial Number is 1A3F-12C9
 Directory of  A:\LESSONS

.            <DIR>     07-15-89  11:39a
..           <DIR>     07-15-89  11:39a
SAMPLE   TXT       29 07-15-89  11:06a
        3 File(s)    319488 bytes free

C:\>_
```

Step 3: Examine the Other XCOPY Parameters

Several other parameters can be used with the XCOPY command in addition to /S. The following table lists all of them.

Parameter	Action
/A	Copies only those files whose archive attribute is turned on. Does not change the archive attribute after copying.
/D:*date*	Copies only those files created or last modified on or after the specified *date*.
/E	Copies any subdirectories beneath the specified source disk or directory, even if they contain no files. This parameter, if used, must be used with /S.
/M	Same as /A, but turns off the archive attribute after copying.
/P	Prompts you for confirmation before each file is copied.
/S	Copies nonempty subdirectories beneath the specified source disk or directory.
/V	Verifies each copy to be identical to the original.
/W	Waits for you to press a key before copying files.

Practice

1. Try each of the following commands and explain exactly what they do. Answer **n** for no to each prompt to leave your diskette in drive A unchanged.

Type   **xcopy *.* a: /p /a**
Press   **Enter**
Type   **xcopy *.* a: /p /d:01-01-89**
Press   **Enter**
Type   **xcopy *.* a: /w /p /m**
Press   **Enter**

2. The XCOPY command can copy an entire diskette to another diskette, even if the source and target diskettes are different types, as long as the target diskette has enough room. For example, if you have a 5¼-inch floppy drive A and a 3½-inch floppy drive B, you would have to use XCOPY instead of DISKCOPY to duplicate a 5¼-inch diskette on a 3½-inch diskette. Even if you have only one floppy drive, you can use XCOPY to duplicate an entire diskette. Unlike DISKCOPY, however, XCOPY cannot automatically format a diskette. To copy an entire diskette with XCOPY, get an extra formatted diskette and execute the following command:

Type   **xcopy a: b: /s /e**
Press   **Enter**

Note that this command will work even if you don't have a floppy drive B installed in your computer. DOS has the ability to "pretend" that drive A is temporarily drive B to complete such commands. It will prompt you when to insert the diskette for drive A or for drive B. Just swap the source and target diskettes in drive A. When you are finished, use DIR to examine the disk in drive A.

Lesson 13: Updating Sets of Files

Suppose you have identical copies of the file SAMPLE.TXT in various subdirectories on your hard disk and you want to update them all with a new copy of SAMPLE.TXT stored on a floppy disk. Although you cannot do this with a single COPY command, you can use a single REPLACE command. REPLACE is an external DOS command that is used to update previous versions of files.

Step 1: Prepare the Floppy Disk

Let's create an updated version of the file SAMPLE.TXT on the diskette in drive A. Then execute the following command to create a new SAMPLE.TXT:

Type   **copy con a:sample.txt**
Press **Enter**

Now, do the following to add the text to SAMPLE.TXT in drive A:

Type   **This is the new sample text file.**
Press **Enter**
Press **F6**
Press **Enter**

Step 2: Replace the Hard Disk Files

Suppose you had several copies of SAMPLE.TXT on the hard disk in different subdirectories. (You don't, but it doesn't matter for this example.) Execute the following command to replace all copies of SAMPLE.TXT on the hard disk with the new version from the floppy disk in drive A:

Type   **replace a:sample.txt c:\ /s**
Press **Enter**

The /S parameter tells the REPLACE command to search through all subdirectories of the target for files to replace. To see what you have done, execute this command:

Type   **type c:\lessons\sample.txt**
Press **Enter**

Your screen should look like Figure 18.

Step 3: Add Files to the Target Disk

The REPLACE command can also be used to copy files that exist on the source disk, but not on the target disk, to the target disk. Execute the following commands to move back into the LESSONS subdirectory on the hard disk and rename a few of the files:

Type   **cd lessons**
Press **Enter**
Type   **ren sample.txt part1.txt**
Press **Enter**
Type   **ren sample2.txt part2.txt**
Press **Enter**
Type   **ren sample3.txt example.txt**
Press **Enter**

*Figure 18 Replacing Files
on the Hard Disk*

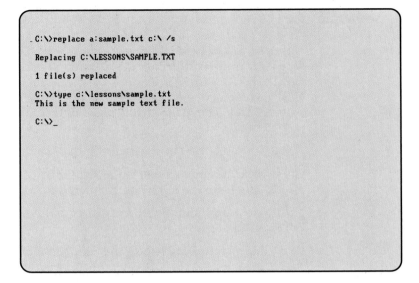

```
_C:\>replace a:sample.txt c:\ /s

Replacing C:\LESSONS\SAMPLE.TXT

1 file(s) replaced

C:\>type c:\lessons\sample.txt
This is the new sample text file.

C:\>_
```

Now your LESSONS subdirectory on the hard disk contains the files PART1.TXT, PART2.TXT and EXAMPLE.TXT. The floppy disk in drive A does not contain files with these three names. Suppose you wanted to copy *only* those files with different names from C to A. Execute this command:

> Type **replace *.* a: /a**
> Press **Enter**

The /A is a parameter that tells the REPLACE command to add files from the source to the target, but only those that don't already exist in the target. To see the result, execute this command:

> Type **dir a:**
> Press **Enter**

Your screen should look like Figure 19.

Step 4: Examine the Other REPLACE Parameters

Several other parameters can be used with the REPLACE command. The following table lists all of them.

Parameter	Action
/A	Adds new files to the target instead of replacing existing files. Cannot be used with /S or /U.
/P	Prompts you for confirmation before each file is replaced.
/R	Replaces read-only files as well as regular files.
/S	Searches all subdirectories on the target disk to replace matching files. Cannot be used with /A.
/U	Replaces only those target files that are older than their matching source files. Cannot be used with /A.
/W	Waits for you to press a key before replacing or adding files.

Figure 19 Using REPLACE to Add Files

```
Adding A:\PART1.TXT

Adding A:\PART2.TXT

Adding A:\EXAMPLE.TXT

3 file(s) added

C:\LESSONS>dir a:

 Volume in drive A has no label
 Volume Serial Number is 1A3F-12C9
 Directory of  A:\

SAMPLE   TXT        35 07-15-89  11:45a
SAMPLE2  TXT       113 07-15-89  11:08a
SAMPLE3  TXT       143 07-15-89  11:09a
COMMAND  BAK     37557 12-19-88  12:00a
LESSONS      <DIR>       07-15-89  11:39a
PART1    TXT        35 07-15-89  11:45a
PART2    TXT       113 07-15-89  11:08a
EXAMPLE  TXT       143 07-15-89  11:09a
         8 File(s)        316416 bytes free

C:\LESSONS>_
```

Practice   Make sure you are in the LESSONS subdirectory on the hard disk and execute the following command to change the EXAMPLE file:

Type   **copy part1.txt+part2.txt example.txt**
Press **Enter**

Execute this command and explain what it does:

Type   **replace *.* a: /w /p /r /u**
Press **Enter**

Press any key to continue and answer **y** for yes to the prompt.

Lesson 14: Transferring the DOS System Files

When you format a system diskette with the /S parameter as you learned in Lesson 9 of Beginning DOS, DOS copies two hidden system files to the newly formatted disk. These files, along with the command processor, COM-MAND.COM, let you boot up your computer from that disk. It is also possible to format a diskette and leave space for the system files to be transferred later. This is sometimes done by individuals and companies that transfer software or data to others. It is not legal to give away or sell DOS without a license from IBM or Microsoft, so you are not supposed to distribute boot-up disks. You can, however, format a disk so that the recipient can transfer his or her own copy of DOS to that disk. The SYS command makes this possible. The SYS command is also used for upgrading to a new version of DOS. SYS, which is an external command, will not work if you are running DOS from a network.

Step 1: Format a Diskette with the /B Parameter

Execute this command to format a diskette to which DOS can be transferred later:

Type   **format a: /b**
Press **Enter**

Insert the diskette you have been using into drive A and press the **Enter** key. When the format procedure is finished, press **Enter** to skip typing a volume label and enter **n** for no in response to the prompt asking if you want to format another disk. As you can see from Figure 20, DOS reserved 73,728 bytes for the system. The hidden system files, however, have not yet been transferred to this space.

Step 2: Transfer the Hidden System Files

To transfer the hidden system files, execute this command:

Type   **sys a:**
Press   **Enter**

When DOS is finished, it will display the message "System transferred," but if you examine the disk with the DIR command, no files will appear in the directory. This is because the system files are hidden.

Step 3: Copy the File COMMAND.COM

One more step is necessary in order to be able to boot up your computer from this diskette. Execute the following command to copy the DOS command processor from the root directory of your hard disk to the diskette in drive A:

Type   **copy c:\command.com a:**
Press   **Enter**

The diskette in drive A can now be used to boot up the computer.

Practice   1. Reboot your computer from the system diskette you just created. Enter the current date and time. Use DIR to examine the directory of your diskette. The procedure you followed in this lesson achieves the same result as using the /S parameter with the FORMAT command.

Figure 20 Using the /B Parameter with FORMAT

```
C:\LESSONS>format a: /b
Insert new diskette for drive A:
and press ENTER when ready...

Format complete

Volume label (11 characters, ENTER for none)?

    362496 bytes total disk space
     73728 bytes used by system
    288768 bytes available on disk

      1024 bytes in each allocation unit
       282 allocation units available on disk

Volume Serial Number is 283D-13CC

Format another (Y/N)?n
C:\LESSONS>_
```

2. Now, reboot your computer from the hard disk. Enter the date and time if necessary. Change the DOS prompt so it displays the current drive and directory, if it does not already do so.

Lesson 15: Comparing Files and Disks

Keeping one or more copies of important files or disks is prudent. After you make a copy of an especially important file or diskette, you might want to check it to make sure that it is identical to the original. Although errors are rare, a bit or byte can get scrambled during the copy procedure if the VERIFY option is turned off. DOS has two external commands, COMP and DISKCOMP, that compare files and diskettes, respectively. These commands can also be used if you forget whether two files or disks are identical. Note: DISKCOMP will not work if you are running DOS from a network.

Step 1: Compare Two Files

Change to your LESSONS subdirectory if you are not already there. Use the directory command to examine the files inside LESSONS. It should contain a file named COMMAND.BAK, which you created in Lesson 9. Let's see if COMMAND.BAK in the LESSONS subdirectory is identical to COMMAND.COM in the root directory of your hard disk. Execute this command:

Type   **comp command.bak c:\command.com**
Press **Enter**

Your screen should look like Figure 21. The files are identical, so DOS reports that the "Files compare OK." Press **n** for no in response to the prompt asking if you want to compare more files. If the files had been different sizes or if any bytes had been different, DOS would have told you.

Figure 21 Using COMP to Compare Two Files

```
C:\LESSONS>comp command.bak c:\command.com


C:COMMAND.BAK and C:\COMMAND.COM

EOF mark not found
Files compare OK
Compare more files (Y/N) ?_
```

Step 2: Compare Two Diskettes

The DISKCOMP command is used to compare the contents of two diskettes. For example, if your computer has two floppy drives, A and B, that are the same type, put a diskette in each one and compare them with this command:

Type   **diskcomp a: b:**
Press   **Enter**

If your computer has only one floppy disk drive, like many hard disk systems, try this command instead:

Type   **diskcomp a: a:**
Press   **Enter**

DOS will then prompt you when to insert each diskette. If the two diskettes are identical, then DOS will display "Compare OK." Otherwise, "Compare error" messages will be displayed that report where mismatches were found. When it is finished, DISKCOMP will ask you if you want to compare another diskette. Type **n** for no.

Practice

1. Let's see what COMP does if two files are different. Try this command:

   Type   **comp part1.txt part2.txt**
   Press   **Enter**

   The COMP command determines immediately that the files are different sizes, so they cannot be identical. It doesn't examine them any further.

2. Now let's try comparing two files that are the same size, but different in some other way. Follow these instructions to create a file similar, but not identical, to PART1.TXT:

   Type   **copy con partx.txt**
   Press   **Enter**
   Type   **This is the old sample text file.**
   Press   **Enter**
   Press   **F6**
   Press   **Enter**

   Compare PART1.TXT with PARTX.TXT with this command:

   Type   **comp part1.txt partx.txt**
   Press   **Enter**

   Since COMP is typically used by programmers, the results are given in hexadecimal (base 16) ASCII codes. For example, the letter "n" is represented as 6E and "o" is 6F. COMP shows three differences between the two files: the letters "n e w" versus "o l d."

Lesson 16: Displaying and Changing a Volume Label

DOS calls the name of a disk the **volume label.** This name, which is optional, can be helpful when trying to identify a disk.

Step 1: Display a Volume Label

One way to see the volume label of a disk is to use the DIR command. Another way is to use the internal command VOL. Try this:

Type **vol**
Press **Enter**

DOS will display the volume label of the disk in your default drive. You can get the volume label of a disk other than the one in your default drive by specifying the disk drive letter. For example, put a formatted diskette into drive A and execute this command:

Type **vol a:**
Press **Enter**

DOS will respond with the volume label of the diskette in drive A.

Step 2: Change a Volume Label

DOS versions 4.0 and newer automatically ask you to supply a volume label whenever you format a disk. With earlier DOS versions, you can use the /V parameter to have the FORMAT command prompt you for a volume label. You can also specify a new volume label or change an existing one with the LABEL command. LABEL is an external command; it does not work if you are running DOS from a network. To see how it works, put a formatted diskette in drive A and execute this command:

Type **label a:**
Press **Enter**

DOS will report the current volume label and allow you to enter a new name, which can be up to 11 characters long.

Type **sample**
Press **Enter**

To see the new volume label of the diskette, execute this command:

Type **vol a:**
Press **Enter**

Figure 22 shows the result.

Practice

1. If you specify the new volume label right after the LABEL command, DOS won't prompt you. Try this command:

   Type **label a:example**
   Press **Enter**

   Use DIR or VOL to examine the new volume label.

2. You can also delete an existing volume label. Try the following:

   Type **label a:**
   Press **Enter**
   Press **Enter**
   Type **y**

Figure 22 Using LABEL to Change a Disk's Name

```
C:\LESSONS>label a:
Volume in drive A has no label
Volume Serial Number is 283D-13CC
Volume label (11 characters, ENTER for none)? sample


C:\LESSONS>vol a:

 Volume in drive A is SAMPLE
 Volume Serial Number is 283D-13CC

C:\LESSONS>_
```

3. VER is an internal DOS command similar to VOL. It is used to find out the version of DOS you are using, in case you don't know or forget. Try it:

   Type   **ver**
   Press **Enter**

Lesson 17: Displaying and Changing the Date and Time

If no AUTOEXEC.BAT file is present in the root directory of the startup disk, DOS will prompt you to enter the new date and time whenever you boot up or reboot the computer. If an AUTOEXEC.BAT file is present, DOS will not prompt you for the date and time unless the commands DATE and TIME are in AUTO-EXEC.BAT. DATE and TIME are internal commands that let you see and change the current date and time kept by the computer's real-time clock. Most micro-computers sold today have a battery that keeps the real-time clock operating even when the computer is off, so you don't need to execute DATE and TIME every time you boot up. Nevertheless, you can still use DATE and TIME to see the current date and time. In addition, DATE and TIME are sometimes needed to correct the internal clock, such as when changing to or from daylight saving time. It is important to set your computer to the correct date and time so that you know when files were created or last changed.

Step 1: Execute the DATE Command

To see the current date kept by your computer, without changing it, execute this command:

   Type   **date**
   Press **Enter** (2 times)

Step 2: Change the Date

One way to change the current date is to execute the DATE command without any parameters. DOS will prompt you to enter the new date. Another way to change the date is to specify the new date after the DATE command before you press Enter. For example, execute this command:

Type   **date 1-1-90**
Press   **Enter**

Now, use the DATE command without any parameters to see the date you set. Notice how DOS automatically figures out the correct day of the week.

When you specify a new date, you must use only numbers: 1–12 for the month, 1–31 for the day, and 80–79 or 1980–2079 for the year. The month, day, and year entries may be separated with hyphens (-) or slashes (/).

Step 3: Execute the TIME Command

To see the current time kept by your computer, without changing it, execute this command:

Type   **time**
Press   **Enter** (2 times)

Step 4: Change the Time

One way to change the current time is to execute the TIME command without any parameters. DOS will prompt you to enter the new date. Another way to change the time is to specify the new time after the TIME command before you press Enter. For example, execute this command:

Type   **time 14:22:13.45**
Press   **Enter**

Now, use the TIME command without any parameters to see the time you set (see Figure 23). Notice that the new time starts ticking as soon as you enter it.

When you specify a new time, you must use the 24-hour format. If you like, you can specify a new time accurate to hundredths of seconds. The command you just executed sets the time to 22 minutes, 13.45 seconds past 14 hundred hours (2 P.M.). You don't have to enter the seconds or hundredths of seconds. If the time is exactly on the hour, you don't have to enter the minutes. Any portion of the time you omit will be set to zero.

Practice
1. Use the DATE command to reset the correct date.
2. Use the TIME command to reset the correct time.
3. Check the current date and time again.

Lesson 18: Displaying a Memory Report

Starting with version 4.0, DOS includes MEM, an external command that presents a memory report. This report displays the amount of memory used and free. It can also specify the location, size, and name of each program or data area

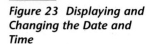

Figure 23 Displaying and Changing the Date and Time

```
C:\>date
Current date is Sun 07-16-1989
Enter new date (mm-dd-yy):

C:\>date 1-1-90

C:\>date
Current date is Mon 01-01-1990
Enter new date (mm-dd-yy):

C:\>time
Current time is 10:41:11.84a
Enter new time:

C:\>time 14:22:13.45

C:\>time
Current time is  2:22:15.09p
Enter new time:

C:\>_
```

currently loaded into memory. MEM can provide more detailed and technical information about memory usage than CHKDSK.

Step 1: Execute the MEM Command

If you don't have DOS 4.00 or newer, you cannot use MEM. Otherwise, execute this command:

Type **mem**
Press **Enter**

Figure 24 shows the result, although your report may have different numbers, depending on the amount of RAM installed and the programs that have been loaded in your computer.

Figure 24 Using MEM to Display a Memory Report

```
C:\>mem


     655360 bytes total memory
     655360 bytes available
     521248 largest executable program size

C:\>_
```

Step 2: Use the /PROGRAM Parameter

The MEM command has an optional parameter that will also display the programs loaded into memory. Execute this command:

Type   **mem /program**
Press   **Enter**

The resulting report will be longer and contain technical details concerning the location, name, and size of each program and data area in memory.

Practice   MEM has one other optional parameter, /DEBUG, that provides even more detailed information than the /PROGRAM parameter. The /DEBUG parameter presents technical facts of interest mainly to assembly language programmers, but you can still try it. Execute this command:

Type   **mem /debug**
Press   **Enter**

The /PROGRAM and /DEBUG parameters cannot be used at the same time.

Lesson 19: Reassigning, Joining, and Substituting Drives

DOS has three external commands that influence the use of disk drives and subdirectories, namely ASSIGN, JOIN, and SUBST. These commands can be handy when working with programs that require certain disks to be in certain drives, when programs don't allow you to specify paths, or when paths get too long. JOIN and SUBST do not work when running DOS from a network.

Step 1: Execute the ASSIGN Command

The ASSIGN command lets you change the drive letter associated with a disk drive. It is sometimes used with application programs developed before hard disks were common. A program, for example, may only work with diskette drives A and B. With ASSIGN, however, you may be able to trick the program into thinking that your hard disk is drive A. Make sure you are at the root directory of your hard disk and then execute this command:

Type   **assign a = c**
Press   **Enter**

To see the result, execute this command:

Type   **dir a:**
Press   **Enter**

DOS will present the directory of the hard disk, not the diskette in drive A. It "thinks" the hard disk is drive A, even though the DOS prompt still reports your current drive and directory as C:\ (see Figure 25).

To change all drives back to their original assignments, execute this command:

Type   **assign**
Press   **Enter**

Figure 25 Using ASSIGN to
Change a Drive's Letter

```
C:\>assign a = c

C:\>dir a:

 Volume in drive A is HARD DISK
 Volume Serial Number is 3324-07CC
 Directory of  A:\

CONFIG   SYS       146 07-09-89   1:22p
COMMAND  COM     37557 12-19-88  12:00a
DOS      <DIR>        07-09-89   1:23p
LESSONS  <DIR>        07-12-89   4:01p
AUTOEXEC BAT       256 01-01-80  12:03a
        5 File(s)   19652608 bytes free

C:\>_
```

In practice, you should avoid using ASSIGN if at all possible because it disguises the true type of the disk drive. Microsoft suggests that you use an equivalent SUBST command instead, which we will discuss shortly, because ASSIGN may not be compatible with future versions of DOS.

Step 2: Execute the JOIN Command

The JOIN command lets you treat an entire disk as if it were a subdirectory on another disk. You can then work with files on multiple disks as if they were part of one subdirectory on one disk. Let's try an example. Make sure you are at the root directory of your hard disk. Create a new subdirectory by executing this command:

Type   **md diska**
Press **Enter**

Put a formatted diskette in drive A. Then execute this command:

Type   **join a: diska**
Press **Enter**

To see the result, execute these commands:

Type   **join**
Press **Enter**
Type   **dir diska**
Press **Enter**

Figure 26 shows the result. When the JOIN command is entered without any parameters, it displays the current drives and subdirectories that are joined. The DIR command presents the files on the floppy disk, in this case just COMMAND.COM, as if they were in the DISKA subdirectory on the hard disk.

You use the /D parameter to undo a previous JOIN command. Execute the following commands to disconnect the join and remove the DISKA subdirectory:

Type   **join a: /d**
Press **Enter**

*Figure 26 Using JOIN to
Treat a Disk as a
Subdirectory*

```
C:\>md diska

C:\>join a: diska

C:\>join
A: => C:\DISKA

C:\>dir diska

 Volume in drive C is HARD DISK
 Volume Serial Number is 3324-07CC
 Directory of  C:\DISKA

COMMAND  COM     37557 12-19-88  12:00a
            1 File(s)   19650560 bytes free

C:\>_
```

Type   **rd diska**
Press **Enter**

Step 3: Execute the SUBST Command

SUBST is the opposite of the JOIN command; it lets you treat a subdirectory as if it were a disk in a separate drive. For example, let's substitute the imaginary drive letter D for your LESSONS subdirectory. If you have a real disk drive D in your computer, choose a different letter. Make sure you are at the root directory of your hard disk and execute these commands:

Type   **subst d: lessons**
Press **Enter**
Type   **subst**
Press **Enter**
Type   **dir d:**
Press **Enter**

SUBST entered without any parameters reports the substitutions that have been made. As Figure 27 shows, the subdirectory C:\LESSONS can now be referred to as simply D:.

You use the /D parameter to cancel a previous substitution. For example, execute the following command:

Type   **subst d: /d**
Press **Enter**

Note that the following DOS commands do not work on drives used in the JOIN or SUBST commands: BACKUP, CHKDSK, DISKCOMP, DISKCOPY, FDISK, FORMAT, LABEL, RECOVER, RESTORE, and SYS.

Practice

The MS-DOS 4.01 *User's Reference* manual suggests that you use the SUBST command instead of ASSIGN. Repeat Step 1 of this lesson, except execute the following command instead of the ASSIGN command:

Type   **subst a: c:**
Press **Enter**

Figure 27 Using SUBST to Treat a Subdirectory as a Disk

```
C:\>subst d: lessons

C:\>subst
D: => C:\LESSONS

C:\>dir d:

 Volume in drive D is HARD DISK
 Volume Serial Number is 3324-07CC
 Directory of  D:\

.            <DIR>      07-15-89  11:06a
..           <DIR>      07-15-89  11:06a
PART1    TXT        35 07-15-89  11:45a
PART2    TXT       113 07-15-89  11:08a
EXAMPLE  TXT       149 07-15-89  11:48a
COMMAND  BAK     37557 12-19-88  12:08a
PARTX    TXT        35 07-15-89   2:49p
        7 File(s)   19652608 bytes free

C:\>_
```

When you are finished examining the directory, use the SUBST command with the /D parameter to restore the original drive assignments.

Lesson 20: Learning More About the PRINT Command

PRINT is a sophisticated command that can print one or more files in the background while you continue your work with DOS. This limited multitasking ability is called **spooling.** Several PRINT parameters allow you to fine-tune this spooling capability on your computer.

Step 1: Examine the First Time PRINT Parameters

Several of the PRINT parameters may be used only the first time you execute the PRINT command after booting up. These parameters set the stage for the way PRINT will work for the rest of your DOS session. You have already used the PRINT command since you booted up, so don't try the following parameters. Just read and try to understand the explanations.

Parameter	*Action*
/D:*device*	Specifies the device name of the printer to be used by PRINT. The default is PRN or LPT1, the printer connected to the first parallel port on your computer. LPT2, LPT3, and COM1 through COM4 are device names of other parallel ports and serial ports to which a printer might be connected. If you don't specify the /D parameter, DOS will prompt you for the device name the first time you use the PRINT command.
/B:*size*	Sets the size in bytes of the memory buffer to be used for data to be printed. The minimum and default value is 512. The maximum value is 1634. Larger values enable PRINT to work faster, but use more memory.

/U:*ticks*	Specifies how long in clock ticks PRINT should wait before giving up for a printer that is still busy. The minimum and default value is 1. The maximum value is 255.
/M:*ticks*	Specifies the number of clock ticks it can take to print a character. The value can range from 1 to 255. The default value is 2.
/S:*time*	Specifies the time interval PRINT must wait before getting the attention of the CPU. The value can range from 1 to 255. The default value is 8.
/Q:*number*	Specifies the number of files that can be held in the **print queue,** the list of files to be printed in the background. The number can range from 4 to 32. The default number is 10.

Step 2: Print Several Files

The remaining parameters to the PRINT command can be used any time, not just the first time PRINT is executed for a given DOS session. Change to your LESSONS subdirectory on the hard disk. If you have a printer, turn it on, but take it off line. In other words, press the On Line button so that the On Line light turns off. This will simulate a busy printer. Execute the following commands:

Type	**print part1.txt**
Press	**Enter**
Type	**print part2.txt**
Press	**Enter**
Type	**print example.txt**
Press	**Enter**

Figure 28 shows the result. Each time you execute a PRINT command, the file is placed in the queue and the DOS prompt returns.

Figure 28 Placing Files in the Print Queue

```
C:\LESSONS>print part1.txt

   C:\LESSONS\PART1.TXT is currently being printed

C:\LESSONS>print part2.txt

   C:\LESSONS\PART1.TXT is currently being printed
   C:\LESSONS\PART2.TXT is in queue

C:\LESSONS>print example.txt
Errors on list device indicate that it
may be off-line. Please check it.

   C:\LESSONS\PART1.TXT is currently being printed
   C:\LESSONS\PART2.TXT is in queue
   C:\LESSONS\EXAMPLE.TXT is in queue

C:\LESSONS>_
```

Step 3: Use the /C Parameter

The /C parameter removes a file from the print queue. Execute this command:

Type   **print part2.txt /c**
Press   **Enter**

PART2.TXT will not be printed.

Step 4: Use the /T Parameter

To remove all the files from the print queue, use the /T parameter like this:

Type   **print /t**
Press   **Enter**

Step 5: Use the /P Parameter

Press your printer's On Line button. The final PRINT parameter /P adds a file to the print queue. This default option is assumed if you don't specify any parameters. For example, try this command:

Type   **print example.txt /p**
Press   **Enter**

Executing the above command is the same as executing this command:

Type   **print example.txt**
Press   **Enter**

In either case, the file EXAMPLE.TXT will be printed.

Summary

- *Using the DOS editing and function keys.* Delete, Insert, Escape, and F1 through F6 perform various editing functions on the DOS command line.

- *Setting the BREAK option.* The BREAK command changes the status of the BREAK option, OFF or ON, which controls when Ctrl-Break will cancel a program.

- *Working with subdirectories.* MD or MKDIR creates a new subdirectory, CD or CHDIR moves into a subdirectory, TREE displays the structure of a disk, and RD or RMDIR removes an empty subdirectory.

- *Using the PATH and APPEND commands.* PATH sets up a directory search path for BAT, COM, and EXE files. APPEND sets up a directory search path for all other files.

- *Changing the DOS prompt.* PROMPT followed by one or prompt codes, such as pg, changes the DOS prompt.

- *Backing up and restoring disks and files.* BACKUP backs up all or part of a hard disk onto floppy diskettes. RESTORE copies files from backup diskettes onto a hard disk.

- *Recovering files from damaged disks.* RECOVER attempts to salvage data from a damaged disk.

- *Using the prompt option when erasing files.* The ERASE (or DEL) command's /P parameter causes DOS to ask for confirmation before erasing each file.

- *Appending files and copying files to devices.* The COPY command can be used to append two or more files together. It can also be used to copy data directly to devices such as displays and printers.

- *Setting the VERIFY option.* The VERIFY command changes the status of the VERIFY option OFF or ON, which controls error checking whenever writing data to a disk.

- *Changing file attributes.* The ATTRIB command can change the status of a file's read-only and archive attributes.

- *Copying groups of files.* XCOPY is often faster and more flexible than COPY for duplicating files, subdirectories, and disks.

- *Updating sets of files.* REPLACE is used to update existing files or add new files from one disk to another.

- *Transferring the DOS system files.* If a disk has been formatted with the /B parameter, SYS can transfer the hidden DOS system files to that disk.

- *Comparing files and disks.* COMP checks two files to see if they are identical. DISKCOMP checks two diskettes to see if they are identical.

- *Changing volume labels.* LABEL can display or change the name of a disk.

- *Changing the current date and time.* DATE and TIME can display or change the current date and time kept by the computer.

- *Displaying a memory report.* MEM can present a more detailed and technical memory report than CHKDSK.

- *Reassigning, joining, and substituting drives.* ASSIGN can change the drive letter associated with a disk drive. JOIN can tell DOS to treat an entire disk as if it were a subdirectory on another disk. SUBST can tell DOS to treat a subdirectory as if it were a disk in a separate drive.

- *Printing multiple files.* PRINT can print one or more files in the background. The /P, /C, and /T parameters add or remove files from the print queue.

Key Terms

As an extra review of this chapter, try defining the following terms.

archive attribute	path
ASCII file	print queue
binary file	read-only attribute
file attribute	root directory
hierarchical	spooling
incremental backup	volume label

Multiple Choice

Choose the best selection to complete each statement.

1. Which keys would you press to repeat the previous DOS command?
   - (a) F1 and then Enter
   - (b) F2 and then Enter
   - (c) F3 and then Enter
   - (d) Escape and then Enter

2. Which key would you press to skip over a character from the previous DOS command?
   - (a) Insert
   - (b) Delete
   - (c) Escape
   - (d) F1

3. What keypresses are influenced by the BREAK command?
   - (a) Alt-Break
   - (b) Ctrl-Break
   - (c) Alt-Num Lock
   - (d) Ctrl-Num Lock

4. Which item cannot be contained in a subdirectory?
   - (a) file
   - (b) subdirectory
   - (c) DOS external command
   - (d) disk

5. Every disk has a single main directory known as the
   - (a) root directory
   - (b) prime directory
   - (c) subdirectory
   - (d) master directory

6. Which expression is a valid path?
   - (a) c: hard disk lessons
   - (b) a:\lessons/c:
   - (c) c:\lessons\part1
   - (d) c:/lessons/part1

7. Which DOS command is used to create a new subdirectory?
   - (a) MD
   - (b) CD
   - (c) RD
   - (d) TREE

8. Which DOS command displays the subdirectory structure of a disk?
   - (a) MD
   - (b) CD
   - (c) RD
   - (d) TREE

9. What must be done before you can remove a subdirectory?
   - (a) execute DIR
   - (b) execute TREE
   - (c) delete all files in the subdirectory
   - (d) delete all files in the root directory

10. Which command is used to establish a subdirectory search path for BAT, COM, and EXE files?
    - (a) APPEND
    - (b) PATH
    - (c) TREE
    - (d) SEARCH

11. Which prompt codes would you use with the PROMPT command to have the DOS prompt always display the current path?
    - (a) Hello
    - (b) pg
    - (c) dg
    - (d) vq

12. Which command would back up the entire contents of the hard disk to diskettes in drive A?
    - (a) backup c: a: /s
    - (b) backup c:\lessons*.* a: /s
    - (c) backup a: c: /s
    - (d) backup hard disk a:

13. Which command is used to salvage files from damaged diskettes?
    - (a) RESTORE
    - (b) RECOVER
    - (c) COPY
    - (d) SYS
14. Of the following commands, which is the safest to use?
    - (a) del *.*
    - (b) erase *.*
    - (c) erase ????????.*
    - (d) erase *.* /p
15. Which device name stands for the keyboard or display screen?
    - (a) CON
    - (b) PRN
    - (c) LPT1
    - (d) COM1
16. Which command appends two files to form a third?
    - (a) append file1 + file2 file3
    - (b) copy file1 + file2 file3
    - (c) xcopy file1 + file2 file3
    - (d) diskcopy file1 + file2 file3
17. Which command makes it impossible to delete the file SAMPLE.TXT?
    - (a) attrib +r sample.txt
    - (b) attrib +a sample.txt
    - (c) attrib −r sample.txt
    - (d) attrib −a sample.txt
18. Which command will read as many files as it can into memory first, before copying them?
    - (a) copy a:*.* c:
    - (b) xcopy a:*.* c:
    - (c) copy a:*.* c: /all
    - (d) mem a:*.* c:
19. Which command will copy only those files from the disk in drive A that don't already exist on the disk in drive C?
    - (a) copy a:*.* c: /a
    - (b) xcopy a:*.* c: /a
    - (c) append a:*.* c: /a
    - (d) replace a:*.* c: /a
20. What command must have been used on a diskette before you can use the SYS command to copy the DOS system files to it?
    - (a) TREE
    - (b) APPEND
    - (c) FORMAT /S or FORMAT /B
    - (d) FORMAT /V

Fill-In

1. The simplest path is _____, which represents the root directory of the default drive.
2. You can copy files into a _____ just as if it were a separate disk.
3. The _____ command tells DOS the directories to be searched for files that have extensions other than BAT, COM, or EXE.
4. The _____ command lets you change the DOS prompt.
5. Unlike COPY, the _____ command can automatically use as many diskettes as needed to save the files from a hard disk.
6. The _____ command reinstates files that have been saved with the BACKUP command.
7. The _____ parameter of the ERASE (or DEL) command tells DOS to ask for confirmation before erasing each file.
8. You can use _____ names such as CON and PRN as if they were file names in commands such as COPY.

9. The _____ parameter of the COPY command tells DOS to verify that the copy has been made successfully with no errors.

10. Another term for text file is _____ file.

11. A _____ file is a file that contains programs or data that are not encoded as ASCII characters.

12. The _____ attribute indicates whether a file has been changed since it was last saved with the BACKUP command.

13. Unlike the COPY command, _____ can be instructed to copy files from all the subdirectories in the source disk or directory.

14. The _____ command is used to update previous versions of files.

15. The _____ command is used to compare the contents of two diskettes.

16. The _____ command lets you change the name of a disk.

17. Starting with version 4.0, DOS included _____, an external command that can present a memory report more detailed than CHKDSK.

18. The ASSIGN command lets you change the drive _____ associated with a disk drive.

19. The _____ command, which is the opposite of the JOIN command, lets you treat a subdirectory as if it were a disk in a separate drive.

20. The /T parameter of the PRINT command removes all files from the print _____ .

Short Problems

1. Change to your LESSONS subdirectory on the hard disk if you are not already there. Use the ATTRIB command to turn on the read-only attribute for every file in the subdirectory. Hint: you can use the global file name character * to do this with a single command. Now try to erase every file in the LESSONS subdirectory. When you are finished, turn off the read-only attributes of all the files in the LESSONS subdirectory.

2. Put a formatted floppy disk in drive A. Back up the contents of the LESSONS subdirectory using the /L parameter to create a log file. Don't specify a file name after the /L. When the BACKUP command is finished, a file named BACKUP.LOG will exist in the root directory of your hard disk. Examine this file with the TYPE command. As you can see, BACKUP.LOG lists the date and time of the backup, as well as the backup disk number and full path and name of each backed-up file.

3. You can create many interesting and useful DOS prompts with the PROMPT command. For example, try the following command:

   Type   **prompt Date = $d Time = t_pg**
   Press **Enter**

   Press **Enter** a few times to see the result. When you are finished, change the DOS prompt back to the way it was.

4. Insert a formatted floppy disk into drive A. If the LESSONS subdirectory isn't your current directory, change to it. Now, use the DIR command to see a directory listing of the LESSONS subdirectory. Notice that . and .. appear as the first two entries in the listing. These are special DOS designations for your current directory and the parent of your current directory. For example,

execute the following command to see a listing of the directory immediately above your current directory, which, in this case, happens to be the root directory of hard disk C:

> Type **dir ..**
> Press **Enter**

The . designation is equivalent to *.*, meaning your entire directory. Execute this command to see how it works:

> Type **xcopy . a:**
> Press **Enter**

This command will copy all of the files in your current directory, which happens to be LESSONS, to the disk in drive A.

5. Use the COPY command to copy all the files in your DOS subdirectory to a diskette in drive A. It doesn't matter if they all won't fit. Try to time, either with a watch or by counting, approximately how long this takes. Now, turn on the VERIFY option and then repeat the same COPY operation, timing the procedure in the same way. Does turning verification on cause the COPY command to take longer? Turn off the VERIFY option when you are finished.

6. Use the DATE command to find out what day of the week July 4, 2026 will fall on.

7. Create a new subdirectory named TEXT inside your LESSONS subdirectory. Copy all files with an extension of TXT from your LESSONS subdirectory to the LESSONS\TEXT subdirectory. Use the TREE command to display the structure of the LESSONS subdirectory. Then change to the LESSONS\TEXT subdirectory.

8. Make sure you are inside the LESSONS\TEXT subdirectory. You should have the files PART1.TXT, PART2.TXT, PARTX.TXT, and EXAMPLE.TXT inside the subdirectory. Create a new EXAMPLE.TXT file with the COPY command by appending PART2.TXT to PARTX.TXT. Use the TYPE command to examine the new EXAMPLE.TXT file.

9. Erase every file inside the LESSONS\TEXT subdirectory. Use the /P parameter to have DOS prompt you before erasing each file. Answer **y** for yes each time.

10. Use DIR to confirm that the LESSONS\TEXT subdirectory is empty. Move back to its parent subdirectory, LESSONS, by using the .. designation with the CD command. Remove the LESSONS\TEXT subdirectory, but leave the LESSONS subdirectory intact. Use DIR to confirm what you have done.

ADVANCED DOS

In This Chapter

Preview

The Beginning and Intermediate DOS chapters taught you most of what the average computer user needs to know about DOS. This chapter proceeds to more advanced DOS topics. You may not need all of the commands and features presented in this chapter, but many of them can make your work easier, faster, and less tedious. The more you learn about DOS, the better you will understand and use your microcomputer hardware and application software.

After studying this chapter, you will know how to

- redirect output and input.
- use DOS filters and piping.
- use batch files.
- use batch processing commands.
- set up a configuration file.
- partition and format a hard disk.
- execute several other DOS commands.
- use the DOS Shell.

Getting Started

You've already learned how to start DOS and use its most common features and commands. This chapter assumes you have completed all of the lessons and exercises of the previous two chapters. It also assumes that you have a computer with a hard disk and DOS 3.30, 4.00, or 4.01 installed on it in a subdirectory named DOS. The screens in this chapter were created with MS-DOS 4.01. To work the following lessons, boot up or reboot your computer if you have not already done so.

Lesson 1: Redirecting Output and Input

An interesting and useful aspect of DOS is its ability to redirect input or output information. Input usually comes from the keyboard or a file. Output usually goes to the display screen, printer, or a file. Some DOS commands that work with files can also receive input from or send output to peripheral devices, such as the keyboard, display, or printer. This can be done by using DOS device names such as CON and PRN in place of file names. CON stands for the console, which refers to the keyboard and display screen, and PRN refers to the printer.

Step 1: Redirect Output to the Printer

Redirection lets you change the normal source or destination of information processed by a DOS command. For example, the DIR command normally sends its output to the display screen. You can, however, instruct DOS to have DIR send its output to the printer. If you have a printer, turn it on, make sure it is on line and loaded with paper, and execute this command:

Type **dir >prn**
Press **Enter**

The directory should print instead of being displayed on your screen. The > (greater than sign) is the DOS symbol for redirecting output. It tells the DIR command to send its output to the device or file whose name follows, which, in this case, is the printer.

Redirecting the output to the printer works for most DOS commands. As another example, try this command:

Type **chkdsk >prn**
Press **Enter**

Step 2: Redirect Output to a File

You can also redirect the output of a DOS command to a text file instead of the display screen or printer. Simply type a valid file name after the redirection symbol. Change to your LESSONS subdirectory if you are not already in it and execute this command:

Type **dir >dirlist**
Press **Enter**

This time, the output of the DIR command goes to a file named DIRLIST. Since this file did not already exist in your LESSONS subdirectory, DOS created it. If a file of that name had existed, however, DOS would have overwritten its contents with the directory listing. Now, execute the following two commands to see a list of the files in your subdirectory and to display the contents of the DIRLIST file:

Type **dir**
Press **Enter**
Type **type dirlist**
Press **Enter**

Your screen should look like Figure 1. The directory listing in the file DIRLIST contains an entry for DIRLIST with a size of 0 bytes because DOS created the file before it actually performed the DIR.

Figure 1 Output of DIR Redirected to DIRLIST

```
PART1     TXT        35 07-15-89  11:45a
PART2     TXT       113 07-15-89  11:08a
EXAMPLE   TXT       149 07-15-89  11:48a
COMMAND   BAK     37557 12-19-88  12:00a
PARTX     TXT        35 07-15-89   2:49p
DIRLIST            471 07-18-89  10:36a
          8 File(s)  19650560 bytes free

C:\LESSONS>type dirlist

Volume in drive C is HARD DISK
Volume Serial Number is 3324-07CC
Directory of  C:\LESSONS

          <DIR>        07-12-89   4:01p
..        <DIR>        07-12-89   4:01p
PART1     TXT        35 07-15-89  11:45a
PART2     TXT       113 07-15-89  11:08a
EXAMPLE   TXT       149 07-15-89  11:48a
COMMAND   BAK     37557 12-19-88  12:00a
PARTX     TXT        35 07-15-89   2:49p
DIRLIST              0 07-18-89  10:35a
          8 File(s)  19650560 bytes free

C:\LESSONS>_
```

Step 3: Redirect and Append Output to a File

The > redirection symbol creates a new file or overwrites an existing file if it is followed by a file name. You can, however, tell DOS to append the output of a command to an existing file instead of overwriting its contents. Execute these commands:

Type **chkdsk >>dirlist**
Press **Enter**
Type **type dirlist**
Press **Enter**

Your screen should look like Figure 2. The >> redirection symbol adds the output of the CHKDSK command to the end of the DIRLIST file instead of overwriting it. If DIRLIST did not already exist, however, the >> symbol would tell DOS to create it.

Step 4: Redirect Input to a Command

DOS can also redirect the input to a command or program, but this is less common than redirecting output. Several DOS commands and many programs require the user to enter responses to prompts. In some cases, you can avoid having to enter these responses every time by putting them all in a text file and then redirecting that text file as input to the command or program.

For example, suppose that you want DOS to display the time, but you don't want to change it. If you don't specify a new time on the command line when you execute TIME, DOS will prompt you for the new time. You must press Enter to go on even if you don't want to change the time. You can, however, put your response in a text file beforehand and then redirect the input from that file to the TIME command. First, create a text file containing the carriage return generated by the Enter key. Execute these commands:

Type **copy con enter.txt**
Press **Enter**

Figure 2 Output of
CHKDSK Redirected and
Appended to DIRLIST

```
PART1    TXT       35 07-15-89  11:45a
PART2    TXT      113 07-15-89  11:08a
EXAMPLE  TXT      149 07-15-89  11:48a
COMMAND  BAK    37557 12-19-88  12:00a
PARTX    TXT       35 07-15-89   2:49p
DIRLIST            0 07-18-89  10:35a
         8 File(s)  19650560 bytes free

Volume HARD DISK   created 01-01-1980 12:28a
Volume Serial Number is 3324-07CC

   21204992 bytes total disk space
      73728 bytes in 3 hidden files
       6144 bytes in 2 directories
    1474560 bytes in 75 user files
   19650560 bytes available on disk

       2048 bytes in each allocation unit
      10354 total allocation units on disk
       9595 available allocation units on disk

     655360 total bytes memory
     521248 bytes free

C:\LESSONS>_
```

Figure 3 Input Redirected from ENTER.TXT

```
C:\LESSONS>copy con enter.txt

^Z
        1 File(s) copied

C:\LESSONS>time <enter.txt
Current time is 10:58:13.35a
Enter new time:

C:\LESSONS>_
```

Press   **Enter**
Press   **F6**
Press   **Enter**

The file ENTER.TXT now contains the carriage return character. To use ENTER.TXT as input to TIME, execute this command:

Type   **time <enter.txt**
Press   **Enter**

The < (less than sign) is the DOS symbol for redirecting input. After you enter this command, your screen should look like Figure 3. The TIME command displays the current time, but instead of waiting for you to enter the new time, it takes its input from the file ENTER.TXT and immediately returns to the DOS prompt.

Because it eliminates the need for you to enter responses, redirecting input is most often used for commands and programs that are run automatically from batch files.

Practice

1. If you are using DOS 4.00 or newer and have a printer, execute the MEM command with the /PROGRAM parameter, but redirect its output to the printer.

2. If you have a printer, change to the root directory and execute the TREE command with the /F parameter, but redirect its output to the printer. Change back to the LESSONS subdirectory.

3. You can use the ENTER.TXT file you created in this lesson as input to other commands. For example, redirect it as input to the DATE command.

Lesson 2: Using DOS Filters and Piping

A DOS **filter** is a command that normally reads input from the keyboard, changes it in some way, and then presents it as output to the display screen. Three DOS commands act as filters: FIND, MORE, and SORT. These commands work only with text. If you redirect the input, a filter can also accept input from a text file or a program. Similarly, you can redirect the output from a filter to a printer, file, or program.

In addition to redirection, DOS has a feature called piping that can be used with filter commands. **Piping,** symbolized by the | (vertical bar), allows you to take the output of one command, which would normally go to the display screen, and feed it as input to another command.

Step 1: Searching Files for Lines of Text

The DOS FIND filter searches a file for lines that contain a specified word or phrase and presents them as output. For example, suppose you want to find all the lines that contain the word "bytes" in the file DIRLIST. Execute the following command:

Type **find "bytes" dirlist**
Press **Enter**

Figure 4 shows the result. Note that the FIND command will locate only those lines with exact matches of the word or phrase you specify. In other words, uppercase and lowercase letters are considered different.

The FIND command has three parameters that can be useful:

Parameter	Action
/V	Displays only those lines *not* containing the specified word or phrase.
/C	Displays only the number of lines that contain a match, not the actual lines themselves.
/N	Precedes each line it finds with its relative line number in the file.

Figure 4 The FIND Command

```
C:\LESSONS>find "bytes" dirlist

---------- DIRLIST
        8 File(s)   19650560 bytes free
 21204992 bytes total disk space
    73728 bytes in 3 hidden files
     6144 bytes in 2 directories
  1474560 bytes in 75 user files
 19650560 bytes available on disk
     2048 bytes in each allocation unit
   655360 total bytes memory
   521248 bytes free

C:\LESSONS>_
```

Step 2: Displaying Output One Screen at a Time

The MORE command accepts input and then presents it as output, but only one screen at a time. This filter is almost always used with redirected or piped input from another command or file.

For example, some directories contain so many files that they scroll by too quickly to read when you use the DIR command. If your hard disk has a DOS subdirectory, execute this command:

Type   **dir c:\dos | more**
Press   **Enter**

Your screen should look like Figure 5. The output of the DIR command has been piped into the MORE filter instead of being displayed directly on the screen. MORE presents the same output, but pauses after a screen is full and displays the message "-- More --" at the bottom of the screen. Press a key, such as **Enter** or **Space Bar,** when you are ready to continue. MORE will present the rest of the directory, one screen at a time. Press a key to continue until you see the DOS prompt again.

The MORE filter can receive its input from a text file as well as from a command. Try this command to display DIRLIST and pause after each screen:

Type   **more <dirlist**
Press   **Enter**

The text file DIRLIST is redirected as the input to the MORE filter. Press a key to continue.

Step 3: Sorting Text

SORT is another DOS filter. This command receives input text, sorts the lines alphabetically or numerically, then displays the sorted text as output. SORT is often used with redirection, piping, and other DOS commands. The SORT filter

Figure 5 Output Piped into the MORE Filter

```
Volume in drive C is HARD DISK
Volume Serial Number is 3324-07CC
Directory of  C:\DOS

.            <DIR>      07-09-89   1:23p
..           <DIR>      07-09-89   1:23p
DOSSHELL BAT      196 07-09-89   1:22p
COMMAND  COM    37557 12-19-88  12:00a
COUNTRY  SYS    12806 10-06-88  12:00a
DISKCOPY COM    10396 10-06-88  12:00a
DISPLAY  SYS    15692 10-06-88  12:00a
FDISK    EXE    60935 12-19-88  12:00a
FORMAT   COM    22859 10-06-88  12:00a
KEYB     COM    14727 10-06-88  12:00a
KEYBOARD SYS    23328 10-06-88  12:00a
REPLACE  EXE    19415 10-06-88  12:00a
SYS      COM    11456 10-06-88  12:00a
ASSIGN   COM     5753 10-06-88  12:00a
ATTRIB   EXE    18263 10-06-88  12:00a
CHKDSK   COM    17787 10-06-88  12:00a
COMP     COM     9459 10-06-88  12:00a
DEBUG    COM    21574 10-06-88  12:00a
DISKCOMP COM     9857 10-06-88  12:00a
-- More --_
```

is often used to present an alphabetical directory listing. If you have a DOS subdirectory on your hard disk, execute this command:

Type **dir c:\dos | sort | more**
Press **Enter**

Figure 6 shows the result. The output of the DIR command is piped into the SORT filter, which rearranges the lines alphabetically. The output of the SORT filter is then piped into the MORE filter, which presents the sorted listing one screen at a time.

SORT is also used to rearrange text files. Let's create a sorted copy of the file DIRLIST in another file named DIRSORT. Execute these commands:

Type **sort <dirlist >dirsort**
Press **Enter**
Type **type dirsort**
Press **Enter**

Figure 7 shows the result. The lines from the file DIRLIST were redirected as input to the SORT filter. The sorted listing was redirected as output to the newly created file DIRSORT.

The SORT command has two useful parameters:

Parameter	Action
/R	Sorts the input in descending order (from Z to A, then from 9 to 0).
/+n	Sorts the input beginning with the character in column n, where n is some number. If you do not use this parameter SORT assumes column 1.

Practice

1. Execute each of the following commands and explain what it does:

Type **find /v "bytes" dirlist**
Press **Enter**

Figure 6 Output Piped into SORT and MORE

```
        68 File(s)   19644416 bytes free
   Directory of  C:\DOS
   Volume in drive C is HARD DISK
   Volume Serial Number is 3324-07CC
   .          <DIR>      07-09-89   1:23p
   ..         <DIR>      07-09-89   1:23p
   4201     CPI      6404 10-06-88  12:00a
   4208     CPI       720 10-06-88  12:00a
   5202     CPI       370 10-06-88  12:00a
   ANSI     SYS      9105 10-06-88  12:00a
   APPEND   EXE     11154 10-06-88  12:00a
   ASSIGN   COM      5753 10-06-88  12:00a
   ATTRIB   EXE     18263 10-06-88  12:00a
   BACKUP   COM     36880 10-06-88  12:00a
   CHKDSK   COM     17787 10-06-88  12:00a
   COMMAND  COM     37557 12-19-88  12:00a
   COMP     COM      9459 10-06-88  12:00a
   COUNTRY  SYS     12806 10-06-88  12:00a
   DEBUG    COM     21574 10-06-88  12:00a
   DISKCOMP COM      9857 10-06-88  12:00a
   DISKCOPY COM     10396 10-06-88  12:00a
   DISPLAY  SYS     15692 10-06-88  12:00a
   -- More --_
```

Figure 7 Redirected Input and Output for SORT

```
     2048 bytes in each allocation unit
     6144 bytes in 2 directories
     9595 available allocation units on disk
    10354 total allocation units on disk
    73728 bytes in 3 hidden files
   521248 bytes free
   655360 total bytes memory
  1474560 bytes in 75 user files
 19650560 bytes available on disk
 21204992 bytes total disk space
Directory of  C:\LESSONS
Volume in drive C is HARD DISK
Volume Serial Number is 3324-07CC
         .        <DIR>       07-12-89    4:01p
         ..       <DIR>       07-12-89    4:01p
COMMAND   BAK       37557 12-19-88   12:00a
DIRLIST               0 07-18-89   10:35a
EXAMPLE   TXT       149 07-15-89   11:48a
PART1     TXT        35 07-15-89   11:45a
PART2     TXT       113 07-15-89   11:08a
PARTX     TXT        35 07-15-89    2:49p
Volume HARD DISK   created 01-01-1980 12:28a
Volume Serial Number is 3324-07CC

C:\LESSONS>_
```

Type	**find /c "bytes" dirlist**
Press	**Enter**
Type	**find /n "bytes" dirlist**
Press	**Enter**
Type	**find /v/c "bytes" dirlist**
Press	**Enter**
Type	**find /v/n "bytes" dirlist**
Press	**Enter**

2. Change to the root directory. Try the following command and explain what it does:

Type	**tree /f | find ".EXE"**
Press	**Enter**

How is it different from DIR *.EXE? Change back to the LESSONS subdirectory.

3. Execute each of the following commands and explain what it does:

Type	**sort /r < dirlist**
Press	**Enter**
Type	**dir c:\dos | sort /+14 | more**
Press	**Enter**

Hint for the second command: the file size appears in the directory listing after column 14.

Lesson 3: Using Batch Files

A **batch file** is a text file that contains a list of commands or programs to be run. Batch files are usually created with a text editor or word processing program, but you can easily create short ones using the COPY command and the CON device name. Every batch file must have an extension of BAT. A batch file is invoked by typing its filename, without the extension, and pressing the Enter key. When this is done, DOS executes each command or program listed in the batch file, one at a time. DOS includes features that enable experienced users to construct complex and very helpful batch files. Even if you never make your own batch files, you will undoubtedly use some made by others or included with application packages. As an example, let's create and use a simple batch file.

Step 1: Create the Batch File

Batch files are usually created with a text editor or word processor. Short ones, however, can be easily created with the COPY command. Make sure LESSONS is your current subdirectory. Execute these commands to create a simple batch file named SHOW.BAT:

Type	**copy con show.bat**
Press	**Enter**
Type	**cls**
Press	**Enter**
Type	**dir *.txt**
Press	**Enter**
Type	**type example.txt**
Press	**Enter**
Press	**F6**
Press	**Enter**

Note that the CLS, DIR, and TYPE commands were not executed when you pressed Enter because they are text in the file SHOW.BAT. They were not passed to the DOS command processor.

Step 2: Execute the Batch File

Running a batch file is the same as executing a command or running an application program. You type its filename (without the extension) and press the Enter key. To run your newly created batch file, execute this command:

Type	**show**
Press	**Enter**

Figure 8 shows the result. The commands inside the file SHOW.BAT were executed as if you had entered them directly from the keyboard.

Most commands and programs that you can run directly from the DOS prompt can be put inside a batch file. Batch files allow you to automate frequently executed series of commands. They also allow experts to set up complex sequences of commands to be run by novices. For example, many new application programs must be installed on your system before you can use them. In some cases, this installation process can be quite involved. Most software developers, therefore, include one or more batch files that make the installation process easier for users.

Step 3: Examine the AUTOEXEC.BAT File

The most commonly used batch file is a special one named AUTOEXEC.BAT—the auto-execute batch file. Each time you boot up your computer, DOS searches the root directory of the default drive for this AUTOEXEC.BAT file. If no AUTOEXEC.BAT is file present, DOS simply asks you to supply the current date and time, and then displays its prompt. If, on the other hand, AUTOEXEC.BAT is found, that batch file is automatically executed. DOS will not prompt you for the

Figure 8 The SHOW Batch File

```
C:\LESSONS>dir *.txt

 Volume in drive C is HARD DISK
 Volume Serial Number is 3324-07CC
 Directory of  C:\LESSONS

PART1     TXT        35 07-15-89   11:45a
PART2     TXT       113 07-15-89   11:08a
EXAMPLE   TXT       149 07-15-89   11:48a
PARTX     TXT        35 07-15-89    2:49p
ENTER     TXT         2 07-18-89   10:57a
         5 File(s)   19644416 bytes free

C:\LESSONS>type example.txt
This is the new sample text file.
A text file contains only letters, numbers,
punctuation marks, and other symbols that
appear on the keyboard.

C:\LESSONS>
C:\LESSONS>_
```

date and time if it finds AUTOEXEC.BAT, unless the DATE and TIME commands appear in AUTOEXEC.BAT.

Since the AUTOEXEC.BAT file is automatically invoked every time you boot up your computer, it is ideal for listing commands and programs you always run when you first turn on your machine. PATH, APPEND, and PROMPT, for example, are often put into the AUTOEXEC.BAT file to be executed each time the computer is booted. Most DOS users eventually set up their own AUTO-EXEC.BAT files or have someone else help them do so. You can examine the contents of the AUTOEXEC.BAT file on your computer by executing this command:

Type   **type c:\autoexec.bat**
Press **Enter**

Figure 9 shows a typical AUTOEXEC.BAT file; yours might be different. Some of the commands, such as VERIFY, PATH, APPEND, PROMPT, VER, and PRINT, should be familiar to you. You will learn about the other commands shown in Figure 9 in this chapter.

Practice

1. Create a batch file named NOW.BAT that displays the current date and time and immediately returns to the DOS prompt without prompting you to enter a new date and time. Hint: redirect input from the ENTER.TXT file you created in Lesson 1. Execute NOW.BAT a couple of times to see that it works.

2. Create a batch file named WHAT.BAT that displays the DOS version and the volume label of the default disk. Execute WHAT.BAT a couple of times to see that it works.

3. Although AUTOEXEC.BAT is executed automatically every time you boot up the computer, you can also execute it manually like any other batch file. Change to the root directory and execute AUTOEXEC.BAT. Then change back to the LESSONS subdirectory.

Figure 9 A Typical AUTO-
EXEC.BAT File

```
C:\LESSONS>type c:\autoexec.bat
@ECHO OFF
SET COMSPEC=C:\DOS\COMMAND.COM
VERIFY OFF
PATH C:\DOS
APPEND /E
APPEND C:\DOS
PROMPT $P$G
C:\DOS\GRAPHICS
VER
PRINT /D:LPT1

C:\LESSONS>_
```

Lesson 4: Using Batch Processing Commands

Any command or program you can invoke from the keyboard can be executed from inside a batch file. In addition, DOS has a special set of internal commands known as **batch processing commands** that can add power and flexibility to batch files. Batch processing commands are normally executed only from within batch files. Let's examine batch files in more detail and demonstrate the batch processing commands designed especially for them.

Step 1: Use Replaceable Parameters

Most computer users find that they occasionally repeat the same, or nearly the same, command sequence over and over. In some cases, you can reduce repetitive typing by creating a batch file with a very short name that contains the command sequence. For example, make sure you are in your LESSONS subdirectory, and execute these commands:

Type   **copy con d.bat**
Press **Enter**
Type   **dir | sort | more**
Press **Enter**
Press **F6**
Press **Enter**

You have created a batch file named D.BAT that contains the DIR | SORT | MORE sequence of commands. To execute this batch file:

Type   **d**
Press **Enter**

This batch file can save you a lot of typing if you often execute the commands it contains, but what if you want to use it on some other directory? You can make this batch file much more flexible by using a **replaceable parameter.** This is a special code you insert into your batch file that lets you pass information to that batch file while it is running. To demonstrate, let's redo the D.BAT file. Execute these commands:

> Type   **copy con d.bat**
> Press **Enter**
> Type   **dir %1 | sort | more**
> Press **Enter**
> Press **F6**
> Press **Enter**

The %1 you have typed into the batch file is a replaceable parameter. When you execute the batch file, the %1 will be replaced by whatever you type on the command line after the D. For example, execute this command:

> Type   **d c:\dos**
> Press **Enter**

The computer will display a sorted listing of the DOS subdirectory on your hard disk, one screen at a time. The C:\DOS you typed after the D replaced the %1 in the batch file. Now you can use your D.BAT file to list any directory on any disk, simply by typing a different path after the D. You can even type nothing after the D to get a listing of your current directory. DOS allows you to use up to nine such replaceable parameters, from %1 to %9, in any single batch file command.

Step 2: Use the CALL Batch Command

A batch file can contain any command you can type at the DOS prompt, even the name of another batch file. For example, execute the following commands to create a new batch file named DO_D.BAT:

> Type   **copy con do_d.bat**
> Press **Enter**
> Type   **type d.bat**
> Press **Enter**
> Type   **d**
> Press **Enter**
> Type   **type d.bat**
> Press **Enter**
> Press **F6**
> Press **Enter**

Now, execute your new batch file:

> Type   **do_d**
> Press **Enter**

Your screen should look like Figure 10. If you look closely, you will see that DO_D.BAT did not do what you might have expected. It did the first TYPE D.BAT and then executed D.BAT all right, but it did not execute the second TYPE D.BAT. This is because when D.BAT ended, so did DO_D.BAT. It appears that invoking one batch file from within another only works when the inside one is at the end. This is sometimes called **chaining** batch files.

The CALL batch file command, however, allows you to invoke one batch file from within another batch file without ending the first batch file. This is some-

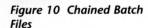

Figure 10 Chained Batch Files

```
C:\LESSONS>dir | sort | more


       13 File(s)   19638272 bytes free
 Directory of   C:\LESSONS
 Volume in drive C is HARD DISK
 Volume Serial Number is 3324-07CC
 .              <DIR>      07-12-89    4:01p
 ..             <DIR>      07-12-89    4:01p
 COMMAND  BAK    37557 12-19-88   12:00a
 D        BAT       22 07-18-89    3:12p
 DIRLIST          923 07-18-89   10:39a
 DIRSORT          923 07-18-89   12:06p
 DO_D     BAT       27 07-18-89    3:19p
 ENTER    TXT        2 07-18-89   10:57a
 EXAMPLE  TXT      149 07-15-89   11:48a
 PART1    TXT       35 07-15-89   11:45a
 PART2    TXT      113 07-15-89   11:08a
 PARTX    TXT       35 07-15-89    2:49p
 SHOW     BAT       34 07-18-89    2:18p

 C:\LESSONS>
 C:\LESSONS>_
```

times known as **nesting** batch files. Let's redo DO_D.BAT. Execute the following commands:

Type   **copy con do_d.bat**
Press   **Enter**
Type   **type d.bat**
Press   **Enter**
Type   **call d**
Press   **Enter**
Type   **type d.bat**
Press   **Enter**
Press   **F6**
Press   **Enter**

Now, execute your new DO_D.BAT file:

Type   **do_d**
Press   **Enter**

This time, DO_D.BAT will execute the second TYPE D.BAT as well, as shown in Figure 11.

Step 3: Use the ECHO Batch Command

Normally, the commands in a batch file are displayed, or echoed, to the screen just as if you had entered them from the command line. The ECHO command lets you turn this echoing off and back on again. It can also be used to display a message on the screen from within a batch file. To demonstrate the ECHO command, execute the following commands to create a new batch file named E.BAT:

Type   **copy con e.bat**
Press   **Enter**
Type   **@echo off**
Press   **Enter**
Type   **echo Your current directory:**

Figure 11 CALL Used to Nest Batch Files

```
        13 File(s)   19638272 bytes free
Directory of  C:\LESSONS
Volume in drive C is HARD DISK
Volume Serial Number is 3324-07CC
           <DIR>      07-12-89    4:01p
 ..        <DIR>      07-12-89    4:01p
COMMAND  BAK    37557 12-19-88   12:00a
D        BAT       22 07-18-89    3:12p
DIRLIST          923 07-18-89   10:39a
DIRSORT          923 07-18-89   12:06p
DO_D     BAT       32 07-18-89    3:22p
ENTER    TXT        2 07-18-89   10:57a
EXAMPLE  TXT      149 07-15-89   11:48a
PART1    TXT       35 07-15-89   11:45a
PART2    TXT      113 07-15-89   11:08a
PARTX    TXT       35 07-15-89    2:49p
SHOW     BAT       34 07-18-89    2:18p

C:\LESSONS>
C:\LESSONS>type d.bat
dir %1 | sort | more

C:\LESSONS>
C:\LESSONS>_
```

Press   **Enter**
Type   **dir**
Press   **Enter**
Press   **F6**
Press   **Enter**

Now, try the batch file you have just created:

Type   **e**
Press   **Enter**

Figure 12 shows the result. The @ (at-sign) preceding the first ECHO command tells DOS not to display that batch file line on the screen. The second ECHO

Figure 12 The ECHO Batch Command

```
        1 File(s) copied

C:\LESSONS>e
Your current directory:

   Volume in drive C is HARD DISK
   Volume Serial Number is 3324-07CC
   Directory of  C:\LESSONS

 .         <DIR>      07-12-89    4:01p
 ..        <DIR>      07-12-89    4:01p
PART1    TXT       35 07-15-89   11:45a
PART2    TXT      113 07-15-89   11:08a
EXAMPLE  TXT      149 07-15-89   11:48a
COMMAND  BAK    37557 12-19-88   12:00a
PARTX    TXT       35 07-15-89    2:49p
DIRLIST          923 07-18-89   10:39a
ENTER    TXT        2 07-18-89   10:57a
DIRSORT          923 07-18-89   12:06p
SHOW     BAT       34 07-18-89    2:18p
D        BAT       22 07-18-89    3:12p
DO_D     BAT       32 07-18-89    3:22p
E        BAT       46 07-18-89    3:28p
        14 File(s)  19638272 bytes free
C:\LESSONS>_
```

does not need to be preceded by a @ because echoing has already been turned off by the previous command. Note that with echoing turned off, only the output of the DIR command is presented on the screen, not the DIR command itself.

Step 4: Repeat a Command On a Set of Files

DOS has a batch command that lets you repeat an action on a set of files. The FOR command is similar to the counted loop commands found in high-level programming languages, such as BASIC and Pascal. Suppose you want to display the contents of every batch file in your current directory. Let's create a batch file that can do this. Execute the following commands:

> Type **copy con type_all.bat**
> Press **Enter**
> Type **for %%f in (*.bat) do type %%f**
> Press **Enter**
> Press **F6**
> Press **Enter**

Now, try this batch file:

> Type **type_all**
> Press **Enter**

Figure 13 shows the result. DOS has repeated the TYPE command on every batch file in your current directory. The %%f symbol in the TYPE_ALL.BAT file is like a variable that holds a different file name each time the FOR command repeats. It repeats for each file that matches the *.BAT file specification and uses the TYPE command to display the contents of that file on the screen.

Step 5: Use the IF and GOTO Batch Commands

The IF and GOTO commands allow you to alter the order in which batch file commands are executed, based on the result of a condition. This is sometimes called **branching.** Like the FOR command, IF and GOTO are similar to statements

Figure 13 The FOR Batch Command

```
C:\LESSONS>type SHOW.BAT
cls
dir *.txt
type example.txt

C:\LESSONS>type D.BAT
dir %1 | sort | more

C:\LESSONS>type DO_D.BAT
type d.bat
call d
type d.bat

C:\LESSONS>type E.BAT
@echo off
echo Your current directory:
dir

C:\LESSONS>type TYPE_ALL.BAT
for %%f in (*.bat) do type %%f


C:\LESSONS>
C:\LESSONS>_
```

found in high-level programming languages, such as BASIC and Pascal. Complex and extremely useful batch files can be set up with these commands, but let's keep our example simple. Suppose you wanted to create a batch file that just tells you if any TXT files are in a directory. Execute the following commands:

Type   `copy con any_txt.bat`
Press **Enter**
Type   `@echo off`
Press **Enter**
Type   `if not exist %1\*.txt goto notfound`
Press **Enter**
Type   `echo At least one .TXT file is in %1.`
Press **Enter**
Type   `goto end`
Press **Enter**
Type   `:notfound`
Press **Enter**
Type   `echo No .TXT files are in %1.`
Press **Enter**
Type   `:end`
Press **Enter**
Press **F6**
Press **Enter**

Let's discuss what this batch file does before you try it. First, it turns off echoing. Notice that it has one replaceable parameter, %1, that is used in two places. This parameter will be the path of the directory to be checked; it must be typed by the user when ANY_TXT.BAT is executed. The IF command tells DOS to branch to the "notfound" label if no .TXT files exist in the specified directory. In this context, a **label** is simply a place for a GOTO command to branch to; it must be present later in the batch file on its own line preceded by a : (colon). If at least one .TXT file is present in the specified directory, the first ECHO message will be displayed, the batch file will branch to the "end" label, and then it will terminate. If no .TXT files were found, only the second ECHO message will be displayed.

Now, execute the following commands to try your ANY_TXT.BAT file:

Type   `any_txt \lessons`
Press **Enter**
Type   `any_txt \dos`
Press **Enter**
Type   `any_txt \`
Press **Enter**

Figure 14 shows the result.

Step 6: Use the PAUSE Batch Command

In some batch files, it may be necessary for the user to change disks or perform some other action. The PAUSE command lets you suspend the execution of a batch file until the user is ready and presses a key to continue. Execute the following commands to create a simple example:

Type   `copy con dir_a.bat`
Press **Enter**

Figure 14 The IF and
GOTO Batch Commands

```
C:\LESSONS>copy con any_txt.bat
@echo off
if not exist %1\*.txt goto notfound
echo At least one .TXT file is in %1.
goto end
:notfound
echo No .TXT files are in %1.
:end
^Z
        1 File(s) copied

C:\LESSONS>any_txt \lessons
At least one .TXT file is in \lessons.
C:\LESSONS>any_txt \dos
At least one .TXT file is in \dos.
C:\LESSONS>any_txt \
No .TXT files are in \.
C:\LESSONS>_
```

Type   **@echo off**
Press   **Enter**
Type   **echo Please put a disk into drive A.**
Press   **Enter**
Type   **pause**
Press   **Enter**
Type   **dir a:**
Press   **Enter**
Press   **F6**
Press   **Enter**

To try your new batch file, execute this command and follow the directions:

Type   **dir_a**
Press   **Enter**

Figure 15 shows the result, but your screen may be different, depending on the diskette you inserted into drive A.

Step 7: Use the REM Command to Add Comments

In some ways, a batch file is like a program created with a high-level language, such as BASIC or Pascal. Most programming languages provide a way for you to document your programs by adding comments. These statements don't tell the computer to do anything; they just let you describe how your program works. Adding comments can help you identify and remember what you did when you created your program. They are also invaluable to anyone who may be trying to understand your work. REM is the DOS batch file comment command. To see how it works, execute the following commands:

Type   **copy con r.bat**
Press   **Enter**
Type   **rem This batch file demonstrates the REM command.**
Press   **Enter**

*Figure 15 The PAUSE
Batch Command*

```
C:\LESSONS>copy con dir_a.bat
@echo off
echo Please put a disk into drive A.
pause
dir a:
^Z
        1 File(s) copied

C:\LESSONS>dir_a
Please put a disk into drive A.
Press any key to continue . . .


  Volume in drive A has no label
  Volume Serial Number is 283D-13CC
  Directory of  A:\

COMMAND  COM    37557 12-19-88  12:00a
        1 File(s)    252928 bytes free
C:\LESSONS>_
```

Type	**rem Remarks (comments) are displayed if ECHO is ON.**
Press	**Enter**
Type	**@echo off**
Press	**Enter**
Type	**rem If ECHO is turned OFF, remarks won't be displayed.**
Press	**Enter**
Press	**F6**
Press	**Enter**

Now, execute your new batch file:

Type	**r**
Press	**Enter**

Your screen should look like Figure 16. Note that even if remarks aren't displayed, they are still in the batch file and can be viewed if you TYPE it or examine it with a text editor or word processor. REM commands are also sometimes used to **comment out,** or temporarily shut off, batch file commands that you may want to activate again later.

Step 8: Use the SHIFT Batch Command

You have learned that you can pass information to a batch file by using replaceable parameters. Usually, batch files are limited to handling a maximum of ten replaceable parameters, symbolized by %0 through %9. The SHIFT command, however, lets you have more than ten replaceable parameters in the unlikely event you would ever need that many. Every time the SHIFT command is executed in a batch file, all parameters on the command line are shifted one position to the left. In other words, the %1 parameter will replace the %0 parameter, the %2 parameter will replace the %3 parameter, and so on. Once SHIFT is executed, you cannot go backward and retrieve the former %0 parameter. SHIFT is a some-

Figure 16 The REM Batch Command

```
C:\LESSONS>copy con r.bat
rem This batch file demonstrates the REM command.
rem Remarks (comments) are displayed if ECHO is ON.
@echo off
rem If ECHO is turned OFF, remarks won't be displayed.
^Z
        1 File(s) copied

C:\LESSONS>r

C:\LESSONS>rem This batch file demonstrates the REM command.

C:\LESSONS>rem Remarks (comments) are displayed if ECHO is ON.
C:\LESSONS>_
```

what exotic command that is rarely needed. Nevertheless, here is an example of its use. Execute the following commands:

Type	**copy con supert.bat**
Press	**Enter**
Type	**@echo off**
Press	**Enter**
Type	**:again**
Press	**Enter**
Type	**for %%f in (%1 %2 %3 %4 %5 %6 %7 %8 %9) do type %%f**
Press	**Enter**
Type	**for %%x in (1 2 3 4 5 6 7 8 9) do shift**
Press	**Enter**
Type	**if not "%1"=="" goto again**
Press	**Enter**
Press	**F6**
Press	**Enter**

This rather complex batch file, named SUPERT.BAT, is essentially a super TYPE command that can accept any number of individual file names on the command line, as long as the total length of the command line does not exceed 127 characters. The first FOR command reads in each of the first nine replaceable parameters and tries to TYPE it out as a file name. The second FOR command performs nine SHIFT commands in a row to load in the next nine file names. The IF statement branches to the "again" label if the first file name is not blank, in which case the entire process is repeated again. SUPERT.BAT ends when no more file names are on the command line.

Suppose you have 20 files named A, B, C, and so on to T. You can use SUPERT to type them all out with one command. Execute the following command even though you don't have files named A to T. (The TYPE command will just say "File not found" for each file.)

Type	**supert a b c d e f g h i j k l m n o p q r s t**
Press	**Enter**

Your screen should look like Figure 17. If you did have 20 files named A through T, SUPERT.BAT would have displayed them all on the screen, one after the other. SUPERT.BAT can handle any number of replaceable parameters. If it weren't for the SHIFT command, it could handle no more than ten.

Practice

1. Use your D.BAT file to generate a directory listing of the root directory. Use it again on your current subdirectory.
2. Try the TYPE_ALL.BAT file again, now that you have more batch files in your LESSONS subdirectory.
3. Use DIR to get a directory of your LESSONS subdirectory. Then use SUPERT.BAT in one command to type out any three batch files and any three text files in the LESSONS subdirectory. Remember: a command line can take up more than one line (just keep typing) as long as it contains no more than 127 characters. Notice how SUPERT.BAT runs all the files together on the screen.

Lesson 5: Setting Up the Configuration File

The configuration file CONFIG.SYS is a special text file that DOS looks for in the root directory of the default disk when you boot up. It contains special commands that set up your system in a certain way and is usually created when you install DOS or a new application package. You may, however, have to create or modify the CONFIG.SYS file yourself if you ever add new hardware or software to your system.

Step 1: Examine Your CONFIG.SYS File

Change back to the root directory of your hard disk and examine the contents of your CONFIG.SYS file by executing these commands:

Type **cd **
Press **Enter**

Figure 17 The SHIFT Batch Command

```
C:\LESSONS>supert a b c d e f g h i j k l m n o p q r s t
File not found - A
File not found - B
File not found - C
File not found - D
File not found - E
File not found - F
File not found - G
File not found - H
File not found - I
File not found - J
File not found - K
File not found - L
File not found - M
File not found - N
File not found - O
File not found - P
File not found - Q
File not found - R
File not found - S
File not found - T
C:\LESSONS>_
```

DOS120 *Advanced DOS*

Type   **type config.sys**
Press **Enter**

Figure 18 shows a typical CONFIG.SYS file, but yours is probably different. If DOS replies with the message "File not found," then you do not have a CON-FIG.SYS file. This means that when DOS boots up on your computer, it uses the default configuration settings.

Step 2: Explore the Configuration Commands

You are not going to change your CONFIG.SYS file in this lesson. If you have one already set up on your computer, it contains the commands you need for your particular arrangement of hardware and software. Usually, CONFIG.SYS is created or modified with a text editor or word processor. It can also be created by copying the output of the console to the file CONFIG.SYS.

Instead of actually changing your CONFIG.SYS file, let's just briefly discuss the special commands that can be put there. Note that the following commands (except for BREAK) cannot be entered from the DOS prompt; they work only in the CONFIG.SYS file when the computer boots up. Some configuration commands are often used, while others are more technical and are rarely used on most systems. The DOS configuration commands are as follows.

Command	*Action*
BREAK = x	This command controls whether or not DOS will stop a command or program from completing its task if Ctrl-Break (or Ctrl-C) is pressed. BREAK = OFF tells DOS to terminate a program only during screen, keyboard, and printer reads and writes if Ctrl-Break is pressed. BREAK = ON tells DOS to terminate a program also during disk reads and writes.
BUFFERS = n	A **disk buffer** is an area of memory DOS uses to temporarily hold data being read from or written to a disk. Increasing the number of buffers may increase performance, but it uses more memory. There is no definite rule for what n should be; use a value suggested by the documentation of the software package you use most often.
COUNTRY = xxx	DOS can be set up to use international conventions for date, time, currency, and character set. This command can be omitted if you want to use the settings for the United States. Otherwise, enter the country code xxx, which you can look up in the DOS reference manual.
DEVICE = *file*	A **device driver** is a file that contains the programming code needed to attach and use a special device such as a nonstandard disk drive, memory board, mouse, monitor, or printer. This file is usually provided by the manufacturer of the device. The *file* name, which has an extension of SYS, must be specified along with any parameters indicated by the manufacturer.

Figure 18 A Typical CONFIG.SYS File

```
C:\LESSONS>cd \

C:\>type config.sys
BREAK=ON
BUFFERS=20
FILES=20
LASTDRIVE=E
SHELL=C:\DOS\COMMAND.COM /P /E:256
DEVICE=C:\DOS\ANSI.SYS
INSTALL=C:\DOS\FASTOPEN.EXE C:=(50,25)

C:\>_
```

Command

DRIVEPARM = /x

Action

This command allows you to define parameters for disk or tape drives when you start DOS, overriding the default device settings. You can specify the drive number, type of drive, number of read/write heads, number of sectors, and number of tracks. For example, suppose you want to set up an internal tape drive as drive D configured to write 20 tracks of 40 sectors per track. Here is the command you would use:

DRIVEPARM = /D:3 /F:6 /H:1 /S:40 /T:20
The /D:3 specifies the tape drive as drive D. The /F:6 specifies that the device is a tape drive. The /H:1 specifies one read/write head. The /S:40 and /T:20 specify 40 sectors and 20 tracks.

FCBS = x,y

A **file control block (FCB)** is a data structure used by early versions of DOS to manage open files. If you have an old application program that requires file control blocks, you can use the FCBS command in CONFIG.SYS to specify the number of files that can be open at one time (x) and the number of opened files that DOS cannot close automatically (y).

FILES = n

By default, DOS can have only eight files open at a time. But many sophisticated software packages, especially data base managers, must have more than eight files open at a time. The FILES command lets you increase the maximum number of open files by specifying a larger n, such as 20.

INSTALL = file

This command can be used to execute certain DOS commands that should be executed only once. It is preferable to put these commands in CONFIG.SYS

Command	Action
	rather than in AUTOEXEC.BAT because AUTO-EXEC.BAT can be executed more than once after the computer is booted up. The *file* name after INSTALL must be one of the following: FASTOPEN.EXE, KEY.EXE, NLSFUNC.EXE, or SHARE.EXE. You will learn what these DOS commands do later in this chapter.
LASTDRIVE = *x*	By default, DOS supports only five drives, A through E. In order to create and access drives with letters beyond E, you must put the LASTDRIVE command in CONFIG.SYS and specify *x*, where *x* is the letter of the last drive you wish to access. For example, suppose you want to use the SUBST command to treat a subdirectory as if it were disk drive Z. You would have to put the command LAST-DRIVE = Z in your CONFIG.SYS file and then reboot before you could execute the SUBST command to create the virtual drive Z.
REM	The CONFIG.SYS file can be cryptic, especially to DOS novices. Fortunately, DOS versions 4.0 and newer include a REM configuration command. The REM configuration command allows you to add comments to CONFIG.SYS, just as the REM batch command allows you to add comments to batch files. REM is also handy for temporarily commenting out commands in CONFIG.SYS that you expect to reinstate later. To comment out a command in CONFIG.SYS, you simply insert REM and a space in front of it and then reboot. DOS will ignore that command as a comment.
SHELL = *file*	COMMAND.COM is the program that processes the DOS commands you enter. The SHELL configuration command lets you install an alternate command processor program. It also lets you install COMMAND.COM as your command processor, but with certain additional parameters specified. For example, examine the SHELL command that appears in Figure 18. It tells DOS to install the COMMAND.COM in the DOS subdirectory as the command processor with an environment size of 256 bytes. (You will learn about environment size later in this chapter.)
STACKS = *n,s*	When a hardware interrupt occurs, such as a key-press, the computer saves what it was doing in a data structure known as a **stack.** The STACKS configuration command lets you set the number (*n*) and size (*s*) of the internal stacks DOS will use when handling hardware interrupts. A hardware or software situation that causes many interrupts in a short period of time might necessitate increasing the number and size of the internal stacks with the STACK command.

`Practice`   1. Type out the CONFIG.SYS file in the root directory of your startup disk and explain what each command does. Skip Practice exercise 2 if you already have a CONFIG.SYS file.

2. If you already have a CONFIG.SYS file in your root directory, do NOT do this exercise. Only if no CONFIG.SYS file is present in your root directory, create one by following these instructions:

Type	`copy con config.sys`
Press	**Enter**
Type	`break=on`
Press	**Enter**
Type	`buffers=20`
Press	**Enter**
Type	`files=20`
Press	**Enter**
Type	`lastdrive = z`
Press	**F6**
Press	**Enter**

Reboot your computer to execute the configuration commands in the new CONFIG.SYS file.

Lesson 6: Partitioning and Formatting Hard Disks

A **partition** is a separate section of a hard disk that may contain its own operating system. Every hard disk must contain at least one partition and may contain as many as four. A DOS partition must be created on a hard disk before DOS can be installed on it and before it can be formatted as a startup disk. This procedure has already been done on your computer. Partitioning and formatting the hard disk is often done by computer retailers, so you may not have to do it even if you buy a new computer. Nevertheless, you should be familiar with this process if you ever have to reconfigure your hard disk.

Step 1: Use the FDISK Command

FDISK is an external command that presents a series of menus to help you partition a hard disk for DOS. FDISK does not work if you are running DOS from a network. You must use FDISK if you want to do one of the following procedures:

- Create a primary DOS partition
- Create an extended DOS partition
- Create a logical DOS drive
- Set the active partition
- Delete a DOS partition or logical drive
- Display information about a partition
- Configure an additional hard drive

The primary DOS partition is the part of the hard disk where DOS is installed. You boot up from the primary DOS partition. In most cases, one DOS partition, the primary partition, will be on a hard disk. Very large hard disks, however, may contain extended DOS partitions configured as extra logical drives. This was common before DOS 4.00, which first allowed hard disks larger than 32 megabytes to be used as a single drive. For example, if you have an 80-megabyte hard disk and you want to run DOS 3.3, you would need to set up a primary DOS partition and two extended DOS partitions. The primary DOS partition of 32 megabytes would be set up as drive C. The extended DOS partitions, each of 24 megabytes, would be set up as logical drives D and E. They are called logical because they are treated as different drives even though they are actually part of the same drive. DOS versions 4.00 and newer allow partitions to be larger than 32 megabytes, so using extended partitions is optional.

After the DOS partitions have been created, you also use FDISK to select the active partition. The active partition is the one that contains the operating system and the files you access when you turn on or reboot your computer. For example, you could set up a large hard disk with a partition for DOS and a partition for XENIX, a variant of the UNIX operating system. Only one of these partitions could be active at a time, however. The XENIX partition would have to be set up after booting up the computer from a XENIX startup diskette.

Let's use FDISK to display partition information about your hard disk.

Type **fdisk**
Press **Enter**

Figure 19 shows the FDISK menu that appears on the screen. Do NOT choose options 1, 2, or 3 unless you are absolutely sure of what you are doing. Creating or changing DOS partitions destroys all existing files on a hard disk. You should reconfigure a hard disk with FDISK only if it is a new, empty disk or if you have backup copies of all the files on the disk. Choose option 4 to display partition information:

Type **4**
Press **Enter**

The FDISK command will present a screen that reveals information about the partitions on your hard disk. Figure 20 shows a computer that has only one DOS

Figure 19 The FDISK Menu

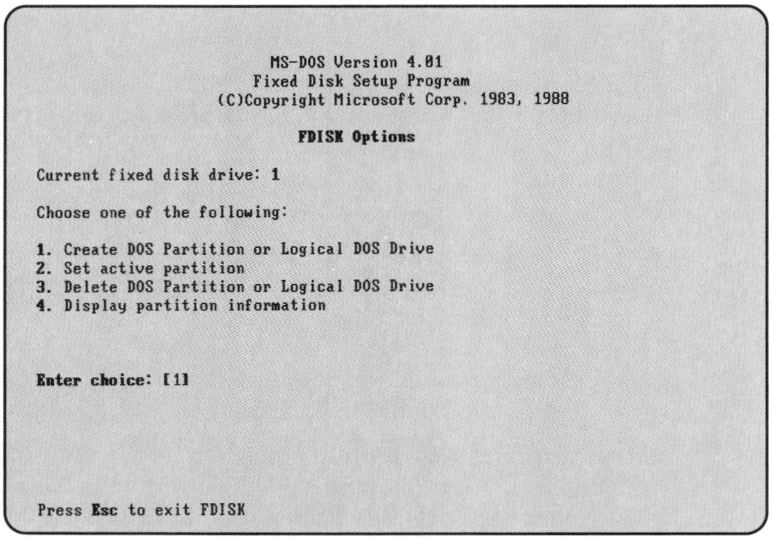

```
                    MS-DOS Version 4.01
                  Fixed Disk Setup Program
              (C)Copyright Microsoft Corp. 1983, 1988

                        FDISK Options

  Current fixed disk drive: 1

  Choose one of the following:

  1. Create DOS Partition or Logical DOS Drive
  2. Set active partition
  3. Delete DOS Partition or Logical DOS Drive
  4. Display partition information



  Enter choice: [1]




  Press Esc to exit FDISK
```

*Figure 20 Partition Infor-
mation Displayed by FDISK*

```
                          Display Partition Information

     Current fixed disk drive: 1

     Partition Status   Type    Size in Mbytes   Percentage of Disk Used
       C: 1        A    PRI DOS       20             100%




     Total disk space is   20 Mbytes (1 Mbyte = 1048576 bytes)








     Press Esc to return to FDISK Options
```

partition, the primary and active partition, with a size of 20 megabytes. Now, do the following to leave FDISK and return to the DOS prompt:

> Press **Escape** (2 times)

Step 2: Use the FORMAT Command

If you were setting up a new hard disk or reconfiguring an old one, you would still have to format each partition you created with FDISK. DON'T do this now, but you would use the FORMAT command with the /S parameter on hard disk C to create the startup disk. Then you would format any extended DOS partitions configured as logical drives.

Warning: you should not use the FDISK and FORMAT commands on a hard disk unless you know *exactly* what you are doing because you can lose all the files on the disk.

Practice Use the DIR and CHKDSK commands to examine the root directories of all the DOS partitions set up as hard drives on your computer.

Lesson 7: Learning About Other DOS Commands

In the Beginning and Intermediate DOS chapters and in the previous lessons of this chapter, you have examined the most commonly used DOS commands. There are other DOS commands, however, we have not yet covered. Some of the remaining ones are rarely used by most people; some are quite technical. Let's briefly discuss these other DOS commands.

Step 1: Examine the CHCP Command

DOS versions 3.30 and newer use code pages to determine which country's character set is to be displayed on the screen or sent to the printer. A **code page** is a conversion table that tells DOS how to translate data stored as numeric values into letters, numbers, punctuation, and other symbols to be displayed or printed. Each country's code page is assigned a different number. The United States' code page, number 437, is the default. Unless you live in a country other than the United States or speak a language other than English, you don't have to worry about code pages. You can, however, see or change your code page number with the internal command CHCP. For example, execute this command:

Type   **chcp**
Press   **Enter**

DOS will respond with the message

```
Active code page: 437.
```

Step 2: Examine the COMMAND Command

The DOS command processor is the program that translates and acts on the commands you enter. COMMAND.COM is the command processor that comes with DOS. It is automatically invoked when you boot up DOS and includes all internal commands, such as DIR and COPY. COMMAND is an external command that lets you invoke a second command processor or load a customized command processor. For example, for security purposes you can create a version of COMMAND.COM that does not include the ERASE (or DEL) command, and load this modified command processor with the COMMAND command. Most people seldom use the COMMAND command directly, but it is sometimes used by application programs to let the user execute a DOS command from within the program. For example, try this command:

Type   **command /c chkdsk**
Press   **Enter**

This command starts a new command processor under the current program, executes the CHKDSK command, and returns to the first command processor.

Step 3: Examine the CTTY Command

The internal command CTTY lets you change your terminal, the device from which you issue DOS commands and see the results. Normally, your terminal is the console, which consists of your computer's keyboard and display screen. The CTTY command can be used, for example, to transfer control of your computer to a separate terminal or workstation connected to the serial port. Most people rarely use CTTY.

Step 4: Examine the EXE2BIN Command

You may have noticed that two kinds of files can be executed as commands besides batch files: EXE files and COM files. The differences between these two kinds of files are somewhat technical. A COM file may load slightly faster than an equivalent EXE file, but it can be no larger than 64K. The external command EXE2BIN allows a skilled assembly language programmer to convert an EXE file to a COM file.

Step 5: Examine the EXIT Command

The EXIT command allows you to terminate a second command processor installed with the COMMAND command and return to the primary command processor. As you will learn later in this chapter, EXIT is also used to return from the DOS Shell to the DOS prompt.

Step 6: Examine the FASTOPEN Command

FASTOPEN is an external command that decreases the amount of time needed to gain access to frequently used files and directories. It works only on hard disks, but will not work when running DOS from a network.

DOS can take a long time to search for a file if your hard disk contains many levels of subdirectories. FASTOPEN maintains a list in memory of your most recently used directory and file locations. If you repeatedly reference a particular file or directory, DOS will be able to find it more quickly by looking up its location in memory instead of checking the disk. If FASTOPEN has not already been executed in your AUTOEXEC.BAT file or INSTALLed in the CONFIG.SYS file, you can improve the performance of your hard disk C by doing this:

Type **fastopen c:**
Press **Enter**

Step 7: Examine the GRAFTABL Command

Many older IBM-compatible computers are equipped with a relatively low-resolution Color Graphics Adapter (CGA). These machines display certain graphics characters poorly in graphics modes unless you use the external command GRAFTABL. Executing GRAFTABL will load an extended character set that looks better in programs that use the CGA graphics modes.

Step 8: Examine the GRAPHICS Command

In the Beginning DOS chapter you learned that pressing the Print Screen Key (or Ctrl-PrtSc on older IBM PC and AT keyboards) will send a copy of your current screen to the printer. By default, this works only with text screens. You can also print graphics screens, however, if you first execute the external command GRAPHICS. This will load the instructions DOS needs to be able to reproduce a graphics screen on your printer. GRAPHICS should be executed only once, so it is often put in the AUTOEXEC.BAT file.

Step 9: Examine the KEYB Command

The external command KEYB is used to load a keyboard translation table for a specific country. It should be executed only once, so it generally appears in the AUTOEXEC.BAT file or is run with the INSTALL command in CONFIG.SYS. If you live in the United States or speak English, you will probably never have to use this command.

Step 10: Examine the MODE Command

The external command MODE can be used to control certain aspects of the printer, serial interface, and display screen. It has many parameters and many possible variations. Fortunately, most of today's application software takes care of setting up these devices, so you probably won't have to use MODE. If you have a color graphics display, however, you can easily demonstrate one aspect of the MODE command.

Type **mode co40**
Press **Enter**

This command tells DOS to display 40 characters across your color screen. Use the DIR command to see how this looks. When you are finished, execute the following command to change your display back to 80 columns:

Type **mode co80**
Press **Enter**

Step 11: Examine the NLSFUNC Command

NLSFUNC is another external command that is used to load country-specific information for DOS. It supports international language features and code pages. Again, if you live in the United States or speak English, you will probably never use this command.

Step 12: Examine the SELECT Command

With DOS 4.00 and newer versions, the external command SELECT is an easy-to-use menu-driven facility for installing DOS on a hard or floppy disk and creating the AUTOEXEC.BAT and CONFIG.SYS files (see the Software Installation appendix). With earlier DOS versions, SELECT is a more limited command that uses prompts to let you install DOS with country-specific keyboard layout, date, and time formats.

Step 13: Examine the SET Command

There is a special area in memory called the **DOS environment** that contains variables, values, and text used by some programs. It is sort of like a scratch pad for DOS. The internal command SET lets you view and change the contents of the DOS environment. For example, execute the following command:

Type **set**
Press **Enter**

Figure 21 shows a typical result. The COMSPEC line displays the full path and file specification of your default command processor. The PATH, APPEND, and PROMPT lines should be familiar; the DOS environment stores the current settings.

You can also use the SET command to change items in the DOS environment, such as new settings for PATH or PROMPT. For example, execute the following command:

Type **set prompt=Hello$g**
Press **Enter**

This changes the DOS prompt just as the PROMPT command does. Change the prompt back to the way it was before with this command:

Type **set prompt=pg**
Press **Enter**

Figure 21 The DOS Environment Displayed by SET

```
C:\>set
COMSPEC=C:\DOS\COMMAND.COM
PATH=C:\DOS
APPEND=C:\DOS
PROMPT=$P$G

C:\>_
```

Step 14: Examine the SHARE Command

SHARE is an external command that instructs DOS to allow file sharing and locking. **File sharing** is when two or more people or programs are using the same file at the same time. **File locking** is the opposite of file sharing—only one person or program can use a file or part of a file at a time. The SHARE command is generally used only on local area networks.

Practice

1. Have DOS display your current code page number on the screen.

2. Check the amount of memory you have free by executing the CHKDSK or MEM command. Then start a new command processor by executing this command:

   Type **command**
   Press **Enter**

   Check the amount of memory you have free again by executing CHKDSK or MEM. The amount should be less than before because a secondary command processor is now loaded into memory. Return to the previous command processor by executing this command:

   Type **exit**
   Press **Enter**

   Use CHKDSK or MEM once again to see that you now have the original amount of memory free.

3. Make sure you are at the root directory of your hard disk. Use the SET command to examine the current DOS environment. Then use SET to change your search PATH to just the root directory of the hard disk. Try to execute the CHKDSK command. Why doesn't it work? Use SET to change the search path back to the DOS subdirectory. Try the CHKDSK command again.

Lesson 8: Using the DOS Shell

Starting with DOS version 4.00, IBM and Microsoft included an enhancement to the operating system's user interface called the **DOS Shell.** This feature allows you to complete common DOS tasks by selecting options from menus instead of entering commands at the DOS prompt. Novices sometimes find it easier to use the DOS Shell than ordinary DOS commands.

We have not used the DOS Shell in this book so far. It wasn't offered with previous versions of DOS, and most people are still using regular DOS commands. Nevertheless, it is worthwhile to take a brief look at this new user interface. If you have DOS 4.00 or a newer version, you might find that you prefer using the DOS Shell. If you don't have DOS 4.00 or a newer version, skip this lesson.

Step 1: Invoke the DOS Shell

The DOS Shell is an option; you can choose whether or not to use it. DOS can be installed so that the DOS Shell is activated every time you turn on the computer. This is done by putting the DOSSHELL command in the AUTOEXEC.BAT file. DOSSHELL.BAT is a batch file created when DOS is installed that starts the DOS Shell. If DOS is installed without putting DOSSHELL in the AUTO-EXEC.BAT file, you can still use the DOS Shell by entering this command yourself. Execute the following command to activate the DOS Shell from the DOS prompt:

Type   **dosshell**
Press   **Enter**

Figure 22 shows the first screen you see in the DOS Shell—the Start Programs screen. (Note: Your screens may look slightly different if your computer has a color graphics display.)

Figure 22 The Start Programs Screen

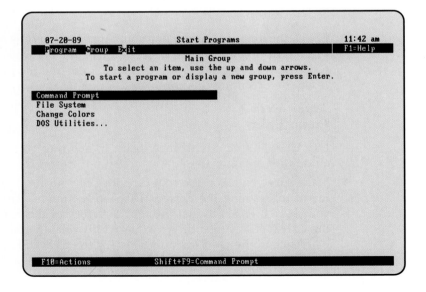

Step 2: Examine the DOS Utilities Menu

From the Start Programs screen you can run programs, customize the DOS Shell menus, change the screen colors, and manage your files and subdirectories. For example, several common DOS tasks are available under the heading DOS Utilities. To position the reverse-video highlight bar on this heading and select it, do this:

Press **Down Arrow** (3 times)
Press **Enter**

Figure 23 shows the new screen that appears—the DOS Utilities menu. The options that appear in this menu correspond to some DOS commands. If you want to copy a diskette, for instance, you would position the highlight bar on the second option in this menu and press the Enter key. The DOS Shell would then prompt you for more information about making the copy. Although this menu contains only a few DOS functions, other commands can be added as options or appear as options inside other menus.

Step 3: Examine the File System Screen

Now, let's go back to the Start Programs screen.

Press **Escape**

Your screen should look like Figure 22 again. The File System option in the Main Group is another useful feature of the DOS Shell. To select this option, follow these directions

Press **Up Arrow** (2 times to highlight File System)
Press **Enter**

DOS will read information from the disk. Then the File System screen will show your current disk and subdirectory path (see Figure 24). The left side of the screen presents a chart that shows the structure of the current disk. The right side of

Figure 23 The DOS Utilities Menu

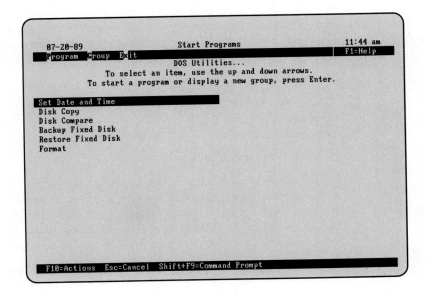

Figure 24 The File System Screen

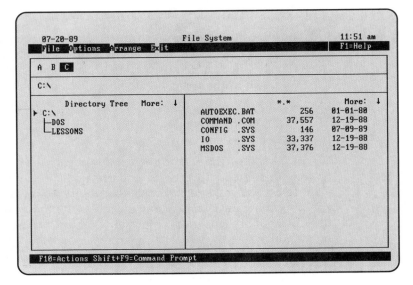

```
 07-20-89                    File System                   11:51 am
╔═══════════════════════════════════════════════════════╤═══════════╗
║ File  Options  Arrange  Exit                           │ F1=Help   ║
╟───────────────────────────────────────────────────────┴───────────╢
║  A  B  C                                                            ║
╟────────────────────────────────────────────────────────────────────╢
║  C:\                                                                ║
╟────────────────────────────────────────────────────────────────────╢
║     Directory Tree     More: ↓       AUTOEXEC.BAT    *.*    More: ↓  ║
║ ▶ C:\                                AUTOEXEC.BAT     256   01-01-80 ║
║   ├─DOS                              COMMAND .COM  37,557   12-19-88 ║
║   └─LESSONS                          CONFIG  .SYS     146   07-09-89 ║
║                                      IO      .SYS  33,337   12-19-88 ║
║                                      MSDOS   .SYS  37,376   12-19-88 ║
║                                                                     ║
╟────────────────────────────────────────────────────────────────────╢
║  F10=Actions  Shift+F9=Command Prompt                               ║
╚═══════════════════════════════════════════════════════════════════╝
```

the screen shows the files in the currently selected directory, including the hidden files. Right now, the root directory of hard disk C is depicted. You should recognize the files AUTOEXEC.BAT, COMMAND.COM, and CONFIG.SYS. The two additional entries, IO.SYS and MSDOS.SYS, are the hidden MS-DOS system files in the root directory of the hard disk. (If you are running IBM DOS, the two hidden system files will be named IBMBIO.COM and IBMDOS.COM instead.)

Step 4: Try Other DOS Shell Features

Although we've only briefly introduced the DOS Shell, you should see that it can be an easy system for novices to use. There are many features of the DOS Shell we have not covered. For example, the DOS Shell can be set up to present more attractive screens if your computer has a high-resolution graphics adapter and display. It can also work with a mouse, which simplifies the process of selecting options from menus. Unlike DOS from the command prompt, the DOS Shell provides comprehensive help information. To get help at any time, do this:

Press **F1**

A help box containing information relevant to your current activity will be displayed on the screen. When you are finished reading the help information, you can return to the File System screen by pressing the Escape key:

Press **Escape** (2 times)

The DOS Shell is very flexible, since it allows you to create new menus and add any programs you like as options. Existing menus can be modified by adding options, deleting options, and copying options from other menus. So although the DOS Shell can make it easier for a novice to use the operating system at a very basic level, it also offers complex features for more advanced users.

Practice Use the DOS Shell help facility to read about all the options in all of the menus. Remember, you press the F10 key to move to the menu bar and the arrow keys to move between and within menus. Pressing F1 will bring up a help box about the currently selected item.

Summary

- *Redirecting output and input.* The > symbol redirects output from the screen to a device or file. The >> symbol redirects and appends output. The < symbol redirects input from a file instead of from the keyboard.

- *Using DOS filters and piping.* FIND, MORE, and SORT are filters that work with text input. The | symbol pipes output from one program into another program.

- *Using batch files.* A batch file is a text file with a BAT extension that contains DOS commands to be run. AUTOEXEC.BAT is a special batch file automatically executed every time the computer is booted.

- *Using batch processing commands.* Replaceable parameters, CALL, ECHO, FOR, IF, GOTO, PAUSE, REM, and SHIFT can greatly enhance the flexibility and power of batch files.

- *Setting up a configuration file.* CONFIG.SYS is a special text file in the root directory that contains configuration commands to set up the computer.

- *Partitioning and formatting a hard disk.* The FDISK command presents a series of menus to divide a hard disk into sections called partitions. A hard disk must be formatted after it has been partitioned.

- *Executing other DOS commands.* Other DOS commands include CHCP, COMMAND, CTTY, EXE2BIN, EXIT, FASTOPEN, GRAFTABL, GRAPHICS, KEYB, MODE, NLSFUNC, SELECT, SET, and SHARE.

- *Using the DOS Shell.* The DOS Shell, included with DOS versions 4.00 and newer, is a user-friendly interface that presents options in menus instead of requiring commands to be entered at the DOS prompt. It is invoked by executing the DOSSHELL.BAT file.

Key Terms

As an extra review of this chapter, try defining the following terms.

batch file	file locking
batch processing commands	file sharing
branching	filter
chaining	label
code page	nesting
comment out	partition
device driver	piping
disk buffer	redirection
DOS environment	replaceable parameter
DOS Shell	stack
file control block (FCB)	

Multiple Choice

Choose the best selection to complete each statement.

1. Which of the following characters tells DOS to redirect the output of a command to a file or device?

   (a) >   (b) <

   (c) | (d) $

2. Which of the following characters tells DOS to pipe the output of one command into another command?

   (a) >   (b) <

   (c) | (d) $

3. Which of the following commands is NOT a filter?

   (a) FIND   (b) MORE

   (c) COPY   (d) SORT

4. What is the name of the DOS configuration file?

   (a) AUTOEXEC.BAT   (b) CONFIG.SYS

   (c) VDISK.SYS   (d) CONFIG.BAT

5. Which of the following commands may appear only in the configuration file?

   (a) DEVICE   (b) ASSIGN

   (c) JOIN   (d) APPEND

6. Which command would you use to nest batch files?

   (a) EXIT   (b) CALL

   (c) COMMAND   (d) JOIN

7. Every batch file must have an extension of

   (a) BAK.   (b) BAT.

   (c) COM.   (d) EXE.

8. Which of the following commands is usually found only in batch files?

   (a) DEVICE   (b) COMMAND

   (c) ECHO   (d) DIR

9. Which batch file command repeats an action on a set of files?

   (a) MORE   (b) IF

   (c) APPEND   (d) FOR

10. Which of the following commands basically does nothing?

    (a) DIR   (b) CHKDSK

    (c) PROMPT   (d) REM

11. Which of the following configuration commands may increase disk performance, but use more memory?

    (a) BREAK   (b) BUFFERS

    (c) COUNTRY   (d) DEVICE

12. Which configuration command is used to install device drivers?

    (a) DEVICE   (b) INSTALL

    (c) DRIVEPARM   (d) FCBS

13. Which command must you use in CONFIG.SYS before you can create and access disk drive Z?

    (a) FILES
    — (b) LASTDRIVE
    (c) DRIVEPARM
    (d) STACKS

14. A separate section of a hard disk that may contain its own operating system is called a

    — (a) partition.
    (b) sector.
    (c) track.
    (d) cylinder.

15. Which command must be used on a new hard disk before it is formatted?

    (a) ASSIGN
    (b) BACKUP
    — (c) FDISK
    (d) SELECT

16. Which command presents the current code page number?

    — (a) CHCP
    (b) DIR
    (c) CHKDSK
    (d) NLSFUNC

17. Which command terminates a second command processor or returns from the DOS Shell to the DOS prompt?

    (a) CALL
    — (b) EXIT
    (c) JOIN
    (d) REPLACE

18. Which command displays the contents of the DOS environment?

    (a) DIR
    (b) CHKDSK
    (c) MEM
    — (d) SET

19. What is the name of the first screen you see after starting the DOS Shell?

    — (a) Start Programs
    (b) DOS Utilities
    (c) File System
    (d) Exit Program

Fill-In

1. The _____ symbol is used to redirect and append the output of a command to a file.

2. The _____ filter accepts input and then presents it as output, one screen at a time.

3. The SORT filter is often used with piping and _____.

4. The _____ command is used in CONFIG.SYS to set the maximum number of files that can be open at a time.

5. You can pass information to a running batch file by using a _____ parameter.

6. Chaining is when you invoke a _____ file as the last command in a batch file.

7. The _____ and _____ commands are used to branch within a batch file.

8. You can suspend the execution of a batch file until the user presses a key by inserting the _____ command.

9. To insert a comment in a batch file or CONFIG.SYS, you precede the line with _____.

10. The FDISK command is used to set up DOS _____.

11. If you want the Print Screen key to work on graphics screens, you must first execute the _____ command.

12. _____ is the command processor that comes with DOS.
13. The _____ command can be used to transfer control of your computer to a separate terminal connected to a serial port.
14. The _____ command decreases the amount of time needed to gain access to frequently used files and directories.
15. The _____ command is a menu-driven facility for installing DOS on a disk and creating AUTOEXEC.BAT and CONFIG.SYS.
16. The _____ command is generally used only on local area networks to prevent two programs from using the same file at the same time.
17. To start the DOS Shell, you type _____ and press the Enter key.
18. The DOS Shell was first introduced with DOS version _____.

Short Problems

1. Use the DIR command, piping, and the FIND filter with the /V parameter to display a directory listing of all the files in the LESSONS subdirectory that do NOT have the extension BAT.
2. Use the DIR command, piping, and the FIND filter with the /C parameter to display a count of the number BAT files in the LESSONS subdirectory.
3. Use the DIR command, piping, and the SORT filter to display a listing of the current directory, with the files arranged in order of increasing file size.
4. Create a batch file named T.BAT that will clear the screen and then TYPE the file specified on the command line. (Hint: Use a replaceable parameter for the file name.) Try T.BAT a few times.
5. Create a batch file named HELP.BAT that turns echoing off, clears the screen, and then uses ECHO commands to present a brief description of how to execute a batch file.
6. Use the COPY command to create a text file called NAMES1.TXT containing the last names of ten of your friends. Type each name on a separate line and enter the names in random order. When you are finished, redirect NAMES1.TXT into the SORT filter and redirect the output to create a new file called NAMES2.TXT, which will contain the names arranged in alphabetical order. Compare the contents of NAME1.TXT and NAME2.TXT with the TYPE command.
7. Create a batch file named REPEAT.BAT that repeats the DIR command forever. (Hint: use the GOTO command to branch to a label placed before the DIR command in the batch file.) Execute the REPEAT batch file. You can stop it at any time by pressing Ctrl-Break and then answering yes when DOS prompts you to terminate the batch job.
8. The MODE command can display the status of all devices installed in your system. Execute the MODE command without any parameters and examine the output.
9. If you have the DOS Shell, invoke it and then format a diskette by using the Format option from the DOS Utilities menu.

BEGINNING WORDPERFECT

In This Chapter

Preview

A word processor is a computer system that helps you type, edit, store, and print documents. Memos, letters, term papers, reports, contracts, articles, and book chapters are all examples of documents that can be produced with a word processing package. The typical word processor consists of a microcomputer, printer, and word processing software package. Systems of this type are common today and are helping all kinds of people with their daily writing chores. Students, educators, authors, scientists, business people, professionals, and office workers are some of the people who use word processing systems. Word processing packages, also called word processors, are perhaps the most popular type of software used on microcomputers. And WordPerfect is the most popular word processing package, with versions sold for all kinds of microcomputers, including IBMs and IBM-compatibles, Apple IIs and Apple Macintoshes, Commodore Amigas, and Atari STs. In this chapter and the next two chapters, you will learn to use WordPerfect 5.1 for IBM and IBM-compatible microcomputers.

After studying this chapter, you will know how to

- start WordPerfect.
- use the editing screen.
- use pull-down menus and the mouse.
- execute function key commands and get help.
- enter text into a document.
- move the cursor.
- insert new text.
- overwrite mistakes.
- delete mistakes.
- search for and replace text.
- save a document in a disk file.
- check spelling.
- mark, move, copy, and delete blocks of text.
- cancel commands and restore deletions.
- underline, boldface, and otherwise format characters.
- set margins, tab stops, justification, line spacing, and line height.
- center text.
- format pages.
- print a document.
- edit an existing document.
- exit WordPerfect.

Getting Started

Although WordPerfect is a large and sophisticated software package, you can easily learn to use it for basic word processing tasks. WordPerfect may be set up in different ways in different computer classrooms, but you are most likely to use the package in one of two arrangements:

1. on a microcomputer with a hard disk and WordPerfect installed in a subdirectory named WP51 or WP and a path set up so that WordPerfect can be run from any disk or subdirectory.

2. on a microcomputer connected to a local area network with WordPerfect installed on the network file server.

Insight

What Is the Secret to WordPerfect's Success?

Even though you've read and re-read the manual, pressed every key combination you can think of, and asked all your friends, your new word processing software is laughing at you. You haven't even managed to set it up, much less write your term paper. What do you do now?

WordPerfect Corporation, maker of WordPerfect word processing software, has an answer: lifetime, toll-free support for everyone who buys its products. The company has a fleet of support operators on the payroll who answer phoned-in questions Monday through Friday from 7 a.m. to 6 p.m. and Saturday from 8 a.m. to noon, Mountain Standard Time. The monthly telephone tab for this service tops $300,000.

"It's truly unlimited support," says Stan Mackay, head of Word-Perfect's support group. "We don't even ask for user numbers. We want to help them, unhassled."

Each support worker specializes in either installation; features; printers; the company's other software, including DataPerfect, Library, and PlanPerfect; the Amiga and Atari versions; the Apple Macintosh version; or general questions. Callers hear three levels of recordings, and the goal is to answer the phone in two minutes and never to let anyone languish on hold for more than 45 minutes. That's not exactly lightning fast, but apparently OK to the people who make the 80,000 calls that come in every month.

Of course, no system is perfect. When WordPerfect 5.0 and WordPerfect for the Macintosh were released within days of one another, so many people called in that all toll-free lines into Utah were knocked out, disabling the telemarketing centers for American Express, Delta Air Lines, and others.

This extensive customer support is a major reason for the astonishing success of the Orem, Utah-based company. Other reasons are its marketing savvy and, as is often the case with software stars, a measure of good timing.

Sources: Christine Strehlo, "What's So Special About WordPerfect?" *Personal Computing*, March 1988, pp. 100–116. Daniel J. Rosenbaum, "Evolutionary Strategy Pays Off for WordPerfect," *PC World*, December 1988, pp. 82–86.

Although WordPerfect 5.1 can be installed on floppy disks, this is seldom done because ten diskettes are required to hold the entire package. Even the minimum configuration requires two diskettes for the WordPerfect program itself, another diskette for the spelling checker, and one more for the thesaurus. In addition, your computer must have two 720K or larger diskette drives to run WordPerfect 5.1 from floppy disks. So, most people run WordPerfect from a hard disk or a network.

The following lessons assume you have a microcomputer with a hard disk. If you are running WordPerfect 5.1 from diskettes or from a local area network, you may need additional directions from your instructor on how to start the program, but you still should be able to do the following lessons.

Lesson 1: Running WordPerfect

You're all ready to start word processing, but first you must boot up your computer and run WordPerfect.

Step 1: Boot Up the Computer

Start up your computer as you learned in Lesson 1 of the Beginning DOS chapter.

Step 2: Prepare Subdirectory or Diskette for Documents

The WordPerfect program is usually stored in its own subdirectory on a hard disk or network. It is best to prepare a separate subdirectory or diskette for the document files you will create in the following lessons. If you want to keep your documents on the hard disk, create a subdirectory called LESSONS, if you don't already have one, that you can use to store your files. If you want to keep your documents on a separate floppy disk, obtain a formatted diskette with room for your files. If you are running on a network, your instructor may have other directions for you to follow.

Step 3: Switch to the LESSONS Subdirectory or Diskette

If you have a microcomputer with a hard disk, WordPerfect should already be installed in its own subdirectory named WP51 or WP (see Appendix B, Software Installation). The following lessons assume that a path has been set up so that you can run WordPerfect from any disk or subdirectory. If you have a LESSONS subdirectory on the hard disk for your files, switch to it with this DOS command:

Type   **cd c:\lessons**
Press   **Enter**

If you want to store your documents on a separate floppy disk, insert the diskette into the A drive and execute this DOS command:

Type   **a:**
Press   **Enter**

If your computer is connected to a local area network, you may have to follow other directions from your instructor before actually starting WordPerfect.

Step 4: Invoke WordPerfect

Once you are in the proper disk drive directory, running WordPerfect is easy.

Type   **wp**
Press   **Enter**

Figure 1 The WordPerfect Copyright Screen

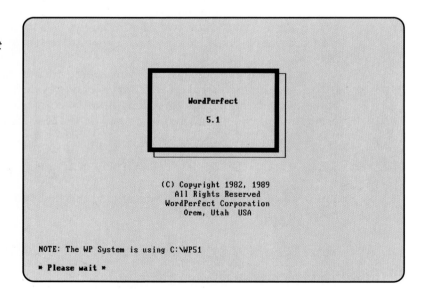

```
                          WordPerfect

                             5.1




                    (C) Copyright 1982, 1989
                       All Rights Reserved
                    WordPerfect Corporation
                        Orem, Utah  USA


NOTE: The WP System is using C:\WP51

* Please wait *
```

It will take a few seconds for WordPerfect to be loaded from the disk into memory. Then your screen will look like Figure 1, which displays the copyright information for WordPerfect.

Practice   Reboot your computer:

Press   **Ctrl-Alt-Del**

Follow the steps of this lesson to start WordPerfect again.

Lesson 2: The Editing Screen

The copyright notice will disappear after a few moments, and WordPerfect will display the almost empty screen shown in Figure 2. This is WordPerfect's editing screen, where you enter, view, and modify text.

Step 1: Examine the Cursor

Look at the upper left corner of the screen. You should see the blinking under-score, known as the **cursor**, which marks your current position within the doc-ument. The cursor indicates where text will be inserted, deleted, or changed in some way.

Step 2: Examine the Status Line

The **status line**, shown at the bottom of the screen, displays messages and warnings from WordPerfect. Right now, the status line indicates that you are working on document one (of a possible two) and that your position within the document is 1 inch from the left edge and 1 inch from the top edge of page 1. WordPerfect already has default margins, tab stops, and line spacing set up. To create a document, all you have to do is begin typing.

Figure 2 The Editing Screen

Doc 1 Pg 1 Ln 1" Pos 1"

Step 3: Examine the Text Area

The rest of the screen, from the cursor down to the status line, is the **text area**. This is the space in which you will enter text and edit your document.

 Practice

Follow these instructions and notice how the status line changes:

Type   **Hello**
Press   **Backspace** (5 times)

Lesson 3: Using Pull-Down Menus and the Mouse

Before version 5.1, WordPerfect commands and menus were executed either by pressing a function key alone or by pressing the Shift, Control, or Alternate key with a function key. WordPerfect 5.1 includes a new pull-down menu system that you can use instead of or in addition to the original function key interface. A **pull-down menu** is a list of options that appears when its name is selected from the **menu bar**, which is a list of the names of pull-down menus across the top of the screen.

Step 1: Display the Menu Bar

As you can see from Figure 2, the menu bar does not automatically appear on the screen. You can display the menu bar by holding down the Alternate key and typing an equal sign.

Press   **Alt-=**

Figure 3 shows the menu bar that appears on the screen. The File option is currently selected, as indicated by the highlight block.

Suppose you change your mind about pulling down a menu. You can easily back out of the pull-down menu system one menu at a time by pressing Escape,

Figure 3 The WordPerfect Pull-Down Menu Bar

File Edit Search Layout Mark Tools Font Graphics Help

Doc 1 Pg 1 Ln 1" Pos 1"

Space Bar, or F1 (the Cancel key). Pressing F7 (the Exit key) lets you exit all the way out of the pull-down menu system in one operation.

Press   **F7**

The menu bar will disappear.

Step 2: Pull Down a Menu

So far, you have only displayed the menu bar. Now, let's pull down a menu.

Press   **Alt-=**
Press   **Down Arrow**

The File menu will appear with the Retrieve option selected (see Figure 4). You can select a different menu by pressing the Right Arrow or Left Arrow key. For example, select the Help menu:

Press   **Left Arrow**

See how the highlight wraps around to the other side of the menu bar. You can also use the Right Arrow key:

Press   **Right Arrow** (10 times)

The Help menu should be on the screen again.

Note that each menu name has a letter that appears in a color brighter than or different from the rest of the letters. This letter, often the first letter, is the mnemonic (easy to remember) letter associated with the menu. When the menu bar is on the screen with no menu pulled down, you can type a particular menu's mnemonic letter to select that menu quickly. For example, back out of the Help menu and then display the Edit menu:

Press   **Escape**
Type   **e**

The Edit menu will appear on the screen. Now, display the Help menu again:

Press   **Escape**
Type   **h**

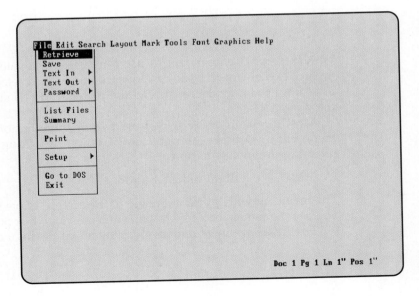

Figure 4 The File Menu

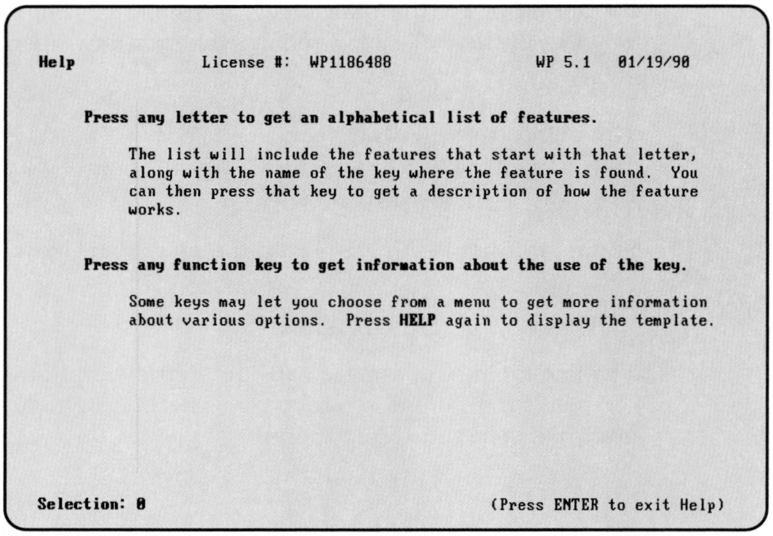

Figure 5 The Help Screen

```
Help                License #:  WP1186488          WP 5.1   01/19/90

      Press any letter to get an alphabetical list of features.

         The list will include the features that start with that letter,
         along with the name of the key where the feature is found.  You
         can then press that key to get a description of how the feature
         works.


      Press any function key to get information about the use of the key.

         Some keys may let you choose from a menu to get more information
         about various options.  Press HELP again to display the template.




    Selection: 0                             (Press ENTER to exit Help)
```

Step 3: Execute an Option

Once a menu is on the screen, you can execute an option by highlighting the option and pressing the Enter key, or by typing the option's mnemonic letter. Right now, the Help option is highlighted in the Help menu. Highlight the Template option:

> Press   **Down Arrow** (2 times)

Now if you press the Enter key, WordPerfect will execute the Template option. Let's execute the Help option instead.

> Type   **h**

WordPerfect immediately executes the Help option. Figure 5 shows the result. When you have finished reading the Help screen, return to the editing screen:

> Press   **Enter**

Step 4: Using the Mouse

WordPerfect 5.1 allows you to use a mouse to activate the menu bar, display menus, execute menu options, move the cursor, and select text. If your computer does not have a mouse, just read the material in this step without performing the operations.

Most IBM-compatible mice have two or three buttons. You can display the menu bar by clicking the right mouse button. **Clicking** is briefly pressing and releasing the mouse button.

> Click   **Right mouse button**

The menu bar will appear at the top of the screen. Move the mouse around until you see the mouse pointer—a small reverse-video box on the screen (see Figure 6). The mouse pointer mimics the movement of the mouse on the screen. To pull down a menu, move the mouse pointer on top of a menu name and click the left mouse button. For example, let's pull down the Help menu.

Point to   **Help**
Click   **Left mouse button**

The Help menu will appear. To select an option in a menu, move the mouse pointer on top of the option and click the left mouse button. Execute the Help option in the Help menu:

Point to   **Help**
Click   **Left mouse button**

When you have finished reading the Help screen, return to the editing screen:

Press   **Enter**

You can also pull down a menu and select an option at once by **dragging**— holding down a mouse button while moving the mouse. For example, follow these directions to pull down the File menu and execute the Exit option:

Click   **Right mouse button**
Point to   **File**
Hold   **Left mouse button**
Drag to   **Exit**
Release   **Left mouse button**

This operation executes the Exit command, which asks you if you want to save your document and then asks if you want to return to DOS. Answer No to both questions:

Type   **n**
Type   **n**

WordPerfect will return to the editing screen.

If you have the menu bar or a menu on the screen and you want to back out of it, you can either click the right mouse button again, or drag the mouse

Figure 6 The Mouse Pointer

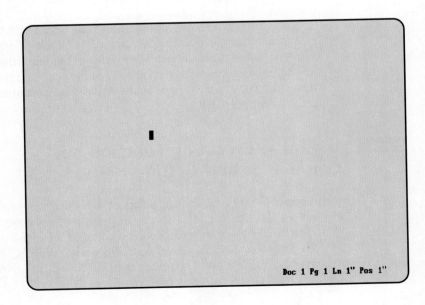

Doc 1 Pg 1 Ln 1" Pos 1"

pointer with the left mouse button held down to an empty part of the screen and then release the button. Try these operations:

Click	**Right mouse button** (3 times)
Point to	**File**
Hold	**Left mouse button**
Drag to	**Empty part of the screen**
Release	**Left mouse button**

WordPerfect will return to the editing screen.

Practice

1. Display the menu bar, pull down the File menu, and execute the Exit option. Do not save your document but do return to DOS. Then start WordPerfect again.

2. Display the menu bar and pull down the File menu. Then perform these operations:

Press	**Page Down**
Press	**Page Up**
Press	**Escape**
Press	**End**
Press	**Home**
Press	**Left Arrow**
Press	**F1**

Page Down moves the highlight to the last option in the current menu; Page Up moves to the first option. When the menu bar is on the screen without a menu pulled down, the End key moves the highlight to the rightmost menu name; pressing the Home key followed by the Left Arrow key moves the highlight to the leftmost menu name. The F1 key returns to the editing screen from the menu bar.

3. Display the menu bar and pull down the Edit menu. Notice that some of the options, such as Copy and Delete, have square brackets ([and]) around them. These brackets mean that the option cannot be selected at this time. Copy, for example, cannot be selected because no text has been marked yet to be copied.

   Also notice that some options, such as Select and Comment, are followed by a little triangle pointing to the right. Each of these options displays a submenu when it is selected. For example, highlight the Select option. Another little menu appears with the options Sentence, Paragraph, Page, Tabular Column, and Rectangle. When you have finished examining the submenu, return to the editing screen.

Lesson 4: Executing Function Key Commands and Getting Help

Pull-down menus and mouse support are new, easy-to-use features of Word-Perfect 5.1. Earlier versions of the program had only the function key interface. With the function key interface, each command is executed by pressing a function key (F1 to F10 or F12) by itself, or along with a Shift, Control, or Alternate key. WordPerfect 5.1 lets you use either the pull-down menu interface or the function key interface to execute any command.

Figure 7 List of Word-Perfect Features Beginning with B

```
Features [B]                            WordPerfect Key   Keystrokes

Backspace (Erase)                       Backspace         Backspace
Backup Directory Location               Setup             Shft-F1,6
Backup Files, Automatic                 Setup             Shft-F1,3,1,1
Backup Options                          Setup             Shft-F1,3,1
Backward Search                         <-Search          Shft-F2
Base Font                               Font              Ctrl-F8,4
Base Font (Document)                    Format            Shft-F8,3,3
Base Font (Printer)                     Print             Shft-F7,s,3,5
Baseline Placement for Typesetters      Format            Shft-F8,4,6,5
Beep Options                            Setup             Shft-F1,3,2
Binding Offset                          Print             Shft-F7,b
Binding Offset (Default)                Setup             Shft-F1,4,8,1
Black and White, View Document In       Setup             Shft-F1,2,5,1
Block                                   Block             Alt-F4
Block, (Assign Variable w/Block On)     Macro Commands    Ctrl-PgUp
Block, Append (Block On)                Move              Ctrl-F4,1,4
Block, Center (Block On)                Center            Shft-F6
Block, Comment (Block On)               Text In/Out       Ctrl-F5
Block Copy (Block On)                   Move              Ctrl-F4,1,2
Block Copy (Block On)                   Block Copy        Ctrl-Ins
More... Press b to continue.

Selection: 0                                    (Press ENTER to exit Help)
```

Step 1: Invoke the Help Command

In the previous lesson, you learned how to execute the Help command from a pull-down menu. Now, let's execute the Help command with a function key. WordPerfect's on-line help facility can be used to answer many questions about the package without having to refer to the manual. To invoke the Help command, do this:

Press   **F3**

WordPerfect will present the screen shown in Figure 5 again. Simply type a letter of the alphabet (A–Z) to see a list of all the features that begin with that letter. For example, to view the WordPerfect features that begin with the letter *B*, do this:

Type   **b**

Figure 7 shows the result. When you have finished with the help facility, you can press either the Enter key or the Space Bar to return to the editing screen.

Press   **Enter**

Step 2: Display the Keyboard Template

When you purchase WordPerfect, you get a **keyboard template** that lists the most common commands. This plastic guide fits over or near the function keys on the keyboard and is invaluable for beginning users. (A cardboard keyboard template is included inside the back cover of this book.) If you don't have the keyboard template, however, you can see an on-screen version by doing this:

Press   **F3** (2 times)

Figure 8 shows the result. While the help facility is active, you can get additional information about any function key simply by pressing the key. For example, do this:

Press   **F7**

Figure 8 On-Screen Key-board Template

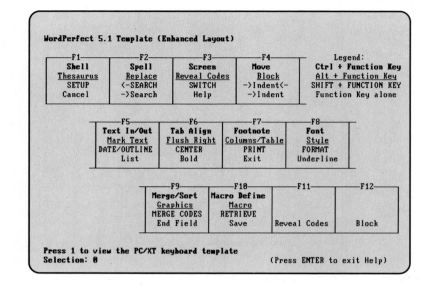

Figure 9 shows the help screen presented when you press the F7 key, referred to by WordPerfect as the Exit key. This is the command you use to exit WordPerfect and return to DOS. When you have finished with the help facility, return to the editing screen by doing this:

Press   **Enter**

Practice 1. Invoke the Help facility and display the commands that begin with the letter F. When you have finished reading the list, return to the editing screen.

2. Invoke the Help facility and display the on-screen keyboard template. When you have finished reading the list, return to the editing screen.

Figure 9 Help Screen for F7

```
Exit

      Gives you the option to save your document and then allows you to either
      exit WordPerfect or clear the screen.

      Exit is also used to exit from editing headers, styles, footnotes, etc.

      When you are in screens other than editing screens, pressing Exit leaves
      menus and will normally take you back to the normal editing screen (you
      may need to press Exit more than once).




Selection: 0                                        (Press ENTER to exit Help)
```

3. Execute the Exit command. Answer No to the two prompts that follow, which ask whether you want to save the document and whether you want to exit WordPerfect.

Lesson 5: Entering Text

The process of entering the text with a word processor is similar to typing on a typewriter. There are, however, a few important differences that make using a word processor much easier. To illustrate how to use WordPerfect, let's create a memo. This memo, from the personnel department of a company to its employees, will explain company policy on employee sick leave.

Step 1: Type the Heading

As we said before, WordPerfect initially places the cursor in the first column of the first line of the first page. To create a new document, simply type the words and punctuation. Don't be concerned if you make some typing errors. You will learn how to fix mistakes later. To start out, follow these instructions:

Type	**To: All Employees**
Press	**Enter**
Type	**From: Personnel Department**
Press	**Enter**
Type	**Re: Sick Leave**
Press	**Enter**

At this point, your screen should look like Figure 10.

Step 2: Type the Body of the Memo

If you had to press Enter at the end of every line typed with a word processor, it wouldn't be all that much better than typing text with an electric typewriter. All word processing programs, however, have a feature called **word wrap** that

Figure 10 Memo Heading

```
To:  All Employees
From:  Personnel Department
Re:  Sick Leave
_




                                        Doc 1 Pg 1 Ln 1.5" Pos 1"
```

eliminates having to press Enter most of the time. The word processing program detects when you are approaching the right margin. If you type a word that extends beyond the right margin, that word is automatically shifted, or wrapped around, to the beginning of the next line. In other words, the word processing program inserts a **soft return** just before the wrapped word. You can then continue typing on the new line without having to press the Enter key. Word wrap significantly speeds up typing because it eliminates constantly having to check the screen to make sure you don't overrun the right margin. You need only press the Enter key when you want to insert a **hard return**, which forces a new line or begins a new paragraph. For example, insert a hard return to space down a line by doing this:

Press   **Enter**

Now, to see how word wrap works, type the rest of the memo without pressing the Enter key:

> **Full-time employees are entitled to twelve working days of sick leave each year. Time taken off is charged against these twelve days and at the end of the year the unused balance is carried forward. Sick leave should only be used for an employee's illness or doctor's appointments. It is essential that accurate records are kept because employees are entitled to payment for one half of their unused sick days when they resign or retire.**

When you have finished, your screen should look like Figure 11.

Practice   Use the Backspace key to erase the last sentence of the memo. Notice how the cursor automatically moves up to the end of the previous line when necessary. Retype the last sentence, watching the screen to see what happens when a word wrap occurs. Remember: Do not press the Enter key. The words will wrap automatically.

Figure 11 Word Wrap Automatically Begins New Lines

```
To:  All Employees
From:  Personnel Department
Re:  Sick Leave

Full-time employees are entitled to twelve working days of sick
leave each year.  Time taken off is charged against these twelve
days and at the end of the year the unused balance is carried
forward.  Sick leave should only be used for an employee's illness
or doctor's appointments.  It is essential that accurate records
are kept because employees are entitled to payment for one-half of
their unused sick days when they resign or retire._




                                              Doc 1 Pg 1 Ln 2.67" Pos 6"
```

Lesson 6: Moving the Cursor

You must be able to move the cursor to change existing text and to see different parts of a long document. Fortunately, there are many ways to move the cursor, the most common of which are quick, direct, and easy.

Step 1: Use the Arrow Keys

All IBM and IBM-compatible keyboards have at least one set of arrow keys. In many programs, including WordPerfect, the simplest way to move the cursor is to press an arrow key. For example, try the following actions:

Press   **Up Arrow** (to move up one line)
Press   **Down Arrow** (to move down one line)
Press   **Left Arrow** (to move back one space)
Press   **Right Arrow** (to move forward one space)

To move the cursor rapidly, you can simply hold down an arrow key for more than a second without releasing it. The computer will simulate repeating the key press ten times per second. Try these actions:

Press   **Left Arrow** (and hold for 5 seconds)
Press   **Right Arrow** (and hold for 5 seconds)

You can also hold down the Control key and press Left Arrow or Right Arrow to move the cursor a word at a time. Try these key presses to move the cursor to the beginning of the word to the left, and then to the beginning of the word to the right:

Press   **Ctrl-Left Arrow**
Press   **Ctrl-Right Arrow**

Step 2: Use Scrolling and Paging

Your document is quite short, but many documents are too long to fit entirely on the screen. Scrolling and paging commands let you change the part of your document displayed on the screen. One simple way to scroll the screen is to press the Up Arrow or Down Arrow key even after the cursor reaches the top or bottom edge of the text area. This won't work on your document because all of it fits on a single screen. If there were more lines above or below, however, pressing Up Arrow or Down Arrow after reaching the edge would scroll the screen and move the cursor to the next line.

The Grey Plus (+) and Grey Minus (−) keys on the numeric keypad are used to move the cursor an entire screen at a time. Try this:

Press   **Grey Plus**

Grey Plus moves the cursor down to the last line of the current screen. If your document were too long to fit entirely on the screen, pressing the Grey Plus key again would move the cursor down through the next screen. Now try this:

Press   **Grey Minus**

Grey Minus moves the cursor up to the first line of the current screen. If you had more text above your current screen, pressing the Grey Minus key again would move the cursor up through the previous screen.

Paging is like scrolling an entire page at a time. The Page Down and Page Up keys are used to move between pages. Try this:

Press   **Page Down**

The cursor will move to the first line of the next page. Since your document has only one page, pressing Page Down merely moves the cursor to the end of the document. Now try this:

Press   **Page Up**

The Page Up key moves the cursor to the first line of the previous page. Again, since your document has only one page, pressing Page Up simply moves the cursor to the beginning of the document.

Step 3: Use the End and Home Keys

End and Home are the two other cursor movement keys on all IBM-compatible keyboards. Try this:

Press   **End**

The End key moves the cursor to the end of the current line.

In WordPerfect, the Home key is used with other keys to perform various cursor movements. For example, follow these directions:

Press   **Home**
Press   **Left Arrow**

Home followed by Left Arrow moves the cursor to the left edge of the current screen—in other words, the beginning of the current line. Now try this:

Press   **Home**
Press   **Right Arrow**

Home followed by Right Arrow moves the cursor to the right edge of the current screen. You can also use the Home key and the Down Arrow or Up Arrow key to move the cursor to the end or beginning of your document. Follow these directions:

Press   **Home** (2 times)
Press   **Down Arrow**
Press   **Home** (2 times)
Press   **Up Arrow**

Pressing Home twice followed by the Down Arrow key moves the cursor to the end of the document. Pressing Home twice followed by the Up Arrow key moves the cursor to the beginning of the document.

Step 4: Use the Go To Command

Another sequence of key presses lets you move to a particular page number in a WordPerfect document. Since your current document fits entirely on a single page, the Go To command would be of little use. Nevertheless, you can still try it:

Press   **Ctrl-Home**

WordPerfect will display the prompt *Go to* on the status line. Then you enter the page number to which you want to go:

Type	**1**
Press	**Enter**

WordPerfect will move the cursor to the top of that page.

Step 5: Use the Mouse

WordPerfect 5.1 allows you to use a mouse to move the cursor easily and quickly. If your computer does not have a mouse, just read the material in this step without performing the operations.

You can move the cursor to any character on the screen by moving the mouse pointer to the character and then clicking the left mouse button. For example, suppose you want to move the cursor to the *E* in *Employees*.

Point to	**E in *Employees***
Click	**Left mouse button**

If you want to scroll to a part of the document that is not currently on the screen, hold down the right mouse button, and then drag the mouse pointer off the edge of the screen in the direction that you want to go. Release the mouse button to stop scrolling. For example, suppose you want to move the cursor to the beginning of the document.

Hold	**Right mouse button**
Drag to	**Upper left corner of screen**
Release	**Right mouse button when scrolling stops**

Practice Try the following key presses and explain what each one does:

Up Arrow	**Down Arrow**
Left Arrow	**Right Arrow**
Ctrl-Left Arrow	**Ctrl-Right Arrow**
Grey Plus	**Grey Minus**
Page Up	**Page Down**
Home, Left Arrow	**Home, Right Arrow**
Home, Home, Up Arrow	**Home, Home, Down Arrow**
Ctrl-Home	**End**

Lesson 7: Inserting Text

WordPerfect, like most word processing software, has two basic typing modes: insert and typeover. By default, WordPerfect has insert mode turned on when you open a document. This means that to insert new material into a document, you just move the cursor to the location where you want the insertion to occur and begin typing. The new characters you type push any existing characters to the right. As an example, let's insert some new text into the memo you've typed.

Step 1: Move the Cursor

Suppose you want to insert the word *cumulative* between the words *twelve* and *working* in the first line of the memo. Use any of the cursor movement keys described in Lesson 6 to put the cursor beneath the *w* in the word *working*.

Figure 12 Text Inserted in a Document

```
To:  All Employees
From:  Personnel Department
Re:  Sick Leave

Full-time employees are entitled to twelve cumulative working days
of sick leave each year.  Time taken off is charged against these
twelve days and at the end of the year the unused balance is
carried forward.  Sick leave should only be used for an employee's
illness or doctor's appointments.  It is essential that accurate
records are kept because employees are entitled to payment for one-
half of their unused sick days when they resign or retire.




                                                Doc 1 Pg 1 Ln 1.5" Pos 1"
```

Step 2: Type the New Text

Since WordPerfect uses insert mode by default, all you have to do is type the new text to be inserted.

Type	**cumulative**
Press	**Space Bar**
Press	**Up Arrow**

Notice how WordPerfect automatically re-forms the paragraph and wraps words to fit within the margins when you move the cursor. Your screen should now look like Figure 12.

Practice   Insert the word *mistake* anywhere in the document. Then use the Backspace key to remove it.

Lesson 8: Overwriting Mistakes

One of the benefits of using a word processor is the ease with which you can make corrections. Since no one is perfect, typing errors are bound to occur—as you may have already discovered. In addition, you may have to go back and change a word or phrase that you already entered. One way to make corrections is by typing over existing text.

Step 1: Move the Cursor

Suppose that employees are only entitled to eleven days of sick leave. You must change the word *twelve* to *eleven* in the memo. Using the cursor movement keys described in Lesson 6, put the cursor beneath the *t* in the first *twelve*.

Figure 13 Word Corrected in Typeover Mode

```
To:  All Employees
From:  Personnel Department
Re:  Sick Leave

Full-time employees are entitled to eleven_cumulative working days
of sick leave each year.  Time taken off is charged against these
twelve days and at the end of the year the unused balance is
carried forward.  Sick leave should only be used for an employee's
illness or doctor's appointments.  It is essential that accurate
records are kept because employees are entitled to payment for one-
half of their unused sick days when they resign or retire.




Typeover                                    Doc 1 Pg 1 Ln 1.67" Pos 5.2"
```

Step 2: Change to Typeover Mode

Insert mode is on by default. To switch, or toggle, between insert and typeover mode, you use the Insert key.

> Press   **Insert**

When you change to typeover mode, WordPerfect displays the word *Typeover* in the status line. Now, any characters you type will replace the existing characters in the same positions.

Step 3: Make the Correction

With the cursor at the beginning of the word *twelve*, do this:

> Type   **eleven**

Your screen should now look like Figure 13.

Practice   Change from typeover mode to insert mode. Change back to typeover mode.

Lesson 9: Deleting Mistakes

Another common way to make corrections and modifications is to delete text.

Step 1: Move the Cursor

Before text can be deleted, the cursor must be moved to the first character to be erased. Let's change the eleven sick days to ten. The first three letters of *eleven* can simply be overwritten with *ten*. Move the cursor to the first *e* in *eleven* and do this:

> Type   **ten**

*Figure 14 Characters
Erased with the Delete Key*

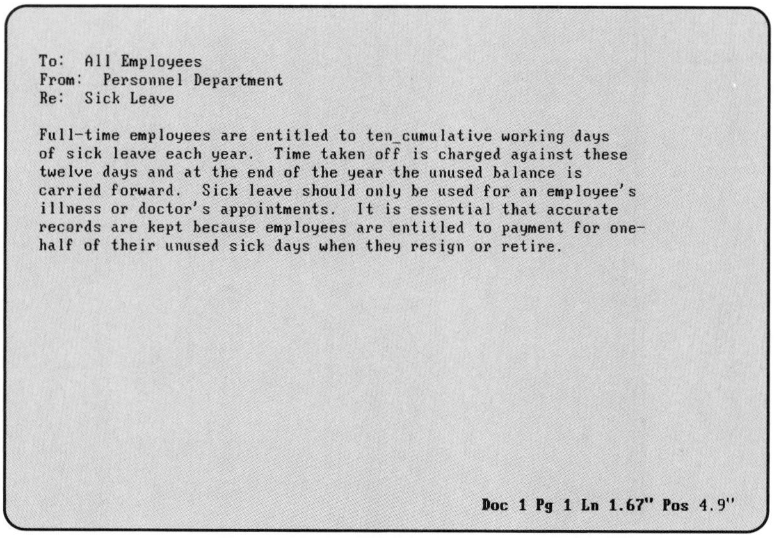

```
To:  All Employees
From:  Personnel Department
Re:  Sick Leave

Full-time employees are entitled to ten_cumulative working days
of sick leave each year.  Time taken off is charged against these
twelve days and at the end of the year the unused balance is
carried forward.  Sick leave should only be used for an employee's
illness or doctor's appointments.  It is essential that accurate
records are kept because employees are entitled to payment for one-
half of their unused sick days when they resign or retire.




                                        Doc 1 Pg 1 Ln 1.67" Pos 4.9"
```

The cursor should now be at the *v*. Change to insert mode by doing this:

Press   **Insert**

Step 2: Use the Delete Key

The Delete (Del) key removes the character at the cursor and shifts all characters to the right of the cursor to the left one space. To remove the characters *ven*, do this:

Press   **Delete** (3 times)

Your screen should now look like Figure 14.

Step 3: Use the Backspace Key

The Delete key removes the character at the current cursor location. Another way to erase text is to use the Backspace key. This key removes the character to the immediate left of the cursor. For example, erase the *ten* like this:

Press   **Backspace** (3 times)

Make sure insert mode is turned on and restore the memo to its original state:

Type   **twelve**

Step 4: Delete an Entire Word

WordPerfect also makes it easy to erase an entire word. Position the cursor on the first character of the word *twelve*. To delete the entire word and the following space, do this:

Press   **Ctrl-Backspace**

Now, make sure insert mode is turned on and put the word back again:

Type   **twelve**
Press   **Space Bar**

Figure 15 An Entire Line Deleted

```
To:  All Employees
From:  Personnel Department

Full-time employees are entitled to twelve cumulative working days
of sick leave each year.  Time taken off is charged against these
twelve days and at the end of the year the unused balance is
carried forward.  Sick leave should only be used for an employee's
illness or doctor's appointments.  It is essential that accurate
records are kept because employees are entitled to payment for one-
half of their unused sick days when they resign or retire.




                                        Doc 1 Pg 1 Ln 1.33" Pos 1"
```

Step 5: Delete an Entire Line

WordPerfect has an even more drastic command that lets you erase an entire line all at once. Move the cursor up to the beginning of the third line in the memo, the one that reads *Re: Sick Leave.*

Press	**Ctrl-End**
Press	**Delete**

All the text from the current cursor location to the end of the line will be deleted. Pressing the Delete key erases the hard return and causes the lines of text below to move up to fill in the empty space, as shown in Figure 15.

Needless to say, Ctrl-End should be used carefully. Unfortunately, you need the deleted line for the remaining lessons, so do this:

Type	**Re: Sick Leave**
Press	**Enter**

Although WordPerfect has several other commands for deleting text, Delete, Backspace, Ctrl-Backspace, and Ctrl-End are the most frequently used.

Practice   Use each of the following keys to remove text from the memo: Delete, Backspace, Ctrl-Backspace, and Ctrl-End. Then restore the memo to its original state.

Lesson 10: Searching and Replacing

The memo you've typed is fairly short, so making corrections throughout the entire document isn't too difficult. But you may have to modify much longer documents. In some cases, the same mistake is made in several places in the document. Most word processors have features that help you locate specific portions of text and change them if necessary.

Step 1: Find Text

You may have noticed that the word *twelve* is used twice in the memo. If you found out that employees are really entitled to only eleven days of sick leave, you would have to change both instances of *twelve* to *eleven*. In this case, you could simply look through the memo to make sure there are no more occurrences of *twelve* to change. If the document were much longer, however, you would have to scan through many pages of text, and you might miss a *twelve* or two. Fortunately, WordPerfect has a search command that can find text quickly and accurately. This feature can be used to make corrections or merely to locate every place in a document where a certain word or phrase is mentioned.

Execute the following commands to move the cursor to the beginning of the document and then search forward for the word *twelve*:

Press	**Home** (2 times)
Press	**Up Arrow**
Press	**Alt-=**
Type	**sf**
Type	**twelve**
Press	**F7**

The Search Forward command will advance the cursor just past the next location of the word *twelve*. If it cannot find the word you tell it to search for, WordPerfect will display **NotFound** on the status line. Another way to execute the Search Forward command is to press F2.

Step 2: Modify the Text

In many cases, you search for a piece of text because you want to change it or some text around it. Now that you've found *twelve*, change it to *eleven* like this:

Press	**Backspace** (6 times)
Type	**eleven**

Step 3: Repeat the Search

Particular words or phrases are often repeated, especially in a long document. You can tell WordPerfect to find the next occurrence of the word or phrase without having to retype it. Execute the Search Next command:

Press	**Alt-=**
Type	**sn**

This action repeats the previous search operation, advancing the cursor to the next location of the word *twelve*. Change this *twelve* to *eleven* too.

Press	**Backspace** (6 times)
Type	**eleven**

Step 4: Find and Replace Text

Since it is often necessary to find and then change a word or phrase, WordPerfect can do both at once. Execute the Replace command in the Search menu to find each *eleven* and change it back to *twelve*:

Press	**Home** (2 times)
Press	**Up Arrow**

Figure 16 Prompt to Con-firm Each Replacement

```
To:  All Employees
From:  Personnel Department
Re:  Sick Leave

Full-time employees are entitled to eleven cumulative working days
of sick leave each year.  Time taken off is charged against these
eleven days and at the end of the year the unused balance is
carried forward.  Sick leave should only be used for an employee's
illness or doctor's appointments.  It is essential that accurate
records are kept because employees are entitled to payment for one-
half of their unused sick days when they resign or retire.




w/Confirm? No (Yes)
```

Press	**Alt-=**
Type	**sr**
Press	**Enter**
Type	**eleven**
Press	**F7**
Type	**twelve**
Press	**F7**

The Replace command displays the message shown in Figure 16. Here WordPerfect is asking if you want to confirm or cancel each replacement. If you answer *Yes*, WordPerfect will prompt you before replacing each occurrence of the text. If you answer *No*, or just press Enter, WordPerfect will automatically replace every occurrence of the text without confirmation. This is known as a **global search and replace**. Since you indicated a global search and replace, WordPerfect changed every *eleven* to *twelve* throughout the entire document, without stopping for confirmation. Another way to execute the Replace command is to press Alt-F2.

Practice

1. Move the cursor to the beginning of the document. Use the Search Forward command to locate each occurrence of the word *sick*. Try the function key interface (press F2) instead of selecting Forward from the Search menu.

2. Move the cursor to the beginning of the document. Use the Replace command with confirmation to change each occurrence of the word *sick* to *ill*. Try the function key interface (press Alt-F2) instead of selecting Replace from the Search menu. Now, use the Replace command without confirmation to change each *ill* back to *sick*. Notice how WordPerfect is clever enough to preserve capitalization.

Lesson 11: Saving the Document

Word processing programs are useful not only because they make it easier to enter and edit text, but also because they let you save documents on disks. While you are editing a document, it is kept in the computer's primary memory, which gives the software quick access. The contents of primary memory are lost when the computer is turned off, so you should periodically save a document to disk as you work on it, even if it is not finished. This guards against losing all of your work if the power should fail or if you make a drastic mistake. Saving a document in a disk file gives you a more permanent copy of your work that can be stored for future reference, printed out later, or retrieved and modified. A long document, such as an article or a book chapter, can be created and edited a little at a time. Corrections, updates, and new versions can be made without having to retype everything. A document stored on a disk is much more compact and useful than the same document printed on paper. So, before we go on, let's save the memo in a disk file.

Step 1: Invoke the Save Command

Pull down the File menu and execute WordPerfect's Save command:

Press	**Alt-=**
Press	**Down Arrow**
Type	**s**

Another way to execute the Save command is to press its function key, F10. This command allows you to copy the memo to a disk file, yet continue working on it. If you want to save your documents to a floppy disk instead of the hard disk, insert a formatted floppy disk into drive A.

Step 2: Enter the File Name

WordPerfect will prompt you for the name of the document to be saved, as shown in Figure 17. You can enter any valid DOS file name. If you are working from a hard disk and want to save the memo in the current subdirectory (which should be LESSONS) do this:

Type	**memo.doc**
Press	**Enter**

Figure 17 Name the Document to be Saved

```
To:  All Employees
From:  Personnel Department
Re:  Sick Leave

Full-time employees are entitled to twelve cumulative working days
of sick leave each year.  Time taken off is charged against these
twelve days and at the end of the year the unused balance is
carried forward.  Sick leave should only be used for an employee's
illness or doctor's appointments.  It is essential that accurate
records are kept because employees are entitled to payment for one-
half of their unused sick days when they resign or retire.




Document to be saved: _
```

If you want to save your document in a file on the diskette in drive A, do this instead:

Type   **a:memo.doc**
Press   **Enter**

The document will then be copied to the disk under the name MEMO.DOC and WordPerfect will return to the editing screen. Notice that the left side of the status line now displays the path and name of your document file.

Practice   You can save a document as many times as you like while you are working on it, even if you have not finished creating it. Each time you save a document, the version on the screen and in memory will replace the version on the disk. Execute the Save command again, but this time use the function key interface:

Press   **F10**
Press   **Enter**
Type   **y**

Notice how WordPerfect suggests the file name you used last time, so you don't have to retype the name every time you save the document. For safety, the program also prompts you before replacing the old version.

Lesson 12: Checking Spelling

One of WordPerfect's most useful features is its spelling checker. Let's put a misspelled word in the memo to use as an example. Go to the second line and remove an *n* from the word *Personnel*.

Step 1: Invoke the Spelling Checker

Pull down the Tools menu and execute the Spell command to invoke the spelling checker:

Press   **Alt-=**
Type   **te**

Another way to execute this command is to press Ctrl-F2. WordPerfect will then present the Check menu shown in Figure 18. To check the entire memo, select the Document option:

Type   **d**

Note that you can select an option from a WordPerfect menu that appears at the bottom of the screen either by typing a number or a mnemonic letter.

After the dictionary has been loaded from the disk into memory, the spelling checker begins to examine each word in your document to see if it is in the dictionary.

Step 2: Correct Spelling Mistakes

When WordPerfect finds a word it doesn't recognize, it highlights the word, suggests possible replacements, and displays the Not Found menu at the bottom

*Figure 18 The Spelling
Check Menu*

```
To:  All Employees
From:  Personel Department
Re:  Sick Leave

Full-time employees are entitled to twelve cumulative working days
of sick leave each year.  Time taken off is charged against these
twelve days and at the end of the year the unused balance is
carried forward.  Sick leave should only be used for an employee's
illness or doctor's appointments.  It is essential that accurate
records are kept because employees are entitled to payment for one-
half of their unused sick days when they resign or retire.




Check: 1 Word; 2 Page; 3 Document; 4 New Sup. Dictionary; 5 Look Up; 6 Count: 0
```

of the screen, as shown in Figure 19. To replace *personel* automatically with the second suggested correction, *personnel*, do this:

Type   **b**

WordPerfect will then check the rest of the memo, find it to be correct, and give you a word count. Press any key to return to the editing screen.

In most longer documents, WordPerfect would likely encounter several more words not in its dictionary. Not all of these would necessarily be misspellings. The spelling checker, for example, cannot recognize many proper names, technical terms, and slang. Nor can it recognize some forms of correctly spelled words. In these cases, you can choose the Skip Once option or the Skip option from the Not Found menu. If you choose Skip Once, WordPerfect will leave the

*Figure 19 The Not Found
Menu*

```
To:  All Employees
From:  Personel Department
Re:  Sick Leave

Full-time employees are entitled to twelve cumulative working days
of sick leave each year.  Time taken off is charged against these
twelve days and at the end of the year the unused balance is
carried forward.  Sick leave should only be used for an employee's
illness or doctor's appointments.  It is essential that accurate
records are kept because employees are entitled to payment for one-
half of their unused sick days when they resign or retire.
                                    Doc 1 Pg 1 Ln 1.17" Pos 1.7"

A. personal            B. personnel




Not Found: 1 Skip Once; 2 Skip; 3 Add; 4 Edit; 5 Look Up; 6 Ignore Numbers: 0
```

word intact and go on, but it will stop at the next occurrence of the word. If you choose Skip, the program will ignore all occurrences of the word for the rest of the document.

If the spelling checker cannot suggest a correction for a misspelled word, you can choose the Edit option from the Not Found menu and correct the word yourself.

Practice

1. A spelling checker cannot find in its dictionary every correctly spelled word, especially names. Insert your last name somewhere in the document. Then execute a spelling check. Select the Skip option from the Not Found menu. Delete your name after you have finished.

2. The spelling checker can be used to check an individual word in your document. Move the cursor to the word *Department*. Invoke the spelling checker, but this time select the Word option from the Check menu. If the word is spelled correctly, WordPerfect will simply advance the cursor to the next word. You can continue to check the words one by one. Exit the spelling checker and return to the editing screen:

   Press   **F7**

3. You can also use the spelling checker to look up a word that is not in the document. Invoke the spelling checker, but this time select the Look Up option. Enter a purposely misspelled word and see if WordPerfect can suggest the appropriate correction. Try another misspelled word if you like. When you have finished, exit the spelling checker and return to the editing screen:

   Press   **F7** (2 times)

Lesson 13: Working with Blocks of Text

In addition to individual characters, words, and lines, most word processing packages let you specify and manipulate blocks of text. In WordPerfect, a **block** is a section of text that can be of any size—from a single character to an entire document. Once a block is designated, or marked, it can be moved, copied, or deleted.

Step 1: Mark a Block

You're going to need more text in your document to illustrate better WordPerfect's block commands. Move the cursor to the end of the document and insert a blank line:

   Press   **Home** (2 times)
   Press   **Down Arrow**
   Press   **Enter** (2 times)

Now, type this paragraph without pressing Enter:

   Full-time employees earn twenty-four working days of vacation per year. These are in addition to official company holidays and must be used by the end of each year. Accurate records of vacation leave taken must be kept because employees will be paid for their unused days when they resign or retire.

Figure 20 A Marked Block

```
To:  All Employees
From:  Personnel Department
Re:  Sick Leave

Full-time employees are entitled to twelve cumulative working days
of sick leave each year.  Time taken off is charged against these
twelve days and at the end of the year the unused balance is
carried forward.  Sick leave should only be used for an employee's
illness or doctor's appointments.  It is essential that accurate
records are kept because employees are entitled to payment for one-
half of their unused sick days when they resign or retire.

Full-time employees earn twenty-four working days of vacation per
year.  These are in addition to official company holidays and must
be used by the end of each year.  Accurate records of vacation
leave taken must be kept because employees will be paid for their
unused days when they resign or retire.
```

Block on   **Doc 1 Pg 1 Ln 4" Pos**

Leave a blank line at the end of the document:

Press   **Enter** (2 times)

The paragraph you just typed is the block you're going to work with. To mark the block, move the cursor to the first character in the paragraph and then pull down the Edit menu and execute the Block command:

Press   **Up Arrow** (6 times)
Press   **Alt-=**
Type   **eb**

Another way to execute the Block command is to press Alt-F4. The message *Block on* will flash on and off in the status line. Move the cursor just past the last character to be included in the block, in this case, the end of the document:

Press   **Home** (2 times)
Press   **Down Arrow**

As the cursor moves, the text in the block will change to reverse video (dark characters against a light background) as shown in Figure 20. You can increase or reduce the size of the marked block by simply moving the cursor.

If you have a mouse, you can use another method to mark a block. First, move the mouse pointer to the beginning of the block. Then hold down the left mouse button and drag the mouse pointer to the character just past the end of the block. Release the mouse button. The marked block will appear highlighted.

To unmark a marked block with the mouse, simply click the left mouse button.

Step 2: Move a Block

Once a block has been marked, it's easy to move it to another position in the document. Suppose you want to put the vacation leave paragraph before the sick leave paragraph. First, pull down the Edit menu and execute the Move (Cut) command:

Press	**Alt-=**
Type	**em**

Now, move the cursor to the first character in the sick leave paragraph, and press Enter:

Press	**Up Arrow** (8 times)
Press	**Enter**

The marked block will be removed from its original position and inserted in the new location, as shown in Figure 21.

Step 3: Copy a Block

Sometimes it's useful to copy text from one location to another. You might need an exact duplicate or a version that's only slightly different. Instead of retyping the text in the new location, you can mark a block, copy the text, then make any necessary modifications. This can save time when you are working on documents that contain repeated sections of text.

Just for practice, let's make a copy of the vacation leave paragraph and put it at the end of the memo. Although the duplicate paragraphs won't make sense in your particular document, the exercise will demonstrate how to copy a block.

First, mark the block to be copied, in this case the first paragraph. If the cursor is not already at the first character of the paragraph, move it there. Then do this:

Press	**Alt-=**
Type	**eb**
Press	**Down Arrow** (6 times)

Figure 21 Second Paragraph Moved

```
To:  All Employees
From:  Personnel Department
Re:  Sick Leave

Full-time employees earn twenty-four working days of vacation per
year.  These are in addition to official company holidays and must
be used by the end of each year.  Accurate records of vacation
leave taken must be kept because employees will be paid for their
unused days when they resign or retire.

Full-time employees are entitled to twelve cumulative working days
of sick leave each year.  Time taken off is charged against these
twelve days and at the end of the year the unused balance is
carried forward.  Sick leave should only be used for an employee's
illness or doctor's appointments.  It is essential that accurate
records are kept because employees are entitled to payment for one-
half of their unused sick days when they resign or retire.

C:\LESSONS\MEMO.DOC                      Doc 1 Pg 1 Ln 1.67" Pos 1"
```

Figure 22 First Paragraph Copied at End of Document

```
To:  All Employees
From:  Personnel Department
Re:  Sick Leave

Full-time employees earn twenty-four working days of vacation per
year.  These are in addition to official company holidays and must
be used by the end of each year.  Accurate records of vacation
leave taken must be kept because employees will be paid for their
unused days when they resign or retire.

Full-time employees are entitled to twelve cumulative working days
of sick leave each year.  Time taken off is charged against these
twelve days and at the end of the year the unused balance is
carried forward.  Sick leave should only be used for an employee's
illness or doctor's appointments.  It is essential that accurate
records are kept because employees are entitled to payment for one-
half of their unused sick days when they resign or retire.

Full-time employees earn twenty-four working days of vacation per
year.  These are in addition to official company holidays and must
be used by the end of each year.  Accurate records of vacation
leave taken must be kept because employees will be paid for their
unused days when they resign or retire.


C:\LESSONS\MEMO.DOC                           Doc 1 Pg 1 Ln 4" Pos 1"
```

Now, pull down the Edit menu again, execute the Copy command, move the cursor to the end of the document, and press Enter:

Press	**Alt-=**
Type	**ec**
Press	**Home** (2 times)
Press	**Down Arrow**
Press	**Enter**

WordPerfect will duplicate the vacation leave paragraph at the end of the document, as shown in Figure 22.

Step 4: Delete a Block

You now have two copies of the vacation leave paragraph, but you need only one for this memo. This is a good opportunity to try deleting a block. Instead of deleting every character, word, or line in a paragraph, you can erase the whole thing at once. For example, mark the first vacation leave paragraph as a block and then delete it:

Press	**Home** (2 times)
Press	**Up Arrow**
Press	**Down Arrow** (4 times)
Press	**Alt-=**
Type	**eb**
Press	**Down Arrow** (6 times)
Press	**Delete**

WordPerfect will display the prompt

Delete block? No (Yes)

Since you are sure that you want to delete the marked block, answer *Yes*:

Type	**y**

Figure 23 shows the result.

Figure 23 Paragraph Deleted

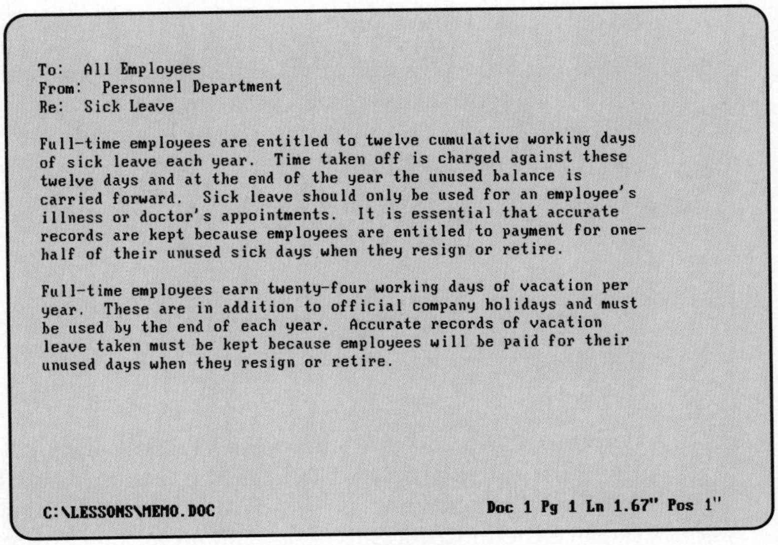

```
To:  All Employees
From:  Personnel Department
Re:  Sick Leave

Full-time employees are entitled to twelve cumulative working days
of sick leave each year.  Time taken off is charged against these
twelve days and at the end of the year the unused balance is
carried forward.  Sick leave should only be used for an employee's
illness or doctor's appointments.  It is essential that accurate
records are kept because employees are entitled to payment for one-
half of their unused sick days when they resign or retire.

Full-time employees earn twenty-four working days of vacation per
year.  These are in addition to official company holidays and must
be used by the end of each year.  Accurate records of vacation
leave taken must be kept because employees will be paid for their
unused days when they resign or retire.



C:\LESSONS\MEMO.DOC                        Doc 1 Pg 1 Ln 1.67" Pos 1"
```

Practice

1. Mark the heading of the memo (the first three lines) as a block.
2. Copy the marked block to the end of the memo.
3. Mark the lines you just copied as a block and then delete it.

Lesson 14: Canceling Commands

At one time or another, everyone who uses a word processing package makes a mistake deleting text or executing some other command. Fortunately, WordPerfect has an Undelete command in the Edit menu that can restore accidentally erased text. It also has a Cancel key that can perform the same operation or stop an executing command. The Cancel key, the F1 function key, can do the following:

- Return from a WordPerfect menu or cancel your response to a WordPerfect prompt before the response is final.
- Turn off, or unmark a marked block.
- Restore any of the three most recently deleted text items.

Whenever you erase text, whether a single character or an entire block, WordPerfect temporarily stores that text in a special area of memory. Up to three deletions are saved, allowing you to reverse a delete command. For example, suppose you accidentally delete the last paragraph in the memo.

Step 1: Delete the Paragraph

Mark the last paragraph as a block and delete it by following these instructions:

Press	**Home** (2 times)
Press	**Down Arrow**
Press	**Up Arrow** (6 times)
Press	**Alt-=**
Type	**eb**
Press	**Down Arrow** (6 times)
Press	**Delete**
Type	**y**

Step 2: Set the Cursor

Now, suppose you realize your mistake and want the deleted paragraph back. First, you would move the cursor to the place where you want to insert the restored text. In this case, the cursor is already at the correct location, so you don't have to move it.

Step 3: Execute the Undelete Command or Press Cancel

Pull down the Edit menu and execute the Undelete command.

Press	**Alt-=**
Type	**eu**

Another way to do this is to press F1, the Cancel key. WordPerfect will display the most recently deleted item in the text area and the Undelete menu at the bottom of the screen, as shown in Figure 24. Execute the Restore option to retrieve the most recently deleted item at the current cursor location:

Type	**r**

The deleted text will be reinstated. To restore a previously deleted item, you would type 2 or P to select Previous Deletion, until the text you want to restore is displayed in reverse video in the text area.

Step 4: Save the Document

To preserve the changes you have made so far, save the document to your disk:

Press	**Alt-=**
Type	**fs**
Press	**Enter**
Type	**y**

Figure 24 The Undelete Menu

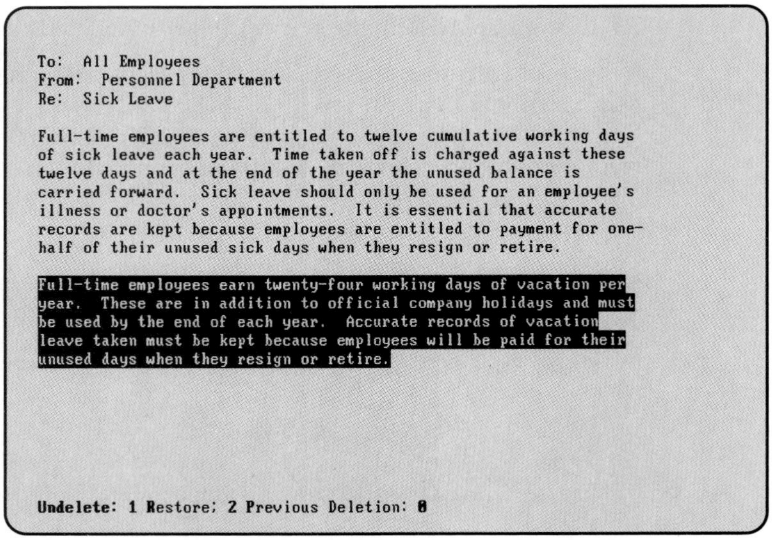

```
To:  All Employees
From:  Personnel Department
Re:  Sick Leave

Full-time employees are entitled to twelve cumulative working days
of sick leave each year.  Time taken off is charged against these
twelve days and at the end of the year the unused balance is
carried forward.  Sick leave should only be used for an employee's
illness or doctor's appointments.  It is essential that accurate
records are kept because employees are entitled to payment for one-
half of their unused sick days when they resign or retire.

Full-time employees earn twenty-four working days of vacation per
year.  These are in addition to official company holidays and must
be used by the end of each year.  Accurate records of vacation
leave taken must be kept because employees will be paid for their
unused days when they resign or retire.




Undelete: 1 Restore; 2 Previous Deletion: 0
```

Practice   Press F1, the Cancel key. Select the second option from the Undelete menu to examine the previous deletion. You don't want to insert this text back into your document, so cancel the Undelete command:

Press   **F7**

Lesson 15: Formatting Characters

Formatting a document means specifying how it will look when it is printed. True what-you-see-is-what-you-get (WYSIWYG) word processing software has an exact correspondence between the screen and the printed page. WordPerfect is not a WYSIWYG word processing package; some formatting specifications show up on the display screen, but others become evident only when the document is printed. WordPerfect has many features that let you format characters, lines, and entire pages. Let's start with the character formatting options.

Step 1: Underline Text

WordPerfect offers several ways to emphasize characters in a document. Let's add an underlined heading before the sick leave paragraph. First, make sure insert mode is turned on. Then follow these instructions:

Press   **Home** (2 times)
Press   **Up Arrow**
Press   **Down Arrow** (4 times)
Press   **F8**
Type   **Sick Leave**
Press   **F8**
Press   **Enter** (2 times)

The F8 key turns underline on and off. On the screen, underlined text may appear underlined, highlighted, or in a different color, depending on the type of monitor you have and the way that WordPerfect has been set up (see Figure 25). When the document is printed, however, the heading *Sick Leave* will be underlined.

Figure 25 Underlined Text

```
To:  All Employees
From:  Personnel Department
Re:  Sick Leave

Sick Leave

Full-time employees are entitled to twelve cumulative working days
of sick leave each year.  Time taken off is charged against these
twelve days and at the end of the year the unused balance is
carried forward.  Sick leave should only be used for an employee's
illness or doctor's appointments.  It is essential that accurate
records are kept because employees are entitled to payment for one-
half of their unused sick days when they resign or retire.

Full-time employees earn twenty-four working days of vacation per
year.  These are in addition to official company holidays and must
be used by the end of each year.  Accurate records of vacation
leave taken must be kept because employees will be paid for their
unused days when they resign or retire.

C:\LESSONS\MEMO.DOC                          Doc 1 Pg 1 Ln 2" Pos 1"
```

Step 2: Boldface Text

WordPerfect makes it just as easy to boldface text. Follow these directions to add a boldfaced heading before the vacation leave paragraph:

Press	**Home** (2 times)
Press	**Down Arrow**
Press	**Up Arrow** (6 times)
Press	**F6**
Type	`Vacation Leave`
Press	**F6**
Press	**Enter** (2 times)

The F6 key turns boldface on and off. On the screen, boldfaced text appears in brighter characters, in a different color, or in reverse video, depending on your monitor and the way in which WordPerfect has been set up (see Figure 26). When the document is printed, however, the *Vacation Leave* heading will be boldfaced.

Step 3: Using other Character Formats

Underline and boldface are the two most commonly used character formats, but WordPerfect also provides other options. Follow these directions to activate the Font menu and select the Appearance option:

Press	**Alt-=**
Type	**oa**

The Appearance submenu shown in Figure 27 will appear on the screen. In addition to boldface and underline, this menu also lists double underline, italics, outline, shadow, small capitals, redline, and strikeout character formats. Exit the menu when you have finished examining it:

Press	**F7**

Figure 26 Boldfaced Text

```
To:  All Employees
From:  Personnel Department
Re:  Sick Leave

Sick Leave

Full-time employees are entitled to twelve cumulative working days
of sick leave each year.  Time taken off is charged against these
twelve days and at the end of the year the unused balance is
carried forward.  Sick leave should only be used for an employee's
illness or doctor's appointments.  It is essential that accurate
records are kept because employees are entitled to payment for one-
half of their unused sick days when they resign or retire.

Vacation Leave

Full-time employees earn twenty-four working days of vacation per
year.  These are in addition to official company holidays and must
be used by the end of each year.  Accurate records of vacation
leave taken must be kept because employees will be paid for their
unused days when they resign or retire.

C:\LESSONS\MEMO.DOC                        Doc 1 Pg 1 Ln 3.67" Pos 1"
```

Figure 27 The Font Appearance Menu

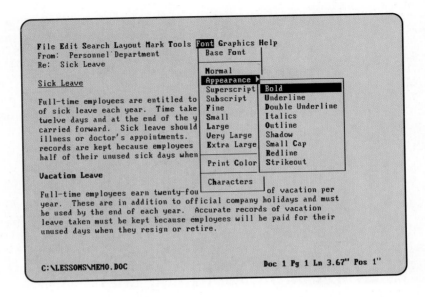

Step 4: Save the Document

To preserve the changes you have made so far, save the document to your disk:

Press	**Alt-=**
Type	**fs**
Press	**Enter**
Type	**y**

Practice

1. In Steps 1 and 2, you formatted new characters as you typed them. You can also format existing text. Find the word *essential* in the first paragraph of the memo and move the cursor to the beginning of the word. Mark this word as a block. Now underline the word:

Press	**F8**

2. Certain combinations of character formats are allowed. For example, text can be underlined and boldfaced. Mark the word *essential* in the first paragraph as a block again. This time, boldface the word:

Press	**F6**

   The word *essential* should now appear underlined and boldfaced.

3. Choose some other word in the memo and mark it as a block. Pull down the Font menu and select the Appearance option:

Press	**Alt-=**
Type	**oa**

   Select a character format option other than underline or boldface for the marked word. The appearance of the word may or may not change on the screen, depending on the type of monitor you have. It will be printed in the format you selected, however, if your printer is capable of producing it.

4. In WordPerfect, character formatting is indicated by hidden codes stored before and after the formatted text. You turn off character formatting by

deleting these codes. Let's turn off the formatting you turned on in the previous Practice exercises. Move the cursor to the space just before the word *essential* in the first paragraph, and do this:

Press	**Right Arrow**
Press	**Delete**

WordPerfect will ask you if you want to delete the underline code.

Type	**y**

Now, turn off the boldface:

Press	**Delete**
Type	**y**

Use what you have learned to turn off the character format you turned on in Practice exercise 3.

Lesson 16: Formatting Lines

Like most word processing packages, WordPerfect has a number of features that control the appearance of lines, paragraphs, and other sections of text. The most common formatting operations allow you to change margins, set tab stops, set justification, set line spacing, set line height, and center text.

Step 1: Change Margins

WordPerfect initially sets both the left and right margins of a document at one inch from the edge of the paper. Although these margins are usually adequate, you may need to change them for some documents. Let's change the left and right margins of the memo to 1.25 inch. First, move the cursor to the beginning of the document, where you want the new margins to begin:

Press	**Home** (2 times)
Press	**Up Arrow**

Next, pull down the Layout menu (see Figure 28) and select the Line option to display the Line menu (see Figure 29):

Press	**Alt-=**
Type	**LL**

Another way to activate the Line menu is to press Shift-F8 and then type L. Now, select the Margins option and enter the new left and right margin measurements:

Type	**m**
Type	**1.25"**
Press	**Enter**
Type	**1.25"**
Press	**Enter**

Press the Exit key to leave the Line menu and return to the editing screen:

Press	**F7**

The new margins will be established, as shown in Figure 30. They will remain in effect in this document unless you change them later.

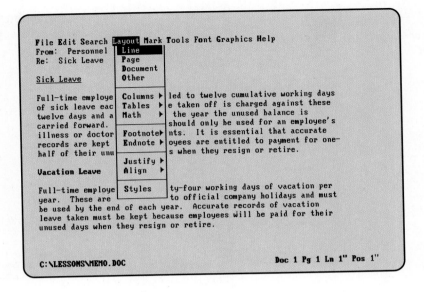

Figure 28 The Layout Menu

Step 2: Set Tab Stops

Like typewriters, computer keyboards have at least one Tab key. When this key is pressed, the cursor advances to some preset location. By default, WordPerfect initially sets tab stops at half-inch intervals. For example, move the cursor to the next tab stop:

Press   **Tab**

If insert mode is turned on, pressing the Tab key pushes any existing characters to the right; if typeover mode is turned on, the Tab key moves the cursor over

Figure 29 The Layout Line Menu

```
Format: Line

    1 - Hyphenation                      No

    2 - Hyphenation Zone - Left          10%
                           Right         4%

    3 - Justification                    Full

    4 - Line Height                      Auto

    5 - Line Numbering                   No

    6 - Line Spacing                     1

    7 - Margins - Left                   1"
                  Right                  1"

    8 - Tab Set                          Rel: -1", every 0.5"

    9 - Widow/Orphan Protection          No


Selection: 0
```

Figure 30 New Margins Have Been Set

```
To:  All Employees
From:  Personnel Department
Re:  Sick Leave

Sick Leave

Full-time employees are entitled to twelve cumulative working days
of sick leave each year.  Time taken off is charged against these
twelve days and at the end of the year the unused balance is
carried forward.  Sick leave should only be used for an employee's
illness or doctor's appointments.  It is essential that accurate
records are kept because employees are entitled to payment for one-
half of their unused sick days when they resign or retire.

Vacation Leave

Full-time employees earn twenty-four working days of vacation per
year.  These are in addition to official company holidays and must
be used by the end of each year.  Accurate records of vacation
leave taken must be kept because employees will be paid for their
unused days when they resign or retire.


C:\LESSONS\MEMO.DOC                              Doc 1 Pg 1 Ln 1" Pos 1.25"
```

existing text. If Insert mode was turned on when you pressed Tab, remove the Tab:

Press	**Backspace**

To view or change the current tab settings, pull down the Layout menu, select the Line option, and then select the Tab Set option:

Press	**Alt-=**
Type	**LL**
Type	**t**

Figure 31 shows the Tab Set menu. The dotted line near the bottom of the screen is a **ruler line** showing the current tab stops. Each *L* denotes a left-justified tab

Figure 31 The Tab Set Menu

```
To:  All Employees
From:  Personnel Department
Re:  Sick Leave

Sick Leave

Full-time employees are entitled to twelve cumulative working
days of sick leave each year.  Time taken off is charged
against these twelve days and at the end of the year the
unused balance is carried forward.  Sick leave should only be
used for an employee's illness or doctor's appointments.  It
is essential that accurate records are kept because employees
are entitled to payment for one-half of their unused sick days
when they resign or retire.

Vacation Leave

Full-time employees earn twenty-four working days of vacation
per year.  These are in addition to official company holidays
and must be used by the end of each year.  Accurate records of
..L....L....L....L....L....L....L....L....L....L....L....L....L.
  !    ^    !    ^    !    ^    !    ^    !    ^    !    ^    !    ^
  0"      +1"      +2"      +3"      +4"      +5"      +6"      +7"
Delete EOL (clear tabs); Enter Number (set tab); Del (clear tab);
Type; Left; Center; Right; Decimal; .= Dot Leader; Press Exit when done.
```

stop. You can use the Left Arrow and Right Arrow keys to move the cursor within the ruler line, and delete existing tab stops with the Delete key. You can add a new tab stop at any position by typing one of the following characters:

L	Inserts a left-justified tab stop, which aligns text along the left side at the tab stop.
C	Inserts a centered tab stop, which centers text at the tab stop.
R	Inserts a right-justified tab stop, which aligns text along the right side at the tab stop.
D	Inserts a decimal tab stop, which aligns numbers by their decimal points at the tab stop.

If you like, you can also delete the existing tab stops in the ruler line by pressing Ctrl-End and insert all new tab stops. For now, just leave the tab stops where they are. Exit the Tab Stop menu and return to the editing screen:

Press	**F7** (2 times)

Step 3: Change to Left Justification

Justification refers to the alignment of text. WordPerfect has four types of justification: left, right, full, and center. Full justification is turned on by default, which aligns text to both the left and right margins. If necessary, **soft spaces** are automatically generated by the word processor and inserted between words to give the text a block look. (**Hard spaces** are inserted only when you press the Space Bar.) Although WordPerfect's full justification feature is turned on, the on-screen text is not displayed as justified. Full justification becomes evident only when the document is printed. Text that is full-justified looks best when it is produced by a printer that can do **proportional spacing**, which allots different amounts of space for different characters. The combination of full justification and proportional spacing produces text similar to the typeset material in this book.

If your printer cannot do proportional spacing, it is better to use left justification. The resulting text will have a ragged right margin similar to that of typewritten text. To change to left justification for the memo, pull down the Layout menu, select the Line option, select the Justification option, and then select the Left option:

Press	**Home** (2 times)
Press	**Up Arrow**
Press	**Alt-=**
Type	**LL**
Type	**j**
Type	**L**
Press	**F7**

Left justification will now be turned on from the cursor position to the end of the document, but the appearance of text on the screen will not change.

The two other types of justification are right and center. Right justification aligns text to the right margin; it is handy for placing the return address and date at the right side of a letter. Center justification centers text between the left and right margins; it is often used for centering multi-line headings and titles.

Step 4: Set Line Spacing

Word processing packages allow you to determine the line spacing for documents. By default, WordPerfect's line spacing is set to 1. In other words, lines are automatically single spaced. This means that no blank lines are left between successive lines of text whenever a word wrap occurs or whenever you press the Enter key. Double spacing leaves one blank line between successive lines of text, triple spacing leaves two blank lines, and so on.

Suppose you want your document to be double-spaced. First you move the cursor to where you want double spacing to begin. Then you pull down the Layout menu, select the Line option, select the Line Spacing option, and specify the line spacing. Follow these directions:

Press	**Home** (2 times)
Press	**Up Arrow**
Press	**Alt-=**
Type	**LL**
Type	**s**
Type	**2**
Press	**Enter**
Press	**F7**

The memo will be double-spaced, as shown in Figure 32. Any new text you type from the current cursor location to the end of the document will also be double-spaced.

Since memos are usually single-spaced, change the line spacing from 2 back to 1:

Press	**Alt-=**
Type	**LL**
Type	**s**
Type	**1**
Press	**Enter**
Press	**F7**

Figure 32 Double-Spaced Memo

```
To:  All Employees

From:  Personnel Department

Re:  Sick Leave


Sick Leave


Full-time employees are entitled to twelve cumulative

working days of sick leave each year.  Time taken off is

charged against these twelve days and at the end of the year

the unused balance is carried forward.  Sick leave should

only be used for an employee's illness or doctor's

appointments.  It is essential that accurate records are

C:\LESSONS\MEMO.DOC                    Doc 1 Pg 1 Ln 1" Pos 1.25"
```

Step 5: Set Line Height

In WordPerfect, the distance between lines of printed text is called **line height**. This is not the same as line spacing. *Line height* is measured from the bottom of one line to the bottom of the next line below. *Line spacing* is one plus the number of blank lines left between successive lines of text. Normally, WordPerfect automatically assigns a line height appropriate for the font you are using. You can, however, adjust the line height to create documents that must meet exact publishing specifications.

WordPerfect's default line height yields 6 lines of text per vertical inch, which is the standard line height of most typewriters. To change line height, you pull down the Layout menu, select the Line option, select the Line Height option, select the Fixed option, and then enter a new line height measurement. Follow these directions:

Press	**Alt-=**
Type	**LL**
Type	**h**
Type	**f**

WordPerfect will then display the current line height in inches. Let's just leave it at 0.167", which is about ⅙-inch. Return to the editing screen:

Press	**F7** (2 times)

Step 6: Center Text

Many documents require certain headings or other text to be centered between the left and right margins. To do this manually is tedious. Fortunately, WordPerfect, like most word processing packages, can automatically center text. All you have to do is pull down the Layout menu, select the Align option, and then select the Center option. You can also center a line using the function key interface by pressing Shift-F6.

Let's center the headings above the two paragraphs in our memo. Follow these instructions to center the heading *Sick Leave*:

Press	**Home** (2 times)
Press	**Up Arrow**
Press	**Down Arrow** (4 times)
Press	**Alt-=**
Type	**Lac**
Press	**Left Arrow**
Press	**Down Arrow**

Now, center the *Vacation Leave* heading:

Press	**Down Arrow** (10 times)
Press	**Alt-=**
Type	**Lac**
Press	**Down Arrow**

Your screen should look like Figure 33.

You can also center a new line of text as you type it. You would simply move the cursor to the left margin of the new line, execute the Center option from the Layout Align menu or press Shift-F6 to move the cursor to the center of the line, type the text, and press Enter.

Figure 33 Centered Headings

```
To:  All Employees
From:  Personnel Department
Re:  Sick Leave

                        Sick Leave

Full-time employees are entitled to twelve cumulative
working days of sick leave each year.  Time taken off is
charged against these twelve days and at the end of the year
the unused balance is carried forward.  Sick leave should
only be used for an employee's illness or doctor's
appointments.  It is essential that accurate records are
kept because employees are entitled to payment for one-half
of their unused sick days when they resign or retire.

                       Vacation Leave

Full-time employees earn twenty-four working days of
vacation per year.  These are in addition to official
company holidays and must be used by the end of each year.
Accurate records of vacation leave taken must be kept
because employees will be paid for their unused days when
they resign or retire.

C:\LESSONS\MEMO.DOC                    Doc 1 Pg 1 Ln 3.67" Pos 1.25"
```

Step 7: Save the Document

To preserve the changes you have made so far, save the document to your disk:

Press	**Alt-=**
Type	**f s**
Press	**Enter**
Type	**y**

Practice

1. Move the cursor to the beginning of the document. Change the left and right margins to 2 inches. Move the cursor down 7 lines. See how the text is reformatted within the new margins. Change them back to 1.25 inches.

2. Triple space your entire document and see how it looks. Then change line spacing back to 1.

3. Type the heading *Unpaid Leave* at the end of the memo, centering it as you type it. When you have finished, delete the heading from the document.

Lesson 17: Formatting Pages

Page formatting features affect entire pages of text. WordPerfect has several commands that let you specify how pages are laid out. Although you don't need to change any of the default page format settings for our simple memo, you may need to change them for other documents. Let's look at the commands that control paper size and type, top and bottom margins, page breaks, and page numbering.

Step 1: Set the Paper Size and Type

Standard letter-size paper is 8½ inches wide and 11 inches long. Given a standard line height of 6 lines per inch, the number of lines on letter-size paper is 6 times

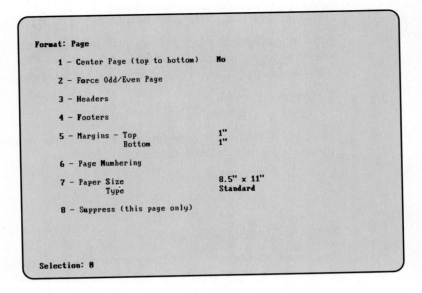

Figure 34 The Layout Page Menu

11, or 66. WordPerfect's default paper size is 8½ by 11 inches, but this can be changed. First, pull down the Layout menu and then select the Page option:

Press   **Alt-=**
Type   **Lp**

WordPerfect will display the Page menu (see Figure 34). Now, select the Paper Size option:

Type   **s**

Here you could select a different paper size and type (see Figure 35). Let's leave it at 8½ by 11 inches and return to the editing screen:

Press   **F7** (2 times)

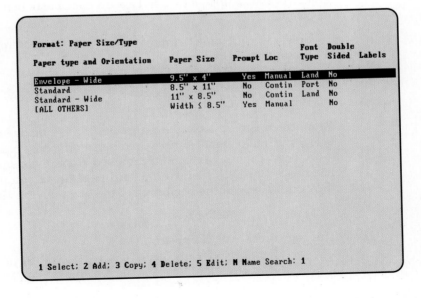

Figure 35 The Paper Size/ Type Menu

Step 2: Set the Top and Bottom Margins

Most documents are printed with some blank space at the top and bottom of every page. By default, WordPerfect leaves one-inch top and bottom margins. You can change these settings from the Layout Page menu:

Press	**Alt-=**
Type	**Lpm**

Here you could enter new top and bottom margin measurements. Let's leave them at one inch. Return to the editing screen:

Press	**F7** (3 times)

Step 3: Start a New Page

The actual number of lines of text printed on a page depends on several factors. For example, WordPerfect's default line height is ⅙ inch. The default page length is 11 inches (66 lines), with a top margin of 1 inch (6 lines) and a bottom margin of 1 inch (6 lines). That leaves 66 minus 12, or 54, as the default number of lines of text printed on a page.

As you type text with WordPerfect, the word wrap feature automatically starts new lines. WordPerfect also automatically starts new pages. Assuming the default page-format settings are in effect, a soft page break is inserted after every 54 lines you type. A **soft page break** is a division between two pages automatically generated by the word processing software. It is symbolized on the screen by a horizontal line of dashes. This line is not actually printed on paper; it simply indicates the place where a new page will begin.

Although WordPerfect's automatic page break feature is convenient, you may sometimes want to have a page with fewer than 54 lines. A new page can be forced by inserting a **hard page break**. This is a division between two pages that is manually generated by the user. It is symbolized on the screen by a horizontal line of equal signs. You can begin a new page at any point within a document by pulling down the Layout menu, selecting the Align option, and then selecting the Hard Page option. Another way to insert a hard page break is to press Ctrl-Enter. As an example, let's insert a hard page break between the two paragraphs in the memo:

Press	**Home** (2 times)
Press	**Up Arrow**
Press	**Down Arrow** (15 times)
Press	**Alt-=**
Type	**Lap**

Your screen should look like Figure 36. If this document were printed, the text below the line of equal signs would begin on a new page.

A hard page break can be removed from a document with the Delete or Backspace key. Let's remove the hard page break you just inserted. Make sure the cursor is still at the beginning of the line with the *Vacation Leave* heading.

Press	**Backspace**

The page break will disappear.

*Figure 36 A Hard Page
Break*

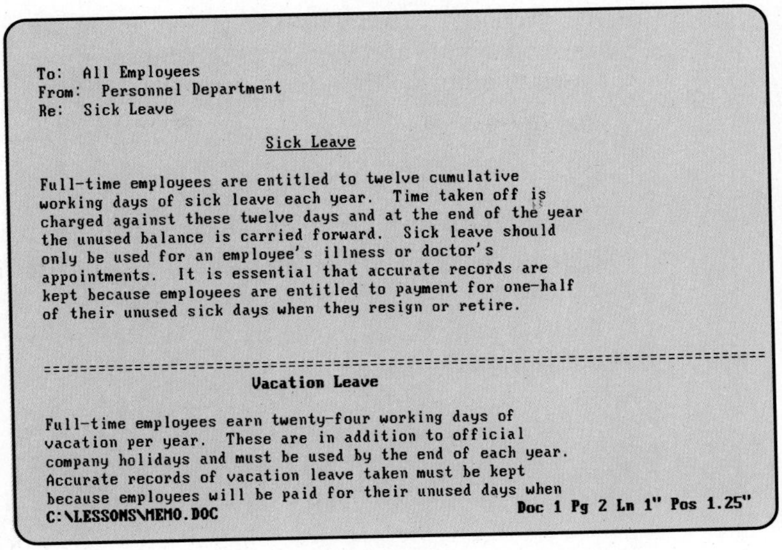

```
To:  All Employees
From:  Personnel Department
Re:  Sick Leave

              Sick Leave

Full-time employees are entitled to twelve cumulative
working days of sick leave each year.  Time taken off is
charged against these twelve days and at the end of the year
the unused balance is carried forward.  Sick leave should
only be used for an employee's illness or doctor's
appointments.  It is essential that accurate records are
kept because employees are entitled to payment for one-half
of their unused sick days when they resign or retire.


===============================================================================
              Vacation Leave

Full-time employees earn twenty-four working days of
vacation per year.  These are in addition to official
company holidays and must be used by the end of each year.
Accurate records of vacation leave taken must be kept
because employees will be paid for their unused days when
C:\LESSONS\MEMO.DOC                          Doc 1 Pg 2 Ln 1" Pos 1.25"
```

Step 4: Set the Page Numbering

WordPerfect automatically keeps track of page numbers while you work on a document and displays the current page number on the screen in the status line (see Figure 36). But WordPerfect does not print page numbers unless you tell it to do so. Although we don't need a page number on our single-page memo, let's see how you would turn on printed page numbering. Pull down the Layout menu, select the Page option, select the Page Numbering option, and then select the Page Number Position option:

Press   **Alt-=**
Type   **Lpnp**

WordPerfect will display the Page Number Position menu on the screen as shown in Figure 37. Here you would select a page number position option. For example,

*Figure 37 The Page
Numbering Menu*

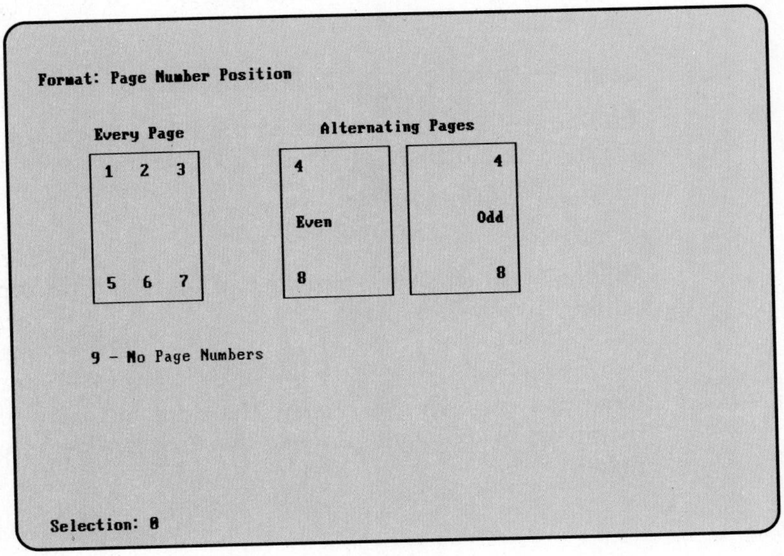

if you wanted a page number to appear in the top right corner of every page, you would type 3 and then press F7. Since you don't need page numbering in the memo, return to the editing screen:

Press   **F7**

1. Change the paper size to Envelope - Wide. Then change it back to Standard.
2. Change the top and bottom margins to 2 inches. Then change them back to 1 inch.
3. Insert a page break in the memo before the first paragraph. Now, remove the page break.

Lesson 18: Printing a Document

You've entered, formatted, proofread, and corrected your document. You're satisfied with your work and now it's time to produce the final product. You're ready to print your document on paper.

Step 1: Save the Document

It is a good idea to save your document before printing.

Press   **Alt-=**
Type   **f s**
Press   **Enter**
Type   **y**

Step 2: Prepare the Printer

Make sure the printer is connected to the computer and turned on. Also, make sure that paper is loaded and aligned to the top of a new page. Finally, make sure that the printer's On Line light is lit. (If it isn't, press the On Line button.)

Step 3: Invoke the Print Command

Pull down the File menu, select the Print option to display the Print menu (see Figure 38), and then select the Full Document option:

Press   **Alt-=**
Type   **fpf**

When WordPerfect has finished printing the document, it will return to the editing screen.

Note that you can also display the Print menu by pressing Shift-F7. Print the memo again, but this time use the function key interface to display the Print menu.

Figure 38 The Print Menu

```
Print

    1 - Full Document
    2 - Page
    3 - Document on Disk
    4 - Control Printer
    5 - Multiple Pages
    6 - View Document
    7 - Initialize Printer


Options

    S - Select Printer                      Epson FX-86e
    B - Binding Offset                      0"
    N - Number of Copies                    1
    U - Multiple Copies Generated by        WordPerfect
    G - Graphics Quality                    Medium
    T - Text Quality                        High




Selection: 0
```

Lesson 19: Returning to DOS

When you have finished working with WordPerfect, you will exit the program and return to DOS.

Step 1: Invoke the Exit Option

Pull down the File menu and select the Exit option to tell WordPerfect that you either want to work on a different document or return to DOS:

Press	**Alt-=**
Type	**fx**

Another way to do this is to press F7, the Exit key.

Step 2: Save the Document

WordPerfect will ask you if you want to save the document. Unless you are just viewing a document that you don't want to change, you should answer *Yes*. If you have never saved this document before, you must enter a file name. If you have saved this document before, as we have done several times in this chapter, WordPerfect will suggest the current name. You can press Enter to choose this name, or type a new name if you want to save the document to a different file. If you choose the same name, WordPerfect will ask if you want to replace the existing document file with the version on your screen, and you should answer yes.

Type	**y**
Press	**Enter**
Type	**y**

Step 3: Confirm the Exit

WordPerfect will copy the document to the disk and then display the prompt

Exit WP? No (Yes)   (**Cancel** to return to document)

Here the program is asking you if you really want to return to DOS, and it assumes you do not. If you press F1, the Cancel key, you can return to editing your document. If you type N or press Enter, you can begin a new document. Exit WordPerfect:

    Type   **y**

You should see the DOS prompt on your screen.

Practice   Start up WordPerfect. Then exit to DOS again, but this time press F7 instead of selecting Exit from the File menu.

Lesson 20: Editing an Existing Document

Word processors make it so easy to store documents in disk files that editing an existing document is a common procedure. Any time you want to examine, modify, or update a previously stored document, all you have to do is tell WordPerfect to retrieve the file.

Step 1: Specify the Document When Loading WordPerfect

At this point you should be at the DOS prompt because you exited WordPerfect at the end of the last lesson. Before you can edit an existing document, you must make sure its file is stored on an accessible disk. The location of the document file depends on your default directory or the path and name you chose when you last saved the document. Your document may be on the diskette in drive A or B, on your hard disk C, or on a network file server disk.

    If you know the name and location of the document file you want to edit, you can start WordPerfect and load the document at the same time. If you are using a computer with a hard disk, and LESSONS, which contains MEMO.DOC, is your current subdirectory, execute this command:

    Type   **wp memo.doc**
    Press   **Enter**

If you are in a subdirectory other than LESSONS, you can preface the filename with its full path:

    Type   **wp c:\lessons\memo.doc**
    Press   **Enter**

If you are running WordPerfect on a computer with no hard disk and you saved the memo on the diskette in drive A, execute this command instead:

    Type   **wp a:memo.doc**
    Press   **Enter**

Your document will be loaded into memory along with WordPerfect, where you can view or edit it.

Step 2: Use the List Files Screen

Another way to edit an existing document is to retrieve its file from within WordPerfect. Exit WordPerfect and return to DOS. Start WordPerfect again with this command:

Type   **wp**
Press   **Enter**

Now, pull down the File menu and select the List Files option:

Press   **Alt-=**
Type   **ff**

Another way to do this is to press F5. WordPerfect will suggest your current drive and directory. If LESSONS is already your current directory, accept it as the subdirectory you want to use:

Press   **Enter**

If you are running WordPerfect from a subdirectory other than LESSONS, do this:

Type   **c:\lessons**
Press   **Enter**

If your document is on the diskette in drive A, do this instead:

Type   **a:**
Press   **Enter**

The List Files screen will appear (see Figure 39). This screen shows the files in the specified directory and presents the List Files menu. Your screen may look somewhat different, depending on the drive or directory you specified.

To load an existing document, use the arrow keys to move the reverse video highlight bar to its file name. Locate MEMO.DOC and highlight it. Then select the Retrieve option:

Type   **r**

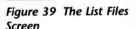

Figure 39 The List Files Screen

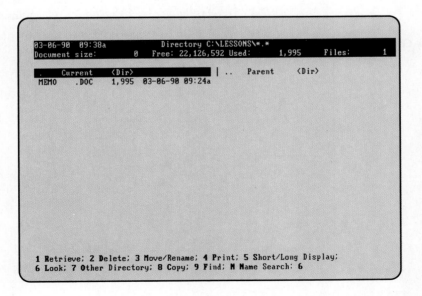

```
03-06-90  09:38a              Directory C:\LESSONS\*.*
Document size:         0  Free: 22,126,592 Used:       1,995   Files:        1

   .    Current    <Dir>         |  ..    Parent    <Dir>
MEMO     .DOC    1,995  03-06-90 09:24a




















 1 Retrieve; 2 Delete; 3 Move/Rename; 4 Print; 5 Short/Long Display;
 6 Look; 7 Other Directory; 8 Copy; 9 Find; N Name Search: 6
```

WordPerfect will load the file into memory and present the memo on the editing screen.

Step 3: Edit the Document

Sometimes you load an existing document file just to read it. Other times you actually want to correct, update, or modify the contents. Let's make a couple of additions to the memo:

Press	**Enter**
Press	**Up Arrow**
Type	**Date:** (today's date)
Press	**Down Arrow** (3 times)
Press	**Space Bar**
Type	**and Vacation Leave**

Except for the date, your screen should look like Figure 40.

Step 4: Exit WordPerfect and Save the File

Pull down the File menu, select the Exit option, and save the updated memo document:

Press	**Alt-=**
Type	**fx**
Type	**y**
Press	**Enter**
Type	**y**
Type	**y**

You should see the DOS prompt again.

Practice 1. Start WordPerfect and load your MEMO.DOC file. Change the date to tomorrow's date. Exit WordPerfect, saving the updated file.

Figure 40 The Completed Memo

```
Date:  March 6, 1990
To:  All Employees
From:  Personnel Department
Re:  Sick Leave and Vacation Leave_

                    Sick Leave

Full-time employees are entitled to twelve cumulative
working days of sick leave each year.  Time taken off is
charged against these twelve days and at the end of the year
the unused balance is carried forward.  Sick leave should
only be used for an employee's illness or doctor's
appointments.  It is essential that accurate records are
kept because employees are entitled to payment for one-half
of their unused sick days when they resign or retire.

                   Vacation Leave

Full-time employees earn twenty-four working days of
vacation per year.  These are in addition to official
company holidays and must be used by the end of each year.
Accurate records of vacation leave taken must be kept
because employees will be paid for their unused days when
they resign or retire.
C:\LESSONS\MEMO.DOC                    Doc 1 Pg 1 Ln 1.5" Pos 4.65"
```

Real World

The Men Behind WordPerfect

Alan Ashton was so happy with his company's profits in 1987 that he took everyone—the whole company—to Hawaii for a week.

Ashton's goal was that his WordPerfect Corporation would make $100 million in profits, double the 1986 figure. On December 22, 1987, the figure stood at $100.3 million in sales. What's more, the company he cofounded has achieved record sales and profits every year since it was created in 1980.

Its success in large part is due to the success of its WordPerfect word processing software. Word-Perfect is currently the world's best-selling word processing program. The White House, Congress, and law offices all over the world use it.

Who are the people who took a company to such dizzying heights in just seven years?

Ashton, president and chief executive officer, owns 49.9 percent of the stock in this private company. A former Brigham Young University professor, he is a Mormon who brings strong values and a sense of family to work with him. He is, according to employees, a father figure so down-to-earth that only recently did he reluctantly trade his pickup truck for a Cadillac. But he's a father figure with incredible drive—a tough combination to beat. Bruce Bastian founded the company along with Ashton and is now an equal partner with him. Also a Mormon and a former college professor, Bastian now serves as chairman of the board and president of Word-Perfect's highly successful international division.

The man who holds the tie-breaking 0.2 percent of the com-

pany stock is Pete Peterson. Back when the company was called Satellite Software International, Peterson was hired to keep the books. He quit the next day because there were no books.

There were also other problems, including no business license and very sketchy records. But when Ashton and Bastian realized that this man with a psychology degree knew what he was doing, they hired him back. Peterson uses a South American saying to describe the situation: "In the land of the blind, the one-eyed man is king."

Source: Christine Strehlo, "What's So Special About WordPerfect?" *Personal Computing*, March 1988, pp. 100–116.

2. Start WordPerfect without loading MEMO.DOC. Display the List Files screen and examine your WordPerfect subdirectory (WP or WP51). Look at other subdirectories or diskettes from the List Files screen. When you have finished, exit WordPerfect and return to DOS.

Summary

- *Starting WordPerfect.* From DOS, type WP and press Enter.

- *The editing screen.* The cursor marks the place where text will be inserted. The status line indicates the document, page number, and line and column position.

- *Using pull-down menus and the mouse.* Press Alt-= to display the menu bar. Press an arrow key or type a mnemonic letter to pull down a menu or select an option in a menu. Move the mouse to move the mouse pointer. Click the right mouse button to display the menu bar. Click the left mouse button to select the item at the mouse pointer. Point to a menu name and drag to pull down the menu.

- *Executing function key commands and getting help.* Most commands can also be executed by pressing a function key alone or by pressing the Shift, Control, or Alternate key with a function key. Help is obtained by pressing F3.

- *Entering text.* Simply type the text, pressing Enter only to force a new line or start a new paragraph.

- *Moving the cursor.* Arrow keys move up, down, left, and right. Ctrl-Left Arrow and Ctrl-Right Arrow move an entire word at a time. Grey Plus and Grey Minus move an entire screen at a time. Page Up and Page Down move an entire page at a time. End moves to the end of a line. Home, Left Arrow moves to the beginning of a line and Home, Right Arrow moves to the end of a line. Home, Home, Up Arrow moves to the beginning of the document and Home, Home, Down Arrow moves to the end of the document. Ctrl-Home moves to a particular page number.

- *Inserting new text.* Set the cursor, make sure insert mode is on, and type the text.

- *Overwriting mistakes.* Switch to typeover mode by pressing Insert and type over mistakes.

- *Deleting mistakes.* The Delete key removes the character at the cursor. The Backspace key removes the character to the left of the cursor. Ctrl-Backspace deletes an entire word. Ctrl-End deletes an entire line.

- *Searching for and replacing text.* Execute the Forward option in the Search menu (or press F2) to find text. Execute the Replace option in the Search menu (or press Alt-F2) to find and change text.

- *Saving a document.* Execute the Save option in the File menu (or press F10) to save a document to a disk file.

- *Checking spelling.* Execute the Spell option in the Tools menu (or press Ctrl-F2) to invoke the spelling checker.

- *Working with blocks of text.* Execute the Block option in the Edit menu (or press Alt-F4) to mark a block. Execute the Move or Copy command in the Edit menu to move or copy a marked block. Press Delete to erase a marked block.

- *Canceling commands.* Execute the Undelete option in the Edit menu (or press F1) to cancel a command in progress or restore a deletion.

- *Formatting characters.* Press F8 to underline text. Press F6 to boldface text. Execute the Appearance option from the Font menu to choose other character formats.

- *Formatting lines.* Execute the Line option from the Layout menu (or press Shift-F8 and then type L) to set left and right margins, tab stops, justification, line spacing, and line height. Pull down the Layout menu, select Align, and then select Center (or just press Shift-F6) to center text.

- *Formatting pages.* Execute the Page option from the Layout menu to set paper size and type, top and bottom margins, and page numbering. Pull down the Layout menu, select the Align option, and then select the Hard Page option (or just press Ctrl-Enter) to force a page break.

- *Printing a document.* Execute the Print option from the File menu (or press Shift-F7) to activate the Print menu, and then select the Full Document option.

- *Editing an existing document.* Type the document name on the command line when starting WordPerfect. Another way to load a document is to execute the List Files option from the File menu (or just press F5) and then select the file you want to retrieve.

- *Exiting WordPerfect.* Execute Exit from the File menu (or press F7) and answer the prompts to return to DOS.

Key Terms

As an extra review of this chapter, try defining the following terms.

block	menu bar
clicking	proportional spacing
cursor	pull-down menu
dragging	ruler line
global search and replace	soft page break
hard page break	soft return
hard return	soft space
hard space	status line
keyboard template	text area
line height	word wrap

Multiple Choice

Choose the best selection to complete each statement.

1. When you start WordPerfect without loading a document, the only thing on the editing screen, except for the cursor, is the
   - (a) Start Up menu.
   - (b) ruler line.
   - (c) status line.
   - (d) Help facility.

2. Which keys would you press to see an on-screen version of the WordPerfect function key template?
   - (a) F1, F1
   - (b) F3, F3
   - (c) F3, F7
   - (d) Alt-F3

3. What is inserted into your document when you press the Enter key?
   - (a) hard return
   - (b) soft return
   - (c) hard page break
   - (d) soft page break

4. What feature eliminates having to press Enter at the end of every line?
   - (a) full justification
   - (b) proportional spacing
   - (c) word wrap
   - (d) auto-hyphenation

5. Which keys would you press to move the cursor to the beginning of the next word to the right?
   - (a) Right Arrow
   - (b) Shift-Right Arrow
   - (c) Ctrl-Right Arrow
   - (d) Home-Right Arrow

6. You can move the cursor to the beginning of a document by pressing
   (a) Ctrl-End.
   (b) End, End, Down Arrow.
   (c) Ctrl-PgDn.
   (d) Home, Home, Up Arrow.

7. Pressing the Insert key toggles the
   (a) delete mode.
   (b) insert mode.
   (c) line spacing.
   (d) tab settings.

8. Pressing the Delete key deletes the character
   (a) at the current cursor location.
   (b) to the immediate right of the cursor.
   (c) to the immediate left of the cursor.
   (d) farthest from the cursor.

9. Pressing Ctrl-Backspace
   (a) deletes the word to the left of the cursor.
   (b) deletes the word at the cursor.
   (c) moves the cursor to the beginning of the line.
   (d) moves the cursor to the end of the line.

10. One operation that WordPerfect cannot do to a marked block is
    (a) copy it.
    (b) reverse it.
    (c) delete it.
    (d) move it.

11. Which Search menu option would you use to repeat the previous search operation?
    (a) Next
    (b) Forward
    (c) Backward
    (d) Previous

12. To force a page break, you can press
    (a) Alt-P.
    (b) Ctrl-Enter.
    (c) Ctrl-PgDn.
    (d) Alt-End.

13. Power failures, voltage fluctuations, system crashes, and unknown WordPerfect bugs are all good reasons to periodically
    (a) print your document.
    (b) edit your document.
    (c) retrieve your document.
    (d) save your document.

14. Including a file name after the WP when you start WordPerfect
    (a) prints that file.
    (b) automatically loads that file.
    (c) periodically saves that file.
    (d) deletes that file.

15. Which key would you press to restore the most recently deleted word or phrase?
    (a) Ctrl-U
    (b) F1
    (c) Ctrl-End
    (d) Escape

16. Which two character-formatting options can each be used by pressing a single function key?
    (a) italics and outline
    (b) shadow and strikeout
    (c) underline and boldface
    (d) double underline and small capitals

17. What are the default WordPerfect settings for left and right margins?
    (a) 1″ and 1″
    (b) 1.25″ and 1″
    (c) 1″ and 2″
    (d) 0″ and 1″

18. How many blank lines are left between double-spaced lines?
    (a) 0   (b) 1
    (c) 2   (d) 3
19. What keys can you press to activate the Print menu?
    (a) Shift-F7   (b) Ctrl-P
    (c) Ctrl-F1   (d) Shift-PrtSc
20. What key can you press to exit WordPerfect and return to DOS?
    (a) F1   (b) F3
    (c) F5   (d) F7

Fill-In

1. To start WordPerfect, you type _____ and press Enter.
2. The line at the bottom of the WordPerfect editing screen is called the _____.
3. Pressing _____ and then _____ moves the cursor to the left edge of the screen.
4. Pressing F3 brings up WordPerfect's _____ facility.
5. _____ is the key you press to move the cursor to the end of the current line.
6. Set justification to _____ to align text to both the left and right margins.
7. Word processors have a feature called _____ that eliminates having to press Enter at the end of each line.
8. Pressing Enter generates what's known as a _____ return.
9. The _____ keys include the Home, End, Page Up, Page Down, and arrow keys.
10. If insert mode is turned on, pressing the Insert key switches to _____ mode.
11. To overwrite mistakes, you must first turn insert mode _____.
12. Backspace, Delete, Ctrl-Backspace, and Ctrl-End are all examples of commands that _____ text.
13. Existing text can be centered between the left and right margins by pressing _____.
14. A _____ is any section of text, from a single character to a whole document, that can be marked and treated as a single entity.
15. A global _____ and _____ operation is used to change automatically every occurrence of a word or phrase.
16. By default, WordPerfect sets both the top and bottom page margins to _____.
17. When left justification is used, you get a _____ right margin.
18. If the spelling checker stops on a word that is not misspelled, you can use the _____ or _____ option to continue.
19. When you _____ a document, WordPerfect copies it from primary memory to a disk file.
20. In WordPerfect, page numbering is turned _____ by default.

Short Problems

1. Start up WordPerfect without loading an existing document. Type the following text. Press **Enter** only once, after the last line.

   The next meeting of the EZ Systems Board of Managers will be held at 7:00 P.M. on November 19, 1989 in Room 217 of Champaign Federal Savings. This is an important meeting, so please try to attend.

2. Move the cursor to the top of the document and type the following lines. Press **Enter** after each line.

   To: Board of Managers
   From: David Franklin, Secretary
   Re: Next meeting

3. Press the **Enter** key again to leave a blank line before the paragraph. Move the cursor to the top of the document, and do this:

Type	**M E M O**
Press	**Enter**

   Boldface, underline, and center this title.

4. Move the cursor to the last line of the memo and delete it with a single command. Restore the text you've deleted with the Cancel command.

5. Mark *EZ Systems* as a block of text and copy it before the *Board of Managers* after the *To:*.

6. Move the cursor to the top of the file. Use the search and replace command to change *Managers* to *Directors* throughout the entire document.

7. Move the cursor to the beginning of the document and set the left and right margins to 1½ inches.

8. Change the tab stops so that they occur at 1-inch intervals.

9. Change justification to Left for this memo.

10. Go back and double space the entire document (use the Line Spacing option from the Layout Line Format menu).

11. Save the document in a disk file named MEETING.DOC, but don't exit WordPerfect.

12. If your computer is equipped with a printer, make sure it is turned on and on-line, and print this memo.

13. Use WordPerfect's on-line help facility to get a list of all the features that begin with *A*. Select a different letter and try it again. Now try learning more about the function keys.

Long Problems

1. Use WordPerfect to create a letter to be sent to three different software companies requesting information about the word processor they sell. Use the same basic letter, but tailor it to each company and its product. Save each version in its own disk file and print out all three. If you have no word processors in mind, use these three:

WordPerfect
WordPerfect Corp.
1555 North Technology Way
Orem, UT 84057

Microsoft Word
Microsoft Corp.
16011 N.E. 36th Way
Redmond, WA 98073

WordStar
WordStar International Corp.
33 San Pablo Ave.
San Rafael, CA 94903

2. Use WordPerfect to write a paper for one of your classes or a report for your company. Be sure to follow any format guidelines specified.

3. Look in a newspaper or placement office listing for a position you might apply for. Prepare a realistic resume and cover letter for this job with WordPerfect. Be sure to use underlining and boldface where appropriate.

4. Investigate three different word processing programs. Use WordPerfect to prepare a report that compares their features.

5. Use WordPerfect to create your academic schedule for this semester. List the days, times, classes, buildings, rooms, and instructors.

6. Create a weekly appointment calendar with WordPerfect. Print out several copies for the next few weeks.

7. Write a letter with WordPerfect to a company praising or criticizing their product or service.

8. Use WordPerfect to write a letter to WordPerfect Corporation detailing some of the things you like or dislike about their word processing package. You can use the address given in Problem 1.

9. Create an address and phone listing of your friends and acquaintances using WordPerfect.

10. Create a quick reference guide to DOS with WordPerfect. In other words, list each DOS command along with a brief description of what it does and how to invoke it.

11. Use WordPerfect to create a quick reference guide to WordPerfect. List the commands and operations that you think are most important to remember.

12. Take a week's worth of notes from a class you are taking and redo them with WordPerfect. Try to do more than just type them as is. Organize, rearrange, and reword the material if you can. Do you think using a word processor can improve your notes?

13. As you redo your notes for Problem 12, keep in mind any questions you might have about the material. Write a letter to your professor in which you outline your questions. If possible, copy sections or even direct quotes from your notes and include them in your letter.

14. Perhaps you have an item that you would like to sell through a newspaper ad, such as a musical instrument, bicycle, car, couch, television, stereo, or computer. You might be looking for a roommate or have an apartment to sublet. Use WordPerfect to design a classified ad to place in your school or local newspaper.

15. Choose a current event or local news item that interests you and use WordPerfect to write a letter expressing your views on it to the editor of your school or town newspaper.

Intermediate WordPerfect

In This Chapter

Preview

In the previous chapter you learned the basics of WordPerfect, the most popular microcomputer word processing package. This chapter continues your exploration of WordPerfect with slightly more advanced topics.

After studying this chapter, you will know how to

- manage documents with the List Files menu.
- create longer documents.
- use additional cursor movement commands.
- use additional delete commands.
- work with formatting codes.
- use the built-in thesaurus.
- split the screen into two windows.
- indent paragraphs.
- create tables with tab stops.
- align numbers to tab stops.
- move text flush right.
- insert the current date automatically.
- center text on a page.
- create a document summary.
- use passwords.
- import and export text files.
- execute a DOS command within WordPerfect.

Getting Started

You've already learned how to start WordPerfect and use its most common features and commands. This chapter assumes you have completed all of the lessons and exercises in the Beginning WordPerfect chapter. Furthermore, it assumes that you have a computer with a hard disk and WordPerfect 5.1 installed so that the program can be run from any subdirectory. It also assumes you have a subdirectory named LESSONS in which to store your document files.

Lesson 1: Managing Documents

WordPerfect makes it easy to create new documents, retrieve existing documents, save and search for documents, as well as delete, rename, copy, and print documents. You can also change the default directory and examine the contents of a directory or file. All of these features are available as pull-down menu options, function key commands, or options in the List Files menu.

Step 1: Start WordPerfect

If you are not already running WordPerfect, switch to the LESSONS subdirectory and start the program:

Type	**cd\lessons**
Press	**Enter**
Type	**wp**
Press	**Enter**

Step 2: Retrieve a Document By Name

In the previous chapter, you learned how to load an existing document file by specifying the file name on the command line when starting WordPerfect or by selecting the file from the List Files screen and executing the Retrieve option. If you know the location and name of the document file you want, a third method exists to retrieve it. Suppose you want to work on the MEMO.DOC file in the LESSONS subdirectory. Pull down the File menu and Execute the Retrieve option:

Press	**Alt-=**
Type	**fr**

Another way to invoke the Retrieve command is to press Shift-F10. Either way, WordPerfect will display the prompt

```
Document to be retrieved:
```

Enter the path and name of the document file:

Type	**c:\lessons\memo.doc**
Press	**Enter**

The document will be loaded into memory and displayed on the screen in the text area.

Step 3: Starting a New Document

If you have finished looking at or working on a document, you can clear the screen to start a new document without actually exiting WordPerfect and restarting the program. Suppose you have either already saved the current document or don't want to save it. Pull down the File menu, execute the Exit option, and answer *No* to both prompts:

Press	**Alt-=**
Type	**fx**
Type	**n**
Type	**n**

WordPerfect will not save the file and will not return to DOS, but will clear the screen so you can start a new document. Another way to perform this procedure is to press F7, the Exit key.

Step 4: Execute the List Files Command

The screen and menu presented by the List Files command provide many options for managing your documents. This command lets you see the names of the files stored on a disk or in a subdirectory. It also lets you retrieve, delete, rename, copy, and print files. Pull down the File menu and execute the List Files option to examine your default directory, which should be the subdirectory C:\LESSONS:

Press	**Alt-=**
Type	**ff**
Press	**Enter**

You can also execute the List Files command directly by pressing F5. WordPerfect will display the directory of C:\LESSONS and present the List Files menu at the bottom of the screen.

*Figure 1 The List Files
Menu*

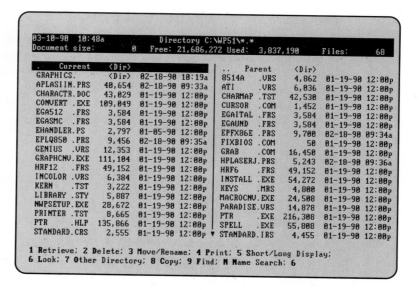

Step 5: Select the Other Directory Option

You can look at any disk or subdirectory from the List Files menu. Select the
Other Directory option:

Type	**o**

WordPerfect will display the prompt

New directory = C:\LESSONS

Here the program is presenting the current path and is asking you to enter the
path of the other directory you want to examine. Specify the WordPerfect 5.1
subdirectory:

Type	**c:\wp51**
Press	**Enter** (2 times)

The list of files will change to reveal the contents of the WP51 subdirectory, as
shown in Figure 1. Note: If your WordPerfect subdirectory is WP or has some
other name, use that name instead of WP51 throughout this chapter and the next
chapter. After you have finished examining the WP51 subdirectory, switch back
to the LESSONS subdirectory:

Type	**o**
Type	**c:\lessons**
Press	**Enter** (2 times)

Step 6: Select the Look Option

Look is the default option of the List Files menu. This option lets you examine
the contents of a directory, which you have just done. The Look option also
allows you to examine the contents of a file without actually loading that file into
the editing screen. Let's look at the file MEMO.DOC. Use the Down Arrow key
to highlight the file name and select the Look option:

Highlight	**MEMO.DOC**
Type	**L**

*Figure 2 MEMO.DOC Pre-
sented with the List Files
Look Option*

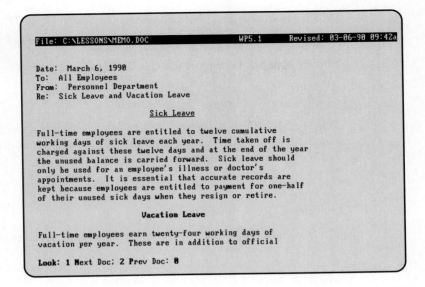

Your screen should look like Figure 2. The file MEMO.DOC is presented, but
you can only look at it, not edit it. If the file is too long to fit on a single screen,
you can use the cursor movement keys to see the rest of it. When you have
finished examining the file, press the Exit key:

Press   **F7**

Step 7: Select the Retrieve Option

You have already learned to use the Retrieve option, but let's try it again. The
file name MEMO.DOC should already be highlighted, so just select the Retrieve
option:

Type   **r**

WordPerfect will load the file into memory and present it on the editing screen.
Unlike using the Look option, using the Retrieve option lets you edit the document.
  Now, clear the screen and execute the List Files command again:

Press   **Alt-=**
Type   **fx**
Type   **n**
Type   **n**
Press   **Alt-=**
Type   **ff**
Press   **Enter**

Step 8: Select the Copy Option

You can use the Copy option of the List Files menu to duplicate a file. The
duplicate can be created either in the same directory or in a different directory.
If it is in the same directory as the original, the duplicate must be given a different
name. Let's copy the file MEMO.DOC and name the duplicate MEMO.BAK. First,
highlight the file MEMO.DOC and then select the Copy option:

Highlight   **MEMO.DOC**
Type   **c**

WordPerfect will display the prompt

```
Copy this file to:
```

Simply enter the name of the duplicate to be created:

Type	**memo.bak**
Press	**Enter**

The file MEMO.BAK will be created in the current directory. Unfortunately, the List Files screen isn't updated, so highlight the current directory and execute the Look option to see what you have done:

Highlight	**. Current ⟨Dir⟩**
Type	**L**
Press	**Enter**

The file MEMO.BAK will now appear in the directory listing shown on the screen.

Step 9: Select the Move/Rename Option

The Move/Rename option of the List Files menu can be used to move a file to a different subdirectory or change the name of a file. Let's rename MEMO.BAK to MEMO.OLD. First, highlight MEMO.BAK. Then select the Move/Rename option:

Highlight	**MEMO.BAK**
Type	**m**

WordPerfect will display the prompt

```
New name: C:\LESSONS\MEMO.BAK
```

To move the file, you would edit the path. To rename the file, simply enter the new name:

Type	**memo.old**
Press	**Enter**

The file MEMO.BAK will become MEMO.OLD in the LESSONS subdirectory.

Step 10: Select the Print Option

In the previous chapter you learned how to print a document from the editing screen. You can also print a document that is not currently loaded into memory from the List Files menu. Let's print MEMO.OLD. Make sure your printer is turned on, loaded with paper, and on-line. Highlight the file to be printed. Then select the Print option from the List Files menu:

Type	**p**

WordPerfect will display the prompt

```
Page(s): (All)
```

Select the default option to print all of the pages:

Press	**Enter**

The document will be sent to the printer.

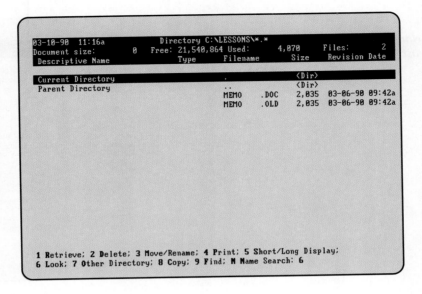

Figure 3 The Long Display Feature

Step 11: Select the Short/Long Display Option

WordPerfect can present the list of files in two formats: Short Display and Long Display. Short Display is the default format, which you see now on the List Files screen. The file list is displayed with two file names on each line. Each file or directory is identified by its name and the date and time it was last changed. The file sizes are also displayed.

Long Display has only one file name on each line. For example, switch to Long Display:

Type	**sL**
Press	**Enter**

Figure 3 shows the result. The Long Display feature is handy for organizing a large collection of document files. You can assign a Type to a group of similar documents and then use the Find option in the List Files menu to restrict your display to only those files. In addition, the Descriptive Name column lists the optional long document name that you can assign to a document. The short, DOS file name is restricted to eight characters plus a three-character extension. A long document name can consist of up to 68 characters, the first 30 of which will appear in the Descriptive Name column of the List Files screen. We will discuss long document names further in the next chapter when we show how to customize WordPerfect with the Environment Setup menu. The Descriptive Name column will be blank for those files with only DOS names.

Now, switch back to Short Display:

Type	**ss**
Press	**Enter**

Step 12: Select the Name Search Option

The Name Search option in the List Files menu allows you to highlight a file name by typing its name instead of using the arrow keys to move through the list. When you type the first letter of the file name, the highlight moves to the

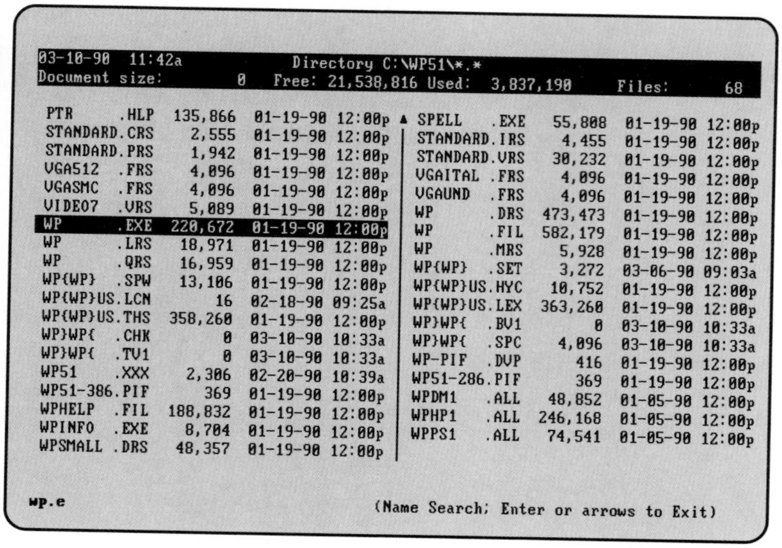

Figure 4 The Name Search Option of the List Files Menu

```
03-10-90  11:42a                  Directory C:\WP51\*.*
Document size:          0   Free: 21,538,816 Used:  3,837,190    Files:      68

   PTR     .HLP  135,866  01-19-90 12:00p ▲ SPELL   .EXE   55,808  01-19-90 12:00p
   STANDARD.CRS    2,555  01-19-90 12:00p | STANDARD.IRS    4,455  01-19-90 12:00p
   STANDARD.PRS    1,942  01-19-90 12:00p | STANDARD.VRS   30,232  01-19-90 12:00p
   VGA512  .FRS    4,096  01-19-90 12:00p | VGAITAL .FRS    4,096  01-19-90 12:00p
   VGASMC  .FRS    4,096  01-19-90 12:00p | VGAUND  .FRS    4,096  01-19-90 12:00p
   VIDEO7  .VRS    5,089  01-19-90 12:00p | WP      .DRS  473,473  01-19-90 12:00p
   WP      .EXE  220,672  01-19-90 12:00p | WP      .FIL  582,179  01-19-90 12:00p
   WP      .LRS   18,971  01-19-90 12:00p | WP      .MRS    5,928  01-19-90 12:00p
   WP      .QRS   16,959  01-19-90 12:00p | WP{WP}  .SET    3,272  03-06-90 09:03a
   WP{WP}  .SPW   13,106  01-19-90 12:00p | WP{WP}US.HYC   10,752  01-19-90 12:00p
   WP{WP}US.LCN       16  02-18-90 09:25a | WP{WP}US.LEX  363,260  01-19-90 12:00p
   WP{WP}US.THS  358,260  01-19-90 12:00p | WP}WP{  .BV1        0  03-10-90 10:33a
   WP}WP{  .CHK        0  03-10-90 10:33a | WP}WP{  .SPC    4,096  03-10-90 10:33a
   WP}WP{  .TV1        0  03-10-90 10:33a | WP-PIF  .DVP      416  01-19-90 12:00p
   WP51    .XXX    2,306  02-20-90 10:39a | WP51-286.PIF      369  01-19-90 12:00p
   WP51-386.PIF      369  01-19-90 12:00p | WPDM1   .ALL   48,852  01-05-90 12:00p
   WPHELP  .FIL  188,832  01-19-90 12:00p | WPHP1   .ALL  246,168  01-05-90 12:00p
   WPINFO  .EXE    8,704  01-19-90 12:00p | WPPS1   .ALL   74,541  01-05-90 12:00p
   WPSMALL .DRS   48,357  01-19-90 12:00p |

 wp.e                               (Name Search; Enter or arrows to Exit)
```

first file name that begins with that letter. As you type more letters of the file name, the highlight moves to the next file name that matches what you have typed so far. You can usually highlight the file name you want by typing just a few characters. To see how the Name Search option works, first switch to the WP51 subdirectory:

Type   **o**
Type   **c:\wp51**
Press   **Enter** (2 times)

The WP51 subdirectory displayed on your screen contains many files. Suppose you want to find the file named WP.EXE. Instead of scrolling through the long list with the arrow keys to highlight WP.EXE, use the Name Search option:

Type   **n**
Type   **wp.e**

Each file name character you type moves the highlight to the next matching file name. By the time you type the *e,* the file WP.EXE is highlighted (see Figure 4). Return to the List Files menu:

Press   **Enter**

Now, change back to the LESSONS subdirectory:

Type   **o**
Type   **c:\lessons**
Press   **Enter** (2 times)

Step 13: Mark Files

In some cases it is necessary to perform an operation on a group of files. For example, you may want to copy, delete, or print several files at once. WordPerfect allows you to mark each file you want on the List Files screen with an asterisk (*). After the files are marked, you can select Copy, Delete, or Print from the List

Files menu. Let's see how to mark and unmark files. First, move the highlight to the file MEMO.OLD. Then mark the file with an asterisk:

Highlight   **MEMO.OLD**
Type   *

An asterisk will appear in the directory listing immediately before the file name. Now mark MEMO.DOC too. If you have a printer connected to your computer, select the Print option:

Type   **p**
Type   **y**

Both files will be printed.

   To unmark a file, simply repeat the process by highlighting the file name and typing another asterisk. The asterisk will disappear from the directory listing. Unmark MEMO.DOC and MEMO.OLD.

Step 14: Select the Find Option

Find is a powerful List Files option that lets you display only those files that meet specific conditions. For example, you can display all those files that contain the word *vacation*. Select the Find option:

Type   **f**

WordPerfect will present a menu that lists several types of searches:

   1 Name This option searches for files by name.

   2 Doc Summary This option searches document summaries for the specified word pattern. A *document summary* is a collection of information about a document. You will learn how to create document summaries later in this chapter.

   3 First Pg This option searches only the first page or the first 4000 characters of documents for the specified word pattern.

   4 Entire Doc This option searches entire documents for the specified word pattern.

   5 Conditions This option allows you to enter criteria to conduct a more detailed search.

   6 Undo This option works like Undelete does in the normal editing screen. Once a search has been completed, it allows you to restore the file list to the way it was before the search.

Let's use the Entire Doc option:

Type   **e**

WordPerfect will display the prompt

   Word pattern:

Now you specify the text you want to search for. You can use a question mark (?) to represent any single character and an asterisk (*) to represent any group of characters. These **wild-card characters** work just like the DOS global file name characters ? and *. In our simple example, however, you don't need wild-card characters because you are just searching for documents that contain the word *vacation*. Specify the word pattern:

Type   **vacation**
Press   **Enter**

WordPerfect will search through all the documents in the current directory and display those documents that contain the word *vacation*. Since MEMO.DOC and MEMO.OLD are duplicates that both contain the word *vacation*, both files are displayed in the list.

Step 15: Select the Delete Option

The Delete option in the List Files menu lets you erase files. Let's delete MEMO.OLD. First, highlight MEMO.OLD. Then select the Delete option:

Highlight   **MEMO.OLD**
Type   **d**

WordPerfect will display the prompt

Delete <u>**C:\LESSONS\MEMO.OLD?**</u> No (Yes)

If you are sure you want to delete the file, answer yes:

Type   **y**

The file will be erased from the disk and removed from the List Files screen. Now, exit the List Files screen and return to the editing screen:

Press   **F7**

Practice

1. Execute the List Files command. Put a formatted diskette in drive A. Select the Other Directory option and examine the contents of the diskette in drive A.
2. Use the Other Directory option to switch to the root directory of the hard disk. Highlight the file CONFIG.SYS and select the Look option to examine its contents. Press the Exit key (F7) to return to the List Files screen.
3. From the List Files screen, switch to the LESSONS subdirectory. Copy the file MEMO.DOC and name the duplicate NOTE.DOC.
4. Use the Look option to examine the contents of NOTE.DOC.
5. Retrieve NOTE.DOC into the editing screen. Make a change to the file and then save it. Execute the List Files command again.
6. Rename NOTE.DOC to NOTE.OLD.
7. Print NOTE.OLD.
8. Delete NOTE.OLD. Exit the List Files screen and return to the editing screen.

Lesson 2: Creating a Longer Document

To illustrate more of WordPerfect's capabilities, you need a more substantial document. In this lesson, you will create a simple newsletter for a fictional business, Paddle and Portage Canoe Outfitters.

Step 1: Type the Heading

The top of the newsletter will present the centered address and phone number of the business. Follow these instructions:

Press	**Shift-F6**
Type	**Paddle and Portage Canoe Outfitters**
Press	**Enter**
Press	**Shift-F6**
Type	**Box 555**
Press	**Enter**
Press	**Shift-F6**
Type	**Grand Marais, MN 55604**
Press	**Enter**
Press	**Shift-F6**
Type	**(218) 555-1234**
Press	**Enter** (2 times)

Step 2: Type the Title

The title of the newsletter will also be centered. Follow these instructions:

Press	**Shift-F6**
Type	**NEWSLETTER**
Press	**Enter**
Press	**Shift-F6**
Type	**1991**
Press	**Enter** (2 times)

Step 3: Type the First Section

Each section of the newsletter will have an underlined heading.

Press	**F8**
Type	**New Outfitting Post**
Press	**F8**
Press	**Enter**

Type the paragraph without pressing Enter at the end of each line:

This winter we completed our new outfitting facility. It will house our office, staff kitchen, retail sales, and equipment storage area. Located close to the lake for easy access, this new building will give us the room we need to help serve you better.

Space down for the next section:

Press	**Enter** (2 times)

Step 4: Type the Next Section

Follow these directions:

Press	**F8**
Type	**Sport Shows**
Press	**F8**

Press	**Enter**
Type	**This year we will be attending the following sport shows:**
Press	**Enter** (2 times)
Type	**Jan 23--Feb 1**
Press	**Enter**
Type	**Chicagoland Show, O'Hare Exposition Center**
Press	**Enter** (2 times)
Type	**Feb 14--Feb 22**
Press	**Enter**
Type	**Greater Northwest Sport Show, Minneapolis Auditorium**
Press	**Enter** (2 times)
Type	**Mar 13--Mar 22**
Press	**Enter**
Type	**Milwaukee Sentinel Sport Show, MECCA Building**
Press	**Enter** (2 times)
Type	**If you can, stop by and say "Hi." Remember our SPECIAL BONUS RATES for sport show reservations.**
Press	**Enter** (2 times)

Step 5: Save the Document So Far

It is a good idea to save your document periodically on a disk as you are creating it, even if it is not finished. Save the document in your current subdirectory, which should be LESSONS, and name it NEWS.DOC:

Press	**Alt-=**
Type	**fs**
Type	**news.doc**
Press	**Enter**

Step 6: Type the Rest of the Document

Follow these directions to type the rest of the newsletter:

Press	**F8**
Type	**New Regulations**
Press	**F8**
Press	**Enter**

Type this paragraph:

Only Ontario's Quetico Provincial Park has changed regulations for this season. Reservations for Quetico camping permits will be accepted no sooner than January 19. Written reservations may be made 21 days in advance of trip departure. Phone reservations may be made from 21 days prior to and up to the date of departure. As always, we will handle all permit reservations for our guests.

Press	**Enter** (2 times)
Press	**F8**

Type	**Equipment Improvements**
Press	**F8**
Press	**Enter**

Type this paragraph:

Our most exciting equipment addition this year is a new Super-Lite Badger canoe. It weighs, believe it or not, slightly over 40 pounds. We feel that this new 17-foot Badger canoe is ideal for wilderness tripping. It's stable, safe, and much easier to paddle and portage.

Press	**Enter**
Press	**Tab**

Type this paragraph:

Last year we field tested several nylon packs and found one in particular that offered several advantages. Lighter and dryer than canvas Duluth packs, we will be incorporating these new nylon packs into our equipment line beginning this year. The Super-Lite Badger canoes and nylon packs will be available on a first-come, first-serve basis.

Press	**Enter** (2 times)
Press	**F8**
Type	**Trail Food Improvements**
Press	**F8**
Press	**Enter**

Type this paragraph:

We have replaced the Ham and Potatoes with Meatballs and Gravy, the Beef Stromboli with Chicken Stew 'N Dumplings, and the Buttermilk Pancakes with Blueberry Pancakes. These are all taste improvements, not cost savings, so our Trail Food will be even better this year.

Press	**Enter** (2 times)
Press	**F8**
Type	**Trips**
Press	**F8**
Press	**Enter**

Type this paragraph:

This fall we took a trip into the Cherry Lake area for some lake trout fishing. We had our usual quota of rain, but did enjoy two beautiful crisp autumn days. Mornings we awoke to clear, deep blue skies with heavy, white steam rising from Cherry Lake. It was almost like being in a shaving commercial. On shore we could look up into the blue sky, but as we paddled into the steam we disappeared into white nothingness. It was a trip we'll long remember.

Press	**Enter**
Press	**Tab**

Type this paragraph:

> **We extended our camping into winter this year with several overnight trips in December. From our house we have easy access to about 15 kilometers of cross-country ski trails that lead to Boundary Waters Canoe Area campsites. After setting up a base camp, we would typically venture out for exploring and ice fishing. Nothing like twenty below temperatures to get you moving in the morning!**

Press	**Enter** (2 times)
Press	**F8**
Type	**A Final Note...**
Press	**F8**
Press	**Enter**

Type this paragraph:

> **After having our best year ever, we want to thank all of you for your friendship and patronage and wish you a happy and prosperous New Year. We look forward to seeing you this spring, summer, or fall.**

Press	**Enter** (2 times)
Type	**Becky and Bob Johnson, owners/operators**
Press	**Enter**
Type	**Paddle and Portage Canoe Outfitters**
Press	**Enter**

Step 7: Check Your Work

Read over the document you have created and make sure it contains no errors. Use what you have learned in the previous chapter to correct any typographical errors you may have made.

Step 8: Save the Completed Document

Now that the document is finished, you must save it on a disk. Pull down the File menu, execute the Save command, and replace your previous version of NEWS.DOC:

Press	**Alt-=**
Type	**fs**
Press	**Enter**
Type	**y**

Step 9: Move to the Beginning

Move the cursor up to the beginning of the document:

Press	**Home** (2 times)
Press	**Up Arrow**

Your screen should look like Figure 5.

*Figure 5 The Completed
Newsletter*

```
              Paddle and Portage Canoe Outfitters
                          Box 555
                   Grand Marais, MN  55684
                       (218) 555-1234

                         NEWSLETTER
                           1991

New Outfitting Post
This winter we completed our new outfitting facility.  It will
house our office, staff kitchen, retail sales, and equipment
storage area.  Located close to the lake for easy access, this new
building will give us the room we need to help serve you better.


Sport Shows
This year we will be attending the following sport shows:


Jan 23--Feb 1
Chicagoland Show, O'Hare Exposition Center


Feb 14--Feb 22
Greater Northwest Sport Show, Minneapolis Auditorium


Mar 13--Mar 22
C:\LESSONS\NEWS.DOC                          Doc 1 Pg 1 Ln 1" Pos 1"
```

Practice

1. Use the spelling checker to inspect further the newsletter for typographical errors. Tell the spelling checker to skip proper names that are not in the dictionary, such as Marais, Chicagoland, O'Hare, Quetico, Stromboli, and Becky.
2. Move the cursor back to the beginning of the document.

Lesson 3: Learning More Cursor-Movement Commands

In the previous chapter you learned several ways to move the cursor within a WordPerfect document. This lesson covers a few other cursor-movement commands.

Step 1: Move to the Bottom and Top of the Screen

Pressing Home once followed by an arrow key moves the cursor to that end of the text on the screen. Home, Left Arrow moves the cursor to the left edge of the screen and Home, Right Arrow moves the cursor to the right edge of the screen. You can also move to the bottom edge and top edge of the current screen. Execute this command:

Press   **Home**
Press   **Down Arrow**

The cursor will jump to the bottom edge of the current screen in the same column, or close to the same column, as its original position. If you repeat the command, the cursor will advance to the bottom of the next screen. Pressing Home, Down Arrow is the same as pressing Grey Plus. Now, execute the opposite command:

Press   **Home**
Press   **Up Arrow**

The cursor will jump to the top of the current screen. Pressing Home, Up Arrow is the same as pressing Grey Minus.

Step 2: Move a Specified Number of Lines

WordPerfect lets you move up or down a specified number of lines. Suppose you want to move the cursor down 12 lines. Follow these instructions:

Press	**Escape**
Type	**12**
Press	**Down Arrow**

The cursor will move down 12 lines, just as if you had pressed Down Arrow 12 times. Now, move up 6 lines with this command:

Press	**Escape**
Type	**6**
Press	**Up Arrow**

Repeat this command to move the cursor up another 6 lines.

Step 3: Move a Specified Number of Characters

In fact, the Escape key can be used in this manner with other cursor movement keys as well. Suppose you want to move the cursor right 20 characters. Execute this command:

Press	**Escape**
Type	**20**
Press	**Right Arrow**

The cursor will move to the right 20 characters just as if you had pressed Right Arrow 20 times. Now, try the opposite command:

Press	**Escape**
Type	**20**
Press	**Left Arrow**

Step 4: Move a Specified Number of Screens or Pages

The Escape key can also be used to rapidly scroll or page. For example, try this command:

Press	**Escape**
Type	**3**
Press	**Grey Plus**

The cursor will move down three screens, just as if you had pressed Grey Plus three times. Now, try a repeated paging command:

Press	**Escape**
Type	**2**
Press	**Page Up**

The cursor will move up two pages, in this case to the top of the document.

Step 5: Move to a Specific Character

A variation of the Go To feature, executed by pressing Ctrl-Home, lets you position the cursor to the immediate right of the first occurrence of a particular character. For example, move the cursor to the beginning of the first line of the newsletter. Suppose you want to advance the cursor just past the *C* in the word *Canoe*. Execute this command:

Press	**Ctrl-Home**
Type	**C**

The cursor will be placed on the *a* following the *C* in the word *Canoe*.

Practice

1. Move the cursor to the beginning of the document.
2. Advance the cursor 10 characters to the right, then move the cursor 5 characters to the left. (Don't press the arrow keys repeatedly.)
3. Move the cursor down 10 lines without repeatedly pressing Down Arrow.
4. Advance the cursor to the next occurrence of the letter *R*.
5. Move the cursor down 4 screens, then move the cursor back up 4 screens. Now, move the cursor to the beginning of the line.

Lesson 4: Learning More Delete Commands

WordPerfect provides several commands for deleting text. You have already learned the most common methods in the previous chapter.

Step 1: Delete to Word Boundary

Suppose you want to delete just part of a word. WordPerfect lets you erase characters from the current cursor location to the beginning or end of a word. For example, move the cursor to the letter *f* in the word *Outfitters* in the first line of the newsletter. Delete the first part of the word:

Press	**Home**
Press	**Backspace**

The *Out* part of the word will be deleted. Now, restore what you have deleted:

Press	**F1**
Type	**r**

This time, try deleting the latter part of the word:

Press	**Home**
Press	**Delete**

The *fitters* part of the word will be deleted. Restore what you have deleted:

Press	**F1**
Type	**r**

Figure 6 The Delete to End of Page Prompt

```
              Paddle and Portage Canoe Outfitters
                          Box 555
                   Grand Marais, MN  55604
                      (218) 555-1234
                        NEWSLETTER
                          1991

New Outfitting Post
This winter we completed our new outfitting facility.  It will
house our office, staff kitchen, retail sales, and equipment
storage area.  Located close to the lake for easy access, this new
building will give us the room we need to help serve you better.

Sport Shows
This year we will be attending the following sport shows:

Jan 23--Feb 1
Chicagoland Show, O'Hare Exposition Center

Feb 14--Feb 22
Greater Northwest Sport Show, Minneapolis Auditorium

Mar 13--Mar 22
Delete Remainder of page? No (Yes)
```

Figure 6 The Delete to End of Page Prompt

Step 2: Delete Several Lines

You can use the Escape key to repeat the Delete to End of Line command and erase several lines at once. For example, move the cursor to the beginning of the paragraph beneath the title New Outfitting Post. Delete four lines by executing this command:

Press	**Escape**
Type	**4**
Press	**Ctrl-End**

The four lines will disappear from the screen. Now, restore the lines you have deleted:

Press	**F1**
Type	**r**

Step 3: Delete to End of Page

WordPerfect provides an even more drastic command that lets you delete the text from the current cursor position to the end of the page. Execute this command:

Press	**Ctrl-PgDn**
Type	**y**

After you answer *Yes* to the prompt (see Figure 6), WordPerfect will delete the rest of the text on the current page. Now, restore what you have erased:

Press	**F1**
Type	**r**

Practice 1. Select a long word in the newsletter. Move the cursor into the middle of the word. Delete the first half of the word. Restore what you have deleted. Then delete the second half of the word. Again, restore what you have deleted.

Figure 7 Formatting Codes Revealed

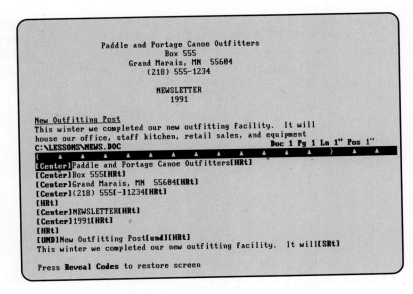

2. Delete ten lines of text from the newsletter with one command. Restore the lines you have deleted.

3. Delete half of the second page of the newsletter. Restore what you have deleted. Move the cursor to the beginning of the document.

Lesson 5: Working with Codes

Whenever you press the Enter key, WordPerfect inserts a **code** in your document that tells the display or printer to start a new line. Although this code does not appear on the screen, it is stored in your document like any other character. WordPerfect has many such hidden formatting codes. Codes are inserted whenever you press the Tab key, underline text, center text, change margins, or execute any of a number of commands that change a document's appearance. Codes not only control how the document should look on the screen, they tell the printer how to print the document. Learning about codes helps you understand and control the way in which WordPerfect formats text.

Step 1: Reveal Codes

By default, codes are hidden from view to simplify the editing screen. You can display codes along with the text at any time, however, by pulling down the Edit menu and executing the Reveal Codes option. Do this now:

Press   **Alt-=**
Type   **er**

Another way to reveal codes is to press Alt-F3, the Reveal Codes key. Your screen should look like Figure 7. The top part of the screen is the normal view of the document with codes hidden. The bar across the middle of the screen is a ruler line that indicates the current left margin (open brace {), the tab stops (triangles), and the right margin (close brace}). If the margins do not fall on tab stops, as they do on your screen, they will be marked by square brackets ([and]) instead of braces. The portion of the screen below the ruler line reveals the codes, which are bright characters enclosed in square brackets, and the text in ordinary characters. For example, [Und] is the code that turns underlining on and off. It appears in uppercase [UND] when turned on and lowercase [und] when turned off.

WordPerfect has nearly 120 different formatting codes. The following table lists a few of the most common codes.

Code	Description
[-]	Hard hyphen inserted by pressing - key
[Bold]	Boldface on or off
[Center]	Begin centering text
[HPg]	Hard page break inserted by Ctrl-Enter
[HRt]	Hard return inserted by pressing Enter
[SPg]	Soft page break inserted by WordPerfect
[SRt]	Soft return inserted by word wrap
[Tab]	Advance to next left-aligned tab stop
[Und]	Underline on or off

Step 2: Examine the Document

With Reveal Codes turned on, use the Down Arrow key to examine the document. Notice how the Reveal Codes cursor, a reverse video block, moves as you press the Down Arrow key. Look up the codes you see in the previous table and try to understand what they mean.

Step 3: Delete Codes

Codes are special characters that you can insert and delete. For example, to remove centering or underlining, you simply delete the appropriate codes. Although you don't have to reveal codes to delete them, revealing codes does make it easier to see what is happening. For example, let's uncenter the first line in the newsletter. Move the cursor to the first [Center] code in the file and then delete it:

Press   **Delete**

The [Center] code will disappear and the text will shift to the left edge of the screen. Now, restore the code you have deleted:

Press   **F1**
Type   **r**

You can also delete codes to remove underlining and remove hard returns [HRt] to join lines or paragraphs.

Step 4: Hide Codes

Revealing codes displays two views of the same document, but you can see only eleven lines above the ruler and twelve lines below. You can leave codes revealed for as long as you like, but most users prefer to turn them on only when needed. When you have finished working with codes, you can hide them again:

Press	**Alt-=**
Type	**er**

You can also press the Reveal Codes key, Alt-F3, to turn off the display of codes. The editing screen will return to full size, the ruler line will disappear, and codes will be hidden again.

Practice

1. Reveal codes.
2. Remove the underline from the heading New Outfitting Post. Restore the underline by marking the heading as a block and then pressing the underline key (F8).
3. Move the cursor down to the end of the first paragraph after the heading Equipment Improvements. Remove the hard return and the following tab to join the two paragraphs. Restore the hard return and tab. Move the cursor to the beginning of the document.
4. Use the help facility to read more about the Reveal Codes command:

Press	**F3**
Press	**Alt-F3**

   When you have finished reading the help screen, return to the document:

Press	**Enter**

5. Hide codes.

Lesson 6: Using the Thesaurus

Like most modern word processing packages, WordPerfect includes a built-in thesaurus program that can help you select just the right word for a situation. The WordPerfect thesaurus can examine a word already in your document or a word that you enter and display a list of synonyms (words with the same or similar meaning) and antonyms (words with the opposite meaning).

Step 1: Move the Cursor to the Desired Word

The thesaurus feature is very easy to use. For example, suppose you want to see alternatives to the word *house* in the second sentence of the New Outfitting Post paragraph. First, move the cursor anywhere within the word *house*.

Step 2: Execute the Thesaurus Command

After you have selected the word you want to look up, pull down the Tools menu and execute the Thesaurus option:

Press	**Alt-=**
Type	**th**

Another way to invoke the thesaurus is to press Alt-F1.

Figure 8 The Thesaurus Screen

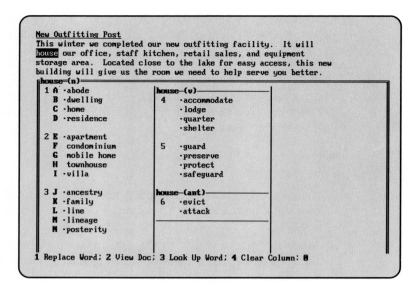

```
New Outfitting Post
This winter we completed our new outfitting facility.  It will
house our office, staff kitchen, retail sales, and equipment
storage area.  Located close to the lake for easy access, this new
building will give us the room we need to help serve you better.
house=(n)
  1 A ·abode             house=(v)
    B ·dwelling            4  ·accommodate
    C ·home                   ·lodge
    D ·residence              ·quarter
                             ·shelter
  2 E ·apartment
    F  condominium        5  ·guard
    G  mobile home           ·preserve
    H  townhouse             ·protect
    I ·villa                 ·safeguard

  3 J ·ancestry          house-(ant)
    K ·family             6  ·evict
    L ·line                  ·attack
    M ·lineage
    N ·posterity


1 Replace Word; 2 View Doc; 3 Look Up Word; 4 Clear Column: 0
```

Step 3: Examine the Thesaurus Screen

Your screen should look like Figure 8. In this case, *house* is the **headword**, a word that can be looked up in the thesaurus. The words under the headword, called references, are divided into nouns (n), verbs (v), adjectives (a), and antonyms (ant). No adjectives are available for *house*. References preceded by a dot are other headwords that can also be looked up in the thesaurus. The references are collected into numbered groups of words with the same meaning. Six groups of references are available for *house*. The Reference menu is the column of capital letters preceding the references. The Thesaurus menu is the list of four options across the bottom of the screen. Presently, the Reference menu is on the first column of words: abode, dwelling, home, residence, and so on. You can move the Reference menu from column to column by pressing Right Arrow and Left Arrow. For example, move the Reference menu to the second column of references:

Press   **Right Arrow**

The column of capital letters will move over so that the word *accommodate* is A, *lodge* is B, *quarter* is C, and so on.

Step 4: Replace the Word

If you find a word in the list of references that you like, you can tell WordPerfect to replace the word you have looked up. Suppose you want to replace *house* with *accommodate*. Select the Replace Word option from the Thesaurus menu and then type the letter of the word you want:

Type   **1**
Type   **a**

Figure 9 *References for Two Headwords Displayed*

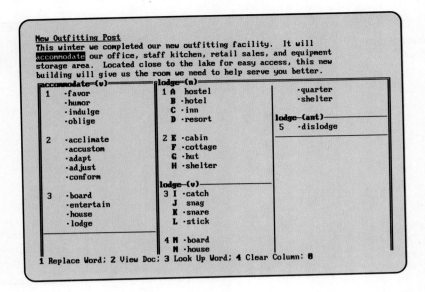

The word *house* will automatically be replaced with *accommodate*.

Step 5: Look Up Other Words

Invoke the thesaurus again:

Press	**Alt-=**
Type	**th**

This time, *accommodate* is the headword. While the thesaurus is on the screen, you can use three methods to look up other words. The first method is to select the Look Up Word option and enter the word you want. Suppose you want to look up the word *lodge*.

Type	**3**
Type	**lodge**
Press	**Enter**

WordPerfect will display references for *lodge* in addition to the references for *accommodate* already on the screen (see Figure 9).

Step 6: Specify a Letter

Another way to look up a word while in the thesaurus is to type the letter next to a headword marked with a dot. Suppose you want to look up the word *board*, which is preceded by the letter *M*.

Type	**m**

Figure 10 References for Three Headwords Displayed

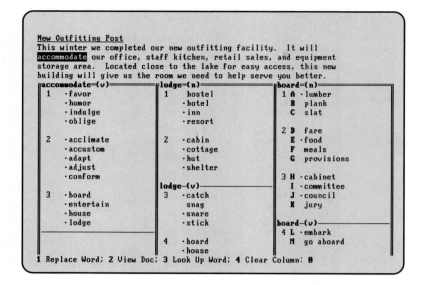

```
New Outfitting Post
This winter we completed our new outfitting facility.  It will
accommodate our office, staff kitchen, retail sales, and equipment
storage area.  Located close to the lake for easy access, this new
building will give us the room we need to help serve you better.
accommodate-(v)         lodge-(n)              board-(n)
  1  ·favor             1   hostel            1 A ·lumber
     ·humor                 ·hotel              B  plank
     ·indulge                ·inn               C  slat
     ·oblige                ·resort
                                              2 D  fare
  2  ·acclimate        2   ·cabin              E ·food
     ·accustom             ·cottage            F  meals
     ·adapt                ·hut                G  provisions
     ·adjust               ·shelter
     ·conform                                3 H ·cabinet
                      lodge-(v)                 I ·committee
  3  ·board           3   ·catch               J ·council
     ·entertain            snag                 K  jury
     ·house                ·snare
     ·lodge                ·stick          board-(v)
                                              4 L ·embark
                      4   ·board               M  go aboard
                          ·house
 1 Replace Word; 2 View Doc; 3 Look Up Word; 4 Clear Column: 0
```

WordPerfect will display references for *board* in addition to the references for *lodge* and *accommodate* already on the screen (see Figure 10). You can move down or up within columns to see more references by pressing the Down Arrow or Up Arrow keys.

Step 7: Use the View Doc Option

The third way to look up other words while using the thesaurus is to select the View Doc option, move the cursor to another word in the document, and then execute the Thesaurus function key command.

Type   **2**

The cursor will move to the top of the screen where four lines of the document are displayed. You can now move the cursor within the document while the thesaurus remains on the screen. Move the cursor to the word *office* and then execute the Thesaurus command:

Press   **Alt-F1**

The thesaurus screen will clear to reveal only the references for *office*.

Step 8: Clear a Column

One more option is in the Thesaurus menu at the bottom of the screen: Clear Column. This option is handy for clearing the contents of a column to make room for the references of another word.

Type   **4**

The column of references for the headword *office* will clear. You now have three empty columns in the thesaurus screen for looking up other words.

Step 9: Exit the Thesaurus

If you replace a word from the thesaurus, WordPerfect will automatically return to the editing screen. You can also exit the thesaurus without replacing a word.

Press   **F7**

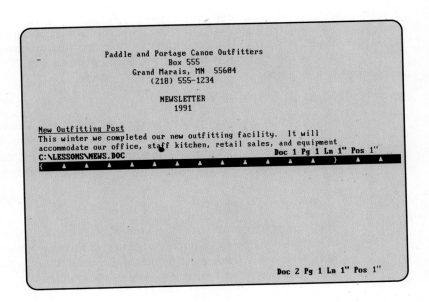

Figure 11 Split-Screen Windows

1. Move the cursor to the word *room* in the New Outfitting Post paragraph and invoke the thesaurus.
2. Tell the thesaurus to replace the word *room* with *space*.
3. Invoke the thesaurus again. Use the Look Up Word option to look up any words you like. When you have finished, exit the thesaurus and move the cursor to the beginning of the document. Save the document to preserve any changes you have made.

Lesson 7: Working with Windows

WordPerfect's Window feature allows you to split the display into two separate document editing screens, each with its own status line. You can then show two different areas of the same document or work on two different documents at the same time. The Window feature is especially handy for referring to one part of a document while working on another part or for copying text from one document to another.

Step 1: Split the Screen

Suppose you want to create a new document while looking at an existing document. You can split the screen into two windows. Pull down the Edit menu, select the Window option, and specify the number of lines to be in the window:

Press	**Alt-=**
Type	**ew**
Type	**11**
Press	**Enter**

Another way to split the screen is to press Ctrl-F3 to execute the Screen command and then type 1 to choose the Window option. Figure 11 shows the result. The top window, which is eleven lines, contains the NEWS.DOC document. It has its own status line at the bottom. A ruler line showing the current margin and tab stop settings separates the two windows. The bottom window, also eleven lines, is empty. In it you can create a new document. Notice that the bottom status line indicates that it is for document number 2.

Step 2: Switch Windows

The top window, which contains the cursor, is the active window. The ruler line reflects the settings in this window and the tab stop triangles point up. The commands you execute and the text you enter affect only this window. Before you can work in the bottom window, you must switch to it. Execute the Switch command:

Press   **Shift-F3**

The cursor will move into the bottom window and the tab stop arrows in the ruler line will point down. Any text you enter or commands you execute will now affect only the bottom window. To go back up to the first window, execute the Switch command again:

Press   **Shift-F3**

Step 3: Copy the Letterhead

Let's create a new document in the bottom window that will be a letter to a customer who inquired about Paddle and Portage Canoe Outfitters' sport show schedule. Fortunately, some of the text can be copied from the newsletter instead of being retyped.

Mark the letterhead at the top of the newsletter as a block of text:

Press   **Home** (2 times)
Press   **Up Arrow**
Press   **Alt-=**
Type   **eb**
Press   **Down Arrow** (4 times)

Pull down the Edit menu and execute the Copy option:

Press   **Alt-=**
Type   **ec**

Position the cursor in the bottom window where you want to copy the block by executing the Switch command and then pressing Enter:

Press   **Shift-F3**
Press   **Enter**

The letterhead will be copied from NEWS.DOC in the top window to the new document in the bottom window (see Figure 12).

Step 4: Type the Letter

Follow these instructions to type the letter in the bottom window:

Press   **Home** (2 times)
Press   **Down Arrow**
Press   **Enter**
Type   **January 2, 1990**
Press   **Enter** (2 times)

Figure 12 The Letterhead Copied to the Bottom Window

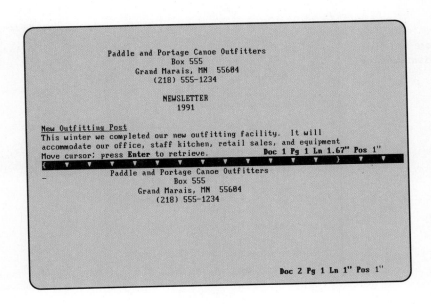

```
              Paddle and Portage Canoe Outfitters
                           Box 555
                   Grand Marais, MN  55604
                       (218) 555-1234

                        NEWSLETTER
                           1991

New Outfitting Post
This winter we completed our new outfitting facility.  It will
accommodate our office, staff kitchen, retail sales, and equipment
Move cursor; press Enter to retrieve.        Doc 1 Pg 1 Ln 1.67" Pos 1"
{   ▼     ▼     ▼     ▼     ▼     ▼     ▼     ▼     ▼     }   ▼     ▼
              Paddle and Portage Canoe Outfitters
_                          Box 555
                   Grand Marais, MN  55604
                       (218) 555-1234




                                          Doc 2 Pg 1 Ln 1" Pos 1"
```

Type	**Mr. Richard Holmes**
Press	**Enter**
Type	**444 Adams Street**
Press	**Enter**
Type	**Green Bay, WI 54301**
Press	**Enter** (2 times)
Type	**Dear Mr. Holmes:**
Press	**Enter** (2 times)
Type	**Here is our sport show schedule for 1991.**
Type	**We hope to see you soon!**
Press	**Enter** (5 times)
Type	**Sincerely,**
Press	**Enter** (4 times)
Type	**Bob Johnson**
Press	**Enter**

Step 5: Copy the Schedule

Notice that the sport show schedule was purposely omitted from the letter. Instead of retyping the sport show schedule, you can copy it from the newsletter. Follow these directions:

Press	**Up Arrow** (8 times)
Press	**Shift-F3**
Press	**Home** (2 times)
Press	**Up Arrow**
Press	**Down Arrow** (17 times)
Press	**Alt-=**
Type	**eb**
Press	**Down Arrow** (11 times)
Press	**Alt-=**
Type	**ec**
Press	**Shift-F3**
Press	**Enter**

Figure 13 More Text Copied to the Bottom Window

```
Chicagoland Show, O'Hare Exposition Center

Feb 14--Feb 22
Greater Northwest Sport Show, Minneapolis Auditorium

Mar 13--Mar 22
Milwaukee Sentinel Sport Show, MECCA Building

If you can, stop by and say "Hi." Remember our SPECIAL BONUS RATES
for sport show reservations.

Move cursor; press Enter to retrieve.          Doc 1 Pg 1 Ln 5.67" Pos 1"
{   ▼   ▼   ▼   ▼   ▼   ▼   ▼   ▼   ▼   ▼   ▼   ▼   }   ▼   ▼
Here is our sport show schedule for 1991.  We hope to see you soon!

Jan 23--Feb 1
Chicagoland Show, O'Hare Exposition Center

Feb 14--Feb 22
Greater Northwest Sport Show, Minneapolis Auditorium

Mar 13--Mar 22
Milwaukee Sentinel Sport Show, MECCA Building

                                         Doc 2 Pg 1 Ln 3.5" Pos 1"
```

The sport show schedule and the two sentences that follow it will be copied to the letter in the bottom window (see Figure 13).

Step 6: Save the Letter

Move the cursor to the top of the letter and examine it for typographical errors. After you are sure that it is correct, save the file in the default directory and name it HOLMES.DOC.

Press	**Alt-=**
Type	**fs**
Type	**holmes.doc**
Press	**Enter**

Step 7: Clear the Bottom Window

After the letter has been saved, you can clear the bottom window and use it to view some other document. Pull down the File menu and execute the Exit option:

Press	**Alt-=**
Type	**fxny**

The bottom window will be cleared and the cursor will be moved into the top window. Move the cursor to the beginning of the document:

Press	**Home** (2 times)
Press	**Up Arrow**

Step 8: View the Same Document in the Bottom Window

The Window feature can also be used to view two different parts of the same document. This capability is especially handy for long documents if you have to refer to distant sections at the same time. Follow these directions to switch to the bottom window and retrieve NEWS.DOC:

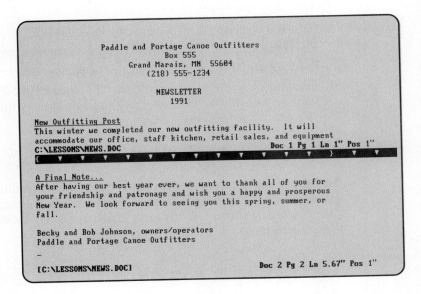

Figure 14 The Same Document In Two Windows

Press	**Shift-F3**
Press	**Alt-=**
Type	**fr**
Type	**news.doc**
Press	**Enter**

The newsletter will be loaded into the bottom window. Now you can look at two different parts of the same document. Move to the end of the newsletter in the bottom window:

Press	**Home** (2 times)
Press	**Down Arrow**

As Figure 14 shows, the beginning of the newsletter appears in the top window and the end of the newsletter appears in the bottom window.

Step 9: Close a Window

Suppose you have finished working on two different sections of the same document or two different documents and want to close one of the windows. First, switch to the window you want to close. In our case, the cursor should already be in the bottom window, which is the window we want to close. Pull down the File menu and execute the Exit option without saving the file:

Press	**Alt-=**
Type	**fxny**

The document will disappear from the window, but the screen will still be split. The cursor will move to the window containing text. To remove the empty window, expand the other window to 24 lines so that it fills the entire screen:

Press	**Alt-=**
Type	**ew**
Type	**24**
Press	**Enter**

A single window will expand to fill the entire screen.

1. Split the screen into two windows of equal size.
2. Retrieve the document MEMO.DOC into the bottom window.
3. Switch back and forth between the windows, examining their contents.
4. Exit and close the second window. The document NEWS.DOC should be on your screen. Move the cursor to the beginning of the newsletter.

Lesson 8: Indenting Paragraphs

Indenting refers to moving text away from the margin toward the center of the page. Several types of paragraph indentation are commonly used in documents. WordPerfect lets you use the first line indent, left indent, double indent, and hanging indent.

Step 1: Start a New Document

To illustrate paragraph indentation with WordPerfect, exit NEWS.DOC and create a new document:

Press   **Alt-=**
Type   **fxnn**

Your editing screen should now be empty.

Step 2: Indent the First Line of a Paragraph

The **first line indent** moves only the first line of the paragraph in from the left margin. This is done by pressing the Tab key before typing the paragraph.

Press   **Tab**

Now type the text:

```
This paragraph illustrates the first line indent.  Only
the first line of the paragraph is moved from the left
margin toward the center of the page.
```

Press   **Enter** (2 times)

Step 3: Indent Paragraphs from the Left Margin

The **left indent** moves all lines of the paragraph in from the left margin. Pull down the Layout menu, select the Align option, and then select the Indent -> option:

Press   **Alt-=**
Type   **Lai**

Another way to invoke the left indent feature is to press F4. Now type the text:

```
This paragraph illustrates the left indent, in which all
lines are moved from the left margin toward the center
of the page.  Pressing F4 creates a temporary left
```

```
margin one tab stop in from the permanent left margin.
Words will automatically wrap to the indented left
margin.
```

Press   **Enter** (2 times)
Press   **F4** (2 times)

Type this text:

```
Each time you press F4, the temporary left margin moves
in another tab stop toward the center of the page.
```

Press   **Enter** (2 times)

Step 4: Indent Paragraphs from Both Margins

A paragraph can be indented from both the left and right margins. This is sometimes called a double indent. Pull down the Layout menu, select the Align option, and then select the Indent -><- option:

Press   **Alt-=**
Type   **Lan**

Another way to execute a double indent is to press Shift-F4. Now type the text:

```
This paragraph is indented from both the left and right
margins.  All lines are moved in from both margins
toward the center of the page.
```

Press   **Enter** (2 times)
Press   **Shift-F4** (2 times)

Type this text:

```
Each time you press Shift-F4, the temporary left and
right margins move in another tab stop toward the center
of the page.
```

Press   **Enter** (2 times)

Step 5: Create a Hanging Indent

A **hanging indent** occurs when all lines of a paragraph except for the first are indented from the left margin. It is created by performing a left indent followed by a margin release.

Press   **Alt-=**
Type   **Lai**
Press   **Alt-=**
Type   **Lam**

Another way to create a hanging indent is to press F4 (left indent) followed by Shift-Tab (margin release). Now type the text:

```
This paragraph illustrates the hanging indent.  The
first line of the paragraph stays at the left margin,
```

**Figure 15 Paragraph
Indentation**

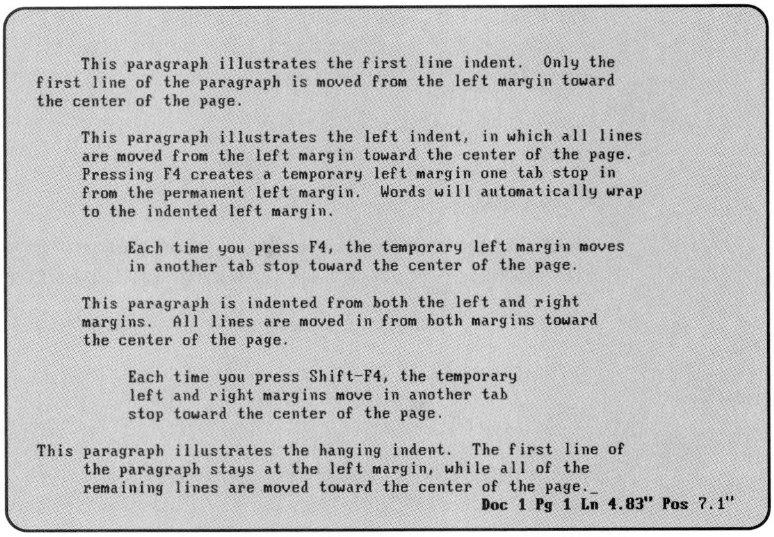

```
        This paragraph illustrates the first line indent.  Only the
    first line of the paragraph is moved from the left margin toward
    the center of the page.

        This paragraph illustrates the left indent, in which all lines
    are moved from the left margin toward the center of the page.
    Pressing F4 creates a temporary left margin one tab stop in
    from the permanent left margin.  Words will automatically wrap
    to the indented left margin.

            Each time you press F4, the temporary left margin moves
        in another tab stop toward the center of the page.

        This paragraph is indented from both the left and right
    margins.  All lines are moved in from both margins toward
    the center of the page.

            Each time you press Shift-F4, the temporary
        left and right margins move in another tab
        stop toward the center of the page.

    This paragraph illustrates the hanging indent.  The first line of
        the paragraph stays at the left margin, while all of the
        remaining lines are moved toward the center of the page._
                                    Doc 1 Pg 1 Ln 4.83" Pos 7.1"
```

**while all of the remaining lines are moved toward the
center of the page.**

Your screen should look like Figure 15.

Step 6: Save the Document

Save the new document you have created in a file named INDENT.DOC in the
current subdirectory.

Press	**Alt-=**
Type	**fs**
Type	**indent.doc**
Press	**Enter**

Practice

1. Move the cursor to the beginning of the INDENT.DOC document, and then
   execute the Reveal Codes command. Scroll through the document and examine the indentation codes. You should be able to understand what they mean.
   Try deleting one of the indentation codes and see what happens. Then restore
   the deleted code. Execute the Reveal Codes command again to return to the
   regular editing screen.

2. Use the help facility to read about the Left Indent command:

Press	**F3**
Press	**F4**

   Then use the help facility to read about the Double Indent (Shift-F4) and the
   Margin Release (Shift-Tab) commands.

Lesson 9: Using Tab Stops to Create Tables

Tab stops allow you to position text precisely within a line. They are often used for aligning text or numbers in a table. Tab stops should always be used instead of pressing the Space Bar to align items vertically in a table because the size of a space varies from font to font. To align items in a table, you press the Tab key to insert a tab code and move the cursor to the next tab stop.

Initially, WordPerfect has a tab stop set at every half-inch position. But you can change these tab stop settings by pulling down the Layout menu, selecting the Line option, and then selecting the Tab Set option.

To illustrate the use of tab stops, let's add a short table to NEWS.DOC that presents the current outfitting rates.

Step 1: Retrieve NEWS.DOC

Clear the editing screen and retrieve the newsletter document by executing these commands:

Press	**Alt-=**
Type	**fxnn**
Press	**Alt-=**
Type	**fr**
Type	**news.doc**
Press	**Enter**

Step 2: Move the Cursor

Let's insert the new table between the Trail Food Improvements paragraph and the Trips paragraph. A quick way to move the cursor is to use the Search command:

Press	**Alt-=**
Type	**sf**
Type	**Trips**
Press	**F7**
Press	**Up Arrow**

The cursor should now be on the blank line just before the Trips paragraph.

Step 3: Insert the Heading

The table will be entitled Current Outfitting Rates, so insert this underlined heading:

Press	**Enter**
Press	**F8**
Type	**Current Outfitting Rates**
Press	**F8**
Press	**Enter**

*Figure 16 The New Tab
Stop Settings*

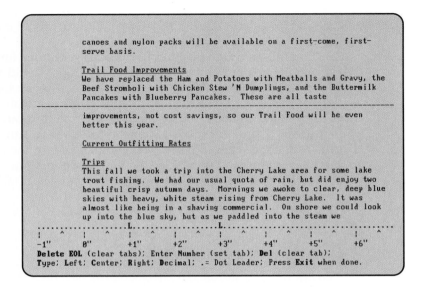

*Figure 16 The New Tab
Stop Settings*

Step 4: Change the Tab Stop Settings

A left-aligned tab stop lines up the left edge of text to the tab stop. This is the default and most commonly used type of tab stop. Let's insert left-aligned tab stops at the 1-inch and 3-inch positions from the current left margin. These tab stops will then affect all text at and below the cursor. Follow these directions:

Press	**Alt-=**
Type	**LLt**
Press	**Home** (2 times)
Press	**Left Arrow**
Press	**Ctrl-End**
Type	**1**
Press	**Enter**
Type	**3**
Press	**Enter**

At this point, your screen should look like Figure 16. Pressing Home, Home, Left Arrow moves the cursor to the absolute left edge of the ruler line, which is at the left edge of the paper. Pressing Ctrl-End deletes all of the default tab stops to the right of the cursor on the ruler line. By default, tab stops are measured relative to the left margin. WordPerfect also lets you specify absolute tab stops, which are measured from the left edge of the paper. Relative tab stops are more convenient if you change margins or arrange text into multiple columns. Left-aligned tab stops are inserted by entering the desired line position. Since left-aligned is the default type of tab stop, the L is inserted automatically in the ruler line. You can also press Right Arrow or Left Arrow to move the cursor within the ruler line to select the desired tab stop position and then type the appropriate letter: L for left-aligned, C for center-aligned, R for right-aligned, and D for decimal-aligned. Short Problem 4, at the end of this chapter, illustrates the use of dot leader tabs.

*Figure 17 The Current
Outfitting Rates Table*

```
canoes and nylon packs will be available on a first-come, first-
serve basis.

Trail Food Improvements
We have replaced the Ham and Potatoes with Meatballs and Gravy, the
Beef Stromboli with Chicken Stew 'N Dumplings, and the Buttermilk
Pancakes with Blueberry Pancakes.  These are all taste
--------------------------------------------------------------------
improvements, not cost savings, so our Trail Food will be even
better this year.

Current Outfitting Rates
          Number In Party    Rate Per Person Per Day
          1 to 3 persons     $31.00
          4 to 6 persons     $29.25
          7 to 9 persons     $28.50

Trips
This fall we took a trip into the Cherry Lake area for some lake
trout fishing.  We had our usual quota of rain, but did enjoy two
beautiful crisp autumn days.  Mornings we awoke to clear, deep blue
skies with heavy, white steam rising from Cherry Lake.  It was
almost like being in a shaving commercial.  On shore we could look
up into the blue sky, but as we paddled into the steam we
C:\LESSONS\NEWS.DOC                        Doc 1 Pg 2 Ln 2.33" Pos 1"
```

Now, press the Exit key twice to finalize your new tab stops and return to the editing screen:

Press   **F7** (2 times)

Step 5: Enter the Table

Follow these directions to enter the Current Outfitting Rates table:

Press	**Tab**
Type	**Number In Party**
Press	**Tab**
Type	**Rate Per Person Per Day**
Press	**Enter**
Press	**Tab**
Type	**1 to 3 persons**
Press	**Tab**
Type	**$31.00**
Press	**Enter**
Press	**Tab**
Type	**4 to 6 persons**
Press	**Tab**
Type	**$29.25**
Press	**Enter**
Press	**Tab**
Type	**7 to 9 persons**
Press	**Tab**
Type	**$28.50**
Press	**Enter**

Your screen should look like Figure 17.

Step 6: Reset Default Tab Stops Below the Table

Changing tab stops affects all text at and below the current cursor location. But you don't want the rest of the document to have the same tab stops as the table. So, you must reset the default tab stops below the table. Follow these directions:

Press	**Alt-=**
Type	**LLt**
Type	**-1,0.5**
Press	**Enter**
Press	**F7** (2 times)

This will set a tab stop at every half inch position beginning at position −1, the left edge of the page measured relative to the current left margin.

Step 7: Save the Document

Save the document to the disk to preserve the changes you have made:

Press	**Alt-=**
Type	**fs**
Press	**Enter**
Type	**y**

Practice

1. Use the Reveal Codes command to examine the Tab Set codes that appear before and after the Current Outfitting Rates table. When you have finished, execute the Reveal Codes command again to return to the full editing screen.

2. Using tabs is better than using spaces to align text and numbers in columns. One reason is that different characters are different widths in some fonts, so columns may not line up when the document is printed if you have used the Space Bar to align text on the screen. Another reason to use tabs is that they make it easy to change the position of columns later. For example, move the cursor to the beginning of the line just below the heading Current Outfitting Rates. Activate the Tab Set menu:

Press	**Alt-=**
Type	**LLt**

Delete the tab stop at the +1-inch position by moving the cursor there and pressing the Delete key. Insert a new left-aligned tab stop at the +1.5-inch position. Delete the tab stop at the +3-inch position and insert a new one at the +3.5-inch position. Exit the Tab Set menu and return to the editing screen. The entire table will be shifted a half inch to the right.

3. Execute the Reveal Codes command again. Note that WordPerfect simply inserted a new Tab Set code for the new tab stop settings you created in the previous exercise. You can remove that Tab Set code and revert to the previous tab stop settings:

Press	**Left Arrow**
Press	**Delete**

The table will shift back to the left a half-inch. Execute the Reveal Codes command again to return to the full editing screen. Move the cursor to the beginning of the document.

Lesson 10: Using the Tab Align Feature

The numbers in the Current Outfitting Rates table line up nicely, but only because they all have the same number of characters. Numbers with fewer or more digits would not line up on the decimal points. In such cases, you can use a decimal tab stop instead of a left-aligned tab stop. Another alternative is to use the Tab Align feature. To illustrate this feature, let's insert another table that lists the Paddle and Portage 1990 fishing records.

Step 1: Move the Cursor

Let's insert the new table after the Current Outfitting Rates table. Move the cursor to the end of the last line of the table. By inserting the new table here, you use the same tab stop settings as the Current Outfitting Rates table.

Step 2: Insert the Heading

The table will be entitled *1990 Fishing Records*, so do this:

Press	**Enter** (2 times)
Press	**F8**
Type	**1990 Fishing Records**
Press	**F8**
Press	**Enter**

Step 3: Enter the Table

Now, enter the table as follows:

Press	**Tab**
Type	**Bluegill**
Press	**Ctrl-F6**
Type	**3.00 lbs.**
Press	**Enter**
Press	**Tab**
Type	**Large Mouth Bass**
Press	**Ctrl-F6**
Type	**20.25 lbs.**
Press	**Enter**
Press	**Tab**
Type	**Northern Pike**
Press	**Ctrl-F6**
Type	**42.33 lbs.**
Press	**Enter**
Press	**Tab**
Type	**Sunfish**
Press	**Ctrl-F6**
Type	**2.20 lbs.**
Press	**Enter**
Press	**Tab**
Type	**Walleye**
Press	**Ctrl-F6**
Type	**25.00 lbs.**

Figure 18 The Numbers Aligned with the Tab Align Command

```
improvements, not cost savings, so our Trail Food will be even
better this year.

Current Outfitting Rates
          Number In Party      Rate Per Person Per Day
          1 to 3 persons       $31.00
          4 to 6 persons       $29.25
          7 to 9 persons       $28.50

1990 Fishing Records
          Bluegill              3.00 lbs.
          Large Mouth Bass     20.25 lbs.
          Northern Pike        42.33 lbs.
          Sunfish               2.20 lbs.
          Walleye              25.00 lbs._

Trips
This fall we took a trip into the Cherry Lake area for some lake
trout fishing.  We had our usual quota of rain, but did enjoy two
beautiful crisp autumn days.  Mornings we awoke to clear, deep blue
skies with heavy, white steam rising from Cherry Lake.  It was
almost like being in a shaving commercial.  On shore we could look
up into the blue sky, but as we paddled into the steam we
disappeared into white nothingness.  It was a trip we'll long
C:\LESSONS\NEWS.DOC                        Doc 1 Pg 2 Ln 3.33" Pos 4.8"
```

Your screen should look like Figure 18. In each line of the table, you pressed Ctrl-F6 instead of Tab before typing the number. This keypress executes the Tab Align command, which lines up text or numbers on an alignment character. The default alignment character is the period or decimal point. When you press Ctrl-F6, the cursor moves to the next tab stop and WordPerfect displays the prompt

    Align char = .

This prompt tells you the default alignment character and lets you change it. For entering numbers, you want the period to be the alignment character so you can ignore the prompt. Characters you type at the tab stop move left until the alignment character is typed, or until Ctrl-F6, Tab, or Enter are pressed. Characters typed after the alignment character move to the right, as they normally do. The result is that all numbers line up on their decimal points at the tab stop.

Another way to invoke the Tab Align feature is to pull down the Layout menu, select the Align option, and then select the Tab Align option. This sequence of menu selections may be easier to remember, but pressing Ctrl-F6 is faster for entering data. You can, of course, use whichever method you prefer.

Step 4: Save the Document

Save the document to the disk to preserve the changes you have made:

Press   **Alt-=**
Type   **f s**
Press   **Enter**
Type   **y**

Practice   1. Execute the Reveal Codes command and examine the table you have just entered. Each [DEC TAB] code indicates a hard decimal tab inserted when you executed the Tab Align command. Return to the normal editing screen.

2. Invoke the help facility and read about the Tab Align command:

Press   **F3**
Press   **Ctrl-F6**

When you have finished, return to the editing screen:

Press   **Enter**

3. Insert another line in the 1990 Fishing Records table:

Lake Trout 50.00 lbs.

Save the document to the disk. Move the cursor to the beginning of the document.

Lesson 11: Using the Flush Right Feature

The Flush Right feature lets you easily align text to the right margin. This feature is especially handy for typing the return address and date in a letter. Let's see how this feature works in the HOLMES.DOC letter you created in Lesson 7.

Step 1: Clear the Screen

Exit NEWS.DOC and clear the screen:

Press   **Alt-=**
Type   **fxnn**

Step 2: Retrieve the Letter

Pull down the File menu and execute the Retrieve option to load the document HOLMES.DOC and display it on the editing screen:

Press   **Alt-=**
Type   **fr**
Type   **holmes.doc**
Press   **Enter**

Step 3: Type a New Line Flush Right

The letterhead at the top of the document HOLMES.DOC is centered. Let's delete the first line and retype it flush right. The cursor should already be at the beginning of the first line of HOLMES.DOC. Delete to the end of the line:

Press   **Ctrl-End**

Now, pull down the Layout menu, select the Align option, execute the Flush Right option and retype the line:

Press   **Alt-=**
Type   **Laf**
Type   **Paddle and Portage Canoe Outfitters**

Another way to invoke the Flush Right feature is to press Alt-F6. Notice how the cursor moves to the right margin when you execute Flush Right and how

Figure 19 Letterhead and Date Moved Flush Right

```
                         Paddle and Portage Canoe Outfitters
                                           Box 555
                                   Grand Marais, MN  55604
                                      (218) 555-1234

                                       January 2, 1990

Mr. Richard Holmes
444 Adams Street
Green Bay, WI  54301

Dear Mr. Holmes:

Here is our sport show schedule for 1991.  We hope to see you soon!

Jan 23--Feb 1
Chicagoland Show, O'Hare Exposition Center

Feb 14--Feb 22
Greater Northwest Sport Show, Minneapolis Auditorium

Mar 13--Mar 22
Milwaukee Sentinel Sport Show, MECCA Building

C:\LESSONS\HOLMES.DOC                           Doc 1 Pg 1 Ln 2" Pos 1"
```

the text you type moves to the left. Since a hard return already exists at the end of the line, move to the beginning of the next line without pressing Enter:

Press	**Right Arrow**

Step 4: Move an Existing Line Flush Right

The Flush Right feature can also move an existing line of text to the right margin. Let's move the second line of the letterhead flush right. First, uncenter the line by deleting the Center code:

Press	**Delete**

Now, move the line flush right:

Press	**Alt-=**
Type	**Laf**
Press	**Down Arrow**

The end of the second line will be aligned to the right margin.

Step 5: Move a Block Flush Right

You can move several lines of text flush right by first marking them as a block. Execute the following commands:

Press	**Home**
Press	**Left Arrow**
Press	**Alt-=**
Type	**eb**
Press	**Down Arrow** (4 times)
Press	**Alt-=**
Type	**Laf**
Type	**y**

The rest of the letterhead and date will move flush right as shown in Figure 19.

Step 6: Save the Document

Save the document to the disk to preserve the changes you have made:

Press	**Alt-=**
Type	**f s**
Press	**Enter**
Type	**y**

Practice

1. Execute the Reveal Codes command and examine the text you have just moved. When an individual line is moved flush right, the [Flsh Rgt] code appears at the beginning. When a block of several lines is moved flush right, WordPerfect switches to right justification for those lines, as indicated by the [Just:Right] code. After the lines, WordPerfect switches back to the type of justification that was in effect before, which was Full, as indicated by the [Just:Full] code.

2. Move the cursor to the [Flsh Rgt] code before the first line and delete it. See how the line moves back to the left margin. Move the first line flush right again, but this time try the function key command:

Press	**Alt-F6**
Press	**Down Arrow**

Execute the Reveal Codes command to return to the normal editing screen.

3. Execute the Help command and read about the Flush Right command:

Press	**F3**
Press	**Alt-F6**

When you have finished reading the description, return to the editing screen:

Press	**Enter**

Lesson 12: Using the Date Options

WordPerfect's Date options lets you insert the current date into your document as text or as a code that is automatically updated and converted to text whenever the document is retrieved or printed. This feature is handy for letters, memos, and other documents that must display the current date. As an example, let's use the Date command to insert the date into the HOLMES.DOC letter. Note that in order for the Date command to work, your computer's clock must be set to the correct date. If the current date is not maintained by a built-in battery, you must use the DOS DATE command to specify the correct date when you boot up.

Step 1: Delete the Existing Date

First, delete the date that you have already typed into the document. Move the cursor to the line that contains the date and delete to the end of the line:

Press	**Home** (2 times)
Press	**Up Arrow**
Press	**Down Arrow** (5 times)
Press	**Ctrl-End**

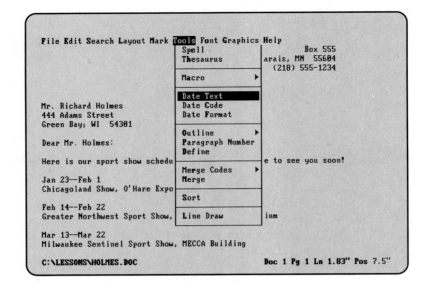

Figure 20 The Date Text Option in the Tools Menu

Step 2: Select the Date Text Option from the Tools Menu

To insert the current date as text, just as you would type it yourself, pull down the Tools menu, select the Date Text option (see Figure 20), and move the cursor:

Press	**Alt-=**
Type	**t t**
Press	**Down Arrow**

The current date will be inserted into the document, flush against the right margin.

Step 3: Select the Date Code Option

The date you inserted in the previous step is ordinary text. It will not change to reflect the current date if you retrieve or print the letter tomorrow. If you want the date in the letter to be current whenever it is retrieved or printed, you must use the Date Code option from the Tools menu. Follow these directions to delete the date text and insert the date code instead:

Press	**Up Arrow**
Press	**Home**
Press	**Left Arrow**
Press	**Ctrl-End**
Press	**Alt-=**
Type	**tc**
Press	**Down Arrow**

The result looks the same as in the previous step, but the date you see will change if you retrieve or print the letter in the future.

Step 4: Select the Date Format Option

The Date Format option in the Tools menu lets you change the way the date is displayed. Pull down the Tools menu and execute the Date Format option:

Press	**Alt-=**
Type	**tf**

Figure 21 The Date
Format Menu

```
Date Format

   Character    Meaning
       1        Day of the Month
       2        Month (number)
       3        Month (word)
       4        Year (all four digits)
       5        Year (last two digits)
       6        Day of the Week (word)
       7        Hour (24-hour clock)
       8        Hour (12-hour clock)
       9        Minute
       0        am / pm
     %,$        Used before a number, will:
                    Pad numbers less than 10 with a leading zero or space
                    Abbreviate the month or day of the week

   Examples:  3 1, 4        = December 25, 1984
              %6 %3 1,  4   = Tue Dec 25, 1984
              %2/%1/5 (6)   = 01/01/85 (Tuesday)
              $2/$1/5 ($6)  =  1/ 1/85 (Tue)
              8:90          = 10:55am


Date format: 3 1, 4
```

Figure 21 The Date Format Menu

The Date Format menu will appear on the screen (see Figure 21). The default date format is presented at the bottom of the screen. The format code 3 1, 4 means the month (word) followed by the day of the month, a comma, and all four digits of the year. The Date Format menu gives you a great deal of flexibility in specifying how the date is to appear when you use the Date Text or Date Code features. Return to the editing screen without changing the date format:

Press   **F7** (2 times)

Step 5: Save the Document

Save the document to the disk to preserve the changes you have made:

Press   **Alt-=**
Type   **f s**
Press   **Enter**
Type   **y**

Practice

1. Execute the Reveal Codes command to examine the date code. Note that no text is actually stored in the document, just the code [Date:3 1, 4], which specifies the format in which to present the current date. Return to the full editing screen.

2. Try moving the cursor within the date. You will find that WordPerfect treats the date as a single character because it is really a date code. You can delete it, but not change it.

3. Delete the date code in the letter. Pull down the Tools menu and select the Date Format option. Change the date format and insert a new date code:

Type   **2/1/5**
Press   **Enter**
Type   **c**

Observe the new date format. Now delete the date code, change the date format back to the way it was, and insert a new date code.

4. You can also execute the Date Text, Date Code, and Date Format features using the function key interface.

Press	**Shift-F5**

This key press activates the Date/Outline menu, which contains Date Text, Date Code, and Date Format as the first three options. Return to the editing screen:

Press	**F7**

Lesson 13: Centering Text on a Page

Short letters and memos often look better when they are centered from top to bottom on a page. Centering from top to bottom is also used for title pages. The Center Page feature makes it easy to center text on a page when it is printed.

Step 1: Move Cursor Before All Codes

To center text on a page, you must move to the very beginning of the document, before any codes that may be hidden. Pressing the Home key three times followed by an Up Arrow or Left Arrow key moves the cursor ahead of any codes at the beginning of a document or line. Execute this command:

Press	**Home** (3 times)
Press	**Up Arrow**

Step 2: Select the Center Page Option

Pull down the Layout menu, select the Page option, select the Center Page option, select Yes to change the setting, and then execute the Exit command:

Press	**Alt-=**
Type	**Lpcy**
Press	**F7**

The document will not look any different on the screen, but it will be centered vertically on the page when it is printed.

Step 3: Print the Document

To see the result of using the Center Page option, print the letter:

Press	**Alt-=**
Type	**fpf**

Practice

1. Execute the Reveal Codes command. The first code in the document is [Center Pg], which tells WordPerfect to center the text vertically on the page when printed. Return to the full editing screen.

2. Turn off the Center Page option for this document. You can either delete the [Center Pg] code or change the Center Page setting in the Layout Page menu.

3. Another way to change the Center Page setting is to press Shift-F8, select Page, and then select Center Page. Execute the Help command and read about the Center Page option:

Figure 22 The Initial Document Summary Screen

```
Document Summary

        Revision Date  03-15-90 09:43a

1 - Creation Date  03-17-90 09:00a

2 - Document Name
    Document Type

3 - Author
    Typist

4 - Subject

5 - Account

6 - Keywords

7 - Abstract




Selection: 0                    (Retrieve to capture; Del to remove summary)
```

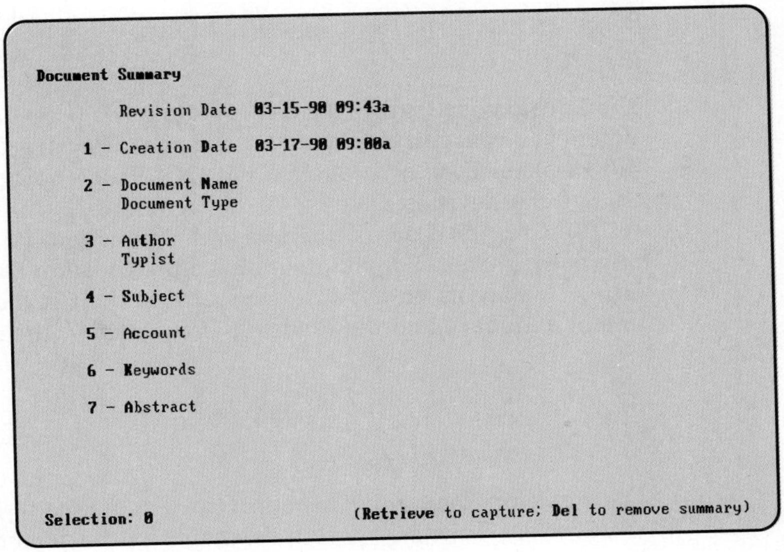

Press	**F3**
Press	**Shift-F8**
Type	**pc**

When you have finished reading the description, return to the editing screen:

Press	**Enter**

Lesson 14: Adding a Document Summary

DOS file names, such as HOLMES.DOC, are limited to eight characters plus a three-character extension. Even if you try to use mnemonic file names, remembering important details about your documents can become difficult, especially if you collect a large number of documents over a long period of time. Fortunately, WordPerfect lets you create a summary for each document that contains the revision and creation dates, the document name, the type of document, the author, the typist, the subject, the account, any keywords, and a short abstract of the document. Document summaries are displayed on the List Files screen and let you quickly determine the contents of a file without actually retrieving it. Document summaries also let you narrow the scope of a search when you use the Find option in the List Files menu. As an example, let's add a document summary to HOLMES.DOC.

Step 1: Select the Summary Option

A document summary can be created or edited from any place in a document. Pull down the Layout menu, select the Document option, and then select the Summary option:

Press	**Alt-=**
Type	**Lds**

WordPerfect will display the Document Summary screen, as shown in Figure 22.

Step 2: Examine the Revision Date and Creation Date

The Revision Date shows the date and time when the document was last changed. Whenever you edit and save a document, WordPerfect automatically updates the Revision Date according to the DOS date and time. You cannot manually change the Revision Date.

The Creation Date is the date and time when the document summary was originally created. So, you might have the Creation Date later than the Revision Date. This seems odd, but remember that the Creation Date refers to the document summary and the Revision Date refers to the document itself.

Step 3: Enter the Document Name and Document Type

The Revision Date and Creation Date have already been entered for you by WordPerfect. To enter a descriptive name for the document, select the Document Name option and type the name:

Type	**n**
Type	**Letter to Richard Holmes**
Press	**Enter**

You may use up to 68 characters in a long document name. After you enter the Document Name, the cursor moves to Document Type. Here you can enter up to 20 characters to describe the type of the document. You are free to make up your own document types. For example, you might classify this document as Correspondence.

Type	**Correspondence**
Press	**Enter**

Step 4: Enter the Author and Typist

The next two items on the Document Summary screen are Author and Typist. Select the Author option, enter Bob Johnson's name as the author, and enter your name as the typist:

Type	**t**
Type	**Bob Johnson**
Press	**Enter**
Type	**(your name)**
Press	**Enter**

Step 5: Enter the Subject

To enter the subject of the document, select the Subject option and enter the information:

Type	**s**
Type	**Sport Show Schedule**
Press	**Enter**

*Figure 23 The Completed
Document Summary
Screen*

```
Document Summary

         Revision Date  03-15-90 09:43a

  1 - Creation Date   03-17-90 09:00a

  2 - Document Name   Letter to Richard Holmes
      Document Type   Correspondence

  3 - Author          Bob Johnson
      Typist          Ernie Colantonio

  4 - Subject         Sport Show Schedule

  5 - Account

  6 - Keywords        Holmes, Schedule

  7 - Abstract          Paddle and Portage Canoe Outfitters;  Box 555;
                      Grand Marais, MN  55604; (218) 555 1234;    Mr.
                      Richard Holmes; 444 Adams Street; Green Bay, WI
                      54301; Dear Mr. Holmes:  Here is our sport show
                      schedule for 1991.  We hope to see you soon!; Jan 23

  Selection: 0                        (Retrieve to capture; Del to remove summary)
```

Step 6: Examine the Account Option

The Account option on the Document Summary screen lets you enter information that will identify the account or department under which the document
should be filed. This option might be used by a large business or organization
with several departments. You can leave it blank.

Step 7: Enter the Keywords

The Keywords option lets you specify one or more words to label a document.
When you use the Find option on the List Files screen, you can then search for
Keyword entries in document summaries. Let's enter two keywords for this
document.

Type	**k**
Type	**Holmes, Schedule**
Press	**Enter**

Step 8: Enter the Abstract

An abstract is a brief summary of a document's contents. WordPerfect lets you
store up to 780 characters in an Abstract entry. You can type your own abstract,
or press the Retrieve key to have WordPerfect automatically enter the first 400
characters in the document as the abstract. Let's use the second method.

Press	**Shift-F10**
Type	**y**

The document summary for HOLMES.DOC is now complete (see Figure 23).

Step 9: Exit the Document Summary Screen

To save the document summary and return to the editing screen, press the Exit key:

Press   **F7**

Step 10: Save the Document

Save the document, along with its summary, to the disk to preserve the changes you have made:

Press   **Alt-=**
Type   **f s**
Press   **Enter**
Type   **y**

Practice
1. Display the document summary for HOLMES.DOC on your screen. You can select the Summary option from the File menu, or select the Document option from the Layout menu and then execute the Summary option. When you have finished examining the Document Summary, press the Exit key (F7) to return to the editing screen.
2. Pull down the File menu, execute the List Files option, and specify the subdirectory C:\LESSONS. Select the Short/Long Display option and change to Long Display. Notice the long document name and the document type for HOLMES.DOC are now shown on the List Files screen.
3. Execute the Find option from the List Files menu and then select the Doc Summary option. Specify the following word pattern:

    Type   **Schedule**
    Press   **Enter**

WordPerfect will find the word *Schedule* in the document summary of HOLMES.DOC and highlight the file on the List File screen. If you were searching for this file, you could then examine or retrieve it. Exit the List Files screen and return to the editing screen.

Lesson 15: Using Passwords

WordPerfect lets you add a password to a document to prevent unauthorized users from retrieving or printing the document. This password feature can be handy when WordPerfect is used on a system that contains sensitive documents and is shared by several users. As an example, let's add a password to HOLMES.DOC.

Step 1: Retrieve the Document

A document must be on the normal editing screen before you can add a password to it. So, if you are not already editing the document, you must retrieve it. HOLMES.DOC should already be on your editing screen. If it is not, retrieve it from the disk.

Figure 24 The Password Submenu

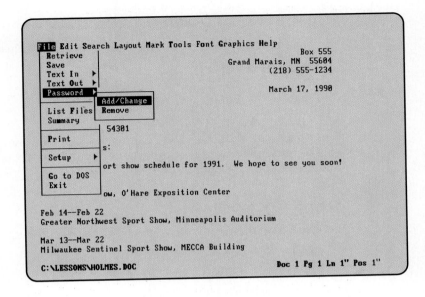

Step 2: Select the Password Option from the File Menu

Pull down the File menu and select the Password option:

Press	**Alt-=**
Type	**fw**

WordPerfect will display the submenu shown in Figure 24. Execute the Add/Change option to create a new password:

Type	**a**

Step 3: Enter the Password Twice

WordPerfect will prompt you to enter the password at the bottom of the screen. You can enter a word or phrase up to 24 characters long. Choose a password that you will remember, but won't be obvious to others. Let's use *secret* as our password for HOLMES.DOC. It's not a very good password, but it will serve as an example.

Type	**secret**
Press	**Enter**

The characters you type will not appear on the screen. This is a security feature that prevents someone from looking at your screen and seeing your password as you type it. WordPerfect will prompt you to enter your password again to make sure you have typed it correctly the first time.

Type	**secret**
Press	**Enter**

Step 4: Save the Document

You must save the document to the disk to save the password with the document.

Press   **Alt-=**
Type   **f s**
Press   **Enter**
Type   **y**

The document HOLMES.DOC is now locked. No one, not even you, will be able to retrieve or print it without entering the correct password. So, you must remember your password.

Step 5: Try the Password

Let's see how the password works. Exit the document:

Press   **Alt-=**
Type   **f x n n**

Now, try to retrieve HOLMES.DOC:

Press   **Alt-=**
Type   **f r**
Type   **holmes.doc**
Press   **Enter**

WordPerfect will display the prompt:

```
Enter Password (HOLMES.DOC):
```

Just to see what will happen, type the wrong password:

Type   **hello**
Press   **Enter**

Notice that the password does not appear on the screen as you type it. When you enter an incorrect password, WordPerfect will display an error message telling you the file is locked. It will then prompt you for another file name and suggest HOLMES.DOC again. This time, enter the correct password:

Press   **Enter**
Type   **secret**
Press   **Enter**

If you typed the password correctly, the document will be retrieved on the editing screen.

Step 6: Remove the Password

Suppose you don't want to keep a document private anymore. If the document is on the editing screen, you can remove the password from the file. Execute the Password option from the File menu and then select the Remove option:

Press   **Alt-=**
Type   **f w r**

The file HOLMES.DOC is no longer locked.

Practice

1. Lock HOLMES.DOC with a password of your own choosing. Save the file and exit WordPerfect.

2. Start WordPerfect and load HOLMES.DOC from the DOS command line. You must enter the correct password for WordPerfect to retrieve the file.

3. Exit HOLMES.DOC but do not exit WordPerfect. Activate the List Files screen and try to print HOLMES.DOC. You must enter the correct password.

4. Retrieve HOLMES.DOC on the editing screen. Remove your password from the document and then save HOLMES.DOC to the disk.

Lesson 16: Importing and Exporting Text Files

WordPerfect 5.1 stores documents in specially-formatted files, as do most application software. The files used by different packages or even different releases of the same package are not necessarily compatible. Fortunately, many popular application packages can now retrieve files from other packages and save files in formats that can be read by other packages. This is called importing and exporting. **Importing** is reading, and if necessary, translating data originally created with some other program. **Exporting** is writing data in a format that can be accepted by a different program.

WordPerfect 5.1 imports WordPerfect 5.0 and 4.2 documents automatically. You simply retrieve them as you would a WordPerfect 5.1 document. In addition, WordPerfect 5.1 can import DOS text files and spreadsheet files from programs such as Lotus 1-2-3, Microsoft Excel, and PlanPerfect.

WordPerfect 5.1 can export WordPerfect 5.0 and 4.2 documents, PlanPerfect spreadsheets, DOS text files, and generic word processor files, a special type of text file. In this lesson, we will import and export text files. We will discuss importing and exporting spreadsheet files in the next chapter.

A text file or ASCII file is a file that contains no special formatting codes—only letters, numbers, punctuation marks, spaces, tabs, and carriage returns. Text files are used for DOS batch files, the CONFIG.SYS file, programming language source code files, and some types of data files. In addition, text files are sometimes used to store documents in a generic format that can be read by other programs and word processing packages. Text files can be imported by using the Text In option in the File menu; they can be exported by using the Text Out option. Let's see how these options work.

Step 1: Clear the Editing Screen

Exit your current document and clear the editing screen:

Press   **Alt-=**
Type   **fxnn**

Step 2: Import a Text File

Suppose you want to examine or edit AUTOEXEC.BAT, the auto-execute batch file in the root directory of the hard disk. Pull down the File menu and select the Text In option:

Press   **Alt-=**
Type   **f i**

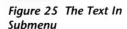

Figure 25 The Text In Submenu

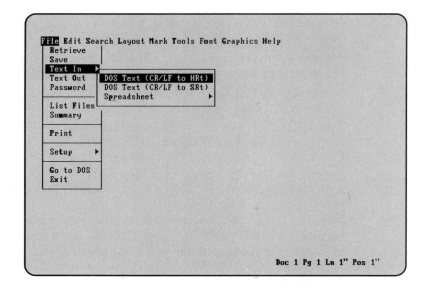

WordPerfect will display the submenu shown in Figure 25. The first option in this submenu will convert each carriage return/line feed pair (CR/LF) in the text file into a WordPerfect hard return code (HRt). If the file you are importing is going to remain a text file, then this is the option you should use.

The second option will convert each carriage return/line feed pair (CR/LF) into a WordPerfect soft return code (SRt). This is the option you should use if you want to convert a text file into a WordPerfect document file.

The third option is used to import and link to spreadsheet files.

Since we want to retrieve AUTOEXEC.BAT, which will remain a DOS text file, select the first option:

Type   **h**

WordPerfect will prompt you for the document to be retrieved. Since AUTO-EXEC.BAT is in the root directory, enter its path before its name:

Type   **c:\autoexec.bat**

The file AUTOEXEC.BAT will be loaded into the editing screen (see Figure 26). Since AUTOEXEC.BAT files are often different on different computers, your screen will probably not match Figure 26.

Step 3: Save a Text File

You could now edit the file AUTOEXEC.BAT with WordPerfect, but don't change it. Since it is not a document, you should not use formatting features such as margins, underlining, flush right, and so on. You could, however, insert, typeover, and delete text. Suppose you have finished editing the file. You save it to the disk with the Text Out option in the File menu.

Press   **Alt-=**
Type   **fo**

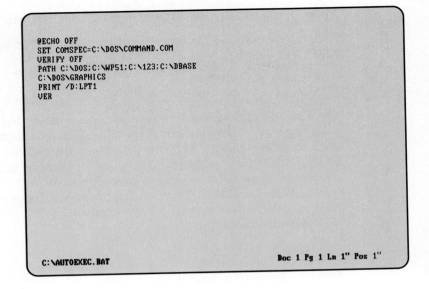

Figure 26 *The Imported Text File AUTOEXEC.BAT*

WordPerfect will present the submenu shown in Figure 27. In this case, you should use the DOS Text option.

Type	**t**
Press	**Enter**
Type	**y**

The file AUTOEXEC.BAT will be saved as a DOS text file. Clear the editing screen:

Press	**Alt-=**
Type	**fxnn**

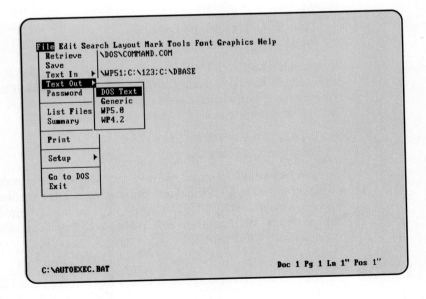

Figure 27 *The Text Out Submenu*

Step 4: Examine the Other Text Out Options

Let's briefly examine the other Text Out options. Pull down the File menu and select Text Out:

Press	**Alt-=**
Type	**fo**

The Generic option lets you save a document so that the general format is preserved without WordPerfect-specific codes. For example, spaces would be used to center, indent, and flush right text instead of WordPerfect formatting codes. This option might be used to save a WordPerfect document in a file to be read by some other word processing package.

The WP5.0 and WP4.2 options let you save a document in a file that can be read by WordPerfect version 5.0 or version 4.2.

Return to the editing screen:

Press	**F7**

Step 5: Export a Text File

Suppose you want to save the document HOLMES.DOC as a text file or a generic word processing file to be used in a different program. You could use the DOS Text or Generic options of the Text Out submenu. Let's try the DOS Text option.

Press	**Alt-=**
Type	**fr**
Type	**holmes.doc**
Press	**Enter**
Press	**Alt-=**
Type	**fot**
Type	**holmes.txt**
Press	**Enter**

You have loaded HOLMES.DOC as a WordPerfect document, and then exported HOLMES.TXT as a DOS text file. Let's exit to DOS and examine the results.

Press	**Alt-=**
Type	**fxny**
Type	**type holmes.doc**
Press	**Enter**

If you use the DOS TYPE command to examine the file HOLMES.DOC, you will see all kinds of funny characters, but not the letter. You are seeing the WordPerfect formatting codes, one of which tells DOS to stop displaying the file. Now, examine the DOS text file HOLMES.TXT.

Type	**type holmes.txt**
Press	**Enter**

The file looks fairly normal because the WordPerfect formatting codes have been stripped out. The generic word processing format for this particular file would be very similar. HOLMES.TXT could now be loaded into another word processing program, such as Microsoft Word, and then formatted, printed, and saved in Microsoft Word format.

Practice   1. Start WordPerfect and use the Text In option in the File menu to retrieve the text file CONFIG.SYS from the root directory of the hard disk. Without chang-

Figure 28 The Secondary DOS Command Processor Prompt

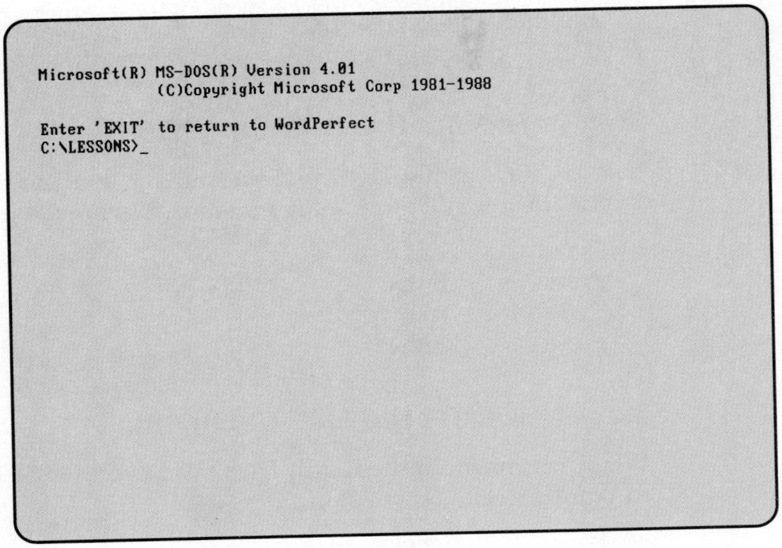

```
Microsoft(R) MS-DOS(R) Version 4.01
             (C)Copyright Microsoft Corp 1981-1988

Enter 'EXIT' to return to WordPerfect
C:\LESSONS>_
```

ing the file, save it to the disk as a DOS Text file with the Text Out option in the File menu.

2. Clear the editing screen and retrieve NEWS.DOC. Export this document as a generic word processing file named NEWS.GEN. Exit WordPerfect and use the DOS TYPE command to examine the contents of NEWS.GEN. When you have finished examining the file, delete NEWS.GEN (but don't delete NEWS.DOC).

Lesson 17: Executing a DOS Command within WordPerfect

Like many of today's application packages, WordPerfect lets you execute one or more DOS commands without actually exiting the program. The Go to DOS option in the File menu keeps WordPerfect in memory while control is passed to a secondary DOS command processor. When you have finished performing DOS commands, you execute the DOS EXIT command and return to Word-Perfect, which is still in memory. This handy feature, for example, can be used to check a disk, format a diskette, or copy files without exiting WordPerfect.

Step 1: Execute the Go to DOS Option

If you are not already running WordPerfect, start the program from DOS and load a document such as NEWS.DOC:

| Type | **wp news.doc** |
| Press | **Enter** |

Suppose you want to execute CHKDSK or some other DOS command without exiting WordPerfect. Pull down the File menu, select Go to DOS, and then execute the Go to DOS option:

| Press | **Alt-=** |
| Type | **fgg** |

WordPerfect will load a secondary DOS command processor and display a message telling you how to get back to the program (see Figure 28).

Another way to go to DOS from within WordPerfect is to press the Shell key (Ctrl-F1) and then select the Go to DOS option.

Step 2: Execute the DOS Commands

You are now at the DOS prompt and can execute any DOS commands, but WordPerfect is still dormant in memory. Execute the following DOS commands:

Type	**chkdsk**
Press	**Enter**
Type	**dir**
Press	**Enter**

Step 3: Execute the EXIT Command

When you have finished with DOS, you execute the EXIT command to return to WordPerfect:

Type	**exit**
Press	**Enter**

The computer will immediately return to the editing screen, just where you left off when you executed the Go to DOS option.

Practice

1. Execute the Go to DOS option and return to DOS. Theoretically, you can now execute any DOS command and even start an application package. In reality, you are limited by the amount of memory installed in your computer. Try running WordPerfect from the secondary command processor. You will probably get the DOS error message:

   ```
   Program too big to fit in memory
   ```

   The reason is that you already have WordPerfect in memory along with a secondary DOS command processor.

2. If you are running DOS version 4 or newer, execute this command:

Type	**mem /program**
Press	**Enter**

   You should see WP, which stands for WordPerfect, in the list of programs in memory.

3. Execute the DOS EXIT command to return to WordPerfect. This will discard the secondary DOS command processor. Exit WordPerfect the usual way and return to the primary DOS command processor.

Summary

- *Managing documents with the List Files menu.* Pull down the File menu and select List Files. Then select an option to change the directory, look at a file, retrieve a file, copy a file, move or rename a file, print a file, see long file names, select a file name, search for files, or delete a file.

- *Using additional cursor movement commands.* Pressing Home, Down Arrow moves the cursor to the bottom edge of the screen. Home, Up Arrow moves to the top edge. Pressing Escape, typing a number, and then pressing a cursor movement key repeats that key the specified number of times. Pressing Ctrl-Home and then typing a character advances the cursor just past the next occurrence of that character.

- *Using additional delete commands.* Pressing Home, Backspace deletes to the beginning of a word. Home, Delete erases to the end of a word. Pressing Escape, typing a number, and pressing Ctrl-End deletes the specified number of lines. Ctrl-PgDn deletes to the end of the page.

- *Working with formatting codes.* Pull down the Edit menu and select Reveal Codes (or press Alt-F3) to reveal or hide formatting codes. Press the Delete key to remove a code.

- *Using the built-in thesaurus.* Move the cursor to the word to be looked up and pull down the Tools menu and select Thesaurus (or press Alt-F1) to invoke the thesaurus.

- *Splitting the screen into two windows.* Pull down the Edit menu and select Window (or press Ctrl-F3), and specify the number of lines to split the screen into two windows. Press Shift-F3 to move the cursor into the other window.

- *Indenting paragraphs.* Press Tab for a first-line indent, press F4 for a left indent, press Shift-F4 for a double indent, and press F4 followed by Shift-Tab for a hanging indent. You can also pull down the Layout menu, select Align, and then select the type of indentation.

- *Creating tables with tab stops.* Pull down the Layout menu, select Line, and then select Tab Set to change the default tab stops.

- *Aligning numbers to tab stops.* Press Ctrl-F6 to execute the Tab Align command, which advances to the next tab stop and aligns text or numbers on an alignment character, usually the period.

- *Moving text flush right.* Pull down the Layout menu, select Align, and then select Flush Right (or press Alt-F6) to execute the Flush Right command, which lets you type new text or move existing text flush against the right margin.

- *Inserting the current date automatically.* Pull down the Tools menu and then select Date Text, Date Code, or Date Format.

- *Centering text on a page.* Move the cursor before all codes, pull down the Layout menu, select Page, select Center Page, and select Yes to center text vertically on a page.

- *Creating a document summary.* Pull down the Layout menu, select Document, and then select Summary to enter or edit document summary information.

- *Using passwords.* Pull down the File menu and select Password to add or remove a password to lock a file.

- *Importing and exporting text files.* Pull down the File menu and then select Text In or Text Out to import or export text files.

- *Executing a DOS command within WordPerfect.* Pull down the File menu and then select Go to DOS (or press Ctrl-F1) to execute one or more DOS commands. Use the EXIT command to return to WordPerfect.

Key Terms

As an extra review of this chapter, try defining the following terms.

code
exporting
first line indent
hanging indent
headword
importing
indenting
left indent
wild-card characters

Multiple Choice

Choose the best selection to complete each statement.

1. Which File menu option do you execute to clear the screen to start work on a new document?
   (a) Retrieve   (b) Save
   (c) Cancel   (d) Exit

2. Which File menu option would you use to examine the files in a subdirectory, retrieve a file, copy a file, or delete a file?
   (a) Summary   (b) Password
   (c) List Files   (d) Go to DOS

3. ASCII files, also known as text files, differ from document files in that they contain no
   (a) carriage returns.   (b) special formatting codes.
   (c) punctuation marks. (d) numbers.

4. Which key or character do you type to mark a file on the List Files screen?
   (a) asterisk (*)   (b) F1
   (c) F10   (d) ampersand (&)

5. Which sequence of key presses will move the cursor to the top edge of the current screen?
   (a) Ctrl-Home   (b) Ctrl-Up Arrow
   (c) Home, Up Arrow   (d) Home, Left Arrow

6. Which sequence of keystrokes will move the cursor down five lines?
   (a) Down Arrow, 5   (b) Escape, 5, Down Arrow
   (c) F1, 5, Down Arrow   (d) Home, Home, Home, Home, Home, Down Arrow

7. Which sequence of keystrokes will advance the cursor just past the next occurrence of the letter *x*?
   (a) Ctrl-Home, x   (b) Home, Home, x
   (c) Right Arrow, x   (d) F3, x

8. Which sequence of key presses will delete characters from the cursor to the end of the word?
   (a) Home, Backspace
   (b) Home, Delete
   (c) Home, Right Arrow
   (d) Delete-Right Arrow

9. What do you press to reveal or hide formatting codes?
   (a) Alt-C
   (b) Alt-PgDn
   (c) Alt-F3
   (d) Ctrl-F3

10. One way to invoke the thesaurus is to move the cursor to the word you want to look up and then press
    (a) Alt-F1.
    (b) Alt-T.
    (c) F1.
    (d) F3.

11. Which menu do you pull down to select the option to display two windows?
    (a) File
    (b) Layout
    (c) Edit
    (d) Tools

12. Which type of paragraph indentation moves all lines toward the center of the page except for the first line?
    (a) first line indent
    (b) left indent
    (c) double indent
    (d) hanging indent

13. By default, WordPerfect has a tab stop set every
    (a) half inch.
    (b) inch.
    (c) inch and a half.
    (d) two inches.

14. Which feature is an alternative to using decimal tab stops?
    (a) Tab
    (b) Tab Align
    (c) Indent
    (d) Flush Right

15. Which feature is used to type text aligned to the right margin?
    (a) Tab
    (b) Tab Align
    (c) Indent
    (d) Flush Right

16. Which code indicates a page break generated by the user?
    (a) [HRt]
    (b) [SRt]
    (c) [HPg]
    (d) [Tab]

17. Which option from the Tools menu do you select to insert a date that will always show the current date whenever the document is retrieved or printed?
    (a) Date Text
    (b) Date Code
    (c) Date Format
    (d) Outline

18. Which menu can you use to create a document summary?
    (a) Edit
    (b) Search
    (c) Layout
    (d) Tools

19. Which File menu option do you execute to retrieve an ASCII file, such as AUTOEXEC.BAT or CONFIG.SYS?
    (a) Retrieve
    (b) Save
    (c) Text Out
    (d) Text In

20. Which File menu option do you execute to return temporarily to DOS while keeping WordPerfect loaded in memory?
    (a) Exit
    (b) Text Out
    (c) Go to DOS
    (d) Save

Fill-In

1. The _____ option of the List Files menu lets you examine the contents of a file or subdirectory.

2. The Find option of the List Files menu lets you _____ files that meet specific conditions.

3. The _____ key lets you repeat a cursor-movement command a number of times.

4. A WordPerfect document contains special _____ that specify how the document is to be formatted.

5. The built-in _____ can examine a word in your document or a word that you enter, and display a list of synonyms and antonyms.

6. The _____ option of the Edit menu lets you split the display into two separate document-editing screens, each with its own status line.

7. The _____ command, executed by pressing Shift-F3, allows you to move the cursor from one window to the other.

8. _____ refers to moving text away from the margin toward the center of the page.

9. A hanging indent is created by performing a left indent followed by a _____.

10. The default and most commonly used type of tab stop is the _____ tab stop.

11. The Tab Align command, executed by pressing Ctrl-F6, lines up text or numbers on an _____ character, usually the period.

12. The _____ feature is especially handy for typing the return address and date against the right margin in a letter.

13. You can move several lines of text against the right margin at once if you first mark the lines as a _____.

14. If you want the date in a document to be updated whenever it is retrieved or printed, you must use the Date _____ option from the Tools menu.

15. The Date _____ option in the Tools menu lets you change the way the date is displayed.

16. Press the _____ key three times and then press Up Arrow to move the cursor ahead of any codes at the beginning of a document.

17. Adding a Document _____ lets you maintain detailed information about a document, including the revision and creation dates, the document name, the subject, the author, the typist, keywords, and an abstract.

18. The _____ option in the File menu lets you save a document in a generic format that can be used by word processors other than WordPerfect.

19. The _____ option in the File menu lets you return temporarily to the DOS prompt.

20. The DOS _____ command is used to return to WordPerfect from a secondary command processor.

Short Problems

1. Start WordPerfect if you are not already running the program. The Escape key can be used to repeat a character or some WordPerfect features a specified number of times. The default number is 8, but you can change this value.

You have already learned to use the Escape key to repeat certain cursor movements. Now use the Escape key to type the letter A twenty times:

Press	**Escape**
Type	**20**
Type	**a**

The Escape key can also be used with the Delete key. Move the cursor to the beginning of the line and use the Escape key with Delete to remove the first ten letters.

2. Normally, WordPerfect displays only the status line below the text area on the editing screen. Some people like to have a ruler line also displayed on the screen to see the current margins and tab stop settings. You can use the Window option of the Edit menu to present a ruler line at the bottom of the screen.

Press	**Alt-=**
Type	**ew**
Type	**23**
Press	**Enter**

Setting the window size to 23 lines displays the ruler line below the status line at the bottom of the screen. Note that you have really opened two windows, but only one window fits on the screen at a time. You can move to the other window with the Switch command (Shift-F3), and edit a different document or view a different part of the same document.

3. The Date Text and Date Code options can insert the current time as well as the date into your document. Pull down the Tools menu and select the Date Format option. Change the format to

3   1, 4   8:90

Select the Date Text or Date Code option and observe the result.

4. WordPerfect has four styles of tabs you can set: left, center, right, and decimal. In addition, the program has a dot leader feature that can fill in the blank space preceding a tab stop with periods. Pull down the Layout menu, select the Line option, and then select the Tab Set option to display the Tab Set menu on your screen. Clear the default tab settings by deleting to the end of the line. Set a left tab stop at +1 inch and a right tab stop at +5 inches. With the cursor still at the +5-inch position, type a period to specify a dot leader for the right tab stop. Return to the editing screen. Enter these lines:

Press	**Tab**
Type	**John Anderson**
Press	**Tab**
Type	**555-1234**
Press	**Enter**
Press	**Tab**
Type	**Melissa Smith**
Press	**Tab**
Type	**555-2468**
Press	**Enter**

5. Now try the center and decimal tab styles. Activate the Tab Set menu and clear the current tab stops. Set a center tab stop at +3 inches and a decimal tab stop at +5 inches. Enter these lines:

Press	**Tab**
Type	**Advertising**
Press	**Tab**
Type	**$1,236.22**
Press	**Enter**
Press	**Tab**
Type	**Office Supplies**
Press	**Tab**
Type	**$287.15**
Press	**Enter**

6. Invoke the thesaurus and select the Look Up Word option. (If the cursor is at the beginning of a new line, the Look Up Word option will be selected automatically.) Look up the word *wonderful*. Select the Look Up Word option again and try these words: *powerful* and *unusual*.

7. Obtain a new diskette or one that can be reformatted. Execute the Go to DOS option from the File menu to return temporarily to DOS without exiting WordPerfect. Put the diskette in drive A. Execute the FORMAT A: command to format the diskette. Copy the file NEWS.DOC from the LESSONS subdirectory to the diskette. Execute the EXIT command to return to WordPerfect.

8. Clear the screen and retrieve MEMO.DOC. Center the document vertically on the page and then print it.

9. Use the Print option from the List Files menu to print the document INDENT.DOC.

10. You have already created a document summary for HOLMES.DOC. Now create document summaries for the files MEMO.DOC, INDENT.DOC, and NEWS.DOC. Note that you have to retrieve a document into the editing screen before you can add a document summary.

Long Problems

1. Use what you have learned about the Date Text and Right Flush features to create a letter of complaint to a company about inadequate service you may have received or an inferior product you may have purchased.

2. Create a table of contents for this chapter, using a right tab stop with a dot leader to align all the page numbers at the right margin.

3. Reproduce a page from the Glossary in this book, using ½-inch hanging indents. Each term along with its definition should be a single paragraph. Remember to boldface the terms.

4. Reproduce the following table of information about the United States. Use tab stops, not spaces, to align the columns. Use left tab stops for the State and Capital columns, a center tab stop for the Admitted column, and a right tab stop for the Size Rank column.

State	Capital	Admitted	Size Rank
Alabama	Montgomery	1819	29
Alaska	Juneau	1959	1
Arizona	Phoenix	1912	6
Arkansas	Little Rock	1836	27
California	Sacramento	1850	3
Colorado	Denver	1876	8
Connecticut	Hartford	1788	48
Delaware	Dover	1787	49
District of Columbia	Washington	—	51
Florida	Tallahassee	1845	22
Georgia	Atlanta	1788	21
Hawaii	Honolulu	1959	47
Idaho	Boise	1890	13
Illinois	Springfield	1818	24
Indiana	Indianapolis	1816	38
Iowa	Des Moines	1846	25
Kansas	Topeka	1861	14
Kentucky	Frankfort	1792	37
Louisiana	Baton Rouge	1812	31
Maine	Augusta	1820	39
Maryland	Annapolis	1788	42
Massachusetts	Boston	1788	45
Michigan	Lansing	1837	23
Minnesota	St. Paul	1858	12
Mississippi	Jackson	1817	32
Missouri	Jefferson City	1821	19
Montana	Helena	1889	4
Nebraska	Lincoln	1867	15
Nevada	Carson City	1864	7
New Hampshire	Concord	1788	44
New Jersey	Trenton	1787	46
New Mexico	Santa Fe	1912	5
New York	Albany	1788	30
North Carolina	Raleigh	1789	28
North Dakota	Bismarck	1889	17
Ohio	Columbus	1803	35
Oklahoma	Oklahoma City	1907	18
Oregon	Salem	1859	10
Pennsylvania	Harrisburg	1787	33
Rhode Island	Providence	1790	50
South Carolina	Columbia	1788	40
South Dakota	Pierre	1889	16
Tennessee	Nashville	1796	34
Texas	Austin	1845	2
Utah	Salt Lake City	1896	11
Vermont	Montpelier	1791	43
Virginia	Richmond	1788	36
Washington	Olympia	1889	20
West Virginia	Charleston	1863	41
Wisconsin	Madison	1848	26
Wyoming	Cheyenne	1890	9

5. Use the Text Out option to create the following DOS batch file for changing to the LESSONS subdirectory and starting WordPerfect. Name the file W.BAT when you save it.

```
cd c:\lessons
wp %1
cd c:\
```

6. Create an inventory of your personal property. Use tab stops to arrange the data into columns. Use a decimal tab stop for the column listing the cost of each item.

7. Use successively nested left and right indentation to reproduce the following paragraphs. Turn on justification for this document and print it when you have finished.

Supercomputers are extremely fast mainframes that execute billions of instructions per second and can serve hundreds of users simultaneously. They cost between $5 million and $20 million each. Only a few hundred supercomputers are operating in the world today.

Mainframes are big, powerful, fast, expensive computers. They execute many millions of instructions per second, can serve hundreds of users at the same time, and cost between $100,000 and $20 million. A mainframe computer may be as small as one or two file cabinets or large enough to fill an entire room.

Minicomputers are medium-sized computers that serve several users simultaneously or control complex equipment. The smallest minicomputers are about the same size as floor-standing microcomputers; the largest may be as big as one or two file cabinets. Minicomputers cost between $15,000 and $500,000.

Workstations are small, powerful computers generally used by only one person at a time. They are superior to microcomputers in their ability to perform complex calculations, display sharp and colorful graphics, and communicate with other computers. Workstations range in price from $4000 to $100,000.

Microcomputers are small enough to fit on a desk and are almost always used by one person at a time. The CPU usually consists of a single microprocessor chip. Prices range from $100 to $15,000.

8. Create a list of all the college courses you have taken, when you took them, the instructor (if you remember), and the grade you received. Use tab stops to align the columns.

9. Create a list of the LP records, cassette tapes, and compact discs you own. Include the title, artist, and type of media. Use tab stops to align the columns.

10. Create a document that lists each menu in the WordPerfect menu bar along with its options. Use tab stops to align the columns.

ADVANCED WORDPERFECT

In This Chapter

Preview

The previous two chapters taught you most of what the average user needs to know about WordPerfect. This chapter proceeds to more advanced word processing topics. You may not need all of the commands and features presented in this chapter, but many of them can make your work easier, quicker, and less tedious. Learning more about WordPerfect can help you create more complex and attractive documents.

After studying this chapter, you will know how to

- use the Print menu.
- hyphenate words.
- avoid orphans and widows.
- avoid splitting paragraphs between pages.
- use the Font menu.
- add headers and footers.
- create text columns.
- add footnotes and endnotes.
- sort text.
- use the Math feature.
- use the Tables feature
- outline a document.
- generate a table of contents.
- generate an index.
- add graphics.
- use macros.
- create form letters.
- use styles.
- use the Equation Editor.
- customize WordPerfect.

Getting Started

You've already learned how to start WordPerfect and use its most common features and commands. This chapter assumes you have completed all of the lessons and exercises in the Beginning and Intermediate WordPerfect chapters. Furthermore, it assumes that you have a computer with a hard disk and WordPerfect 5.1 installed so that the program can be run from any subdirectory. It also assumes that you have a subdirectory named LESSONS in which to store your document files. To work the following lessons, boot up your computer, change to the LESSONS subdirectory, and start WordPerfect.

Lesson 1: Using the Print Menu

In the two previous chapters you used the Full Document option of the Print menu to print your documents. Full Document is the most commonly used option, but the Print menu's other options can be handy in some circumstances.

Step 1: Retrieve NEWS.DOC

Retrieve the newsletter document:

Press	**Alt-=**
Type	**fr**
Type	**news.doc**
Press	**Enter**

Step 2: Execute the Print Command

Pull down the File menu and execute the Print command:

Press	**Alt-=**
Type	**fp**

Your screen should look like Figure 1.

Step 3: Prepare the Printer

Make sure the printer is connected to the computer and turned on. Also, make sure that paper is loaded and aligned to the top of a new page. Finally, make sure that the printer's On Line light is lit. (If it isn't, press the On Line button.)

Step 4: Select the Page Option

You already know how to use Full Document, the first option in the Print menu. The second option, Page, lets you print the single page in which the cursor is located. At this point, the cursor should be in the first page of NEWS.DOC. Print the current page:

Type	**p**

Only the first page will be printed. WordPerfect will then return to the editing screen.

Figure 1 The Print Menu

```
Print

     1 - Full Document
     2 - Page
     3 - Document on Disk
     4 - Control Printer
     5 - Multiple Pages
     6 - View Document
     7 - Initialize Printer


Options

     S - Select Printer                        Epson FX-86e
     B - Binding Offset                        0"
     N - Number of Copies                      1
     U - Multiple Copies Generated by          WordPerfect
     G - Graphics Quality                      Medium
     T - Text Quality                          High




Selection: 0
```

Step 5: Select the Document on Disk Option

When you choose the Full Document or Page option, the document currently on the editing screen is printed. The Document on Disk option lets you print a document other than the one you are editing. Suppose you want to print MEMO.DOC without retrieving it. Activate the Print menu, select the Document on Disk option, and enter the name of the document to be printed:

Press	**Alt-=**
Type	**fpd**
Type	**memo.doc**
Press	**Enter**

WordPerfect displays the prompt

    Page(s): (All)

You can enter a page number or range of pages, or simply press the Enter key to print the entire document.

Press	**Enter**

The document MEMO.DOC will be printed and the Print menu will remain on the screen.

Step 6: Select the Control Printer Option

If you use the Full Document option, WordPerfect returns to the editing screen and lets you work while the document is printing. You can also return to the editing screen from the Print menu after selecting the Document on Disk option. In fact, you can choose Document on Disk several times and specify several documents to be printed. WordPerfect stores the names of the documents you have sent to the printer in a **print queue**, or waiting line of print jobs. The Printer Control option of the Print menu lets you manage these print jobs. Let's see how it works.

Press your printer's On Line button to take it off line (the On Line light should be off). This will prevent the printer from printing while you examine the print queue. The Print menu should be displayed on your screen. Follow these instructions to load two files into the print queue and then select the Control Printer option:

Type	**d**
Type	**memo.doc**
Press	**Enter** (2 times)
Type	**d**
Type	**news.doc**
Press	**Enter** (2 times)
Type	**c**

Information about your print jobs and the Printer Control menu will appear on the screen (see Figure 2). The messages displayed on the screen can diagnose most printing problems and help you solve them. The menu provides options for controlling your print jobs. The Cancel option lets you terminate one or more print jobs. The Rush Job option changes the priority of a document in the print queue. The Display Jobs option presents all of the print jobs if they are not already shown on the screen. The Go (start printer) option restarts the printer after it

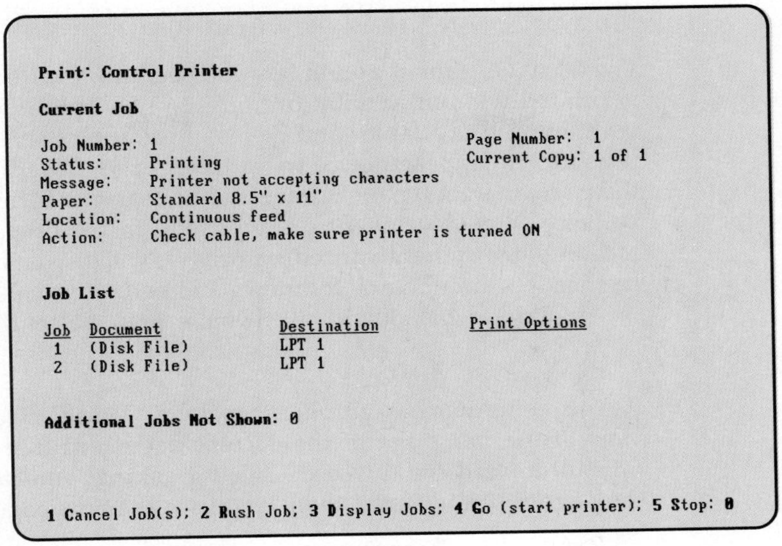

Figure 2 The Printer Control Menu

```
Print: Control Printer

Current Job

Job Number: 1                              Page Number:  1
Status:      Printing                      Current Copy: 1 of 1
Message:     Printer not accepting characters
Paper:       Standard 8.5" x 11"
Location:    Continuous feed
Action:      Check cable, make sure printer is turned ON


Job List

Job  Document              Destination        Print Options
 1   (Disk File)           LPT 1
 2   (Disk File)           LPT 1


Additional Jobs Not Shown: 0



 1 Cancel Job(s); 2 Rush Job; 3 Display Jobs; 4 Go (start printer); 5 Stop: 0
```

has been halted to change a cartridge or after using the Stop option. The Stop option halts the printer, without canceling any print jobs, to let you handle a paper jam, ribbon change, or some other problem.

Cancel all of the print jobs and return to the editing screen:

Type	**c**
Type	**∗**
Type	**y**
Press	**F7**

Press your printer's On Line button again. Part of the first document may still be printed, because many printers have their own internal memory buffer. WordPerfect cannot control text that has already been sent to a printer's buffer. You can, however, shut off the printer while it is still off-line to clear the buffer, wait a few seconds, and then turn it on again.

Step 7: Select the Multiple Pages Option

The Multiple Pages option of the Print menu allows you to specify which pages of the current document are to be printed. Activate the Print command and select the Multiple Pages option:

Press	**Alt-=**
Type	**fpm**

WordPerfect displays the prompt

Page(s): (All)

You can enter a page number or range of pages, or simply press the Enter key to print the entire document. Let's not print the document again. Delete the (All) and press the Exit key to cancel the print job and return to the editing screen:

Press	**Delete**
Press	**F7**

Step 8: Select the View Document Option

The View Document option lets you see how your document will look when it is printed without actually printing it. This option works best on a computer with a graphics adapter and display. A graphics screen can show as closely as possible the appearance of the printed page, including the position of text on the page, margins, page numbers, and character formats such as underline and boldface. View Document can be useful in the preparation of documents that include some of the advanced features we will discuss later in this chapter, including headers and footers, footnotes and endnotes, columns, and graphics.

The Print menu should be on your screen. Select the View Document option:

Type   **v**

If your computer has graphics capability, WordPerfect will present a full-page view of the first page of the current document (see Figure 3). Although it is difficult to read the tiny text, called **greeking**, you can easily see the layout of the page. Use the Page Down key to see the next page in the document:

Press   **Page Down**

Now, return to the first page:

Press   **Page Up**

The View Document menu at the bottom of the screen presents several options for showing a page. The default option, Full Page, shows an entire page of the document on the screen, using greeking to represent text. Try the 100% option, which presents the page in the actual size it would be if it were printed:

Type   **1**

Figure 4 shows the result. If the entire page does not fit on the screen, you can use the arrow keys to see other parts of the page:

Press   **Right Arrow**
Press   **Down Arrow** (4 times)

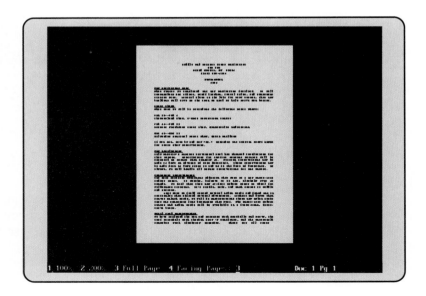

*Figure 3 View Document
Showing the Full Page*

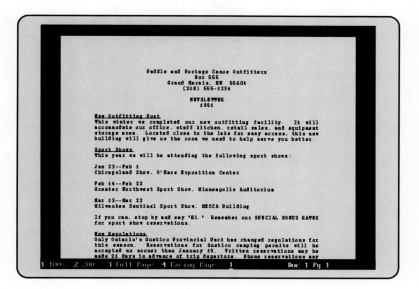

Figure 4 View Document Showing the Actual Size Page

Now, return to the top of the document:

Press	**Home** (2 times)
Press	**Up Arrow**

The 200% option presents a page twice its actual size.

Type	**2**

Your screen should look like Figure 5. You can use the arrow keys and other cursor movement keys to see different parts of the document.

The last option in the View Document menu, Facing Pages, is used to display odd-numbered pages on the right and even-numbered pages on the left. Note

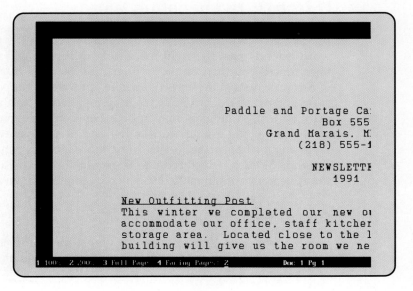

Figure 5 View Document Showing the Page Twice Actual Size

that you cannot edit text in the View Document screen, only examine it. Press the Exit key to return to document editing screen:

Press　　　　**F7**

Step 9: Examine the Other Print Options

Activate the Print menu again:

Press　　　　**Alt-=**
Type　　　　**fp**

Several other options are available in the Print menu. Option number 7, Initialize Printer, is normally used only with certain laser printers to load software fonts. The Select Printer option is used to connect a new printer to your computer or choose another connected printer. The Binding Offset option lets you leave space along the edges of pages that are to be bound into a book. You can print several copies of the same document with the Number of Copies option. Some printers and network software can automatically generate multiple copies after a document has been sent the first time. The Multiple Copies Generated By option lets you specify whether WordPerfect or your printer or network software is to create the multiple copies.

The last two options in the menu, Graphics Quality and Text Quality, allow you to control the resolution and speed of printing. High quality looks the best, but it also takes the longest to print. In addition to High and Medium quality settings, WordPerfect also has Draft, which prints a fast, rough copy. The Do Not Print option is also available for printing text and graphics separately.

Practice

1. With NEWS.DOC on your editing screen, print HOLMES.DOC.
2. Use the View Document option to examine the bottom half of the second page of NEWS.DOC. Use the 200% option to magnify the page.
3. Change the Number of Copies option to print two copies of MEMO.DOC with the Document on Disk option.

Lesson 2: Hyphenating Words

By default, word wrap moves an entire word to the next line whenever that word extends past the right margin. WordPerfect will not split words between lines unless you turn on the hyphenation feature. **Hyphenation** is the division of certain words at the ends of lines to improve the appearance of text. Hyphenation is most useful when text is fully justified. If hyphenation is turned off for justified text, large gaps may appear between the words on some lines. These gaps occur when a long word at the end of a line is wrapped to the next line. Hyphenation can make justified text more attractive by splitting long words at the ends of lines, which reduces large gaps between words. It can also improve the appearance of unjustified text by reducing the raggedness of the right margin.

Step 1: Move the Cursor

Before turning on hyphenation, you must move the cursor to the place where you want hyphenation to begin. In most cases, this place will be the beginning of the document.

Press   **Home** (2 times)

Press   **Up Arrow**

Step 2: Turn On Full Justification

Hyphenation is most often used with full justification. Pull down the Layout menu, select Justify, and then select Full to turn on full justification for the newsletter:

Press   **Alt-=**

Type   **Ljf**

The appearance of text on the screen will not change, but the text will be fully justified when it is printed or examined with View Document.

Step 3: Turn On Hyphenation

Hyphenation is turned off by default. To turn it on, pull down the Layout menu, select Line, select Hyphenation, and then select Yes.

Press   **Alt-=**

Type   **LLyy**

Press   **F7**

When hyphenation is on, WordPerfect uses three criteria to decide when and how to hyphenate a word: the hyphenation zone, the hyphenation dictionary, and the Hyphenation Prompt.

The hyphenation zone is an area around the right margin that WordPerfect examines to determine if a word should be hyphenated. You can change the size of the hyphenation zone, but its default setting is adequate for most documents.

The hyphenation dictionary is the list of words that WordPerfect consults when attempting to hyphenate a word. Two hyphenation dictionaries are available. One is an internal dictionary built into WordPerfect. The other, much larger dictionary is kept on the disk in the files WP{WP}US.LEX and WP{WP}US.HYC. WordPerfect is usually set up to consult the larger hyphenation dictionary on the disk.

WordPerfect sometimes needs your help in placing the hyphen when attempting to split a word. The Hyphenation Prompt lets you specify how often WordPerfect should ask for assistance by selecting one of three options: Never, When Required, and Always. The Never option tells WordPerfect to hyphenate words automatically according to the rules in the hyphenation dictionary. If a word is not in the dictionary, WordPerfect will wrap the entire word to the next line without asking you for assistance. The When Required option, which is the default Hyphenation Prompt setting, tells WordPerfect to ask for assistance only when a word is not in the hyphenation dictionary. The Always option tells WordPerfect to prompt you for assistance at every word to be hyphenated.

Step 4: Scroll Through the Document

In order to hyphenate an existing document, you must scroll through it. Since the When Required option is on, WordPerfect will beep and prompt you for help only when it tries to split a word that it cannot find in the hyphenation dictionary. Use the Down Arrow key to move the cursor through the document:

Press   **Down Arrow** (to the end of the document)

WordPerfect will automatically hyphenate *improvements* in the Trail Food Improvements paragraph and *disappear* in the Trips paragraph. Since both of these words are in the hyphenation dictionary, WordPerfect has no difficulty hyphenating them without your assistance.

If WordPerfect cannot find a word in the hyphenation dictionary, it will present the word and suggest where to insert the hyphen. It will tell you to position the hyphen, which you can do with the Left Arrow or Right Arrow key, and then press Escape.

Step 5: Hyphenate While Entering New Text

Hyphenation also works while you are entering new text. To see it in action, move the cursor to the word *improvements* in the Trail Food Improvements paragraph and delete it:

Press	**Home** (2 times)
Press	**Up Arrow**
Press	**Alt-=**
Type	`sf`
Type	`taste improvements`
Press	**F7**
Press	**Ctrl-Backspace**

Retype the word and see how it is hyphenated automatically:

Type	`improvements,`
Press	**Space Bar**

Your screen should look like Figure 6.

Step 6: View the Document

The best way to see the full result of hyphenation and justification is to print the document or use the View Document feature.

Press	**Alt-=**
Type	`fpv1`
Press	**Page Up**
Press	**Down Arrow** (10 times)

Your screen should look like Figure 7. When you have finished examining the page, return to the editing screen:

Press	**F7**

Step 7: Turn Off Hyphenation

Move the cursor to the beginning of the document and turn off hyphenation:

Press	**Home** (2 times)
Press	**Up Arrow**
Press	**Shift-F8**
Type	**LLyn**
Press	**F7**

Figure 6 Hyphenated Word

```
particular that offered several advantages.  Lighter and dryer than
canvas Duluth packs, we will be incorporating these new nylon packs
into our equipment line beginning this year.  The Super-Lite Badger
canoes and nylon packs will be available on a first-come, first-
serve basis.

Trail Food Improvements
We have replaced the Ham and Potatoes with Meatballs and Gravy, the
Beef Stromboli with Chicken Stew 'N Dumplings, and the Buttermilk
Pancakes with Blueberry Pancakes.  These are all taste improve-
--------------------------------------------------------------------
ments, not cost savings, so our Trail Food will be even better this
year.

Current Outfitting Rates
     Number In Party       Rate Per Person Per Day
     1 to 3 persons        $31.00
     4 to 6 persons        $29.25
     7 to 9 persons        $28.50

1990 Fishing Records
     Bluegill              3.00 lbs.
     Large Mouth Bass     20.25 lbs.
     Northern Pike        42.33 lbs.
C:\LESSONS\NEWS.DOC                    Doc 1 Pg 2 Ln 1" Pos 1.7"
```

Practice

1. Move the cursor to the beginning of the document and turn on hyphenation.
2. Use the Down Arrow key to scroll through the entire document.
3. Use the View Document feature to examine the document. Return to the editing screen, move the cursor to the beginning of the document, and leave hyphenation turned on.

Lesson 3: Avoiding Orphans and Widows

The page formatting settings determine how many lines of text will appear on a page. WordPerfect simply counts the number of lines and inserts a soft page break wherever necessary. Some paragraphs, however, may be divided inappropriately between pages. An **orphan** is the last line of a paragraph that appears

Figure 7 Hyphenation and Justification

at the top of a page. A **widow** is the first line of a paragraph that appears at the bottom of a page. Both orphans and widows are considered poor form because they can confuse the reader. It is better to have two lines from a paragraph at the top or bottom of a page. Fortunately, WordPerfect can automatically eliminate orphans and widows.

Step 1: Examine the Document

The document NEWS.DOC does not contain any orphans or widows. We can, however, easily create an orphan as an example for this lesson. Delete the blank line before the Trail Food Improvements paragraph:

Press	**Home** (2 times)
Press	**Up Arrow**
Press	**Page Down**
Press	**Up Arrow** (5 times)
Press	**Delete**

The word *year* is now all by itself at the top of the second page (see Figure 8). This is the worst kind of orphan and it should not appear in the final document.

Step 2: Move the Cursor

Before eliminating orphans and widows from an entire document, you must move the cursor to the beginning.

Press	**Home** (2 times)
Press	**Up Arrow**

Step 3: Turn On Widow and Orphan Protection

Pull down the Layout menu, select the Line option, select the Widow/Orphan Protection option, and then select Yes:

Press	**Alt-=**
Type	**LLwy**
Press	**F7**

Step 4: Examine the Document

Examine the document again to see if the orphan has been eliminated.

Press	**Page Down**
Press	**Up Arrow** (5 times)

As you can see from Figure 9, the page break has been inserted one line earlier so that two lines from the end of the paragraph appear at the top of the second page.

Now, insert the blank line you removed before the Trail Food Improvements paragraph:

Press	**End**
Press	**Enter**

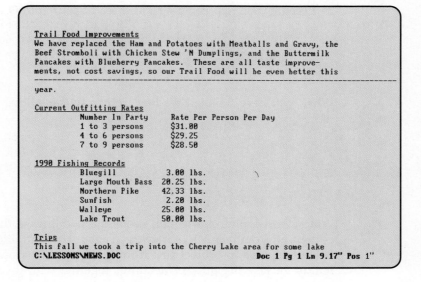

Figure 8 An Orphan at the Top of the Second Page

Step 5: Save the Document

Save the document to the disk to preserve the changes you have made:

Press	**Alt-=**
Type	**fs**
Press	**Enter**
Type	**y**

Practice 1. Move the cursor to the beginning of NEWS.DOC and execute the Reveal Codes command. Note the [Hyph On] code, which indicates that hyphenation is turned on, and the [W/O On] code, which indicates that widow and orphan protection is turned on. Return to the full editing screen.

Figure 9 The Orphan Has Been Eliminated

```
serve basis.
Trail Food Improvements
We have replaced the Ham and Potatoes with Meatballs and Gravy, the
Beef Stromboli with Chicken Stew 'N Dumplings, and the Buttermilk
Pancakes with Blueberry Pancakes.  These are all taste improve-
-----------------------------------------------------------------------
ments, not cost savings, so our Trail Food will be even better this
year.

Current Outfitting Rates
          Number In Party      Rate Per Person Per Day
          1 to 3 persons       $31.00
          4 to 6 persons       $29.25
          7 to 9 persons       $28.50

1990 Fishing Records
          Bluegill             3.00 lbs.
          Large Mouth Bass    20.25 lbs.
          Northern Pike       42.33 lbs.
          Sunfish              2.20 lbs.
          Walleye             25.00 lbs.
          Lake Trout          50.00 lbs.

Trips
C:\LESSONS\NEWS.DOC                          Doc 1 Pg 1 Ln 9" Pos 1"
```

2. Execute the Help command and read about widow and orphan protection:

Press	**F3**
Press	**Shift-F8**
Type	**L**
Type	**w**

When you have finished reading, return to the editing screen:

| Press | **Space Bar** |

Lesson 4: Using the Conditional End of Page Feature

Widow and orphan protection keeps the two lines at the beginning or end of a paragraph from being split between pages. The Conditional End of Page feature is another way to protect text from being split between pages. This feature is handy for keeping titles or headings together with their first paragraphs or for preventing tables from being split between pages.

Step 1: Move the Cursor to the Line Above

Suppose you want to keep the three lines at the end of the Trail Food Improvements paragraph from being split between pages. The first step is to move the cursor to the line before the lines you want to keep together.

Press	**Home** (2 times)
Press	**Up Arrow**
Press	**Page Down**
Press	**Up Arrow** (2 times)

Step 2: Select the Conditional End of Page Option

Pull down the Layout menu, select the Other option, and then select the Conditional End of Page option:

| Press | **Alt-=** |
| Type | **Loc** |

Step 3: Enter the Number of Lines

WordPerfect will prompt you for the number of lines to keep together (see Figure 10). Enter the number and exit the menu:

Type	**3**
Press	**Enter**
Press	**F7**

Step 4: Move the Cursor

The page break will not actually change position until you move the cursor.

| Press | **Down Arrow** (2 times) |

The last three lines of the paragraph will be kept together after the page break (see Figure 11).

*Figure 10 Conditional End
of Page Prompt*

```
Format: Other

   1 - Advance

   2 - Conditional End of Page

   3 - Decimal/Align Character      .
       Thousands' Separator         ,

   4 - Language                     US

   5 - Overstrike

   6 - Printer Functions

   7 - Underline - Spaces           Yes
                   Tabs             No

   8 - Border Options




Number of Lines to Keep Together: _
```

Practice
1. Execute the Reveal Codes command. Note the code [CndlEOP:3], which indicates the Conditional End of Page option has been set for the three lines below the current line. Delete this code to turn the option off. Return to the full editing screen and move the cursor to the beginning of the document.
2. Execute the Help command and read about the Conditional End of Page option. When you have finished, return to the editing screen.

Lesson 5: Using the Font Menu

WordPerfect has the ability to use different fonts and change the size, appearance, and color of text. Whether or not you can actually use these features depends on your computer and printer. Nevertheless, let's examine the options of the Font menu.

*Figure 11 Last Three Lines
of the Paragraph Kept
Together*

```
Beef Stromboli with Chicken Stew 'N Dumplings, and the Buttermilk
---------------------------------------------------------------
Pancakes with Blueberry Pancakes.  These are all taste improve-
ments, not cost savings, so our Trail Food will be even better this
year.

Current Outfitting Rates
         Number In Party    Rate Per Person Per Day
         1 to 3 persons     $31.00
         4 to 6 persons     $29.25
         7 to 9 persons     $28.50

1990 Fishing Records
         Bluegill            3.00 lbs.
         Large Mouth Bass   20.25 lbs.
         Northern Pike      42.33 lbs.
         Sunfish             2.20 lbs.
         Walleye            25.00 lbs.
         Lake Trout         50.00 lbs.

Trips
This fall we took a trip into the Cherry Lake area for some lake
trout fishing.  We had our usual quota of rain, but did enjoy two
beautiful crisp autumn days.  Mornings we awoke to clear, deep blue
C:\LESSONS\NEWS.DOC                        Doc 1 Pg 2 Ln 1.17" Pos 1"
```

Step 1: Clear the Editing Screen

Exit NEWS.DOC and start a new document to illustrate the capabilities of the Font menu:

Press	**Alt-=**
Type	**fxnn**

Step 2: Activate the Font Menu

Pull down the Font menu:

Press	**Alt-=**
Type	**o**

Figure 12 shows the result.

Step 3: Select the Base Font Option

The Base Font option of the Font menu displays the fonts available with your printer and allows you to change the font you are using.

Type	**o**

Figure 13 shows the result for an Epson FX-86e dot-matrix printer. The list you see on your screen may be different. The font highlighted and marked with an asterisk is the base font, the default typeface used for normal characters. If more fonts are available than fit on the screen, they can be viewed by pressing Up Arrow or Down Arrow to scroll through the list. The list presents the name of each font and its size. Sizes are given in points (pt) or characters per inch (CPI). A **point** is a typographic measure equal to about 1/72-inch. Ten characters per inch (10 CPI), the most common default size, is equivalent to the type produced by pica typewriters. Elite typewriters produce 12-CPI type. The abbreviation PS stands for *proportionally spaced*, which refers to fonts that use different amounts of horizontal space for each character.

Figure 12 The Font Menu

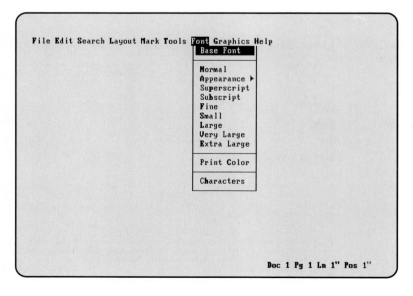

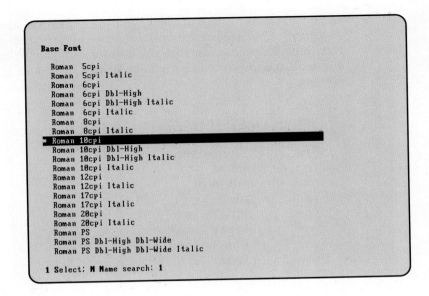

Figure 13 The Base Font Menu for the Epson FX-86e Printer

The two options at the bottom of the screen allow you to select a different base font or search through the list for a particular font name. Let's just leave the base font the same. Press the Exit key to leave the Base Font menu:

Press   **F7**

Step 4: Select the Normal Option

The Normal option of the Font menu turns off all size and appearance attributes for the next characters you type. It returns to the default character size and format. Activate the Font menu and select the Normal option:

Press   **Alt-=**
Type   **on**

Step 5: Select the Appearance Option

Activate the Font menu and select the Appearance option:

Press   **Alt-=**
Type   **oa**

WordPerfect will display the Appearance submenu, which has nine options: Bold, Underline, Double Underline, Italics, Outline, Shadow, Small Cap, Redline, and Strikeout. This menu allows you to change character formats, as you learned in the Beginning WordPerfect chapter. Leave the Appearance submenu:

Press   **Escape**

Step 6: Try the Size Options

The next seven options in the Font menu deal with the height of characters or their relative position in a line: Superscript, Subscript, Fine, Small, Large, Very Large, and Extra Large. While these options do not change the appearance of text on the screen, they do allow you to change the size of text in the printed document. The Superscript and Subscript options also change the position of text. Superscript characters are small and raised, like [this], and subscript characters are small and lowered, like [this]. Follow these directions to try all of the font size options:

Type	**p**
Type	**Superscript**
Press	**Right Arrow**
Type	**characters**
Press	**Enter**
Press	**Alt-=**
Type	**ob**
Type	**Subscript**
Press	**Right Arrow**
Type	**characters**
Press	**Enter**
Press	**Alt-=**
Type	**of**
Type	**Fine characters**
Press	**Right Arrow**
Press	**Enter**
Press	**Alt-=**
Type	**os**
Type	**Small characters**
Press	**Right Arrow**
Press	**Enter**
Press	**Alt-=**
Type	**oL**
Type	**Large characters**
Press	**Right Arrow**
Press	**Enter**
Press	**Alt-=**
Type	**ov**
Type	**Very Large characters**
Press	**Right Arrow**
Press	**Enter**
Press	**Alt-=**
Type	**oe**
Type	**Extra Large characters**
Press	**Right Arrow**
Press	**Enter**
Press	**Alt-=**
Type	**on**

Selecting each of these options inserts codes into the document before and after the text you type, just like the Underline command. Pressing the Right Arrow key after typing text in a particular size moves the cursor past the second size code and returns to the default size. To see what you have done, use the View Document feature:

Press	**Alt-=**
Type	**fpv2**

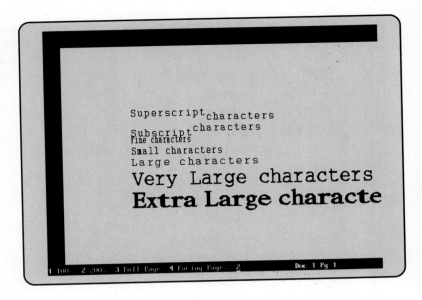

*Figure 14 Font Sizes on
the View Document Screen*

Your screen should look like Figure 14. When you have finished examining the view, return to the editing screen:

Press	**F7**

If you like, you can also print the document.

Press	**Alt-=**
Type	**fpf**

Note that some of the sizes may turn out the same, depending upon your printer. A dot-matrix printer, for example, may have only two or three different sizes. A laser printer, on the other hand, can probably produce all of the different character sizes.

Step 7: Select the Print Color Option

If you have a color printer, you can use the Print Color option to change the color of printed text.

Press	**Alt-=**
Type	**oc**

Most printers cannot produce colors, only black and white. If you have a color printer, however, the table presented by the Print Color option lets you compose print colors by specifying the mixture percentages of the primary colors red, green, and blue. Leave the table the same and return to the editing screen:

Press	**F7**

Step 8: Select the Characters Option

WordPerfect lets you include in your documents more than 1700 characters that do not appear on the keyboard. These special characters are listed in an appendix in the WordPerfect reference manual. They are divided into character sets. Each character set has a number, and each character in a character set has a number. The Character option in the Font menu invokes the Compose feature, which lets you access these special characters. For example, suppose you want to include a large filled bullet symbol in your document. First, clear your screen:

Press	**Alt-=**
Type	**fxnn**

Now, follow these directions to enter the code for a large filled bullet, which is character number 0 in character set number 4.

Press	**Alt-=**
Type	**oh**
Type	**4,0**
Press	**Enter**

WordPerfect will insert a code in your document that indicates a large bullet is to be printed. The character you see on the screen, however, may not appear exactly as it will be printed.

Press	**Space Bar**
Type	**Large Filled Bullet**
Press	**Enter**

Try a few other special characters:

Press	**Alt-=**
Type	**oh**
Type	**4,23**
Press	**Enter**
Press	**Space Bar**
Type	**Copyright Symbol**
Press	**Enter**
Press	**Alt-=**
Type	**oh**
Type	**6,18**
Press	**Enter**
Press	**Space Bar**
Type	**Sigma**
Press	**Enter**
Press	**Alt-=**
Type	**oh**
Type	**6,19**
Press	**Enter**
Press	**Space Bar**
Type	**Infinity**
Press	**Enter**

The best way to see what you have done is to invoke the View Document screen:

Press	**Alt-=**
Type	**fpv2**

Figure 15 shows the result. When you have finished looking at the view, return to the editing screen:

Press	**F7**

Figure 15 Special Characters on the View Document Screen

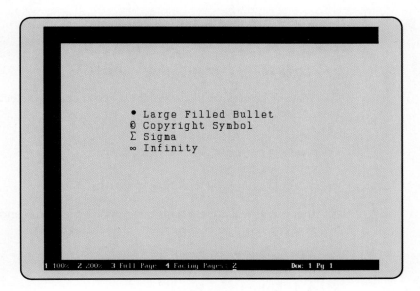

Practice

1. Move the cursor to the beginning of the document and execute the Reveal Codes command. Examine the codes for the special characters. Return to the editing screen.

2. Reproduce these expressions in your document:
   H_2O
   2×10^3
   $e = mc^2$

3. Use the Help facility to read about all of the Font menu options. When you have finished, return to the editing screen.

4. Change the base font, type some new text, and print out the document to see the result. Then change the base font back to what it was before. Clear the screen without saving the document:

Press	**Alt-=**
Type	**fxnn**

Lesson 6: Adding Headers and Footers

A **header** is one or more lines of text printed at the top of every page. A **footer** is one or more lines of text printed at the bottom of every page. Headers and footers are most often used to print titles, chapters, page numbers, or other identification on every page. WordPerfect makes it easy to create headers and footers.

Step 1: Retrieve NEWS.DOC

As an example, let's add a header to the document NEWS.DOC. Your editing screen should be empty. If it is not, use the File Exit command to clear it. Then retrieve NEWS.DOC:

Press	**Alt-=**
Type	**fr**

Type	**news.doc**
Press	**Enter**

Step 2: Select the Headers Option

To create a header, pull down the Layout menu, select the Page option, and then select the Headers option:

Press	**Alt-=**
Type	**Lph**

Step 3: Select the Header

Another menu will appear with two options: Header A and Header B. WordPerfect lets you create up to two headers. Select Header A:

Type	**a**

Step 4: Select the Pages

Another menu will appear with five options: Discontinue, Every Page, Odd Pages, Even Pages, and Edit. Select the Every Page option to have the header printed at the top of every page:

Type	**p**

Step 5: Enter the Header Text

The screen will temporarily clear so you can enter the text of the header. Suppose you want the header to be *Newsletter* followed by the page number. Follow these instructions:

Type	**Newsletter**
Press	**Space Bar**
Press	**Ctrl-B**
Press	**F7** (2 times)

The Ctrl-B is a code that tells WordPerfect to insert the current page number.

Step 6: Print or View the Document

Headers show up only when the document is printed or examined with View Document. If you have a printer, you can print the document:

Press	**Alt-=**
Type	**fpf**

Or you can use the View Document feature:

Press	**Alt-=**
Type	**fpv1**

The header will appear in the upper left corner of every page (see Figure 16). Return to the editing screen:

Press	**F7**

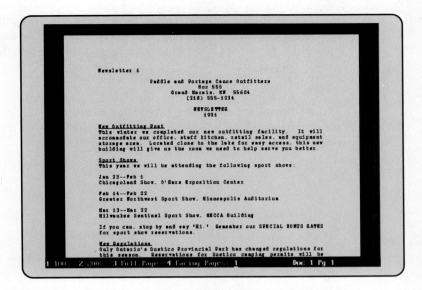

Figure 16 The Header at the Top of the Page

Step 7: Examine the Other Options

Pull down the Layout menu and select Page:

Press	**Alt-=**
Type	**Lp**

The process for creating footers is the same, except you choose the Footers option after you select Page from the Layout menu. Select the Footers option and then select Footer A:

Type	**f a**

The Discontinue option allows you to remove an existing header or footer. The Edit option allows you to make changes to an existing header or footer. Return to the editing screen:

Press	**F7**

Practice

1. Discontinue the header you have created for NEWS.DOC.
2. Create a footer for NEWS.DOC. Print the document or examine it with View Document.
3. Use the Edit option to alter the footer in some way.
4. Discontinue the footer.

Lesson 7: Creating Text Columns

WordPerfect can create two types of text columns in a printed document: newspaper-style and parallel. **Newspaper-style columns** contain text that continues from the bottom of one column on the left to the top of the next column on the right on the same page. **Parallel columns** contain text that continues in the same column on the next page. Columns are often used in newsletters, magazines, newspapers, and for narrow lists of items in books. As an example, let's reformat NEWS.DOC so that it contains two newspaper-style columns.

Step 1: Move the Cursor

The first step is to move the cursor to the place in the document where columns are to begin. In NEWS.DOC, columns should begin on the line that contains the title *New Outfitting Post*.

Press	**Home** (2 times)
Press	**Up Arrow**
Press	**Down Arrow** (8 times)

Step 2: Turn On Automatic Hyphenation

It is usually necessary to hyphenate some words when text is arranged in columns. Let's change the hyphenation prompt to *Never* so that WordPerfect will automatically hyphenate all words it finds in the hyphenation dictionary. Any words not found will be moved automatically to the next line. Pull down the File menu, select Setup, select Environment, select Prompt for Hyphenation, and then select *Never*:

Press	**Alt-=**
Type	**ftepn**
Press	**F7**

Now, turn on hyphenation if it is not already turned on:

Press	**Alt-=**
Type	**LLyy**
Press	**F7**

Step 3: Define the Columns

Next, you must tell WordPerfect the number of columns you want and their spacing on the page. Pull down the Layout menu, select Columns, and then select Define:

Press	**Alt-=**
Type	**Lcd**

WordPerfect will display the Text Column Definition menu, as shown in Figure 17. The default type of columns is newspaper-style, with two three-inch-wide columns spaced ½-inch apart. These default settings are fine for our example, so tell WordPerfect to accept them:

Press	**F7** (2 times)

Step 4: Turn On Columns

The columns are now defined, but you still have to turn them on. Pull down the Layout menu, select Columns, and then select On:

Press	**Alt-=**
Type	**Lco**

Figure 17 The Text Column Definition Menu

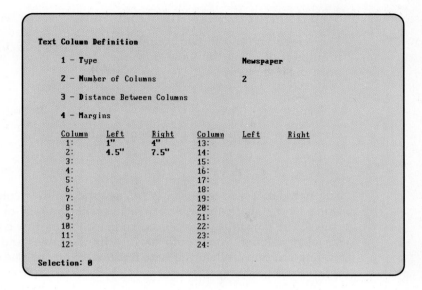

```
Text Column Definition

  1 - Type                              Newspaper

  2 - Number of Columns                 2

  3 - Distance Between Columns

  4 - Margins

  Column    Left      Right     Column    Left      Right
    1:       1"        4"         13:
    2:       4.5"      7.5"       14:
    3:                            15:
    4:                            16:
    5:                            17:
    6:                            18:
    7:                            19:
    8:                            20:
    9:                            21:
   10:                            22:
   11:                            23:
   12:                            24:

Selection: 0
```

After you turn on columns, any new text you type will automatically be arranged in columns. You can turn off columns at any time by pulling down the Layout menu, selecting Columns, and then selecting Off. Then you can type text that you don't want split into columns.

Step 5: Scroll Through the Text

Now that columns are turned on, you can use the Down Arrow key to scroll through the text and WordPerfect will create the columns on your screen.

Press	**Down Arrow** (to the end of the document)

When you have finished, move to the beginning of the left column:

Press	**Home** (2 times)
Press	**Up Arrow**
Press	**Down Arrow** (8 times)

Step 6: Move to the Other Column

The normal cursor movement commands work only within the current column. You must use a variation of the Go To command to move to another column. Execute this command to move to the right column:

Press	**Ctrl-Home**
Press	**Right Arrow**

Now, move back to the left column:

Press	**Ctrl-Home**
Press	**Left Arrow**

Note the change in the status bar as the cursor moves from one column to the other.

Step 7: Print or View the Document

The screen shows the two columns, but you can see the document better by printing it or using the View Document feature. If you have a printer, you can print the document:

Press **Alt-=**
Type **fpf**

Or you can use the View Document feature:

Press **Alt-=**
Type **fpv1**

The newsletter will appear in two newspaper-style columns (see Figure 18). Don't worry about the tables, which do not line up or are split between the pages. The tab stops were set too wide for the narrow columns. If this were an actual newsletter, you would have to fix the tables and any other minor formatting problems. When you have finished examining the View Document screen, return to the editing screen:

Press **F7**

Step 8: Exit and Retrieve NEWS.DOC

Let's abandon the columns you have created and leave NEWS.DOC the way it was before this lesson. Exit the file without saving it and then retrieve NEWS.DOC again:

Press **Alt-=**
Type **fxnn**
Press **Alt-=**
Type **fr**
Type **news.doc**
Press **Enter**

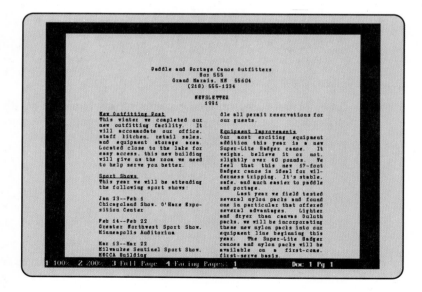

Figure 18 Two Newspaper-Style Text Columns

Practice	Invoke the Help facility and read about the commands and options you have used in this lesson.

Lesson 8: Adding Footnotes and Endnotes

Anyone who has written a term paper or technical report has faced the problem of placing footnotes. A **footnote** is a numbered comment or explanation at the bottom of a page. Footnotes are used to list sources or provide more detailed information about items in the text. A footnote must appear at the bottom of the page that contains its number. Placing footnotes at the bottom of the appropriate pages is difficult with a typewriter and some word processing programs. If text is added or deleted, existing footnotes may have to be moved to a different page. Fortunately, WordPerfect automatically numbers footnotes and keeps them at the bottom of the appropriate page. An **endnote** is similar to a footnote, except that comments are collected and placed at the end of the document instead of at the bottom of each page. You can have footnotes and endnotes in the same document. Although newsletters usually don't have footnotes or endnotes, let's add a footnote to NEWS.DOC just to see how they work.

Step 1: Move the Cursor

The cursor must be moved to the location in the document where the note number is to be inserted. Let's put a footnote number at the end of the New Outfitting Post paragraph.

Press	**Home** (2 times)
Press	**Up Arrow**
Press	**Down Arrow** (12 times)
Press	**End**

Step 2: Execute the Footnote Command

Footnotes and endnotes can be created from the Layout menu. Pull down the Layout menu and select Footnote:

Press	**Alt-=**
Type	**Lf**

Step 3: Create the Footnote

WordPerfect will present a submenu that has four options: Create, Edit, New Number, and Options. Select the Create option to begin creating the footnote:

Type	**c**

WordPerfect will present a special screen for editing footnotes. The footnote number, in this case 1, is automatically created. Simply type the text of the footnote:

Type	**See last year's newsletter for a photo.**

Figure 19 The Footnote Text

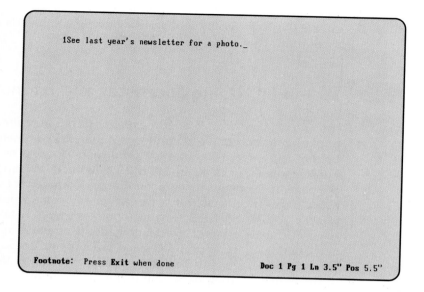

Your screen should look like Figure 19. Press the Exit key to save the footnote and return to the document editing screen:

Press   **F7**

Step 4: View the Document

When you return to the editing screen, you can immediately see the footnote number WordPerfect placed at the end of the first paragraph. The footnote text, however, only appears when the document is printed or examined with View Document. Use the View Document feature to look at the footnote you have created:

Press   **Alt-=**
Type   **fpv1**
Press   **Grey Plus**

Your screen should look like Figure 20. The footnote appears at the bottom of the first page beneath a line separating it from the document text. Return to the editing screen:

Press   **F7**

Step 5: Examine Other Options

Creating endnotes is just like creating footnotes, except that you select the End-note option instead of the Footnote option from the Layout menu. In addition, you have to tell WordPerfect where you want the endnotes placed in the doc-ument. This is done by moving the cursor to the desired location, pulling down the Layout menu, selecting Endnote, and then selecting the Placement option.

To edit existing footnotes or endnotes, you select the Edit option from the Footnote or Endnote submenu. The New Number option lets you start num-bering notes with a new number. This option is useful when you have a document broken up between two files and you want the note numbers in the second file

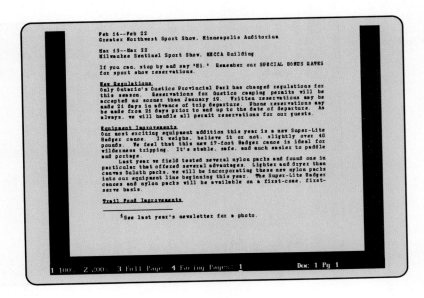

Figure 20 The Footnote Has Been Added at the Bottom

to continue after the numbers in the first file instead of starting from 1. The Options option in the Footnote or Endnote submenu lets you specify attributes such as footnote spacing and the numbering style.

Practice

1. Add the following footnote at the end of the New Regulations paragraph:

   `Write to the Ontario Ministry of Natural Resources for more information.`

2. Add a couple of endnotes and place them at the end of the document. Use the View Document feature to examine the endnotes you have created.

3. Delete all the footnotes and endnotes you have created by deleting each note number in the document text. Answer *Yes* to the confirmation prompt displayed by WordPerfect each time you delete a note number. Move the cursor to the beginning of the document.

Lesson 9: Sorting Text

Sorting is arranging items in some particular order. WordPerfect makes it easy to sort lines of text or paragraphs. This feature is handy for alphabetizing names or any list of words or phrases. Sorting is also used to arrange numbers, such as dates and ZIP codes, into ascending or descending order. As an example, let's sort the list of fishing records on the second page of NEWS.DOC.

Step 1: Mark the Lines As a Block

The first step is to mark the lines of text to be sorted as a block. Follow these directions to move the cursor with the Search command and then mark the fishing records as a block:

Press	**Home** (2 times)
Press	**Up Arrow**
Press	**Alt-=**

Figure 21 The Sort Menu

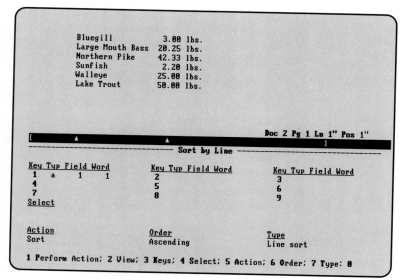

Type	**sf**
Type	**Bluegill**
Press	**F2**
Press	**Home**
Press	**Left Arrow**
Press	**Alt-=**
Type	**eb**
Press	**Down Arrow** (6 times)

The table of fishing records will be marked as a block and displayed in reverse video.

Step 2: Select Sort from the Tools Menu

The table of fish names and records is almost sorted. The only name out of order is Lake Trout. Let's sort the table by fish name. Pull down the Tools menu and select Sort:

Press	**Alt-=**
Type	**ts**

WordPerfect will display the Sort menu shown in Figure 21. Each line in the marked block is a **record** to be sorted. Each word separated by tabs or spaces is a **field**. The **key** is a field on which the records are to be sorted. WordPerfect lets you specify up to nine keys, but in most cases you need only one. The key in this case will be the first word of the fish names. But because all of the lines in this table begin with a tab, you must tell WordPerfect that the second field in each record is to be the key. Select the Keys option and change the key field from 1 to 2:

Type	**k**
Press	**Right Arrow**
Type	**2**
Press	**F7**

The default sort order is Ascending, which will sort items in alphabetical order from A to Z. Select the Perform Action option to complete the sort:

Type   **p**

The table will be rearranged, with Lake Trout coming after Bluegill.

Practice
1. Sort the Fishing Records table in descending order. Select the Order option from the Sort menu and then select the Descending option.
2. Sort the Fishing Records table in ascending order again. Save NEWS.DOC to the disk to preserve the changes you have made. Move the cursor to the beginning of the document.

Lesson 10: Using the Math Feature

WordPerfect has two features that enable you to perform calculations in your documents: Math and Tables. The Math feature lets you total numbers arranged in columns designated by tab stops. The Tables feature, introduced in Word-Perfect 5.1, lets you quickly organize information into columns and rows without using tab stops. Like a spreadsheet program, the Tables feature makes it easy to perform calculations on numbers arranged in rows and columns. This lesson will show you how to use the Math feature to compute subtotals, totals, and grand totals. The next lesson will explore the Tables feature.

Step 1: Clear the Screen

Exit the current document to clear the editing screen:

Press   **Alt-=**
Type   **fxnn**

Our simple example will use the Math feature to subtotal the Sales and Rentals figures of a business for each month, total each quarter, and then calculate a grand total for the year.

Step 2: Set Up the Tab Stops

The Math feature uses tab stops to designate columns. The simplest way to use the Math feature is to calculate subtotals, totals, and grand totals down the tab columns. The space between the left margin and the first tab stop is not counted as a math column, so it can contain text labels that explain the numbers. The default tab stop settings are too close together for most math columns. Pull down the Layout menu, select Line, select Tab Set, clear the current tab stop settings, and insert a decimal tab stop three inches from the left margin:

Press   **Alt-=**
Type   **LLt**
Press   **Ctrl-End**
Type   **3**
Press   **Enter**
Type   **d**
Press   **F7** (2 times)

Step 3: Turn On the Math Feature

Our simple example will have only one column of numbers. All subtotals, totals, and grand totals will be calculated down this column. If you want different types of columns or need to calculate across columns, you must pull down the Layout menu, select Math, select Define, and then complete the Math Definition screen. We don't have to define the columns for our example, but we do have to turn on the Math feature. First, move the cursor to the position where you want the calculations to begin. Since your cursor is already at the beginning of a new document, simply pull down the Layout menu, select Math, and then select On:

Press	**Alt-=**
Type	**Lmo**

WordPerfect will return to the editing screen, and the word *Math* will appear in the lower left corner of the screen to remind you that the Math feature is turned on.

Step 4: Enter the Labels, Numbers, and Functions

The space between the left margin and the first tab stop is not used by the Math feature, so you can use it to enter the labels that describe each number. The tab column holds the numbers and the functions that perform the calculations. Each function is designated by a symbol:

+	Subtotals the numbers above
=	Totals all subtotals above
*	Computes a grand total of all totals above

Follow these directions to enter the labels, numbers, and functions:

Type	**January**
Press	**Enter**
Type	**Sales**
Press	**Tab**
Type	**$568.25**
Press	**Enter**
Type	**Rentals**
Press	**Tab**
Type	**$1,245.93**
Press	**Enter**
Type	**Subtotal**
Press	**Tab**
Type	**$+**
Press	**Enter** (2 times)
Type	**February**
Press	**Enter**
Type	**Sales**
Press	**Tab**
Type	**$693.50**
Press	**Enter**
Type	**Rentals**
Press	**Tab**
Type	**$1,082.67**

Press	**Enter**
Type	**Subtotal**
Press	**Tab**
Type	**$+**
Press	**Enter** (2 times)
Type	**March**
Press	**Enter**
Type	**Sales**
Press	**Tab**
Type	**$721.80**
Press	**Enter**
Type	**Rentals**
Press	**Tab**
Type	**$1,163.69**
Press	**Enter**
Type	**Subtotal**
Press	**Tab**
Type	**$+**
Press	**Enter** (2 times)
Type	**First Quarter**
Press	**Tab**
Type	**$=**
Press	**Enter** (2 times)
Type	**Year-to-Date**
Press	**Tab**
Type	**$***
Press	**Enter**

To save typing, we have entered just the first quarter. You could enter the remaining months and quarters between the First Quarter and Year-to-Date rows. Your screen should look like Figure 22. Check your work against this figure and correct any errors.

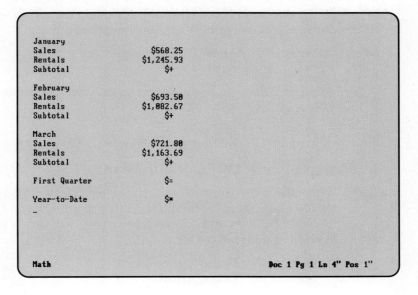

Figure 22 The Labels, Numbers, and Functions

Figure 23 The Function Results Have Been Computed

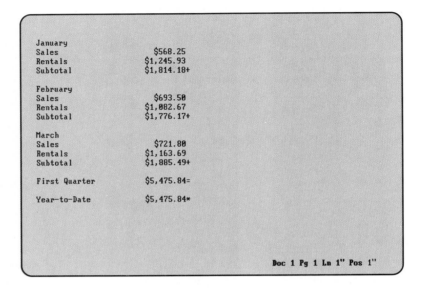

```
January
Sales                    $568.25
Rentals                $1,245.93
Subtotal               $1,814.18+

February
Sales                    $693.50
Rentals                $1,082.67
Subtotal               $1,776.17+

March
Sales                    $721.80
Rentals                $1,163.69
Subtotal               $1,885.49+

First Quarter          $5,475.84=

Year-to-Date           $5,475.84*

                                     Doc 1 Pg 1 Ln 1" Pos 1"
```

Step 5: Perform the Calculations

When the Math feature is turned on and you type a function symbol (+, =, or *), the character appears on the screen, but a code is actually inserted into the document. The results of the functions do not appear until you tell WordPerfect to perform the calculations. Pull down the Layout menu, select Math, and then select Calculate:

Press   **Alt-=**
Type   **Lmc**

Move to the beginning of the document:

Press   **Page Up**

Your screen should look like Figure 23. The subtotals, total, and grand total have been calculated by WordPerfect. The function symbols (+, =, and *) still appear on the screen, but they will not be printed. You can confirm this by printing the document or using the View Document feature:

Press   **Alt-=**
Type   **fpv1**

When you have finished examining the View Document screen, return to the editing screen:

Press   **F7**

Step 6: Turn Off the Math Feature

When you have finished performing calculations, you can turn off the Math feature and resume normal text editing in your document. Move the cursor to the end of the section that contains math, pull down the Layout menu, select Math, and then select Off:

Press   **Home** (2 times)
Press   **Down Arrow**

Press   **Alt-=**
Type   **Lmf**

The Math feature will be turned off at the current cursor location.

Step 7: Save the Document

Save your document in a file named SALES.DOC.

Press   **Alt-=**
Type   **fs**
Type   **sales.doc**
Press   **Enter**

Practice

1. Activate the Reveal Codes screen, scroll through the document, and find the following codes: [Math On], [+], [=], [*], and [Math Off]. When you have finished examining the codes, return to the full editing screen.
2. Change the January Sales figure to $699.25 and tell WordPerfect to recalculate the totals. (Pull down the Layout menu, select Math, and then select Calculate.)
3. Make up and enter Sales and Rentals figures for the remaining months of the year. Enter your new rows above the Year-to-Date row. Be sure to compute totals for the second, third, and fourth quarters. Tell WordPerfect to perform the calculations, save your document, and then print it.

Lesson 11: Using the Tables Feature

The new Tables feature introduced in WordPerfect 5.1 provides an easy way to create rows and columns of data without having to use tabs. This feature is also handy for creating tabular forms such as invoices. Let's use the Tables feature to make part of a simple income statement for a business such as Paddle and Portage Canoe Outfitters.

Step 1: Clear the Screen

Exit the current document to clear the editing screen:

Press   **Alt-=**
Type   **fxnn**

Step 2: Set Up the Table

A table consists of rows, which run horizontally, and columns, which run vertically. The maximum number of columns you can have in a table is 32; the maximum number of rows is 32,765. Columns are labeled with letters A, B, C, D, and so on. Rows are labeled with numbers 1, 2, 3, 4, and so on. Each intersection of a row and a column is a **cell** in which you can enter text, a number, or a formula. A **formula** is an expression that tells WordPerfect how to perform a calculation. Each cell has its own label indicating its column and row. For example, A1 is the cell at the intersection of the first column and the first row. C10 is the cell at the intersection of the third column and the tenth row. A table in WordPerfect is like a worksheet in a spreadsheet program.

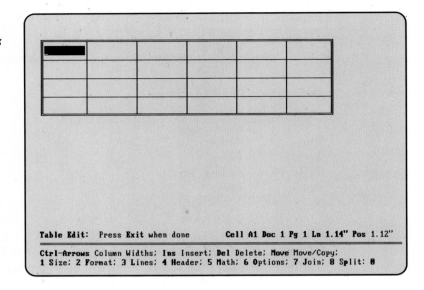

*Figure 24 The New Blank
Table*

To create a new table, pull down the Layout menu, select Tables, and then
select Create:

Press   **Alt-=**
Type   **Ltc**

WordPerfect will prompt you for the number of columns, suggesting 3 as the
default. Our income statement requires six columns.

Type   **6**
Press   **Enter**

Next, WordPerfect will prompt you for the number of rows, suggesting 1 as the
default. Our income statement requires four rows.

Type   **4**
Press   **Enter**

WordPerfect will display the blank table on the Table Edit screen (see Figure 24).
The Table Edit screen lets you adjust the structure of the table.

Step 3: Enter the Data

You cannot enter data into the table on the Table Edit screen. You must switch
to normal text editing mode by pressing the Exit key.

Press   **F7**

Follow these directions to enter the data into the table:

Press   **Right Arrow**
Type   **Jan-Mar**
Press   **Right Arrow**
Type   **Apr-Jun**
Press   **Right Arrow**

Type	**Jul-Sep**
Press	**Right Arrow**
Type	**Oct-Dec**
Press	**Right Arrow**
Type	**Sales**
Press	**Right Arrow**
Type	**1,523.25**
Press	**Right Arrow**
Type	**1,459.50**
Press	**Right Arrow**
Type	**1,752.75**
Press	**Right Arrow**
Type	**1,543.00**
Press	**Right Arrow** (2 times)
Type	**Rentals**
Press	**Right Arrow**
Type	**1,787.50**
Press	**Right Arrow**
Type	**1,294.50**
Press	**Right Arrow**
Type	**1,037.00**
Press	**Right Arrow**
Type	**1,111.25**
Press	**Right Arrow** (2 times)
Type	**Total**

Step 4: Enter the Formulas and Functions

Now you must enter the formulas and functions to calculate the totals. Pull down the Layout menu, select Tables, and select Edit to go back to the Table Edit screen:

Press	**Alt-=**
Type	**Lte**

Move the cursor to cell F2:

Press	**Home** (2 times)
Press	**Up Arrow**
Press	**Down Arrow**
Press	**End**

To total the Sales figures across the second row, you must add cells B2, C2, D2, and E2. Select Math, select Formula, and then enter the formula to add these cells:

Type	**mf**
Type	**b2+c2+d2+e2**
Press	**Enter**

The result will be computed and displayed in the cell. Now, copy this formula down to the two cells below the current cell:

Type	**mpd2**
Press	**Enter**

Figure 25 The Completed Table

	Jan-Mar	Apr-Jun	Jul-Sep	Oct-Dec	Total
Sales	1,523.25	1,459.50	1,752.75	1,543.00	6,278.50
Rentals	1,787.50	1,294.50	1,037.00	1,111.25	5,230.25
Total	3,310.75	2,754.00	2,789.75	2,654.25	11,508.75

=B4+C4+D4+E4   Cell F4 Doc 1 Pg 1 Ln 1.98" Pos 6.41"

Move to cell B4 and enter the + function to total the numbers above it:

Press	**Left Arrow** (4 times)
Press	**Down Arrow** (2 times)
Type	**m+**

Now, copy this function to the three columns to the right:

Type	**mpr3**
Press	**Enter**

Step 5: Recalculate All Formulas

Tell WordPerfect to recalculate the table so that the grand total in the lower right corner is updated:

Type	**mc**

Narrow the first column and widen the last column so that the grand total fits on one row:

Press	**Left Arrow**
Press	**Ctrl-Left Arrow**
Press	**End**
Press	**Ctrl-Right Arrow**

Return to the editing screen:

Press	**F7**

Your screen should look like Figure 25.

Step 6: Save the Document

Save the document in a file named TABLE.DOC:

Press	**Alt-=**
Type	**fs**
Type	**table.doc**
Press	**Enter**

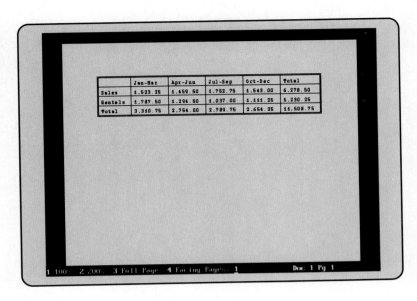

Figure 26 The Table on the View Document Screen

	Jan-Mar	Apr-Jun	Jul-Sep	Oct-Dec	Total
Sales	1,523.25	1,469.50	1,752.75	1,543.00	6,278.50
Rentals	1,787.50	1,294.50	1,037.00	1,111.25	5,230.25
Total	3,310.75	2,754.00	2,789.75	2,654.25	11,508.75

1 100%   2 200%   3 Full Page   4 Facing Pages: 1   Doc: 1 Pg 1

Step 7: View the Document

Examine your table on the View Document screen:

Press	**Alt-=**
Type	**fpv1**

Your screen should look like Figure 26. If you like, you can print the document. Return to the editing screen:

Press	**F7**

The Tables feature has many capabilities we have not explored. For example, you can insert and delete rows and columns, change the justification of data within cells, specify the number of digits to appear to the right of the decimal points, change the row height, reposition the table on the page, shade cells, and change the type of lines around the table.

Practice

1. Change the Jan-Mar Rentals figure to $1,344.25 and tell WordPerfect to recalculate the table. (Pull down the Layout menu, select Tables, select Edit, Math, and then select Calculate.)

2. Move to column B and right justify its contents by selecting the Format Column Justify Right option:

Type	**fLjr**

Repeat this procedure for columns C through F.

3. Move the cursor to cell F4, which contains the grand total. Boldface the number in this cell by executing the Format Cell Attributes Appearance Bold option:

Type	**fcaab**

Return to the editing screen and save the document. Examine your table on the View Document screen or print it out.

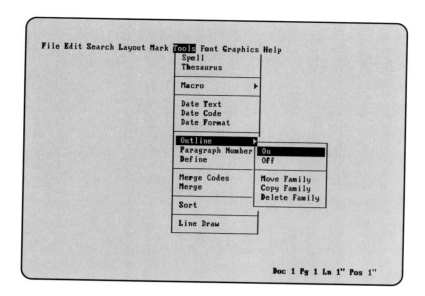

Figure 27 The Outline Submenu

Lesson 12: Outlining a Document

An outline is an invaluable tool for organizing topics before you type the text of a document. Many word processing programs include outlining facilities to help you plan your documents. WordPerfect's Outline feature is simple and easy to use. Let's illustrate this helpful feature by creating part of the outline of a quick reference guide to WordPerfect.

Step 1: Clear the Screen

Exit the current document to clear the editing screen:

Press   **Alt-=**
Type   **fxnn**

Step 2: Select the Outline Option

Pull down the Tools menu and select the Outline option:

Press   **Alt-=**
Type   **to**

WordPerfect will display the Outline submenu shown in Figure 27. Select the On option to turn on the Outline feature:

Type   **o**

WordPerfect will display the word *Outline* on the status line to indicate the Outline feature is turned on.

Step 3: Enter the Outline

The default outline style used by WordPerfect can be summarized as follows: I., A., 1., a., (1), (a), 1), and a). In other words, the first level headings are assigned Roman numerals, the second level headings are assigned capital letters, the third level headings are assigned Arabic numerals, and so on. Up to eight heading levels can be used. The first level headings begin at the left margin. You press the Tab key to move in to the next level heading. Headings are automatically numbered or lettered by WordPerfect. Follow these directions to enter part of the outline of our quick reference guide:

Press	**Enter**
Press	**Space Bar**
Type	**Function Key Commands**
Press	**Enter**
Press	**Tab**
Press	**Space Bar**
Type	**F1 Key Commands**
Press	**Enter**
Press	**Tab**
Press	**Space Bar**
Type	**Cancel (F1)**
Press	**Enter**
Press	**Space Bar**
Type	**Thesaurus (Alt-F1)**
Press	**Enter**
Press	**Space Bar**
Type	**Shell (Ctrl-F1)**
Press	**Enter**
Press	**Space Bar**
Type	**Setup (Shift-F1)**
Press	**Enter**
Press	**Shift-Tab**
Press	**Space Bar**
Type	**F2 Key Commands**
Press	**Enter**

Your screen should look like Figure 28. You can edit an outline and add or delete headings. You can press Shift-Tab to move back to a previous heading level after pressing Tab too many times.

Figure 28 The Outline

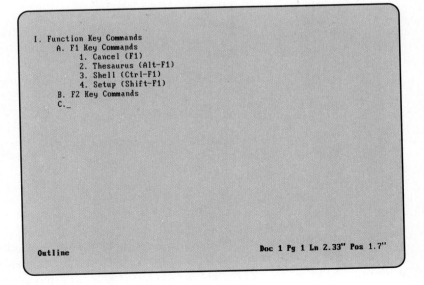

```
I. Function Key Commands
   A. F1 Key Commands
      1. Cancel (F1)
      2. Thesaurus (Alt-F1)
      3. Shell (Ctrl-F1)
      4. Setup (Shift-F1)
   B. F2 Key Commands
   C._



Outline                              Doc 1 Pg 1 Ln 2.33" Pos 1.7"
```

Step 4: Use the Family Options

Move to the second line of the outline, pull down the Tools menu, and select the Outline option:

Press	**Home** (2 times)
Press	**Up Arrow**
Press	**Down Arrow** (2 times)
Press	**Alt-=**
Type	**to**

Examine the three options at the bottom of the Outline submenu: Move Family, Copy Family, and Delete Family. An outline *family* is the line on which the cursor is located, plus any subordinate levels. For example, since the cursor is on the second line of your outline, the current outline family is

A. F1 Key Commands

    1. Cancel (F1)

    2. Thesaurus (Alt-F2)

    3. Shell (Ctrl-F1)

    4. Setup (Shift-F1)

The Move Family, Copy Family, and Delete Family options let you move, copy, and delete entire outline families at a time. These options are handy for editing an outline because they automatically update the outline numbers and letters. For example, try the Move Family option:

Type	**m**

WordPerfect will highlight the family as a block and display the prompt

Press **Arrows** to move family; **Enter** when done.

Move the family to level B:

Press	**Down Arrow**
Press	**Enter**

Now, move the family back up to level A:

Press	**Alt-=**
Type	**tom**
Press	**Up Arrow**
Press	**Enter**

The Copy Family and Delete Family work similarly.

Step 5: Turn Off the Outline Feature

When you have finished creating your outline, pull down the Tools menu, select Outline, and then select Off:

Press	**Alt-=**
Type	**tof**

WordPerfect will remove the word *Outline* from the status line, indicating that the Outline feature has been turned off.

Practice

1. Turn on the Outline feature again and enter headings that go below *F2 Key Commands*:

   ```
   Search Forward (F2)
   Replace (Alt-F2)
   Spell (Ctrl-F2)
   Search Backward (Shift-F2)
   ```

2. Turn off the Outline feature. Save the document in a file named OUTLINE.DOC.

Lesson 13: Generating a Table of Contents

Many long documents, such as reports and books, require a table of contents. The purpose of a table of contents is to list the chapter titles and other headings along with their page numbers. WordPerfect, like many advanced word processing packages, can automatically generate a table of contents. All you have to do is mark the headings to be included in the table of contents, define a numbering style for the table, and tell WordPerfect to generate the table. The headings will be copied from the existing text and the correct page numbers will be inserted by the program. Although it is rather short, let's generate a table of contents for the document NEWS.DOC.

Step 1: Retrieve NEWS.DOC

Clear the editing screen and retrieve the document NEWS.DOC:

Press	**Alt-=**
Type	**fxnn**
Press	**Alt-=**
Type	**fr**
Type	**news.doc**
Press	**Enter**

Step 2: Mark a Heading as a Block

Each title or heading from the document to be included in the table of contents must be marked as a block and then flagged as a table entry. Follow these steps to mark the New Outfitting Post heading as a block:

Press	**Down Arrow** (8 times)
Press	**Alt-=**
Type	**eb**
Press	**End**

Step 3: Mark the Block as a Table of Contents Entry

Now, flag the marked block as a table of contents entry. Pull down the Mark menu and select Table of Contents:

Press	**Alt-=**
Type	**mc**

WordPerfect will display the prompt

```
ToC Level:
```

Up to five levels of headings can be created in the table of contents. In this simple document, all of the table of contents entries will be at the first level.

Type	**1**
Press	**Enter**

Step 4: Mark the Remaining Headings

Repeat the two previous steps for the remaining headings in the document. First, mark each heading as a block. Then pull down the Mark menu, select Table of Contents, and enter 1 as the ToC level.

Step 5: Insert a New Page for the Table of Contents

The table of contents will come before the text of the document. So, move the cursor to the beginning of the document, insert a new page, and type a title for the table:

Press	**Home** (2 times)
Press	**Up Arrow**
Press	**Ctrl-Enter**
Press	**Up Arrow**
Type	`Paddle and Portage Newsletter`
Press	**Enter**
Type	`Table of Contents`
Press	**Enter** (2 times)

Step 6: Define the Table of Contents

After the headings have been marked and a page has been inserted for the table of contents, you must define a numbering style for the table of contents. Pull down the Mark menu, select Define, select Table of Contents, and then accept the default settings for defining the table of contents:

Press	**Alt-=**
Type	**mdc**
Press	**Enter**

When the table is generated, WordPerfect will use one level of headings and present page numbers flush right with dot leaders.

Step 7: Generate the Table

The final step is to tell WordPerfect to generate the table of contents. Pull down the Mark menu, select Generate, and then select Generate Tables, Indexes, Cross-References, etc.:

Press	**Alt-=**
Type	**mggy**

Move to the beginning of the document:

Press	**Home** (2 times)
Press	**Up Arrow**

Your screen should look like Figure 29.

Figure 29 The Generated Table of Contents

```
Paddle and Portage Newsletter
Table of Contents

New Outfitting Post. . . . . . . . . . . . . . . . . . . . .   2

Sport Shows. . . . . . . . . . . . . . . . . . . . . . . .   2

New Regulations. . . . . . . . . . . . . . . . . . . . . .   2

Equipment Improvements . . . . . . . . . . . . . . . . . .   2

Trail Food Improvements. . . . . . . . . . . . . . . . . .   2

Current Outfitting Rates . . . . . . . . . . . . . . . . .   3

1990 Fishing Records . . . . . . . . . . . . . . . . . . .   3

Trips. . . . . . . . . . . . . . . . . . . . . . . . . . .   3

A Final Note.... . . . . . . . . . . . . . . . . . . . . .   3

=========================================================================
                    Paddle and Portage Canoe Outfitters
C:\LESSONS\NEWS.DOC                            Doc 1 Pg 1 Ln 1" Pos 1"
```

Practice

1. Move the cursor to the New Outfitting Post heading in the document on page 2. Execute the Reveal Codes command and examine the codes that mark the heading as a table of contents entry.

2. You can remove a heading from the table of contents as follows. Delete the code [Mark:ToC,1] in front of the heading New Outfitting Post. Execute the Reveal Codes command again to return to the full editing screen. Move the cursor to the beginning of the document. Repeat Step 7 in this lesson to regenerate the table of contents. The new table of contents will omit the heading New Outfitting Post.

3. Mark the heading New Outfitting Post as a table of contents entry again. Then regenerate the table of contents.

Lesson 14: Generating an Index

An index lists important terms and their page numbers in alphabetical order at the end of a document. Generating an index with WordPerfect is similar to generating a table of contents. As an example, let's create an index containing a few terms for the document NEWS.DOC.

Step 1: Move the Cursor to a Term

If a term to be included in the index is a single word, you can simply move the cursor to the word. If the term is a phrase, it must be marked as a block. Move the cursor to the word *building* in the New Outfitting Post paragraph:

Press	**Alt-=**
Type	**sf**
Type	**building**
Press	**F2**
Press	**Left Arrow**

Step 2: Select the Index Option

To flag the word as an index entry, pull down the Mark menu and select the Index option:

Press   **Alt-=**
Type   **mi**

WordPerfect will display the prompt

Index heading: Building

At this point, you can enter a more descriptive index entry or simply press the Enter key twice to accept the entry as is and without a subheading:

Press   **Enter** (2 times)

Step 3: Mark the Remaining Index Entries

To create a comprehensive index, you would have to go through the entire document and mark all the significant terms. For the purpose of this example, however, just mark each of the following terms by moving the cursor to the term and repeating Step 2:

Shows

Regulations

Equipment

Food

Rates

Fishing

Trips

Step 4: Insert a New Page for the Index

The index will come after the text of the document. So, move the cursor to the end of the document, insert a new page, and type a title for the index:

Figure 30 The Generated Index

```
After having our best year ever, we want to thank all of you for
your friendship and patronage and wish you a happy and prosperous
New Year.  We look forward to seeing you this spring, summer, or
fall.

Becky and Bob Johnson, owners/operators
Paddle and Portage Canoe Outfitters

=================================================================
Newsletter Index

Building . . . . . . . . . . . . . . . . . . . . . . . . . . .2
Equipment. . . . . . . . . . . . . . . . . . . . . . . . . . .2
Fishing. . . . . . . . . . . . . . . . . . . . . . . . . . . .2
Food . . . . . . . . . . . . . . . . . . . . . . . . . . . . .3
Rates. . . . . . . . . . . . . . . . . . . . . . . . . . . . .2
Regulations. . . . . . . . . . . . . . . . . . . . . . . . . .3
Shows. . . . . . . . . . . . . . . . . . . . . . . . . . . . .2
Trips. . . . . . . . . . . . . . . . . . . . . . . . . . . . .3



C:\LESSONS\NEWS.DOC                           Doc 1 Pg 4 Ln 1.33" Pos 1"
```

Press	**Home** (2 times)
Press	**Down Arrow**
Press	**Ctrl-Enter**
Type	`Newsletter Index`
Press	**Enter** (2 times)

Step 5: Define the Index

After the entries have been marked and a page has been inserted for the index, you must define a numbering style. Pull down the Mark menu, select Define, select Index, and then accept the default settings for defining the index:

Press	**Alt-=**
Type	**mdi**
Press	**Enter** (2 times)

When the index is generated, WordPerfect will list the page numbers flush right with dot leaders.

Step 6: Generate the Index

The final step is to tell WordPerfect to generate the index. Pull down the Mark menu, select Generate, and then select Generate Tables, Indexes, Cross-References, etc.:

Press	**Alt-=**
Type	**mggy**

Your screen should look like Figure 30.

Practice

1. Mark a few more terms as index entries. Try some phrases instead of single words. Remember that you must mark a phrase as a block before you can mark it as an index entry. Also, try entering a slightly different entry when WordPerfect prompts you for the index heading.

2. Move the cursor to a term you have marked as an index entry. Execute the Reveal Codes command and examine the code that designates a term as an index entry. You can delete the index code to unmark the term as an index entry. Return to the full editing screen.

3. Regenerate the index. Save the document to preserve the changes you have made.

Lesson 15: Adding Graphics

With WordPerfect you can incorporate horizontal and vertical lines, boxes, and pictures in documents. These features can greatly improve the appearance of documents such as newsletters, reports, ads, and tutorials. This lesson will introduce some of WordPerfect's graphics capabilities. In order to use them, however, you will need a computer with a graphics display or a dot-matrix or laser printer.

Step 1: Insert a Horizontal Line

The simplest application of graphics in a document is to add horizontal or vertical lines. Even basic elements such as lines can improve the appearance of a document. Horizontal lines are often used to separate sections of text. Let's insert

Figure 31 The Horizontal Line

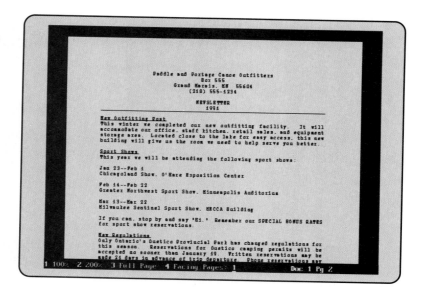

a horizontal line between the heading and first paragraph of the newsletter. First, move the cursor to the proper position and insert a blank line:

Press	**Home** (2 times)
Press	**Up Arrow**
Press	**Page Down**
Press	**Down Arrow** (7 times)
Press	**Enter**
Press	**Up Arrow**

The cursor is now where you want the horizontal line to go. Pull down the Graphics menu, select Line, and then select Create Horizontal:

Press	**Alt-=**
Type	**gLh**

WordPerfect will present the Horizontal Line menu, which lets you specify the position, length, width, and gray shading of the line. The default settings are for a thin black line extending from the left margin to the right margin. Accept these settings and return to the editing screen:

Press	**Enter**

The line will be inserted, but you can see it only if you print the document or use the View Document feature.

Press	**Alt-=**
Type	**fpv1**

Your screen should look like Figure 31. When you have finished examining your work, return to the editing screen.

Press	**F7**

Step 2: Insert a Vertical Line

Vertical lines are often used to separate columns of text. Let's insert a vertical line between the columns of the Current Outfitting Rates table. Move the cursor between the columns in the first line of the table:

Figure 32 The Vertical Line

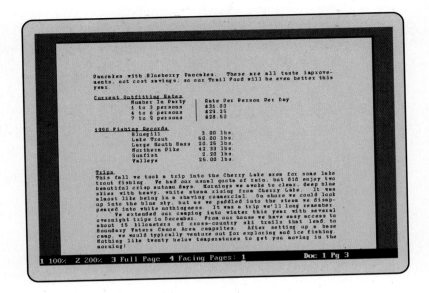

Figure 32 The Vertical Line

Press	**Alt-=**
Type	**sf**
Type	**Number In Party**
Press	**F2**

Look in the status line. The cursor is 3.5 inches from the left edge of the paper. The next column begins 4 inches from the left edge of the paper. So, 3.75 inches from the left edge would be a good place to put the vertical line. Since the table is only four lines long and six lines equals an inch, the line should be about 0.67 inches long. Pull down the Graphics menu, select Line, and then select Create Vertical:

Press	**Alt-=**
Type	**gLv**

WordPerfect will present the Vertical Line menu on the screen. Follow these directions to specify a vertical line 0.67 inches long positioned 3.75 inches from the left edge of the paper:

Type	**h**
Type	**s**
Type	**3.75**
Press	**Enter**
Type	**v**
Type	**s**
Press	**Enter**
Type	**L**
Type	**0.67**
Press	**Enter** (2 times)

To see the vertical line you have created, use the View Document feature:

Press	**Alt-=**
Type	**fpv1**

Your screen should look like Figure 32. When you have finished examining your work, return to the editing screen:

Press	**F7**

Step 3: Insert a Box Around Text

Text is often enclosed in a box to draw the reader's eye. As an example, let's enclose the letterhead of the newsletter in a box. First, move the cursor to the first line of the letterhead and insert a blank line:

Press	**Home** (2 times)
Press	**Up Arrow**
Press	**Page Down**
Press	**Enter**

Insert another blank line after the letterhead and move back up to the top of the page:

Press	**Down Arrow** (4 times)
Press	**Enter**
Press	**Grey Minus**

Pull down the Graphics menu, select Text Box, and then select Options:

Press	**Alt-=**
Type	**gbo**

WordPerfect will display a menu of options for designing a text box. By default, a text box has no sides. Follow these directions to add thick lines to the sides of the box:

Type	**b**
Type	**t**
Type	**t**
Press	**F7** (3 times)

Pull down the Graphics menu again, select Text Box, and then select Create:

Press	**Alt-=**
Type	**gbc**

WordPerfect will display the Text Box Definition menu. Specify the position and size of the box as follows:

Type	**h**
Type	**c**
Type	**s**
Type	**b**
Type	**4**
Press	**Enter**
Type	**1**
Press	**Enter**
Type	**w**
Type	**n**
Press	**F7**

WordPerfect will return to the editing screen, but you will not see the box. You must print the document or use the View Document feature to see the box you have created:

Press	**Alt-=**
Type	**fpv1**

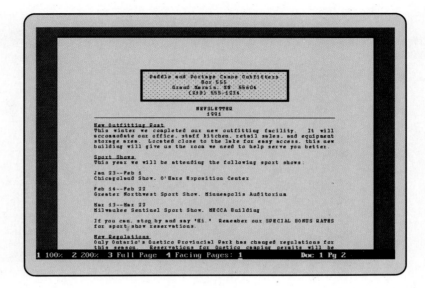

Figure 33 The Text Box

Figure 33 shows the result. Note that the inside of the box is lightly shaded, due to the default Grey Shading setting of 10%. When you have finished examining your work, return to the editing screen:

Press	**F7**

Step 4: Insert a Picture

You cannot create pictures with WordPerfect, but you can import images created with many painting, drawing, and graphing packages. In fact, WordPerfect comes with a number of sample graphics files on the diskette labeled Graphics. These files are identified by the extension *WPG*, which stands for WordPerfect Graphics format. This lesson assumes that you have at least one of these WPG files on your hard disk in the WP51 subdirectory. As an example, let's insert a picture on a new page before the index. The graphics file we will use is TROPHY.WPG, which contains a drawing of a trophy. If you like, you can substitute another WPG file or a picture file from some other program, such as PC Paintbrush, Microsoft Windows Paint, or Lotus 1-2-3. Use the List Files command to examine your disk to find the name of a graphics file if you are not going to use TRO-PHY.WPG in the WP51 subdirectory.

Move the cursor to the end of the page before the index and insert a new page:

Press	**Home** (2 times)
Press	**Down Arrow**
Press	**Page Up**
Press	**Ctrl-Home**
Press	**Down Arrow**
Press	**Ctrl-Enter**

Pull down the Graphics menu, select Figure, and then select Create:

Press	**Alt-=**
Type	**gfc**

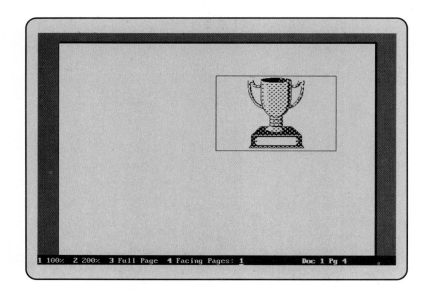

**Figure 34 The Picture
from TROPHY.WPG**

WordPerfect will display the Figure Definition screen. All of the default settings are fine for our example, but you must specify the name of the graphics file.

Type	**f**
Type	**\wp51\trophy.wpg**
Press	**Enter**
Press	**F7**

If you do not have TROPHY.WPG in your WP51 subdirectory, type the path and name of a graphics file you do have. When WordPerfect returns to the editing screen, you will not see the picture. You must print the document or use the View Document feature to see the picture you have inserted.

Press	**Alt-=**
Type	**fpv1**

Your screen should look like Figure 34. If you print the document, the picture will appear much nicer because the printer has a higher resolution than the screen. When you have finished examining your work, return to the editing screen:

Press	**F7**

WordPerfect has many other options for inserting graphics into your documents. You can resize pictures, specify their exact position on the page, and wrap text around them. You can also automatically number figures and create captions for them.

Practice

1. Insert a horizontal line in the newsletter after the line *Becky and Bob Johnson.*

2. Insert a vertical line in the newsletter separating the columns of the Fishing Records table.

3. Use the List Files command to see the names of any WPG files you may have in your WP51 subdirectory. Choose a name and insert this picture file into

the newsletter. Print the document or examine it with the View Document feature.

4. Use the Reveal Codes command to examine the document. Graphic elements such as lines, boxes, and pictures can be removed by deleting their codes. Delete the code for the picture you just inserted and examine the newsletter with the View Document feature.

Lesson 16: Using Macros

A *macro* is a sequence of keystrokes that can be recorded, stored, and replayed. The keystrokes may include function keys, menu selections, and ordinary text. Macros are handy for automating frequent actions that require many keystrokes. For instance, suppose you must often type the phrase *Paddle and Portage Canoe Outfitters* in a document. WordPerfect lets you assign this entire phrase to an abbreviated command, such as Alt-P. Once you define the macro, you can simply press Alt-P instead of typing the phrase. Instead of having to type 35 characters, you need only press two keys at the same time. The phrase will be automatically inserted at the current cursor location. You can use the macro as often as you like. As an example, let's create such a macro.

Step 1: Move the Cursor

When you create a macro, the keys you press will be executed. So, you must first move the cursor to the place where you want to perform the action the first time. In this case, you can move the cursor to the end of the document:

Press	**Home** (2 times)
Press	**Down Arrow**

Step 2: Name the Macro

Before you can use a macro, you must name it and then record it. Pull down the Tools menu, select Macro, and then select Define:

Press	**Alt-=**
Type	**tad**

Another way to do this is to press Ctrl-F10. WordPerfect will display the prompt:

    Define Macro:

This is where you choose a name for the macro. You can enter a name up to eight characters long, press Enter to have WordPerfect choose a name for you, or hold down the Alternate key and type any letter from A to Z. The last method is the easiest to use, but you get only a single letter with which to name your macro. Name your macro Alt-P, for Paddle and Portage:

Press	**Alt-P**

Step 3: Describe the Macro

WordPerfect will display the prompt

    Description:

Now you can enter an optional explanation of the function of your macro. A description is helpful for complex macros, but our simple example hardly requires a comment. Leave the description blank:

Press	**Enter**

Step 4: Record the Macro

The macro recorder will be turned on and WordPerfect will display a blinking *Macro Def* message on the status line. Now you press the keys that will make up the macro—the keystrokes that will be activated when you press Alt-P later. To specify our simple macro, type the phrase and then execute the Macro Define command again:

Type	`Paddle and Portage Canoe Outfitters`
Press	**Alt-=**
Type	**tad**

Step 5: Use the Macro

The macro can now be used anywhere in the document. To see how it works, move down a line and execute the macro:

Press	**Enter**
Press	**Alt-P**

The phrase *Paddle and Portage Canoe Outfitters* will be inserted at the current cursor location. Try it again:

Press	**Enter**
Press	**Alt-P**

This simple macro merely inserts text, but it can save you a lot of time if you must type the same phrase over and over again. Remember that macros can record any series of keys, including commands and menu selections. They can be a powerful tool for repeating complex sequences of commands.

Practice

1. Create a macro named Alt-N to type your name. Try the macro a number of times.

2. Create a macro named Alt-B to move the cursor to the beginning of the document and then execute the List Files command on the current directory. Exit the List Files menu, move the cursor to the end of the document, and try the macro you have created.

Lesson 17: Creating Form Letters

WordPerfect's Merge feature allows you to print form letters or other personalized text by combining a document with a data file. This feature, sometimes called **mail-merge**, is very useful to businesses and organizations that send letters or bills to various individuals. As an example, let's modify the document HOLMES.DOC, which you created in the previous chapter, so that it can be used to print personalized form letters to a number of different customers.

Step 1: Create the Address File

Form letters are generated by combining names and addresses from a data file with a generic letter. The letter contains codes that indicate where the names and addresses are to go. The data file is sometimes called the **secondary merge file** or **address file**. Let's create the address file first. Execute the Exit command and save the current file to clear the screen:

Press	**Alt-=**
Type	**fxy**
Press	**Enter**
Type	**y**
Type	**n**

Suppose form letters are to be sent to four customers. The address file will consist of one record for each customer. Each record consists of five fields: the name, street address, city, state, and ZIP code. Each field is typed on its own line and is terminated by pressing F9, which inserts an {END FIELD} merge code and a hard return. A record is terminated by pulling down the Tools menu, selecting Merge Codes, and selecting End Record, which inserts an {END REC-ORD} merge code and a hard page break. Follow these directions to enter the four customer records:

Type	**Oscar Griffith**
Press	**F9**
Type	**805 Florida**
Press	**F9**
Type	**Urbana**
Press	**F9**
Type	**IL**
Press	**F9**
Type	**61801**
Press	**F9**
Press	**Alt-=**
Type	**tre**
Type	**George Carver**
Press	**F9**
Type	**906 Busey**
Press	**F9**
Type	**Brainerd**
Press	**F9**
Type	**MN**
Press	**F9**
Type	**56401**
Press	**F9**
Press	**Alt-=**
Type	**tre**
Type	**David Banks**
Press	**F9**
Type	**604 Armory**
Press	**F9**
Type	**Green Bay**
Press	**F9**

Figure 35 The Address File

```
{END RECORD}
============================================================================
George Carver{END FIELD}
906 Busey{END FIELD}
Brainerd{END FIELD}
MN{END FIELD}
56401{END FIELD}
{END RECORD}
============================================================================
David Banks{END FIELD}
604 Armory{END FIELD}
Green Bay{END FIELD}
WI{END FIELD}
54305{END FIELD}
{END RECORD}
============================================================================
Susan Young{END FIELD}
1104 Grand{END FIELD}
Anchorage{END FIELD}
AK{END FIELD}
99502{END FIELD}
{END RECORD}
============================================================================

Field: 1                                        Doc 1 Pg 5 Ln 1" Pos 1"
```

Type	**WI**
Press	**F9**
Type	**54305**
Press	**F9**
Press	**Alt-=**
Type	**tre**
Type	**Susan Young**
Press	**F9**
Type	**1104 Grand**
Press	**F9**
Type	**Anchorage**
Press	**F9**
Type	**AK**
Press	**F9**
Type	**99502**
Press	**F9**
Press	**Alt-=**
Type	**tre**

At this point, your screen should look like Figure 35. Save the document in a file named CUSTOMER:

Press	**Alt-=**
Type	**fs**
Type	**customer**
Press	**Enter**

Step 2: Create the Primary File

The **primary file** is the text of the form letter containing special merge codes. In this case, you can simply modify the existing document HOLMES.DOC to create the primary file. Clear the screen and retrieve HOLMES.DOC:

Press	**Alt-=**
Type	**fxnn**

Press	**Alt-=**
Type	**fr**
Type	**holmes.doc**
Press	**Enter**

Move the cursor to the line that contains *Mr. Richard Holmes* and delete to the end of the line:

Press	**Down Arrow** (7 times)
Press	**Ctrl-End**

Instead of an explicit name, you will insert a merge code that stands for the first field of the data file, which contains the customer's name. Pull down the Tools menu, select Merge Codes, select Field, and then enter the number of the field to be merged:

Press	**Alt-=**
Type	**trf1**
Press	**Enter**

When the letter is merged with the address file, the {FIELD} 1~ merge codes will be replaced with customer names. Now, follow these directions to delete the remaining address items and replace them with the appropriate merge codes:

Press	**Home**
Press	**Left Arrow**
Press	**Down Arrow**
Press	**Ctrl-End**
Press	**Alt-=**
Type	**trf2**
Press	**Enter**
Press	**Home**
Press	**Left Arrow**
Press	**Down Arrow**
Press	**Ctrl-End**
Press	**Alt-=**
Type	**trf3**
Press	**Enter**
Type	**,**
Press	**Space Bar**
Press	**Alt-=**
Type	**trf4**
Press	**Enter**
Press	**Space Bar** (2 times)
Press	**Alt-=**
Type	**trf5**
Press	**Enter**
Press	**Home**
Press	**Left Arrow**
Press	**Down Arrow** (2 times)
Press	**Right Arrow** (5 times)
Press	**Ctrl-End**
Press	**Alt-=**
Type	**trf1**
Press	**Enter**
Type	**:**

Figure 36 The Primary File

```
                                    Paddle and Portage Canoe Outfitters
                                                    Box 555
                                          Grand Marais, MN  55604
                                              (218) 555-1234

                                              March 31, 1990

{FIELD}1~
{FIELD}2~
{FIELD}3~, {FIELD}4~  {FIELD}5~

Dear {FIELD}1~:_

Here is our sport show schedule for 1991.  We hope to see you soon!

Jan 23--Feb 1
Chicagoland Show, O'Hare Exposition Center

Feb 14--Feb 22
Greater Northwest Sport Show, Minneapolis Auditorium

Mar 13--Mar 22
Milwaukee Sentinel Sport Show, MECCA Building

C:\LESSONS\HOLMES.DOC                   Doc 1 Pg 1 Ln 2.83" Pos 1.8"
```

When you have finished, your screen should look like Figure 36. Save the document in a file named LETTER.DOC:

Press	**Alt-=**
Type	**fs**
Type	**letter.doc**
Press	**Enter**

Step 3: Merge the Primary File and Address File

The address file and primary file are now complete. When they are merged, WordPerfect will substitute items from the address file for the {FIELD}1~ through {FIELD}5~ merge codes in the letter. A new document will be created containing four separate letters, each one addressed to a different customer. Clear the screen, pull down the Tools menu, select Merge, and enter the names of the primary and secondary merge files:

Press	**Alt-=**
Type	**fxnn**
Press	**Alt-=**
Type	**tm**
Type	**letter.doc**
Press	**Enter**
Type	**customer**
Press	**Enter**

Move to the beginning of the document and then move the cursor down a few lines:

Press	**Home** (2 times)
Press	**Up Arrow**
Press	**Down Arrow** (7 times)

Figure 37 A Generated Form Letter

```
                         Paddle and Portage Canoe Outfitters
                                       Box 555
                               Grand Marais, MN  55604
                                  (218) 555-1234

                                  March 31, 1990


     Oscar Griffith
     805 Florida
     Urbana, IL  61801

     Dear Oscar Griffith:

     Here is our sport show schedule for 1991.  We hope to see you soon!

     Jan 23--Feb 1
     Chicagoland Show, O'Hare Exposition Center

     Feb 14--Feb 22
     Greater Northwest Sport Show, Minneapolis Auditorium

     Mar 13--Mar 22
     Milwaukee Sentinel Sport Show, MECCA Building

                                  Doc 1 Pg 1 Ln 2.17" Pos 1"
```

Your screen should look like Figure 37. Examine the other three letters:

Press	**Page Down**
Press	**Page Down**
Press	**Page Down**

You could now save the new document or print it to produce the four separate letters.

Practice

1. Clear the screen without saving the document containing the four form letters. Retrieve the CUSTOMER file and add another record:

    Richard Holmes
    444 Adams Street
    Green Bay
    WI
    54301

    Save the updated CUSTOMER file and clear the screen. Note that you can add any number of records to the address file.

2. Merge LETTER.DOC with the new CUSTOMER file to create five form letters.

3. Print the full document to output the five form letters.

Lesson 18: Using Styles

A **style** is a collection of formatting codes and, possibly, text that can be created, saved, and inserted into documents to automate formatting and provide a consistent appearance to documents. Styles are often used for book chapters, newsletters, and other long documents whose format settings are used over and over again. For example, three styles might be used for a book. One style could include the margin and tab stop settings and be inserted at the beginning of each chapter. Another style could contain formatting codes for the chapter headings. A third style could include formatting codes for the multiple choice questions that appear at the end of each chapter. As an example, let's create a style that sets margins, justification, and tab stops.

Step 1: Clear the Screen

Clear your current editing screen:

Press	**Alt-=**
Type	**fxnn**

Step 2: Name the Style

Pull down the Layout menu, select Styles, select Create, select Name, and then enter a name for the style:

Press	**Alt-=**
Type	**Lscn**
Type	**Settings**
Press	**Enter**

Step 3: Select the Style Type

Two types of styles are available, paired and open. A **paired style** type has a beginning and ending code. A style to underline text, for example, would be a paired style because a code is required before and after the underlined text. An **open style** has just a beginning code and is often used to set formats for an entire document. A style to set margins, justification, and tab stops would be an open style. Select Open as the type of the style:

Type	**to**

Step 4: Describe the Style

The style description is text that explains the purpose of the style. This description appears in the Styles menu to help you remember what the style does. Enter a description for the style:

Type	**d**
Type	**Margins, justification, and tab stop settings**
Press	**Enter**

Step 5: Enter the Codes

A style can contain WordPerfect codes and text. To include codes in a style, you select the Codes option and then execute the commands to create those codes. Follow these directions to enter the codes to set margins, justification, and tab stops:

Type	**c**
Press	**Shift-F8**
Type	**L**
Type	**m**

Figure 38 The Styles Menu

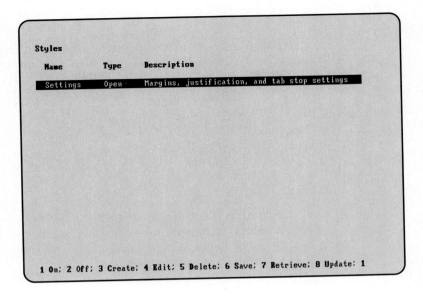

Styles		
Name	**Type**	**Description**
Settings	Open	Margins, justification, and tab stop settings

1 On; 2 Off; 3 Create; 4 Edit; 5 Delete; 6 Save; 7 Retrieve; 8 Update: 1

Type	**1.25**
Press	**Enter**
Type	**1.25**
Press	**Enter**
Type	**j**
Type	**L**
Type	**t**
Press	**Home** (2 times)
Press	**Left Arrow**
Press	**Ctrl-End**
Type	**L**
Type	**0,1**
Press	**Enter**
Press	**F7** (4 times)

WordPerfect will return to the Styles menu, shown in Figure 38. The Settings style that you have created will set the left and right margins to 1.25 inches, set justification to Left, and set tab stops at 1-inch intervals beginning at the left edge of the page.

Step 6: Save the Style

By default, a style is saved with the document in which it was created. You can, however, save the styles you create separately and use them in any document. Select the Save option and then enter a file name to hold your styles:

Type	**s**
Type	**styles**
Press	**Enter**

The style Settings is now saved in a file named STYLES. Return to the editing screen:

Press	**F7**

Step 7: Use the Style

After you have created and saved a style, you can use it in any document. Move the cursor to the place where the style is to be inserted, pull down the Layout menu, select Styles, and retrieve the style file:

Press	**Home** (2 times)
Press	**Up Arrow**
Press	**Alt-=**
Type	**Lsr**
Type	**styles**
Press	**Enter**
Type	**y**

WordPerfect will present the Styles menu. In this case, only one style is listed. You can, however, create and save a number of different styles. Then you would use Up Arrow or Down Arrow to highlight the style you want to use. When the style is highlighted, select the On option:

Type	**o**

The Settings style is now inserted at the beginning of the current document. You don't have to set the margins, justification, and tab stops individually. Any time you need these particular format settings, you can simply retrieve the STYLES file and select the Settings style.

Practice

1. Execute the Reveal Codes command to confirm that the Settings style has indeed been inserted. When you have finished, return to the full editing screen.

2. Pull down the Layout menu and select the Line option to confirm that the margins, justification, and tab stops have indeed been set. When you have finished, return to the editing screen.

Lesson 19: Using the Equation Editor

WordPerfect 5.1 includes a powerful new feature called the Equation Editor that lets you create, display, and print mathematical and scientific expressions. The program provides more than 300 commonly-used mathematical symbols and commands. Let's use this feature to include a mathematical expression in a document.

Note: The Equation Editor requires a graphics display to show expressions on the screen. If your computer cannot display graphics, however, you can still print equations on a dot-matrix, ink-jet, or laser printer. This lesson assumes you have a computer that can display graphics.

Step 1: Clear the Screen

Clear your current editing screen:

Press	**Alt-=**
Type	**fxnn**

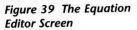

Figure 39 The Equation Editor Screen

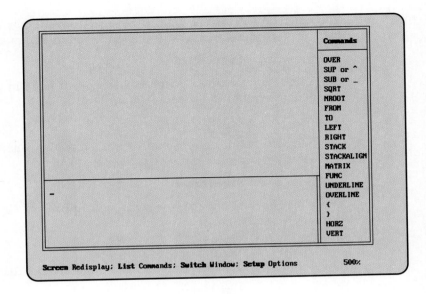

Step 2: Enter Normal Text

As an example, let's create a document that includes the quadratic formula, an algebraic expression used to solve equations that involve one or more squared quantities. Start out by typing an introductory sentence in normal text:

Type	**The quadratic formula gives the solutions to any quadratic equation:**
Press	**Enter** (3 times)

Step 3: Activate the Equation Editor

Pull down the Graphics menu, select Equation, select Create, and then select Edit:

Press	**Alt-=**
Type	**gece**

WordPerfect will display the Equation Editor screen, which has three main parts: the Display window on top, the Editing window on the bottom, and the Equation Palette on the right side (see Figure 39).

Step 4: Examine the Equation Palette

To create an equation, you type characters from the keyboard or select symbols and commands from the Equation Palette. Right now, you are in the Editing window. You can switch to the Equation Palette by pressing the List key (F5):

Press	**F5**

Now you can use the Down Arrow or Up Arrow key to highlight a command or symbol in the current menu and read the brief description that appears in the lower left corner of the screen:

Press	**Down Arrow** (several times)
Press	**Up Arrow** (several times)

The Equation Palette has eight menus. The current menu is Commands, which lists actions to help you set up your expressions. Examine the other menus:

Press   **Page Down**

The Large menu contains symbols that appear large in equations, such as the summation symbol and the integral symbol.

Press   **Page Down**

The Symbols menu contains many common mathematical symbols, such as the division sign, not equal sign, and therefore symbol.

Press   **Page Down**

The Greek menu contains lowercase and uppercase Greek letters, which are commonly used in math and science.

Press   **Page Down**

The Arrows menu contains arrows and other symbols used in expressions.

Press   **Page Down**

The Sets menu contains symbols used in set notation, such as member and not a member.

Press   **Page Down**

The Other menu lists a few other symbols.

Press   **Page Down**

The Functions menu lists trigonometric and other mathematical functions.

Press   **Page Down**

To select an item from the Equation Palette and enter it into the Editing window, you highlight the item you want and press the Enter key. Let's not select anything right now. To switch from the Equation Palette to the Editing window without entering anything, simply press the Exit key (F7) or Escape.

Press   **F7**

Step 5: Type the Equation

If you know the Equation Palette commands and symbols you need, you can type your equation directly into the Editing window without picking items from the Equation Palette. Type this expression to create the quadratic formula:

Type   `x = {-b plusminus sqrt {b^2-4ac}} over {2a}`

Step 6: Display the Equation

The Display window lets you see an enlarged view of how your equation will look when it is printed. Press the Screen key (Ctrl-F3 or F9) to display the equation:

Press   **Ctrl-F3**

Your screen should look like Figure 40.

Figure 40 The Completed Quadratic Formula

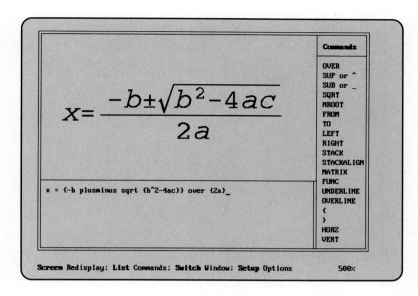

Step 7: Return to the Normal Editing Screen

When you are satisfied that your equation is correct, you can leave the Equation Editor and return to the normal editing screen.

Press   **F7** (2 times)

Step 8: View or Print the Document

The equation will not appear on the normal editing screen. You will see only an Equation box because the equation is a graphic element. To see the final result, use the View Document feature or print the document:

Press   **Alt-=**
Type   **fpv**

When you have finished examining the View Document screen, return to the editing screen:

Press   **F7**

Step 9: Save the Document

Save your document in a file named EQUATION.DOC:

Press   **Alt-=**
Type   **fs**
Type   **equation.doc**
Press   **Enter**

Practice Enter the following expression into the Equation Editor to create an equation that represents the definition of the derivative:

f'(x) = lim from h to 0 {f(x+h)-f(x)} over h

View and print your equation. Save your document.

Figure 41 The Setup Submenu

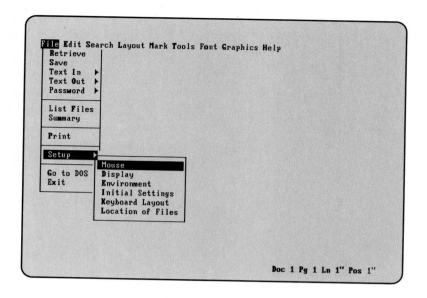

```
File Edit Search Layout Mark Tools Font Graphics Help
  Retrieve
  Save
  Text In    ▶
  Text Out   ▶
  Password   ▶

  List Files
  Summary

  Print

  Setup      ▶
                 Mouse
  Go to DOS      Display
  Exit           Environment
                 Initial Settings
                 Keyboard Layout
                 Location of Files




                                          Doc 1 Pg 1 Ln 1" Pos 1"
```

Lesson 20: Customizing WordPerfect

When you start WordPerfect, you can begin typing immediately. The program has already been set up for speed and efficiency. The default settings in effect are adequate for most users. You can, however, tailor WordPerfect to your specific needs by using the Setup option from the File menu to change various settings. These changes will then remain in effect each time you start WordPerfect. Let's examine the settings you can change with the Setup option.

Step 1: Clear the Screen

Clear your current editing screen:

>Press   **Alt-=**
>Type   **fxnn**

Step 2: Examine the Setup Submenu

To examine or change various WordPerfect options, pull down the File menu and select Setup:

>Press   **Alt-=**
>Type   **ft**

The program will display the Setup submenu, shown in Figure 41.

Step 3: Examine the Mouse Setup Screen

Select the Mouse option:

>Type   **m**

WordPerfect will display the Mouse Setup screen, which lets you specify how your mouse will operate. Return to the Setup submenu:

Press   **F7**
Press   **Alt-=**
Type   **f t**

Step 4: Examine the Display Setup Screen

Select the Display option:

Type   **d**

WordPerfect will present the Display Setup screen, which lets you specify what kind of display you have, what colors you want to use, how you want the menus displayed, and how you want the View Document and editing screens displayed. Return to the Setup submenu:

Press   **F7**
Press   **Alt-=**
Type   **f t**

Step 5: Examine the Environment Setup Screen

Select the Environment option:

Type   **e**

WordPerfect will display the Environment Setup screen, which lets you specify whether the program should automatically save your document to the disk at timed intervals, when it should beep, the rate at which a key will repeat when it is held down, whether the program should automatically create a document summary, whether the program should format documents for printing when they are saved, the default hyphenation dictionary and prompt, and the units of measure to use (inches, centimeters, points, and so on). Return to the Setup submenu:

Press   **F7**
Press   **Alt-=**
Type   **f t**

Step 6: Examine the Initial Settings Setup Screen

Select the Initial Settings option:

Type   **i**

WordPerfect will display the Initial Settings Setup screen, which lets you specify the default date format, the equation options, whether to format retrieved documents for the default printer, any initial codes to appear at the beginning of every document, the default repeat value, the table of authorities options, and the default print options. Return to the Setup submenu:

Press   **F7**
Press   **Alt-=**
Type   **f t**

Step 7: Examine the Keyboard Layout Setup Screen

Select the Keyboard Layout option:

    Type   **k**

WordPerfect will display the Keyboard Layout Setup screen, which lets you remap your keyboard. In other words, it lets you assign WordPerfect features, characters, and macros to almost any key on the keyboard. This is sometimes done to make WordPerfect mimic another word processing program. Return to the Setup submenu:

    Press   **F7**
    Press   **Alt-=**
    Type   **f t**

Step 8: Examine the Location of Files Setup Screen

Select the Location of Files option:

    Type   **L**

WordPerfect will display the Location of Files Setup screen, which lets you specify default disk directories for backup files; keyboard and macro files; thesaurus, spelling checker, and hyphenation dictionary files; printer files; style files; graphic files; and document files.

Step 9: Exit the Program

This concludes the WordPerfect lessons. Exit the program and return to DOS:

    Press   **F7**
    Press   **Alt-=**
    Type   **fxny**

Practice   Use the Help facility to read more about the various Setup command options.

Summary

- *Using the Print menu.* Pull down the File menu, select Print, and then select Full Document, Page, Document on Disk, Control Printer, Multiple Pages, View Document, Initialize Printer, Select Printer, Binding Offset, Number of Copies, Multiple Copies Generated By, Graphics Quality, or Text Quality.

- *Hyphenating words.* Pull down the Layout menu, select Line, select Hyphenation, and then select Yes.

- *Avoiding orphans and widows.* Pull down the Layout menu, select Line, select Widow/Orphan Protection, and then select Yes.

- *Avoiding splitting paragraphs between pages.* Pull down the Layout menu, select Other, and then select Conditional End of Page.

- *Using the Font menu*. Pull down the Font menu and then select Base Font, Normal, Appearance, Superscript, Subscript, Fine, Small, Large, Very Large, Extra Large, Print Color, or Characters.

- *Adding headers and footers*. Pull down the Layout menu, select Page, and then select Headers or Footers.

- *Creating text columns*. Pull down the Layout menu, select Columns, select Define, and specify the column settings. Then pull down the Layout menu, select Columns, select On, and type the text. Press Ctrl-Home followed by an arrow key to move to another column.

- *Adding footnotes and endnotes*. Pull down the Layout menu, select Footnote or Endnote, select Create, and type the note.

- *Sorting text*. Mark the lines to be sorted as a block, pull down the Tools menu, select Sort, specify the keys, specify the sort order, and select Perform Action.

- *Using the Math feature*. Set up tab stops for columns of numbers, pull down the Layout menu, select Math, select On, enter the data, enter the functions ($+$, $=$, and $*$), pull down the Layout menu, select Math, and then select Calculate.

- *Using the Tables feature*. Pull down the Layout menu, select Tables, select Create, and enter the number of rows and columns. Enter data on the normal editing screen and formulas on the Table Edit screen.

- *Outlining a document*. Pull down the Tools menu, select Outline, and enter the headings. Press Tab to move in to the next level heading and Shift-Tab to move out to the previous level heading.

- *Generating a table of contents*. Mark each heading as a block, pull down the Mark menu, select Table of Contents, and enter the heading level. Pull down the Mark menu, select Define, and select Table of Contents. Pull down the Mark menu, select Generate, and then select Generate Tables.

- *Generating an index*. Move the cursor to each word to be in the index, pull down the Mark menu, and select Index. Pull down the Mark menu, select Define, and select Index. Pull down the Mark menu, select Generate, and then select Generate Tables.

- *Adding graphics*. Pull down the Graphics menu, and then select Line, Text Box, or Figure.

- *Using macros*. Pull down the Tools menu, select Macro, select Define, name the macro, describe the macro, and record the macro. Use the macro by pressing Alternate along with its key.

- *Creating form letters*. Create the address file, separating fields by pressing F9 and terminating records by pulling down the Tools menu, selecting Merge Codes, and selecting End Record. Create the primary file, inserting merge codes by pulling down the Tools menu, selecting Merge Codes, selecting Field, and then entering the number of the field. Pull down the Tools menu, select Merge, and then enter the names of the primary and address files to generate the form letters.

- *Using styles*. Pull down the Layout menu, select Styles, select Create, specify the name, type, description, and codes of the style, and then save the style. Pull down the Layout menu, select Styles, select Retrieve, enter the file name, highlight the style name, and select On.

- *Using the Equation Editor.* Pull down the Graphics menu, select Equation, select Create, select Edit, type the expression or choose items from the Equation Palette, and press Ctrl-F3 to display the equation.

- *Customizing WordPerfect.* Pull down the File menu, select Setup, and then select Mouse, Display, Environment, Initial Settings, Keyboard Layout, or Location of Files.

Key Terms

As an extra review of this chapter, try defining the following terms.

endnote
field
footer
footnote
greeking
header
hyphenation
key
macro
mail-merge
newspaper-style columns
open style
orphan
paired style
parallel columns
point
primary file
print queue
record
secondary merge file (address file)
sorting
style
widow

Multiple Choice

Choose the best selection to complete each statement.

1. WordPerfect lets you specify several documents to be printed by using a
   - (a) display adapter.
   - (b) function key.
   - (c) print queue.
   - (d) View Document feature.

2. Which feature do you use to see how your document will look when it is printed?
   - (a) Setup
   - (b) Reveal Codes
   - (c) Screen
   - (d) View Document

3. Which feature can make justified text more attractive by reducing large gaps between words?
   - (a) hyphenation
   - (b) indentation
   - (c) mail-merge
   - (d) word wrap

4. What term is used to describe the last line of a paragraph that appears at the top of a page?

   (a) orphan
   (b) widow
   (c) header
   (d) footer

5. Which feature is handy for keeping titles or headings together with their first paragraphs?

   (a) Merge
   (b) Block
   (c) Mark Text
   (d) Conditional End of Page

6. Which menu do you use to change the size of characters?

   (a) File
   (b) Edit
   (c) Font
   (d) Tools

7. One or more lines of text printed at the top of every page is called a(n)

   (a) orphan.
   (b) widow.
   (c) header.
   (d) footer.

8. Which type of column continues text from the bottom of one column on the left to the top of the next column on the right on the same page?

   (a) parallel
   (b) newspaper-style
   (c) horizontal
   (d) vertical

9. A numbered comment or explanation at the bottom of a page is a(n)

   (a) footnote.
   (b) endnote.
   (c) header.
   (d) footer.

10. Which of the following sequences is an example of descending sort order?

    (a) A to Z
    (b) Z to A
    (c) 0 to 9
    (d) X, Y, Z

11. What is the most common use of the WordPerfect Math feature?

    (a) computing π (pi)
    (b) computing square roots
    (c) adding columns of numbers
    (d) multiplying columns of numbers

12. After the Outline feature is turned on, which key do you press to move in to the next level heading?

    (a) Enter
    (b) Shift
    (c) Space Bar
    (d) Tab

13. After a phrase has been marked as a block, what menu do you use to flag it as a table of contents or index entry?

    (a) File
    (b) Edit
    (c) Tools
    (d) Mark

14. How do you remove a term from an index?

    (a) Execute the Cancel command.
    (b) Execute Reveal Codes and delete the index code.
    (c) Execute the Macro command and delete the line.
    (d) Execute the Merge command.

15. Which menu do you use to insert lines and boxes into a document?

    (a) Font
    (b) Graphics
    (c) Edit
    (d) Tools

16. Which file name extension identifies the sample graphics files that come with WordPerfect?

    (a) GRA   (b) DOC

    (c) PIX   (d) WPG

17. Which key, along with a letter key, is often used to name and execute WordPerfect macros?

    (a) Alternate   (b) Control

    (c) Shift   (d) Tab

18. Which feature allows you to create personalized form letters?

    (a) List Files   (b) Macro

    (c) Merge   (d) Style

19. Which term describes a collection of formatting codes that can be created, saved, and inserted into documents to provide a consistent appearance?

    (a) Format   (b) Macro

    (c) Outline   (d) Style

20. What menu do you use to change WordPerfect's default initial settings?

    (a) Tools Outline   (b) Edit Window

    (c) Layout Document   (d) File Setup

Fill-In

1. The View Document option of the _____ menu allows you to see on the screen how your document will look when it is printed.

2. Hyphenation is most useful when text is fully _____.

3. To avoid orphans and widows, pull down the _____ menu, select the Line option, and then select the Widow/Orphan Protection option.

4. The Conditional End of Page feature is a way to keep text from being _____ between pages.

5. The _____ option of the Font menu displays the fonts available with your printer and allows you to change the font you are using.

6. A _____ or _____ is often used to print a title, chapter number, page number, or other identification on every page.

7. Press _____ and then Right Arrow to move the cursor to the right column in a document set up with newspaper-style or parallel columns.

8. An _____ is similar to a footnote, except that comments are collected and placed at the end of the document instead of at the bottom of each page.

9. The _____ option is handy for alphabetizing names or any list of words or phrases.

10. After math columns have been defined and the math feature has been turned on, the math function _____ is inserted below a column of numbers to tell WordPerfect to compute their subtotal.

11. An _____ is an invaluable tool for organizing topics before you type the text of a document.

12. A table of contents entry is flagged by pulling down the _____ menu and selecting the Table of Contents option.

13. Generating an _____ with WordPerfect is similar to generating a table of contents.

14. Text may be enclosed in a box by pulling down the _____ menu and selecting the _____ option.

15. The Figure option of the Graphics menu lets you insert a previously created _____ in your document.

16. A macro is a sequence of _____ that can be recorded, stored, and replayed.

17. The Merge feature allows you to combine a primary file, containing text and merge codes, with an address file, containing fields and records, to create _____ letters.

18. An _____ style has just a beginning code and is often used to set formats for an entire document.

19. You can tailor WordPerfect to your specific needs by pulling down the File menu and selecting the _____ option to change various default settings.

20. You use the _____ option from the Setup Environment submenu to have the cursor position on the status line reported in column and line numbers instead of inches.

Short Problems

1. Start WordPerfect and retrieve the file MEMO.DOC. Activate the Print menu and change the Text Quality option to Draft. Print the file and compare its quality to previous printouts of the memo. Change the Text Quality option back to High.

2. Clear the screen and retrieve NEWS.DOC. Use the Conditional End of Page feature to ensure that no headings are separated from their paragraphs.

3. Clear the screen. Use the Base Font option of the Font menu to create a document that demonstrates at least five different fonts available with your printer. Print the document to see the results.

4. Clear the screen. Type the following words, pressing **Enter** after each one:

```
couch
zebra
donkey
turtle
frog
apple
gate
vine
ball
uncle
horse
whistle
elephant
x-ray
ivy
reindeer
kangaroo
parrot
lobby
```

```
neighbor
soda
melody
```

Use the Sort feature to alphabetize this list of words.

5. Clear the screen. Use the Graphics Line options to create a sheet for playing Tic-Tac-Toe. Print two copies using the Number of Copies option in the Print menu.

6. Clear the screen. Use the Graphics Figure option to import one or two WPG files. Examine the pictures with View Document. Activate the Print menu, set Graphics Quality to High, and print the document.

7. Clear the screen. Use the math feature to add up the following column of numbers:

```
16.34
25.00
127.35
57.70
50.00
75.00
22.00
19.97
906.51
209.12
```

8. Create a macro named Alt-D that will move the cursor to the end of the document and execute the Reveal Codes command. Return to the full editing screen, move the cursor to the beginning of the document, and try your new macro.

9. Create a style named Letterhead that will set the left and right margins to 1.5 inches. In addition, have the style insert a centered letterhead containing your name and address, and the current date flush right two lines below the letterhead. Save the style in a file named LHEAD. Clear the screen, pull down the Layout menu, select Styles, retrieve LHEAD, and apply the Letterhead style to your new document.

10. Pull down the File menu, select Setup, select Environment, select Units of Measure, and change the status line display so that it reports the current cursor position in line and column numbers. Return to the editing screen, move the cursor, and observe the status line. Now, change the setting back to inches.

Long Problems

1. Create a quick reference guide to WordPerfect that includes all of the commands covered in this chapter and the previous two chapters.

2. Use WordPerfect's Outline feature to organize the topics of a term paper, report, speech, or presentation you must do for school or work.

3. Use WordPerfect to type a term paper or report, complete with footnotes or endnotes, for school or work.

4. Use the Line options of the Graphics menu to create a calendar page for the month of January.

5. Create an address file containing ten friends' names and addresses. Remember to separate each field by pressing F9 and terminate each record by pulling down the Tools menu, selecting Merge Codes, and then selecting End Record. Create a primary file that contains the text and appropriate merge codes of an invitation to your birthday party. Use the Merge feature to generate and print the form letters for all ten friends.

6. Suppose you are moving. Create a form letter informing your friends of your new address. You can use the address file you created in the previous exercise.

7. Select an article from a newspaper or magazine. Reproduce this article in a WordPerfect document with two newspaper-style columns.

8. Create a document that demonstrates how text can wrap around a picture. Import a WPG file. Examine the picture with View Document. Make up a couple of paragraphs to go with the picture and type the text so that it wraps around the picture. Print the document when you have finished.

9. Suppose you want to sell your stereo, bike, car, or some other possession. Use what you have learned about drawing lines and text boxes and changing character sizes to create an attractive and eye-catching flyer to put up on bulletin boards.

10. Use what you have learned about the Equation Editor to create, display, and print the following expressions:

$$A = \pi r^2$$

$$\sin^2\Theta + \cos^2\Theta = 1$$

$$PowerRule: \quad \frac{d}{dx}(x^r) = rx^{r-1}$$

$$\int \frac{dx}{\sqrt{a^2 - x^2}} = \sin^{-1}\frac{x}{a}$$

(End-of-Section Exercises begin on the next page.)

END-OF-SECTION EXERCISES

True or False

1. WP is the command you enter to start WordPerfect from DOS. _____

2. The cursor marks your current position within a document, and indicates where text will be inserted, deleted, or changed in some way. _____

3. The WordPerfect status line, shown at the top of the screen, lists the names of all pull-down menus. _____

4. WordPerfect has always had a pull-down menu system. _____

5. When you start WordPerfect, you must select either the pull-down menu system or the function key interface; you cannot use both. _____

6. WordPerfect 5.1 includes mouse support. _____

7. The word wrap feature automatically generates a soft return when the word you are typing will not fit on the current line. _____

8. The simplest way to move the cursor is to press an arrow key. _____

9. The Page Up and Page Down keys are used to move the cursor an entire screen at a time. _____

10. In WordPerfect, the Home key is pressed and released one or more times before pressing another key to move the cursor. _____

11. WordPerfect has two basic typing modes: insert and typeover. _____

12. The Delete key and the Backspace key both remove the character at the current cursor location. _____

13. WordPerfect does not allow deleting an entire word or line at a time. _____

14. The Replace command is better than the Search command for correcting a consistent misspelling throughout a document. _____

15. Your document will be lost unless you save it to disk before you turn off the computer or before the power goes out. _____

16. You must enter a valid DOS file name the first time you save a WordPerfect document. _____

17. You may save a document as many times as you like, even if you are not finished creating it. _____

18. The WordPerfect spelling checker recognizes all proper names, slang, and technical terms. _____

19. In WordPerfect, a block is a section of text that can contain no less than a single word and no more than a page. _____

20. A block can be copied, moved, or deleted. _____

21. WordPerfect lets you restore any of the three most recently deleted text items. _____

22. You can boldface text with the press of a function key. _____

23. WordPerfect provides only underline and boldface character formats. _____

24. WordPerfect initially sets the top, bottom, left, and right margins to one inch. _____

25. WordPerfect initially sets tab stops at one inch intervals. _____

26. WordPerfect allows four types of tab stops: left, centered, right, and decimal. _____

27. Full justification, which is turned on by default, aligns text to both the left and right margins. _____

28. Full justification looks worse when it is used with hyphenation and proportional spacing. _____

29. Line spacing, like justification, does not appear on the editing screen, but only when the document is printed. _____

30. WordPerfect requires you to center text manually. _____

31. WordPerfect asks if you want to save your document whenever you try to exit the program and return to DOS. _____

32. One way to retrieve an existing document is to use the List Files screen. _____

33. The List Files screen provides many options for managing WordPerect documents. _____

34. The Escape key lets you repeat a key press any number of times. _____

35. WordPerfect embeds hidden formatting codes in documents to represent hard and soft returns, hard and soft page breaks, margin changes, tab stop settings, character formats, and centering. _____

36. Unfortunately, you can never reveal WordPerfect's hidden formatting codes. _____

37. The WordPerfect thesaurus displays synonyms, antonyms, and the definition of the selected headword. _____

38. WordPerfect's Window feature lets you split the display into two separate document editing screens, each with its own status line. _____

39. The Window feature does not let you copy or move text from one document to another. _____

40. To create a hanging indent in WordPerfect, you perform a left indent followed by a margin release. _____

41. WordPerfect lets you insert the current date into a document as text or as a code that is automatically updated whenever the document is retrieved or printed. _____

42. WordPerfect has no provision for recording a document name that is longer than an ordinary DOS file name. _____

43. If you forget the password that you have entered to lock a document, you can call WordPerfect Corporation's technical support department for a way to reveal the password. _____

44. WordPerfect 5.1 can import Lotus 1-2-3 spreadsheet files without having to convert them to ASCII files first. _____

45. WordPerfect cannot be used to create or edit DOS text files such as AUTOEXEC.BAT and CONFIG.SYS. _____

46. You can execute a DOS command, such as FORMAT or CHKDSK, without actually exiting WordPerfect. _____

47. The View Document feature lets you see how your document will look when it is printed before actually printing it. _____

48. Hyphenation is most useful when text is fully justified. _____

49. An orphan is the last line of a paragraph that appears at the bottom of a page. _____

50. The Conditional End of Page feature is often used to keep titles with their first paragraphs or to prevent tables from being split between pages. _____

51. The number, size, and kind of fonts you can use with WordPerfect depend ultimately on your printer. _____

52. The point is a typographic measure equal to about one inch. _____

53. A proportionally spaced font uses the same amount of horizontal space for each character. _____

54. WordPerfect can produce only those characters you see on your keyboard. _____

55. A footer is usually printed at the top of every page. _____

56. Parallel columns contain text that continues from the bottom of one column on the left to the top of the next column on the right on the same page. _____

57. WordPerfect lets you have footnotes and endnotes in the same document. _____

58. The WordPerfect Sort feature can be used to alphabetize words or arrange numbers into ascending or descending order. _____

59. You must use a tab stop to list numbers to be totaled with the WordPerfect Math feature. _____

60. The Tables feature introduced in WordPerfect 5.1 works somewhat like a mini-spreadsheet program. _____

61. The Right Arrow key moves to the next heading level when the Outline feature is turned on. _____

62. WordPerfect can automatically generate a table of contents, providing you first mark the headings to be included and define a numbering style. _____

63. Generating an index with WordPerfect is not at all like generating a table of contents. _____

64. WordPerfect lets you incorporate diagonal lines and circles in documents. _____

65. WordPerfect can import images created by many painting, drawing, and graphics packages. _____

66. WordPerfect graphics files are identified by the extension WPG. _____

67. A macro may not include function keys or menu selections. _____

68. A macro can be used to store a long phrase that must be entered frequently. _____

69. Before you can print a set of form letters, you must create the primary file, which contains the letter, and the secondary merge file, which contains the names and addresses. _____

70. The primary file contains special merge codes that indicate where items from the address file are to be placed. _____

71. In WordPerfect, a style can automate formatting and provide a consistent appearance to documents such as book chapters, newsletters, and memos. _____

72. The Equation Editor has been included in all versions of WordPerfect. _____

Matching

Match each term with the phrase that best describes it.

_____ 1. widow
_____ 2. primary file
_____ 3. ASCII file
_____ 4. clicking
_____ 5. sorting
_____ 6. word wrap
_____ 7. Ctrl-Backspace
_____ 8. formula
_____ 9. Exit
_____ 10. Ctrl-End
_____ 11. left indent
_____ 12. block
_____ 13. macro

_____ 14. Flush Right
_____ 15. soft page break
_____ 16. View Document
_____ 17. password
_____ 18. code
_____ 19. status line
_____ 20. Cancel
_____ 21. pull-down menu
_____ 22. full justification
_____ 23. Home, Left Arrow
_____ 24. headword
_____ 25. Insert
_____ 26. Home, Home, Up Arrow

a. The WordPerfect name for the F7 key, used to leave a menu or return to DOS.
b. The WordPerfect name for the F1 key, used to reinstate a previous deletion.
c. A sequence of keystrokes that can be recorded, stored, and replayed.
d. A feature that lets you see how a document will look when it is printed.
e. A setting that aligns text to both the left and right margins.
f. The first line of a paragraph that appears at the bottom of a page.
g. Arranging items in some particular order.
h. An expression that indicates how a calculation is to be performed.
i. The text of a form letter, which contains special merge codes.
j. A hidden formatting instruction embedded in a document.
k. A word that can be looked up in the thesaurus.
l. A way to move all lines of a paragraph in from the left margin.
m. A feature that aligns text to the right margin quickly and easily.
n. A way to prevent unauthorized users from retrieving or printing a document.
o. A text file that contains no special formatting codes.
p. The area at the bottom of the WordPerfect editing screen that displays messages and warnings.
q. A list of options that appears when its name is selected.
r. Briefly pressing and releasing a mouse button.
s. A word processing freature that eliminates having to press the Enter key at the end of every line.
t. The key that switches to or from typeover mode.
u. Key presses that will erase an entire word.
v. Key presses that will erase an entire line.
w. A section of text, from a single character to an entire document, that can be marked and manipulated as a unit.
x. A division between two pages automatically generated by WordPerfect.
y. Key presses that will move the cursor to the beginning of the current line.
z. Key presses that will move the cursor to the beginning of the current document.

Short Problems

1. Reproduce and print the following letter on your computer using WordPerfect. Note that the letter is centered from top to bottom on the page and it is justified. Be sure to use underline and boldface where indicated.

International Securities, Inc.
103 Madison Square
Kansas City, MO 64141

Dear Ms. Jones:

We believe you will find the International Gold Trust to be the most secure, most economical, and most convenient way to invest in pure gold.

As you will see in the accompanying prospectus, the International Gold Trust offers a combination of benefits found <u>nowhere</u> else. It has all the advantages that only a full-time investment in pure gold can provide, together with all the convenience and security of a mutual fund.

After you review the prospectus, if you need additional information, please call us toll-free at our corporate office, **1-800-555-5142**. We will welcome your call. Of course, there is absolutely no obligation.

To invest in the International Gold Trust, simply complete the enclosed Account Application and mail it in the postage-paid envelope provided.

We hope you will join us soon as an investor in the International Gold Trust.

Sincerely,

Carolyn J. Stowers
President

2. Reproduce and print the following document on your computer using WordPerfect. Note that the top and bottom margins are 1 inch, and the left and right margins are 1.5 inches. Full justification is used. Use the Small font size and appropriate tab stops to duplicate the listing from the *Wall Street Journal*. Use boldface and italics where indicated.

How to Read Mutual Fund Quotations

Mutual fund prices are listed in the financial section of many newspapers, including the *Wall Street Journal*. Funds are listed alphabetically, unless they are part of a major fund group, in which case they appear under the group heading. For example, here is part of a typical listing from the *Wall Street Journal*:

	NAV	Offer Price	NAV Chg
Mutl Beac	24.68	N.L.	+ .04
Mutl BnFd	16.37	17.89	+ .03
Mutual of			
Omaha Funds			
Amer	10.03	N.L.	...
Growth	9.05	9.84	- .04
Income	9.58	10.41	- .01
Tax Free	11.06	12.02	+ .02
Mutl Fd	24.81	N.L.	+ .04
Mut Ql Shars	74.39	N.L.	+ .06
NtlAvia Tc	13.89	14.58	- .01
Natl Ind	15.56	N.L.	...

The fund names are extremely abbreviated, but they are not difficult to recognize with a little practice.

NAV is the net asset value per share for each fund, calculated at the close of business on the given day. It also refers to the price that the fund pays for shares redeemed on that day. In other words, the net asset value is how much each share is worth.

Offer Price is the price paid by investors who bought shares on that day. It is the net asset value plus the commission or *load*. In other words, the offer price is how much you would pay for a share.

The abbreviation *N.L.* stands for *No Load*, meaning that the offer price is the same as the net asset value. A no-load fund charges no commission (sales charge) for the purchase of shares.

The **NAV Chg** column shows the change in net asset value compared with the previous day. A plus sign means the value went up, and a minus sign means the value went down. An ellipsis in the column means that the value did not change.

Some quotation listings use the terms *Bid* and *Asked* instead of *NAV* and *Offer Price*. These are somewhat outdated terms. The idea is that the mutual fund will bid a certain price to buy your shares from you when you redeem them, and it will ask a certain price when you want to purchase shares.

3. Reproduce and print the following newsletter on your computer using WordPerfect. You may have some minor differences due to your printer. Use a text box with 10% grey shading for the heading. Use two newspaper-style columns for the main body of text. Use different font sizes, boldface, and italics where indicated.

The Amateur Investor
Special Report #5

The Amateur Investor, Inc.   (414) 555-5362
Box 555, Abrams, WI 54101

Mutual Funds Demystified

Those fortunate enough to have hundreds of thousands of dollars to invest can hire professional advisors to manage their stock portfolios. The rest of us have mutual funds.

A **mutual fund** is a company that manages its shareholders' investments toward a stated objective. The objective may be to invest in stocks for capital appreciation, bonds for regular income, or a combination of these and other investments. Many small investors can pool their money into a large fund organized and managed by professionals. Each investor holds shares in the pool, according to the amount contributed. So, even if you have only $500, you can invest in stocks or bonds and benefit from the advice of professional money-managers.

Why a Mutual Fund?
Mutual funds offer three major advantages over buying individual stocks or bonds:

1. *Diversification.* Each dollar you invest buys a share in the fund's entire portfolio, which typically consists of the stocks or bonds of hundreds of companies.

2. *Management.* Each fund has a professional manager, often assisted by a staff of investment analysts, who decides which stocks or bonds to buy and sell and when to do so.

3. *Liquidity.* Most funds issue new shares and redeem existing shares on demand. You can easily invest more or sell your shares for cash at any time. The price of a share equals the current market value of the fund's entire investments divided by the number of outstanding shares (the **net asset value** or **NAV**), plus any sales charges. Funds with no sales or redemption charges are called no-load funds.

Types of Funds
The mutual fund manager's job is to buy and sell stocks or bonds in keeping with the fund's stated goals. As an investor, you must choose a mutual fund that meets your goals. There are many types of mutual funds, but here are the main categories:

* *Capital appreciation.* Stocks with fast-rising profits for maximum growth.
* *Growth.* Profitable, but well-established stocks for moderate growth.
* *Growth and income.* Growth stocks that also pay large dividends.
* *Balanced.* A mix of stocks and bonds to conserve capital.
* *Fixed income.* Primarily bonds and related securities with predictable yields.
* *International.* Securities outside the U.S market for foreign diversification.
* *Gold.* Gold stocks, coins, and bullion as a hedge against inflation.

4. Reproduce and print the following document on your computer using WordPerfect. Do not use tabs. After typing the title and first sentence, define and turn on three parallel columns. Use WordPerfect's default margin settings for the three parallel columns. Be sure to turn on automatic hyphenation before you begin typing the columns. Use boldface where indicated. Press Ctrl-Enter when you are finished typing each column entry to start the next column. Note how WordPerfect wraps words automatically within each column.

A Concise Guide to Mortgages

This guide is taken from material prepared by the Federal Trade Commission.

Type	**Description**	**Considerations**
Fixed-rate mortgage	Fixed interest rate, usually long-term; equal monthly payments of principal and interest until debt is paid in full.	Offers stability and long-term tax advantages. Interest rates may be higher than with other types of financing. New fixed rates are rarely assumable.
Adjustable-rate mortgage	Interest rate changes are based on a financial index, resulting in possible changes in your monthly payments, loan term, and/or principal. Some plans have rate or payment caps.	Readily available. Starting interest rate is slightly below market, but payments can increase sharply and frequently if index increases. Payment caps prevent wide fluctuations in payments but may cause negative amortization (your debt actually increases). Rate caps limit amount total debt can expand.
Renegotiable-rate mortgage (rollover)	Interest rate and monthly payments are constant for several years; changes possible thereafter. Long-term mortgage.	Less frequent changes in interest rate offer some stability.
Balloon mortgage	Monthly payments based on fixed interest rate; usually short-term; payments may cover interest only with principal due in full at term end.	Offers low monthly payments but possibly no equity until loan is fully paid. When due, loan must be paid off or refinanced. Refinancing poses high risk if rates climb.

5. Reproduce and print the following document on your computer using WordPerfect's Outline feature. First, center and boldface the title. Then, turn on the Outline feature and press the Enter key. As you type the outline, remember that the Tab key advances to the next outline level and Shift-Tab moves back out to the previous level.

A Short Course in Mutual Funds

```
I. Introduction
II. Defining Your Investment Goals
      A. Growth
      B. Risks and Rewards
III. The Main Advantages of Mutual Funds
      A. Professional Management
      B. Diversification
      C. Quantity Trading
IV. Other Advantages of Mutual Funds
      A. Liquidity
      B. Fund Switching
      C. Convenience and Service
      D. Simplified Retirement Plans
      E. Strict Regulation
      F. Full Disclosure
      G. Simplified Accounting
V. Disadvantages of Mutual Funds
      A. No Choice of Individual Securities
      B. No Personal Broker
      C. Lower Risk, Less Potential Gain
      D. Fees
      E. Complacency
VI. Types of Mutual Funds
      A. Money Market Funds
      B. Bond Funds
            1. Taxable
            2. Tax-exempt
      C. Common Stock Funds
            1. Aggressive Growth
            2. Growth
            3. Growth and Income
            4. Income
      D. Balanced Funds
      E. International Funds
      F. Other Specialized Funds
            1. Gold
            2. Options
VII. Picking the Right Mutual Fund
      A. Load Funds
      B. No-load Funds
      C. 12b-1 Plans
VIII. Understanding Net Asset Value
IX. Evaluating Performance
      A. Payment of Dividends
      B. Payment of Capital Gains Distributions
      C. Increase in Net Asset Value
X. Reading the Prospectus and Financial Report
      A. Diversified and Non-diversified Funds
      B. Management
      C. Management Fees
      D. Fund Expenses
```

6. Reproduce and print the following document on your computer using WordPerfect. The two headings are centered and boldfaced. The world map image is in a WordPerfect graphics file named GLOBE2-M.WPG, which is included with the WordPerfect 5.1 package. It will most likely be in the WP51 subdirectory or in a subdirectory named GRAPHICS under the WP51 subdirectory. Ask your instructor if you cannot find the file. Pull down the Graphics menu, select Figure, select Create, and then enter GLOBE2-M.WPG as the file name. You don't have to change any of the default options. Turn on hyphenation and enter the text of the paragraph, which will automatically appear to the left of the figure. Don't forget the footnote. Use italics where indicated. To create the table, use a right tab stop at 1 inch, a left tab stop at 2 inches, and a right tab stop at 6 inches. Use the default options of the Graphics Line Create Horizontal command to generate the three horizontal lines in the table.

Global Population On the Rise

The global population growth rate has reversed its 20-year decline and is now on the up-swing. New figures show the rate at 1.8 percent, up from 1.7 percent in 1988. In part, this rise reflects continued declines in death rates in some regions not matched by similar trends in birthrates. In some countries, such as China and India, and in parts of Africa, birthrates actually have risen somewhat according to *World-Watch* magazine, published by Worldwatch Institute, Washington, D.C.[1]

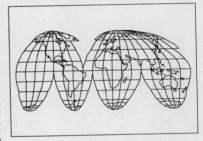

World's 20 Most Populous Countries: 1989

Rank	Country	Population
1	China	1,103,900,000
2	India	835,000,000
3	USSR	289,000,000
4	United States	248,800,000
5	Indonesia	184,600,000
6	Brazil	147,400,000
7	Japan	123,200,000
8	Nigeria	115,300,000
9	Bangladesh	114,700,000
10	Pakistan	110,400,000
11	Mexico	86,700,000
12	Vietnam	66,800,000
13	Philippines	64,900,000
14	West Germany	61,500,000
15	Italy	57,600,000
16	United Kingdom	57,300,000
17	France	56,100,000
18	Thailand	55,600,000
19	Turkey	55,400,000
20	Egypt	54,800,000

Source: 1989 World Population Data Sheet of the Population Reference Bureau, Inc.

---

[1] *The 1990 Information Please Almanac* (Boston: Houghton Mifflin Company, 1989), p. 140.

Beginning Lotus 1-2-3

In This Chapter

Preview

The original 1-2-3 program was conceived by Mitch Kapor, founder of Lotus Development Corporation, in 1982. By that time Kapor had already teamed up with a programmer named Jonathan Sachs, who helped develop the software. Lotus 1-2-3 was first released in the fall of 1982. One year later, its sales had reached 53 million dollars. Designed specifically for the then new IBM Personal Computer, 1-2-3 was a best-seller because of its power, flexibility, and ease of use. The second major version of 1-2-3, which was released in 1985, sold extremely well. In 1989, after a long wait by computer industry standards, Lotus finally delivered two new releases of its venerable software: Lotus 1-2-3 Release 2.2 for low-end IBM-compatible microcomputers that use the 8088 or 8086 chip, and Lotus 1-2-3 Release 3.0 for more powerful machines that use the 80286 or 80386 chip. Despite increased competition from other powerful spreadsheet packages, such as Microsoft Excel and SuperCalc5, Lotus 1-2-3 remains the best-selling spreadsheet package, with at least 65 percent of the market. In this chapter and the next two chapters, you will learn to use Lotus 1-2-3. Most of the lessons can be completed with any version of 1-2-3, Release 2.0 or newer. A few lessons address special and advanced features introduced with Lotus 1-2-3 Release 2.2 and Release 3.1.

After studying this chapter, you will know how to

- start 1-2-3.
- create a worksheet.
- use 1-2-3 menus.
- save a worksheet.
- print a worksheet.
- quit 1-2-3.
- retrieve an existing worksheet.
- get help.
- move around a worksheet.
- edit cells.
- change column widths.
- delete and insert columns and rows.
- copy and move cells.
- format cells.
- undo commands.
- use formulas.
- use functions.

Getting Started

Although Lotus 1-2-3 is a large and sophisticated software package, it is easy to learn to use for basic spreadsheet tasks. Lotus 1-2-3 might be set up several different ways at your particular computer installation. You are most likely to use the package in one of three possible arrangements:

1. On a microcomputer with two floppy drives and 1-2-3 installed on several diskettes

2. On a microcomputer with a hard disk and 1-2-3 installed in a subdirectory named 123 or 123R3 (for Release 3.1)

3. On a microcomputer connected to a local area network with 1-2-3 installed on the network file server

Insight

Which Lotus Spreadsheet Software Is Right for Me?

The release of Lotus 1-2-3's new 2.2 and 3.1 versions has created an embarrassment of riches for Lotus customers.

Spreadsheet users who, in the past, automatically reached for Lotus 1-2-3 now have to decide which Lotus version to use, or whether to drop Lotus and head for Microsoft's or some other company's product.

"It's a complex and difficult decision," said one spreadsheet user. "Before, it was much simpler. Then your choices were: stay put, change to release 3.1, or go to a third product. Now, you've got four choices. It makes the decision either very

complex or very easy. If all you've got is 8088 machines, it's pretty easy. For those who don't, it's much more complex. Most of us are in that boat."

Which version to use depends on the customer's microprocessor and graphics adapter support. Lotus designed release 3.1 for computers using Intel's 80286 and 80386 chips. Release 2.2 was designed for first-generation computers, which have smaller memory capabilities. But what about companies with different generations of computers?

There are other considerations as well. Version 2.2 is a direct descendant of 2.01. Release 3.1, writ-

ten in C language, has a new format that prevents it from being used with existing 1-2-3 add-in packages. To further complicate matters, there is some confusion about how easy it is to upgrade from 2.2 to 3.1.

Many customers are taking a wait-and-see attitude about the new Lotus releases. Changing software is too expensive to base on a snap judgement, and in many cases, may also require an even more costly hardware upgrade.

Source: Bob Francis, "Muddy Waters," *Datamation,* July 15, 1989, pp. 31–32.

You may need some additional direction from your instructor on how to start Lotus 1-2-3, but once you get situated, you should be able to do the following lessons.

Lesson 1: Running 1-2-3

You are all ready to start working with spreadsheets, but first you must boot up your computer and run 1-2-3.

Step 1: Boot Up the Computer

If your computer is not already turned on and running DOS, boot it up as you learned to do in the Beginning DOS chapter.

Step 2: Prepare Diskette or Subdirectory for Files

The Lotus 1-2-3 software is stored on its own diskettes or in its own subdirectory on a hard disk or network. It is best to prepare a separate diskette or subdirectory for the files you will create in the following lessons. If your computer has only floppy drives, obtain a formatted diskette with room for your files and insert it into drive B. If your computer has a hard disk, create a subdirectory called LESSONS, if you don't already have one, that you can use to store your files. If you are running on a network, your instructor may have other directions for you to follow.

Step 3: Insert the System Disk or Switch to the LESSONS Subdirectory

If you have a system with only floppy drives, remove the DOS startup diskette from drive A and replace it with the Lotus 1-2-3 diskette labeled "System Disk." The diskette to hold your data files should be in drive B. Go on to Step 4.

If you have a microcomputer with a hard disk, 1-2-3 should already be installed in its own subdirectory, named 123 or 123R3 for Release 3.1 (see Appendix C, Software Installation). The following lessons assume that a path has been set up so that you can run 1-2-3 from any subdirectory and that you have a LESSONS subdirectory on the hard disk for your files. Switch to the LESSONS subdirectory with this DOS command:

Type **cd c:\lessons**
Press **Enter**

If your computer is connected to a local area network, you may have to follow other directions from your instructor before actually starting 1-2-3.

Step 4: Invoke 1-2-3

Once you are in the proper disk drive directory, running 1-2-3 is easy.

Type **123**
Press **Enter**

It will take a few moments for 1-2-3 to be loaded from the disk into memory. A screen presenting the 1-2-3 logo and copyright information will appear (see Figure 1).

Most of the Lotus 1-2-3 figures you will see in this book have been created with Release 2.2. Some figures have been created with Release 3.1 to illustrate features available only in that version of 1-2-3. Except where indicated, all of the spreadsheet lessons can be completed with any version of 1-2-3, Release 2.0 or newer, although your screen may differ slightly from the figures you see in this book.

Figure 1 Lotus 1-2-3
Copyright Screen

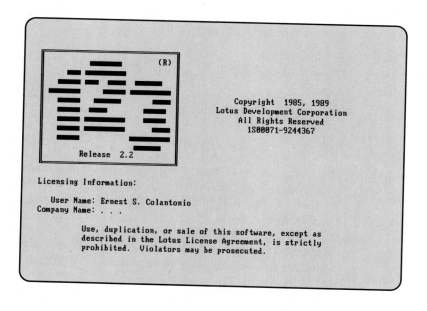

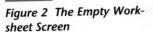 Reboot your computer and start 1-2-3 again.

Lesson 2: Creating a Worksheet

As a simple example, let's use Lotus 1-2-3 to create a small budget worksheet. A **worksheet** is simply a table of data arranged into rows and columns. In the context of a spreadsheet program, **data** can be numbers, labels, or formulas. A **number** is a numeric quantity, such as 100, 52.34, or 0.05. A **label** is any kind of text, such as a title, heading, name, or address. A **formula** is an expression that tells the spreadsheet program to perform a calculation, such as 100 + 200.

Step 1: Examine the Worksheet Screen

After the copyright screen disappears, 1-2-3 presents the empty worksheet screen shown in Figure 2. The letters A through H across the top represent columns. The numbers 1 through 20 along the left side represent rows. Although you can see only 8 columns and 20 rows at the moment, the whole worksheet is actually much larger than this. Imagine the columns continuing out beyond the right edge of the screen and the rows continuing down below the bottom. A Lotus 1-2-3 worksheet has a maximum of 256 columns and 8,192 rows. The first 26 columns are labeled A through Z. The next 26 are labeled AA through AZ, the next 26 are labeled BA through BZ, and so on up to IV. The rows are simply numbered 1 through 8192.

Each intersection of a row and a column is called a cell. The **cell** is the basic unit of storage in a worksheet—where you put a number, label, or formula. Each cell is designated by its column letter(s) and row number. For example, A1 refers to the cell located at the intersection of the first column and the first row. This column-row designation is known as the **cell address** or **cell reference** because it uniquely identifies and locates each storage unit.

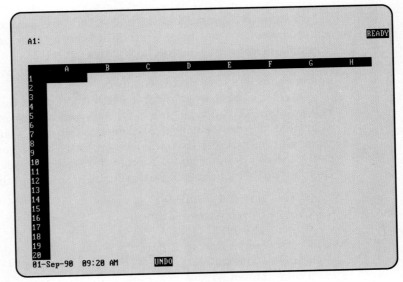

Figure 2 The Empty Worksheet Screen

Lotus 1-2-3 can refer to 256 × 8,192 or 2,097,152 cells, but you cannot actually store data in all of these cells at once. The absolute number of cells you can fill depends on the amount of memory installed in your computer and several other factors. For example, on a microcomputer equipped with 640K of memory, you can fill around 40,000 cells with numbers before you run out of memory. Lotus 1-2-3 addresses more cells than you can possibly fill so that you can place your data in convenient locations.

As you can see in Figure 2, all of the cells are initially blank. The **cell pointer** is the highlighted bar that indicates the **current cell,** the place in the worksheet where you can enter data, perform a calculation, or initiate a command. The blinking underscore within the cell pointer is the cursor. When you start a new worksheet, A1 is the current cell.

The space at the top of the screen above the column letters is known as the **control panel.** It displays cell information, command choices, command descriptions, messages, and the mode in which 1-2-3 is operating. The address of the current cell appears in the upper left corner of the control panel. The blank space to the right of the current cell address indicates that the cell is empty. The highlighted block in the upper-right corner of the control panel is the **mode indicator,** which describes the current operating mode. Right now, the mode indicator displays READY, telling you that 1-2-3 is waiting for you to enter data or initiate a command.

Now look at the bottom of the screen. The lower left corner of the screen displays the current date and time. Lotus 1-2-3 Release 2.2 also shows the UNDO indicator, which tells you that you can use the Undo feature to cancel the last operation you performed. You will learn more about the Undo feature later in this chapter.

Step 2: Enter the Labels

Our simple budget worksheet will have text labels in column A and numbers in column C. Any text you enter that does not resemble a number or formula is assumed by 1-2-3 to be a label. To be more precise, a label is any text that does not begin with one of the following characters:

    0 1 2 3 4 5 6 7 8 9 . + - ($ # @

If you want to begin a label, such as an address or phone number, with one of these characters, you must precede it with a **label prefix character.** This is a symbol, such as an apostrophe ('), that tells 1-2-3 to treat the characters that follow it as a label, not as a number or formula. You will learn more about label prefix characters later in this chapter.

To enter a label, type its characters, then press the Enter key or move the cell pointer. As you type, the characters will appear in the control panel. The characters are not actually stored in the cell until you press the Enter key or move the cell pointer. If you make a mistake before you press the Enter key or move the cell pointer, you can press the Backspace key to erase the characters, then retype them. Follow these directions to enter the labels into your worksheet:

Type **Monthly Budget**
Press **Down Arrow** (2 times)
Type **INCOME**
Press **Down Arrow** (2 times)
Type **EXPENSES**
Press **Down Arrow**

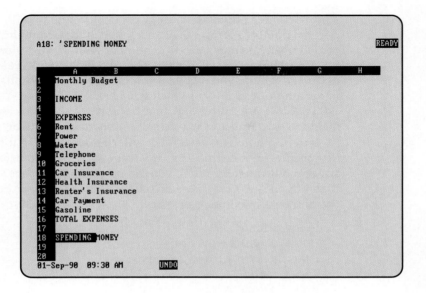

Figure 3 Labels Entered into the Worksheet

Type	**Rent**
Press	**Down Arrow**
Type	**Power**
Press	**Down Arrow**
Type	**Water**
Press	**Down Arrow**
Type	**Telephone**
Press	**Down Arrow**
Type	**Groceries**
Press	**Down Arrow**
Type	**Car Insurance**
Press	**Down Arrow**
Type	**Health Insurance**
Press	**Down Arrow**
Type	**Renter's Insurance**
Press	**Down Arrow**
Type	**Car Payment**
Press	**Down Arrow**
Type	**Gasoline**
Press	**Down Arrow**
Type	**TOTAL EXPENSES**
Press	**Down Arrow** (2 times)
Type	**SPENDING MONEY**
Press	**Enter**

Your screen should look like Figure 3.

Step 3: Enter the Numbers

Lotus 1-2-3 assumes an entry to be a number if it begins with one of the following characters:

0 1 2 3 4 5 6 7 8 9 . + - $ (

You may enter numbers without decimal points (like 10, −22, or 1234) or with decimal points (like .5, −0.12, or 11.123). You may not include spaces or commas in a number. You may precede a number with + or $, or enclose it in parentheses, but these characters will not be displayed in the worksheet. In addition to normal decimal notation, you may also enter numbers in scientific (exponential) notation. For example, 4.32E+05 (which equals 432,000) and −2.54E−05 (which equals −0.0000254) are both valid number entries. Using scientific notation lets you include very large and very small numbers in your worksheet.

Entering numbers is just like entering labels; type them and press the Enter key or move the cell pointer. If you make a mistake before you press the Enter key or move the cell pointer, you can press the Backspace key to erase the number, then retype it. Follow these directions to move the cell pointer to C3, then enter the numbers into your worksheet:

Press	**Home**
Press	**Right Arrow** (2 times)
Press	**Down Arrow** (2 times)
Type	**2000**
Press	**Down Arrow** (3 times)
Type	**650**
Press	**Down Arrow**
Type	**125**
Press	**Down Arrow**
Type	**15**
Press	**Down Arrow**
Type	**75**
Press	**Down Arrow**
Type	**200**
Press	**Down Arrow**
Type	**50**
Press	**Down Arrow**
Type	**50**
Press	**Down Arrow**
Type	**15**
Press	**Down Arrow**
Type	**200**
Press	**Down Arrow**
Type	**50**
Press	**Down Arrow**

Your screen should look like Figure 4.

Step 4: Enter the Formulas

A formula is an expression that tells the spreadsheet program to perform a calculation. It can include arithmetic operators (such as + and −), cell addresses, and functions. A **function** is a predefined formula that performs a useful operation, such as computing a sum or a square root. Lotus 1-2-3 has many functions, some of which we will discuss later in this chapter.

Our budget worksheet needs two formulas: one to compute the total expenses and the other to compute the spending money. At this point, C16 should be the current cell. Enter this formula to compute the total expenses:

Type	**@sum(c6..c15)**
Press	**Enter**

Figure 4 Numbers Entered into the Worksheet

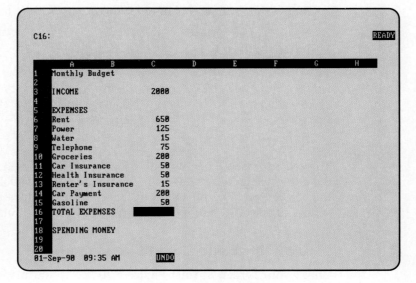

The @ character, which must begin every function name, tells 1-2-3 that the following word is a function, not a label. The @SUM function adds the contents of a range of cells. A **range** is simply a block of adjacent cells, indicated by the address of the upper left cell, two periods, and the address of the lower right cell. The range C6..C15, for example, refers to cells C6, C7, C8, C9, C10, C11, C12, C13, C14, and C15. Note that function names and cell addresses may be entered in either uppercase or lowercase letters.

Your screen should look like Figure 5. The control panel reports that cell C16 actually contains the formula @SUM(C6..C15), but the computed result of that formula, the value 1430, is displayed in the worksheet.

Figure 5 A Formula Entered into the Worksheet

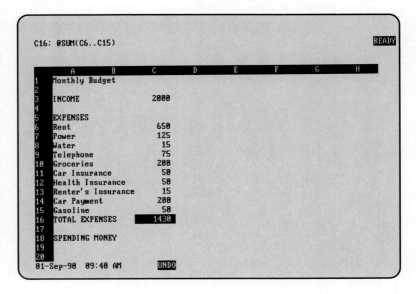

Follow these directions to enter the other formula for this worksheet:

Press **Down Arrow** (2 times)
Type   **+c3–c16**
Press   **Enter**

This formula tells 1-2-3 to subtract the total expenses result from the income figure. It begins with a plus sign because a formula must begin with one of these characters:

0 1 2 3 4 5 6 7 8 9 . + - (@ # $

The cell address C3 begins with a C. If you don't begin the formula with one of the above characters, 1-2-3 will assume the entry is a label and will not perform the calculation. The plus sign in front of the C3 does not change the result, it simply enables 1-2-3 to recognize the entry as a formula.

Step 5: Check and Correct Your Work

Check your screen against Figure 6 to see if you made any mistakes entering labels, numbers, or formulas. To correct a mistake, move the cell pointer with the arrow keys to the erroneous cell, retype the entry, and press the Enter key.

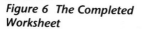

1. Move the cell pointer to a formula. Compare the contents of the control panel with the result you see displayed in the worksheet cell.

2. Move the cell pointer to a label. Notice the label prefix character displayed in front of the label in the control panel. The apostrophe (') is the default label prefix character automatically put in front of the label by 1-2-3. It appears in the control panel but not in the worksheet cell.

Figure 6 The Completed Worksheet

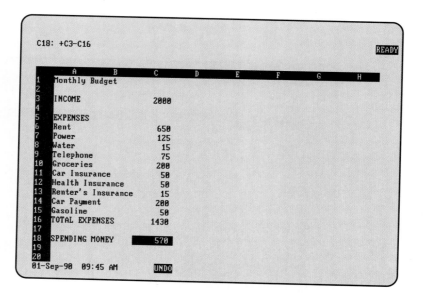

Lesson 3: Using 1-2-3 Menus

To accomplish many tasks in 1-2-3, you must select commands from menus. Commands allow you to work with, rearrange, and otherwise manipulate data stored in worksheet cells. In addition, you use commands to control the appearance, disk storage, and output of 1-2-3 worksheets. This lesson will briefly describe how to use the 1-2-3 command menus. Other lessons in this chapter and the next two chapters will cover the most important commands in more detail.

Step 1: Activate the Main Menu

Lotus 1-2-3 uses a system of pop-up menus that appear in the control panel only when activated. No menu appears in Figure 6, because 1-2-3 is in READY mode. Switch to MENU mode and display the Main menu in the control panel:

Type   /

Typing a forward slash key activates the Main menu of commands, shown in Figure 7. The mode indicator changes to MENU, and the second line of the control panel displays a list of commands. A highlighted block, known as the **menu pointer,** shows the command that will be invoked if you press the Enter key. The third line of the control panel displays information relevant to the highlighted command. In many cases this information is a list of additional options available when you invoke the highlighted command. For example, Worksheet is the command currently highlighted. If you press the Enter key, 1-2-3 will present the list of options in the third line of the control panel: Global, Insert, Delete, Column, Erase, Titles, Window, Status, Page, and Learn.

Step 2: Highlight a Command and Press Enter

One way to select a command from a menu is to position the menu pointer on the command you want and press the Enter key. For example, select the File command:

Press   **Right Arrow** (4 times)
Press   **Enter**

The menu of File commands will be activated. This method of selecting commands is often preferred by beginners because they can see information about a command on the third line of the control panel before they choose it.

Step 3: Return From a Menu

In many cases, you can return to a previous menu without executing a command. Suppose you have changed your mind about executing a command from the File menu. You can return to the Main menu from the File menu by pressing the Escape key.

Press   **Escape**

You can exit the Main menu and return to READY mode by pressing the Escape key again.

Press   **Escape**

The Main menu will disappear and the second and third lines of the control panel will be cleared.

Figure 7 The Main Menu

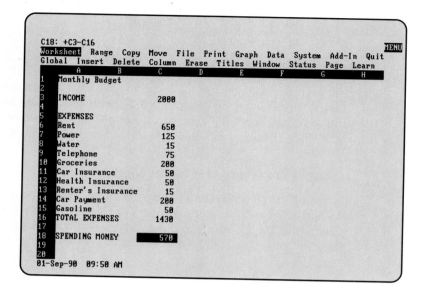

```
C18: +C3-C16                                                    MENU
Worksheet Range Copy Move File Print Graph Data System Add-In Quit
Global  Insert  Delete  Column  Erase  Titles  Window  Status  Page  Learn
        A         B         C         D         E         F         G         H
1  Monthly Budget
2
3  INCOME                2000
4
5  EXPENSES
6  Rent                   650
7  Power                  125
8  Water                   15
9  Telephone               75
10 Groceries              200
11 Car Insurance           50
12 Health Insurance        50
13 Renter's Insurance      15
14 Car Payment            200
15 Gasoline                50
16 TOTAL EXPENSES        1430
17
18 SPENDING MONEY         570
19
20
01-Sep-90  09:50 AM
```

Step 4: Type the First Letter of a Command

Activate the Main menu again:

> Type   /

The second way to select a command from a menu is to type the first letter of the command. Each 1-2-3 menu is carefully designed so that every command begins with a different letter. Select the File option by typing its first letter:

> Type   **f**

Typing the first letter of a command is usually faster than moving the menu pointer and pressing the Enter key, but you don't get a chance to read the description of the command in the third line of the control panel. Users who are familiar with 1-2-3 menus often prefer to select commands this way. Now, exit the File menu and the Main menu and return to READY mode:

> Press   **Escape** (2 times)

Practice

1. Activate the Main menu.
2. Select the Print command by moving the menu pointer and pressing the Enter key, then exit the Print menu without executing a command.
3. Select the Range command by typing its first letter, then exit the Range menu and the Main menu to return to READY mode.

Lesson 4: Saving a Worksheet

The worksheet you see on the screen is held temporarily in memory. If you shut off your computer or the power goes out, the worksheet will be lost. To avoid losing your work, you must save your worksheet in a disk file. Saving a worksheet creates a more permanent copy of your work that can be later printed or retrieved and modified. You can create large worksheets a little at a time and make corrections, updates, and new versions without having to retype all of the entries.

You must save your worksheet before you leave 1-2-3 to use another application package. It is also prudent to save your worksheet every fifteen minutes or so as you work. By periodically saving your worksheet, you will guard against losing all of your work if you make a drastic mistake or a power failure occurs.

Step 1: Execute the File Save Command

The File Save command copies the current worksheet to a disk file. Execute the File Save command:

Type **/fs**

Step 2: Enter the File Name

Lotus 1-2-3 will prompt you to enter the name of the file to save. Let's name the worksheet file BUDGET. If your computer has a hard disk and you are working from the LESSONS subdirectory, enter the file name:

Type **budget**
Press **Enter**

If your computer has only floppy disk drives and you want to store the worksheet on the diskette in drive B, follow these directions instead:

Press **Escape**
Type **b:budget**
Press **Enter**

Lotus 1-2-3 Release 2.0 and Release 2.2 will store the worksheet in a file named BUDGET.WK1. The WK1 file name extension identifies worksheet files. Lotus 1-2-3 Release 3.1 will add the extension WK3 instead of WK1.

Practice You can save your worksheet as many times as you like. After you name and save the worksheet the first time, 1-2-3 will remember the name, so the next time you save the worksheet you won't have to enter it again. Execute the File Save command and press Enter without typing the file name again. Lotus 1-2-3 will present a menu with three options: Cancel, Replace, and Backup. Select the Replace command to replace the file on the disk with the current worksheet. Note: Lotus 1-2-3 Release 2.0 does not present the Backup option.

Lesson 5: Printing a Worksheet

In many cases, a spreadsheet program is used to produce a finished worksheet printed on paper. Now that you have saved your worksheet, you may want to print it. If your computer is not connected to a printer, read this lesson and examine the figure without actually performing the steps.

Step 1: Execute the Print Command

The first step is to execute the Print command from the Main menu.

Type **/p**

Step 2: Choose Printer or File

The Print command provides two options: Printer and File. Lotus 1-2-3 Release 3.1 has a few other options as well. The Printer option will send the output directly to the printer. The File option will create a text file that can be printed later or used in another application, such as a word processing package. If you have a printer, select the Printer option:

Type   **p**

Step 3: Specify the Range

The program will display the Print Printer menu shown in Figure 8. Lotus 1-2-3 Release 2.2 will also present the Print Settings sheet, which shows the current values of various parameters, such as margins and page length. Before you can print a worksheet, you must tell 1-2-3 the range of cells you want to print. Select the Range option:

Type   **r**

The program will prompt you to enter the print range. You can specify a range two ways. The first method is to type the range and press the Enter key. For example, to specify your entire worksheet

Type   **a1..c18**
Press   **Enter**

The other way to specify the range is to use POINT mode to highlight the range. To use POINT mode, move the cell pointer to the first cell in the range, type a period to anchor the cell pointer, move to the last cell in the range, then press the Enter key. If you would like to try the pointing method, follow these directions:

Type   **r**
Press   **Home**
Type   **.**
Press   **Right Arrow** (2 times)
Press   **Down Arrow** (17 times)
Press   **Enter**

Most 1-2-3 commands accept either of these two methods of specifying a range.

Step 4: Prepare the Printer

Make sure the printer is connected to the computer and turned on. Also, make sure that paper is loaded and aligned to the top of a new page. Finally, make sure that the printer's On Line light is lit. (If it isn't, press the On Line button.)

Step 5: Select the Go Option

To begin printing, select the Go option from the Print Printer menu:

Type   **g**

The worksheet will be printed.

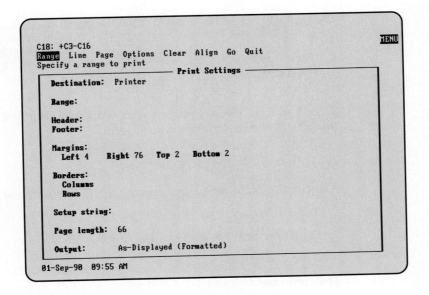

Figure 8 The Print Printer Menu and Print Settings Sheet

Step 6: Select the Page Option

If you like, you can tell 1-2-3 to have the printer advance to the top of the next page. Select the Page option from the Print Printer menu:

Type **p**

Step 7: Select the Quit Option

When you are finished printing, select the Quit option to exit the Print Printer menu and return to READY mode:

Type **q**

Practice
1. Print only this range from your worksheet: A1..A18.
2. Select the File option of the Print menu to produce a text file of your entire worksheet instead of sending it directly to the printer. Enter BUDGET as the file name. Precede the filename with B: if you have only floppy drives and want to put the file on the diskette in drive B. Lotus 1-2-3 will automatically add the file name extension PRN, indicating that it is a file to be printed.

Lesson 6: Quitting 1-2-3

You have entered, saved, and printed a worksheet. Suppose you are finished with Lotus 1-2-3 for now and want to return to DOS.

Step 1: Save the Worksheet

Although you have already saved your worksheet, you should save it again before you quit 1-2-3. This preserves the page settings created when you printed the worksheet. In addition, saving your worksheet before quitting records any changes you might have made since the previous save, and it is a good habit to form. Execute the File Save command:

Type   **/fs**
Press   **Enter**
Type   **r**

Since you have already named your worksheet the first time you saved it, you don't have to enter the file name again.

Step 2: Execute the Quit Command

Activate the Main menu and execute the Quit command:

Type   **/q**

You must confirm the quit by selecting the Yes option:

Type   **y**

The computer will exit 1-2-3 and return to DOS.

Practice

Start Lotus 1-2-3. Enter a number in cell A1. Do not save the worksheet. Execute the Quit Yes command. If you are running Lotus 1-2-3 Release 2.0, the program will immediately return to DOS. You are out of luck if you intended to save the worksheet but forgot to do so. If you are running Release 2.2 or 3.1, however, the program will display the prompt

WORKSHEET CHANGES NOT SAVED! End 1-2-3 anyway?

This warning is a welcome safety feature that tells you when you are attempting to quit without having saved your worksheet. If you really do want to save your worksheet, you can select No and then execute the File Save command. In this case, you do not want to save your worksheet, so select Yes and return to DOS.

Lesson 7: Retrieving an Existing Worksheet

Retrieving an existing worksheet is a very common procedure. You can easily examine, modify, or update a previously saved worksheet. Let's start 1-2-3 again and retrieve the BUDGET worksheet.

Step 1: Start 1-2-3

In the previous lesson, you quit 1-2-3 and returned to DOS. Start the program again:

Type   **123**
Press   **Enter**

Lotus 1-2-3 will display a new worksheet screen.

Step 2: Execute the File Retrieve Command

To load a previously saved worksheet, execute the File Retrieve command:

Type   **/fr**

Step 3: Select the File

Lotus 1-2-3 will prompt you for the name of the file to retrieve. The mode indicator will change to FILES, and the names of the worksheet files and the subdirectories in your current directory will be listed across the third line of the control panel (see Figure 9). If the file you want to retrieve is in the current directory, the easiest way to retrieve it is to use Left Arrow or Right Arrow to highlight it and press the Enter key. Alternatively, you can type the name of the file and press Enter. If you want to retrieve a file from a different disk or directory, press the Escape key twice, then enter the entire path and file name.

> Highlight   **BUDGET.WK1** (or **BUDGET.WK3** for Release 3.1)
> Press   **Enter**

The worksheet will be loaded from the disk into memory and presented on the screen. The cell pointer will appear in the position it occupied when the worksheet was saved.

Practice

Change any cell in the BUDGET worksheet, but do not save the worksheet. Then execute the File Retrieve command and select the BUDGET worksheet. Lotus 1-2-3 Releases 2.0, 2.2, and 3.1 will all retrieve the file and overwrite the worksheet you have in memory without issuing a warning or confirmation prompt. You will lose the worksheet on the screen if you have not saved it whenever you retrieve an existing worksheet. Unfortunately, the designers of Lotus 1-2-3 did not add a safety feature for this situation. Always make sure you have either saved or will not need the worksheet on your screen before you retrieve an existing worksheet.

Lesson 8: Getting Help

Lotus 1-2-3 has an excellent on-line help facility that lets you retrieve information about the current command or choose from an index of topics. In many cases, using the help facility is faster and easier than consulting the printed reference manual.

Step 1: Highlight a Command

The Lotus 1-2-3 help system is **context-sensitive,** which means that it will provide information relevant to your current operation. For example, activate the Main menu:

> Type   **/**

The Worksheet command should be highlighted.

Step 2: Insert Help Disk If Necessary

If you are running Lotus 1-2-3 from a hard disk or a network, skip this step. If your computer has only two floppy drives and the file 123.HLP is not on the System Disk, remove the System Disk from drive A and replace it with the Help Disk.

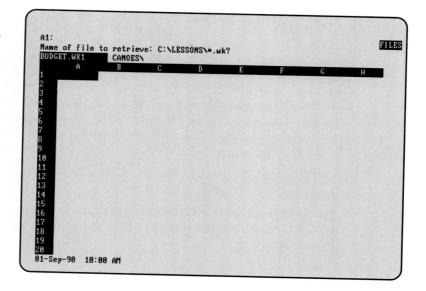

Figure 9 The File Retrieve Command

Step 3: Press the F1 Key

The help facility is activated by pressing the F1 function key.

> Press   **F1**

Figure 10 shows the result. The screen provides information about the Main menu and selecting commands. The topic Worksheet Commands is highlighted. You can use the arrow keys to highlight another topic or press the Enter key to read about the highlighted topic.

> Press   **Enter**

Lotus 1-2-3 will display another help screen with more detailed information about the topic you selected (see Figure 11).

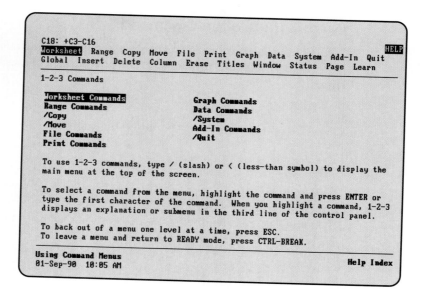

Figure 10 Main Menu Help Screen

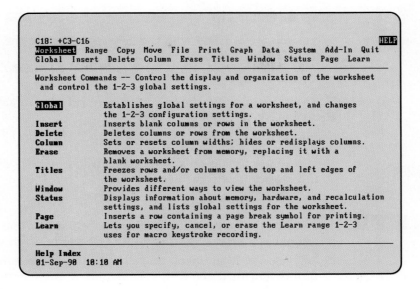

Figure 11 Worksheet Command Help Screen

Step 4: View the Help Index

You can see an index of the available help topics at any time. Highlight the Help Index topic at the bottom of the screen and press Enter:

Press   **Up Arrow**
Press   **Enter**

Figure 12 shows the Help Index. You can highlight any topic in this index and press the Enter key to see more information about it.

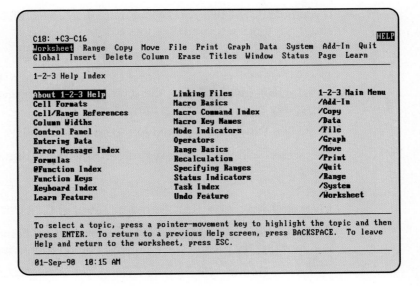

Figure 12 The Help Index

Step 5: Exit Help

When you are finished with the help facility, press the Escape key to return to what you were doing:

Press   **Escape**

The Main menu should be on your screen with the Worksheet option highlighted. Return to READY mode:

Press   **Escape**

If your computer has only two floppy drives, remove the Help Disk from drive A and replace it with the System Disk.

Practice

1. Activate the help facility, display the help index, and select the topic entitled "About 1-2-3 Help." Return to READY mode when you are finished.
2. Activate the Main menu and execute the File command. Activate the Help facility and read about the commands in the File menu. Return to READY mode when you are finished.

Lesson 9: Moving Around a Worksheet

Lotus 1-2-3 lets you move the cell pointer easily to any of the more than 2 million cells it can address. You have already used a few of the **pointer movement keys** that move the cell pointer. Let's examine the pointer movement keys in more detail.

Step 1: Move the Cell Pointer One Cell at a Time

The arrow keys move the cell pointer one cell at a time. Try each arrow key:

Press   **Right Arrow**
Press   **Left Arrow**
Press   **Down Arrow**
Press   **Up Arrow**

If you hold down an arrow key for more than a second, its action will be repeated about ten times a second. Try this action:

Press   **Right Arrow** (hold for about two seconds)

The cell pointer will rapidly travel to the right. When it goes past the left edge of the screen into column I, the screen will scroll to reveal more columns. Now try rapidly moving the cell pointer down:

Press   **Down Arrow** (hold for about five seconds)

The screen will scroll to reveal more rows when the cell pointer moves into row 21.

Step 2: Move the Cell Pointer Several Cells at a Time

Other pointer movement keys let you move the cell pointer several cells at a time. For example, try each of the following pointer movement keys:

Press   **Home**

The Home key always moves the cell pointer to A1.

Press **Page Down**
Press **Page Up**

The Page Up and Page Down keys move the cell pointer an entire screen (usually 20 rows) up or down at a time.

Press **Tab** (or **Ctrl-Right Arrow**)
Press **Shift-Tab** (or **Ctrl-Left Arrow**)

The Tab and Ctrl-Right Arrow keys both move the cell pointer an entire screen to the right. The Shift-Tab and Ctrl-Left Arrow keys both move the cell pointer an entire screen to the left.

Press **End**
Press **Down Arrow**
Press **End**
Press **Right Arrow**
Press **End**
Press **Up Arrow**
Press **End**
Press **Left Arrow**

Pressing and releasing the End key followed by an arrow key moves the cell pointer to the next intersection of a blank cell and a nonblank cell in that direction.

Press **End**
Press **Home**

Pressing End followed by pressing Home moves the cell pointer to the lowest rightmost nonblank cell in the worksheet.

Step 3: Move to a Particular Cell

Lotus 1-2-3 also provides an easy way to move to a particular cell address. Suppose you want to move to cell AB2015.

Press **F5**

The F5 function key invokes the Go To feature. The program will display the prompt

```
Enter address to go to:
```

And it will suggest the current cell address. Enter the address of the cell to which you want to move:

Type **ab2015**
Press **Enter**

The cell pointer will move immediately to that cell.

Practice

1. With a single keypress, move the cell pointer to A1.
2. Move the cell pointer right two screens.
3. In the most direct manner, move the cell pointer to the lowest rightmost cell possible in a 1-2-3 worksheet, cell IV8192.

Lesson 10: Editing Cells

Suppose you make a typing error but don't discover your mistake until after you have pressed the Enter key or moved the cell pointer. Or suppose you want to modify or update the existing contents of a cell. Lotus 1-2-3 makes it easy to edit cells.

Step 1: Retype an Entry

One way to edit the existing contents of a cell is to retype the entire entry. Suppose the power bill is $130 instead of $125. Move the cell pointer to C7 and retype the entry:

Press   **F5**
Type   **c7**
Press   **Enter**
Type   **130**
Press   **Enter**

Notice how the worksheet recomputes the formula results automatically. Total expenses increases by 5 and spending money decreases by 5 as soon as you change 125 to 130 for the power bill.

Step 2: Edit an Existing Entry

If an existing entry is long or complex and you don't need to change it entirely, retyping it can be tedious and can introduce errors. Fortunately, you can edit the contents of a cell without retyping the entire entry. As an example, let's change the label in cell A14 to *Car Loan Payment*. Follow these directions:

Press   **F5**
Type   **a14**
Press   **Enter**
Press   **F2**
Press   **Left Arrow** (7 times)
Type   **Loan**
Press   **Space Bar**
Press   **Enter**

First, you move the cell pointer to the cell you want to edit. Then you activate the EDIT mode by pressing the F2 key. Lotus 1-2-3 will display the existing entry in the second line of the control panel with a cursor at the end. You can use the Left Arrow, Right Arrow, Backspace, and Delete keys to move the cursor and erase characters. By default, any character you type will be inserted into the entry. To type over existing characters, you must press the Insert key. When you are finished editing the entry, press the Enter key to store it in the cell and return to READY mode. The following table summarizes the actions of certain keys in EDIT mode.

Key	*Action*
Enter	Stores entry and returns to READY mode
Backspace	Erases character to left of cursor
Delete	Erases character at cursor
Escape	Erases entire entry

Insert	Toggles insert/overwrite mode
Home	Moves cursor to first character of entry
End	Moves cursor to last character of entry
Left Arrow	Moves cursor left one character
Right Arrow	Moves cursor right one character
Tab	Moves cursor right five characters
Ctrl-Right Arrow	Moves cursor right five characters
Shift-Tab	Moves cursor left five characters
Ctrl-Left Arrow	Moves cursor left five characters
Up Arrow	Stores entry and moves up one row
Down Arrow	Stores entry and moves down one row
Page Up	Stores entry and moves up one screen
Page Down	Stores entry and moves down one screen

Step 3: Save the Worksheet

After you edit a worksheet, you should save it to preserve your changes. Execute the File Save command:

Type	**/f s**
Press	**Enter**
Type	**r**

Practice

1. Use EDIT mode to change the entry in cell A11 from *Car Insurance* to *Auto Insurance*.
2. Move the cell pointer to C18. Use EDIT mode to change the formula to $(C3 - C16)$. Can you explain why this formula is equivalent to $+C3 - C16$?

Lesson 11: Changing Column Widths

The default width of columns in Lotus 1-2-3 is nine characters. Although this width is fine in many cases, you may have to change the width of a column. In the BUDGET worksheet, some of the labels in column A appear to have over-lapped into column B. This overlapping does not present a problem, since column B is empty. Keep in mind, however, that the labels really are in column A. Although characters appear to be in column B on the screen, column B is still empty. You can confirm this by moving the cell pointer to cell A13 then B13 and viewing the contents of the cells displayed in the control panel. Let's widen column A so that it can hold all of the labels in the BUDGET worksheet.

Step 1: Move the Cell Pointer into the Column

Move the cell pointer to a cell in the column to be widened or narrowed. Move to cell A1:

Press **Home**

Step 2: Execute the Worksheet Column Set-Width Command

The width of a single column can be changed with the Worksheet Column Set-Width command:

Type   /wcs

Step 3: Enter the Width In Characters

Lotus 1-2-3 will prompt you to enter the column width, which must be between 1 and 240 characters, and it will suggest the current width of 9 characters. Change the column width to 25:

Type   **25**
Press   **Enter**

Column A will widen to 25 characters, as shown in Figure 13. Notice that the width of the column now appears in square brackets in the control panel, between the current cell address and the contents of the current cell.

Step 4: Save the Worksheet

After you modify a worksheet, you should save it to preserve your changes. Execute the File Save command:

Type   **/fs**
Press   **Enter**
Type   **r**

Practice

1. Execute the Worksheet Column Reset-Width command to change the width of column A back to the default width.
2. Execute the Worksheet Column Set-Width command to change the width of column A to 25 again.

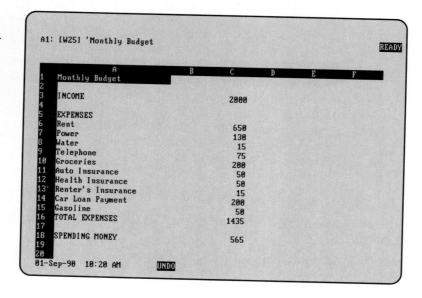

Figure 13 Column A Widened to 25 Characters

Lesson 12: Deleting and Inserting Columns and Rows

Lotus 1-2-3 provides commands for deleting and inserting columns and rows. As examples, let's delete a column and insert a row in the BUDGET worksheet.

Step 1: Delete a Column

Since you widened column A, you no longer need a blank column B. You can easily delete it. Move the cell pointer to column B and execute the Worksheet Delete Column command:

Press　**Home**
Press　**Right Arrow**
Type　**/wdc**

Lotus 1-2-3 will prompt you for the range of columns to delete, and it will suggest the current column. Since you want to delete only the current column

Press　**Enter**

The contents of column B will disappear and all the columns to the right will be shifted over to the left. The former column C is now column B. Note that the cell addresses in formulas are automatically adjusted to account for this move. For example, move to cell B16 and examine the formula to compute total expenses in the control panel:

Press　**F5**
Type　**b16**
Press　**Enter**

Before you deleted column B, the formula in C16 was @SUM(C6..C15). After you deleted column B, 1-2-3 shifted the contents of column C into column B, and it changed the formula to @SUM(B6..B15). If you examine the formula in cell B18, you will see a similar adjustment.

The process for deleting a row is similar. Move the cell pointer to the row to be removed and then execute the Worksheet Delete Row command.

Step 2: Insert a Row

Suppose you forgot to include the cable television bill in your budgeted expenses. You can easily insert a new row and then enter the data. Move the cell pointer to the row where you want the inserted row to appear, then execute the Worksheet Insert Row command:

Press　**F5**
Type　**a10**
Press　**Enter**
Type　**/wir**
Press　**Enter**

The former row 10 and all the rows below it will be shifted down. A blank row now appears as row 10. Enter the new data for this row:

Type　**Cable TV**
Press　**Right Arrow**
Type　**15**
Press　**Enter**

The new row occurs between the first and last cells in the range specified in the total expenses formula. So, the range in the formula is automatically changed to B6..B16 from B6..B15, which it was before the row was inserted. The total expenses increase by 15, and the spending money decreases by 15. Move to cell B17 to see the adjusted formula:

Press   **F5**
Type   **b17**
Press   **Enter**

Your screen should look like Figure 14.

The process for inserting a column is similar. You move the cell pointer to the column where the new column is to be added, then execute the Worksheet Insert Column command.

Step 3: Save the Worksheet

After you modify a worksheet, you should save it to preserve your changes. Execute the File Save command:

Type   **/fs**
Press   **Enter**
Type   **r**

Practice

1. Insert a new column B.
2. Insert a new row 13.
3. Delete the blank column B.
4. Delete the blank row 13.

Lesson 13: Copying and Moving Cells

Lotus 1-2-3 makes it easy to copy the contents of cells. The Copy command can reduce repetitive typing. As an example, let's copy a range of cells in the BUDGET worksheet. A Practice exercise will illustrate the use of the Move command, which is very similar to the Copy command.

Step 1: Execute the Copy Command

Examine your BUDGET worksheet. Suppose column B contains the numbers and formulas for a single month and you want to show another month in column C. Most of the numbers will be the same, so the easiest way to enter the data in column C is to copy the contents of column B. Execute the Copy command:

Type   **/c**

Step 2: Specify the Source Range

Lotus 1-2-3 will prompt you to enter the range of cells to copy from. Specify the source range:

Type   **b3..b19**
Press   **Enter**

Figure 14 Column B Deleted and Row 10 Inserted

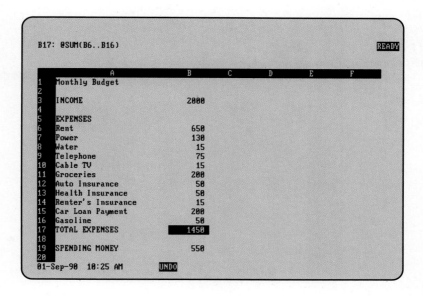

Step 3: Specify the Target Range

Next the program will prompt you to enter the range of cells to copy to. Specify the target range:

Type **c3..c19**
Press **Enter**

Lotus 1-2-3 will copy the cells from B3 through B19 to cells C3 through C19.

Step 4: Examine the Screen

Move the cell pointer to C17:

Press **F5**
Type **c17**
Press **Enter**

Your screen should look like Figure 15. Examine the formula in cell C17. When 1-2-3 copies formulas, it automatically adjusts the cell references. So, the formula in cell C17 sums the numbers in cells C6 through C16.

Step 5: Save the Worksheet

After you modify a worksheet, you should save it to preserve your changes. Execute the File Save command:

Type **/fs**
Press **Enter**
Type **r**

Practice

1. Copy the contents of cells A1 through A19 to cells D1 through D19, then delete column D.
2. The Move command is like the Copy command, except that the source cells are erased. Activate the Main menu, execute the Move command, and move

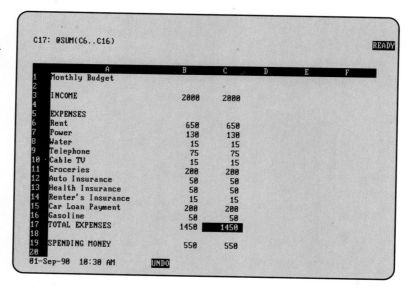

Figure 15 *Cells From Column B Copied to Column C*

the contents of cells C3 through C19 to cells E3 through E19, then move them back to column C.

Lesson 14: Cell Formatting

Lotus 1-2-3 offers an assortment of cell formatting options for tailoring the appearance of a worksheet. For example, you can left justify, center, or right justify labels within their columns. Numbers and formula results can be displayed as currency values, as percentages, with a fixed number of decimal places, or in scientific notation. In this lesson, you will learn how to use label prefix characters and how to format numbers as currency values.

Step 1: Left Justify a Label

The default label prefix character is the apostrophe ('), which aligns labels with the left edge of the cell. Whenever you type an entry that 1-2-3 recognizes as a label, an apostrophe is automatically inserted at the beginning. For example, move to cell A1 and examine the control panel:

Press   **Home**

The label *Monthly Budget* is preceded by an apostrophe.

In most cases, you don't have to type the apostrophe, because it will be added automatically by 1-2-3. But if a label must begin with one of these characters, you must type the label prefix character yourself:

0 1 2 3 4 5 6 7 8 9 . + - ($ # @

For example, enter a new left-justified label in cell A1:

Type   **'1991 Budget**
Press **Enter**

Step 2: Center a Label

The caret (^) label prefix character centers a label within its cell. For example, center the label *EXPENSES* in cell A5:

Press   **F5**
Type   **a5**
Press   **Enter**
Type   **^EXPENSES**
Press   **Enter**

The label *EXPENSES* will be centered in cell A5.

Step 3: Right Justify a Label

The quotation mark (") label prefix character aligns a label with the right edge of its cell. For example, enter right-justified labels in cells B2 and C2:

Press   **F5**
Type   **b2**
Press   **Enter**
Type   **"Jan**
Press   **Right Arrow**
Type   **"Feb**
Press   **Enter**

Step 4: Fill a Cell

The backslash (\) label prefix character fills a cell with the characters that follow it. It is often used to fill cells with hyphens (-), equal signs (=), or underscores (_) as dividing lines in a worksheet. For example, create a horizontal line of hyphens across cells A18 through C18:

Press   **F5**
Type   **a18**
Press   **Enter**
Type   **\ –**
Press   **Right Arrow**
Type   **\ –**
Press   **Right Arrow**
Type   **\ –**
Press   **Enter**

Your screen should look like Figure 16. Note that cells A18 through C18 appear filled with hyphens, even though each cell contains only \-.

Step 5: Format a Range as Currency

Lotus 1-2-3 offers several ways to format numbers and formula results. The default format is General, which displays no trailing zeros to the right of the decimal point, displays no commas separating thousands, and uses a minus sign to indicate negative values. A common numeric format for financial worksheets is Currency. This format displays the currency symbol, separates thousands with commas, and uses parentheses to indicate negative values. Let's format the numbers in columns B and C as currency values. Execute the Range Format Currency

Figure 16 The \ Label Prefix Character

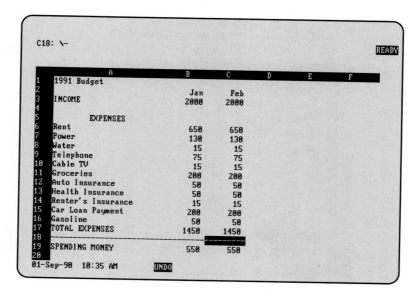

```
C18: \-                                                           READY

          A                B       C       D       E       F
1  1991 Budget
2
3  INCOME                 Jan     Feb
                          2000    2000
4
5           EXPENSES
6  Rent                    650     650
7  Power                   130     130
8  Water                    15      15
9  Telephone                75      75
10 Cable TV                 15      15
11 Groceries               200     200
12 Auto Insurance           50      50
13 Health Insurance         50      50
14 Renter's Insurance       15      15
15 Car Loan Payment        200     200
16 Gasoline                 50      50
17 TOTAL EXPENSES         1450    1450
18
19 SPENDING MONEY          550     550
20
01-Sep-90  10:35 AM            UNDO
```

command, specify the number of decimal places as two, and then specify the range of cells to be formatted:

Type	**/rfc**
Press	**Enter**
Type	**b3..c19**
Press	**Enter**

Examine the screen. Cells B3, C3, B17, and C17 are filled with asterisks. This means that the cells are not wide enough to hold the numbers in the format you specified. Widen columns B and C:

Press	**F5**
Type	**b1**
Press	**Enter**
Type	**/wcs**
Type	**10**
Press	**Enter**
Press	**Right Arrow**
Type	**/wcs**
Type	**10**
Press	**Enter**
Press	**Home**

Your screen should now look like Figure 17.

Step 6: Save the Worksheet

After you modify a worksheet, you should save it to preserve your changes. Execute the File Save command:

Type	**/fs**
Press	**Enter**
Type	**r**

Figure 17 Values Formatted as Currency

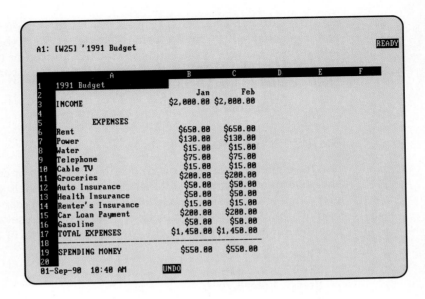

```
A1: [W25] '1991 Budget                                           READY

         A              B          C          D       E       F
1  1991 Budget
2                       Jan        Feb
3  INCOME           $2,000.00  $2,000.00
4
5        EXPENSES
6  Rent               $650.00    $650.00
7  Power              $130.00    $130.00
8  Water               $15.00     $15.00
9  Telephone           $75.00     $75.00
10 Cable TV            $15.00     $15.00
11 Groceries          $200.00    $200.00
12 Auto Insurance      $50.00     $50.00
13 Health Insurance    $50.00     $50.00
14 Renter's Insurance  $15.00     $15.00
15 Car Loan Payment   $200.00    $200.00
16 Gasoline            $50.00     $50.00
17 TOTAL EXPENSES   $1,450.00  $1,450.00
18 ─────────────────────────────────────
19 SPENDING MONEY     $550.00    $550.00
20
01-Sep-90  10:40 AM      UNDO
```

Practice

1. Move to cell B3 and examine the control panel. The cell actually contains 2000 but the value $2,000.00 is displayed in the worksheet. Changing a cell's format changes the way the number is displayed in the worksheet, not the data itself. For example, execute the Range Format Currency command and specify zero decimal places for the current cell. Enter the value 1250.25 in B3. Lotus 1-2-3 will display 1250.25 as $1,250, but it still stores the value as 1250.25 and uses the fractional part in calculations. Notice that the value in cell C19 now appears in parentheses because it is a negative value.

2. Change the format of cell B3 back to Currency with two decimal places. Enter 2000 as the value in B3.

Lesson 15: Using the Undo Feature in Releases 2.2 and 3.0

It is easy to make mistakes when using a computer. Fortunately, you can correct typing errors by retyping or editing entries. If you begin to execute a command and then change your mind, you can usually back out of the operation by pressing the Escape key. Recovering accidentally deleted data, however, can be more difficult. A good way to guard against losing data is to regularly save your worksheet to a disk file.

Lotus 1-2-3 Release 2.2 and Release 3.1 also include an Undo feature that lets you reverse the effects of the most recent operation that changed data or worksheet settings. Let's demonstrate this feature by deleting some cells and recovering them with the Undo feature. Note that the Undo feature is not available in Lotus 1-2-3 Release 2.0. If you have Release 2.0, read this lesson without performing the steps.

Step 1: Enable the Undo Feature

Lotus 1-2-3 Release 2.2 has the Undo feature turned on by default. If you see the UNDO indicator at the bottom of the screen, you know that the Undo feature is enabled. Lotus 1-2-3 Release 3.1 has the Undo feature disabled by default. Release

3.1 does not display an UNDO indicator on the screen to tell you if the Undo feature is enabled. If you are using Release 3.1, or if you are using Release 2.2 and do not see the UNDO indicator at the bottom of the screen, execute the Worksheet Global Default Other Undo Enable Quit command to turn on the Undo feature and return to READY mode:

Type   **/wgdoueq**

Step 2: Erase a Range

You have already learned how to delete entire rows or columns with the Worksheet Delete command. The Range Erase command lets you delete the contents of a range of cells. You can use the Range Erase command to erase a single cell, part of a column or row, or a block of adjacent cells in several columns and rows. Use the Range Erase command to delete the contents of cells B6 through C16:

Type   **/re**
Type   **b6..c16**
Press   **Enter**

Cells B6 through C16 will be erased.

Step 3: Use the Undo Feature

Suppose you made a mistake or changed your mind about erasing that data. To invoke the Undo feature, hold down the Alternate key and press the F4 key.

Press   **Alt-F4**

If you are using Lotus 1-2-3 Release 2.2, the data you deleted will be reinstated immediately. If you are using Lotus 1-2-3 Release 3.1, the program will ask you to confirm the Undo operation. Select the Yes option to tell the program to perform the Undo operation:

Type   **y**

Practice   The Undo feature can be used to reverse a command that changes a worksheet setting but does not delete data. For example, use the Range Format command to select the General format for cells B3 through C19, then invoke the Undo feature to reverse your action.

Lesson 16: Using Formulas

As you know, a formula is an expression stored in a cell that tells 1-2-3 to perform a calculation. You have used formulas in this chapter to sum a column of numbers and to subtract one number from another. In fact, formulas can do much more than add and subtract numbers. In this lesson, we will discuss Lotus 1-2-3 formulas in more detail.

Step 1: Create a New Worksheet

To illustrate some of the properties of formulas, let's set up a simple worksheet. First, save the BUDGET worksheet:

Type   **/fs**

Press   **Enter**
Type   **r**

Execute the Worksheet Erase Yes command to clear the worksheet screen and move the cell pointer to A1:

Type   **/wey**

Follow these directions to create a simple worksheet:

Type   **One**
Press   **Down Arrow**
Type   **Two**
Press   **Down Arrow**
Type   **Three**
Press   **Home**
Press   **Right Arrow**
Type   **100**
Press   **Down Arrow**
Type   **200**
Press   **Down Arrow**
Type   **300**
Press   **Down Arrow**

Your screen should look like Figure 18. This new worksheet is only a place for you to try out formulas for this lesson and the next lesson. You do not have to save it to a disk file when you are finished.

Step 2: Enter a Numeric Formula

Lotus 1-2-3 lets you create three basic types of formulas: numeric, string, and logical. A **numeric formula** is a mathematical expression that calculates using numeric values and produces a numeric result. Numeric formulas may include built-in functions and arithmetic operations, such as addition, subtraction, mul-

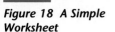

Figure 18 A Simple Worksheet

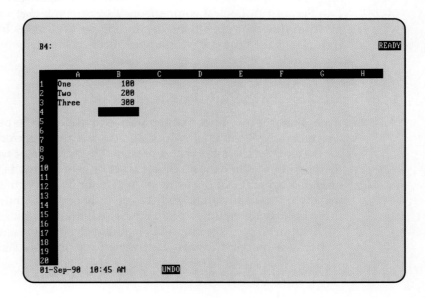

tiplication, and division. The formulas you have used so far in this chapter have all been numeric formulas. Try another numeric formula:

Type   **+b1+b2+b3**
Press   **Enter**

You should see the sum 600 displayed in cell B4.

Step 3: Enter a String Formula

A **string formula** manipulates labels. It may include the **string combination operator** (&), which joins two labels, and certain built-in functions. Although string formulas are used less frequently than numeric and logical formulas, they can be handy in worksheets that manipulate text. Move the cell pointer to C1 and enter a text formula:

Press   **Up Arrow** (3 times)
Press   **Right Arrow**
Type   **+a1&" Hundred"**
Press   **Enter**

This formula tells 1-2-3 to take the label in A1 and combine it with the label in quotation marks. The result is *One Hundred* in cell C1.

Step 4: Enter a Logical Formula

A **logical formula** compares values and produces the result of TRUE, symbolized by the value 1, or FALSE, symbolized by the value 0. Logical formulas may include certain built-in functions and logical operations, such as greater than, less than, and equal to. For example, suppose you want to know if the value in cell B3 is greater than the value in cell B1. Move the cell pointer to C2 and enter a logical formula:

Press   **Down Arrow**
Type   **+b3>b1**
Press   **Enter**

Since 300 is in B3 and 100 is in B1, the result of the logical formula is 1, or TRUE (see Figure 19). Logical comparisons can be combined with logical functions to perform different operations depending on the values in specific cells. Logical formulas make it possible for a worksheet to choose between alternative sets of computations when solving a problem.

Step 5: Try the Arithmetic Operators

An **operator** is a symbol that represents an action to be performed in a formula. An **operand** is a value on which an action is to be performed. The + operator, for example, is a symbol that represents the addition of two numbers, which are the operands. While most operators act on two operands, some operators act on only one operand. In the expression −3, for instance, the − operator stands for negation, not subtraction, and acts on only one operand, the 3. Lotus 1-2-3 has three basic types of operators: arithmetic, string, and logical.

Arithmetic operators perform mathematical operations on numeric operands to produce numeric results. Let's enter a formula to illustrate each arithmetic

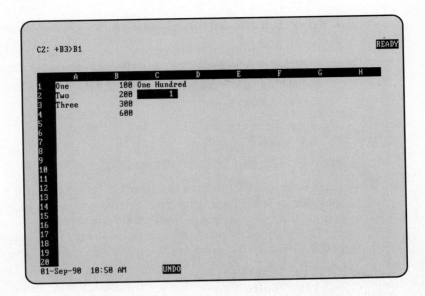

Figure 19 A Logical Formula

operator. After you enter each formula, examine the screen and make sure you understand the result. First, move the cell pointer to C4:

> Press **F5**
> Type **c4**
> Press **Enter**

The addition operator (+) adds two values.

> Type **25+b1**
> Press **Enter**

The subtraction operator (−) subtracts one value from another.

> Type **450−b3**
> Press **Enter**

The negation operator (−) makes a value negative.

> Type **−b1**
> Press **Enter**

The multiplication operator (*) multiplies two values.

> Type **15*b1**
> Press **Enter**

The division operator (/) divides one value by another.

> Type **+b3/b1**
> Press **Enter**

The exponentiation operator (^) takes a value to a power.

> Type **2^3**
> Press **Enter**

This formula takes 2 to the 3rd power, which is 8.

Step 6: Try the String Operator

Lotus 1-2-3 has only one string operator, the string combination operator &. Try an example of a formula that uses the string combination operator:

Type   **+a1&" "&a2&" "&a3**
Press   **Enter**

You should see *One Two Three* in the current cell.

Step 7: Try the Logical Operators

Logical operators produce the result 1 for TRUE or 0 for FALSE. Let's try an example of each logical operator. After you enter each formula, examine the screen and make sure you understand the result.

The = operator produces a result of 1 for TRUE only if its two operands are equal. Otherwise it produces 0 for FALSE.

Type   **+b1=100**
Press   **Enter**

The < operator produces a result of 1 for TRUE only if its first operand is less than its second operand. Otherwise it produces 0 for FALSE.

Type   **100<b1**
Press   **Enter**

The <= operator produces a result of 1 for TRUE only if its first operand is less than or equal to its second operand. Otherwise it produces 0 for FALSE.

Type   **100<=b1**
Press   **Enter**

The > operator produces a result of 1 for TRUE only if its first operand is greater than its second operand. Otherwise it produces 0 for FALSE.

Type   **+b1>100**
Press   **Enter**

The >= operator produces a result of 1 for TRUE only if its first operand is greater than or equal to its second operand. Otherwise it produces 0 for FALSE.

Type   **+b1>=100**
Press   **Enter**

The <> operator produces a result of 1 for TRUE only if its two operands are not equal. Otherwise it produces 0 for FALSE.

Type   **+b1<>100**
Press   **Enter**

The #NOT# operator negates a logical result. It produces 1 for TRUE if its operand was FALSE, or 0 for FALSE if its operand was TRUE.

Press   **Down Arrow**
Type   **#not#c4**
Press   **Enter**

The #AND# operator produces 1 for TRUE only if both of its operands are TRUE. Otherwise it produces 0 for FALSE.

Type   **+c4#and#1**
Press   **Enter**

The #OR# operator produces 0 for FALSE only if both of its operands are FALSE. Otherwise it produces 1 for TRUE.

Type   **+c4#or#1**
Press   **Enter**

Step 8: Understand the Order of Operations

When more than one operator is used in a formula, the operations are executed in a specific order. For example, try this formula:

Type   **+b1+b2/b3**
Press   **Enter**

You might expect the 100 in B1 to be added to the 200 in B2, and the result to be divided by the 300 in B3 to yield 1. In this case, however, the operations do not proceed from left to right. The division is performed before the addition, so the result is 100.6666.

You must understand the order of operations to construct formulas that execute correctly. The table below lists the Lotus 1-2-3 operators in order of priority or precedence. In other words, the ^ operator is executed first and the #AND#, #OR#, or & operator is executed last. Operators that appear on the same line in the table have equal precedence and are executed from left to right in a formula.

Order of Operations

Precedence	Operators	Operations
1	^	Exponentiation
2	–	Negation
3	* /	Multiplication and division
4	+ –	Addition and subtraction
5	= < <= > >= <>	Logical comparisons
6	#NOT#	Logical NOT
7	#AND# #OR# &	Logical AND, logical OR, and string combination

Step 9: Use Parentheses

Although it is important to understand the order of operations, you can eliminate much confusion by using parentheses in your formulas. Expressions in parentheses are evaluated first, regardless of the order of operations. When in doubt about the order of operations, use parentheses to force the order you want. For example, try this formula:

Type   **(b1+b2)/b3**
Press   **Enter**

First, the 100 in B1 is added to the 200 in B2. The sum, 300, is then divided by the 300 in B3 to yield a result of 1 (see Figure 20).

Expressions in parentheses can be nested within other parentheses. The expression inside the innermost set of parentheses is evaluated first. Evaluation

Figure 20 A Formula that Uses Parentheses

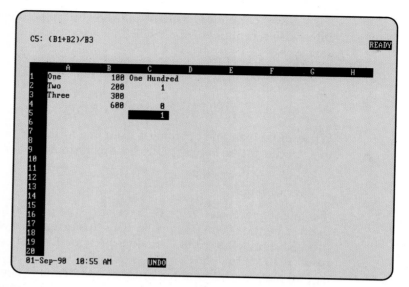

```
C5: (B1+B2)/B3                                                    READY

       A          B       C        D       E       F       G       H
1    One         100  One Hundred
2    Two         200       1
3    Three       300
4                600       0
5                          1
6
7
8
9
10
11
12
13
14
15
16
17
18
19
20
01-Sep-90  10:55 AM          UNDO
```

then proceeds progressively outward. Expressions within parentheses at the same level of nesting are evaluated from left to right.

Practice

1. Enter a formula to divide the result in cell B4 by 3.

2. Enter a formula to test whether the contents of cell B3 is greater than the sum of cells B1 and B2.

3. Enter a formula to add the contents of cells B1, B2, and B3 and divide the sum by 10.

Lesson 17: Using Functions

Lotus 1-2-3 functions are ready-made procedures that you can use to perform complex or common operations. For example, the @SUM function, which you have already used in this chapter, adds the contents of any range of cells. Lotus 1-2-3 provides built-in functions, like those in high-level programming languages such as BASIC or Pascal, so that users don't have to "reinvent the wheel" whenever they need to perform certain routine calculations. Functions make it easier to manipulate data in a worksheet because they provide convenience and accuracy. The built-in functions include many operations users may not know how to do on their own. For instance, do you remember how to compute a square root? Could you figure out how to compute a square root with a Lotus 1-2-3 formula? Fortunately, 1-2-3 has the @SQRT function, which will compute a square root for you.

Some functions perform operations that may be difficult or even impossible to do in any other way. For example, if you had to tally the values in 1,000 cells, you could not do it by adding the individual cells. Even if you wanted to enter all 1,000 cell addresses and plus signs, Lotus 1-2-3 would not let you, because 240 is the maximum number of characters you can enter into a cell. The @SUM function, however, lets you add up the contents of 1,000 cells as easily as 3 cells.

Lotus 1-2-3 has more than 90 different built-in functions. This lesson will introduce only a few of the most commonly used functions. You will learn more functions later. The Lotus 1-2-3 Command Summary appendix at the end of this book lists all of the Lotus 1-2-3 functions.

Step 1: Try Some Mathematical Functions

Mathematical functions compute a numeric result given one or more other numeric values. Let's try a few examples.

Type   **@abs(-25)**
Press   **Enter**

The result should be 25. The @ABS function computes the absolute value of a number. In other words, it converts a negative value to a positive value.

Type   **@int(2.667)**
Press   **Enter**

The result should be 2. The @INT function converts a value to an integer by truncating the fractional part.

Type   **@log(100)**
Press   **Enter**

The result should be 2. The @LOG function computes the base 10 logarithm of a value.

Type   **@mod(7,3)**
Press   **Enter**

The @MOD function returns the remainder (modulus) from a division operation. In this case, the result should be 1, the remainder you get when 7 is divided by 3.

Type   **@rand**
Press   **Enter**

The result could be any number between 0 and 1. The @RAND function returns a random number between 0 and 1. Random numbers are sometimes used in statistics and games.

Type   **@round(2.2468,3)**
Press   **Enter**

The result should be 2.247. The @ROUND function rounds a value to a specified number of decimal places, in this case 3.

Type   **@sqrt(9)**
Press   **Enter**

The result should be 3. The @SQRT function computes the square root of a value.

Step 2: Try Some Trigonometric Functions

Trigonometric functions are mathematical functions that deal with angles. Let's try a few examples.

Type   **@pi**
Press   **Enter**

The result should be 3.141592. The @PI function returns the value of π, the ratio of the circumference of a circle to its diameter.

Type   `@sin(@pi/2)`
Press   **Enter**

The result should be 1. The @SIN function returns the sine of an angle assumed to be expressed in radians. Notice how functions are combined in the above formula.

Type   `@cos(0)`
Press   **Enter**

The result should be 1. The @COS function returns the cosine of an angle assumed to be expressed in radians.

Type   `@tan(@pi/4)`
Press   **Enter**

The result should be 1. The @TAN function returns the tangent of an angle assumed to be expressed in radians.

Step 3: Try Some Statistical Functions

Statistical functions perform calculations on lists of values. These lists may be single values, ranges, or combinations of both. Let's try a few examples. The following examples assume you still have the values 100, 200, and 300 in cells B1, B2, and B3.

Type   `@avg(b1..b3)`
Press   **Enter**

The result should be 200. The @AVG function computes the average (or mean) of a list of values.

Type   `@count(b1..b3)`
Press   **Enter**

The result should be 3. The @COUNT function returns the number of nonblank cells in a list of cells.

Type   `@max(b1..b3)`
Press   **Enter**

The result should be 300. The @MAX function returns the maximum value in a list of values.

Type   `@min(b1..b3)`
Press   **Enter**

The result should be 100. The @MIN function returns the minimum value in a list of values.

Type   `@sum(b1,b1..b3,200)`
Press   **Enter**

The result should be 900. The @SUM function computes the sum of a list of values. This example shows how a list of values can contain individual cells, ranges, and constant values separated by commas.

Step 4: Try Some Financial Functions

Spreadsheet programs are used extensively in accounting, business, and finance. Lotus 1-2-3 provides functions for calculations concerning loans, annuities, and cash flows. Let's try a few examples.

Type   **@pmt(9000,1%,48)**
Press   **Enter**

The @PMT function computes the payment on a loan per payment period for a given principal amount, interest rate, and number of periods. The above formula could represent the monthly payment on a new car loan of $9,000 (the principal), at 1% per month (12% annual) interest rate, for 48 monthly payment periods. If you round the result to two decimal places, the monthly payment would be $237.

Type   **@pv(2000,8%,10)**
Press   **Enter**

The @PV function computes the present value of an investment, given the payment amount, discounted interest rate, and number of periods. Suppose that you have the opportunity to make an investment that will return $2,000 per year for the next ten years. To receive this fixed yearly payment or annuity of $2,000, you must invest $10,000. Is it wise to spend $10,000 today to earn $20,000 over the next ten years? You must compute the present value of the $2000 payments you will receive to decide if the investment is sound. Assume that as an alternative to this annuity, you can earn 8% investing your money in certificates of deposit. This 8% will be the discounted interest rate of the investment. The above

Real World

Temporaries Trained to Use Lotus 1-2-3

Kelly Services, one of the largest agencies of temporary workers in the United States, now provides employees who are spreadsheet literate. Because of the increase in the number of requests for temporary workers with spreadsheet skills, the agency has instituted a nationwide program to teach and certify its qualified employees in the use of programs such as Lotus 1-2-3.

"Depending on the mix of skills identified by our branch offices, we train to meet those needs," explained Carolyn Fryar, senior vice president of Kelly Services. "Software skills include setting the column width and cell display, retrieving a spreadsheet, activating calculations, sending to print, and storing a spreadsheet."

This program, the Kelly PC-Pro System for spreadsheet training, is now available in all 700 Kelly offices in the United States. Trainees receive detailed reference guides for selected spreadsheet programs and a toll-free hotline that they can call to get on-the-job help. Kelly temporaries who qualify for spread-sheet training include those who already have secretarial and word processing skills, or ledger and bookkeeping experience.

As more businesses and organizations acquire microcomputers and spreadsheet programs, their need for skilled employees grows. It seems that familiarity with spreadsheet programs is almost a necessity in today's business world.

Source: Daniel Sommer, "Kelly Trains Temps to Use Spreadsheets," *InfoWorld*, September 28, 1987, p. 48.

formula evaluates this situation. The result of 13,420.16 means that you should be willing to spend $13,420.16 now to receive $20,000 over the next ten years. Since your initial payment is only $10,000, this investment is sound.

Type   @fv(2000,8%,35)
Press   **Enter**

The @FV function computes the future value of an investment, based on a given payment, interest rate, and number of periods. Suppose you plan to deposit $2,000 at the end of each year into your Individual Retirement Account (IRA) for the next 35 years. The average rate of return on your IRA is 8% per year. How much money will you have in your IRA at the end of 35 years? The above formula answers this question. Your nest egg will be worth around $344,633 at the end of 35 years.

Type   @term(2000,8%,500000)
Press   **Enter**

The @TERM function computes the number of payment periods in the term of an investment, given a payment amount, interest rate, and future value amount. Given the scenario presented in the @FV example, how long will it take you to accumulate $500,000 in your IRA? The result of the above formula indicates that it would take a little over 39 and a half years (see Figure 21).

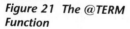**Practice**

1. Calculate the square root of 65536.
2. Calculate the cosine of 2π.
3. Calculate the average of these three numbers: 25.67, 89.46, and 65.32.
4. Calculate the monthly payment on a $50,000 loan with an interest rate of 12% per year (1% per month) and a term of 30 years (360 months).

Figure 21   The @TERM Function

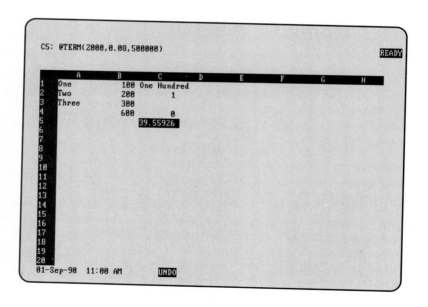

Summary

- *Starting 1-2-3.* Boot up the computer, switch to the proper disk or directory, and enter 123 from DOS.

- *Creating a worksheet.* Enter labels, numbers, and formulas into worksheet cells.

- *Using 1-2-3 menus.* Press / to activate the Main menu. Highlight a command and press Enter or type the command's first letter. Press Escape to return from a menu.

- *Saving a worksheet.* Execute the File Save command and enter the file name.

- *Printing a worksheet.* Execute the Print command, choose Printer or File, specify the range to print, and select the Go option.

- *Quitting 1-2-3.* Save the worksheet, then execute the Quit command from the Main menu.

- *Retrieving an existing worksheet.* Execute the File Retrieve command, then type or select the file name.

- *Getting help.* Press the F1 function key to activate the help facility. Press Escape to exit the help facility.

- *Moving around an existing worksheet.* The pointer movement keys include the arrow keys, Home, Page Up, Page Down, Tab, Ctrl-Right Arrow, Shift-Tab, and Ctrl-Left Arrow. Pressing End followed by an arrow key moves to the next intersection of a blank cell and nonblank cell in that direction. Pressing End followed by Home moves to the lowest rightmost nonblank cell. Pressing F5 prompts you for a cell address to go to.

- *Editing cells.* Retype an entire entry or press F2 to edit an existing entry.

- *Changing column widths.* Move to the column, execute the Worksheet Column Set-Width command, and enter the width.

- *Deleting and inserting columns and rows.* Move to the column or row and execute Worksheet Delete Column, Worksheet Delete Row, Worksheet Insert Column, or Worksheet Insert Row.

- *Copying and moving cells.* Execute the Copy or Move command, specify the source range, and specify the target range.

- *Formatting cells.* The label prefix characters include ' (left justify), ^ (center), " (right justify), and \ (fill a cell). Execute the Range Format command and select an option to format numbers and formula results.

- *Undoing commands.* Press Alt-F4 to invoke the Undo feature (not available in Lotus 1-2-3 Release 2.0).

- *Using formulas.* Three types of formulas can be used: numeric, string, and logical. The arithmetic operators are + (addition), − (subtraction and negation), * (multiplication), / (division), and ^ (exponentiation). The only string operator is &, which combines labels. The logical operators are =, <, >, <=, >=, <>, #NOT#, #AND#, and #OR#. Expression evaluation follows the order of operations unless parentheses are used.

- *Using functions.* Commonly-used mathematical functions include @ABS, @INT, @LOG, @MOD, @RAND, @ROUND, and @SQRT. Trigonometric functions include @PI, @SIN, @COS, and @TAN. Statistical functions include @AVG, @COUNT, @MAX, @MIN, and @SUM. Financial functions include @PMT, @PV, @FV, and @TERM.

Key Terms

As an extra review of this chapter, try defining the following terms.

cell
cell address (cell reference)
cell pointer
context-sensitive
control panel
current cell
data
formula
function
label
label prefix character
logical formula

menu pointer
mode indicator
number
numeric formula
operand
operator
pointer movement keys
range
string combination operator
string formula
worksheet

Multiple Choice

Choose the best selection to complete each statement.

1. Which command do you enter to start Lotus 1-2-3 from the DOS prompt?
   (a) START
   (b) 1-2-3
   (c) 123
   (d) CALC

2. A cell is a
   (a) worksheet row.
   (b) worksheet column.
   (c) column-row intersection.
   (d) piece of data.

3. How are the columns labeled in a 1-2-3 worksheet?
   (a) A to IV
   (b) 1 to 256
   (c) 1 to 8192
   (d) A to Z

4. What are the three types of data that can be entered into worksheet cells?
   (a) headings, text, and labels
   (b) numbers, labels, and formulas
   (c) sums, products, and quotients
   (d) commands, operators, and operands

5. What is an expression that tells 1-2-3 to perform a calculation?
   (a) cell
   (b) address
   (c) formula
   (d) operand

6. Which key do you press to edit the existing contents of a cell?
   (a) Escape
   (b) Delete
   (c) F1
   (d) F2

7. Which key do you press or character do you type to activate the Main menu?
   (a) /
   (b) M
   (c) Escape
   (d) F1

8. How many cells can Lotus 1-2-3 address?
   (a) 256
   (b) 8192
   (c) 10,000
   (d) 2,097,152

9. Which label prefix character do you use to center a label within its cell?

    (a) '

    (b) ^

    (c) "

    (d) \

10. Which of the following numbers is not a valid 1-2-3 entry?

    (a) 0.5

    (b) 100,000

    (c) 4.32E+05

    (d) −11.123

11. What is a predefined formula that performs a useful operation, such as computing a sum or a square root?

    (a) command

    (b) operator

    (c) function

    (d) operand

12. Which of the following expressions is a range?

    (a) A1..B10

    (b) +A1−B10

    (c) @RAND

    (d) /wey

13. Which keys would you press or letters would you type to execute the File Save command?

    (a) Alt-F4

    (b) /fs

    (c) Escape-Home

    (d) \save

14. Which key(s) do you press or letters do you type to invoke the help facility?

    (a) F1

    (b) F2

    (c) /h

    (d) Alt-F4

15. Which key will always move the cell pointer to A1?

    (a) Escape

    (b) Up Arrow

    (c) Shift-Tab

    (d) Home

16. The three basic types of 1-2-3 formulas are

    (a) mathematical, statistical, and financial.

    (b) numeric, string, and logical.

    (c) additive, multiplicative, and exponential.

    (d) micro, mini, and macro.

17. If all of the following operators were in the same formula without parentheses, which operator would be executed first?

    (a) +

    (b) −

    (c) *

    (d) ^

18. Which expression evaluates to 1?

    (a) 100+200/300

    (b) (100+200)/300

    (c) 1/100−99

    (d) 10^1−1

19. Which operator combines two labels?

    (a) +

    (b) *

    (c) &

    (d) @

20. Three examples of financial functions are

    (a) @ABS, @INT, and @LOG.

    (b) @AVG, @MAX, and @SUM.

    (c) @SIN, @COS, and @TAN.

    (d) @PMT, @FV, and @TERM.

Fill-In

1. A worksheet is a table of _____ and _____ of entries.
2. The _____ is the basic unit of storage in a worksheet—where you enter numbers, labels, and formulas.
3. Lotus 1-2-3 can address over two _____ cells.
4. The three lines at the top of the 1-2-3 screen are known as the _____.
5. To move the cell pointer one cell at a time, you would press one of the _____ keys.
6. To move the cell pointer to a particular address, you would press the _____ key.
7. The three types of data you can enter into worksheet cells are numbers, labels, and _____.
8. You can change the existing contents of the current cell by pressing F2 to invoke the _____ mode.
9. Type _____ to activate the Main menu of commands.
10. To select an option from a menu, type its first letter, or move the menu pointer on top of it and press _____.
11. A rectangular block of one or more adjacent cells is called a _____.
12. The _____ command is just like the Copy command, except that it erases the contents of the source range.
13. The _____ copies the worksheet on the screen to a disk file.
14. Press _____ to activate the help facility.
15. _____ formulas produce either TRUE (symbolized by a 1) or FALSE (symbolized by a 0).
16. An _____ is a symbol that represents an action to be performed in a formula.
17. Expressions inside _____ are evaluated first, regardless of the order of operations.
18. As do high-level programming languages, Lotus 1-2-3 provides a set of _____ to perform certain routine calculations.
19. The _____ function truncates the fractional part of a value.
20. The _____ function computes the payment on a loan per payment period for a given principal, interest rate, and term.

Short Problems

1. If you are not already running 1-2-3, start the program. Create and print a simple multiplication table for the numbers 1 through 6. Use these numbers as your row and column labels. Enter only the value 1. All other values in the table should be calculated using formulas.
2. Create a table of the cube root, square root, square, and cube for each whole number value from 1 to 25. List the number in column A, the cube root in column B, the square root in column C, the square in column D, and cube in column E. Enter only the numbers in column A. All other values should be calculated using formulas. Hint: use the exponentiation operator.
3. Use the @RAND function and the Copy command to put random numbers between 0 and 1 into cells A1 through A10. Notice how a different random

number appears in each cell. Move the cell pointer to B1 and enter a formula using the @INT function to convert the random number in cell A1 to an integer between 1 and 6 inclusive. Hint: Try @INT(A1*6)+1. Copy the formula from B1 to cells B2 through B10. This worksheet simulates the throwing of a die ten times.

4. Use the @RAND function and the Copy command to simulate 100 coin tosses. Do this by generating random numbers in cells A1 through A100. Then convert these random numbers into either 0 (for heads) or 1 (for tails). Hint: Try @INT(A1*2) in B1 and copy this formula to cells B2 through B100. Use the @AVG function to compute the mean of the zeros and ones, which will be the probability of getting a tail. It should be near 0.5.

5. Make up twenty exam grades from 0 to 100 and enter them into cells A1 through A20. Use the @MAX function to find the highest grade and the @MIN function to find the lowest grade. Use the @AVG function to calculate the mean grade.

6. Use the @PMT function to calculate the monthly mortgage payment on a $100,000 home loan that has an interest rate of 10% per year and a term of 20 years.

7. You can calculate the number of periods to pay back a loan with the @TERM function if you use a negative value as the future value and take the absolute value of the result. Try the following formula to calculate the number of months it will take to pay back a $100,000 loan with an interest rate of 10% per year making monthly payments of $965.02:

@ABS(@TERM(965.02,10%/12,-100000))

8. You just won $20 million in the new MegaBucks state lottery. You are given two payment options. You can receive 20 annual payments of $1 million at the end of each year, or you can receive an immediate lump sum payment of $8 million. Which option is worth more in today's dollars? Assume that if you accept the 20 annual payments of $1 million, you would invest the money at an interest rate of 8%, compounded annually. Hint: Try @PV(1000000,8%,20). The result will show that the $20 million paid over 20 years is worth $9,818,147.41 in today's dollars. Take the 20 annual payments.

9. Create a worksheet that will compute automobile gas mileage. Put the mileage when the tank is first filled in cell A1, the mileage when the tank is filled the second time in cell A2, and the number of gallons it took to refill the tank in cell A3. Enter a formula to compute the miles per gallon in cell A4.

10. Reproduce the following table in a 1-2-3 worksheet. You will need to use the Worksheet Column Set-Width and the Range Format commands to set up the worksheet to display such large numbers. Use formulas to compute the two totals.

ACCOUNT	THIS YEAR	LAST YEAR
Cash on hand	344,584,904.50	235,452,143.60
Receivables	655,473,321.08	527,004,321.97
Inventories	315,733,211.95	130,982,021.80
Real estate	894,992.20	864,389.10
Equipment	448,993,406.00	406,894,600.00
Sales	772,345,236.75	652,945,870.25
TOTAL		

Long Problems

1. Create a worksheet that lists your major expenditures for the past 12 months. Include items like rent, room and board, or mortgage payments; tuition; power bills; telephone bills; health, automobile, and property insurance; travel expenses; credit card purchases; and so on. Be sure to compute both the row and column totals. Try to use the Copy command to reduce repetitive typing. Use appropriate labels and numeric formatting to improve the clarity and appearance of your worksheet.

2. Create a worksheet listing all of the courses you are taking this semester, along with the number of credit hours and the grade you expect. Also include a column showing the numerical equivalent for each grade you expect (A = 4.0, B = 3.0, C = 2.0, D = 1.0, and F = 0.0). Have your worksheet total your number of hours and your grade points and calculate your grade point average.

3. Suppose you have decided to purchase a new microcomputer system. List eight or ten components and supplies you'll need (computer, display adapter, monitor, disk drives, expansion boards, printer, cables, diskettes, paper, and so on). Enter these headings into column A and estimate an amount for each item in column B. Using ads from computer magazines or information from a local retailer, enter the actual costs for these items into column C. Enter a formula and use the Copy command to calculate the differences between your budgeted and actual costs in column D. Include column totals for each of the numeric columns, and add appropriate column headings.

4. In a small local newspaper the fee for classified advertising is a function of the price charged for the item. The fee is collected only if the item sells. The fee is 10% of the first $100.00 of the advertised price, plus 3% of the second $100.00, plus 2% of the third $100.00, plus 1% of the amount of the advertised price over $300.00. Create a worksheet that will accept the advertised price as input and calculate the advertising fee. Test your worksheet using prices of $140.00 (fee = $11.20) and $750.00 (fee = $19.50).

5. Once upon a time, a king won great acclaim from his subjects by abolishing all taxes. In their place, he told the people that they would have to place one grain of wheat in one square of a checkerboard at the end of the first year. At the end of the second year, they would owe him two grains, placed in the second square. At the end of the third year, they would owe four grains, placed in the third square, and at the end of the fourth year, eight grains in the fourth square, and so on up to the sixty-fourth square of the checkerboard. After that, they would own their land outright and wouldn't have to give up any more wheat. Update this problem using pennies instead of wheat, and produce a worksheet that shows each of the sixty-four years, the amount paid that year, and the total amount paid to date. Does this worksheet help explain the revolt that deposed the king several years later?

6. Assume you own 200 individual student apartments now renting for $110.00 a month. Since all your apartments are currently occupied, your gross is $22,000.00 per month. A real estate agent tells you your rent is way too low, but he further states that if you decide to raise the rent, you would lose one tenant for every $7.50 rent increase. In other words, you would be able to rent only 199 of the apartments at $117.50, 198 apartments at $125.00, and so on. Prepare a worksheet that will list in one column the number of apartments rented, in the second column the rent per apartment, and in the third

column the gross income for that particular combination of number rented and rent per apartment. What does your table suggest the rent should be?

7. Suppose you start a savings account that pays interest at a rate of 6% per year, and interest is paid monthly. In other words, you will receive 0.5% per month on your balance. You decide to begin a systematic savings plan in which you will deposit $10.00 per month. Create a worksheet that will show the amount of interest earned each month and the ending balance each month for a period of five years.

8. Consider the expenses of a typical traveling business person (airline tickets, automobile rental, mileage, meals, lodging, supplies, and so on). Construct a worksheet that keeps track of such expenses for each month of the year. Total all rows and columns and do a grand total.

9. Create a worksheet to maintain and balance your checkbook. Have column A contain the check number, column B the date, column C the payment or withdrawal amount, column D the deposit amount, column E an "x" if the transaction has cleared, and column F a description of the transaction. Leave a few blank rows at the top of the worksheet. In one of these cells, compute the current balance by subtracting the sum of the payments from the sum of the deposits. The first entry in the check register should be a deposit with the beginning balance. Enter at least twenty transactions into your checkbook worksheet and verify the computed balance.

10. Create a worksheet to track your income and taxes. For each month of the past year, list your gross income, federal income taxes withheld, state income taxes withheld, any other withholdings, and your net income. Then total the columns.

INTERMEDIATE LOTUS 1-2-3

In This Chapter

▆ Preview

In Beginning Lotus 1-2-3 you learned the basics of Lotus 1-2-3, the top-selling microcomputer spreadsheet package. This chapter teaches you how to create graphs and manage worksheet data bases using Lotus 1-2-3.

After studying this chapter, you will know how to

- create a bar graph.
- print a graph.
- name a graph.
- create a pie chart.
- create a line graph.
- create a stacked bar graph.
- create an XY graph.
- create a data base worksheet.
- sort a data base worksheet.
- search a data base worksheet.
- extract data from a worksheet.
- use the data base functions.

▆ Getting Started

You've already learned how to start Lotus 1-2-3 and use its most basic features and commands. This chapter assumes you have completed the lessons and exercises in the previous chapter. Furthermore, it assumes that you have a computer with a hard disk and Lotus 1-2-3 installed on it in a subdirectory named 123 or 123R3. A DOS PATH should be set up so that you can run Lotus 1-2-3 from within any subdirectory. You should have a subdirectory named LESSONS in which to store your worksheet files.

▆ Lesson 1: Creating a Bar Graph

VisiCalc, the first spreadsheet program, originally developed for the Apple II computer in 1979, could not produce graphs. Since the introduction of Lotus 1-2-3 for the IBM Personal Computer in 1982, however, graphics capability has been considered an essential component of any serious spreadsheet package. Lotus 1-2-3 can produce several different types of graphs from worksheet data.

Let's create a bar graph that will show a company's sales over a period of years. A **bar graph** is a chart in which numeric values are represented by evenly spaced, thick vertical lines. Bar graphs are useful for comparing different sets of data, such as the sales figures for several different years.

Step 1: Start 1-2-3

If you are not already running Lotus 1-2-3, switch to your LESSONS subdirectory and start the program:

Type   **cd c:\lessons**
Press   **Enter**
Type   **123**
Press   **Enter**

Step 2: Set Up a New Worksheet

In a spreadsheet program, a graph is created from data in a worksheet. So, you must first create the worksheet that contains the data for the graph. Widen column A to 16 characters:

Type   `/wcs16`
Press **Enter**

Change the numeric format of the range B2 to E2 so that numbers are presented as currency values with no decimal places:

Type   `/rfc0`
Press **Enter**
Type   `b2..e2`
Press **Enter**

Step 3: Enter the Data

Follow these directions to enter the data for the graph into the worksheet:

Press **Right Arrow**
Type   **1988**
Press **Right Arrow**
Type   **1989**
Press **Right Arrow**
Type   **1990**
Press **Right Arrow**
Type   **1991**
Press **Home**
Press **Down Arrow**
Type   **Sales (millions)**
Press **Right Arrow**
Type   **55**
Press **Right Arrow**
Type   **115**
Press **Right Arrow**
Type   **150**
Press **Right Arrow**
Type   **210**
Press **Home**

Your screen should look like Figure 1. Check your work against Figure 1 and correct any mistakes you made.

Step 4: Save the Worksheet

It is a good idea to save your worksheet in a disk file before you generate a graph. Execute the File Save command and name the worksheet file SALES:

Type   `/fs`
Type   `sales`
Press **Enter**

Figure 1 The SALES Bar Graph Worksheet

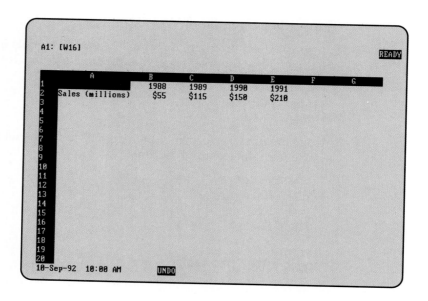

Step 5: Execute the Graph Command

To create a graph, you must execute the Graph command from the Main menu:

Type   **/g**

The Graph menu will appear across the top of the screen (see Figure 2). If you are running Lotus 1-2-3 Release 2.2, the Graph Settings sheet will also appear. Release 2.0 and Release 3.1 do not display a Graph Settings sheet.

Step 6: Select the Type of Graph

Examine the third line of the control panel. Since the Type command is highlighted, the third line of the control panel displays the submenu of options available if you select the Type command. Lotus 1-2-3 Release 2.0 and Release 2.2 let you create five basic types of graphs. Lotus 1-2-3 Release 3.1 lets you create seven basic types of graphs. Select Bar as the type of graph you want to create:

Type   **tb**

Step 7: Specify the X Data Range

In bar, line, and stacked bar graphs, the X data range contains the values or labels that will appear along the horizontal x-axis. In the SALES bar graph, the years should be presented along the x-axis, so select B1 to E1 as the X data range:

Type   **x**
Type   **b1..e1**
Press   **Enter**

Step 8: Specify the A Data Range

Next you must specify the cells that contain the actual numeric data to be graphed along the y-axis. Some graphs may contain as many as six data ranges. In Lotus 1-2-3, these data ranges are specified as A, B, C, D, E, and F. For your simple

Figure 2 The Graph Menu and Graph Settings Sheet

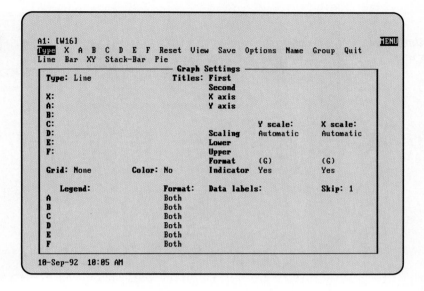

SALES bar graph, only one data range is necessary. Specify the A data range as B2 to E2:

Type   **a**
Type   **b2..e2**
Press   **Enter**

Step 9: Add Titles

Most graphs make little sense unless they have a main title and titles along the axes. Select Options, Titles, and First, and then enter the first line of the graph title:

Type   **otf**
Type   **Beaver Canoe Company**
Press   **Enter**

Enter the second line of the graph title:

Type   **ts**
Type   **Yearly Sales of Aluminum Canoes**
Press   **Enter**

Enter a title for the x-axis:

Type   **tx**
Type   **Year**
Press   **Enter**

Enter a title for the y-axis:

Type   **ty**
Type   **Sales (millions)**
Press   **Enter**

Quit the Options submenu and return to the Graph menu:

Type   **q**

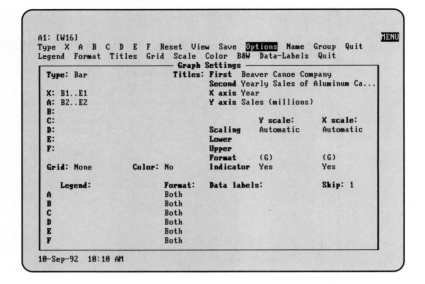

Figure 3 The Completed Graph Settings Sheet

If you are running Lotus 1-2-3 Release 2.2, the graph settings you have specified will be summarized in the Graph Setting sheet on the screen (see Figure 3).

Step 10: View the Graph

If your computer is equipped with a graphics adapter and monitor, you can view the graph you have specified. Select the View option from the Graph menu:

Type   **v**

Your screen should look like Figure 4. When you are finished looking at the graph, you can press any key to return to the Graph menu:

Press   **Escape**

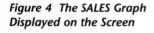

Figure 4 The SALES Graph Displayed on the Screen

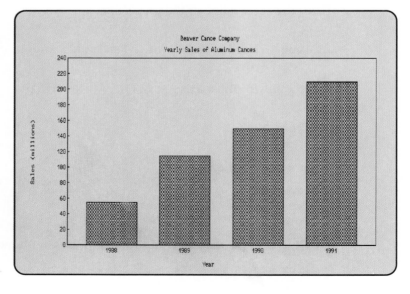

Step 11: Save the Graph

Examine the Graph menu on your screen. The Save option lets you save the graph you have created in a file with a PIC extension. This type of graph file can be printed later with the Lotus PrintGraph program or loaded by another application package, such as a word processor or a graphics program that can accept Lotus PIC files. Select the Save option from the Graph menu to save your graph in a file named SALES.PIC:

    Type   **s**
    Type   **sales**
    Press **Enter**

Quit the Graph menu and return to READY mode:

    Type   **q**

Note that Release 3.1 uses a CGM extension instead of PIC.

Step 12: Save the Worksheet

You have saved the graph to a file named SALES.PIC, but you must also save the worksheet to preserve the graph settings you have specified. Execute the File Save command and replace the worksheet file on the disk:

    Type   **/fs**
    Press **Enter**
    Type   **r**

Practice

1. When you create a graph, you must view it the first time by selecting the View option from the Graph menu. After that, you can use a shortcut from READY mode to view the graph:

    Press **F10**

The F10 key presents the current graph on the screen. Press any key to return to READY mode.

2. Lotus 1-2-3 provides many options for altering the appearance of a graph. For example, you can add horizontal grid lines to your SALES graph to make it easier to determine the exact heights of the bars:

    Type   **/goghqv**

Press any key to return to the graph menu.

3. Save the new graph with grid lines to SALES.PIC and save the SALES worksheet as well.

Lesson 2: Printing a Graph with Release 2.0 or 2.2

If you are running Lotus 1-2-3 Release 2.0 or Release 2.2, you must use a separate program called PrintGraph to print your graphs. Skip this lesson if you are running Lotus 1-2-3 Release 3.1.

Step 1: Exit 1-2-3

Before you can start PrintGraph, you must exit 1-2-3. Make sure that you have saved your worksheet, then

Type   **/qy**

You should see the DOS prompt on your screen.

Step 2: Start PrintGraph

To run the PrintGraph program, execute the PGRAPH command from the DOS prompt:

Type   **pgraph**
Press   **Enter**

The PrintGraph screen will appear (see Figure 5).

Step 3: Change the Hardware Settings

Examine the Hardware Settings on the right side of the screen. You may have to change these settings. If your computer has a hard disk, the Graphs directory should be C:\LESSONS, and the Fonts directory should be C:\123. In addition, a printer should be selected. Follow these directions to change the hardware settings if necessary:

Type   **shg**
Press   **Escape**
Type   **c:\lessons**
Press   **Enter**
Type   **f**
Press   **Escape**
Type   **c:\123**
Press   **Enter**

Figure 5 The PrintGraph Screen

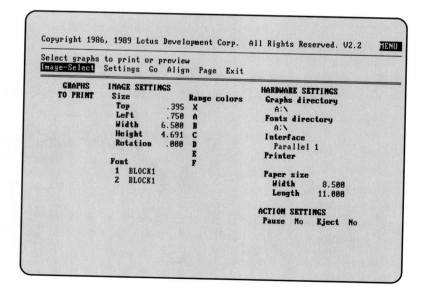

```
Copyright 1986, 1989 Lotus Development Corp.  All Rights Reserved. V2.2   MENU

Select graphs to print or preview
Image-Select  Settings  Go  Align  Page  Exit

  GRAPHS    IMAGE SETTINGS                      HARDWARE SETTINGS
  TO PRINT    Size              Range colors      Graphs directory
              Top       .395   X                    A:\
              Left      .750   A                  Fonts directory
              Width    6.500   B                    A:\
              Height   4.691   C                  Interface
              Rotation  .000   D                    Parallel 1
                               E                  Printer
            Font               F
              1  BLOCK1                           Paper size
              2  BLOCK1                             Width     8.500
                                                   Length   11.000

                                                 ACTION SETTINGS
                                                   Pause  No  Eject  No
```

Now select the printer:

> Type   **p**

A list of the printers connected to your computer will appear, with two options for each printer: Low density and High density. Low density will produce quick, low-quality printouts. High density will produce slow, high-quality printouts. Highlight the printer and density you want to use.

> Press   **Space Bar**
> Press   **Enter**

Quit the Hardware Settings menu and the Settings menu:

> Type   **qq**

Step 4: Select the Image

Execute the Image-Select option from the Main PrintGraph menu:

> Type   **i**

A list of graph (PIC) files will be displayed on the screen.

> Highlight   **SALES**
> Press   **Space Bar**
> Press   **Enter**

Step 5: Prepare the Printer

Make sure the printer is connected to the computer and turned on. Also, make sure that paper is loaded and aligned to the top of a new page. Finally, make sure that the printer's On Line light is lit. (If it isn't, press the On Line button.)

Step 6: Select the Go Option

After you have specified all of the PrintGraph settings you want to use and have prepared the printer, select the Go option to actually print the graph.

> Type   **g**

The graph will be printed.

Step 7: Exit PrintGraph and Start 1-2-3

After the graph has been printed, exit the PrintGraph program, return to DOS, and start 1-2-3 again:

> Type   **ey**
> Type   **123**
> Press   **Enter**

Practice   Use the PrintGraph program to print the SALES graph at the other density setting. If you like, try changing some of the image settings, such as graph size, colors, and font. When you are finished experimenting with PrintGraph, exit the program and start 1-2-3 again.

Lesson 3: Printing a Graph with Release 3.1

If you are running Lotus 1-2-3 Release 3.1, you do not need to use a separate program to print out your graphs. Skip this lesson if you are running Lotus 1-2-3 Release 2.0 or Release 2.2.

Step 1: Execute the Print Printer Image Current Go Command

Printing a graph with Lotus 1-2-3 Release 3.1 is much easier than printing a graph with Release 2.0 or 2.2. You can print the current graph with the Print Printer Image Current Go command without leaving the 1-2-3 program.

Type **/ppicg**

The graph will be produced by the printer.

Step 2: Return to READY Mode

Select the Quit option from the Print menu to return to READY mode:

Type **q**

Practice   You can print the SALES graph to a file instead of directly to the printer, but you must use the Encoded option instead of the File option. Follow these directions to create an encoded file named SALES.ENC that can be printed later from DOS:

Type   **/pe**
Type   **sales**
Press **Enter**
Type   **icg**
Type   **q**

To print SALES.ENC from DOS, exit 1-2-3 and execute this command:

Type   **copy sales.enc prn**
Press **Enter**

When the printer is finished, start 1-2-3 again.

Lesson 4: Naming a Graph

If you change the graph settings in the SALES worksheet, 1-2-3 will produce a different graph. Suppose you want to create a different type of graph from the same worksheet without losing the previous graph. Fortunately, 1-2-3 lets you have several graphs associated with the same worksheet. All you have to do is name your graphs.

Step 1: Retrieve the SALES Worksheet

If the SALES worksheet is not already on your screen, retrieve it from the disk:

Type   **/fr**
Highlight **SALES.WK1** (or **SALES.WK3**)
Press   **Enter**

Step 2: View the Graph

Make sure that the current graph is the one you want to name. In this case, only one graph is associated with the SALES worksheet, but it cannot hurt to check.

Press **F10**

You should see the bar graph on the screen. Return to READY mode:

Press **Escape**

Step 3: Execute the Graph Name Create Command

To associate a name with an existing graph, execute the Graph Name Create command:

Type **/gnc**

Step 4: Enter a Graph Name

Lotus 1-2-3 will prompt you to enter a graph name. You can specify a name up to 15 characters long (14 characters long in Release 2.0).

Type **sales_bar**
Press **Enter**

Return to READY mode:

Type **q**

Step 5: Use a Named Graph

The Graph Name Use command retrieves a named graph and makes it the current graph.

Type **/gnu**

Lotus 1-2-3 will present a menu of graph names. Currently, only one name exists for the SALES worksheet: SALES_BAR. Select this graph:

Highlight **SALES_BAR**
Press **Enter**

The program will display the bar graph on the screen. Press any key to return to the Graph menu, then quit to READY mode:

Press **Escape**
Type **q**

Practice　　If you modify a named graph after you retrieve it, and want to save the changed settings, you must use the Graph Name Create and File Save commands again. Follow these directions:

Type **/gnc**
Highlight **SALES_BAR**
Press **Enter**
Type **q**
Type **/fs**
Press **Enter**
Type **r**

Lesson 5: Creating a Pie Chart

A **pie chart** represents values as wedges of a circle. Pie charts are used to show the parts of a whole. For example, a pie chart might be used to break down total sales into various categories. Let's make a pie chart for Beaver Canoe Company that shows its canoe sales at sport shows, camping stores, boat stores, department stores, and the factory outlet.

Step 1: Create the Worksheet

Let's enter the data for the pie chart in an empty area of the SALES worksheet. Move the cell pointer to A5 and enter the following data:

Press	**F5**
Type	**a5**
Press	**Enter**
Type	**Sport Show**
Press	**Right Arrow**
Type	**10**
Press	**Down Arrow**
Type	**40**
Press	**Left Arrow**
Type	**Camping Store**
Press	**Down Arrow**
Type	**Boat Store**
Press	**Right Arrow**
Type	**60**
Press	**Down Arrow**
Type	**70**
Press	**Left Arrow**
Type	**Department Store**
Press	**Down Arrow**
Type	**Factory Outlet**
Press	**Right Arrow**
Type	**30**
Press	**Enter**

The numbers you have entered represent the sales in millions of dollars at each of the outlets. Your screen should look like Figure 6. Check your work against Figure 6 and correct any mistakes you find.

Step 2: Save the Worksheet

It is a good idea to save your worksheet before you generate the graph. Execute the File Save command:

Type	**/fs**
Press	**Enter**
Type	**r**

Step 3: Execute the Graph Reset Graph Command

Since you already have a graph defined as the current graph, execute the Graph Reset Graph command to clear the settings.

Type	**/grg**

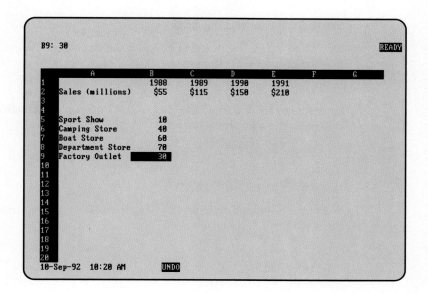

Figure 6 The Pie Chart Data

Step 4: Specify the Type Pie Option

Now tell 1-2-3 that you want to create a pie chart:

Type   **tp**

Step 5: Specify the X Data Range

In a pie chart, the X data range contains the labels for the slices of the pie. Specify the X data range as cells A5 to A9:

Type   **x**
Type   **a5..a9**
Press **Enter**

Step 6: Specify the A Data Range

In a pie chart, the A data range contains the values that will be represented as slices. Specify the A data range as cells B5 to B9:

Type   **a**
Type   **b5..b9**
Press **Enter**

Step 7: Add Titles

Use the Options Titles command to add a two-line title to the pie chart:

Type   **otf**
Type   **Beaver Canoe Company**
Press **Enter**
Type   **ts**
Type   **1991 Sales to Various Outlets**
Press **Enter**

Quit the Options submenu and return to the Graph menu:

Type   **q**

Step 8: View the Graph

Now you can view the graph you have specified. Select the View option from the Graph menu:

Type   **v**

Your screen should look like Figure 7. When you are finished looking at the graph, return to the Graph menu:

Press   **Escape**

Step 9: Save the Graph

Select the Save option from the Graph menu to save your pie chart in a file named PIE.PIC:

Type   **s**
Type   **pie**
Press   **Enter**

Step 10: Name the Graph

Since you now have two graphs associated with the SALES worksheet, you should name the pie chart. Execute the Name Create option and specify SALES_PIE as the name of the graph:

Type   **nc**
Type   **sales_pie**
Press   **Enter**

Quit the Graph menu and return to READY mode:

Type   **q**

Step 11: Save the Worksheet

You have saved the graph to a file named PIE.PIC and named the graph SALES_PIE, but you must also save the worksheet to preserve the graph settings you have specified. Execute the File Save command and replace the worksheet file on the disk:

Type   **/fs**
Press   **Enter**
Type   **r**

Practice   1. If your computer has a monochrome monitor, the pie chart you have created appears quite plain. You can, however, tell 1-2-3 to use different hatch patterns for the pie slices. You can even explode, or pull out, one or more slices for emphasis. These settings are specified by creating a B data range. Follow these directions:

Press   **F5**
Type   **c5**
Press   **Enter**
Type   **1**
Press   **Down Arrow**

Figure 7 The Sales Pie Chart

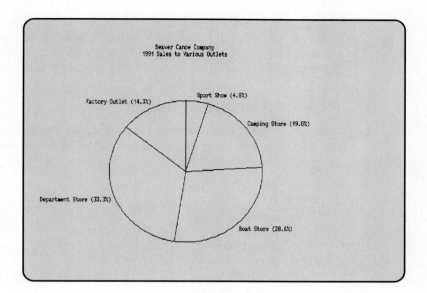

Type	**2**
Press	**Down Arrow**
Type	**103**
Press	**Down Arrow**
Type	**4**
Press	**Down Arrow**
Type	**5**
Press	**Enter**
Type	**/gb**
Type	**c5..c9**
Press	**Enter**
Type	**v**

Each slice now has a different pattern, and the Boat Store slice is exploded. Eight different hatch patterns, numbered 1 through 8, are available in Lotus 1-2-3 Releases 2.0 and 2.2. Release 3.1 has fourteen different hatch patterns. These are the numbers entered in the B data range. To explode a slice, you add 100 to the hatch pattern number in the B data range. So, the Boat Store cell in the B data range signifies hatch pattern 3 added to the 100 that indicates the slice is to be exploded from the pie.

Note that if you have a color monitor and the Graph Options Color option is set, each slice will have a different color instead of a different hatch pattern. You can select the Graph Options B&W option to display a black and white graph and see the hatch patterns.

2. Use the Name Create option to save SALES_PIE again and execute the File Save command to update the worksheet on the disk.

3. Print the new pie chart you have created.

Lesson 6: Creating a Line Graph

A **line graph** represents each data value by a point at an appropriate distance above the horizontal axis. Related points are designated by the same symbol and are connected by line segments. Line graphs are useful for plotting values that change over time. For example, the Beaver Canoe Company could use a line graph to plot the units of three canoe models sold over the past five years. Because line graphs emphasize the continuity of data over time, they are especially handy for identifying trends and making projections.

Step 1: Create the Worksheet

Let's create the line graph we just described for the Beaver Canoe Company. You can enter the data in an empty area of the SALES worksheet. Follow these directions to enter the data:

Press	**F5**
Type	**b12**
Press	**Enter**
Type	**1987**
Press	**Right Arrow**
Type	**1988**
Press	**Right Arrow**
Type	**1989**
Press	**Right Arrow**
Type	**1990**
Press	**Right Arrow**
Type	**1991**
Press	**Down Arrow**
Press	**End**
Press	**Left Arrow**
Type	**Beaver Canoe**
Press	**Right Arrow**
Type	**10000**
Press	**Right Arrow**
Type	**8000**
Press	**Right Arrow**
Type	**7000**
Press	**Right Arrow**
Type	**6500**
Press	**Right Arrow**
Type	**6000**
Press	**Down Arrow**
Press	**End**
Press	**Left Arrow**
Type	**Mohawk Canoe**
Press	**Right Arrow**
Type	**4500**
Press	**Right Arrow**
Type	**5500**
Press	**Right Arrow**
Type	**6000**
Press	**Right Arrow**
Type	**5200**
Press	**Right Arrow**
Type	**5500**
Press	**Down Arrow**
Press	**End**

*Figure 8 The Line Graph
Data*

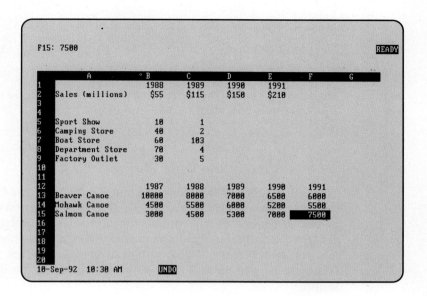

	A	B	C	D	E	F	G
		1988	1989	1990	1991		
1							
2	Sales (millions)	$55	$115	$150	$210		
3							
4							
5	Sport Show	10	1				
6	Camping Store	40	2				
7	Boat Store	60	103				
8	Department Store	70	4				
9	Factory Outlet	30	5				
10							
11							
12		1987	1988	1989	1990	1991	
13	Beaver Canoe	10000	8000	7000	6500	6000	
14	Mohawk Canoe	4500	5500	6000	5200	5500	
15	Salmon Canoe	3000	4500	5300	7000	7500	

F15: 7500   READY

10-Sep-92 10:30 AM   UNDO

Press	**Left Arrow**
Type	**Salmon Canoe**
Press	**Right Arrow**
Type	**3000**
Press	**Right Arrow**
Type	**4500**
Press	**Right Arrow**
Type	**5300**
Press	**Right Arrow**
Type	**7000**
Press	**Right Arrow**
Type	**7500**
Press	**Enter**

The numbers you have entered represent the units sold of each type of canoe for each year. Your screen should look like Figure 8. Check your work against Figure 8 and correct any mistakes you find.

Step 2: Save the Worksheet

It is a good idea to save your worksheet before you generate the graph. Execute the File Save command:

Type	**/fs**
Press	**Enter**
Type	**r**

Step 3: Execute the Graph Reset Graph Command

Since you already have a graph defined as the current graph, execute the Graph Reset Graph command to clear the settings.

Type	**/grg**

Step 4: Specify the Type Line Option

Now tell 1-2-3 that you want to create a line graph:

    Type   **tL**

Incidentally, Line is the default type of graph. If you do not select a graph type, 1-2-3 assumes you want to do a line graph.

Step 5: Specify the Data Ranges

This line graph will have four data ranges: X, A, B, and C. The X data range will contain the years 1987 through 1991. The A data range will contain the unit sales of Beaver canoes, B will contain the unit sales of Mohawk canoes, and C will contain the unit sales of Salmon canoes. The Group option from the Graph menu lets you specify several data ranges at once if they are in consecutive rows or columns. Follow these directions to specify all of the data ranges for the line graph:

    Type   **g**
    Type   **b12..f15**
    Press   **Enter**
    Type   **r**

B12 to F12 is now the X data range, B13 to F13 is the A data range, B14 to F14 is the B data range, and B15 to F15 is the C data range.

Step 6: Add Titles

Use the Options Titles command to add titles to the line graph:

    Type   **otf**
    Type   **Beaver Canoe Company**
    Press   **Enter**
    Type   **ts**
    Type   **Canoe Model Sales Comparison**
    Press   **Enter**
    Type   **tx**
    Type   **Year**
    Press   **Enter**
    Type   **ty**
    Type   **Number of Units Sold**
    Press   **Enter**

Step 7: Specify Lines and Symbols

Let's have the line graph display each point as a symbol and connect the points with lines. A different symbol will be used for each data range. Select the Format Graph Both Quit option:

    Type   **fgbq**

Figure 9 The Line Graph

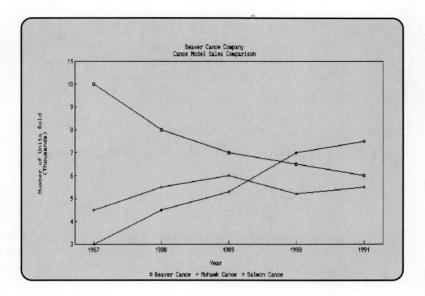

Step 8: Add a Legend

A legend identifies the data range represented by each symbol in the graph. Follow these directions to use the labels in cells A13 through A15 as the legend:

Type   **Lr**
Type   **a13..a15**
Press   **Enter**

Quit the Options submenu and return to the Graph menu:

Type   **q**

Step 9: View the Graph

Now you can view the graph you have specified. Select the View option from the Graph menu:

Type   **v**

Your screen should look like Figure 9. When you are finished looking at the graph, return to the Graph menu:

Press   **Escape**

Step 10: Save the Graph

Select the Save option from the Graph menu to save your line graph in a file named LINE.PIC:

Type   **s**
Type   **line**
Press   **Enter**

Step 11: Name the Graph

Since you now have three graphs associated with the SALES worksheet, you should name the line graph. Execute the Name Create option and specify SALES_LINE as the name of the graph:

Type   **nc**
Type   **sales_line**
Press **Enter**

Quit the Graph menu and return to READY mode:

Type   **q**

Step 12: Save the Worksheet

You have saved the graph to a file named LINE.PIC and named the graph SALES_LINE, but you must also save the worksheet to preserve the graph settings you have specified. Execute the File Save command and replace the worksheet file on the disk:

Type   **/fs**
Press **Enter**
Type   **r**

Practice

1. You can tell Lotus 1-2-3 to label the points in the line graph with their actual values. Labeling the points lets the viewer easily see their exact values. Follow these directions to place labels above the points in the line graph:

Type   **/godg**
Type   **b13..f15**
Press **Enter**
Type   **raqqv**

When you are finished looking at the graph, press any key to return to the Graph menu.

2. Use the Name Create option to save SALES_LINE again and execute the File Save command to update the worksheet on the disk.

3. Print the new line graph you have created.

Lesson 7: Creating a Stacked Bar Graph

A **stacked bar graph** is a variation of the basic bar graph that shows components and total amounts for each category. For example, you could present the unit sales of the three types of canoes for five years in a stacked bar graph. Each bar would represent the total number of units sold in a year. Each bar would be divided into three stacked sections, one section for each type of canoe. Let's create such a graph. You don't have to enter the data because it already exists in the table you created for Lesson 6.

Step 1: Execute the Graph Reset Graph Command

Since you already have a graph defined as the current graph, execute the Graph Reset Graph command to clear the settings.

Type   **/grg**

Step 2: Specify the Type Stack-Bar Option

Now tell 1-2-3 that you want to create a stacked bar graph:

> Type **ts**

Step 3: Specify the Data Ranges

This stacked bar graph will have the same four data ranges as the line graph you created in Lesson 6. Use the Group option to specify the four data ranges:

> Type   **g**
> Type   **b12..f15**
> Press **Enter**
> Type   **r**

Step 4: Add Titles

Use the Options Titles command to add titles to the stacked bar graph:

> Type   **otf**
> Type   **Beaver Canoe Company**
> Press **Enter**
> Type   **ts**
> Type   **Five Year Unit Sales**
> Press **Enter**
> Type   **tx**
> Type   **Year**
> Press **Enter**
> Type   **ty**
> Type   **Number of Units Sold**
> Press **Enter**

Step 5: Add a Legend

A legend identifies the stack pattern that goes with each canoe model. Follow these directions to use the labels in cells A13 through A15 as the legend:

> Type   **Lr**
> Type   **a13..a15**
> Press **Enter**

Quit the Options submenu and return to the Graph menu:

> Type   **q**

Step 6: View the Graph

Now you can view the graph you have specified. Select the View option from the Graph menu:

> Type   **v**

Your screen should look like Figure 10. When you are finished looking at the graph, return to the Graph menu:

> Press **Escape**

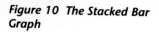

Figure 10 The Stacked Bar Graph

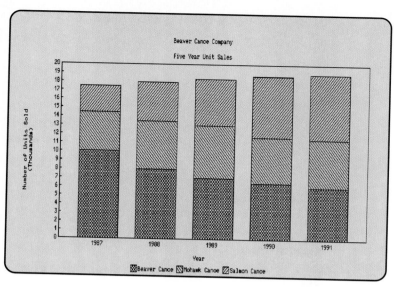

Step 7: Save the Graph

Select the Save option from the Graph menu to save your stacked bar graph in a file named STACK.PIC:

Type **s**
Type **stack**
Press **Enter**

Step 8: Name the Graph

Since you now have four graphs associated with the SALES worksheet, you should name the stacked bar graph. Execute the Name Create option and specify SALES_STACK as the name of the graph:

Type **nc**
Type **sales_stack**
Press **Enter**

Quit the Graph menu and return to READY mode:

Type **q**

Step 9: Save the Worksheet

You have saved the graph to a file named STACK.PIC and named the graph SALES_STACK, but you must also save the worksheet to preserve the graph settings you have specified. Execute the File Save command and replace the worksheet file on the disk:

Type **/fs**
Press **Enter**
Type **r**

Practice 1. You can easily create a bar graph from the same data that will show a separate bar for each canoe model. Execute the Graph Type Bar command, then view the graph you have created. This is a good example of a bar graph with multiple data ranges. When you are finished viewing the graph, change it back to a stacked bar graph, then return to READY mode.

2. Print the stacked bar graph you have created.

Lesson 8: Creating an XY Graph

An **XY graph,** sometimes called a **scatterplot,** shows the relationship between two or more variables. For example, XY graphs can be used to show correlations between sales and profits, price and the number of units sold, and per capita income and life expectancy. Let's create an XY graph that shows the relationship between the price of a canoe and the number of units sold for the Beaver Canoe Company.

Step 1: Create the Worksheet

You can enter the data for this new graph in an empty area of the SALES worksheet. Follow these directions to enter and format the data:

Type	**/rfc0**
Press	**Enter**
Type	**b20..b28**
Press	**Enter**
Press	**F5**
Type	**a19**
Press	**Enter**
Type	**"Units Sold**
Press	**Right Arrow**
Type	**"Price**
Press	**Down Arrow**
Type	**100**
Press	**Down Arrow**
Type	**200**
Press	**Down Arrow**
Type	**300**
Press	**Down Arrow**
Type	**400**
Press	**Down Arrow**
Type	**500**
Press	**Down Arrow**
Type	**600**
Press	**Down Arrow**
Type	**700**
Press	**Down Arrow**
Type	**800**
Press	**Down Arrow**
Type	**900**
Press	**Enter**
Press	**F5**

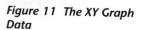

Figure 11 The XY Graph Data

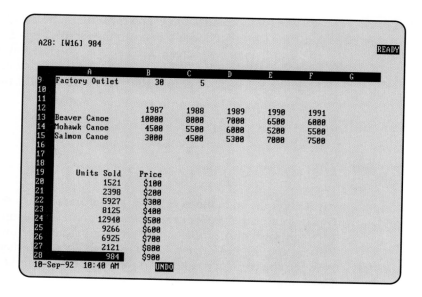

Type	**a20**
Press	**Enter**
Type	**1521**
Press	**Down Arrow**
Type	**2398**
Press	**Down Arrow**
Type	**5927**
Press	**Down Arrow**
Type	**8125**
Press	**Down Arrow**
Type	**12940**
Press	**Down Arrow**
Type	**9266**
Press	**Down Arrow**
Type	**6925**
Press	**Down Arrow**
Type	**2121**
Press	**Down Arrow**
Type	**984**
Press	**Enter**

Your screen should look like Figure 11. Check your work against Figure 11 and correct any mistakes you find.

Step 2: Save the Worksheet

It is a good idea to save your worksheet before you generate the graph. Execute the File Save command:

Type	**/fs**
Press	**Enter**
Type	**r**

Step 3: Execute the Graph Reset Graph Command

Since you already have a graph defined as the current graph, execute the Graph Reset Graph command to clear the settings.

Type **/grg**

Step 4: Specify the Type XY Option

Now tell 1-2-3 that you want to create an XY graph:

Type **tx**

Step 5: Specify the Data Ranges

This XY graph will have two data ranges: X and A. The X data range will contain the values for canoe prices. The A data range will contain the number of units sold at that price. Follow these directions to specify the data ranges for the XY graph:

Type **x**
Type **b20..b28**
Press **Enter**
Type **a**
Type **a20..a28**
Press **Enter**

Step 6: Add Titles

Use the Options Titles command to add titles to the line graph:

Type **otf**
Type **Beaver Canoe Company**
Press **Enter**
Type **ts**
Type **Canoe Price vs. Units Sold**
Press **Enter**
Type **tx**
Type **Price per Canoe (dollars)**
Press **Enter**
Type **ty**
Type **Number of Units Sold**
Press **Enter**

Step 7: Specify Lines and Symbols

Let's have the line graph display each point as a symbol and connect the points with lines. Select the Format Graph Both Quit option:

Type **fgbq**

Quit the Options submenu and return to the Graph menu:

Type **q**

Figure 12 The XY Graph

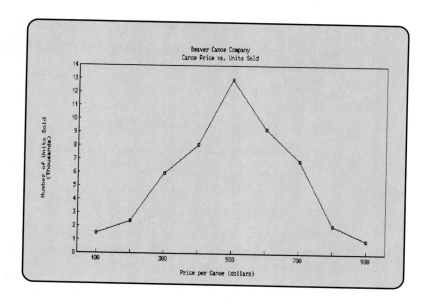

Step 8: View the Graph

Now you can view the graph you have specified. Select the View option from the Graph menu:

Type   **v**

Your screen should look like Figure 12. This graph suggests that people buy more canoes when the price is around $500. Perhaps if they are priced too low, people will think the canoes are poorly constructed and not buy them. If they are priced too high, people cannot afford them. When you are finished looking at the graph, return to the Graph menu:

Press   **Escape**

Step 9: Save the Graph

Select the Save option from the Graph menu to save your line graph in a file named XY.PIC:

Type   **s**
Type   **xy**
Press   **Enter**

Step 10: Name the Graph

Since you now have five graphs associated with the SALES worksheet, you should name the XY graph. Execute the Name Create option and specify SALES_XY as the name of the graph:

Type   **nc**
Type   **sales_xy**
Press   **Enter**

Quit the Graph menu and return to READY mode:

Type   **q**

Step 11: Save the Worksheet

You have saved the graph to a file named XY.PIC and named the graph SALES_XY, but you must also save the worksheet to preserve the graph settings you have specified. Execute the File Save command and replace the worksheet file on the disk:

Type   **/fs**
Press **Enter**
Type   **r**

Practice

1. Change the XY graph so that it displays symbols, but not line segments. Now change the graph to display line segments, but not symbols. Finally, change the XY graph so that it displays both symbols and lines again.
2. Print the XY graph you have created.

Lesson 9: Creating a Data Base Worksheet

A data base is an organized collection of one or more files of related data. A worksheet, which stores data in a table format, can be used as a simple data base. Although a spreadsheet package is no match for a true data base management system such as dBASE IV, you can store, sort, find, and extract data in a worksheet. As an example, let's use Lotus 1-2-3 to set up a personal property inventory.

Step 1: Erase the Worksheet

If the SALES worksheet is still on your screen, execute the Worksheet Erase command to clear it from memory and start with a blank worksheet:

Type   **/wey**

Step 2: Set Up the Worksheet for the Data Base

The data base will be a list of personal property, which you might create for insurance purposes. Column A will hold short item descriptions, column B will hold the purchase dates, and column C will hold the amounts paid. Column C will also be summed, so you can maintain a property value total.

Since column A will hold item descriptions, you should widen it. Execute the Worksheet Column Set-Width command to widen column A to 40 characters:

Type   **/wcs40**
Press **Enter**

Column B will hold dates; widen it to 10 characters and format it to display dates:

Press **Right Arrow**
Type   **/wcs10**
Press **Enter**
Type   **/rfd**
Press **Enter**
Type   **b1..b100**
Press **Enter**

Column C will hold dollar amounts. Widen it to 11 characters and format it to display currency values:

Press	**Right Arrow**
Type	**/wcs11**
Press	**Enter**
Type	**/rfc**
Press	**Enter**
Type	**c1..c100**
Press	**Enter**

Step 3: Enter the Field Names

Each row in a data base worksheet represents a record, which contains all the data about a particular item. Each column in a data base worksheet represents a field, which contains an individual data value for each record. The first row in a data base worksheet must contain the names of the fields. Follow these directions to enter the field names:

Type	**"AMOUNT**
Press	**Left Arrow**
Type	**^DATE**
Press	**Left Arrow**
Type	**^ITEM**
Press	**Down Arrow**

Step 4: Enter the Data

Enter the data from the following table into the worksheet. The items go in column A, the date formulas go in column B, and the amounts go in column C. Note that each date is entered as a formula made up of the @DATE function. This function converts the year, month, and day numbers into a single number that 1-2-3 uses to keep track of dates. You will learn more about date numbers in the next chapter.

Personal Property Data

Item	Date	Amount
Guitar, Yamaha	@date(86,04,13)	363.50
Tent, Eureka	@date(87,06,18)	99.95
Lamp, K-Mart	@date(85,01,15)	39.97
Microwave Oven, Sears	@date(86,03,12)	386.64
Answering Machine, Panasonic	@date(88,03,17)	127.47
Backpack, L.L. Bean	@date(89,08,08)	94.50
Walkman, Sony	@date(88,03,10)	82.31
Television, Sony	@date(89,04,29)	524.75
Skis, Trak Cross Country	@date(88,01,05)	113.45
Ski Boots, Salomon	@date(88,01,05)	81.50
Telephone, AT&T	@date(87,04,15)	87.70
CD Player, Sony	@date(87,10,17)	169.00
Stereo Receiver, JVC	@date(86,10,27)	199.00
Speakers, Avid	@date(86,10,27)	156.00
VCR, Magnavox	@date(86,01,04)	318.74
Popcorn Popper, Westbend	@date(88,01,02)	22.15
File Cabinet, Sears	@date(86,11,19)	78.45

Step 5: Enter the Formula

When you use a worksheet as a data base, you can take advantage of the computational abilities of the spreadsheet program. Adding up the amounts spent on each item in the property inventory is easy.

Press **F5**
Type **c20**
Press **Enter**
Type **@sum(c2..c19)**
Press **Enter**

If you have entered the amounts and the formula correctly, the sum will be $2,945.08. Now enter a label for the total:

Press **Left Arrow**
Press **Left Arrow**
Type **"TOTAL**
Press **Enter**

Your screen should look like Figure 13.

Step 6: Save the Worksheet

Save the worksheet in a disk file before you go on to use the data.

Type **/fs**
Type **property**
Press **Enter**

The worksheet will be saved in a file named PROPERTY.WK1 (or PROPERTY.WK3 if you are using Lotus 1-2-3 Release 3.1).

Figure 13 The Completed Data Base Worksheet

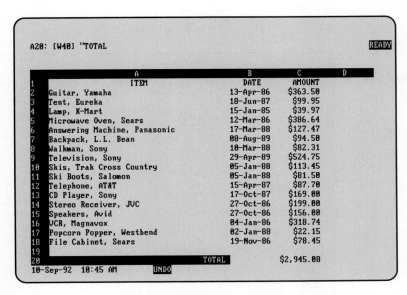

Invoke the Help facility and read about the @DATE function.

Lesson 10: Sorting a Data Base Worksheet

The records in the PROPERTY data base worksheet are arranged in the order in which they were entered. Records would be easier to find if they were sorted into some predictable order. Let's tell 1-2-3 to sort the PROPERTY records by the contents of the ITEM field.

Step 1: Execute the Data Sort Command

Commands for manipulating a data base worksheet are in the Data menu. The Sort command is used to rearrange the records in a data base.

Type   **/ds**

Lotus 1-2-3 will present the Data Sort menu, shown in Figure 14. If you are running Release 2.2, the program will also present the Sort Settings sheet, which displays the current settings of the Sort command.

Step 2: Specify the Data Range to be Sorted

The range to be sorted is called the data range. It should include all the records in the data base, but not the row of field names or the row with the formula for summing the AMOUNT field. Invoke the Data-Range option and specify the range of cells to be sorted:

Type   **d**
Type   **a2..c18**
Press **Enter**

Lotus 1-2-3 will return to the Sort menu.

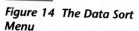

Figure 14 The Data Sort Menu

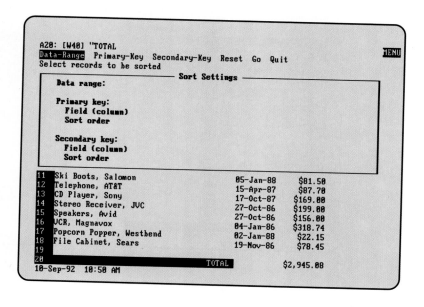

Step 3: Specify a Sort Key

A **key** is a field in a data base used to sort the records. If you want to sort the records on the basis of the contents of the ITEM field, then the ITEM field would be the key. Lotus 1-2-3 lets you specify two keys: the primary key and a secondary key. The **primary key** determines the first sort order. If you want to sort a data base on the basis of only one field, then this field is the primary key. An optional **secondary key** may be specified to determine the order of records after they are sorted first on the primary key. For example, suppose you had a mailing list data base that contained records in which several of the last names were identical. You would probably use the LAST NAME field as the primary key and the FIRST NAME field as the secondary key to sort the records. In the PROPERTY data base worksheet, you need only specify the column containing the ITEM field as the primary key.

Type   **p**
Type   **a1**
Press   **Enter**

Note that you could have specified any cell in the ITEM column to indicate the key.

Step 4: Specify the Sort Order

Lotus 1-2-3 will prompt you to indicate the sort order. You have two choices: descending and ascending. For text, ascending order is alphabetical order from A to Z. Specify the sort order as ascending:

Type   **a**
Press   **Enter**

The program will return to the Sort menu.

Step 5: Execute the Sort

Now you are ready to tell 1-2-3 to sort the records. Invoke the Go option to execute the sort:

Type   **g**

The records will be rearranged on the basis of the contents of the ITEM field, as shown in Figure 15.

Step 6: Save the Worksheet

If you want to keep the data base sorted in this order, you must save it to the disk.

Type   **/fs**
Press   **Enter**
Type   **r**

Practice

1. Sort the PROPERTY data base worksheet by AMOUNT, with the most expensive item listed first. Do not save the worksheet when you are finished.
2. Sort the PROPERTY data base worksheet by DATE and then by AMOUNT. In other words, DATE should be the primary key and AMOUNT should be

**Figure 15 Records Sorted
by ITEM**

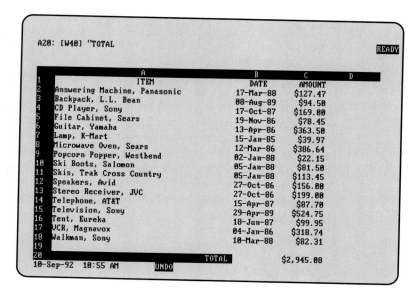

```
A20: [W40] "TOTAL                                                    READY

                        A                        B          C          D
 1                    ITEM                      DATE      AMOUNT
 2  Answering Machine, Panasonic             17-Mar-88   $127.47
 3  Backpack, L.L. Bean                      08-Aug-89    $94.50
 4  CD Player, Sony                          17-Oct-87   $169.00
 5  File Cabinet, Sears                      19-Nov-86    $78.45
 6  Guitar, Yamaha                           13-Apr-86   $363.50
 7  Lamp, K-Mart                             15-Jan-85    $39.97
 8  Microwave Oven, Sears                    12-Mar-86   $386.64
 9  Popcorn Popper, Westbend                 02-Jan-88    $22.15
10  Ski Boots, Salomon                       05-Jan-88    $81.50
11  Skis, Trak Cross Country                 05-Jan-88   $113.45
12  Speakers, Avid                           27-Oct-86   $156.00
13  Stereo Receiver, JVC                     27-Oct-86   $199.00
14  Telephone, AT&T                          15-Apr-87    $87.70
15  Television, Sony                         29-Apr-89   $524.75
16  Tent, Eureka                             18-Jun-87    $99.95
17  VCR, Magnavox                            04-Jan-86   $318.74
18  Walkman, Sony                            10-Mar-88    $82.31
19
20                                          TOTAL        $2,945.08
10-Sep-92  10:55 AM           UNDO
```

the secondary key. Arrange the records so that the oldest item is first. Within each date, list the most expensive item last. Do not save the worksheet when you are finished. Instead, retrieve the PROPERTY worksheet on the disk, which is sorted by ITEM.

Lesson 11: Searching a Data Base Worksheet

Creating a data base is a way to store and organize large quantities of information. One of the most common operations performed on a data base is searching it for one or more records. The PROPERTY data base worksheet contains only 17 records, so finding a particular record would not be difficult. Most data bases, however, have many more records. Imagine trying to find a particular record in a data base with hundreds or even thousands of records. Fortunately, Lotus 1-2-3 has a command that can locate records for you.

Step 1: Set Up the Criteria Range

Suppose you want to search PROPERTY for all items that cost $300 or more. In 1-2-3 you must set up a **query** to search a data base worksheet. The first step is to set up a range in which to enter the **criteria,** which are the search requirements. The criteria range consists of at least two rows: the first row must include one or more field names and the second row must include one or more expressions that specify the field values you want to find. To set up the criteria range, you can copy the field names from the first row to a blank portion of the worksheet. It is a good idea to copy all of the field names, even if you don't need them all at the moment, so that you can easily change the criteria later. Follow these directions to copy the field names to a blank area of the worksheet:

Press   **Home**
Type   **/ca1..c1**
Press   **Enter**
Type   **j1**
Press   **Enter**

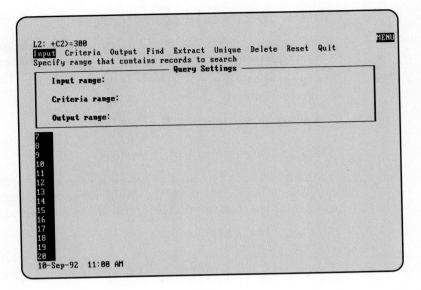

Figure 16 The Data Query Menu

```
L2: +C2>=300                                                      MENU
Input Criteria Output Find Extract Unique Delete Reset Quit
Specify range that contains records to search
                        ─── Query Settings ───
   Input range:

   Criteria range:

   Output range:

7
8
9
10
11
12
13
14
15
16
17
18
19
20
10-Sep-92  11:00 AM
```

Press	**F5**
Type	**j1**
Press	**Enter**

Note that when you use the Copy command, 1-2-3 copies only the cell contents, not cell widths. Consequently, the widths of cells J1 through L1 do not match the widths of cells A1 through C1.

Step 2: Enter the Criterion

You want to search for those records with AMOUNT values equal to at least $300. In this case, the single criterion would be a logical formula that determines if a number in the AMOUNT field is greater than or equal to 300. Follow these directions to enter the criterion in the cell beneath the AMOUNT field name:

Press	**Right Arrow**
Press	**Right Arrow**
Press	**Down Arrow**
Type	**+c2>=300**
Press	**Enter**

Note that you use the cell address of the first entry in the AMOUNT field for the criterion. Lotus 1-2-3 will display 0 in cell L2 as the result of that formula because the value in cell C2 is less than 300.

Step 3: Execute the Data Query Command

To search a data base worksheet, you use options from the Data Query menu.

Type **/dq**

Lotus 1-2-3 will display the Data Query menu. If you are running Release 2.2, it will also display the Query Settings sheet (see Figure 16).

Step 4: Specify the Criteria Range

Now you must tell 1-2-3 to use the criteria range you have set up. Select the Criteria option and specify the location of the cells that make up the criteria range:

Type   **cj1..L2**
Press   **Enter**

The program will return to the Data Query menu.

Step 5: Specify the Input Range

The range of cells you want to search is called the input range. Unlike the data range for a sort command, the input range must include the field names in addition to the data records. Select the Input option and specify the input range:

Type   **ia1..c18**
Press   **Enter**

The program will return to the Data Query menu.

Step 6: Begin the Search

Now that the criteria and input ranges have been specified, you can begin the search for the records that match your criterion. Select the Find option from the Data Query menu:

Type   **f**

The mode indicator will change to FIND, and 1-2-3 will highlight the first record in the input range that matches the criterion in the criteria range (see Figure 17).

Step 7: Continue the Search

When 1-2-3 is in FIND mode, you simply press the Down Arrow key to advance to the next matching record.

Press   **Down Arrow**

You can also use the Up Arrow key to see the previous record that matches the criterion.

Press   **Up Arrow**

Keep pressing the Down Arrow key to see the rest of the records with an AMOUNT greater than or equal to $300:

Press   **Down Arrow** (4 times)

Lotus 1-2-3 will beep if you press Down Arrow or Up Arrow when no more matching records are found.

Note that you can edit cell contents when 1-2-3 is in FIND mode. This is handy for updating only those records that match certain criteria.

Step 8: End the Search

Follow these directions to end the search and move to A1 when you are finished looking at the records:

Press   **Enter**
Type   **q**
Press   **Home**

Figure 17 The First Matching Record Has Been Found

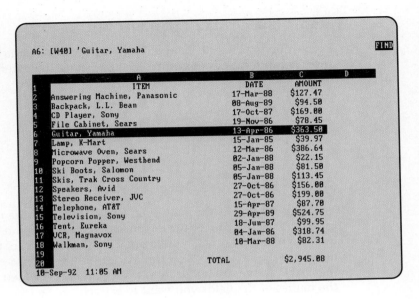

A6: [W40] 'Guitar, Yamaha			FIND

	A	B	C	D
1	ITEM	DATE	AMOUNT	
2	Answering Machine, Panasonic	17-Mar-88	$127.47	
3	Backpack, L.L. Bean	08-Aug-89	$94.50	
4	CD Player, Sony	17-Oct-87	$169.00	
5	File Cabinet, Sears	19-Nov-86	$78.45	
6	Guitar, Yamaha	13-Apr-86	$363.50	
7	Lamp, K-Mart	15-Jan-85	$39.97	
8	Microwave Oven, Sears	12-Mar-86	$386.64	
9	Popcorn Popper, Westbend	02-Jan-88	$22.15	
10	Ski Boots, Salomon	05-Jan-88	$81.50	
11	Skis, Trak Cross Country	05-Jan-88	$113.45	
12	Speakers, Avid	27-Oct-86	$156.00	
13	Stereo Receiver, JVC	27-Oct-86	$199.00	
14	Telephone, AT&T	15-Apr-87	$87.70	
15	Television, Sony	29-Apr-89	$524.75	
16	Tent, Eureka	18-Jun-87	$99.95	
17	VCR, Magnavox	04-Jan-86	$318.74	
18	Walkman, Sony	10-Mar-88	$82.31	
19				
20		TOTAL	$2,945.08	

10-Sep-92   11:05 AM

Step 9: Save the Worksheet

If you will want to use your criteria range and criterion again, you must save the PROPERTY worksheet.

Type   **/fs**
Press **Enter**
Type   **r**

Practice

1. Lotus 1-2-3 offers three special characters that can be used in criteria when searching for text: *, ?, and ~. The * (asterisk) matches any number of characters. For example, *Ski** matches *Ski lodge, Skis, Skit,* and *Skipper.* The ? (question mark) matches any single character. For example, *Ski?* matches *Skis* and *Skit,* but not *Ski lodge* and *Skipper.* The * and ? operate just like the DOS global filename characters. The ~ (tilde) matches any label except the label that follows it. For example, *~Ski* matches every label that does not begin with *Ski.* Use one of these special characters to search PROPERTY for all records that begin with *Ski* in the ITEM field.

2. Search PROPERTY for all records of items purchased after January 1, 1988.

Lesson 12: Extracting Records from a Data Base Worksheet

The Extract option of the Data Query menu lets you copy records that meet your criteria and place them in a range outside the data base. Although the term Extract implies that the records are removed from the original data base, this is not so. The Extract option merely copies the records, leaving the originals intact. This option is handy for working with a subset of a data base. For example, you could extract all records with an AMOUNT greater than or equal to $300, then print only those records.

Step 1: Specify the Criterion

In the previous lesson, you already set up the criteria range as J1 through L2 and the input range as A2 through C18. Enter the criterion again in cell L2:

Press   **F5**
Type   **L2**
Press   **Enter**
Type   **+c2>=300**
Press   **Enter**

Step 2: Set Up the Output Range

The output range is the cells where 1-2-3 will copy the records that match your criteria. The first row of the output range must contain the names of the fields that you want to extract. You do not have to extract all of the fields in the original data base. For example, you can extract only the ITEM and AMOUNT, and not the DATE. Move to a blank area of the worksheet, widen the columns, and enter the names of the fields you want to extract:

Press   **F5**
Type   **j10**
Press   **Enter**
Type   **/wcs40**
Press   **Enter**
Type   **^ITEM**
Press   **Right Arrow**
Type   **/wcs11**
Press   **Enter**
Type   **"AMOUNT**
Press   **Enter**

Step 3: Specify the Output Range

In most cases, you will not know exactly how many records 1-2-3 will find. If you specify the single row containing the field names as the output range, 1-2-3 will use as many rows as necessary for the extracted records. You should make sure you have no existing data below the row you specify. Execute the Data Query Output command and specify the output range:

Type   **/dqoj10..k10**
Press   **Enter**

The program will return to the Data Query menu.

Step 4: Extract the Records

You are now ready to extract the items and amounts of records with amounts greater than or equal to $300. Select the Extract option and then quit the Data Query menu:

Type   **e**
Type   **q**

Your screen should look like Figure 18. At this point, you could print only these records or use them for other calculations.

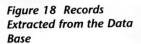

Figure 18 Records Extracted from the Data Base

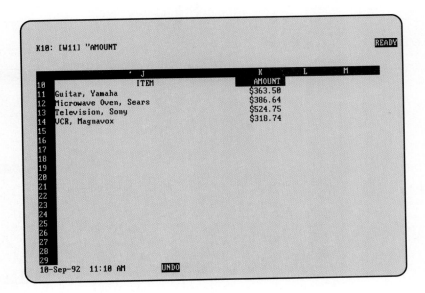

```
K10: [W11] ''AMOUNT                                    READY
                         J               K      L     M
                         ITEM           AMOUNT
10
11 Guitar, Yamaha                       $363.50
12 Microwave Oven, Sears                $386.64
13 Television, Sony                     $524.75
14 VCR, Magnavox                        $318.74
15
16
17
18
19
20
21
22
23
24
25
26
27
28
29
10-Sep-92  11:18 AM         UNDO
```

Practice   Extract the items and amounts of records with a DATE of January 1, 1988, or later. You can use the same output range.

Lesson 13: Using the Data Base Functions

Lotus 1-2-3 has a set of functions designed especially for data base worksheets. The data base functions scan a data base, select the records that match the criteria in the criteria range, then perform calculations on only the selected values. Let's briefly examine the Lotus 1-2-3 data base functions.

Step 1: Try the @DCOUNT Function

Suppose you want to know how many PROPERTY records have an AMOUNT value greater than or equal to $300. The @DCOUNT function counts the non-blank cells in a field of a data base. It considers only those records that meet the specified criteria. Follow these directions to see how @DCOUNT works:

Press **F5**
Type **m10**
Press **Enter**
Type **@dcount(a1..c18,0,j1..L2)**
Press **Enter**

The result should be 4 (see Figure 19). The first parameter of the @DCOUNT function is the input range, which in this case is A1 to C18. The second parameter is the field number. For the data base functions, fields are numbered from the left starting at zero. In this case, it does not matter which field is checked; the 0 refers to the ITEM field. The third parameter of the @DCOUNT function is the criteria range, which is J1 to L2.

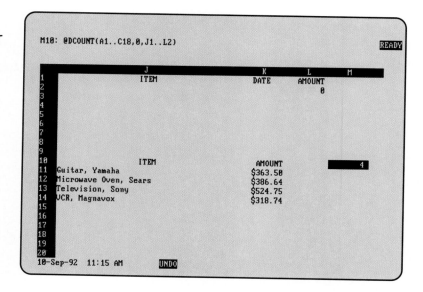

Figure 19 The @DCOUNT Function

Step 2: Try the Other Data Base Functions

Lotus 1-2-3 has six other data base functions. Let's try some of them.

> Type **@davg(a1..c18,2,j1..L2)**
> Press **Enter**

The @DAVG function computes the average value of the specified field, in this case field 2, which is the AMOUNT field. It uses only those records that meet the specified criteria. Hence, the average you see is that of records with amounts greater than or equal to $300.

> Type **@dmax(a1..c18,2,j1..L2)**
> Press **Enter**

The @DMAX function returns the largest value of the specified field given the criteria.

> Type **@dmin(a1..c18,2,j1..L2)**
> Press **Enter**

The @DMIN function returns the smallest value of the specified field given the criteria.

> Type **@dsum(a1..c18,2,j1..L2)**
> Press **Enter**

The @DSUM function computes the sum of the values in the specified field given the criteria.

Two other data base functions are available in Lotus 1-2-3 for computing statistics: @DSTD and @DVAR. The @DSTD function computes the population standard deviation of the values in the specified field given the criteria. The @DVAR function computes the population variance of the values in the specified field given the criteria.

Practice   Change the criterion and use a data base function to compute the average amount of PROPERTY items that cost less than $300.

Summary

- *Creating a bar graph*. Set up the worksheet, select Bar as the graph type, and specify the data ranges.

- *Printing a graph*. Use the PrintGraph program with Lotus 1-2-3 Release 2.0 or 2.2. Execute the Print Printer Image Current Go command with Lotus 1-2-3 Release 3.1.

- *Naming a graph*. Execute the Graph Name Create command to associate a name with the current graph. The Graph Name Use command retrieves a named graph and makes it the current graph.

- *Creating a pie chart*. Set up the worksheet, select Pie as the graph type, and specify the data ranges.

- *Creating a line graph*. Set up the worksheet, select Line as the graph type, and specify the data ranges.

- *Creating a stacked bar graph*. Set up the worksheet, select Stack-Bar as the graph type, and specify the data ranges.

- *Creating an XY graph*. Set up the worksheet, select XY as the graph type, and specify the data ranges.

- *Creating a data base worksheet*. Set up the worksheet so that each column is a field and each row is a record, except for the first row, which must contain the field names.

- *Sorting a data base worksheet*. Execute the Data Sort command, specify the data range, specify one or two keys, specify the sort order, and select the Go option.

- *Searching a data base worksheet*. Set up the criteria range, enter the criteria, execute the Data Query command, specify the criteria and input ranges, and select the Find option to begin the search. Press the Down Arrow key to continue the search and the Enter key to end the search.

- *Extracting data from a worksheet*. Specify the criteria, specify the output range, and execute the Extract option from the Data Query menu.

- *Using the data base functions*. @DCOUNT, @DSUM, @DAVG, @DMIN, @DMAX, @DSTD, and @DVAR are data base functions that scan a data base, select the records that match the specified criteria, and then perform calculations on only the selected values.

Key Terms

As an extra review of this chapter, try defining the following terms.

bar graph	query
criteria	secondary key
line graph	stacked bar graph
pie chart	XY graph (scatterplot)
primary key	

Multiple Choice

Choose the best selection to complete each statement.

1. What is a chart in which numeric values are represented by evenly spaced, thick vertical lines?
   - (a) bar graph
   - (b) pie chart
   - (c) line graph
   - (d) XY graph

2. In a spreadsheet program, a graph is created from data in a
   - (a) data entry form.
   - (b) settings sheet.
   - (c) worksheet.
   - (d) separate file.

3. In bar, line, and stacked bar graphs, the X data range contains the values or labels that will appear along which axis?
   - (a) horizontal
   - (b) vertical
   - (c) diagonal
   - (d) rotational

4. After you have viewed a graph the first time with the View option from the Graph menu, which key can you press to display the current graph on the screen?
   - (a) Escape
   - (b) Enter
   - (c) F1
   - (d) F10

5. If you have Lotus 1-2-3 Release 2.0 or 2.2, what must you do to print a graph?
   - (a) execute /PPICG
   - (b) use the PrintGraph program
   - (c) press Print Screen
   - (d) press Ctrl-Alt-Del

6. Which command retrieves a named graph and makes it the current graph?
   - (a) Graph Name Create
   - (b) Graph Name Reset
   - (c) Graph Name Use
   - (d) Graph Name Delete

7. Which type of graph would you use to show the parts of a whole?
   - (a) bar graph
   - (b) pie chart
   - (c) line graph
   - (d) XY graph

8. In a pie chart, which data range contains the values that will be represented as slices?
   - (a) A
   - (b) B
   - (c) C
   - (d) X

9. In a pie chart, which optional data range can be used to specify hatch patterns and whether slices are to be exploded?
   - (a) A
   - (b) B
   - (c) C
   - (d) X

10. Which type of graph is often used to plot values that change over time as points at appropriate distances above the horizontal axis?
    - (a) bar graph
    - (b) pie chart
    - (c) line graph
    - (d) stacked bar graph

11. What graph feature identifies the data represented by each different symbol, type of line, or pattern in a graph?
    - (a) legend
    - (b) title
    - (c) axis label
    - (d) data label

12. Which type of graph shows components and total amounts for each category?
    (a) bar graph
    (b) line graph
    (c) XY graph
    (d) stacked bar graph
13. Which type of graph is often used to show the correlation between two variables?
    (a) bar graph
    (b) line graph
    (c) XY graph
    (d) stacked bar graph
14. Each row in a data base worksheet represents a
    (a) field.
    (b) record.
    (c) file.
    (d) character.
15. Each column in a data base worksheet represents a
    (a) field.
    (b) record.
    (c) file.
    (d) character.
16. The first row in a data base worksheet must contain the
    (a) first record.
    (b) first field.
    (c) field names.
    (d) record numbers.
17. Which Lotus 1-2-3 menu contains commands for manipulating a data base worksheet?
    (a) Worksheet
    (b) Data
    (c) File
    (d) Range
18. The first sort order is determined by the
    (a) primary key.
    (b) secondary key.
    (b) primary record.
    (d) secondary record.
19. In Lotus 1-2-3, what must you set up to search a data base worksheet?
    (a) data range
    (b) sort order
    (c) query
    (d) output range
20. Which function is not a data base function?
    (a) @DSUM
    (b) @AVG
    (c) @DCOUNT
    (d) @DVAR

Fill-In

1. A _____ graph is a chart in which numeric values are represented by evenly spaced, thick vertical lines.
2. Before you can create a graph, you must first create the _____ that contains the data for the graph.
3. Lotus 1-2-3 Release _____ does not require you to use PrintGraph to print out your graphs.
4. Lotus 1-2-3 lets you have several graphs associated with the same worksheet, if you _____ your graphs.
5. The Graph Name _____ command retrieves a named graph and makes it the current graph.
6. A _____ chart represents values as wedges of a circle.
7. A _____ graph is useful for plotting values that change over time.

8. A _____ bar graph is a variation of the basic bar graph that shows components and total amounts for each category.
9. A(n) _____ graph can be used to show a correlation between price and the number of units sold.
10. The _____ function converts the year, month, and day numbers into a single number that 1-2-3 uses to keep track of dates.
11. The Data _____ command is used to rearrange the records in a worksheet data base.
12. A _____ is a field in a data base used to sort the records.
13. For text, _____ order is simply alphabetical order from A to Z.
14. In 1-2-3, you must set up a _____ to search a data base worksheet.
15. In a query, the _____ range consists of at least two rows: the first row must include one or more field names and the second row must include one or more expressions that specify the field values you want to find.
16. Before you can search for records in a worksheet data base, you must specify the criteria and _____ ranges.
17. When 1-2-3 is in FIND mode, you press the _____ key to advance to the next matching record.
18. The three special characters *, ?, and ~ can be used in criteria when _____ for text.
19. The _____ option of the Data Query menu lets you copy records that meet your criteria and place them in a range outside the data base.
20. The _____ function counts the nonblank cells in a field of a data base worksheet, considering only those records that meet the specified criteria.

Short Problems

1. Retrieve the SALES worksheet you created in Lesson 1. Execute the Graph Name Use command and tell 1-2-3 that you want to use the SALES_BAR graph. Return to the Graph menu and select Options Data-Labels. For the A data range, assign B2..E2 as the range of data labels. Then select the Above option. Return to the Graph menu and view the graph. Assigning data labels in this manner presents the actual value of each bar.
2. If you are running Lotus 1-2-3 Release 2.0 or 2.2, use the PrintGraph program to print the new SALES_BAR graph. Try printing it in a different font.

   If you are running Lotus 1-2-3 Release 3.1, execute the Graph Options Advanced Text First Font command. Then select 2, 4, 5, 6, 7, or 8 to change the font of the first line of the graph title. Repeat the process for the Second and Third graph text groups, then print the graph.
3. Move the cell pointer to a blank area of the SALES worksheet below all data. Execute the Graph Name Table command and use the current cell as the range. Return to READY mode and examine the worksheet. The Graph Name Table command creates a three-column table that lists all named graphs in the worksheet, along with their graph types and titles.
4. View the SALES_PIE graph you created in Lesson 5. Modify the chart so that all slices are exploded. Save and print the new pie chart.
5. View the SALES_LINE graph you created in Lesson 6. Add horizontal and vertical grid lines to the graph. Save and print the new line graph.

6. View the SALES_STACK graph you created in Lesson 7. Add data labels above each bar for all three data ranges. Save and print the new stacked bar graph.

7. View the SALES_XY graph you created in Lesson 8. Add horizontal and vertical grid lines to the graph. Save and print the new XY graph.

8. Erase the current worksheet from the screen and retrieve the PROPERTY data base worksheet you created in Lesson 9. Make up at least ten more records and add them to the worksheet. If you add new records after the last record, you may have to change the range to include the new rows in the formula that computes the sum of the amounts.

9. Sort the PROPERTY worksheet by DATE, with the oldest item appearing first.

10. Set up a query and use a data base function to compute the average amount of PROPERTY items that cost more than $100.

Long Problems

1. Create a worksheet and bar graph to compare tape rentals of movies of various categories for the month of March for Valley Video. Use the following movie categories and numbers of rentals:

   Adventure 222
   Comedy   179
   Foreign   65
   Horror   130
   Mystery   205

   Be sure to create a two-line title for the graph and label both axes. Save the worksheet and print the graph.

2. Create a worksheet and multiple data range line graph to plot the sales of three computer magazines for the years 1985 to 1990. Use different symbols for each magazine, connect the points with line segments, and have 1-2-3 generate a legend. Use the following data for the numbers of thousands of magazines sold per year:

	1985	1986	1987	1989	1990
Megabytes Magazine	200	160	140	130	120
Number Cruncher	90	110	120	104	110
Hardware User	60	90	106	140	150

   Be sure to create a two-line title for the graph and label both axes. Save the worksheet and print the graph.

3. Create a worksheet and pie chart to show the cost-per-unit breakdown for a Beaver Canoe. Use the following data:

   Advertising $69.99
   Labor $99.99
   Materials $219.98
   Packaging $30.00
   Service $79.99

   Be sure to create a two-line title for the chart and label the pie slices. Save the worksheet and print the chart.

4. Suppose Beaver Canoe Company went public in 1988. Create a worksheet and stacked bar graph to compare the components of total capitalization. Use the following data, in millions of dollars, for each fiscal year:

	1988	1989	1990
Stockholder Equity	9	11	14
Long-Term Debt	5	4	4
Short-Term Debt	1	2	3

Be sure to create a two-line title for the graph, generate a legend, and label both axes. Save the worksheet and print the graph.

5. Create a pie chart from the 1990 data in Long Problem 4. Be sure to create a two-line title for the chart and label the pie slices. Save the worksheet and print the chart.

6. Create a worksheet and XY graph to depict the relationship between per capita income (in U.S. dollars) and male life expectancy (in years). Plot per capita income along the X axis and life expectancy along the Y axis. Use the following data:

Country	Per Capita Income	Male Life Expectancy
Afghanistan	$168	40
Australia	$9,914	70
Belgium	$9,827	69
Brazil	$1,523	61
Cambodia	$90	44
Canada	$10,193	69
Denmark	$12,956	71
Ecuador	$1,050	55
Ethiopia	$117	37
France	$7,179	70
West Germany	$11,142	67
Guatemala	$1,083	48
Haiti	$300	47
Honduras	$822	53
India	$150	52
Iran	$2,160	58
Israel	$3,332	72
Italy	$6,914	70
Jamaica	$1,340	65
Japan	$8,460	73
Kenya	$196	56
Kuwait	$11,431	67
Laos	$85	39
Libya	$6,335	51
Mexico	$1,800	62
Nicaragua	$804	51
Norway	$12,432	73
Pakistan	$280	54
Poland	$4,670	66
Singapore	$4,100	68

Country	Per Capita Income	Male Life Expectancy
Spain	$5,500	70
Sweden	$14,821	73
Turkey	$1,300	57
USSR	$2,600	64
USA	$11,675	71

Be sure to create a two-line title for the graph, connect the points with line segments, and label both axes. Save the worksheet and print the graph.

7. Retrieve the worksheet you created in Long Problem 6. Save it in a file with a different name to create a copy of the worksheet and graph. Examine the data and the printed graph. Eliminate those data points that deviate significantly from the pattern. Modify the graph so that Lotus 1-2-3 labels each point. Save the worksheet and print the graph. The moral of this problem: data can be carefully selected and graphs designed to enhance or distort the facts.

8. Create an "electronic Rolodex" with Lotus 1-2-3. Set up the columns and enter the records of a worksheet data base to hold the information you keep in your personal address book. Include fields for last name, first name, address, city, state, ZIP code, and phone number. Sort the data base by last name and then by first name. Print the worksheet when you are finished.

9. Create a data base worksheet to hold the following expense records:

No	Date	Category	Amount	Description
13	03-Mar-90	Freight	$8.75	UPS
4	09-Jan-90	Publications	$3.95	PC Magazine
1	04-Jan-90	Freight	$8.50	Federal Express
3	09-Jan-90	Freight	$2.79	Postage
15	16-Mar-90	Supplies	$5.05	Envelopes
6	14-Jan-90	Supplies	$40.98	Diskettes
20	28-Mar-90	Freight	$13.50	Federal Express
8	02-Feb-90	Software	$49.88	Reflex Plus upgrade
2	04-Jan-90	Freight	$8.50	Federal Express
10	11-Feb-90	Freight	$4.79	Postage Stamps
16	20-Mar-90	Freight	$8.50	Federal Express
11	13-Feb-90	Freight	$9.50	Federal Express
18	22-Mar-90	Publications	$19.95	Using PageMaker
14	04-Mar-90	Publications	$12.70	The Well-Connected PC
5	14-Jan-90	Publications	$3.00	CD-ROM Magazine
9	10-Feb-90	Utilities	$10.04	Telephone calls
17	21-Mar-90	Freight	$8.50	Federal Express
12	21-Feb-90	Freight	$14.50	Federal Express
19	24-Mar-90	Supplies	$35.66	Computer Paper
7	02-Feb-90	Hardware	$18.01	IBM Modem Cable

Sort the records by No or Date and sum the amounts.

10. Use the data base worksheet you created in Long Problem 9. In a blank part of the worksheet, set up queries and use the @DSUM function to compute subtotals for the following expense categories: Freight, Hardware, Publications, Software, Supplies, and Utilities.

ADVANCED
LOTUS 1-2-3

In This Chapter

Preview

The previous two chapters taught you most of what the average user needs to know about Lotus 1-2-3. This chapter proceeds to more advanced spreadsheet topics, including powerful new features found in Lotus 1-2-3 Release 2.2 and Release 3.1. You may not need all of the commands and features presented in this chapter, but many of them can make your work easier, quicker, and less tedious. Learning more about Lotus 1-2-3 can help you create more complex and powerful worksheets.

After studying this chapter, you will know how to

- change worksheet settings.
- freeze titles and use windows.
- hide columns and protect cells.
- change range formats.
- use range names.
- fill a range with a sequence of numbers.
- transpose columns and rows.
- control recalculation and iteration.
- use relative, absolute, and mixed cell references.
- use additional functions.
- use macros.
- use the Release 2.2 Learn feature.
- use the Release 3.1 Record feature.
- use file linking with Release 2.2 and 3.1.
- use three-dimensional worksheets with Release 3.1.

Getting Started

You've already learned how to start Lotus 1-2-3 and use its most basic features and commands. This chapter assumes you have completed the lessons and exercises in Chapters 11 and 12. Furthermore, it assumes that you have a computer with a hard disk and Lotus 1-2-3 installed on it in a subdirectory named 123 or 123R3. A DOS path should be set up so that you can run Lotus 1-2-3 from within any subdirectory. You should have a subdirectory named LESSONS in which to store your worksheet files.

Lesson 1: Changing Worksheet Settings

Worksheet is the first option in the Main menu of Lotus 1-2-3. Selecting Worksheet activates a submenu of options for changing worksheet settings. The Worksheet Global options affect the entire worksheet. Other Worksheet options let you insert and delete columns and rows, set column widths, hide columns, erase the entire worksheet, freeze titles on the screen, split the display into windows, show the current worksheet settings, and insert page breaks into the worksheet. Let's explore some of these options.

Step 1: Start 1-2-3

If you are not already running Lotus 1-2-3, switch to your LESSONS subdirectory and start the program:

Type   **cd c:\lessons**
Press **Enter**
Type   **123**
Press **Enter**

Step 2: Set the Global Format

The Worksheet Global Format command lets you specify the way numeric values are to appear for the entire worksheet. We will discuss the various types of formatting later in this chapter when we cover the Range Format command. For now, let's just change the global format of the worksheet to Currency.

Type   **/wgfc**
Press **Enter**

The default number of decimal places is two. Enter a number into any cell and you will see it formatted as a currency value.

Type   **100**
Press **Enter**

Step 3: Set the Global Label-Prefix

The Worksheet Global Label-Prefix command lets you set the alignment of labels for the entire worksheet. The default label alignment is Left, which means that the apostrophe (') is the default global label-prefix character. Suppose you want all labels to be centered unless you explicitly specify otherwise. Set the global label-prefix to Center, which will automatically use the caret (^) as the label-prefix character.

Type   **/wglc**

Now move the cell pointer and enter a label into any cell.

Press **Right Arrow**
Type   **One**
Press **Enter**

The label will be centered automatically within its cell.

Step 4: Set the Global Column-Width

You already know how to set the column width for the entire worksheet, but let's try it once more. Use the Worksheet Global Column-Width command to set the width of every column to 15 characters.

Type   **/wgc15**
Press **Enter**

Every column will widen to 15 characters.

Step 5: Set the Global Default Directory

By default, 1-2-3 will search the current disk drive directory for files that you want to retrieve and it will place files that you save in that same directory. If you have a DOS PATH statement set up so that you can run 1-2-3 from within any subdirectory, you probably will not have to change this default directory setting. But suppose you want Lotus 1-2-3 to use C:\LESSONS as its default directory for saving and retrieving files, no matter which directory you are in when you start the program. Execute the Worksheet Global Default Directory command and enter the path of the directory you want 1-2-3 to use.

Type   **/wgdd**
Press   **Escape**
Type   **c:\lessons**
Press   **Enter**
Type   **q**

For the rest of your 1-2-3 session, the LESSONS subdirectory will be the default directory. If you want to make this the default directory every time you use 1-2-3, you would execute the Worksheet Global Default Update command.

Step 6: Set the Display of Zero Values

By default, 1-2-3 displays values of zero, whether they are entered as numbers or are the results of formulas. For example, move the cell pointer and enter a zero into a cell.

Press   **Down Arrow**
Type   **0**
Press   **Enter**

As you can see, $0.00 is displayed in cell B2. Suppose you want to suppress the display of zero values. Execute the Worksheet Global Zero Yes command.

Type   **/wgzy**

Examine cell B2. In the worksheet, the cell appears to be empty, but the control panel shows that the cell contains the number 0.

To turn on the display of zero values, execute the Worksheet Global Zero No command.

Lotus 1-2-3 Release 2.2 and Release 3.1 also let you display a label instead of zero values in the worksheet. For example, if you are running Release 2.2 or 3.1, try the Worksheet Global Zero Label command:

Type   **/wgzl**
Type   **(zero)**
Press   **Enter**

The label "*(zero)* will appear instead of zero values in the worksheet.

Step 7: Display the Worksheet Status

The Worksheet Status command displays information about memory use, current global settings, and various hardware options.

Type   **/ws**

Figure 1 shows the result. When you are finished examining the status screen, press any key to return to ready mode.

Press   **Enter**

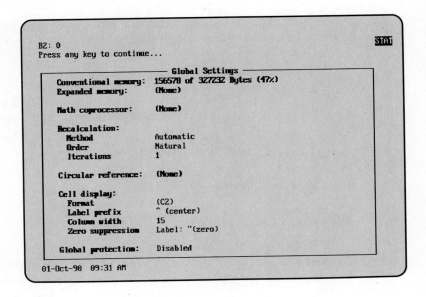

Figure 1 The Worksheet Status Screen

Step 8: Insert Page Breaks

The Lotus 1-2-3 Worksheet Page command lets you insert page breaks into a worksheet. Then when you print the worksheet, a new page will begin after each page break. For example, follow these directions to have row 11 begin at the top of a new page when the worksheet is printed:

Press **F5**
Type **a10**
Press **Enter**
Type **/wp**

A double colon (::) will appear in column A of the row that contains the page break. The rest of the worksheet will move down. No entries should appear in the row containing the page break, because 1-2-3 does not print anything in that row.

You can remove a page break by using the Range Erase command or by overwriting the cell that contains the double colon.

Practice
1. Change the Worksheet Global Format to General.
2. Change the Worksheet Global Label-Prefix to Left.
3. Change the Worksheet Global Column-Width to 12.
4. Turn on the display of zero values.
5. Delete the page break in row 10.

Lesson 2: Freezing Titles and Using Windows

The Worksheet Titles command lets you freeze rows, columns, or both on the screen so you can see them when you scroll the worksheet. Use this command to keep row and column labels on the screen when you work with long or wide worksheets. The Worksheet Windows command lets you split the screen into two horizontal or vertical windows. You can synchronize scrolling in the two windows or scroll them independently. Let's examine these two useful commands.

Step 1: Retrieve the PROPERTY Worksheet

Retrieve the PROPERTY worksheet, which you created in the previous chapter, so that you have a more substantial worksheet on the screen.

Type	**/fr**
Highlight	**PROPERTY.WK1** (or **PROPERTY.WK3**)
Press	**Enter**
Press	**Home**

Step 2: Freeze Horizontal Titles

The PROPERTY worksheet contains only 20 rows. Suppose it were much longer. When you scroll down, the column labels ITEM, DATE, and AMOUNT will disappear off the top of the screen. For example, move the cell pointer down 20 rows.

Press   **Down Arrow** (20 times)

The column labels disappear. The Worksheet Titles Horizontal command lets you freeze these labels on the screen. Move the cell pointer one row below the rows you want to freeze and then execute the Worksheet Titles Horizontal command.

Press	**Home**
Press	**Down Arrow**
Type	**/wth**

The top row is now frozen. It will always remain on the screen. You cannot move the cell pointer into the frozen row with the pointer-movement keys, but you can do so with F5, the Go To key. Try moving the cell pointer with the top row frozen.

Press	**Up Arrow**
Press	**Down Arrow** (25 times)

Notice how row 1 always remains on the screen even as the worksheet scrolls.

Step 3: Freeze Both Titles

The Worksheet Titles command also lets you freeze the vertical titles or both the horizontal and vertical titles. For example, move the cell pointer to B2 and freeze both titles.

Press	**Home**
Press	**Right Arrow**
Type	**/wtb**

Row 1 and column A are now frozen. To see how they remain on the screen, scroll down and right.

Press	**Down Arrow** (25 times)
Press	**Right Arrow** (3 times)

Rows 2 through 8 and column B disappear, but row 1 and column A remain on the screen (see Figure 2).

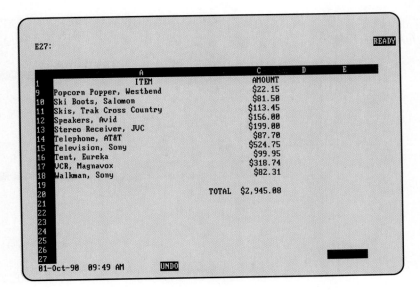

Figure 2 Row 1 and Column A Frozen as Titles

Step 4: Clear the Titles

The Worksheet Titles Clear command lets you unfreeze all existing titles.

> Type   **/wtc**
> Press **Home**

You can now move to row 1 or column A, and they will disappear when the worksheet is scrolled.

Step 5: Split the Screen Into Two Windows

The Worksheet Windows command lets you split the screen into two horizontal or vertical windows so you can view two different parts of the same worksheet. Suppose you want two horizontal windows. Move the cell pointer to the row that you want to be the top of the bottom window, say row 11, and then execute the Worksheet Window Horizontal command.

> Press **Down Arrow (10 times)**
> Type   **/wwh**

Figure 3 shows the result. The top of the second window is marked by the second column border across the middle of the screen. The top window is active and the cell pointer is in A10.

Step 6: Move Between Windows

Right now, you are in the top window. Any vertical pointer movement keys will act only within this window. For example, move the cell pointer down ten cells.

> Press **Down Arrow** (10 times)

Notice that the top window scrolls while the bottom window remains still.

Figure 3 Two Horizontal Windows

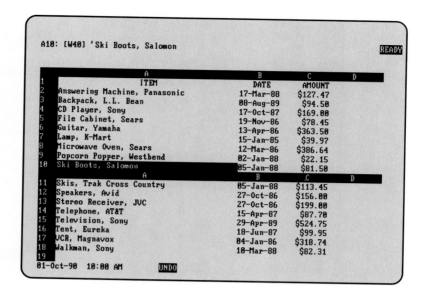

Suppose you want to move to the bottom window. The F6 function key lets you move to the other window. Switch to the bottom window, and move the cell pointer up ten rows.

Press **F6**
Press **Up Arrow** (10 times)

This time, the bottom window will scroll while the top window remains still. Switch to the top window again and move the cell pointer to A1.

Press **F6**
Press **Home**

Step 7: Unsynchronize Windows

By default, windows are synchronized. For vertical windows, this means that the same rows are kept on the screen in both windows when you scroll up or down. For horizontal windows, this means that the same columns will remain on the screen in both windows when you scroll right or left. For example, move the cell pointer to the right.

Press **Right Arrow** (4 times)

The screen will scroll so that the same columns appear in both windows.

You can tell 1-2-3 to allow windows to scroll independently in all directions by executing the Worksheet Window Unsync command.

Type **/wwu**

Now move the cell pointer to the left in the top window.

Press **Left Arrow** (4 times)

Only the top window will scroll to the left. The bottom window will remain still.

Step 8: Clear Windows

When you are finished using windows, you can restore the screen to a single window by executing the Worksheet Window Clear command.

> Type   **/wwc**

The contents and settings of the window that was on the top or the left will expand to occupy the entire screen.

Practice

1. Freeze column A as a vertical title. Move the cell pointer to the right and see how column A always remains on the screen. When you are finished, clear worksheet titles.

2. Move the cell pointer to column B and split the screen into two vertical windows. Tell 1-2-3 to synchronize the windows. Move the cell pointer down 25 rows and see how the two vertical windows scroll together. When you are finished, clear worksheet windows and move the cell pointer to A1.

Lesson 3: Hiding Columns and Protecting Cells

Worksheets often contain sensitive data, such as salaries and grades, that you may not want anyone to see. Lotus 1-2-3 lets you hide columns without erasing the data they contain. Worksheets may also contain data that should not be changed by the average user. Lotus 1-2-3 lets you protect ranges of cells to prevent them from being changed.

If the PROPERTY worksheet is not on your screen, retrieve it.

Step 1: Hide a Column

Suppose you want to keep the AMOUNT values in the PROPERTY worksheet private. The Worksheet Column Hide command lets you conceal the contents of one or more columns. Move to column C and execute the Worksheet Column Hide command.

> Press   **Home**
> Press   **Right Arrow** (2 times)
> Type   **/wch**
> Press   **Enter**

Figure 4 shows the result. Column C appears to have been removed from the worksheet. In fact, it is only hidden.

Step 2: Display a Column

Now suppose you want to see the hidden column. Execute the Worksheet Column Display command and enter a cell address from the hidden column.

> Type   **/wcd**
> Type   **c1**
> Press   **Enter**

The hidden column will reappear in the worksheet.

Figure 4 Column C Has Been Hidden

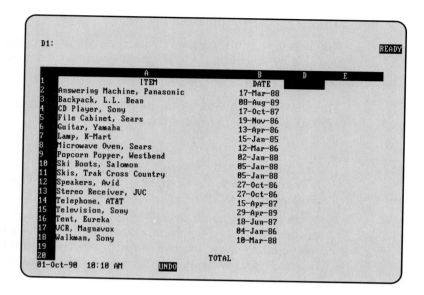

Step 3: Create a Template

A **template** is a general-purpose worksheet in which the user fills in the blanks or changes selected entries to perform a well-defined task. The person who creates the template enters the labels, formulas, and perhaps some constant numbers. The person who uses the template supplies the variables. The template generates the result. For example, you could create a template to compute the monthly payment on a loan, given the principal, interest rate, and term. Follow these directions to create such a template:

Type	**/wey**
Type	**/wgfc**
Press	**Enter**
Type	**/wgc15**
Press	**Enter**
Press	**Right Arrow**
Type	**'<-- Enter the amount of the loan**
Press	**Down Arrow**
Type	**'<-- Enter the annual interest rate**
Press	**Down Arrow**
Type	**'<-- Enter the term in months**
Press	**Down Arrow**
Type	**'<-- This is the monthly payment**
Press	**Left Arrow**
Type	**@pmt(a1,a2/12,a3)**
Press	**Up Arrow**
Type	**/rfga2..a3**
Press	**Enter**

The ERR message you see in cell A4 indicates a division by zero in the formula. It will disappear as soon as numbers are entered into cells A1, A2, and A3.

Step 4: Try the Template

The template is now set up for a user to enter values in cells A1, A2, and A3. Let's try the template.

> Press **Home**
> Type   **4500**
> Press **Down Arrow**
> Type   **12%**
> Press **Down Arrow**
> Type   **24**
> Press **Enter**

The template will calculate the monthly payment to be $211.83.

Step 5: Protect the Worksheet

In this template, only cells A1, A2, and A3 should be changed by the user. The user should not change the labels or the formula. The Worksheet Global Protection Enable command prevents changes being made to all cells. The Range Unprot command can then be used to turn off protection for those cells the user is supposed to change.

> Type **/wgpe**

Now try changing a cell.

> Type   **hello**
> Press **Enter**

Lotus 1-2-3 will beep and display the message

> `Protected cell`

Cancel your attempted change.

> Press **Escape**

Step 6: Unprotect Selected Cells

The template is worthless if no cells can be changed. You must use the Range Unprot command to turn off protection for cells A1 through A3.

> Type   **/rua1..a3**
> Press **Enter**

Now, try changing the amount of the loan to $9,000.

> Press **Home**
> Type   **9000**
> Press **Enter**

Cells A1 through A3 can be changed, but all other cells in the worksheet are protected.

Step 7: Save the Worksheet

Save the template you have created in a worksheet file named LOAN so that you can use it in the future.

> Type   **/fs**
> Type   **loan**
> Press **Enter**

1. The Range Protect command lets you protect one or more cells you have unprotected with the Range Unprot command. For example, suppose the interest rate will never change and you don't want users to alter it. Use the Range Protect command to prevent cell A2 from being changed. Try to change it and see what happens.

2. Protection for the entire worksheet can be turned off with the Worksheet Global Protection Disable command. Use this command to allow changes to all cells in the worksheet.

Lesson 4: Changing Range Formats

Lotus 1-2-3 lets you set the numeric format of one cell, a range of cells, or every cell in the worksheet. So far, you have used General format, which is the default, and Currency format, which is used for dollar amounts. Let's examine each of the formats you can set with the Range Format command.

Step 1: Set Up a New Worksheet

Erase the worksheet from your screen and widen all columns to 15 characters.

Type   **/wey**
Type   **/wgc15**
Press **Enter**

Step 2: Use the General Format

General format displays negative numbers with a leading minus sign, does not use commas to separate thousands, and suppresses trailing zeros after the decimal point. If the number is too large to fit within the column width, scientific notation is used to express the number. When the number of digits to the right of the decimal point exceeds the column width, 1-2-3 displays as many digits as it can. General format is the default numeric format used for all cells unless you specify otherwise. Try General format.

Type   **General**
Press **Right Arrow**
Type   **12345.678**
Press **Down Arrow**
Press **Left Arrow**

Step 3: Use the Fixed Format

Fixed format lets you specify how many decimal places to display, from 0 to 15. Values are rounded or filled out with zeros to fit the exact number of decimal places you specify. Negative numbers have a leading minus sign and commas are not used to separate thousands. Values between −1 and 1 are expressed with a leading zero before the decimal point. Enter a number and use the Range Format Fixed command with two decimal places.

Type   **Fixed**
Press **Right Arrow**
Type   **12345.678**
Press **Enter**

Type	**/rff**
Press	**Enter**
Press	**Enter**
Press	**Down Arrow**
Press	**Left Arrow**

Notice that 12345.678 is rounded to 12345.68 to fit the Fixed format with two decimal places.

Step 4: Use the Scientific Format

Scientific format expresses numbers in exponential notation. It is useful for very large or very small numbers. A number in scientific format has three parts: the mantissa, the letter E, and the exponent. The **mantissa** is the decimal part of the number. The letter E indicates exponential format and separates the mantissa from the exponent. The **exponent** indicates the power of ten to be multiplied by the mantissa to yield the number. For example, 1.5E+02 is equal to 1.5×10^2 or 150. Either the mantissa or the exponent can be negative. For example, $-1.5E-02$ is equal to -1.5×10^{-2} or -0.015. The mantissa can have up to 15 decimal places and the exponent can be any number from -99 to 99. Enter a number and use the Range Format Scientific command with two decimal places.

Type	**Scientific**
Press	**Right Arrow**
Type	**12345.678**
Press	**Enter**
Type	**/rfs**
Press	**Enter**
Press	**Enter**
Press	**Down Arrow**
Press	**Left Arrow**

Notice that 12345.678 is expressed in scientific format as 1.23E+04 with the mantissa rounded to two decimal places.

Step 5: Use the Currency Format

You have already used Currency format, but let's try it again. Numbers are displayed with a currency symbol, such as $, thousands are separated by commas, and up to 15 decimal places can be specified. Negative values are enclosed in parentheses, a common convention in financial worksheets. However, the currency symbol and the expression of negative values in parentheses can be changed with the Worksheet Global Default Other International command. Enter a number and use the Range Format Currency command with two decimal places.

Type	**Currency**
Press	**Right Arrow**
Type	**12345.678**
Press	**Enter**
Type	**/rfc**
Press	**Enter**
Press	**Enter**
Press	**Down Arrow**
Press	**Left Arrow**

The number will be rounded to two decimal places and expressed as $12,345.68.

Step 6: Use the Comma Format

Comma format is essentially the same as Currency format except it does not display the leading currency symbol. Enter a number and use the Range Format , (comma) command with two decimal places.

Type	**Comma**
Press	**Right Arrow**
Type	**12345.678**
Press	**Enter**
Type	**/rf,**
Press	**Enter**
Press	**Enter**
Press	**Down Arrow**
Press	**Left Arrow**

The number will be expressed as 12,345.68.

Step 7: Use the +/− Format

The +/− format displays a horizontal bar of plus signs or minus signs, or a period. It is used to generate crude bar graphs. The number of plus signs or minus signs equals the whole-number value of the entry rounded to the nearest integer. For example, if you enter 5 into a cell in +/− format, five plus signs will be displayed. If you enter −5 instead, five minus signs will be displayed. If the number is between −1 and 1, a period will be displayed. Enter a number and use the Range Format +/− command.

Type	**'+/−**
Press	**Right Arrow**
Type	**5**
Press	**Enter**
Type	**/rf+**
Press	**Enter**
Press	**Down Arrow**
Press	**Left Arrow**

You should see five plus signs instead of the number 5 in cell B6.

Step 8: Use the Percent Format

Percent format displays numbers as percentages with up to 15 decimal places and a trailing percent sign. In other words, a number expressed in Percent format is multiplied by 100. Enter a number and use the Range Format Percent command with two decimal places.

Type	**Percent**
Press	**Right Arrow**
Type	**0.678**
Press	**Enter**
Type	**/rfp**
Press	**Enter**
Press	**Enter**
Press	**Down Arrow**
Press	**Left Arrow**

You should see the number expressed as 67.80%.

Step 9: Use the Date and Time Formats

Lotus 1-2-3 maintains dates and times as numbers that can be used in calculations. Each day between January 1, 1900 and December 31, 2099 is assigned a sequential date number. January 1, 1900 is 1; January 2, 1900 is 2; and so on up to December 31, 2099, which is 73050. The total time in each day is represented by the number 1. The time number for midnight is 0.0; noon is 0.5; and just before midnight is 0.99999. Although these date and time numbers might seem strange, you can perform calculations with them, and 1-2-3 can easily express them in the format you are used to seeing. The Date option of the Range Format menu lets you express date numbers as dates, such as 21-Jun-90, and time numbers as times, such as 02:38:24 PM. Enter a number and use the Range Format Date 1 (DD-MM-YY) command.

Type	**Date**
Press	**Right Arrow**
Type	**33045**
Press	**Enter**
Type	**/rfd1**
Press	**Enter**
Press	**Down Arrow**
Press	**Left Arrow**

You should see the date number 33045 expressed as the date 21-Jun-90 in cell B8. Now, enter a number and use the Range Format Date Time 1 (HH:MM:SS AM/PM) command.

Type	**Time**
Press	**Right Arrow**
Type	**0.61**
Press	**Enter**
Type	**/rfdt1**
Press	**Enter**
Press	**Down Arrow**
Press	**Left Arrow**

You should see the time number 0.61 expressed as the time 02:38:24 PM in cell B9.

Step 10: Use the Text Format

Text format displays formulas in worksheet cells instead of their computed results. This format can be handy for checking formulas in a complex worksheet. Numbers in cells formatted as Text are displayed in General format. Enter a formula and use the Range Format Text command to display that formula instead of its computed result in the worksheet.

Type	**Text**
Press	**Right Arrow**
Type	**+b1+b2**
Press	**Enter**
Type	**/rft**
Press	**Enter**
Press	**Down Arrow**
Press	**Left Arrow**

You should see the formula +B1+B2 in cell B10 instead of the computed result 24691.356.

Step 11: Use the Hidden Format

Hidden format allows you to conceal the contents of one or more cells in the worksheet. The contents of a hidden cell still exist and can be viewed in the control panel unless the cell is protected and global protection is turned on. Enter a number and use the Range Format Hidden command to conceal it.

Type	**Hidden**
Press	**Right Arrow**
Type	**12345.678**
Press	**Enter**
Type	**/rfh**
Press	**Enter**

As Figure 5 shows, cell B11 appears to be empty in the worksheet, but its contents are visible in the control panel.

To reveal hidden cells, you can change their format to anything but Hidden. You can also use the Range Format Reset command to restore the global cell format for those cells.

Step 12: Save the Worksheet

Save the worksheet you have created in a file named FORMATS in case you want to use it again.

Type	**/fs**
Type	**formats**
Press	**Enter**

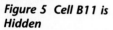

1. Change the format of cell B2 to Fixed format with 0 decimal places. Notice how the number is rounded to 12346.
2. Change the number in cell B6 to −5 and observe the result. Change the number to 0.5 and see what happens. Finally, try entering 50 into the cell. The asterisks indicate that the contents cannot fit within the specified column width. Change the number back to 5.

Figure 5 Cell B11 is Hidden

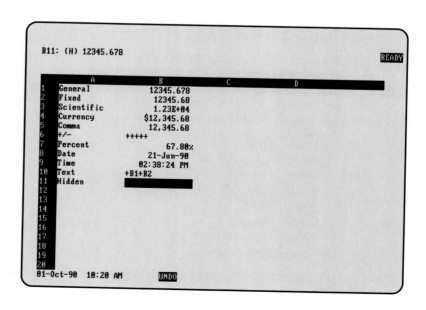

Lesson 5: Using Range Names

You have learned that a range of cells is designated like this: A1..B10. Lotus 1-2-3 also lets you assign a name to a range of cells. Range names can make it much easier to specify ranges in formulas and commands. Let's retrieve the BUDGET worksheet and see how to use range names.

Step 1: Retrieve the BUDGET Worksheet

Execute the File Retrieve command and select the BUDGET worksheet.

Type   **/fr**
Highlight   **BUDGET.WK1** (or **BUDGET.WK3**)
Press   **Enter**

Step 2: Name a Range

The expenses for January are in the range B6..B16. Let's name this range. A range name can be up to 15 characters long. It should not start with a number or resemble a cell address, such as B5. A range name cannot contain spaces or any of these characters:

, ; + * - / & < > { @ #

You can, however, use the underscore (_) character in range names. Execute the Range Name Create command, enter a name, and specify the range.

Type   **/rnc**
Type   **jan_expenses**
Press   **Enter**
Type   **b6..b16**
Press   **Enter**

Step 3: Use the Range Name in a Command

Let's use the range name JAN_EXPENSES to copy the expenses from column B to column D.

Type   **/c**
Type   **jan_expenses**
Press   **Enter**
Type   **d6**
Press   **Enter**

If you don't remember or don't want to type the range name you want to use, you can press the F3 function key to display a menu of range names. For example, follow these directions.

Type   **/c**
Press   **F3**
Highlight   **JAN_EXPENSES**
Press   **Enter**
Type   **e6**
Press   **Enter**

The contents of the JAN_EXPENSES range have been copied to columns D and E.

Step 4: Examine the Other Range Name Options

Activate the Range Name menu and examine the other Range Name options.

> Type   **/rn**

Figure 6 shows the Range Name menu. The Create option lets you change an existing range name as well as create a new one. The Delete option lets you remove a range name. The Labels option lets you assign range names to single-cell ranges, using the labels in adjacent cells as the range names. The Reset option deletes all range names. The Table option creates a two column table that lists all your range names and their corresponding ranges.

> Press   **Escape** (3 times)

1. Move the cell pointer to B17 and examine the formula. Lotus 1-2-3 automatically replaced the B6..B16 in the formula with the range name JAN_EXPENSES.
2. Create range names for the February, March, and April expenses.
3. Move to an empty portion of the worksheet and execute the Range Name Table command. Return to READY mode.

Lesson 6: Filling a Range with a Sequence of Numbers

Sometimes, it is useful to fill a range of cells with a sequence of numbers. For example, suppose you wanted to number each item in your PROPERTY inventory. The Data Fill command makes it easy to generate sequences of numbers.

Step 1: Retrieve the PROPERTY Worksheet

Make PROPERTY your current worksheet.

> Type   **/fr**
> Highlight   **PROPERTY.WK1** (or **PROPERTY.WK3**)

Figure 6 The Range Name Menu

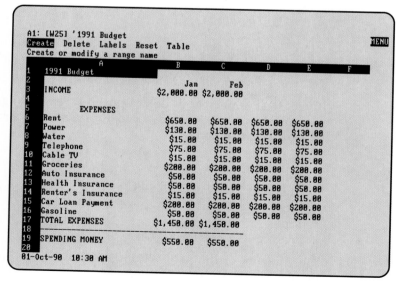

Figure 7 The Data Fill Command Has Numbered the Items

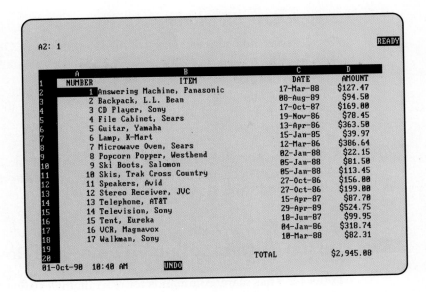

```
A2: 1                                                          READY

        A              B                      C        D
1   NUMBER          ITEM                     DATE     AMOUNT
2        1 Answering Machine, Panasonic    17-Mar-88  $127.47
3        2 Backpack, L.L. Bean             08-Aug-89   $94.50
4        3 CD Player, Sony                 17-Oct-87  $169.00
5        4 File Cabinet, Sears             19-Nov-86   $78.45
6        5 Guitar, Yamaha                  13-Apr-86  $363.50
7        6 Lamp, K-Mart                    15-Jan-85   $39.97
8        7 Microwave Oven, Sears           12-Mar-86  $386.64
9        8 Popcorn Popper, Westbend        02-Jan-88   $22.15
10       9 Ski Boots, Salomon              05-Jan-88   $81.50
11      10 Skis, Trak Cross Country        05-Jan-88  $113.45
12      11 Speakers, Avid                  27-Oct-86  $156.00
13      12 Stereo Receiver, JVC            27-Oct-86  $199.00
14      13 Telephone, AT&T                 15-Apr-87   $87.70
15      14 Television, Sony                29-Apr-89  $524.75
16      15 Tent, Eureka                    18-Jun-87   $99.95
17      16 VCR, Magnavox                   04-Jan-86  $318.74
18      17 Walkman, Sony                   10-Mar-88   $82.31
19
20                                   TOTAL           $2,945.08
01-Oct-90  10:40 AM        UNDO
```

Press	**Enter**
Press	**Home**

Step 2: Insert a New Column A

To number the items in the first column, you must insert a new column A. Execute the Worksheet Insert Column command.

Type	**/wic**
Press	**Enter**

A new blank row A, nine characters wide, will be inserted in the worksheet. Enter a label for the column.

Type	**"NUMBER**
Press	**Down Arrow**

Step 3: Execute the Data Fill Command

We want to fill the range A2..A18 with the numbers 1 through 17. Execute the Data Fill command, specify the fill range, specify the start value, specify the step value, and specify the stop value.

Type	**/df**
Type	**a2..a18**
Press	**Enter**
Type	**1**
Press	**Enter**
Press	**Enter**
Press	**Enter**

Lotus 1-2-3 will fill the range with a sequence of numbers that starts with 1 and increases by 1 in each successive cell (see Figure 7).

Step 4: Save the Worksheet

To preserve the changes you have made, save the PROPERTY worksheet to its disk file.

> Type   **/fs**
> Press   **Enter**
> Type   **r**

Practice   Execute the Worksheet Erase Yes command to clear the PROPERTY worksheet. Use the Data Fill command to load the range A1 to Z1 with the numbers 2, 4, 6, 8, 10, 12, and so on.

Lesson 7: Transposing Columns and Rows

Lotus 1-2-3 has many commands for rearranging existing data. For example, you already know how to use commands such as Move, Copy, Worksheet Insert, and Worksheet Delete. Range Trans is a more specialized command that lets you transpose data from a horizontal arrangement to a vertical arrangement, or vice versa. As an example, let's transpose a table in the SALES worksheet you created in the previous chapter.

Step 1: Retrieve the SALES Worksheet

Make SALES your current worksheet.

> Type   **/fr**
> Highlight   **SALES.WK1** (or **SALES.WK3**)
> Press   **Enter**
> Press   **Home**

Step 2: Transpose a Range

The sales figures in rows 1 and 2 are arranged horizontally, with a year in each column. Let's transpose this table and make a new copy in which the sales figures are arranged vertically. Execute the Range Trans command, specify the FROM range, then specify the first cell of the TO range.

> Type   **/r t**
> Type   **a1..e2**
> Press   **Enter**
> Type   **e5**
> Press   **Enter**

Figure 8 shows the result. The original sales table in cells A1..E2 has been transposed and copied to cells E5..F9.

Practice   Transpose another table in the SALES worksheet. Be sure to specify a TO range in an empty part of the worksheet.

Figure 8 The Transposed Sales Table

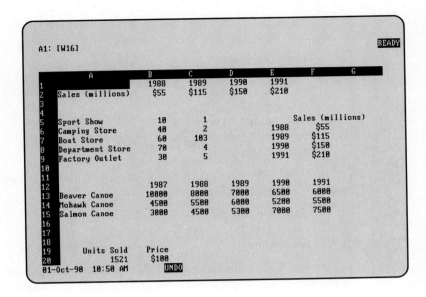

Lesson 8: Controlling Recalculation and Iteration

Spreadsheet programs are useful tools because you can easily change data and recalculate worksheets. Usually, recalculation occurs automatically, and you don't have to worry about it. In some cases, however, you must exercise control over the method and order of recalculation. Lotus 1-2-3 lets you do both.

Most formulas need only be calculated once, unless their data are changed. Some special formulas, however, may have to be recalculated many times to achieve a final result. This repeated recomputation is called **iteration.** It can also be controlled with 1-2-3.

Step 1: Set Up a New Worksheet

Erase the screen and start with a new worksheet.

Type   **/wey**

Step 2: Change the Method of Recalculation

Lotus 1-2-3 has two recalculation methods: Automatic and Manual. **Automatic recalculation** is the default method, used unless you specify otherwise. In Lotus 1-2-3 Release 2.01, automatic recalculation means that every formula in the entire worksheet is recalculated every time any cell is changed. Lotus 1-2-3 Release 2.2 and Release 3.1 use a more sophisticated type of automatic recalculation known as **minimal** or **optimal recalculation.** This feature increases speed by recalculating only those cells that have changed, and the cells that depend on them, since the worksheet was last recalculated.

Even with minimal recalculation, very large worksheets can take a long time to recalculate. The delays can be annoying. Fortunately, Lotus 1-2-3 lets you turn off automatic recalculation and use **manual recalculation** instead. When manual recalculation is turned on, the worksheet is recalculated only when you press

F9, the CALC key. For example, execute the Worksheet Global Recalculation Manual command and create a simple worksheet.

Type	**/wgrm**
Type	**100**
Press	**Down Arrow**
Type	**200**
Press	**Down Arrow**
Type	**+a1+a2**
Press	**Enter**

The formula will be calculated because it was just entered. Try changing cell A2 and see what happens.

Press	**Up Arrow**
Type	**100**
Press	**Enter**

The result in cell A3 remains 300, even though it should be 200. You must press F9, the CALC key, to tell 1-2-3 to recalculate the worksheet.

Press	**F9**

The result in cell A3 will change to 200.

Step 3: Change the Order of Recalculation

Lotus 1-2-3 can perform only one calculation at a time, so it must begin recalculating with a single cell and then proceed throughout the worksheet in some particular order. Early spreadsheet programs, such as VisiCalc, gave you a choice between two orders: column-wise and row-wise recalculation. **Column-wise recalculation** begins with cell A1 and proceeds down column A, goes on to cell B1 and proceeds down column B, and so on. **Row-wise recalculation** also starts at cell A1, but then proceeds to go across row 1, then row 2, and so on. The problem with both of these methods is that they can lead to incorrect results if you are not careful about how you set up your worksheet. For example, erase the worksheet, execute the Worksheet Global Recalculation Columnwise command, and enter the following worksheet.

Type	**/wey**
Type	**/wgrc**
Type	**100+a3**
Press	**Down Arrow**
Type	**200**
Press	**Down Arrow**
Type	**100+a2**
Press	**Enter**

As soon as you finish entering the worksheet, the formulas are calculated for the first time, and you see 100 in A1, 200 in A2, and 300 in A3. Already there is a problem. Cell A1 is supposed to contain 100 plus the value in cell A3. It should contain 400, but it contains only 100. Since the cells were evaluated in the order A1, A2, and A3, nothing was in A3 when cell A1 was originally evaluated. That is why A1 contains only 100. Now, change the contents of cell A2 to 222.

Press	**Up Arrow**
Type	**222**
Press	**Enter**

With either column-wise or row-wise recalculation, the results will be 400 in A1, 222 in A2, and 322 in A3. This is *still* not right. Cell A1 should contain 422. It now contains 400 because 1-2-3 added 100 to the formula result of 300 left in cell A3 after the previous change. Clearly, in some instances neither column-wise nor row-wise recalculation work correctly.

Lotus 1-2-3 solves this problem by using **natural recalculation** unless you specify otherwise. This method recalculates a cell only after evaluating any cells on which it depends. For example, natural recalculation would evaluate our worksheet in this order: A2, A3, then A1. Execute the Worksheet Global Recalculation Natural command and then change cell A2 back to 200.

Type   **/wgrn**
Type   **200**
Press   **Enter**

The results are now computed correctly. Cell A1 displays 400, cell A2 displays 200, and cell A3 displays 300.

Although natural recalculation is best for most worksheets, Lotus 1-2-3 lets you change to column-wise or row-wise so that you can create worksheets in which you have explicit control over the order of recalculation.

Step 4: Create a Direct Circular Reference

As you have just seen, formulas can refer to cells that contain other formulas. In the previous step, cell A1 contains a formula that refers to cell A3, but A3 also contains a formula. Although this might seem unusual and perhaps even a bit confusing, it is really quite common for worksheets to contain formulas that refer to other formulas. As long as natural recalculation is used, there is seldom a problem. One potential difficulty, however, can occur. A **circular reference** results when a formula in a cell is either directly or indirectly dependent on the value in that very same cell. The most obvious example is when you use a formula that refers to the same cell in which it is stored. This is a direct circular reference. For example, move to A1 and enter the following formula.

Press   **Home**
Type   **100+a1**
Press   **Enter**

Lotus 1-2-3 cannot evaluate this formula correctly. It displays the value 100 in A1 because it calculated the formula only once. The CIRC error message appears at the bottom of the screen to indicate the presence of a formula containing a circular reference. Although you could tell Lotus 1-2-3 to recalculate the formula several times, every time it would try to evaluate 100 + A1, the value in A1 would change. No matter how many times it would try, the program could not compute a final result for this formula.

Step 5: Use Iteration

Certain *indirect* circular references, however, can be resolved eventually. An absolute final answer may not be reached, but an approximate result can often be obtained by recalculating the formulas a number of times. This method is called iterative recalculation, or simply iteration, and it can be used to solve certain kinds of problems. For example, just about everyone knows what a square root is, but do you know how to calculate one? We seldom figure square roots by hand anymore because most calculators, spreadsheet packages, and programming languages have built-in functions to compute square roots. Before these tools were available, people looked up square roots in printed tables in math books. So, although you will probably never have to know how to compute a square root, let's demonstrate an interesting way to do it with 1-2-3 without using the built-in @SQRT function.

One method to compute the square root of a number is to repeatedly make better and better estimates until you finally arrive at the correct answer. Follow these directions to create a template that will simulate this method of computing a square root:

Type	**/wey**
Type	**16**
Press	**Right Arrow**
Type	**'<-- Enter the number**
Press	**Down Arrow**
Type	**'<-- "Fudge factor" to avoid division by 0**
Press	**Left Arrow**
Type	**0.000001**
Press	**Down Arrow**
Type	**+a4**
Press	**Right Arrow**
Type	**'<-- Contains the formula +A4**
Press	**Down Arrow**
Type	**'<-- Here is the square root**
Press	**Left Arrow**
Type	**@round((a3+a1/(a3+a2))/2,2)**
Press	**Enter**

Obviously, the square root of 16 is not 8,000,000. By default, 1-2-3 recalculates circular references only once. Execute the Worksheet Global Recalculation Iteration command and enter 50 as the number of times to recalculate circular references. Then press the F9 key to recalculate the worksheet.

Type	**/wgri50**
Press	**Enter**
Press	**F9**

Figure 9 shows the result. This worksheet simulates the process of repeatedly making better square root estimates until an answer close enough to the correct answer is obtained. The formula in cell A3 displays the current result of the formula in cell A4, and the formula in cell A4 uses the current result of the formula in cell A3. This is an indirect circular reference. Each time these formulas are recalculated, the result in cell A4 gets closer to the true square root of the number in cell A1. After many iterations, a final answer is obtained.

Step 6: Save the Worksheet

Save the square root template in case you would like to use it again.

Type	**/fs**
Type	**sqrt**
Press	**Enter**

Practice   Use the template to compute the square roots of some numbers other than 16. For example, try 9, 81, 144, and any other numbers you like.

Figure 9 Iteration Used to Compute a Square Root

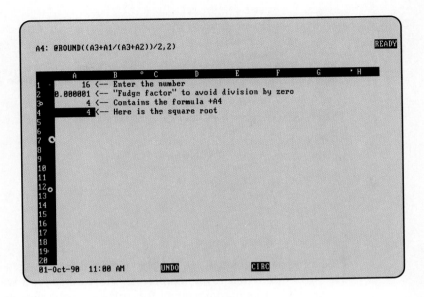

```
A4: @ROUND((A3+A1/(A3+A2))/2,2)                                    READY

        A     B    °  C     D       E      F       G      •H
 1          16 <-- Enter the number
 2   0.000001 <-- "Fudge factor" to avoid division by zero
 3°          4 <-- Contains the formula +A4
 4           4 <-- Here is the square root
 5
 6
 7 o
 8
 9
10
11
12 o
13
14
15
16
17
18
19°
20
01-Oct-90  11:00 AM        UNDO              CIRC
```

Lesson 9: Using Relative, Absolute, and Mixed Cell References

Three types of cell references can be used in a formula: relative, absolute, and mixed. A **relative reference** is a cell address that pertains to a cell's position relative to the current cell. For example, if the current cell is A3 and it contains the formula +A1+A2, the A1 in the formula refers to the cell located two cells above the formula. Lotus 1-2-3 assumes all cell references to be relative unless you specify otherwise. Relative cell references are automatically changed to reflect their new locations when they are moved or copied.

An **absolute reference** is a cell address that does not change when it is moved or copied. This type of cell address is specified by preceding the column and row designations with dollar signs. For example, the absolute reference A1 always refers to cell A1, even if a formula that contains it is moved or copied.

A **mixed reference** is half-relative and half-absolute, in which either a column or a row is absolute, but not both. For example, $A1 is a mixed reference that always means column A, but the row might be changed if this reference is copied or moved. Similarly, A$1 is a mixed cell reference that keeps the row constant.

Let's demonstrate each type of cell reference.

Step 1: Set Up a New Worksheet

Erase the screen and start with a new worksheet.

Type   **/wey**

Step 2: Use Relative References

Cell addresses without dollar signs are assumed to be relative references. For example, follow these directions to create a formula that contains relative references:

Type   **100**
Press   **Down Arrow**
Type   **200**

Press	**Down Arrow**
Type	**+a1+a2**
Press	**Enter**

The cell references in the formula in cell A3 are relative references.

Step 3: Copy Relative References

The Copy command demonstrates the effect of using relative references. Copy cells A1 through A3 to column B.

Type	**/ca1..a3**
Press	**Enter**
Type	**b1**
Press	**Enter**
Press	**Right Arrow**

Examine the formula in cell B3. The original formula was +A1+A2; it was changed to +B1+B2 when it was copied. In most cases, you want cell references to be changed in this manner when formulas are copied or moved.

Step 4: Use an Absolute Reference

In certain situations, however, you may not want a cell reference to be changed when it is copied or moved. For example, you may use a constant value, such as the current interest rate, in several formulas in different places. But you need only store the interest rate once, in a single cell. If you are going to copy or move cells containing formulas that refer to this interest rate, you should use an absolute reference for the cell containing the interest rate. Change the formula in B3 so that it contains an absolute reference to cell A1.

Type	**+a1+b2**
Press	**Enter**

Now change the value in B1 and see how the result of the formula in B3 remains the same because it adds A1 instead of B1 to B2.

Press	**Up Arrow**
Press	**Up Arrow**
Type	**200**
Press	**Enter**

The value displayed in cell B3 should still be 300.

Step 5: Copy An Absolute Reference

Let's see what happens when you copy a formula containing an absolute reference. Copy cells B1 through B3 to column C, then move to cell C3.

Type	**/cb1..b3**
Press	**Enter**
Type	**c1**
Press	**Enter**
Press	**Down Arrow**
Press	**Down Arrow**
Press	**Right Arrow**

Examine the formula in C3 (see Figure 10). The absolute cell reference A1 was not changed, but the relative cell reference was changed to C2.

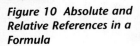

Figure 10 Absolute and Relative References in a Formula

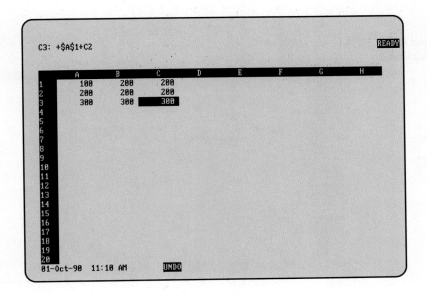

Step 6: Use Mixed Cell References

If you want part of a cell address to remain the same and part to change when you copy or move a formula, you must use a mixed reference. Let's create a small multiplication table of the numbers 0 through 5 to demonstrate the use of mixed cell references. Follow these directions to erase the worksheet and use the Data Fill command to enter the column and row headings of the multiplicands (the numbers to be multiplied):

Type	**/wey**
Type	**/dfb1..g1**
Press	**Enter** (4 times)
Type	**/dfa2..a7**
Press	**Enter** (4 times)

The numbers 0 through 5 should appear in cells B1 through G1 and A2 through A7. Move to cell B2 and enter the multiplication formula containing mixed references.

Press	**Down Arrow**
Press	**Right Arrow**
Type	**+$a2*b$1**
Press	**Enter**

When this formula is copied to the rest of the table, the $A2 mixed reference will keep column A constant, but vary the row. The B$1 mixed reference will vary the column, but keep row 1 constant. To see how these mixed references work, copy the formula in B2 to cells B3 through B7 and C2 through G7, then move to cell G7.

Type	**/c**
Press	**Enter**
Type	**b3..b7**
Press	**Enter**
Type	**/c**
Press	**Enter**

Figure 11 Mixed References in a Multiplication Table

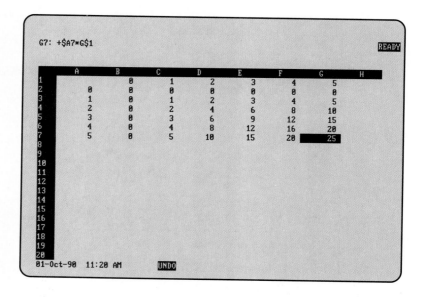

```
G7: +$A7*G$1                                              READY

        A       B       C       D       E       F       G       H
1               0       1       2       3       4       5
2       0       0       0       0       0       0       0
3       1       0       1       2       3       4       5
4       2       0       2       4       6       8       10
5       3       0       3       6       9       12      15
6       4       0       4       8       12      16      20
7       5       0       5       10      15      20      25
8
9
10
11
12
13
14
15
16
17
18
19
20
01-Oct-90   11:20 AM        UNDO
```

Type   **c2..g7**
Press   **Enter**
Press   **F5**
Type   **g7**
Press   **Enter**

Your screen should look like Figure 11. The rest of the multiplication table is easily created with the Copy command, because you used mixed references to keep column A constant for the first multiplicand and row 1 constant for the second multiplicand.

Practice See what happens if you use relative references instead of mixed references in the multiplication table. Change the formula in B2 to +A2*B1. Then copy this formula to cells B3..B7 and C2..G7. Examine some of the copied formulas and try to understand why mixed references are necessary in this case.

Lesson 10: Using Additional Functions

You have already learned to use some of the mathematical, trigonometric, statistical, and financial functions of Lotus 1-2-3. Now let's examine some of the date and time, logical, and string functions.

Step 1: Set Up a New Worksheet

Erase the screen and start with a new worksheet.

Type   **/wey**

Step 2: Try Some Date and Time Functions

Date and time functions help you work with the Lotus 1-2-3 date and time numbers. Let's try a few examples.

Type   **@date(90,12,31)**
Press   **Enter**

The result should be 33238. The @DATE function returns the sequential date number, given the year, month, and day.

Press **Down Arrow**
Type   `@day(a1)`
Press **Enter**

The result should be 31. The @DAY function returns the day, given a date number. The @MONTH and @YEAR functions work similarly.

Press **Down Arrow**
Type   `@time(14,10,20)`
Press **Enter**

The result should be 0.590509, the time number for 2:10:20 PM. The @TIME function returns the 1-2-3 time number, given an hour (0-23), minute (0-59), and second (0-59).

Press **Down Arrow**
Type   `@hour(a3)`
Press **Enter**

The result should be 14. The @HOUR function returns the hour (0-23), given a time number. The @MINUTE and @SECOND functions work similarly.

Press **Down Arrow**
Type   `@now`
Press **Enter**

The @NOW function returns the full serial number for the current date and time.

Step 3: Try Some Logical Functions

Logical functions return values that are dependent on the results of conditional expressions. They essentially allow you to compare values in cells and perform different actions based on the results of those comparisons. Let's try a few examples.

Press **Down Arrow**
Type   `@isnumber(a1)`
Press **Enter**

The result should be 1, which stands for TRUE. The @ISNUMBER function returns 1 (TRUE) if the given value is numeric and 0 (FALSE) if it is a label. The @ISSTRING function is the opposite of @ISNUMBER.

Press **Home**
Press **Right Arrow**
Type   `100`
Press **Down Arrow**
Type   `@if(b1>100,"Big","Small")`
Press **Enter**

You should see "Small" in cell B2. The @IF function evaluates the given logical expression as TRUE or FALSE, and returns the first value if it is TRUE, or the second value if it is FALSE. Since the number in B1 is not greater than 100, the @IF function returns "Small," the second value after the logical expression.

Step 4: Try Some String Functions

String functions manipulate labels. Let's try a few examples.

Press   **Down Arrow**
Type   **@length(b2)**
Press   **Enter**

The result should be 5, the number of characters in "Small," the label in cell B2. The @LENGTH function returns the length of the given string.

Press   **Down Arrow**
Type   **@left(b2,3)**
Press   **Enter**

The result should be "Sma," the first three characters in the label in cell B2. The @LEFT function returns the first *n* characters in a string. The @RIGHT function works similarly, except that it returns the last *n* characters in a string. The @MID function returns *n* characters from the middle of a string, starting at the specified position.

Press   **Down Arrow**
Type   **@upper(b2)**
Press   **Enter**

The result should be "SMALL." The @UPPER function converts the given string to all uppercase characters. The @PROPER function works similarly, except that it capitalizes only the first character in each word in the string.

Press   **Down Arrow**
Type   **@repeat("Hello ",10)**
Press   **Enter**

The result should be "Hello" repeated ten times. The @REPEAT function repeats the given string a specified number of times.

Practice   To see how you might use @NOW, try the following formulas: @YEAR(@NOW), @MONTH(@NOW), @DAY(@NOW), @HOUR(@NOW), @MINUTE(@NOW), @SECOND(@NOW).

Lesson 11: Using Macros

A **macro** is a sequence of keystrokes and special commands that you can create to automate a task. Any task that 1-2-3 can perform can be automated with a macro. When you run a macro, 1-2-3 performs the instructions much faster than you could do them manually. Once a macro has been created, you can use it over and over again. Creating a macro takes planning and time to develop, but it can save a great deal of time in the long run. Macros are used to automate repetitive tasks, reduce keystrokes, simplify complex procedures, guide novices who are unfamiliar with 1-2-3, increase accuracy, and ensure consistency in a worksheet. Let's start with a simple macro that will automatically enter labels into a worksheet.

Step 1: Plan the Macro

A macro is a sequence of keystrokes that you can store, name, and play back over and over again. The first step in creating a macro is to decide what you want it to do. Suppose you want to create a macro that will enter the names of the months of the year across the columns. To plan the macro, think of how you would do this procedure manually. First, you would type *January* and press the Right Arrow key. Then you would type *February* and press the Right Arrow key. After entering the twelve months in this fashion, you would move the cell pointer down to the beginning of the next row. For now, clear the current worksheet and widen all columns to 12 characters.

Type   **/wey**
Type   **/wgc12**
Press   **Enter**

Step 2: Enter the Macro Definition

Before you can use a macro, you must define it. This definition tells 1-2-3 what keystrokes to execute when you run the macro. A macro definition is basically a series of labels stored in an empty part of the worksheet. Usually, a macro definition is stored in cells far below or to the right of the area the actual worksheet is expected to occupy. For this example, move the cell pointer to A100.

Press   **F5**
Type   **a100**
Press   **Enter**

You may type the label entries of a macro definition in any column of cells. Furthermore, you may type more than one macro instruction in any cell, as long as you don't try to enter more than 240 characters in a single cell. Every cell entry in a macro definition must be a label; numbers and formulas will be translated when the macro is run. The entries in a macro definition may consist of any characters you can type on the keyboard. In addition, keys that perform actions instead of displaying characters can also be included in macro definitions. These special keys are specified by entering a symbol or a name enclosed in braces ({ and }). For example, to include a Right Arrow keystroke in a macro definition, you would enter {right}. The following table shows the macro instructions for some common keys.

Macro Instructions for Common Keys

Key	Macro Instruction
Enter	˜(the tilde character)
Down Arrow	{down}
Up Arrow	{up}
Left Arrow	{left}
Right Arrow	{right}
Home	{home}
End	{end}
Page Up	{pgup}
Page Down	{pgdn}
Ctrl-Right Arrow	{bigright}

Macro Instructions for Common Keys (continued)

Key	Macro Instruction
Ctrl-Left Arrow	{bigleft}
F2	{edit}
F5	{goto}
Escape	{esc}
Backspace	{bs}
Delete	{del}

Now, follow these directions to enter the definition of a macro that will enter the months of the year across the columns.

Type   ^January {right}
Press **Down Arrow**
Type   ^February {right}
Press **Down Arrow**
Type   ^March {right}
Press **Down Arrow**
Type   ^April {right}
Press **Down Arrow**
Type   ^May {right}
Press **Down Arrow**
Type   ^June {right}
Press **Down Arrow**
Type   ^July {right}
Press **Down Arrow**
Type   ^August {right}
Press **Down Arrow**
Type   ^September {right}
Press **Down Arrow**
Type   ^October {right}
Press **Down Arrow**
Type   ^November {right}
Press **Down Arrow**
Type   ^December {down}
Press **Down Arrow**
Type   {end} {left}
Press **Enter**

Step 3: Name the Macro

Before you can use a macro, a range name must be assigned to the cells that hold the macro definition. This range name will serve as the macro name. Two types of macro names can be used: a backslash followed by a single letter (such as \A or \M) or a name of up to 15 characters (such as HEADING or MONTHS). The type of name you choose determines how you run the macro. (Note: Lotus 1-2-3 Release 2.01 allows only macro names that consist of a backslash and a single letter.) Follow these directions to name your macro \M:

Type   /rnc
Type   \m

Figure 12 The Completed Macro Definition

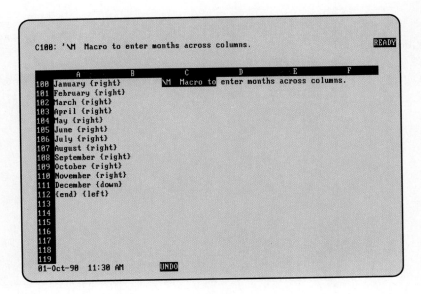

> Press **Enter**
> Type **a100..a112**
> Press **Enter**

Step 4: Document the Macro

It is a good idea to enter the macro name and a brief description beside the macro definition to document the macro for yourself and other users. Complex macros may also have a brief comment beside each macro instruction. Follow these directions to document your macro:

> Press **F5**
> Type **c100**
> Press **Enter**
> Type **'\M Macro to enter months across columns.**
> Press **Enter**

The completed macro is shown in Figure 12.

Step 5: Run the Macro

Now you can use the macro you have created. A macro named with a backslash and a letter is invoked by holding down the Alternate key and typing the letter. Move to cell A2 and run the macro:

> Press **Home**
> Press **Down Arrow**
> Press **Alt-M**

Wasn't that fun? All twelve month labels are entered automatically and the cell pointer returns to the beginning of the next row. Try it again:

> Press **Alt-M**

Your screen should look like Figure 13. You can use the \M macro in any row and as many times as you like.

Figure 13 The Macro Has Been Run Twice

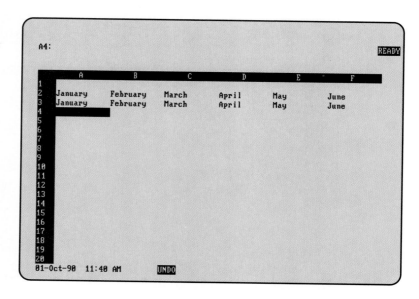

Note: a macro with a long name, such as HEADING or MONTHS, created with Lotus 1-2-3 Release 2.2 or 3.1, is run by pressing Alt-F3, the RUN key, to display a menu of macro names. You then highlight the name of the macro you want to run and press the Enter key.

Step 6: Save the Worksheet

To save the macro you have created, you must save the worksheet.

Type   **/fs**
Type   **months**
Press   **Enter**

Practice   Modify the \M macro so that it always moves the cell pointer to A1 when it is finished entering the months. Test the modified macro to make sure it works correctly.

Lesson 12: Using the Learn Feature with Release 2.2

Lotus 1-2-3 Release 2.2 has an easier way to create macros. (If you are not running Lotus 1-2-3 Release 2.2, just read this lesson without performing its steps.) The **learn feature** lets you have 1-2-3 record your keystrokes as you perform the task you want to automate in order to generate the macro definition. Let's use this method to create a macro to enter today's date in the current cell. This lesson assumes that the global column width has been set to 12 characters.

Step 1: Specify the Learn Range

The **learn range** is the single-column range of cells in your worksheet where 1-2-3 will record your keystrokes and create the macro definition. Since you cannot always be certain how many cells your macro will require, you should reserve more cells than you think you might need. The date macro should require no more than five cells. Execute the Worksheet Learn Range command and specify cells A50 to A55 as the learn range.

Type   **/wlr**
Type   **a50..a55**
Press   **Enter**

Step 2: Turn On the Learn Feature

You must turn on the learn feature so that 1-2-3 knows what keystrokes to record. First, make sure that the cell pointer is not in the learn range. Alt-F5, the LEARN key, is used to turn on the learn feature.

Press   **Alt-F5**

The LEARN indicator will appear at the bottom of the screen.

Step 3: Perform the Task

To record the macro, you perform the task you want to automate. Follow these directions to enter the @NOW function and format the current cell as a date:

Type   **@now**
Press   **Enter**
Type   **/rfd1**
Press   **Enter**

Note that the keystrokes you execute are performed as they are recorded in the learn range.

Step 4: Turn Off the Learn Feature

After you have executed the keystrokes you want to automate, you must turn off the learn feature. Alt-F5, the LEARN key, also turns off the learn feature.

Press   **Alt-F5**

The LEARN indicator will disappear from the bottom of the screen.

Step 5: Name the Macro

The macro definition must be named before you can use it. Move to the learn range:

Press   **F5**
Type   **a50**
Press   **Enter**

Notice cells A50 and A51 are filled with the keystrokes you executed while the learn feature was turned on. Remember that the ~ (tilde) character symbolizes the Enter key. Execute the Range Name Create command to name the macro \D:

Type   **/rnc**
Type   **\d**
Press   **Enter**
Type   **a50..a51**
Press   **Enter**

Step 6: Document the Macro

Move to cell B50 and enter the macro name and a brief description.

Press   **Right Arrow**
Type   **'\D Macro to enter today's date.**
Press   **Enter**

Your screen should look like Figure 14.

Step 7: Run the Macro

Move to cell A5 and run the new macro.

Press   **F5**
Type   **a5**
Press   **Enter**
Press   **Alt-D**

Today's date number will be entered into cell A5 and the cell will be formatted as a date.

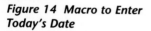 Modify the macro definition so that the cell is formatted to display only the day and month. Hint: use date format number 2.

Lesson 13: Using the Record Feature with Release 3.1

Lotus 1-2-3 Release 3.1 has a feature similar to the Learn feature of Release 2.2 for easily creating macros. (If you are not running Lotus 1-2-3 Release 3.1, just read this lesson without performing its steps.) The **record feature** lets you create a macro by copying keystrokes saved in the **record buffer,** a 512-byte area of

Figure 14 Macro to Enter Today's Date

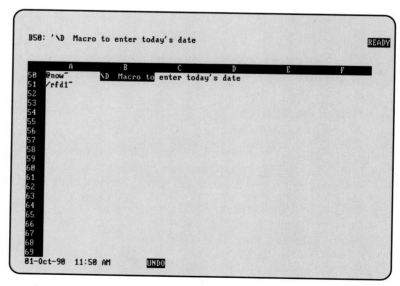

memory in which Lotus 1-2-3 Release 3.1 stores your most recent keystrokes. Let's use this method to create a macro to enter today's date in the current cell. This lesson assumes that the global column width has been set to 12 characters.

Step 1: Erase the Record Buffer

Press Alt-F2, the RECORD key, and select the Erase option to clear the current contents of the record buffer.

Press	**Alt-F2**
Type	**e**

Step 2: Perform the Task

Move the cell pointer to the cell where you want to start the task, and execute the keystrokes you want to automate.

Type	**@now**
Press	**Enter**
Type	**/rfd1**
Press	**Enter**

Today's date number will be entered in the current cell and it will be formatted as a date.

Step 3: Copy the Keystrokes from the Record Buffer

The next step is to copy the keystrokes you just executed from the record buffer to the range in which you want to store the macro definition. Let's store the macro definition in cell A50. Press the RECORD key, select the Copy option, highlight the keystrokes in the buffer, and specify the destination cell.

Press	**Alt-F2**
Type	**c**
Press	**Home**
Press	**Tab**
Press	**End**
Press	**Enter**
Type	**a50**
Press	**Enter**

The recorded keystrokes will be copied into cell A50.

Step 4: Name the Macro

The macro definition must be named before you can use it. Move to the cell containing the macro definition and name it \D:

Press	**F5**
Type	**a50**
Press	**Enter**
Type	**/rnc**
Type	**\d**
Press	**Enter**
Press	**Enter**

Step 5: Document the Macro

Move to cell B50 and enter the macro name and a brief description.

Press	**Right Arrow**
Type	**'\D Macro to enter today's date.**
Press	**Enter**

Step 6: Run the Macro

Move to cell A5 and run the new macro.

Press	**F5**
Type	**a5**
Press	**Enter**
Press	**Alt-D**

Today's date number will be entered into cell A5, and the cell will be formatted as a date.

Practice   Modify the macro definition so that the cell is formatted to display only the day and month. Hint: use date format number 2.

Lesson 14: Linking Worksheets with Releases 2.2 and 3.1

Lotus 1-2-3 Releases 2.2 and 3.1 include a linking feature that allows you to use values from other worksheets in your current worksheet. (If you are running Lotus 1-2-3 Release 2.01, just read this lesson without performing its steps.) Linking is often used to consolidate data from a number of worksheets in a summary worksheet. As an example, let's create a worksheet that uses values from three other worksheets.

Step 1: Create the Three Sales Worksheets

Suppose a business has offices in three cities: New York, Chicago, and Los Angeles. Sales figures from each office are kept in separate worksheets. Follow these directions to create the three sales worksheets:

Type	**/wey**
Type	**/wgc12**
Press	**Enter**
Type	**/wgfc**
Press	**Enter**
Type	**New York**
Press	**Right Arrow**
Type	**Sales**
Press	**Down Arrow**
Type	**99600**
Press	**Enter**
Type	**/fs**
Type	**ny**
Press	**Enter**

Type	**/wey**
Type	**/wgc12**
Press	**Enter**
Type	**/wgfc**
Press	**Enter**
Type	**Chicago**
Press	**Right Arrow**
Type	**Sales**
Press	**Down Arrow**
Type	**88466**
Press	**Enter**
Type	**/fs**
Type	**ch**
Press	**Enter**
Type	**/wey**
Type	**/wgc12**
Press	**Enter**
Type	**/wgfc**
Press	**Enter**
Type	**Los Angeles**
Press	**Right Arrow**
Type	**Sales**
Press	**Down Arrow**
Type	**90800**
Press	**Enter**
Type	**/fs**
Type	**la**
Press	**Enter**

Step 2: Create the Summary Worksheet

Now create a worksheet that will summarize the sales figures from New York, Chicago, and Los Angeles.

Type	**/wey**
Type	**/wgc12**
Press	**Enter**
Type	**/wgfc**
Press	**Enter**
Type	**Sales Summary**
Press	**Down Arrow**
Type	**New York**
Press	**Down Arrow**
Type	**Chicago**
Press	**Down Arrow**
Type	**Los Angeles**
Press	**Down Arrow**
Type	**TOTAL**
Press	**Right Arrow**
Type	**@sum(b2..b4)**
Press	**Up Arrow**

Step 3: Enter Linking Formulas

You create a link between two files by entering a linking formula in the current worksheet that refers to a cell in the other worksheet file. The cell in the other worksheet is called the source cell and the cell in the current worksheet is called the target cell. Once the two files are linked, 1-2-3 copies the value from the source cell to the target cell. A linking formula must have the following format:

> + <<*file name*>>*cell reference*

For example, follow these directions to enter the linking formulas into the summary worksheet:

Type	**+<<la.wk1>>b2**
Press	**Up Arrow**
Type	**+<<ch.wk1>>b2**
Press	**Up Arrow**
Type	**+<<ny.wk1>>b2**
Press	**Enter**

Note: if you are running Lotus 1-2-3 Release 3.1, you should enter LA.WK3, CH.WK3, and NY.WK3 as the worksheet file names.

Your screen should look like Figure 15. Cell B2 contains the sales figure from cell B2 in the worksheet file NY.WK1, cell B3 contains the sales figure from cell B2 in the worksheet file CH.WK1, and cell B4 contains the sales figure from cell B2 in the worksheet file LA.WK1. The formula in cell B5 computes the sum of these values from three different worksheets.

Step 4: Save the Summary Worksheet

Save the summary worksheet in a disk file.

Type	**/fs**
Type	**summary**
Press	**Enter**

Figure 15 Linking Formulas in the Summary Worksheet

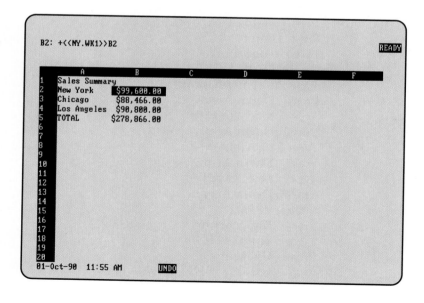

Practice   Retrieve NY.WK1, change the sales figure, and save the updated file. Then retrieve SUMMARY.WK1 and see the result. If the source files are changed, values in target cells are automatically updated when the target file is retrieved.

Lesson 15: Using Three-Dimensional Worksheets with Release 3.0

Three-dimensional worksheets carry linking to its logical extreme: every cell in a worksheet can be linked to corresponding cells in other worksheets. A third dimension creates a kind of "super-worksheet" that is like a stack of conventional worksheets. Perhaps the easiest way to envision a three-dimensional worksheet is as a sequence of pages, each of which is a table of rows and columns. Lotus 1-2-3 Release 3.1 lets you create such multiple-sheet worksheet files. (If you are not running Lotus 1-2-3 Release 3.1, just read this lesson without performing its steps.) Let's create a simple three-dimensional worksheet.

Step 1: Set Up a New Worksheet

The worksheets we will create will hold sales figures for two different years and a summary statement. First, clear your current worksheet and set up the first sales worksheet.

Type	**/wey**
Type	**/wgc12**
Press	**Enter**
Type	**/wgfc**
Press	**Enter**
Type	**Sales 1989**
Press	**Down Arrow**
Press	**Down Arrow**
Press	**Right Arrow**
Type	**^Jan-Mar**
Press	**Right Arrow**
Type	**^Apr-Jun**
Press	**Right Arrow**
Type	**^Jul-Sep**
Press	**Right Arrow**
Type	**^Oct-Dec**
Press	**Right Arrow**
Type	**^TOTAL**
Press	**End**
Press	**Left Arrow**
Press	**Left Arrow**
Press	**Down Arrow**
Type	**Sales**
Press	**Right Arrow**
Type	**4200**
Press	**Right Arrow**
Type	**5000**
Press	**Right Arrow**

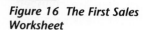

*Figure 16 The First Sales
Worksheet*

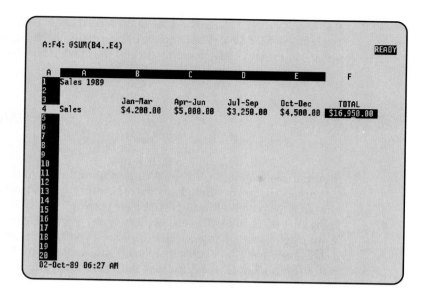

Type	**3250**
Press	**Right Arrow**
Type	**4500**
Press	**Right Arrow**
Type	**@sum(b4..e4)**
Press	**Enter**

Your screen should look like Figure 16.

Step 2: Add New Worksheets to a File

Lotus 1-2-3 always starts with a single worksheet on the screen. You can add up to 255 additional worksheets, depending on how much memory is installed in your computer. When multiple worksheets are loaded into memory, you can work with any one of them or with several at the same time. You can move between multiple worksheets like flipping pages in a notebook. Worksheets are designated by letters. The first worksheet is A, the second is B, and so on up to IV. Examine the upper left corner of the control panel. The full address of the current cell is A:F4, which means row 4 of column F of worksheet A.

You are going to add two new worksheets to the file. The second worksheet will hold the sales figures for 1990, and the third worksheet will summarize the first two worksheets. Execute the Worksheet Insert Sheet After 2 command to add two new worksheets after the current worksheet.

Type	**/wisa2**
Press	**Enter**

Worksheet B will appear on the screen.

Step 3: Change to Perspective View

Lotus 1-2-3 lets you display three consecutive worksheets on your screen at the same time stacked in an upward slope. Execute the Worksheet Window Perspective command.

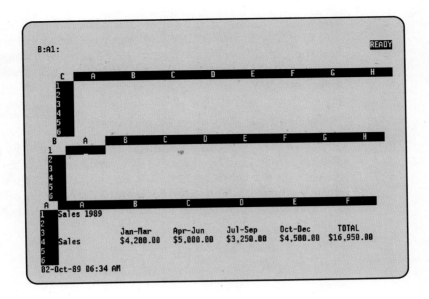

**Figure 17 Perspective
View of Three Worksheets**

Type **/wwp**

Your screen should look like Figure 17.

Step 4: Move Among Worksheets

Right now, worksheet B is your current worksheet. Several keys allow you to move among the multiple worksheets you have loaded. Move to the previous worksheet:

Press **Ctrl-PgDn**

Move to the next worksheet:

Press **Ctrl-PgUp**

Use the GOTO key to move to a particular cell in a particular worksheet:

Press **F5**
Type   **c:d4**
Press **Enter**

Move to cell A:A1:

Press **Ctrl-Home**

Step 5: Format Worksheets Simultaneously

In many cases, you want all of the worksheets in the same file to be formatted the same way. You could format each worksheet individually, but by using GROUP mode, you can format all of the worksheets at once. When you turn on GROUP mode, 1-2-3 changes the format of all the worksheets in the file to match the format of the current worksheet. Make sure A is your current worksheet and execute the Worksheet Global Group Enable command.

Type **/wgge**

The GROUP indicator will appear at the bottom of the screen and worksheets B and C will be formatted like worksheet A. The global column width is now 12 and the global format is Currency for all three worksheets. The GROUP mode remains turned on until you disable it, and the worksheets will continue to format simultaneously.

Step 6: Copy Between Worksheets

You can easily create the second and third worksheets by copying the first worksheet, then making any necessary modifications. To copy the contents of worksheet A to the other two worksheets, specify a three-dimensional range that includes the worksheet letter. For example, execute the following Copy command to duplicate the contents of worksheet A in worksheets B and C.

Type	**/c**
Type	**a:a1..a:f4**
Press	**Enter**
Type	**b:a1..c:f4**
Press	**Enter**

The contents of worksheet A will be copied to worksheets B and C.

Step 7: Modify Worksheet B

Worksheet B will contain the sales figures for 1990. Follow these directions to make the necessary modifications:

Press	**Ctrl-PgUp**
Press	**Home**
Type	**Sales 1990**
Press	**Down Arrow** (3 times)
Press	**Right Arrow**
Type	**4750**
Press	**Right Arrow**
Type	**5200**
Press	**Right Arrow**
Type	**5050**
Press	**Right Arrow**
Type	**6100**
Press	**Right Arrow**

The TOTAL sales for 1990 should be $21,100.00.

Step 8: Modify Worksheet C

Worksheet C will summarize the figures in worksheets A and B. Instead of numbers, worksheet C will contain formulas that sum cells in worksheets A and B. Follow these directions to create the summary worksheet.

Press	**Ctrl-PgUp**
Press	**Home**
Type	**Sales Summary 1989 – 1990**
Press	**Down Arrow** (3 times)
Press	**Right Arrow**
Type	**@sum(a:b4..b:b4)**

Figure 18 The Completed Summary Worksheet

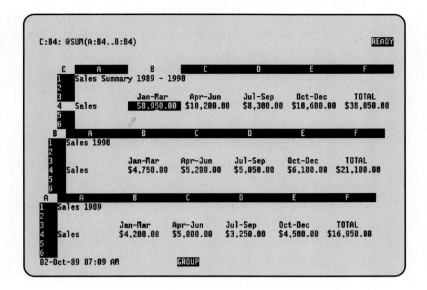

```
C:B4: @SUM(A:B4..B:B4)                                              READY

    C     A         B            C         D         E         F
  1   Sales Summary 1989 - 1990
  2
  3                Jan-Mar    Apr-Jun    Jul-Sep   Oct-Dec     TOTAL
  4   Sales        $8,950.00  $10,200.00 $8,300.00 $10,600.00 $38,050.00
  5
  6
    B     A         B            C         D         E         F
  1   Sales 1990
  2
  3                Jan-Mar    Apr-Jun    Jul-Sep   Oct-Dec     TOTAL
  4   Sales        $4,750.00  $5,200.00  $5,050.00 $6,100.00  $21,100.00
  5
  6
    A     A         B            C         D         E         F
  1   Sales 1989
  2
  3                Jan-Mar    Apr-Jun    Jul-Sep   Oct-Dec     TOTAL
  4   Sales        $4,200.00  $5,000.00  $3,250.00 $4,500.00  $16,950.00
  5
  6
  02-Oct-89 07:09 AM              GROUP
```

Press	**Enter**
Type	**/c**
Press	**Enter**
Type	**c4..f4**
Press	**Enter**

Figure 18 shows the result. Worksheet C summarizes worksheets A and B.

Step 9: Save the File

You must save the file to preserve the worksheets you have created.

Type	**/fs**
Type	**three_d**
Press	**Enter**

All three worksheets will be saved in the file THREE_D.WK3.

Practice   Print all three worksheets at the same time by specifying a three-dimensional print range.

Summary

- *Changing worksheet settings.* The Worksheet Global options affect the entire worksheet. You can change the format, label-prefix, column width, default directory, and the display of zero values. You can also display the worksheet status and insert page breaks.

- *Freezing titles and using windows.* The Worksheet Titles command lets you keep certain rows, columns, or both always on the screen. The Worksheet Windows command lets you split the screen into two horizontal or vertical windows.

- *Hiding columns and protecting cells.* The Worksheet Column Hide command lets you conceal the contents of one or more columns. The Worksheet Global

Protection Enable command prevents changes from being made to any cells. The Range Unprot command can then be used to turn off protection for selected cells.

- *Changing range formats.* The Range Format command lets you set Fixed, Scientific, Currency, Comma, General, +/−, Percent, Date, Text, and Hidden formats for one or more cells.

- *Using range names.* The Range Name Create lets you assign names to ranges to be used in commands and formulas.

- *Filling a range with a sequence of numbers.* The Data Fill command lets you fill a range of cells with a sequence of numbers.

- *Transposing columns and rows.* The Range Trans command lets you rearrange columns as rows or rows as columns.

- *Controlling recalculation and iteration.* The Worksheet Global Recalculation command lets you specify Natural, Columnwise, Rowwise, Automatic, or Manual recalculation. It also lets you set the iteration count for circular references.

- *Using relative, absolute, and mixed cell references.* Relative references change when cells are copied or moved. Absolute references, indicated by a $ in front of both the column letter and row number, always refer to the same address, even if they are copied or moved. Mixed references are half-relative and half-absolute.

- *Using more functions.* Date and time functions include @DATE, @DAY, @MONTH, @YEAR, @TIME, @HOUR, @MINUTE, @SECOND, and @NOW. Logical functions include @ISNUMBER, @ISSTRING, and @IF. String functions include @LENGTH, @LEFT, @RIGHT, @MID, @UPPER, @PROPER, and @REPEAT.

- *Using macros.* Plan the macro, enter the macro definition, and name the macro. Macros named with a \ (backslash) and a letter are run by holding down the Alternate key and typing the letter.

- *Using the Release 2.2 Learn feature.* Lotus 1-2-3 Release 2.2 lets you create a macro definition by specifying the learn range, pressing Alt-F5 to turn on the learn feature, and executing the actions to be automated.

- *Using the Release 3.1 Record feature.* Lotus 1-2-3 Release 3.1 lets you create a macro definition by copying keystrokes saved in the record buffer.

- *Using file linking with Release 2.2 and 3.1.* Lotus 1-2-3 Release 2.2 and 3.1 let you use values from other worksheets in your current worksheet.

- *Using three-dimensional worksheets with Release 3.1.* Lotus 1-2-3 Release 3.1 lets you create multi-page worksheets in a single file.

Key Terms

As an extra review of this chapter, try defining the following terms.

absolute reference	exponent
automatic recalculation	iteration
circular reference	learn feature
column-wise recalculation	learn range

macro
mantissa
manual recalculation
minimal (optimal) recalculation
mixed reference
natural recalculation

record buffer
record feature
relative reference
row-wise recalculation
template

Multiple Choice

Choose the best selection to complete each statement.

1. What options affect the entire worksheet?
   (a) Worksheet Global
   (b) Range Format
   (c) File Save
   (d) Data

2. What command lets you set the alignment of labels for the entire worksheet?
   (a) Worksheet Global Format
   (b) Worksheet Global Column-Width
   (c) Worksheet Global Label-Prefix
   (d) Worksheet Global Protection

3. Which command lets you freeze rows or columns or both on the screen so you can see them even if you scroll the worksheet?
   (a) Worksheet Global Zero
   (b) Worksheet Titles
   (c) Worksheet Window
   (d) Worksheet Page

4. Which command lets you split the screen horizontally or vertically?
   (a) Worksheet Global Zero
   (b) Worksheet Titles
   (c) Worksheet Window
   (d) Worksheet Page

5. Which command lets you conceal the contents of one or more columns?
   (a) Worksheet Global Protection
   (b) Worksheet Global Default
   (c) Worksheet Column Hide
   (d) Range Format Text

6. A general-purpose worksheet in which the user fills in the blanks or changes selected entries to perform a well-defined task is called a
   (a) macro.
   (b) iteration.
   (c) template.
   (d) circular reference.

7. The Worksheet Global Protection Enable command prevents changes being made to
   (a) all cells.
   (b) selected cells.
   (c) cells marked with the Range Prot command.
   (d) no cells.

8. Which Range Format would you use to display a number this way: 25,246.00?
   (a) Fixed
   (b) Scientific
   (c) Currency
   (d) , (comma)

9. Which Range Format would you use to generate crude bar graphs?
   (a) General
   (b) +/−
   (c) Percent
   (d) Text

10. In a Lotus 1-2-3 time number, the total time in each day is represented by the number
    (a) 1.
    (b) 12.
    (c) 24.
    (d) 360.

11. Which command would you use to enter the numbers 1 to 100 in cells A1 to A100?

   (a) Copy
   (b) Move
   (c) Data Fill
   (d) Range Format

12. What is the default method of recalculation?

   (a) Automatic
   (b) Manual
   (c) Column-wise
   (d) Row-wise

13. What is the default order of recalculation?

   (a) Automatic
   (b) Natural
   (c) Column-wise
   (d) Row-wise

14. A formula either directly or indirectly dependent on the value in the same cell results in a(n)

   (a) manual recalculation.
   (b) circular reference.
   (c) absolute reference.
   (d) iteration.

15. Which term describes the repeated recalculation of formulas containing circular references?

   (a) minimal recalculation
   (b) automatic recalculation
   (c) iteration
   (d) absolute reference

16. A cell address that does not change when it is moved or copied is called a(n)

   (a) relative reference.
   (b) absolute reference.
   (c) mixed reference.
   (d) circular reference.

17. The cell address A$1 is an example of a(n)

   (a) relative reference.
   (b) absolute reference.
   (c) mixed reference.
   (d) circular reference.

18. Which function returns the full serial number for the current date and time?

   (a) @DATE
   (b) @TIME
   (c) @NOW
   (d) @HOUR

19. What key(s) would you press to execute a macro named \B?

   (a) Alt-B
   (b) Ctrl-B
   (c) Shift-B
   (d) F5

20. Which of the following expressions is a valid linking formula that refers to cell B5 from the worksheet file NY.WK1?

   (a) +B5<<NY.WK1>>
   (b) +(NY.WK1)B5
   (c) +<<NY.WK1>>B5
   (d) B5{NY.WK1}

Fill-In

1. The Worksheet _____ options affect the entire worksheet.

2. The Range Format _____ command displays formulas in worksheet cells instead of their computed results.

3. Range _____ can make it much easier to specify ranges in formulas and commands.

4. Lotus 1-2-3 Release 2.2 and 3.1 use _____ recalculation to increase speed by recalculating only those cells that have changed, and the cells that depend on them, since the worksheet was last recalculated.

5. A(n) _____ reference results when a formula in a cell is either directly or indirectly dependent on the value in that very same cell.

6. Certain indirect circular references can be eventually resolved through _____.

7. Lotus 1-2-3 assumes all cell addresses to be _____ unless you specify otherwise.

8. The cell address A1 is an example of a(n) _____ reference.

9. If you want part of a cell address to remain the same and part to change when you copy or move a formula, you must use a(n) _____ reference.

10. The _____ function returns the sequential date number, given the year, month, and day.

11. The _____ function evaluates the given logical expression as TRUE or FALSE, and returns the first value if TRUE, or the second value if FALSE.

12. The _____ function lets you repeat the given string a specified number of times.

13. A _____ is a sequence of keystrokes and special commands that you can create to automate a task.

14. In a macro definition, the macro instruction _____ performs the same action as pressing the Right Arrow key.

15. A macro named with the _____ and a letter is executed by holding down the Alternate key and typing that letter.

16. To facilitate the creation of macros, Lotus 1-2-3 Release 2.2 has the _____ feature and Release 3.1 has the _____ feature.

17. The range of cells containing a macro definition must be _____ before the macro can be run.

18. In Lotus 1-2-3 Release 2.2 and 3.1, you can create a _____ between two files by entering a formula in the current worksheet that refers to a cell in the other worksheet file.

19. One way to envision a three-dimensional worksheet is as a sequence of _____, each of which is a table of rows and columns.

20. In Lotus 1-2-3 Release 3.1, multiple worksheets in the same file are designated by _____, like columns.

Short Problems

1. Erase the current worksheet from the screen. Change the Worksheet Global Format to Fixed with two decimal places, the Worksheet Global Label-Prefix to Center, and the Worksheet Global Column-Width to 12 characters.

2. Retrieve the PROPERTY worksheet. Freeze the first row as a horizontal title. Then try scrolling the worksheet down.

3. Split the screen at row 11 into two horizontal windows. Switch to the other window and scroll the worksheet down. When you are finished, clear worksheet windows.

4. Turn on worksheet global protection. Try changing the contents of a cell. When you are finished, disable global protection.

5. Erase the current worksheet from the screen. Change the range format of cells A1 through A5 to scientific notation with two decimal places. Then enter the following numbers into cells A1 through A5: 156,000,000, −25,200, 0.000000381, −0.000000000752, and 4,321,123,321.

6. Erase the current worksheet from the screen. Fill cells A1 through A4095 with only even numbers from 2 through 8190.

7. Erase the current worksheet from the screen. Enter the names of the months of the year in columns B through M, then transpose these names into cells A2 through A13.

8. Retrieve the SQRT worksheet. Enter the formula @SQRT(A1) into cell A10 to check the iterative square root calculation method against the built-in SQRT function. Calculate the square root of 123456. Enter other values to try to "stump" the iterative method. Now try an obviously invalid value of −1 and see what happens.

9. Retrieve the MONTHS worksheet you created in Lesson 11. Modify the \M macro so that it enters the names of the months down a column instead of across a row. Run the macro to make sure it works correctly.

10. If you have Lotus 1-2-3 Release 2.2 or 3.1, retrieve the SUMMARY worksheet you created in Lesson 14 to demonstrate linking. You may want to see the list of linked files when you are working on a summary worksheet. Fortunately, Lotus 1-2-3 lets you do this. Execute the File List Linked command. Press the Enter key when you are finished viewing the list.

Long Problems

1. Suppose you are an instructor who uses 1-2-3 to track your students' grades. You want to post the final grades without displaying the students' names, only their social security numbers. Create the following grades worksheet and hide the names column. Then print the worksheet.

Name	SSN	Grade
Abel	324-32-9974	A
Alexander	322-93-2854	B
Banks	495-89-9832	C
Becker	123-93-8237	A
Calhoon	324-58-9245	D
Carver	258-11-3848	B
Crawford	429-29-2847	C
Daily	199-23-9382	A
Davis	342-21-9284	C
Diamond	415-28-3018	B
Eaton	321-45-8294	B
Edwards	312-29-9285	A

2. A company uses Lotus 1-2-3 to store employee salary information. Create the following worksheet and hide the salary column. Enter a formula in cell C1 to sum the salaries. Although cells may be hidden, they can still be referenced in formulas.

Name	Salary
Abel	$32,500.00
Alexander	$25,000.00
Banks	$30,000.00
Becker	$45,000.00

Name	Salary
Calhoon	$25,000.00
Carver	$20,000.00
Crawford	$35,000.00
Daily	$45,000.00
Davis	$25,000.00
Diamond	$32,250.00
Eaton	$20,000.00
Edwards	$35,000.00

3. Enter the following worksheet. Then transpose the columns and rows.

Year	Sales
1987	$32,500.00
1988	$25,000.00
1989	$30,000.00
1990	$45,000.00
1991	$25,000.00

4. Indirect circular references and iteration are sometimes used in business calculations. For example, suppose you want to calculate a bonus that is ten percent of net profit, and net profit is defined as gross profit minus the bonus. Create a worksheet that contains the following data and formulas:

	A	B
1	Gross Profit	$1,000.00
2	Bonus	10%*B3
3	Net Profit	+B1-B2

Set the Worksheet Global Recalculation Iteration to 50 and recalculate the worksheet to get final answers. The Bonus should be $90.91 and the Net Profit should be $909.09.

5. Create an addition table for the numbers 0 through 5. Enter the numbers 0 through 5 in cells B1 through G1 and cells A2 through A7. Enter a formula that adds the column and row header using mixed references. Use the Copy command to fill out the rest of the table.

6. Create a formula using the @NOW and @DATE functions to calculate the number of days since you were born.

7. Create a macro to widen all columns to 12 characters, set the worksheet global label prefix to Center, and enter the names of the days of the week in columns A through G. If you have Lotus 1-2-3 Release 2.2, use the Learn feature. If you have Lotus 1-2-3 Release 3.1, use the Record feature.

8. Create a macro to format the current cell to display the time in Lotus standard long form (for example 10:22:05 AM) and then enter the time of day.

9. If you have Lotus 1-2-3 Release 2.2 or 3.1, create a separate worksheet for each of the following income statements from different cities. Use formulas to compute the Income figures. Then create a summary worksheet that uses linking to import and sum the Income figures from the three cities.

Boston

Net Sales	$12,000.00
Expenses	$7,350.00
Income	$4,650.00

St. Louis

Net Sales	$11,000.00
Expenses	$6,050.00
Income	$4,950.00

San Diego

Net Sales	$15,000.00
Expenses	$9,250.00
Income	$5,750.00

10. If you have Lotus 1-2-3 Release 3.1, create a multiple-worksheet file that puts each of the following income statements in a separate worksheet. Use formulas to compute the Income figures. Add another worksheet to summarize the data from the three income statements. Save and print your multiple-worksheet file.

Income Statement 1989

Net Sales	$10,000.00
Expenses	$6,350.00
Income	$3,650.00

Income Statement 1990

Net Sales	$13,000.00
Expenses	$8,050.00
Income	$4,950.00

Income Statement 1991

Net Sales	$16,000.00
Expenses	$10,250.00
Income	$5,750.00

END-OF-SECTION EXERCISES

1. Create, save, and print the following income statement worksheet with Lotus 1-2-3. Use formulas to calculate the row and column totals, and use the appropriate cell formats for your numbers and labels.

```
                      Income Statement
---------------------------------------------------------------------
   Item       Jan-Mar      Apr-Jun      Jul-Sep      Oct-Dec      Total
---------------------------------------------------------------------
   INCOME
Sales Income  $10,523.50  $13,459.25  $17,752.00  $11,543.50  $53,278.25
Labor Income   $7,987.25  $11,208.00  $15,489.00  $10,653.00  $45,337.25
   Total      $18,510.75  $24,667.25  $33,241.00  $22,196.50  $98,615.50
---------------------------------------------------------------------
   EXPENSES
Rent           $1,500.00   $1,500.00   $1,500.00   $1,500.00   $6,000.00
Telephone        $750.00     $625.45     $589.32     $782.50   $2,747.27
Utilities        $425.67     $398.25     $450.68     $410.25   $1,684.85
Advertising      $625.00     $625.00     $625.00     $625.00   $2,500.00
Insurance        $500.00                 $500.00               $1,000.00
Vehicles         $712.52   $1,020.50   $1,200.25     $945.67   $3,878.94
Payroll        $7,200.00   $7,200.00   $7,200.00   $7,200.00  $28,800.00
   Total      $11,713.19  $11,369.20  $12,065.25  $11,463.42  $46,611.06
---------------------------------------------------------------------
Net Profit     $6,797.56  $13,298.05  $21,175.75  $10,733.08  $52,004.44
```

2. Create, save, and print the following bar graph from the income statement worksheet you made in Exercise 1.

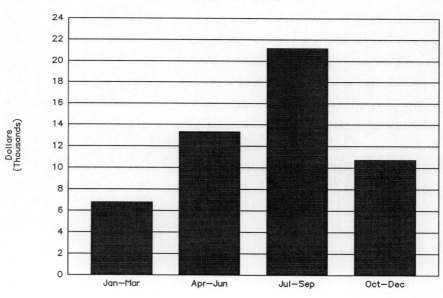

Net Profit

3. Create, save, and print the following pie chart from the income statement worksheet you made in Exercise 1. Chart the expenses from the first quarter, January through March.

Expenses
January through March

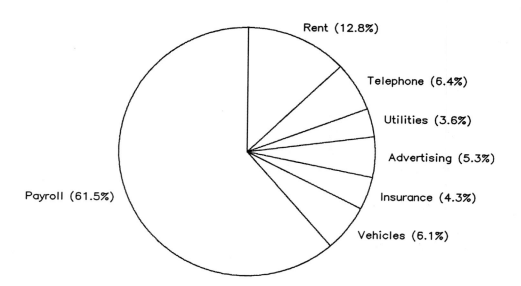

Rent (12.8%)

Telephone (6.4%)

Utilities (3.6%)

Advertising (5.3%)

Insurance (4.3%)

Vehicles (6.1%)

Payroll (61.5%)

4. **Create, save and print the following line graph from the income statement worksheet you made in Exercise 1. Graph the total income for each quarter of the year.**

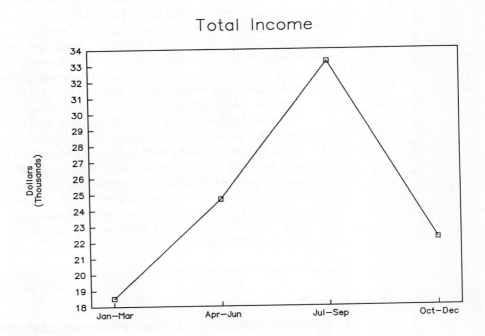

5. Spreadsheet programs are ideal for asking "what if" questions about your data because they can automatically and quickly recalculate all formulas whenever an entry is changed. Once a worksheet has been set up, it's easy to experiment with different values just to see what the results would be.

A common "what if" application of spreadsheet programs is the **break-even analysis,** which determines how many units of a particular product must be sold before the manufacturer shows a profit. Two groups of figures are manipulated in a break-even analysis: fixed costs and variable costs. **Fixed costs** remain generally constant no matter how many units are sold. Factory or office rent, utilities, and advertising expenses are examples of fixed costs. **Variable costs** are directly proportional to the number of units sold. The price of materials, labor, packaging, and shipping are examples of variable costs.

The typical break-even analysis deducts the fixed costs once and then subtracts the per-unit cost for each unit produced. These negative values are balanced against the **net profit,** which is the net sales cost times the number of units sold. As the number of units sold increases, a break-even point will be reached where the total profit equals the negative fixed and variable costs. In this exercise, you will create a break-even analysis worksheet. In the next exercise, you will use it to try out "what if" scenarios.

First, reproduce this worksheet on your Lotus 1-2-3 screen and save it in a file named BREAK:

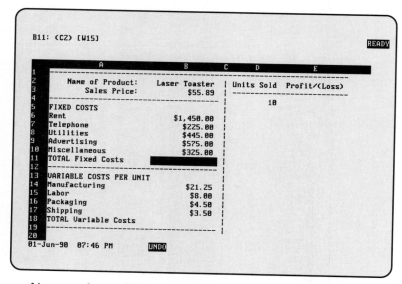

You now have all the labels and numbers entered in the worksheet. Next, enter the formulas, using the @SUM function, to calculate the Total Fixed Costs and Total Variable Costs.

The first cell in the Units Sold column (cell D4) already holds 10, the quantity increment. Each cell below the first cell will increase the units sold by the value of the quantity increment. For example, the second number under Units Sold will be 20, the third number will be 30, the fourth number will be 40, and so on. Enter this formula in cell D5:

d4+d4

Note that this formula contains an absolute reference (D4) and a relative reference (D4). The absolute reference will always refer to cell D4. The relative reference will change when the formula is copied to the cells below.

Now, copy the formula in cell D5 to cells D6 through D20. You should see 170 in cell D20.

Move to cell E4 and enter the following formula to calculate the Profit/(Loss):

(d4*b3) - (b11+(b18*d4))

Make sure that you have typed this formula correctly.

The first part of the formula *(D4*B3)* computes the total income by multiplying the number of units sold by the unit sales price. The second part of the formula *(B11 + (B18*D4))* computes the total costs by adding the total fixed costs to the product of the total variable costs and the number of units.

You should see ($2,833.60) in cell E4. The parentheses around the result means that it is a negative value. This convention is common in financial worksheets. The result of the formula tells you that after producing and selling only 10 Laser Toasters, the company will experience a loss of $2,833.60. More Laser Toasters must be sold to turn a profit. Let's see how many more.

Copy the formula in cell E4 to cells E5 through E20. Your screen should now look like this:

```
E20: (C2) [W15] (D20*$B$3)-($B$11+($B$18*D20))                    READY

            A    ·           B      C    D         E
1    ------------------------------------------------------------
2     Name of Product:   Laser Toaster | Units Sold  Profit/(Loss)
3        Sales Price:        $55.89    | ------------------------
4    ------------------------------    |    10      ($2,833.60)
5    FIXED COSTS                       |    20      ($2,647.20)
6    Rent                  $1,450.00   |    30      ($2,460.80)
7    Telephone               $225.00   |    40      ($2,274.40)
8    Utilities               $445.00   |    50      ($2,088.00)
9    Advertising             $575.00   |    60      ($1,901.60)
10   Miscellaneous           $325.00   |    70      ($1,715.20)
11   TOTAL Fixed Costs     $3,020.00   |    80      ($1,528.80)
12   ------------------------------    |    90      ($1,342.40)
13   VARIABLE COSTS PER UNIT           |   100      ($1,156.00)
14   Manufacturing           $21.25    |   110        ($969.60)
15   Labor                    $8.00    |   120        ($783.20)
16   Packaging                $4.50    |   130        ($596.80)
17   Shipping                 $3.50    |   140        ($410.40)
18   TOTAL Variable Costs    $37.25    |   150        ($224.00)
19   ------------------------------    |   160         ($37.60)
20                                          170         $148.80
01-Jun-90  07:46 PM      UNDO
```

Cell E20 contains the first positive result. So, this break-even analysis tells you that the company must sell between 160 and 170 Laser Toasters at $55.89 each to break even. If 170 Laser Toasters are sold at this price, the company will make a profit of $148.80. Save the completed worksheet.

6. The break-even analysis worksheet you have set up in Exercise 5 presents only one scenario, but you can easily change entries to explore other possibilities. For example, you can change the sales price of the Laser Toaster and see what happens. You can observe how varying the Fixed Costs or Variable Costs will affect the break-even point. You can decrease the quantity increment in cell D4 to get a more detailed analysis, or increase it to get a more general view. You can extend the analysis to cover more units by simply copying the formulas in Columns D and E down into more rows. Try some of these "what if" scenarios:

- *Increase the sales price.* Double the sales price to $111.78. Where is the break-even point now? Change the sales price back to $55.89.

- *Extend the analysis.* Copy the formulas in columns D and E down to row 500.

- *Decrease the quantity increment.* Suppose you want a more detailed analysis. You may want to know exactly how many Laser Toasters must be sold to break even. Change the number in D4 to 1. What is the exact break-even point?

- *Increase the quantity increment.* Change the number in D1 to 50. What happens? Change the increment back to 10.

- *Decrease the sales price.* Change the sales price of Laser Toasters to a more reasonable $35.98. What is the approximate break-even point now?

- *Increase the rent.* What would happen if the company had its rent increased by $100? Enter $1550 in cell B6 to find out. What is the break-even point now?

- *Decrease the manufacturing cost.* Suppose the company adopted new assembly procedures that reduced manufacturing costs by $2.00 per unit? Enter $19.25 in cell B14. What is the break-even point now?

7. Create, save, and print the following mortgage analysis and amortization schedule worksheet. This worksheet could be useful to anyone in the market for a new or refinanced mortgage loan. A **mortgage** is the pledging of property, such as a house, as security for the payment of a debt, often a loan to buy the house. **Amortization** is the process of making payments at regular intervals to pay back or "kill off" a mortgage loan.

The mortgage analysis accepts the **principal** amount of the loan (the amount you initially borrow), the yearly **interest rate** (in percent form), and the **term** of the loan (in years). The worksheet computes the monthly mortgage **payment.** For simplicity, this worksheet assumes a fixed-rate mortgage, in which the interest rate remains constant over the life of the loan.

The amortization schedule is a table showing the starting balance, ending balance, total paid, principal payment, and interest payment amounts for each year over the life of the loan.

Note that the principal amount, interest rate, and term are entered by the user and can be changed to try out "what if" scenarios.

Enter a formula using the @PMT function to calculate the monthly mortgage payment. Use formulas and the Copy command to complete all but the first row of the amortization schedule. Note that the first year's starting balance is the principal amount of the loan, and each subsequent year's starting balance is the previous year's ending balance. Enter a formula using the @PV function to calculate the ending balance. Here are the three parameters you should use in the @PV function:

1. the monthly mortgage payment, which remains constant

2. the monthly interest rate, which is the yearly interest rate divided by 12, which also remains constant

3. the term in months, which is 12 times the term of the loan in years minus the current year

```
Mortgage Analysis

     Principal amount of the loan: $240,000.00
Yearly interest rate, in percent:        10.50%
       Term of the loan, in years:           30
================================================
MONTHLY MORTGAGE PAYMENT:            $2,195.37
```

Year	Starting Balance	Ending Balance	Total Paid	Principal	Interest
1	$240,000.00	$238,798.79	$26,344.49	$1,201.21	$25,143.28
2	$238,798.79	$237,465.20	$26,344.49	$1,333.59	$25,010.91
3	$237,465.20	$235,984.65	$26,344.49	$1,480.55	$24,863.94
4	$235,984.65	$234,340.94	$26,344.49	$1,643.71	$24,700.78
5	$234,340.94	$232,516.08	$26,344.49	$1,824.86	$24,519.63
6	$232,516.08	$230,490.12	$26,344.49	$2,025.96	$24,318.53
7	$230,490.12	$228,240.89	$26,344.49	$2,249.23	$24,095.26
8	$228,240.89	$225,743.79	$26,344.49	$2,497.10	$23,847.39
9	$225,743.79	$222,971.49	$26,344.49	$2,772.29	$23,572.20
10	$222,971.49	$219,893.68	$26,344.49	$3,077.81	$23,266.68
11	$219,893.68	$216,476.69	$26,344.49	$3,416.99	$22,927.50
12	$216,476.69	$212,683.13	$26,344.49	$3,793.56	$22,550.93
13	$212,683.13	$208,471.51	$26,344.49	$4,211.62	$22,132.87
14	$208,471.51	$203,795.75	$26,344.49	$4,675.76	$21,668.73
15	$203,795.75	$198,604.71	$26,344.49	$5,191.04	$21,153.45
16	$198,604.71	$192,841.60	$26,344.49	$5,763.11	$20,581.38
17	$192,841.60	$186,443.37	$26,344.49	$6,398.23	$19,946.26
18	$186,443.37	$179,340.03	$26,344.49	$7,103.33	$19,241.16
19	$179,340.03	$171,453.89	$26,344.49	$7,886.15	$18,458.35
20	$171,453.89	$162,698.66	$26,344.49	$8,755.23	$17,589.26
21	$162,698.66	$152,978.58	$26,344.49	$9,720.08	$16,624.41
22	$152,978.58	$142,187.31	$26,344.49	$10,791.27	$15,553.22
23	$142,187.31	$130,206.80	$26,344.49	$11,980.51	$14,363.99
24	$130,206.80	$116,906.00	$26,344.49	$13,300.80	$13,043.69
25	$116,906.00	$102,139.41	$26,344.49	$14,766.59	$11,577.90
26	$102,139.41	$85,745.49	$26,344.49	$16,393.92	$9,950.57
27	$85,745.49	$67,544.90	$26,344.49	$18,200.59	$8,143.90
28	$67,544.90	$47,338.54	$26,344.49	$20,206.36	$6,138.14
29	$47,338.54	$24,905.38	$26,344.49	$22,433.17	$3,911.33
30	$24,905.38	$0.00	$26,344.49	$24,905.38	$1,439.11

The total paid for each year is the monthly payment times 12. The principal is the starting balance minus the ending balance for each year. The interest is the total paid minus the principal for each year.

8. Create, save, and print the following stacked bar graph from the mortgage analysis and amortization schedule worksheet you made in Exercise 7. The graph uses two data ranges, A and B. For each year over the life of the loan, the amount of principal paid is graphed as the A data range and the amount of interest paid is graphed as the B data range. This graph shows how the proportion of principal to interest changes over the life of the loan.

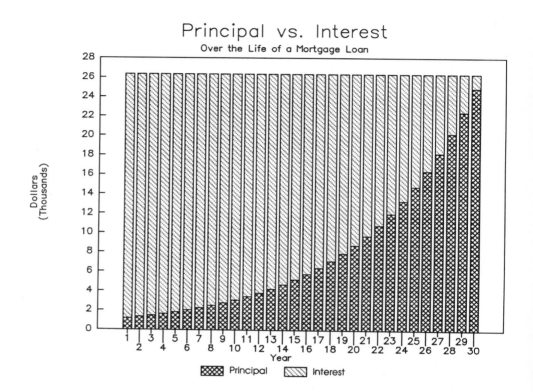

9. Create, save, and print the following Individual Retirement Account (IRA) worksheet. Use formulas and the Copy command to complete all but the first row of the worksheet. The starting balance for the first year is $0.00. To simplify matters, assume that the contribution of $2,000 and the 8.5% interest rate remain constant for 35 years. Use this expression to create a formula to calculate the new balance:

$$((s + c) * i) + s + c$$

where

s = start balance
c = contribution
i = interest rate

The formula calculates on the basis of simple interest by adding the current balance to the yearly contribution, and adding the result multiplied by the yearly interest rate to provide the new balance. Each year's new balance is then carried over to the successive start balance column. This worksheet shows that by contributing $2,000 a year in an IRA that pays 8.50% per year, you will have $418,162.64 in 35 years.

IRA Worksheet

Year	Start Balance	Contribution	Interest Rate	New Balance
1	$0.00	$2,000.00	8.50%	$2,170.00
2	$2,170.00	$2,000.00	8.50%	$4,524.45
3	$4,524.45	$2,000.00	8.50%	$7,079.03
4	$7,079.03	$2,000.00	8.50%	$9,850.75
5	$9,850.75	$2,000.00	8.50%	$12,858.06
6	$12,858.06	$2,000.00	8.50%	$16,120.99
7	$16,120.99	$2,000.00	8.50%	$19,661.28
8	$19,661.28	$2,000.00	8.50%	$23,502.49
9	$23,502.49	$2,000.00	8.50%	$27,670.20
10	$27,670.20	$2,000.00	8.50%	$32,192.17
11	$32,192.17	$2,000.00	8.50%	$37,098.50
12	$37,098.50	$2,000.00	8.50%	$42,421.87
13	$42,421.87	$2,000.00	8.50%	$48,197.73
14	$48,197.73	$2,000.00	8.50%	$54,464.54
15	$54,464.54	$2,000.00	8.50%	$61,264.02
16	$61,264.02	$2,000.00	8.50%	$68,641.47
17	$68,641.47	$2,000.00	8.50%	$76,645.99
18	$76,645.99	$2,000.00	8.50%	$85,330.90
19	$85,330.90	$2,000.00	8.50%	$94,754.03
20	$94,754.03	$2,000.00	8.50%	$104,978.12
21	$104,978.12	$2,000.00	8.50%	$116,071.26
22	$116,071.26	$2,000.00	8.50%	$128,107.32
23	$128,107.32	$2,000.00	8.50%	$141,166.44
24	$141,166.44	$2,000.00	8.50%	$155,335.58
25	$155,335.58	$2,000.00	8.50%	$170,709.11
26	$170,709.11	$2,000.00	8.50%	$187,389.38
27	$187,389.38	$2,000.00	8.50%	$205,487.48
28	$205,487.48	$2,000.00	8.50%	$225,123.92
29	$225,123.92	$2,000.00	8.50%	$246,429.45
30	$246,429.45	$2,000.00	8.50%	$269,545.95
31	$269,545.95	$2,000.00	8.50%	$294,627.36
32	$294,627.36	$2,000.00	8.50%	$321,840.69
33	$321,840.69	$2,000.00	8.50%	$351,367.14
34	$351,367.14	$2,000.00	8.50%	$383,403.35
35	$383,403.35	$2,000.00	8.50%	$418,162.64

10. Create, save, and print the following worksheet to compute areas and volumes. Use these fomulas:

Triangle   Area = 1/2 * base * height

Circle   Area = @pi * radius^2

Cone   Volume = 1/3 * @pi * radius^2 * height

Sphere   Volume = 4/3 * @pi * radius^3

```
        Area and Volume

        Triangle
                Base   =        10
                Height =        20
                Area   =       100

        Circle
                Radius =        10
                Area   = 62.83185

        Cone
                Radius =        10
                Height =        20
                Volume = 2094.395

        Sphere
                Radius =        10
                Volume = 4188.790
```

11. Create, save, and print the following worksheet and line graph to depict the volume and surface area of a sphere as its radius varies from 1 to 20. Use these formulas:

    Volume   = 4/3 * @pi * radius^3

    Surface Area = 4 * @pi * radius^2

```
            Volume and Surface Area of a Sphere

        Radius           Volume        Surface Area
          1                4.189          12.566
          2               33.510          50.265
          3              113.097         113.097
          4              268.083         201.062
          5              523.599         314.159
          6              904.779         452.389
          7             1436.755         615.752
          8             2144.661         804.248
          9             3053.628        1017.876
         10             4188.790        1256.637
         11             5575.280        1520.531
         12             7238.229        1809.557
         13             9202.772        2123.717
         14            11494.040        2463.009
         15            14137.167        2827.433
         16            17157.285        3216.991
         17            20579.526        3631.681
         18            24429.024        4071.504
         19            28730.912        4536.460
         20            33510.322        5026.548
```

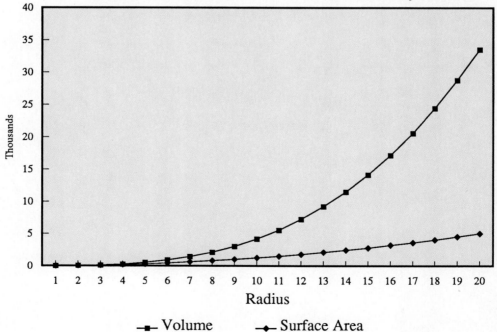

Volume and Surface Area of a Sphere

BEGINNING dBASE IV

In This Chapter

Preview

The original dBASE II program ran on 8-bit CP/M systems and the Apple II family of microcomputers. A version for the IBM Personal Computer soon followed and by 1983 dBASE II had sold more than 200,000 copies. In May 1984, Ashton-Tate released dBASE III, a more powerful successor to dBASE II designed especially for 16-bit computers like the IBM PC family. A year and a half later, dBASE III PLUS was introduced, offering a friendlier menu-driven user interface and local area network support for IBM-compatible microcomputers. A powerful and easy-to-use version for the Apple Macintosh computer, called dBASE Mac, was released in 1987. Finally, in the last quarter of 1988 dBASE IV for IBM-compatibles was unveiled. It boasted a new user interface, more than 300 new commands and functions, and support for Structured Query Language (SQL). Despite increased competition from other software packages, dBASE remains a leading programmable relational data base management system. It is the system against which all others are compared.

After studying this chapter, you will know how to

- start dBASE IV.
- use the Control Center.
- design a data base file.
- enter data base records.
- examine a data base.
- add new records to a data base.
- modify existing data base records.
- delete data base records.
- find data base records.
- modify the data base design.
- sort a data base.
- index a data base.
- generate a data base report.

Getting Started

Although dBASE IV is a large and sophisticated software package, it is not difficult to learn how to use for basic data base management tasks. You are most likely to use the package in one of two possible arrangements:

1. on a microcomputer with a hard disk and the single-user version of dBASE IV installed in a subdirectory named DBASE
2. on a microcomputer connected to a local area network with the multi-user version of dBASE IV installed on the network file server

The dBASE IV package cannot be run unless you have a hard disk or are connected to a local area network. Furthermore, it requires at least 640K of memory. If you are going to run dBASE IV from a network, you may need some additional directions from your instructor on how to start the program.

Lesson 1: Starting dBASE IV

This chapter and the following two chapters assume that dBASE IV has already been installed on your computer and a path has been set up so that you can run the package from any subdirectory.

Step 1: Boot Up the Computer

If your computer is not already on, you must boot it up.

Step 2: Prepare a Subdirectory for Data Files

The dBASE IV package is stored in its own subdirectory on a hard disk or network. It is best to prepare a separate subdirectory for the data files you will create in the following lessons. Create a subdirectory called LESSONS, if you don't already have one, that you can use to store your files. If you are running on a network, your instructor may have other directions for you to follow.

Step 3: Switch to the LESSONS Subdirectory

The dBASE IV package is normally installed so that it can be run from within any subdirectory. Switch to your LESSONS subdirectory:

Type   **cd c:\lessons**
Press   **Enter**

Step 4: Invoke dBASE IV

Once you get situated in the desired subdirectory, simply execute the DBASE command:

Type   **dbase**
Press   **Enter**

The program will present the Ashton-Tate logo for a moment (see Figure 1). Then you will see a screen that identifies the program and the owner and displays Ashton-Tate's License Agreement (see Figure 2). The screen will disappear in a few moments, or you can press Enter to continue:

Press   **Enter**

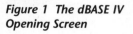

Figure 1 The dBASE IV Opening Screen

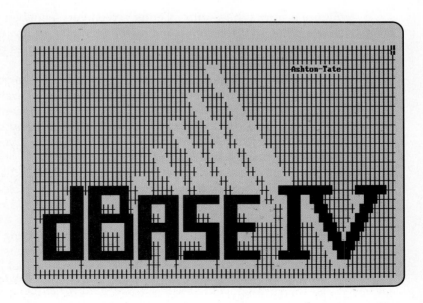

Figure 2 The dBASE IV
Copyright and License
Screen

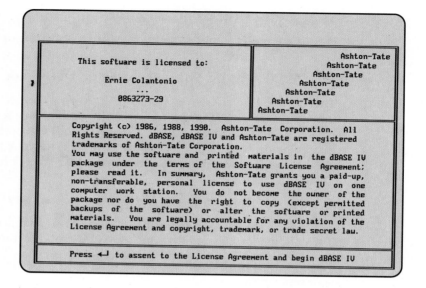

```
This software is licensed to:                          Ashton-Tate
                                                       Ashton-Tate
     Ernie Colantonio                                  Ashton-Tate
          ...                                          Ashton-Tate
     0863273-29                                        Ashton-Tate
                                                       Ashton-Tate
                                                       Ashton-Tate

Copyright (c) 1986, 1988, 1990. Ashton-Tate Corporation. All
Rights Reserved. dBASE, dBASE IV and Ashton-Tate are registered
trademarks of Ashton-Tate Corporation.
You may use the software and printed materials in the dBASE IV
package under the terms of the Software License Agreement;
please read it.   In summary, Ashton-Tate grants you a paid-up,
non-transferable, personal license to use dBASE IV on one
computer work station.   You do not become the owner of the
package nor do you have the right to copy (except permitted
backups of the software) or alter the software or printed
materials.   You are legally accountable for any violation of the
License Agreement and copyright, trademark, or trade secret law.

Press ↵ to assent to the License Agreement and begin dBASE IV
```

Practice   Reboot your computer:

Press   **Ctrl-Alt-Del**

Follow the steps of this lesson to start up dBASE IV again.

Lesson 2: Using the Control Center

The Control Center is the menu system of dBASE IV. It is the means by which you select files and choose the actions you want to perform.

Step 1: Examine the Control Center Screen

Figure 3 shows the Control Center screen you see when you start the program. The top line of the screen contains the menu bar on the left and the time-of-day clock on the right. The **menu bar** contains the names of the menus currently available: Catalog, Tools, and Exit.

A **catalog** is a list of files in dBASE IV. Catalogs help you organize your work. For example, you could have different catalogs for separate offices, departments, or projects. When you start dBASE IV, the Control Center automatically loads the catalog you used last. If you have not created any catalogs yet, dBASE IV creates the first catalog, named UNTITLED.CAT, for you. The Control Center names the current catalog and presents the files it contains in the six panels displayed on the screen. Since you have not yet created any files, the panels are all empty. You cannot choose any existing files, only create new ones.

The six panels correspond to the six types of files you can create with dBASE IV. The Data panel lists data base files, which contain data. The Queries panel lists query files, which contain instructions for viewing or updating data base files. The Forms panel lists form files, which contain custom screen displays for entering, editing, and viewing data. The Reports panel lists report files, which print data in a specified format. The Labels panel lists label files, which print

Insight

Large Data Base Packages vs. File Management Programs

It's like using an elephant gun to kill a flea. Hauling out dBASE IV to solve a simple problem sometimes isn't worth the time or effort.

Anyone who has worked with large-scale data base programs realizes they aren't particularly easy to use. To solve elaborate problems, dBASE IV requires that you develop actual programs in the dBASE language. These programs can be as complex as programs written in BASIC, COBOL, or Pascal.

For simple applications, dBASE IV may be more powerful than necessary. Experts ignore dBASE IV, first, when the problem needs only one file that is not linked to any other files and, second, when the computations are simple and limited to operations such as summing fields or deriving a new field based on calculations of other fields.

A number of flat-file manager programs can provide excellent solutions for situations such as this. Unlike dBASE IV, flat-file manager programs can't link the fields in different files. All the information has to be in a single file. Simple address or customer lists and client billing files are examples.

Two typical file manager programs that meet these needs are PFS:Professional File and PC-File Plus. Each allows the user to define simple file structures, enter and edit data, sort records, search for information, do simple computations, and generate reports, without complex and time-consuming programming.

mailing labels. The Applications panel lists programs that can perform a variety of data base management tasks.

The last line you see in Figure 3 is the **navigation line,** which lists important keystrokes that can be used on the current screen.

Step 2: Activate the Menu Bar

The menu bar contains the titles of the currently available menus. The menus stay out of sight until you want to use them. You press the F10 key to activate the menu bar.

Press **F10**

As Figure 4 shows, "Catalog" will be highlighted in the menu bar, and the Catalog menu will appear below. The menu lists options. The first option is highlighted and a description of its function is given in the **message line,** which appears below the navigation line.

Step 3: Consider a Different Option

To consider a different option, move the highlight bar with the Up Arrow or Down Arrow keys.

Press **Down Arrow**

Notice how the highlight bar moves down and the message line changes. Try it again:

Press **Up Arrow**

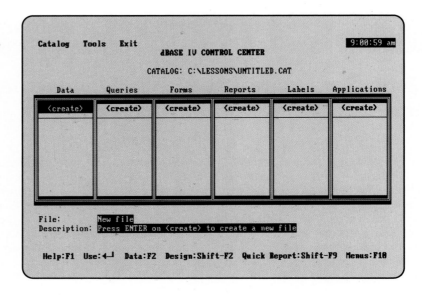

Figure 3 The Control Center Screen

Step 4: Activate a Different Menu

Suppose you want to see the Tools menu. You can move between the titles in the menu bar by pressing the Right Arrow or Left Arrow key.

> Press **Right Arrow**

Now, go back to the Catalog menu:

> Press **Left Arrow**

Another way to activate a menu is to hold down the Alternate key and type the first letter of the menu title. Activate the Exit menu:

> Press **Alt-E**

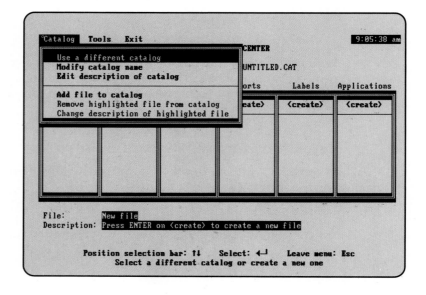

Figure 4 The Catalog Menu

Step 5: Execute a Menu Option

To actually execute a menu option, highlight it and then press the Enter key. For example, execute the Quit to DOS option from the Exit menu on your screen:

Press   **Down Arrow**
Press   **Enter**

The dBASE IV program will terminate and you will return to the DOS prompt. Start up the program again:

Type   **dbase**
Press   **Enter**

You can also select and execute a menu option at once when the menu is active by typing the option's first letter. For example, follow these instructions to activate the Exit menu and execute the Quit to DOS option:

Press   **Alt-E**
Type   **q**

Start up dBASE IV again:

Type   **dbase**
Press   **Enter**

Step 6: Deactivate a Menu

Suppose you activate a menu and then change your mind. You can close a menu and make it disappear by pressing the Escape key. For example, activate the Tools menu and then remove it from the screen:

Press   **Alt-T**
Press   **Escape**

Step 7: Explore the Help System

The dBASE IV package has a comprehensive Help system that can provide on-screen information about any menu, command, or function. You can get Help at any time by pressing the F1 key.

Press   **F1**

The program will present a Help box relevant to your current activity (see Figure 5). Since the highlight bar was on the <create> option in the Data panel, the Help box describes the procedure for creating data base files. If the information does not fit in a single box, you can see more by pressing the F4 key.

Press   **F4**

You can reread a previous box screen by pressing the F3 key.

Press   **F3**

Several options are listed across the bottom of the Help box: CONTENTS, RELATED TOPICS, BACKUP, and PRINT. The CONTENTS option presents a nested table of contents for the Help system. The CONTENTS option should be highlighted, so execute it:

Press   **Enter**

Figure 5 The Help Box

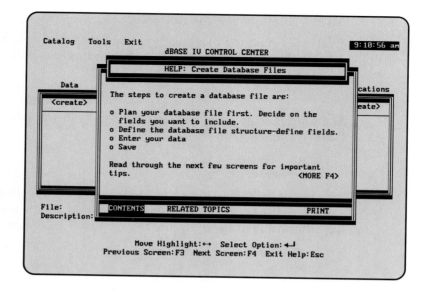

The program will present a table of contents of topics about data base files (see Figure 6). Return to the Help box entitled Create Database Files:

Press   **Enter**

The RELATED TOPICS option presents a list of associated Help boxes.

Press   **Right Arrow**
Press   **Enter**

Remove the Related Topics box:

Press   **Escape**

Figure 6 The Help System Table of Contents

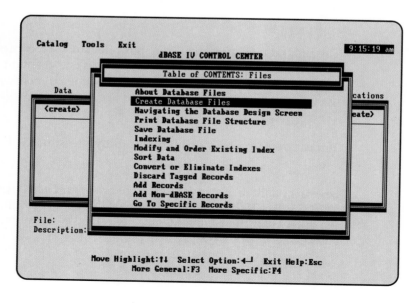

The BACKUP option lets you retrace your steps through the Help system. You can explore related topics or read about unrelated topics from the table of contents and still get back to your original Help box.

> Press **Right Arrow**
> Press **Enter**

PRINT is the last option in the Help box. This option lets you print the current Help box for future reference. Exit the Help system:

> Press **Escape**

Practice

1. Activate the Exit menu.
2. Execute the Quit to DOS command. Restart dBASE IV.
3. Invoke the Help system. Execute the CONTENTS option and select the About Database Files topic. Execute the BACKUP option to return to your original screen. If you have a printer connected to your computer, make sure it is turned on, on-line, and contains paper. Then print the current Help box. When it is finished, exit the Help box and return to the Control Center.

Lesson 3: Designing a Data Base File

A **data base** is one or more related files. A **file** is a collection of records. A **record** is a sequence of fields. And a **field** is simply a single data item, such as a number, character, word, or phrase. As an example, let's create a data base file to contain the Paddle and Portage Canoe Outfitters mailing list of customer names and addresses, shown in Figure 7. Each record in the file will store the data about a single customer. Each field in a record will hold the individual data items, including the customer's first name, last name, address, city, state, and ZIP code. Before you can enter any data, however, you must specify the structure of the records that will make up the data base file. This is called designing the data base.

Step 1: Execute the Create Option in the Data Panel

When you start dBASE IV with the Control Center, a highlight bar is automatically placed on the <create> option in the Data panel. This is the option you execute to design a new data base file.

> Press **Enter**

Step 2: Examine the Data Base Design Screen

The Data Base Design screen will appear after you press the Enter key (see Figure 8). This is where you specify the structure of the new file. Note the new menu bar across the top of the screen containing the titles Layout, Organize, Append, Go To, and Exit. In addition, the reverse video **status bar** now appears as the third line from the bottom, just above the navigation line. It provides information about the operation you have chosen or are about to choose. The status bar lists the type of screen you are in (Database), the path and name of the current file (C:\lessons\<NEW>), and the location of the cursor (Field 1/1).

The table in the center of the screen is where you enter information about the fields that make up the records of the data base file you are designing. The message

```
Bytes remaining: 4000
```

Figure 7 Paddle and Portage Canoe Outfitters Mailing List

Last Name	First Name	Address	City	State	ZIP
Skubic	Mike	321 Gregory	Champaign	IL	61820
Griffith	Oscar	805 Florida	Urbana	IL	61801
Carver	George	906 Busey	Brainerd	MN	56401
Banks	David	604 Armory	Green Bay	WI	54035
Young	Susan	1104 Grand	Anchorage	AK	99502
Mitchell	Dan	310 Paddock	Flagstaff	AZ	86001
Hudson	Henry	1007 Barclay	Akron	OH	44309
Becker	Molly	402 Main	Ann Arbor	MI	48106
Franklin	Melissa	2012 Anderson	Big Bear	CA	92314
Savage	Julian	2209 Philo	Cedar City	UT	84720
Prorok	Brian	502 Chalmers	Fairfax	VA	22030
Underwood	Rhonda	701 Dover	Las Vegas	NV	89114
Hall	Robert	1721 Valley	Ogallala	NE	69153
Davis	Becky	7822 Kostner	Chicago	IL	60652
Alexander	Barbara	102 White	Baltimore	MD	21233
Walden	Roxanne	1010 Bridle	Denver	CO	80202
Quinlan	Kerry	311 Southmoor	Homestead	FL	33030
Irving	Judith	1329 Grandview	Cairo	GA	31728
Diamond	Jim	142 Hazelwood	Belmar	NJ	07719
Kelley	Joyce	805 Randolf	Albany	NY	12207
Garret	Gerald	135 Cedar	Boone	NC	28607
Weaver	Sally	700 Elm	Madison	WI	53705
Tudor	Anthony	909 Crestwood	Duluth	MN	55806
Jenkins	Alfred	605 Willis	Hometown	IL	60456
Calhoon	Carrie	809 Maple	Superior	WI	54880

Figure 8 The Blank Data Base Design Screen

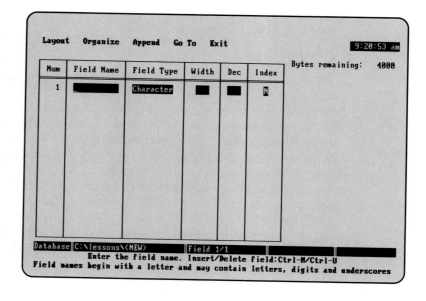

tells you how much room you have left for the record definition. A byte is equivalent to a single character. The maximum size of a single data base record is 4000 bytes.

Each row in the table corresponds to a field and each column specifies an attribute of that field. The Num column gives the field's number, which is automatically generated by dBASE IV and reflects the position of the field within the record.

The Field Name column contains the name you choose for the field. Field names can have up to ten letters, digits, or underscores (_), but the first character must always be a letter. No blanks can be embedded in field names; underscores are often used instead, like this: FIRST_NAME. You can type field names in lowercase letters, but dBASE IV translates all the letters to uppercase.

The Field Type column specifies the type of field to be created. Six types of fields are available:

Character	up to 254 letters, digits, or punctuation marks
Numeric	numbers used for counting or exact calculations
Float	very small or large numbers for calculations
Date	dates of the form mm/dd/yy, such as 01/15/91
Logical	T for True, or F for False
Memo	pointer to a file containing up to 512K of text

The Width column specifies the maximum number of characters or digits that can be stored in the field. Character fields can have a maximum width of 254. Numeric and Float fields can be up to 20 digits wide. The widths for Date, Logical, and Memo fields are entered automatically by dBASE IV. Date fields are 8 characters wide, Logical fields are 1 character wide, and Memo fields are 10 characters wide.

The Dec column is relevant only to Numeric and Float fields. It specifies the number of digits, from 0 to 18, to appear to the right of the decimal point. The width specified for a Numeric or Float field must be at least two greater than the number of decimal places to accommodate the decimal point and a possible minus sign.

The Index column specifies whether the field is to be used to index the file. Indexing, a method of arranging the records in a data base, will be discussed later in this chapter.

Step 3: Decide on the Field Attributes

Before you can actually specify the data base design, you must decide what fields to include. Then for each field you have to choose its name, type, and width. If the field is a numeric value, you must also decide the number of digits to appear to the right of the decimal point. Examine the mailing list in Figure 7. There are six fields: last name, first name, address, city, state, and ZIP code. Naming the fields after the contents is a good idea. More thought must be applied to choosing field widths: you want widths that are not too large because that will waste storage space, yet you want the fields to be wide enough to hold the necessary data. Deciding on the field type is pretty straightforward.

The Paddle and Portage Canoe Outfitters mailing list is a fairly simple example. All of its fields are Character fields. Note that although the fields for address and ZIP code will contain numbers, these numbers are classified as characters because they don't represent quantities and won't be used in calculations. The following field names, field types, and widths can be used for the mailing list:

Field Name	Field Type	Width
LAST_NAME	Character	15
FIRST_NAME	Character	10
ADDRESS	Character	20
CITY	Character	10
STATE	Character	5
ZIP	Character	5

The Dec column will be blank for all fields, and the Index entries will all be N for No.

Step 4: Fill In the Data Base Design Table

Once you have decided on the field names, types, and widths, you can enter them into the empty data base design table. Follow these instructions to fill in the table:

Type	last_name
Press	Enter (2 times)
Type	15
Press	Enter (2 times)
Type	first_name
Press	Enter
Type	10
Press	Enter (2 times)
Type	address
Press	Enter (2 times)
Type	20
Press	Enter (2 times)
Type	city
Press	Enter (2 times)
Type	10
Press	Enter (2 times)
Type	state
Press	Enter (2 times)
Type	5
Press	Enter (2 times)
Type	zip
Press	Enter (2 times)
Type	5
Press	Enter (2 times)

Your screen should look like Figure 9. Note that dBASE IV automatically converts the field names you type into uppercase letters. The program also automatically generates the next field number and fills in Character for the Field Type and N for the Index column. If you want to change these default values, you can either type a different value or press the Space Bar to cycle through the possible selections. Whenever you type an entry that completely fills the allotted space, dBASE IV beeps and jumps to the next entry. This happened when you typed FIRST_NAME, which is 10 characters long, the maximum length of a field name.

*Figure 9 The Completed
Data Base Design Screen*

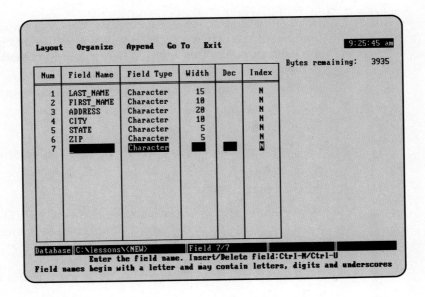

Step 5: Check the Table

Check your table against Figure 9. To correct a mistake, move the cursor to the erroneous entry and then retype it. You can move from column to column by pressing the Enter key. You can go from row to row by pressing Up Arrow or Down Arrow. You can move from character to character by pressing Left Arrow or Right Arrow.

Step 6: Exit the Data Base Design Screen

When you have completed and checked your work, you can leave the Data Base Design screen. Several methods are available:

- Activate the Exit menu and choose the Save Changes and Exit option or the Abandon Changes and Exit option.
- Press Enter when the cursor is at the first empty Field Name column after the last defined field.
- Press Ctrl-End or Ctrl-W.
- Press Escape to abandon the design.

Beginners usually find that selecting an option from a menu is the easiest way to remember what to do, even if it is not the quickest. Activate the Exit menu and choose Save Changes and Exit:

> Press   **Alt-E**
> Type   **s**

A box will appear in which dBASE IV displays the prompt

> Save as :

The program is asking for the name under which you want to save the data base file. Enter a valid DOS file name without an extension:

> Type   **mailing**
> Press **Enter**

Then dBASE IV will create the new file MAILING.DBF and return to the Control Center. The extension DBF stands for Data Base File.

Practice
1. Invoke the Help system. Execute the Contents option and select the topic entitled "Files." Then select the topic entitled "Create Database Files." Read the Help boxes on this topic. When you are finished, return to the Control Center.

2. Highlight the <create> option in Data panel and execute it:

   Press   **Up Arrow**
   Press   **Enter**

   The program will present a new Data Base Design screen.

   Type   **total**
   Press   **Enter**

   Observe how dBASE IV presents the next choice for Field Type each time you press the Space Bar and read the description in the message line:

   Press   **Space Bar** (6 times)

   Return to the Control Center without saving the data base design:

   Press   **Alt-E**
   Type   **a**
   Type   **y**

Lesson 4: Entering Data Base Records

All you have done so far is define the structure of a new data base file; it does not have any data in it yet. You now face the somewhat tedious task of entering the data.

Step 1: Highlight the Data Base File

The Control Center should be on your screen. The highlight bar should be in the Data panel. If MAILING is not highlighted, do this:

   Press   **Down Arrow**

Step 2: Execute the Data Command

When you want to examine, enter, or edit data, you execute the Data command by pressing the F2 key.

   Press   **F2**

Step 3: Examine the Data Entry Form

The dBASE IV program will present the Edit screen shown in Figure 10. The menu bar at the top contains four titles: Records, Organize, Go To, and Exit. A blank data entry form appears below the menu bar. A **form** displays the fields of an individual record on the screen. The default format of a dBASE IV form has a separate line for each field. The field names are listed along the left edge of the screen. Beside each field name is reverse video block where you enter the data for that field. The width of the block reflects the field width you specified

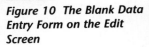

Figure 10 The Blank Data Entry Form on the Edit Screen

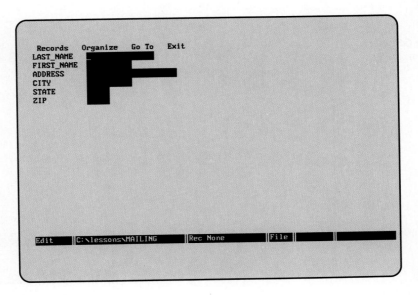

when you designed the data base file. The status bar near the bottom of the screen indicates that you are using the Edit screen, your current file is C:\LESSONS\MAILING.DBF, and no records have been entered yet.

Step 4: Enter the Data for Record 1

Refer to the Paddle and Portage mailing list in Figure 7. Follow these directions to enter the data for the first record:

Type	**Skubic**
Press	**Enter**
Type	**Mike**
Press	**Enter**
Type	**321 Gregory**
Press	**Enter**
Type	**Champaign**
Press	**Enter**
Type	**IL**
Press	**Enter**
Type	**61820**

Don't be alarmed when dBASE IV beeps and seemingly erases what you have just typed. Because the ZIP field is five characters wide and you have typed exactly five characters, the program automatically enters that field, stores the record, advances to the next record, and beeps to signal what it has done.

Step 5: Check the Record for Errors

This automatic advance feature is handy for entering records one after another, but it requires you to go back to the record you have just entered to check its accuracy.

Press **Page Up**

The completed form for the first record will appear on your screen as shown in Figure 11. Check the data for accuracy. To correct a mistake, use the arrow keys

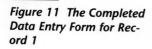

Figure 11 The Completed Data Entry Form for Record 1

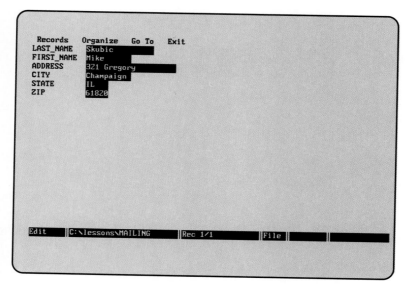

to move the cursor and then retype the entry. You can use the Backspace and Delete keys to erase characters. By default, typeover mode is turned on. You can switch to insert mode by pressing the Insert key. Then you can insert new characters into an entry at the current cursor location. Pressing the Insert key again toggles back to typeover mode. When you are sure the record is correct, advance again to the next record:

> Press **Page Down**

The program will display the prompt

> Add new records? (Y/N)

Answer Y for Yes:

> Type **y**

The program will present the blank data entry form for record number 2 on the screen.

Step 6: Enter the Remaining Records

Now enter the rest of the Paddle and Portage mailing list records from Figure 7. You might prefer to check each record for errors before you type the last digit of the ZIP code field. Then you can avoid having to go back to the previous record, check for errors, advance to the next record, and answer the prompt about adding new records.

After you enter the last record (Carrie Calhoon's) and dBASE IV advances to the next blank record, move back to the previous record:

> Press **Page Up**

This will prevent a blank record from being saved as the last record in your data base file. You should have 25 records in MAILING.DBF.

Step 7: Terminate Data Entry

As you enter each record, dBASE IV adds it to the MAILING.DBF data base file. When you are finished entering records, you can either press Ctrl-End or execute the Exit option from the Exit menu to save your work and return to the Control Center.

> Press   **Ctrl-End**

The Control Center will appear on your screen again.

Practice   Execute the Data command:

> Press   **F2**

Use the Page Up key to examine the forms of the records you have entered. When the first record (Mike Skubic's) is on the screen, return to the Control Center:

> Press   **Escape**

Lesson 5: Examining an Existing Data Base

Now that you have a complete data base, you can examine its contents. One of the major advantages of a data base management package is the flexibility with which you can retrieve previously stored information. A great many different ways to access data bases are available with dBASE IV. In this lesson, we will look at a method that works well with small data bases like the Paddle and Portage Canoe Outfitters' mailing list.

Step 1: Select the Data Base File

The first step is to tell dBASE IV the data base file you want to examine. If you have already been working with the file, as we have been with MAILING.DBF, you can skip this step. Otherwise, you would highlight the name of the file in the Data panel of the Control Center screen. Then you would press Enter to select the file, and press Enter again to tell dBASE IV that you want to open it.

Step 2: Display the Data Base Design

You may want to look at the record structure of a data base you have never seen before or one that you have not worked with for a while. The Design command, invoked by pressing Shift-F2, lets you review the design of a data base.

> Press   **Shift-F2**

The Data Base Design screen will appear with the Organize menu activated. Deactivate the menu to examine the screen:

> Press   **Escape**

Your screen should look like Figure 9 again. When you are finished examining the data base design, activate the Exit menu and select the Abandon Changes and Exit option:

> Press   **Alt-E**
> Type   **a**

The program will return to the Control Center.

Step 3: Use the Browse Screen

The Data command, which is invoked by pressing the F2 key, has two functions. It activates either the Edit screen or the Browse screen. The Edit screen, as you learned in the previous lesson, lets you enter and examine each record in its own form. The Browse screen lets you see data in a **table,** which presents a record in each row and a field in each column. You simply press the F2 key again to switch from the Edit screen to the Browse screen, or from the Browse screen to the Edit screen. For example, activate the Edit screen:

> Press   **F2**

Now, switch to the Browse screen:

> Press   **F2**

Figure 12 shows the result. If your table shows only the last record, use the Page Up key to move to the beginning of the file. In fact, you can move to any record, field, or character in the data base file. The following list summarizes the cursor movement keys available on either the Browse screen or the Edit screen. Try each of them.

Keypress	*Cursor Movement*
Right Arrow	Right one character
Left Arrow	Left one character
Down Arrow	Down one row
Up Arrow	Up one row
Page Down	Next screen
Page Up	Previous screen
End	End of field (Edit) or record (Browse)
Home	Start of field (Edit) or record (Browse)
Tab	Next field
Shift-Tab	Previous field
Enter	Next field
Ctrl-Right Arrow	Start of next word or field
Ctrl-Left Arrow	Start of previous word or field
Ctrl-PgDn	Last record in file
Ctrl-PgUp	First record in file

Move back to the first field of the first record:

> Press   **Ctrl-PgUp**
> Press   **Home**

Practice

1. Switch to the Edit screen:

   > Press   **F2**

   Now try each cursor movement keypress listed in this lesson.
2. Return to the Control Center. Display the data base design of MAILING.DBF.
3. Return to the Control Center. Display the Browse screen for MAILING.DBF. Use the Page Down key to examine all the records, then return to the Control Center again.

Figure 12 The Browse Screen

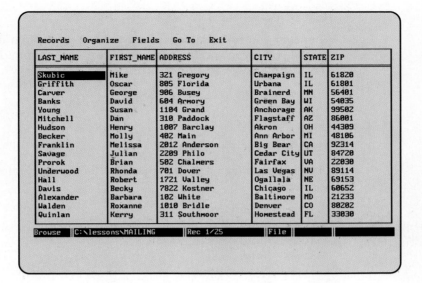

```
  Records   Organize   Fields   Go To   Exit

 ┌─────────────┬──────────┬──────────────┬──────────────┬─────┬──────┐
 │LAST_NAME    │FIRST_NAME│ADDRESS       │CITY          │STATE│ZIP   │
 ├─────────────┼──────────┼──────────────┼──────────────┼─────┼──────┤
 │Skubic       │Mike      │321 Gregory   │Champaign     │IL   │61820 │
 │Griffith     │Oscar     │805 Florida   │Urbana        │IL   │61801 │
 │Carver       │George    │906 Busey     │Brainerd      │MN   │56401 │
 │Banks        │David     │604 Armory    │Green Bay     │WI   │54035 │
 │Young        │Susan     │1104 Grand    │Anchorage     │AK   │99502 │
 │Mitchell     │Dan       │310 Paddock   │Flagstaff     │AZ   │86001 │
 │Hudson       │Henry     │1007 Barclay  │Akron         │OH   │44309 │
 │Becker       │Molly     │402 Main      │Ann Arbor     │MI   │48106 │
 │Franklin     │Melissa   │2012 Anderson │Big Bear      │CA   │92314 │
 │Savage       │Julian    │2209 Philo    │Cedar City    │UT   │84720 │
 │Prorok       │Brian     │502 Chalmers  │Fairfax       │VA   │22030 │
 │Underwood    │Rhonda    │701 Dover     │Las Vegas     │NV   │89114 │
 │Hall         │Robert    │1721 Valley   │Ogallala      │NE   │69153 │
 │Davis        │Becky     │7822 Kostner  │Chicago       │IL   │60652 │
 │Alexander    │Barbara   │102 White     │Baltimore     │MD   │21233 │
 │Walden       │Roxanne   │1010 Bridle   │Denver        │CO   │80202 │
 │Quinlan      │Kerry     │311 Southmoor │Homestead     │FL   │33030 │
 └─────────────┴──────────┴──────────────┴──────────────┴─────┴──────┘
 ┌Browse──┬┬C:\lessons\MAILING───────┬┬Rec 1/25──┬┬File┬┬──────┬┬──────┐
```

Lesson 6: Adding New Records

Most data bases are continually being changed as people use them. For example, as Paddle and Portage Canoe Outfitters gains more customers, new records will have to be added to the mailing list data base file. Adding new records is one of the most common data base operations.

Step 1: Select the Data Base File

At this point, you should be at the Control Center. Before you can add new records, you must tell dBASE IV the data base file you want to add to. If you have already been working with the file, as we have been with MAILING.DBF, you can skip this step. Otherwise, you would highlight the name of the file in the Data panel of the Control Center screen. Then you would press Enter to select the file, and press Enter again to tell dBASE IV that you want to open it.

Step 2: Activate the Edit Screen

Adding new records to an existing data base is essentially the same process as entering records to a new data base. Execute the Data command to activate the Edit screen:

Press **F2**

Step 3: Move to the Last Record

New records are always added after the last record. Move to the last record in the data base file:

Press **Ctrl-PgDn**

Step 4: Advance Past the Last Record

Whenever you try to advance past the last record in a data base file, dBASE IV will ask you if you want to add new records (see Figure 13). Advance to the next record and answer yes to the prompt:

Press   **PgDn**
Type   **y**

Step 5: Enter the Record

A blank data entry form will appear on the screen. Simply enter the data for the new record:

Type   **Eaton**
Press   **Enter**
Type   **Candy**
Press   **Enter**
Type   **2314 Sunset**
Press   **Enter**
Type   **Rantoul**
Press   **Enter**
Type   **IL**
Press   **Enter**
Type   **61866**

Step 6: Terminate Data Entry

As soon as you finish typing the ZIP code, dBASE IV will beep and store the record. A blank data entry form for the next record will appear on the screen. If you have more than one new record to add, you can continue entering them. In our case, only one record is to be added. So, move back to the record you just entered, terminate data entry, and return to the Control Center:

Press   **PgUp**
Press   **Ctrl-End**

Instead of pressing Ctrl-End, you can also select Exit from the Exit menu.

Practice   Activate the Edit screen. Move to the last record in the file. Advance past it. This time, answer no to the prompt asking if you want to add new records. Return to the Control Center.

Lesson 7: Modifying Existing Records

What if a customer moves? His or her record will have to be modified to reflect the change of address. Updating the contents of existing records is another very common data base operation.

Step 1: Select the Data Base File

At this point, you should be at the Control Center. Before you can modify existing records, you must tell dBASE IV the data base file you want to change. If you have already been working with the file, as we have been with MAILING.DBF,

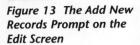

Figure 13 The Add New Records Prompt on the Edit Screen

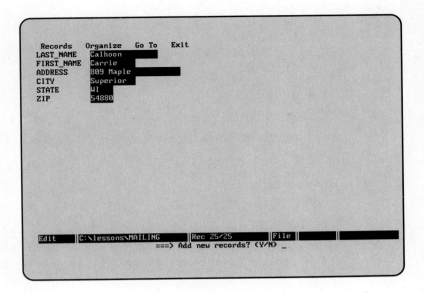

you can skip this step. Otherwise, you would highlight the name of the file in the Data panel of the Control Center screen. Then you would press Enter to select the file, and press Enter again to tell dBASE IV that you want to open it.

Step 2: Activate the Edit Screen

Records can be modified from either the Edit screen or the Browse screen. Let's use the Edit screen. Execute the Data command to activate the Edit screen:

Press **F2**

Step 3: Select the Record

Just as dBASE IV remembers the data base file on which you are working, it also keeps track of the record. Whenever you are using a data base, an invisible pointer is always aimed at a particular record. This current record is the one listed in the status bar after the label *Rec*. The number before the slash is the current record, and the number after the slash is the total number of records in the data base file.

Before you can change a record, you must have its entry form on the Edit screen or see its line on the Browse screen. In a later lesson, you will learn how to tell dBASE IV to locate a specific record. You can, of course, locate a particular record by visually scanning through the data base. This process, however, can be inconvenient and time consuming, especially with large data bases. For this lesson, let's just modify the current record, which should be Candy Eaton's record.

Step 4: Edit the Data

Once the record to be changed is on the screen, you can move the cursor to any field and make corrections. Follow these directions to change the address in Candy Eaton's record:

Press **Down Arrow** (2 times)
Type **1458 Clearwater**

Press   **Enter**
Type   **Gary**
Press   **Delete** (3 times)
Press   **Enter**
Type   **IN**
Press   **Enter**
Type   **46401**

The program will display the prompt

Add new records? (Y/N)

Answer no:

Type   **n**

Note the use of the Delete key to erase existing characters from the field. Three other keypresses can be used to erase characters from a field or other entry. The following table lists the keys you can use to erase characters while editing text.

Key	*Action*
Delete	Erases character at current cursor position
Backspace	Erases character to left of cursor
Ctrl-T	Erases characters from cursor to beginning of next word
Ctrl-Y	Erases characters from cursor to end of field or entry

Step 5: Save the Changes

When you are finished changing records, you can either press Ctrl-End or execute the Exit option from the Exit menu to save your work and return to the Control Center.

Press   **Ctrl-End**

Practice

1. Activate the Browse screen:

    Press   **F2** (2 times)

    Change Candy Eaton's street address to 1459 Clearwater. Save the change and return to the Control Center.

2. Activate the Edit screen:

    Press   **F2** (2 times)

    Change Candy Eaton's street address back to 1458 Clearwater. Save the change and return to the Control Center.

Lesson 8: Deleting Records

Occasionally, records must be completely removed from a data base. In the Paddle and Portage Canoe Outfitters example, customers might not come back for many years or they may not want to receive newsletters in the mail. From time to time, the mailing list data base will have to be purged of these inactive records.

Step 1: Select the Data Base File

At this point, you should be at the Control Center. Before you can delete existing records, you must tell dBASE IV the data base file you want to delete from. If you have already been working with the file, as we have been with MAIL-ING.DBF, you can skip this step. Otherwise, you would highlight the name of the file in the Data panel of the Control Center screen. Then you would press Enter to select the file, and press Enter again to tell dBASE IV that you want to open it.

Step 2: Activate the Edit Screen

Records can be deleted from either the Edit screen or the Browse screen. Let's use the Edit screen. Execute the Data command to activate the Edit screen:

Press   **F2**

Step 3: Select the Record

The next step is to locate the record you want to remove. For this lesson, let's just delete the current record, which should be Candy Eaton's record.

Step 4: Mark the Record For Deletion

Records are deleted in two stages: first you mark them for deletion, then you remove them permanently later. This two-stage process allows you to change your mind before records are permanently deleted. Activate the Records menu and select the option Mark Record For Deletion (see Figure 14):

Press   **Alt-R**
Type   **m**

The record is not actually removed, but the indicator *Del* appears on the right side of the status bar at the bottom of the screen to show that this record is marked for deletion.

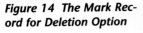

Figure 14 The Mark Record for Deletion Option

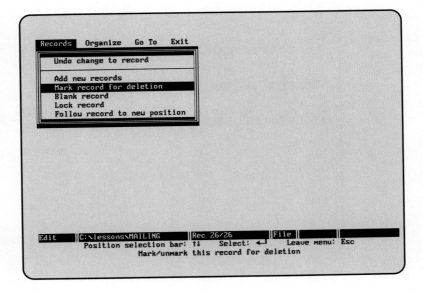

Step 5: Mark Another Record For Deletion

If you have other records to remove, you can mark them for deletion as well. Move to the preceding record, Carrie Calhoon's, and mark it for deletion too:

Press   **Page Up**
Press   **Alt-R**
Type   **m**

Step 6: Remove a Deletion Mark

Suppose you change your mind about deleting Carrie Calhoon's record. You can simply tell dBASE IV to clear the deletion mark. Activate the Records menu and select the option Clear Deletion Mark (see Figure 15):

Press   **Alt-R**
Type   **c**

The deletion mark will be removed and Carrie Calhoon's record will be restored.

Step 7: Save the Changes

When you are finished marking records for deletion, you can either press Ctrl-End or execute the Exit option from the Exit menu to save your work and return to the Control Center.

Press   **Ctrl-End**

Step 8: Permanently Remove the Marked Record

Records marked for deletion are permanently removed from the data base file by displaying the Data Base Design screen, selecting the Erase Marked Records option from the Organize menu (see Figure 16), and confirming the deletion. Before you perform this step, however, you should make sure you really want

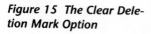

Figure 15 The Clear Deletion Mark Option

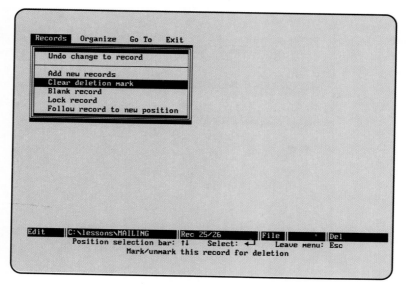

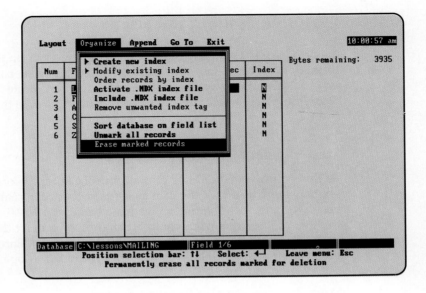

*Figure 16 The Erase
Marked Records Option*

to remove the records marked for deletion. You will not be able to get them back afterwards. Follow these directions to permanently remove Candy Eaton's record:

Press   **Shift-F2**
Type   **e**
Type   **y**

The program will execute a PACK procedure that removes all records marked for deletion, reclaims the disk space used by the deleted records, and renumbers the remaining records. When dBASE IV is finished, save the changes and exit the Data Base Design screen to return to the Control Center:

Press   **Alt-E**
Type   **s**
Press   **Enter**

Practice   1. Activate the Browse screen to confirm that Candy Eaton's record has been removed while Carrie Calhoon's record has been retained.

2. In this lesson you learned that a record can be marked for deletion or a deletion mark can be cleared by selecting an option from the Records menu on the Edit or Browse screen. A shortcut exists for performing both of these operations.

Press   **Ctrl-U**

This keypress will mark the current record for deletion. Note the *Del* indicator on the right side of the status bar. To clear the deletion mark, repeat the keypress:

Press   **Ctrl-U**

When you are finished, return to the Control Center.

Lesson 9: Finding Records

If a data base file is small, you can easily find records on the Browse screen. This method, however, is too slow and tedious for large data bases. Fortunately, dBASE IV provides other ways to find records. You can locate a specific record by its record number, or you can find records containing data that match certain search criteria.

Step 1: Select the Data Base File

At this point, you should be at the Control Center. Before you can find records, you must tell dBASE IV the data base file you want to search. If you have already been working with the file, as we have been with MAILING.DBF, you can skip this step. Otherwise, you would highlight the name of the file in the Data panel of the Control Center screen. Then you would press Enter to select the file, and press Enter again to tell dBASE IV that you want to open it.

Step 2: Activate the Browse Screen

Records can be found from either the Edit screen or the Browse screen. Let's use the Browse screen. Execute the Data command to activate the Browse screen:

Press   **F2**

If the Edit screen appears, press the F2 key again.

Step 3: Go To the First or Last Record

The Go To menu of the Browse and Edit screens lets you quickly reach particular records in a data base file. Activate the Go To menu:

Press   **Alt-G**

Your screen should look like Figure 17. The first two options in the Go To menu let you go to the first or last record in the data base file. Go to the first or top record:

Type   **t**

Selecting Top Record from the Go To menu achieves the same result as pressing Ctrl-PgUp. Now try the Last Record option from the Go To menu:

Press   **Alt-G**
Type   **L**

Carrie Calhoon's record will become the current record.

Step 4: Go To a Particular Record Number

The Record Number option of the Go To menu lets you advance to a particular record number. This option is useful if you happen to know the number of a record you want to find. In most cases, however, you probably won't know the exact record number. Nevertheless, the Record Number option can be handy for moving to an approximate position in a data base file. For example, use the

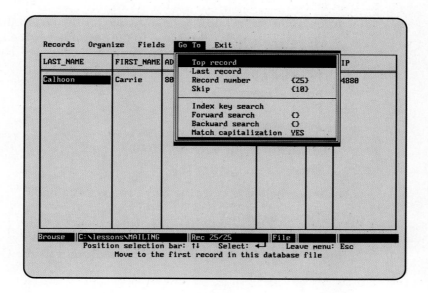

Figure 17 The Go To Menu

Record Number option of the Go To menu to advance to record number 12, which is at about the middle of the MAILING.DBF file:

Press   **Alt-G**
Type   **r**
Press   **Backspace** (2 times)
Type   **12**
Press   **Enter**

Rhonda Underwood's record will be highlighted on the Browse screen. The status line will reveal that the current record number is now 12 out of 25.

Step 5: Skip Forward or Backward

The Skip option of the Go To menu lets you jump forward or backward a given number of records. The default number is 10. Activate the Go To menu and select the Skip option:

Press   **Alt-G**
Type   **s**
Press   **Enter**

Record number 22, Sally Weaver's record, will be highlighted. You can skip backward by specifying a negative number of records.

Press   **Alt-G**
Type   **s**
Press   **Backspace** (2 times)
Type   **−10**
Press   **Enter**

The program will skip backward to record number 12.

Step 6: Search for a Particular Record

In most cases, you will not remember record numbers. Furthermore, browsing is an inefficient way to search large data bases. Fortunately, dBASE IV lets you find records that contain specific data. Suppose you want to find Jim Diamond's record. You can tell dBASE IV to search for the record that contains "Diamond" in the LAST_NAME field. Move to the beginning of the file, move to the LAST_NAME field, activate the Go To menu, and select the Forward Search option:

Press   **Ctrl-PgUp**
Press   **Home**
Press   **Alt-G**
Type   **f**

The program will display the prompt

```
Enter search string:
```

Here is where you enter the name you want to find.

Type   **Diamond**
Press   **Enter**

Jim Diamond's record will be highlighted. Activate the Go To menu again:

Press   **Alt-G**

Note the last option in the menu, Match Capitalization. This option is set to YES, which means that dBASE IV will locate only exact matches. If you had entered "diamond" instead of "Diamond" as the search string, the program would have failed to find Jim Diamond's record. You can turn off the Match Capitalization option if you want dBASE IV to ignore the case of letters when searching for data.

Press   **Escape**

The Backward Search option of the Go To menu is like Forward Search, except that it searches from the current record to the beginning of the file. For example, find the nearest preceding record that contains "Chicago" in its CITY field:

Press   **Tab** (3 times)
Press   **Alt-G**
Type   **b**
Press   **Home**
Press   **Ctrl-Y**
Type   **Chicago**
Press   **Enter**

Becky Davis's record will become the current record. Note that the highlight bar and cursor must be in the field you want to search before you execute the search procedure.

Step 7: Search for a Group of Records

Suppose you want to see the records of all customers from Wisconsin. Follow these directions:

Press   **Tab**
Press   **Ctrl-PgUp**
Press   **Alt-G**
Type   **f**
Press   **Home**
Press   **Ctrl-Y**
Type   **WI**
Press   **Enter**

The program will advance to David Banks's record, the first record that contains "WI" in its STATE field. Execute the Find Next command to advance to the next matching record:

Press **Shift-F4**

Sally Weaver's record will become the current record. Execute the Find Next command again:

Press **Shift-F4**

The program will jump to Carrie Calhoon's record. Execute Find Next once more:

Press **Shift-F4**

The program will wrap around to the beginning of the file and jump to David Banks's record again.

You can also move backward through the group of records that match the search criterion. Try the Find Previous command:

Press **Shift-F3**

The program will jump back to Carrie Calhoon's record.

Step 8: Use the Wildcard Characters ? and *

Two special characters, called **wildcard characters,** can be used in search strings. These characters, ? and *, act like the DOS global file name characters. The question mark (?) matches any single character and the asterisk (*) matches any group of characters.

Suppose you want to find all records from states that begin with the letter *A*. Follow these directions:

Press **Ctrl-PgUp**
Press **Alt-G**
Type **f**
Press **Backspace** (2 times)
Type **A?**
Press **Enter**

The program will advance to Susan Young's record, which has AK in the STATE field. Use the Find Next command to see the other matching record:

Press **Shift-F4**

Dan Mitchell's record, which has AZ in the STATE field, will become the current record.

The asterisk will match any number of characters. Suppose you want to see the records of all customers whose last names begin with W. Follow these instructions:

Press **Ctrl-PgUp**
Press **Home**
Press **Alt-G**
Type **f**
Press **Backspace** (2 times)
Type **W***
Press **Enter**

The program will advance to Roxanne Walden's record. Find the next matching record:

>   Press   **Shift-F4**

Sally Weaver's record will become the current record.

Practice
1. Use the Go To menu to move to the first record in the data base.
2. Advance to record number 15.
3. Use the Backward Search option to find Brian Prorok's record.
4. Find the records of all customers whose first name ends with the letter *e*.

Lesson 10: Modifying the Data Base Design

Occasionally, you need to change the design of a data base file. You might have to change the name, type, or width of a field; add new fields; or delete existing fields. All of these operations can be performed with dBASE IV.

Step 1: Display the Data Base Design Screen

At this point, the Browse screen should still be on your computer. Return to the Control Center and then execute the Design command to display the Data Base Design screen:

>   Press   **Alt-E**
>   Type   **e**
>   Press   **Shift-F2**
>   Press   **Escape**

Step 2: Change a Field Name

Suppose you want to change the name of the ZIP field to ZIP_CODE. Simply move to the ZIP field and edit the name:

>   Press   **Down Arrow** (5 times)
>   Press   **Right Arrow** (3 times)
>   Type   **_CODE**

The field is now named ZIP_CODE. Whenever you change a field name, however, you must activate the Layout menu and select Save This Database File Structure. If you don't execute this option, the data in the former ZIP field will not be copied into the new ZIP_CODE field and you will have to re-enter all of the ZIP codes.

>   Press   **Alt-L**
>   Type   **s**
>   Press   **Enter**

The program will display the prompt

>   Should data be COPIED from backup for all fields? (Y/N)

Answer yes:

>   Type   **y**

The program will then ask if you are sure you want to save the changes. Answer yes again:

> Type   **y**

Step 3: Change a Field Width

You might have noticed that the width of the STATE field is 5, but all state abbreviations are only two letters. This discrepancy wastes three bytes per record. Although three bytes per record may not sound like much, it could add up to a significant waste of disk space if the data base grows very large. Move the cursor to the Width column of the STATE field, and change the 5 to a 2:

> Press   **Up Arrow**
> Press   **Tab** (2 times)
> Type   **2**
> Press   **Enter**

The width of the STATE field is now 2.

Step 4: Add a New Field

You can also add new fields to your data base design. As an example, let's add a numeric field to MAILING.DBF. This new field will be called CHARGES and will hold the customer's charges for the last trip outfitted by Paddle and Portage. Follow these instructions to add the CHARGES field:

> Press   **Home**
> Press   **Down Arrow** (2 times)
> Type   **charges**
> Press   **Enter**
> Press   **Space Bar**
> Press   **Enter**
> Type   **7**
> Press   **Enter**
> Type   **2**
> Press   **Enter**

Your screen should look like Figure 18. Note that you had to specify a value for the Dec column because CHARGES is a numeric field.

Step 5: Save the Changes

Any time you modify the data base design, you must save the changes you have made. Activate the Exit menu and select the Save Changes and Exit option:

> Press   **Alt-E**
> Type   **s**

The program will ask if you are sure you want to save the changes. Answer yes:

> Type   **y**

The program will then copy your data to a file with the new data base design, and return to the Control Center.

Figure 18 The CHARGES Field Added to the Record

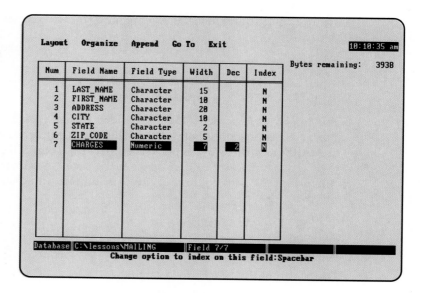

Step 6: Examine the Modified Data Base File

Examine the form of your modified data base file. Execute the Data command twice to display the Edit screen and then move the to first record:

Press **F2** (2 times)
Press **Ctrl-PgUp**

Your screen should look like Figure 19. Note that the CHARGES field is empty except for the decimal point.

Figure 19 The Modified Entry Form Showing the CHARGES Field

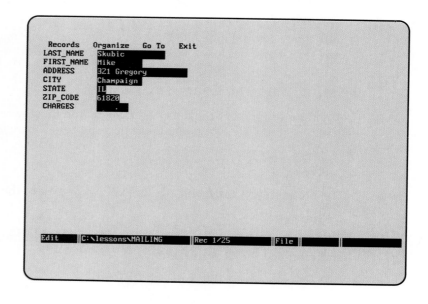

Step 7: Enter the New Field Contents

You have added a new field to the data base design, but you still have to enter the new data. Follow these directions to enter the CHARGES data for Mike Skubic's record:

Press   **Down Arrow** (6 times)
Type   **245.25**

The program will beep and advance to the next record. Now enter the values from the following table into the CHARGES fields of the remaining records.

Last Name	Charges	Last Name	Charges
Griffith	125.00	Davis	457.75
Carver	55.00	Alexander	125.00
Banks	250.00	Walden	250.00
Young	100.00	Quinlan	250.00
Mitchell	25.00	Irving	175.50
Hudson	375.50	Diamond	350.00
Becker	150.00	Kelley	475.00
Franklin	225.25	Garret	125.50
Savage	125.00	Weaver	250.75
Prorok	235.00	Tudor	120.00
Underwood	75.00	Jenkins	225.25
Hall	115.00	Calhoon	150.00

Practice

1. Move to the beginning of the file and activate the Browse screen. The CHARGES field will not fit on the screen completely. Move the cursor to the CHARGES field and the screen will scroll to reveal the entire width of the column.

2. Exit the Browse screen and return to the Control Center. Activate the Data Base Design screen:

Press   **Shift-F2**

Activate the Layout menu and highlight the option Save This Database Structure. Invoke the Help system and read about this option. When you are finished, return to the Control Center.

Lesson 11: Sorting the Data Base

One of the most common operations performed on data bases is sorting them into some particular order. Records are stored in a data base file in the order in which they are entered. This order is reflected by the record number assigned to each record. The records of MAILING.DBF were entered in no particular order. Let's sort them according to the contents of the LAST_NAME field. In this case, LAST_NAME will be the **key**, the field used to sort the records of the data base file.

Step 1: Select the Data Base File

At this point, you should be at the Control Center. Before you can sort records, you must tell dBASE IV the data base file you want to sort. If you have already been working with the file, as we have been with MAILING.DBF, you can skip this step. Otherwise, you would highlight the name of the file in the Data panel of the Control Center screen. Then you would press Enter to select the file, and press Enter again to tell dBASE IV that you want to open it.

Step 2: Display the Data Base Design Screen

Execute the Design command to display the Data Base Design screen:

> Press **Shift-F2**

The program automatically activates the Organize menu when you display the Data Base Design screen of an existing data base file (see Figure 20).

Step 3: Select the Sort Option

The Organize menu should already be on the screen. Select the option Sort Database On Field List:

> Type **s**

Step 4: Specify the Keys

You specify the keys on which to sort the records and the types of sorting to use in the box that appears (see Figure 21). In many cases, just one key will be necessary. You can, however, specify up to ten keys. If you specify more than one key, the sorting is done successively on each key. For example, you might sort a very large mailing list first by state, then by city, then by last name, and then by first name. The records would be arranged alphabetically by state, then by city within each state, then by last name and first name within each city.

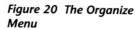

Figure 20 The Organize Menu

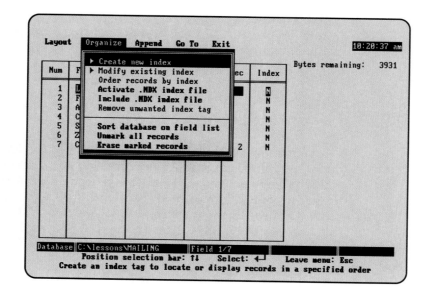

Figure 21 The Sort Key Box

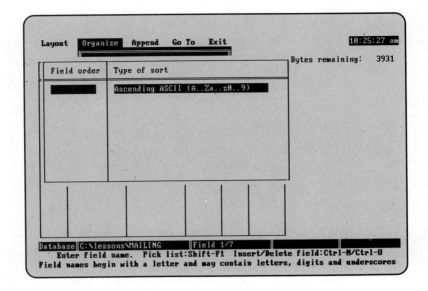

Four different types of sorts are available: ascending ASCII, descending ASCII, ascending dictionary, and descending dictionary. Ascending ASCII is the default type of sort. ASCII stands for American Standard Code for Information Interchange. It is the scheme by which computers encode letters and punctuation marks as numbers. An ascending ASCII sort arranges records by key field contents from 0 to 9 and then alphabetically from A to Z, and it distinguishes between uppercase and lowercase letters. Descending ASCII arranges records in the opposite order, from 9 to 0 and Z to A. Ascending and descending dictionary sorts are not case sensitive. For example, if you choose descending dictionary, all records beginning with the letters *a* or *A* will appear before records beginning with *b* or *B*.

In our simple mailing list data base, you need only sort by LAST_NAME and you can use an ascending ASCII sort. Enter the field name of the key and save your specification:

Type   **last_name**
Press   **Ctrl-End**

Step 5: Specify the New File Name

The program will display the prompt

    Enter name of sorted file:

When dBASE IV sorts a file, it actually creates a new file with the records arranged in the proper order. You will have two versions of the same data base file. So, you must enter a new file name for the sorted data base.

Type   **by_name**
Press   **Enter** (2 times)

A new file named BY_NAME.DBF will be created containing the same records as MAILING.DBF, but the records will be sorted by LAST_NAME.

Step 6: Examine the Sorted File

Return to the Control Center, highlight BY_NAME in the Data panel, and activate the Browse screen to examine the sorted file:

Press   **Alt-E**
Type   **a**
Press   **Down Arrow**
Press   **F2**

The records will appear in alphabetical order by LAST_NAME as shown in Figure 22. Page down to see the rest of the records, then go back to the first record:

Press   **Page Down**
Press   **Page Up**

Practice   Return to the Control Center, display the Data Base Design screen, and highlight the Sort Database On Field List option from the Organize menu. Invoke the Help system and read the Sort Data box. When you are finished, return to the Control Center.

Lesson 12: Indexing the Data Base

Sorting a data base file that has many records is a relatively slow process. It can also take up a lot of disk space because a new copy of the entire file is produced. Several versions of the same data base, each sorted in a different way, can occupy a significant portion of a disk. Another disadvantage of sorting is the problem of updating multiple files. An address change, for example, would have to be made to every sorted version of the same data base file.

Indexing is a convenient alternative to sorting that rearranges record numbers instead of entire records. When you index a data base file, dBASE IV does not

Figure 22 The BY_NAME Data Base on the Browse Screen

LAST_NAME	FIRST_NAME	ADDRESS	CITY	STATE	ZIP_CODE	CHAR
Alexander	Barbara	102 White	Baltimore	MD	21233	125
Banks	David	604 Armory	Green Bay	WI	54035	250
Becker	Molly	402 Main	Ann Arbor	MI	48106	150
Calhoon	Carrie	809 Maple	Superior	WI	54880	150
Carver	George	906 Busey	Brainerd	MN	56401	55
Davis	Becky	7822 Kostner	Chicago	IL	60652	457
Diamond	Jim	142 Hazelwood	Belmar	NJ	07719	350
Franklin	Melissa	2012 Anderson	Big Bear	CA	92314	225
Garret	Gerald	135 Cedar	Boone	NC	28607	125
Griffith	Oscar	805 Florida	Urbana	IL	61801	125
Hall	Robert	1721 Valley	Ogallala	NE	69153	115
Hudson	Henry	1007 Barclay	Akron	OH	44309	375
Irving	Judith	1329 Grandview	Cairo	GA	31728	175
Jenkins	Alfred	605 Willis	Hometown	IL	60456	225
Kelley	Joyce	805 Randolf	Albany	NY	12207	475
Mitchell	Dan	310 Paddock	Flagstaff	AZ	86001	25
Prorok	Brian	502 Chalmers	Fairfax	VA	22030	235

Browse | C:\lessons\BY_NAME | Rec 1/25 | File

change the order of the records and record numbers in the original file. Instead it creates an **index file** that contains two columns of data. One column contains a reference to each record by one or more key values. The other column lists each record number. Suppose you index the MAILING.DBF file by LAST_NAME. The following table shows part of the contents of the index file.

Index Field Data	Record Number
Alexander	15
Banks	4
Becker	8
Calhoon	25
Carver	3
Davis	14
Diamond	19

The last names are arranged in alphabetical order, but the record numbers refer to the order of the records in the original file, MAILING.DBF. Only key data and record numbers are stored in the appropriate order in an index file. The original data base file remains intact and contains the rest of the data.

With large data bases, an index file is usually much smaller than the data base file from which it is created. Indexing a file is therefore faster than sorting a file because less data are copied. As an analogy, think of a library as a data base. Each book on the shelf is like a record. A card catalog is like an index file. Each card in the card catalog just lists data that identify the book, such as title, author, subject, and call number. The call number is like the book's record number. Suppose you want to find books by the author's last name. Which would you rather rearrange: the books themselves or the cards in the card catalog? What if you want to find books by title and subject too? You can maintain several card catalogs with cards arranged differently, yet have just one set of books arranged by call number on the shelves.

As an example, let's index MAILING.DBF by ZIP_CODE.

Step 1: Select the Data Base File

At this point, you should be at the Control Center. Before you can index records, you must tell dBASE IV the data base file you want to index. Highlight MAILING in the Data panel and tell dBASE IV that you want to open this file:

Press   **Down Arrow**
Press   **Enter**
Press   **Enter**

Step 2: Display the Data Base Design Screen

Execute the Design command to display the Data Base Design screen:

Press   **Shift-F2**

The program automatically activates the Organize menu when you display the Data Base Design screen of an existing data base file (see Figure 20).

Step 3: Change Index Setting to Y

The Organize menu should already be on the screen with the Create New Index option highlighted. The easiest way to index a file with dBASE IV, however, does not require you to use this menu. Deactivate the menu to see the full Data Base Design screen:

Press   **Escape**

To index the data base file on the basis of ZIP codes, simply move to the Index column of the ZIP_CODE field and change the setting from N to Y:

Press   **Down Arrow** (5 times)
Press   **Tab** (3 times)
Type   **y**

Step 4: Save the Change

Save the altered data base design and return to the Control Center:

Press   **Alt-E**
Type   **s**

The file MAILING.DBF will be indexed on the basis of ZIP codes.

Step 5: Examine the Indexed File

Activate the Browse screen and move to the first record to examine the indexed file:

Press   **F2**
Press   **Ctrl-PgUp**

The records will appear ordered by ZIP_CODE as shown in Figure 23. Page down to see the rest of the records, then go back to the first record:

Press   **Page Down**
Press   **Page Up**

Practice   1. Index MAILING.DBF on the basis of LAST_NAME instead of ZIP_CODE:

Press   **Escape**
Press   **Shift-F2**
Press   **Escape**
Press   **Tab** (3 times)
Type   **y**
Press   **Down Arrow** (4 times)
Press   **Tab** (3 times)
Type   **n**
Press   **Alt-E**
Type   **s**

2. Activate the Browse screen to examine MAILING.DBF indexed by LAST_NAME. When you are finished, return to the Control Center.

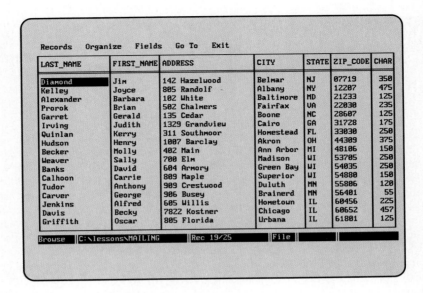

Figure 23 The Records Indexed by ZIP_CODE

```
  Records   Organize   Fields   Go To   Exit

  LAST_NAME       FIRST_NAME ADDRESS           CITY       STATE ZIP_CODE CHAR

  Diamond         Jim        142 Hazelwood     Belmar     NJ    07719    350
  Kelley          Joyce      805 Randolf       Albany     NY    12207    475
  Alexander       Barbara    102 White         Baltimore  MD    21233    125
  Prorok          Brian      502 Chalmers      Fairfax    VA    22030    235
  Garret          Gerald     135 Cedar         Boone      NC    28607    125
  Irving          Judith     1329 Grandview    Cairo      GA    31728    175
  Quinlan         Kerry      311 Southmoor     Homestead  FL    33030    250
  Hudson          Henry      1007 Barclay      Akron      OH    44309    375
  Becker          Molly      402 Main          Ann Arbor  MI    48106    150
  Weaver          Sally      700 Elm           Madison    WI    53705    250
  Banks           David      604 Armory        Green Bay  WI    54035    250
  Calhoon         Carrie     809 Maple         Superior   WI    54880    150
  Tudor           Anthony    909 Crestwood     Duluth     MN    55806    120
  Carver          George     906 Busey         Brainerd   MN    56401     55
  Jenkins         Alfred     605 Willis        Hometown   IL    60456    225
  Davis           Becky      7822 Kostner      Chicago    IL    60652    457
  Griffith        Oscar      805 Florida       Urbana     IL    61801    125

  Browse   C:\lessons\MAILING       Rec 19/25          File
```

3. Close the file MAILING.DBF:

Press   **Enter**
Press   **Enter**

Now, open it again. Highlight MAILING in the Data panel and then do this:

Press   **Enter**
Press   **Enter**

Activate the Browse screen to examine the file. It does not appear to be indexed. What happened? When you close an indexed file or exit dBASE IV and then open that file again, you must explicitly tell the program to order the records by the index. Display the Data Base Design screen, select the Order Records By Index option, and display the Browse screen again:

Press   **Escape**
Press   **Shift-F2**
Type   **o**
Highlight   **LAST_NAME**
Press   **Enter**
Press   **Alt-E**
Type   **a**
Press   **F2**

The file should again appear indexed by LAST_NAME. Return to the Control Center.

Lesson 13: Generating Reports

You have learned how to use the Browse and Edit screens to examine all or part of a data base on your computer display. The dBASE IV program also provides a wide choice of printing options for producing reports. A **report** is simply a listing of the contents of a data base printed on paper. You can print an unformatted list of all the records in a file or selectively print only certain fields and records. Mailing labels, preprinted forms, and custom-formatted reports can all

Real World

Computerizing the City Clerk

In May, 1986, the city clerk's office in Torrance, California, was given a computer terminal hooked up to the city's Digital VAX 11/780 mainframe. Within 24 hours the staff had tossed their pencils out the window and created and installed five data base programs. They were in the world of computers.

How did it happen so fast? Deputy City Clerk Dora Hong, relying on her self-taught knowledge of data base management programming, simply coached the staff members individually. She worked on dBASE syntax structure from the dot prompt on a blank screen, ignoring menu applications.

Hong's pupils were such fast learners that within three months, they had indexed the city council legislative history up to the most recently approved minutes, indexed the city's deeds, and created a new system of records storage based on a "box filing system." Since then, additional terminals have been installed.

There have been long-term benefits as well. First, according to Hong, the data base program has saved the office enormous amounts of time, particularly in summarizing, indexing, and searching for and retrieving information. It once took nearly a week to summarize, categorize, and file city council legislative history, she said. Now that can be done in less than two hours.

In addition, human filing error has been virtually eliminated, staff assignments can be made more flexibly, and staff morale has increased, according to Hong. Service to city departments and the city council has improved because information is indexed and can be quickly and accurately retrieved.

Source: Dora Hong, "Database Management System Benefits City," *The Office*, October 1988, pp. 117–120.

be created with dBASE IV. In this lesson you will learn how to produce a Quick Report of the Paddle and Portage Canoe Outfitters mailing list. The next chapter will present more advanced printing options.

Step 1: Select the Data Base File

At this point, you should be at the Control Center. Before you can create a report, you must tell dBASE IV the data base file you want to print. If you have already been working with the file, as we have been with MAILING.DBF, you can skip this step. Otherwise, you would highlight the name of the file in the Data panel of the Control Center screen. Then you would press Enter to select the file and press Enter again to tell dBASE IV that you want to open it.

Step 2: Prepare the Printer

Make sure the printer is connected to the computer and turned on. Also, make sure that paper is loaded and aligned to the top of a new page. Finally, make sure that the printer's On Line light is lit. (If it isn't, press the On Line button.)

Step 3: Execute the Quick Report Command

The Quick Report command organizes and prints data from the current data base file. It is an easy way to print a complete report from the Control Center without having to design the report layout yourself. The output is similar to what you

Figure 24 The Print Menu

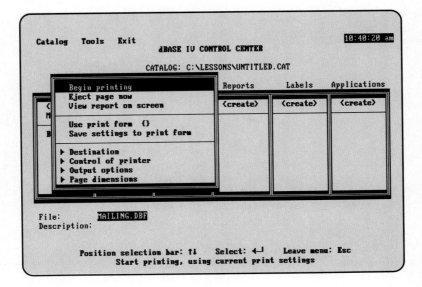

```
  Catalog   Tools   Exit                                    10:40:20 am
                            dBASE IV CONTROL CENTER

                        CATALOG: C:\LESSONS\UNTITLED.CAT

        ┌────────────────────────────┐ Reports    Labels    Applications
        │ Begin printing             │
      < │ Eject page now             │ <create>   <create>   <create>
      M │ View report on screen      │
        │                            │
      B │ Use print form  {}         │
        │ Save settings to print form│
        │                            │
        │ ► Destination              │
        │ ► Control of printer       │
        │ ► Output options           │
        │ ► Page dimensions          │
        └────────────────────────────┘

  File:      MAILING.DBF
  Description:

            Position selection bar: ↑↓    Select: ◄┘    Leave menu: Esc
                    Start printing, using current print settings
```

see on the Browse screen without dividing lines. Execute the Quick Report command:

> Press   **Shift-F9**

Step 4: Print the Report

The Print menu will appear on your screen as shown in Figure 24. You can begin printing immediately. Select the Begin Printing option:

> Type   **b**

The output from the printer should look like Figure 25. Note that the records have been printed in indexed order by LAST_NAME. Also note that dBASE IV automatically totaled the numbers in the CHARGES column.

Practice   Use the Quick Report command to print the BY_NAME data base file.

Summary

- *Starting dBASE IV.* Switch to the desired subdirectory and enter **dbase** from the DOS prompt.

- *Using the Control Center.* Press F10 to activate the menu bar. Highlight menu options with the arrow keys. Activate a menu by holding down the Alternate key and typing the menu title's first letter. Execute a menu option by highlighting it and pressing Enter or typing the first letter. Deactivate a menu by pressing Escape. Invoke Help by pressing F1.

- *Designing a data base file.* Select the <create> option from the Data panel and enter each field's name, type, and width.

- *Entering data base records.* Activate the Edit screen by pressing F2 and enter the data for each field. Terminate data entry by pressing Ctrl-End.

Figure 25 Quick Report of MAILING.DBF Indexed by LAST_NAME

Page No. 1
08/10/89

LAST_NAME	FIRST_NAME	ADDRESS	CITY	STATE	ZIP_CODE	CHARGES
Alexander	Barbara	102 White	Baltimore	MD	21233	125.00
Banks	David	604 Armory	Green Bay	WI	54035	250.00
Becker	Molly	402 Main	Ann Arbor	MI	48106	150.00
Calhoon	Carrie	809 Maple	Superior	WI	54880	150.00
Carver	George	906 Busey	Brainerd	MN	56401	55.00
Davis	Becky	7822 Kostner	Chicago	IL	60652	457.75
Diamond	Jim	142 Hazelwood	Belmar	NJ	07719	350.00
Franklin	Melissa	2012 Anderson	Big Bear	CA	92314	225.25
Garret	Gerald	135 Cedar	Boone	NC	28607	125.50
Griffith	Oscar	805 Florida	Urbana	IL	61801	125.00
Hall	Robert	1721 Valley	Ogallala	NE	69153	115.00
Hudson	Henry	1007 Barclay	Akron	OH	44309	375.50
Irving	Judith	1329 Grandview	Cairo	GA	31728	175.50
Jenkins	Alfred	605 Willis	Hometown	IL	60456	225.25
Kelley	Joyce	805 Randolf	Albany	NY	12207	475.00
Mitchell	Dan	310 Paddock	Flagstaff	AZ	86001	25.00
Prorok	Brian	502 Chalmers	Fairfax	VA	22030	235.00
Quinlan	Kerry	311 Southmoor	Homestead	FL	33030	250.00
Savage	Julian	2209 Philo	Cedar City	UT	84720	125.00
Skubic	Mike	321 Gregory	Champaign	IL	61820	245.25
Tudor	Anthony	909 Crestwood	Duluth	MN	55806	120.00
Underwood	Rhonda	701 Dover	Las Vegas	NV	89114	75.00
Walden	Roxanne	1010 Bridle	Denver	CO	80202	250.00
Weaver	Sally	700 Elm	Madison	WI	53705	250.75
Young	Susan	1104 Grand	Anchorage	AK	99502	100.00
						5055.75

- *Examining a data base.* Press Shift-F2 to see the Data Base Design screen. Press F2 to see the Edit screen or Browse screen.

- *Adding new records.* Activate the Edit screen or Browse screen, advance past the last record, and enter the data for the new records.

- *Modifying records.* Activate the Edit screen or Browse screen and change the data.

- *Deleting records.* Activate the Edit screen or Browse screen and select the Mark Record For Deletion option from the Records menu. Activate the Data Base Design screen and select the Erase Marked Records option to permanently remove marked records.

- *Finding records.* Activate the Edit screen or Browse screen and use the Go To menu.

- *Modifying the data base design.* Press Shift-F2, make the changes, and select Save This Database File Structure from the Layout menu.

- *Sorting a data base.* Press Shift-F2, select the Sort option, specify the keys, and specify the new file name.

- *Indexing a data base.* Change the Index entry of the Data Base Design screen to Y for the field on which the file is to be indexed.

- *Generating reports.* Press Shift-F9 to activate the Print menu and select the Begin Printing option to produce a Quick Report.

Key Terms

As an extra review of this chapter, try defining the following terms.

catalog	menu bar
data base	message line
field	navigation line
file	record
form	report
index file	status bar
indexing	table
key	wildcard character

Multiple Choice

Choose the best selection to complete each statement.

1. A data base file is a collection of
   - (a) rows.
   - (b) columns.
   - (c) records.
   - (d) bits.

2. The dBASE IV menu system is called the
   - (a) dot prompt.
   - (b) Help system.
   - (c) status bar.
   - (d) Control Center.

3. Which keys do you press to activate the Exit menu?
   - (a) Alt-Escape
   - (b) Alt-E
   - (c) Escape
   - (d) F1

4. Which key do you press to invoke the Help system?
   - (a) F1
   - (b) F10
   - (c) Escape
   - (d) Alternate

5. Which of the following terms is not a valid field type?
   - (a) Character
   - (b) Numeric
   - (c) Time
   - (d) Memo

6. Which type of field would you use to store Social Security numbers?
   - (a) Character
   - (b) Numeric
   - (c) Float
   - (d) Logical

7. What is the maximum size of a dBASE IV record?
   (a) 254 bytes   (b) 1000 bytes
   (c) 2500 bytes   (d) 4000 bytes

8. Which of the following characters is not allowed in field names?
   (a) A   (b) 5
   (c) underscore (_)   (d) space

9. Which key do you press to display the Edit screen or Browse screen?
   (a) F1   (b) F2
   (c) F9   (d) F10

10. Which screen lets you see the contents of several records at the same time in a table format?
    (a) Edit screen   (b) Browse screen
    (c) Data Base Design screen   (d) Control Center screen

11. Which key(s) do you press to jump immediately to the first record in a data base file?
    (a) Home   (b) Up Arrow
    (c) Ctrl-Tab   (d) Ctrl-PgUp

12. Which menu do you use to permanently remove records marked for deletion?
    (a) Records on the Edit or Browse screen
    (b) Organize on the Data Base Design screen
    (c) Exit on the Edit or Browse screen
    (d) Exit on the Data Base Design screen

13. How do you add new records to an existing data base?
    (a) Press the Insert key.
    (b) Advance past the last record.
    (c) Select Append from the Fields menu.
    (d) Press F1.

14. How would you jump forward ten records on the Browse screen?
    (a) Press Page Up.
    (b) Select Skip from the Go To menu.
    (c) Select Jump from the Records menu.
    (d) Select Forward Search from the Go To menu.

15. Which keypress does not delete characters?
    (a) Delete   (b) Backspace
    (c) Ctrl-D   (d) Ctrl-Y

16. Which Browse screen menu lets you quickly reach particular records in a data base file?
    (a) Records   (b) Fields
    (c) Go To   (d) Exit

17. Which wildcard character will match any number of characters?
    (a) ?   (b) *
    (c) &   (d) $

18. Record numbers are assigned to records on the basis of
    (a) the order in which they were entered.
    (b) the key field.
    (c) the index expression.
    (d) the field width.
19. Which method of organizing a large data base file is usually slow and takes up a lot of disk space?
    (a) indexing   (b) sorting
    (c) printing   (d) searching
20. Which key(s) execute the Quick Report command and activate the Print menu?
    (a) F1   (b) F2
    (c) Shift-F3   (d) Shift-F9

Fill-In

1. The dBASE IV package cannot be run unless you have a _____ disk or are connected to a local area network.
2. The Control Center is the _____ system of dBASE IV.
3. The menu bar contains the _____ of the currently available menus.
4. One way to activate a menu is to hold down the _____ key and type the first letter of the menu title.
5. You can close a menu and make it disappear by pressing the _____ key.
6. The _____ option lets you retrace your steps through the Help system.
7. A record is a sequence of _____.
8. A byte is equivalent to a single _____.
9. The _____ field type is for counting or exact calculations.
10. A _____ displays the fields of an individual record on the screen.
11. When you are finished entering records, you can either press _____ or execute the Exit option from the Exit menu to save your work.
12. The Data command, which is invoked by pressing the F2 key, activates either the _____ screen or the _____ screen.
13. Whenever you try to advance past the last record in a data base file, dBASE IV will ask you if you want to _____ records.
14. Records can be modified from either the _____ screen or the _____ screen.
15. Records are first _____ for deletion before they are permanently removed from a data base file.
16. If you are at the beginning of a file, you can use the _____ Search option from the Go To menu to find records that contain specific data.
17. The Find Next command, executed by pressing _____, advances to the next record that matches the search criteria.
18. Wildcard characters can be used in search strings to find records containing data with one or more _____ in common.
19. When dBASE IV sorts a file, it actually creates a new _____ with the records arranged in the proper order.
20. A convenient alternative to sorting is _____, which rearranges record numbers instead of entire records.

Short Problems

1. If you are not already running dBASE IV, switch to the LESSONS subdirectory and start the program. Highlight MAILING in the Data panel of the Control Center and tell dBASE IV that you want to use this file.
2. Execute the Data command to display the Browse screen. Move to the last record in the file.
3. Activate the Go To menu and perform a Backward Search to find George Carver's record.
4. Move to the beginning of the MAILING data base file and then move to the STATE field. Activate the Go To menu and perform a Forward Search to find the records of all customers who live in Illinois. Use the Find Next command to view each of these records.
5. Move to the beginning of the MAILING data base file and then move to the CITY field. Activate the Go To menu and perform a Forward Search to find the records of all customers who live in cities that begin with the letter C. Use the Find Next command to view each of these records.
6. Exit the Browse screen and then display the Data Base Design screen. Execute the Order Records by Index option from the Organize menu. Select the LAST NAME index. Activate the Exit menu and select Abandon Changes and Exit. Examine the MAILING data base file on the Browse screen. When you are finished, return to the Control Center.
7. Select the MAILING file in the Data panel and tell dBASE IV that you want to close this file. Then select the BY_NAME file from the Data panel and tell dBASE IV that you want to use this file. Activate the Browse screen to examine the file.
8. Modify Oscar Griffith's address so that it reads "810 Florida" and then return to the Control Center.
9. Index the BY_NAME data base file by STATE. Examine the data base on the Browse screen.
10. Print a Quick Report of the BY_NAME data base indexed by STATE.

Long Problems

1. Create a data base file containing information about your collection of LP records, cassette tapes, and compact discs. Include fields for the title, artist, type of media (LP, tape, or CD), amount paid, and year released. Use a Numeric field for the cost. Index the data base by artist. Print a Quick Report to calculate the total value of your collection.
2. Create a data base file containing your personal property inventory. Include fields for item, serial number, location, date purchased, and amount paid. Use a Date field for the date purchased and Numeric field for the amount paid. Print a Quick Report to calculate the total value of your property.
3. Create an "electronic Rolodex" with dBASE IV. Design and enter the records of a data base file to hold the information you keep in your personal address/phone book. Include fields for name, address, city, state, ZIP code, and phone number. If you like, you can also include fields for work address and phone, birth dates, anniversaries, and any other information you keep. Index the data base by name and print a Quick Report.

4. Suppose you are a teaching assistant for this course. Create a data base file to keep track of grades. Include fields for each student's name, Social Security number, class, section, classroom, meeting day and time, homework grades, test grades, and final letter grade. Make up and enter at least twenty records.

5. Create a data base file that contains information about all of the courses you have taken throughout your college career. Include fields for course title, course number, semester or quarter and year taken, hours or credits earned, instructor, and school (if you have attended more than one).

6. Create a data base file for keeping track of your (or your family's) car expenses. Use a separate record for each month of the year. Include fields for month, taxes, insurance, repairs, gas, oil, parking fees, tolls, speeding tickets, car washes, and any other expenses you can think of.

7. Create a data base file containing your academic schedule for this semester or quarter. Use a separate record for each class. Include fields for class, day, time, building, room, and instructor. Print a Quick Report of your class schedule.

8. Create a data base file that stores information about your textbooks, reference books, and personal books. Include fields for title, author, publisher, copyright date, and cost. Print a Quick Report of your data base.

9. Use a current reference such as *The World Almanac* to create a data base file of information about the fifty states. Include fields for state name, capital city, population, and area in square miles.

10. Don't put away your copy of *The World Almanac* yet. Modify your states data base file so that it includes the names of the governor and the two U.S. senators for each state.

INTERMEDIATE
dBASE IV

In This Chapter

■ **Preview**

In Chapter 4 you learned the basics of dBASE IV, the top-selling microcomputer data base management package. This chapter continues your exploration of dBASE IV, focusing on slightly more advanced topics.

After studying this chapter, you will know how to

- use memo fields.
- create view queries.
- create relational data bases.
- link files.
- create update queries.
- use calculated fields.
- summarize data.
- design custom forms.
- design custom reports.
- create mailing labels.
- use applications.
- use the Catalog menu.
- use the Tools menu.

■ **Getting Started**

You've already learned how to start dBASE IV and use its most basic features and commands. This chapter assumes you have completed all of the lessons and exercises in Chapter 4. Furthermore, it assumes that you have a computer with a hard disk and dBASE IV installed on it in a subdirectory named DBASE. A DOS path should be set up so that you can run dBASE IV from within any subdirectory. You should have a subdirectory named LESSONS in which to store your data base files.

■ **Lesson 1: Using Memo Fields**

Most data base fields contain a single number, word, or phrase. The Memo field type, however, allows you to include a block of text in a data base record. Memo fields can be used to store explanatory notes, descriptions, comments, or other free-form information. For example, you could use a Memo field in a biblio-graphic data base to record your notes about each book. Actually, the text itself is not stored in the Memo field. It is kept in a separate file. The Memo field tells dBASE IV which file contains the text. As an example, let's create a Memo field for the Paddle and Portage Canoe Outfitters data base to list the compliments or complaints made by each customer.

Step 1: Select the Data Base File

If you are not already running dBASE IV, switch to your LESSONS subdirectory and start the program:

Type **cd \lessons**
Press **Enter**
Type **dbase**
Press **Enter**
Press **Enter**

The Control Center screen should be visible, with the highlight bar in the Data panel. Tell dBASE IV that you want to use the MAILING data base file:

Highlight **MAILING**
Press   **Enter**
Press   **Enter**

Step 2: Add a Memo Field to the Design

To add a Memo field to an existing data base file, you must modify the data base design. Execute the Design command to display the Data Base Design screen:

Press   **Shift-F2**
Press   **Escape**

Move past the last field in the record and insert a new Memo field named COMMENTS:

Press   **Down Arrow** (7 times)
Type   **comments**
Press   **Enter**
Type   **m**
Press   **Up Arrow**

Your screen should look like Figure 1. Note that dBASE IV automatically sets the width of a Memo field to 10 bytes. Remember that a Memo field itself does not actually hold any text. It holds only a pointer to a separate, but related file that contains the text. Now, save the changes you have made and return to the Control Center:

Press   **Alt-E**
Type   **s**
Press   **Enter**

Figure 1 Memo Field Added to the Data Base Design

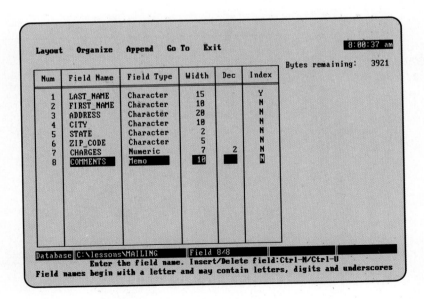

Num	Field Name	Field Type	Width	Dec	Index
1	LAST_NAME	Character	15		Y
2	FIRST_NAME	Character	10		N
3	ADDRESS	Character	20		N
4	CITY	Character	10		N
5	STATE	Character	2		N
6	ZIP_CODE	Character	5		N
7	CHARGES	Numeric	7	2	N
8	COMMENTS	Memo	10		N

Layout   Organize   Append   Go To   Exit   8:00:37 am

Bytes remaining: 3921

Database C:\lessons\MAILING   Field 8/8
Enter the field name. Insert/Delete field:Ctrl-N/Ctrl-U
Field names begin with a letter and may contain letters, digits and underscores

Step 3: Add Data to the Memo Field

Execute the Data command to display the Edit screen:

Press **F2**

If the Browse screen appears, repeat the command to switch to the Edit screen. Move to the first record in the data base file:

Press **Ctrl-PgUp**

Your screen should look like Figure 2. The COMMENTS field contains the word "memo" in lowercase letters. This word is called a **memo marker.** It indicates whether the file associated with the Memo field contains any text. If the word "memo" appears in lowercase letters, the Memo field file is empty. If it appears entirely in uppercase letters, the Memo field file contains text. The memo marker allows you to see if a Memo field file contains text without having to open it.

At this point, all the COMMENTS fields in the MAILING data base file are empty. To enter text in a Memo field file, move the cursor to that field and open it by pressing Ctrl-Home.

Press **Down Arrow** (7 times)
Press **Ctrl-Home**

The dBASE IV program activates its word-wrap editor, shown in Figure 3. This editor works like a simple word processor. It allows you to enter, edit, and to some extent format text in Memo fields and dBASE IV programs. (You will learn about dBASE IV programs in the next chapter.) A ruler line appears below the menu bar across the top of the screen. The left bracket ([) indicates the left margin, and the right bracket (]) indicates the right margin. The dots indicate character positions, the triangles indicate tab stops, and the numbers indicate inch measurements. By default, the line width in Memo fields is set to 65 characters. Word wrap will occur automatically as you type. You can press the arrow keys to move the cursor and the Backspace and Delete keys to erase characters. The Insert key toggles between the insert and typeover modes. Insert mode is turned on by

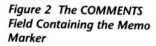

Figure 2 The COMMENTS Field Containing the Memo Marker

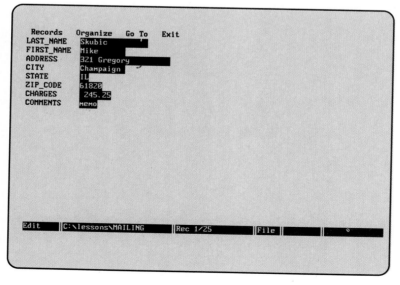

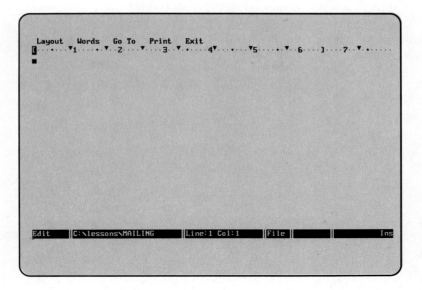

Figure 3 The Word-Wrap Editor

default and is indicated by the abbreviation "Ins," which appears at the right side of the status bar. The Enter key begins a new paragraph. Type the following text, without pressing the Enter key, into the COMMENTS field of Mike Skubic's record:

> **Mike feels that the Beaver canoe is a bit unstable when it is not fully loaded. He likes the nylon Duluth packs. He prefers the Beef Stromboli to the Chicken Stew 'N Dumplings. Next trip, he would like to try a route that does not go through the Silver Falls portage.**

Check your work against Figure 4. If you have made any mistakes, correct them by using the arrow keys to move the cursor and the Delete or Backspace key to erase characters. When you are finished entering or editing text in the Memo field, press Ctrl-End or select the Save Changes and Exit option from the Exit menu.

Press **Alt-E**
Type **s**

The program will return to the Edit screen showing Mike Skubic's record. Note that the memo marker is now "MEMO" in uppercase letters, which indicates that the COMMENTS field contains text.

Step 4: Examine an Existing Memo Field

You cannot see the contents of a Memo field on the Edit screen. Try the Browse screen:

Press **F2**
Press **End**

The result is the same. Only the memo marker "memo" or "MEMO" appears in the COMMENTS field on the Edit or Browse screen. To see the contents of a Memo field, you must move to that field and activate the word-wrap editor.

Press **Ctrl-Home**

*Figure 4 The Completed
COMMENTS Field Contents*

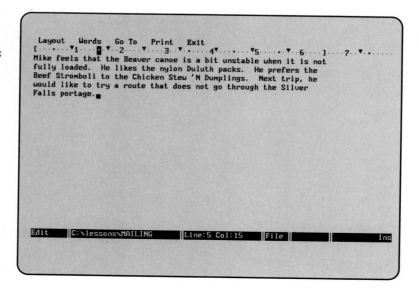

Your screen should look like Figure 4 again. Now you can read or change the contents of the current record's COMMENTS field. Return to the Browse screen:

Press   **Alt-E**
Type   **a**

Practice   1. Switch to the Edit screen. Advance to Oscar Griffith's record and enter the following text in the COMMENTS field.

Oscar loves the Beaver canoe. He prefers the canvas Duluth packs, despite their additional weight. He likes all of the Trail Food.

Save the text and return to the Edit screen.
2. Activate the word-wrap editor again and change "loves" to "hates." Save your work and return to the Edit screen.

Lesson 2: Creating a Simple View Query

In dBASE IV, a **query** is a set of instructions that lets you retrieve, display, organize, or edit data. Two types of queries can be created: view queries and update queries. A **view query** is used to display selected data on the screen. An **update query** is used to add, modify, or delete data in a data base file. Both view queries and update queries can be saved for future use. They are powerful tools for organizing and managing data. In this lesson, you will create and use a simple view query. You will learn to use update queries in a later lesson.

Step 1: Execute <create> in the Queries Panel

A view query accepts one or more data base files as input and creates a view as output. In this context, a **view** is an arrangement of data on the screen. Let's create a simple view query that will display the records of all the customers who

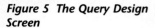

Figure 5 The Query Design Screen

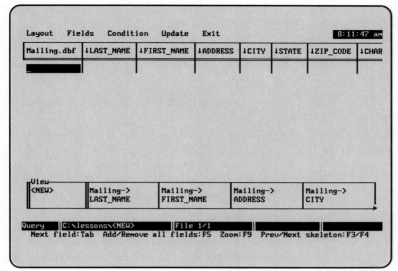

live in Wisconsin. MAILING should be your current data base file. Return to the Control Center, move into the Queries panel, and select the <create> option.

Press **Escape**
Press **Right Arrow**
Press **Enter**

Step 2: Examine the Query Design Screen

The program will present the Query Design screen, shown in Figure 5. Query-by-Example, or QBE, is the approach used by dBASE IV on this screen. QBE is an interactive query language designed to make it easy to tell the data base manager how to retrieve data. The menu bar across the top of the screen contains five titles: Layout, Fields, Condition, Update, and Exit. Just below the menu bar is a **file skeleton,** which is a graphic representation of a data base file. The file skeleton shows the name of the current data base file and the names of all of its fields. You can enter instructions for dBASE IV in the spaces below the names in the file skeleton. Another skeleton is shown near the bottom of the screen above the status bar. This is the **view skeleton,** a graphic representation of the fields that will be presented in the view created by the view query.

Step 3: Move to the STATE Field

Our simple view will present the records of all the customers who live in Wisconsin. Move the highlight bar and cursor to the STATE field:

Press **Tab** (5 times)

The file skeleton will scroll, if necessary, to reveal the fields to the right.

Step 4: Enter the Filter Condition

A **filter condition** is an expression that determines which records are selected for the view. The simplest type of filter condition is an expression that specifies the characters, numbers, or other values to be matched. For example, to select the records of customers who live in Wisconsin, enter "WI" in the space beneath the STATE field name. Note that specific text must be enclosed in quotation marks.

Type   **"WI"**
Press   **Enter**

The program will search MAILING.DBF for the records that contain "WI" in the STATE field.

Step 5: Display the View on the Browse Screen

You can see the view you have created by displaying the Edit or Browse screen. Execute the Data command to display the Browse screen:

Press   **F2** (2 times)

If the Edit screen appears, execute the Data command again. The Browse screen will present only the records of customers from Wisconsin (see Figure 6).

Step 6: Save the View Query

Suppose you want to be able to use the view query you have created again later. You can save it on your disk and use it at any time without having to redefine it. Return to the Query Design Screen, save the changes, enter a name for the query file, and exit back to the Control Center.

Press   **Alt-E**
Type   **t**
Press   **Alt-E**
Type   **s**
Type   **wi**
Press   **Enter**

The dBASE IV program will return to the Control Center. Note that the file named WI.QBE, which contains the view query you just created, appears in the Queries panel (see Figure 7).

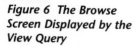

Figure 6 The Browse Screen Displayed by the View Query

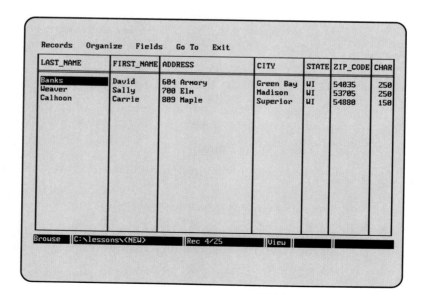

*Figure 7 WI.QBE Added to
the Queries Panel*

```
 Catalog  Tools  Exit                                  8:15:03 am
                           dBASE IV CONTROL CENTER
                        CATALOG: C:\LESSONS\UNTITLED.CAT

      Data        Queries       Forms       Reports      Labels    Applications
  ┌───────────┬───────────┬───────────┬───────────┬───────────┬───────────┐
  │ <create>  │ <create>  │ <create>  │ <create>  │ <create>  │ <create>  │
  │           │    WI     │           │           │           │           │
  │ BY_NAME   │           │           │           │           │           │
  │ MAILING   │           │           │           │           │           │
  │           │           │           │           │           │           │
  │           │           │           │           │           │           │
  │           │           │           │           │           │           │
  └───────────┴───────────┴───────────┴───────────┴───────────┴───────────┘

   File:       WI.QBE
   Description:


   Help:F1  Use:◄┘  Data:F2  Design:Shift-F2  Quick Report:Shift-F9  Menus:F10
```

Step 7: Use an Existing View Query

It is easy to use an existing view query file. Move into the Queries panel and highlight the view query file you want. Since WI.QBE is the last file you used, you don't have to go through these steps now. Simply execute the Data command to display the Edit or Browse screen:

> Press **F2**

The program will use the view query instructions you have saved to present only the records of customers from Wisconsin. When you are finished examining the screen, return to the Control Center:

> Press **Escape**

Practice   Create a view query that presents the MAILING records of customers whose first names begin with the letter *J*. Move the cursor beneath the FIRST_NAME field in the Query Design screen and do this:

> Type   `like "J*"`
> Press **Enter**

The word "like" is a filter condition operator that specifies a pattern match instead of an exact match. Execute the Data command to display the Browse screen. When you are finished, return to the Control Center without saving the view query you have created.

Lesson 3: Creating a Relational Data Base

A **relational data base** is a data base that includes two or more files with at least one field in common. For example, Paddle and Portage Canoe Outfitters might want to keep its mailing list information separate from its accounting information. Right now, the MAILING data base file contains the CHARGES field. A better arrangement would be to put the CHARGES data in a separate data base file along with the customers' names and other accounting information. The two separate files would then be related by the fields they have in common: LAST_NAME and FIRST_NAME. In this lesson, you will learn how to use a view query to derive one data base file from another. The next lesson will teach you how to use a view query to extract information from two separate data base files that are related by at least one common field.

Step 1: Select MAILING.DBF

Move back into the Data panel of the Control Center and select the MAILING data base file if it is not already selected:

Press	**Left Arrow**
Highlight	**MAILING**
Press	**Enter**
Press	**Enter**

Step 2: Create a New View Query

Move into the Queries panel and select the <create> option:

Press	**Right Arrow**
Press	**Enter**

The program will present a new Query Design screen containing MAILING.DBF in the file skeleton and all of the MAILING fields in the view skeleton.

Step 3: Remove the Unwanted Fields from the View

By default, all the fields from MAILING are included in your view. But you want to create a new data base file named ACCOUNT.DBF that will contain only three fields from the MAILING data base file: LAST_NAME, FIRST_NAME, and CHARGES. Later you will remove the CHARGES field from the MAILING data base file and add a new field named BALANCE to the ACCOUNT data base file.

In this step, you will tell dBASE IV which MAILING fields you want to remove from your view. This can be done by moving the highlight bar into each field, then selecting the Remove Field From View option of the Fields menu. Follow these directions to remove the ADDRESS, CITY, STATE, ZIP_CODE, and COMMENTS fields from the view:

Press	**Tab** (3 times)
Press	**Alt-F**
Type	**r**
Press	**Tab**
Press	**Alt-F**
Type	**r**
Press	**Tab**
Press	**Alt-F**
Type	**r**
Press	**Tab**
Press	**Alt-F**
Type	**r**
Press	**Tab** (2 times)
Press	**Alt-F**
Type	**r**

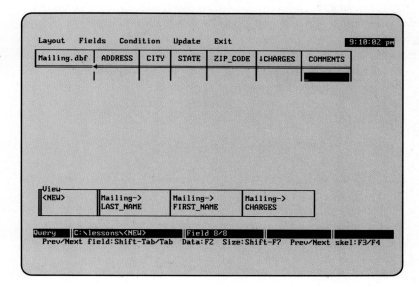

Figure 8 The View Skeleton Containing Only Three Fields

Your screen should look like Figure 8. Examine the view skeleton near the bottom of the screen. It contains only three fields from the MAILING data base file: LAST_NAME, FIRST_NAME, and CHARGES.

Step 4: Sort the Records in the View

Although this step is not absolutely necessary, it will arrange the records in the view in a predictable order. Since you are going to create a new data base file for the records anyway, sorting them in the view will not take up any more disk space. Move the highlight bar back to the LAST_NAME field, select the Sort On This Field option from the Fields menu, and select the Ascending ASCII sort order:

Press **Home**
Press **Tab**
Press **Alt-F**
Type **s**
Press **Enter**

The program will enter the sorting operator Asc1 in the space below the LAST_NAME field in the file skeleton. This operator tells dBASE IV to sort the records in ascending ASCII order when it creates the view.

Step 5: Examine the View

Now you can execute the Data command to display the Browse screen and see the view you have created.

Press **F2**

Figure 9 shows the result. The records are sorted by LAST_NAME. Each record contains three fields: LAST_NAME, FIRST_NAME, and CHARGES.

Figure 9 The View with Records Sorted by LAST_NAME

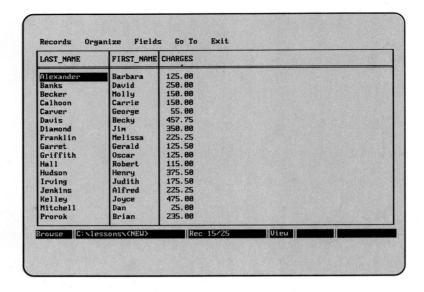

```
 Records    Organize    Fields    Go To    Exit

 LAST_NAME       FIRST_NAME CHARGES

 Alexander       Barbara    125.00
 Banks           David      250.00
 Becker          Molly      150.00
 Calhoon         Carrie     150.00
 Carver          George      55.00
 Davis           Becky      457.75
 Diamond         Jim        350.00
 Franklin        Melissa    225.25
 Garret          Gerald     125.50
 Griffith        Oscar      125.00
 Hall            Robert     115.00
 Hudson          Henry      375.50
 Irving          Judith     175.50
 Jenkins         Alfred     225.25
 Kelley          Joyce      475.00
 Mitchell        Dan         25.00
 Prorok          Brian      235.00

 Browse    C:\lessons\<NEW>        Rec 15/25        View
```

Step 6: Create a Data Base File from the View

A view is just an arrangement of data on the screen. You must tell dBASE IV to create a new data base file named ACCOUNT.DBF from the view you have created. Return to the Query Design screen, select the Write View As Database File option from the Layout menu, and enter the name of the new data base file:

Press	**Alt-E**
Type	**t**
Press	**Alt-L**
Type	**w**
Type	**account**
Press	**Enter** (2 times)

The program will create a new data base file named ACCOUNT.DBF that has the same design and contents as the view. You do not need to save the view query, so abandon the changes and exit to the Control Center:

Press	**Alt-E**
Type	**a**
Type	**y**

Step 7: Remove CHARGES From MAILING.DBF

From now on, the ACCOUNT data base file will contain accounting information for Paddle and Portage Canoe Outfitters, so you can remove the CHARGES field from the MAILING data base file. Move back into the Data panel, highlight MAILING, and execute the Design command to display the Data Base Design screen:

Press	**Left Arrow**
Press	**Shift-F2**
Press	**Escape**

Now, highlight the CHARGES field and remove it from the record structure:

Press   **Down Arrow** (6 times)
Press   **Ctrl-U**

Tell dBASE IV to save the change you have made and return to the Control Center:

Press   **Alt-E**
Type   **s**
Type   **y**

Step 8: Add a New Field to ACCOUNT.DBF

Let's make your relational data base more interesting by adding another field to the ACCOUNT file. This new field, named BALANCE, will hold the amount still owed by the customer. The existing field, CHARGES, holds the total charges, paid or unpaid.

Highlight the ACCOUNT file in the Data panel of the Control Center and execute the Design command to display the Data Base Design screen:

Highlight   **ACCOUNT**
Press   **Shift-F2**
Press   **Escape**

Move past the last field in the record structure and specify the new field:

Press   **Down Arrow** (3 times)
Type   **balance**
Press   **Enter**
Type   **n**
Type   **7**
Press   **Enter**
Type   **2**
Press   **Home**

Your screen should look like Figure 10. Save the modified data base design and return to the Control Center:

Press   **Alt-E**
Type   **s**
Type   **y**

Step 9: Add Data for the BALANCE Field

Now that you have created a new field named BALANCE in the ACCOUNT data base file, you can add the data for each customer. Execute the Data command twice to display the Edit screen and move to the first record in the file:

Press   **F2** (2 times)
Press   **Ctrl-PgUp**

Move the cursor to the BALANCE field and enter Barbara Alexander's data:

Press   **Down Arrow** (3 times)
Type   **55**
Press   **Enter**

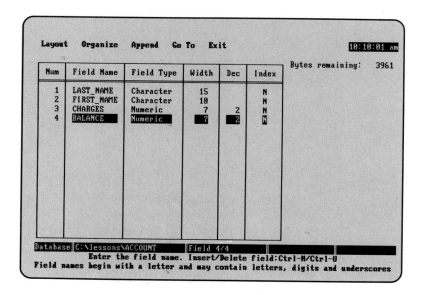

Figure 10 The BALANCE Field Added to ACCOUNT.DBF

The program will advance to the next record. Use the following table to enter the BALANCE figures for the remaining records:

Last Name	Balance	Last Name	Balance
Banks	0.00	Jenkins	0.00
Becker	50.00	Kelley	175.00
Calhoon	25.00	Mitchell	0.00
Carver	0.00	Prorok	0.00
Davis	200.00	Quinlan	50.00
Diamond	0.00	Savage	25.00
Franklin	100.00	Skubic	0.00
Garret	0.00	Tudor	0.00
Griffith	0.00	Underwood	0.00
Hall	0.00	Walden	0.00
Hudson	75.50	Weaver	0.00
Irving	100.00	Young	50.00

Return to the Control Center when you are finished.

Practice

1. Display the Browse screen and check your data entries against the previous table. Correct any errors you made. Return to the Control Center.

2. Create a view that displays only the records of customers who have not paid all of their charges. Move into the Queries panel and select the <create> option to display the Query Design screen. Move the highlight bar to the BALANCE field. Tell dBASE IV that you want to see the records of customers whose BALANCE figures are greater than zero:

   Type   **>0**
   Press   **Enter**

Display the Browse screen to see the view you have created. When you are finished, exit the Query Design screen without saving the view query and return to the Control Center.

Lesson 4: Linking Files

If two or more files have at least one field in common, you can create a view that links the files and displays data from any of them. Suppose you want to see the last names, addresses, ZIP codes, and balances of customers who have not yet paid all of their charges. You can easily retrieve this information from MAIL-ING.DBF and ACCOUNT.DBF with a view query.

Step 1: Create a New View Query

At this point, ACCOUNT.DBF should be your current data base file. From the Control Center, move the highlight bar to the <create> option in the Queries panel, then display the Query Design screen:

    Press   **Enter**

Step 2: Add MAILING.DBF to the Query

The file skeleton for ACCOUNT.DBF is near the top of the screen. In order to retrieve data from MAILING.DBF as well, you must display its file skeleton on the screen. Activate the Layout menu and select the Add File to Query option:

    Press   **Alt-L**
    Type   **a**

A menu box will appear containing the names of the available data base files.

    Highlight   **MAILING.DBF**
    Press   **Enter**

The file skeleton for MAILING.DBF will appear on the screen below the file skeleton for ACCOUNT.DBF (see Figure 11).

Figure 11 Two File Skeletons on the Query Design Screen

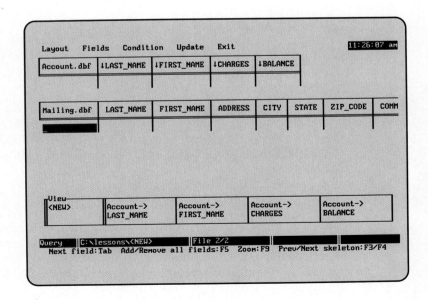

Step 3: Remove All Fields from the View Skeleton

You want only the LAST_NAME, ADDRESS, ZIP_CODE, and BALANCE fields included in the view. The easiest method in this case is to remove all of the fields from the view skeleton and then selectively add the fields you want. Right now, the highlight bar is in the MAILING.DBF file skeleton. You can move to the previous file skeleton by pressing F3 to execute the Prev command, or move to the next file skeleton by pressing F4 to execute the Next command. Move to the ACCOUNT.DBF file skeleton:

Press **F3**

All the fields from ACCOUNT.DBF are currently included in the view skeleton near the bottom of the screen. With the highlight bar beneath the file name, execute the Field command to remove all of the ACCOUNT.DBF fields from the view skeleton:

Press **F5**

The view skeleton will disappear.

Step 4: Add the Desired Fields to the View Skeleton

Now you can add just the fields you want, in the order you want, to the view skeleton. Move the highlight bar beneath the LAST_NAME field in the ACCOUNT.DBF file skeleton and select the Add Field to View option from the Fields menu:

Press **Tab**
Press **Alt-F**
Type **a**

A view skeleton will appear with LAST_NAME from ACCOUNT.DBF as the first field. Follow these directions to add the ADDRESS, ZIP_CODE, and BALANCE fields:

Press **F4**
Press **Tab** (3 times)
Press **Alt-F**
Type **a**
Press **Tab** (3 times)
Press **Alt-F**
Type **a**
Press **F3**
Press **Tab** (3 times)
Press **Alt-F**
Type **a**

The view skeleton now contains LAST_NAME from ACCOUNT.DBF, ADDRESS and ZIP_CODE from MAILING.DBF, and BALANCE from ACCOUNT.DBF (see Figure 12).

Step 5: Enter the Filter Condition

You want to see only those records of customers who have a balance greater than zero. This filter condition can be specified with an expression that contains a **relational operator,** a symbol or word that specifies how items are to be compared. The highlight bar should be beneath the BALANCE field.

Type **>0**
Press **Enter**

Figure 12 Fields from Different Files in the View Skeleton

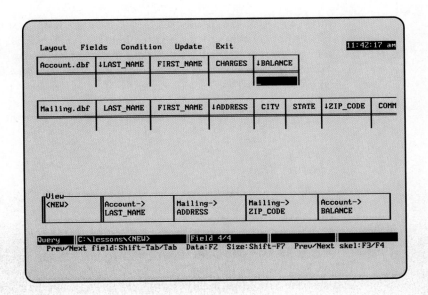

The expression >0 tells dBASE to retrieve only those records with a value greater than zero in the BALANCE field.

Several relational operators are available in addition to > (greater than). The following table lists dBASE IV relational operators.

Operator	Description
>	greater than
<	less than
=	equal
<> or #	not equal
>=	greater than or equal
<=	less than or equal
$	contains
Like	pattern search
Sounds Like	Soundex search

The $ operator is used to retrieve records that contain a specified substring. For example, suppose you want to retrieve all records that contain "New" as part of the contents of the CITY field. You can use the expression *$"New"* as the filter condition.

The Like operator is used to specify search strings that contain wildcard characters (* and ?). For example, the expression *Like "A*"* will find any word or phrase beginning with an uppercase A.

The Sounds Like operator performs Soundex searches. A **Soundex search** finds words that sound like the word you specify. For example, the expression *Sounds Like "jerry"* will find the names Jeri, Jerri, Gerry, and Geri, as well as Jerry.

Step 6: Link the Files

Before you can examine the view, you must link the two data base files by the field they share. This is done by placing the same example variable in the common field, known as the **link field**. An **example variable** is a place holder for the value of a field. It may be up to ten characters long, but must begin with a letter and cannot contain any embedded blanks. For example, you could use the word "name" as an example variable. Follow these directions to enter the same example variable in the LAST_NAME fields and link the ACCOUNT.DBF and MAIL-ING.DBF files:

Press **Home**
Press **Tab**
Type **name**
Press **F4**
Press **Home**
Press **Tab**
Type **name**
Press **Enter**

Note that linking files works best when each possible value in the link field is unique. In our simple example, no two last names are the same, so we can use LAST_NAME as the link field. In the real world, however, a large mailing list data base would probably contain records of several people with common last names, such as Jones or Smith. Such data bases are usually designed with a field for a unique identification number, such as a customer number or Social Security number. This unique field would be included in every related data base file and used as the link field.

Step 7: Examine the View

Execute the Data command to display the Browse screen and examine the view you have created:

Press **F2**

Figure 13 shows the result. The records are sorted by LAST_NAME because the records in ACCOUNT.DBF are sorted by LAST_NAME. The data in the LAST_NAME and BALANCE fields are from ACCOUNT.DBF; the data in the ADDRESS and ZIP_CODE fields are from MAILING.DBF.

Figure 13 The View Linking MAILING.DBF and ACCOUNT.DBF

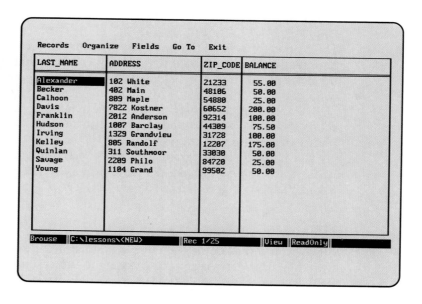

LAST_NAME	ADDRESS	ZIP_CODE	BALANCE
Alexander	102 White	21233	55.00
Becker	402 Main	48106	50.00
Calhoon	809 Maple	54880	25.00
Davis	7822 Kostner	60652	200.00
Franklin	2012 Anderson	92314	100.00
Hudson	1007 Barclay	44309	75.50
Irving	1329 Grandview	31728	100.00
Kelley	805 Randolf	12207	175.00
Quinlan	311 Southmoor	33030	50.00
Savage	2209 Philo	84720	25.00
Young	1104 Grand	99502	50.00

Records   Organize   Fields   Go To   Exit

Browse   C:\lessons\<NEW>   Rec 1/25   View   ReadOnly

Step 8: Save the View Query

You may want to use the view query you have created again. Return to the Query Design screen and save the query in a file named WHO_OWES.QBE:

Press	**Alt-E**
Type	**t**
Press	**Alt-E**
Type	**s**
Type	**who_owes**
Press	**Enter**

The program will return to the Control Center.

Practice   Create a view query that links MAILING.DBF and ACCOUNT.DBF and displays the LAST_NAME, CITY, and CHARGES fields. Examine the view you have created. Return to the Control Center without saving the query to disk.

Lesson 5: Creating an Update Query

An update query allows you to make changes to selected records throughout an entire data base file. You can also use an update query to mark certain records for deletion.

Update queries are often used to make corrections to selected records. For example, suppose you consistently entered an incorrect abbreviation in the STATE field for a particular state. You could correct all the mistakes at once with an update query.

Selected records throughout an entire data base also can be marked for deletion with an update query. You could, for instance, mark all records with "WI" in the STATE field for deletion.

An update query is frequently used to make a consistent change to selected fields throughout a data base. Suppose Paddle and Portage Canoe Outfitters charged a five percent late-payment fee to customers who had not paid all of their charges after a certain period of time. Let's create an update query to increase the value in the BALANCE field by five percent for all customers with a balance greater than zero.

Step 1: Select the Data Base File

The data you want to change is in the ACCOUNT data base file. The Control Center should be on your screen. Tell dBASE IV that you want to use the ACCOUNT data base:

Move	to the Data panel
Highlight	**ACCOUNT**
Press	**Enter** (2 times)

Step 2: Create a New Update Query

Move into the Queries panel and select the <create> option:

Press	**Right Arrow**
Highlight	**<create>**
Press	**Enter**

The program will present a new Query Design screen, with ACCOUNT.DBF in the file skeleton and all of the ACCOUNT fields in the view skeleton.

Step 3: Move to the Field to be Changed

BALANCE is the field to be changed. Move the highlight bar beneath BALANCE in the file skeleton:

Press   **Tab** (4 times)

Step 4: Specify the Update Operation

Now you can tell dBASE IV which update operation you want to perform. Activate the Update menu and select the Specify Update Operation option:

Press   **Alt-U**
Type   **s**

Figure 14 shows the menu that appears on the screen. Four update operations are available: Replace, Append, Mark, and Unmark. The Replace operation substitutes values in a field for all or selected records. The Append operation adds selected records to the current data base file. The Mark operation marks records for deletion based on a condition. The Unmark operation is the opposite of the Mark operation. To increase all of the values in the BALANCE field by five percent, you would use a Replace operation:

Type   **r**

The program will display a box saying that changing the view query to an update query will delete the view skeleton. In other words, the view skeleton is not needed for an update query, because an update query does not produce a view. An update query changes the records in the original data base file stored on the disk. Tell dBASE IV that you want to proceed with creating an update query:

Type   **p**

*Figure 14 The Specify
Update Operation Menu*

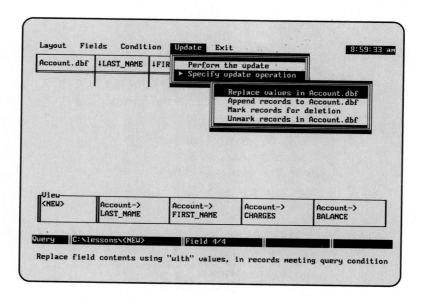

The view skeleton will disappear. Now you can enter a replacement instruction in the BALANCE field of the file skeleton that will increase each nonzero value by five percent. This instruction must begin with the word "with" followed by an expression. Other conditions may then follow to select the records to be updated. Follow these directions:

Type **with balance * 1.05**
Press **Down Arrow**
Type **> 0**
Press **Enter**

Your screen should look like Figure 15.

Step 5: Perform the Update

So far, you have just specified the update operation. Now tell dBASE IV to actually perform the update operation. Activate the Update menu and select Perform the Update:

Press **Alt-U**
Type **p**

When dBASE IV is finished updating the file, it will prompt you to press any key to continue.

Press **Enter**

Step 6: Examine the Data Base File

To see the changes you have made, execute the Data command to display the Browse screen and move to the beginning of the file:

Press **F2**
Press **Ctrl-PgUp**

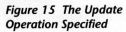

Figure 15 The Update Operation Specified

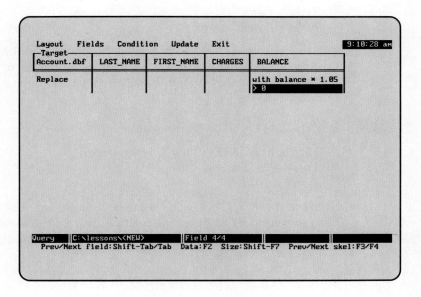

Figure 16 After Performing the Update Query

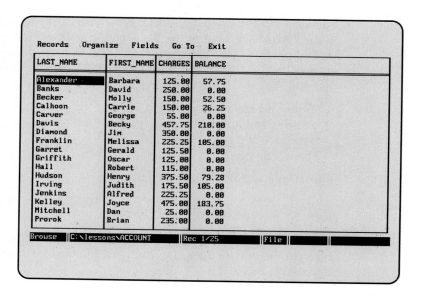

Your screen should look like Figure 16. All of the nonzero BALANCE values have been increased by five percent. For example, Barbara Alexander's balance was $55.00. Now it is $57.75, $2.75 more (five percent of $55.00).

Step 7: Save the Update Query

The update query you have created is one that Paddle and Portage will want to use again. Return to the Query Design screen, save the update query in a file named LATE, and then exit to the Control Center:

Press	**Alt-E**
Type	**t**
Press	**Alt-E**
Type	**s**
Type	**late**
Press	**Enter**

The program will create a file named LATE.UPD on the disk and return to the Control Center (see Figure 17). Note that the names of update query files are preceded by an asterisk (*) in the Queries panel.

Practice   Run the LATE update query again:

Highlight	**LATE** (in the Queries panel)
Press	**Enter** (2 times)
Type	**y**

Examine the ACCOUNT file on the Browse screen. The nonzero balances have been increased by five percent again. Return to the Control Center.

**Figure 17 LATE.UPD Saved
in the Queries Panel**

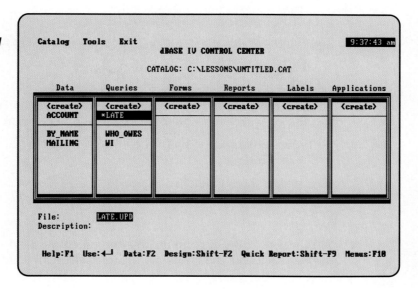

Lesson 6: Using Calculated Fields

A **calculated field** contains the result of an expression instead of a value entered directly in a data base file. Calculated fields are not stored in data base files, but they can be created in views, forms, and reports. For example, suppose you want to see how much each Paddle and Portage customer has paid toward his or her balance so far. This exact information is not stored, but it can be calculated from the CHARGES and BALANCE fields in ACCOUNT.DBF. Let's create a view query that includes a calculated field named PAID, which shows how much each customer has paid so far.

Step 1: Select the Data Base File

The data you want to manipulate is in the ACCOUNT data base file. The Control Center should be on your screen. Tell dBASE IV that you want to use ACCOUNT.DBF if it is not already in use:

Move	to the Data panel
Highlight	**ACCOUNT**
Press	**Enter** (2 times)

Step 2: Create a New View Query

Move into the Queries panel and select the <create> option:

Press	**Right Arrow**
Highlight	**<create>**
Press	**Enter**

The program will present a new Query Design screen with ACCOUNT.DBF in the file skeleton and all of the ACCOUNT fields in the view skeleton.

Step 3: Create the Calculated Field

Activate the Fields menu and select Create Calculated Field:

Press   **Alt-F**
Type   **c**

The program will display the calculated field skeleton between the file skeleton and the view skeleton. Enter the expression to perform the calculation:

Type   **charges - balance**
Press   **Enter**

Your screen should look like Figure 18.

Step 4: Add the Calculated Field to the View

You must tell dBASE IV to include the calculated field you have just created in the view. Activate the Fields menu and select Add Field to View:

Press   **Alt-F**
Type   **a**

The program will prompt you to enter a name for the calculated field.

Type   **paid**
Press   **Enter**

The calculated field, now named PAID, will be added to the right end of the view skeleton.

Step 5: Examine the View

Execute the Data command to display the Browse screen and examine the view you have created:

Press   **F2**

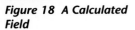

Figure 18 *A Calculated Field*

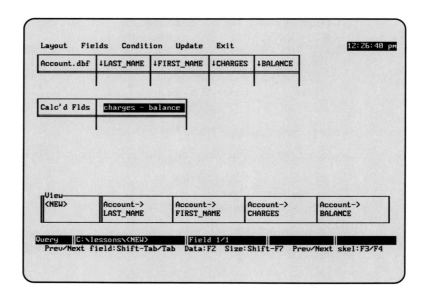

Figure 19 *The View Show-ing the Calculated Field*

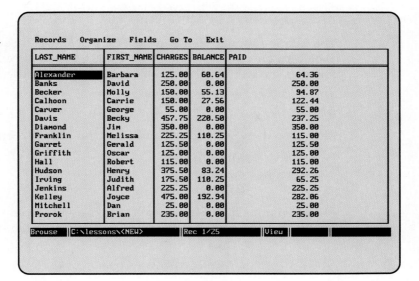

Figure 19 shows the result. For each record, the contents of the PAID field is calculated by subtracting the value in the BALANCE field from the value in the CHARGES field.

Step 6: Return to the Control Center

You do not need to save this view query, so exit the Browse screen and return to the Control Center:

Press **Alt-E**
Type **e**
Type **n**

Practice   Create a view of ACCOUNT.DBF that includes a calculated field named LATE_FEE. Calculate the contents of LATE_FEE by multiplying the contents of BALANCE by 0.05. Display the Browse screen to examine your work. When you are finished, return to the Control Center without saving the view query.

Lesson 7: Summarizing Data

Suppose you want to add up all of the charges and all of the balances in the ACCOUNT data base file. The dBASE IV program provides several **summary operators,** also called **aggregate operators,** for performing such tasks in view queries. Five summary operators are available: SUM, AVG (or AVERAGE), MIN, MAX, and CNT (or COUNT). SUM adds up the values in a column of fields. AVG computes the arithmetic mean of a column of fields. MAX presents the maximum value and MIN presents the minimum value. CNT computes the number of values in a column of fields. Let's use the SUM operator in a view query to add up the values in the CHARGES and BALANCE fields in ACCOUNT.DBF.

Step 1: Select the Data Base File

The data you want to sum is in the ACCOUNT data base file. The Control Center should be on your screen and ACCOUNT should already be the current file. If it is not, you would tell dBASE IV that you want to use ACCOUNT.

Step 2: Create a New View Query

Move into the Queries panel and select the <create> option:

Press	**Right Arrow**
Highlight	**<create>**
Press	**Enter**

The program will present a new Query Design screen with ACCOUNT.DBF in the file skeleton and all of the ACCOUNT fields in the view skeleton.

Step 3: Enter the Summary Operators

You must place the summary operator you want to use in the column of the appropriate field. Move to the CHARGES field and enter the SUM operator:

Press	**Tab** (3 times)
Type	**sum**
Press	**Enter**

Now enter the summary operator in the BALANCE column as well:

Press	**Tab**
Type	**sum**
Press	**Enter**

Your screen should look like Figure 20.

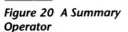

***Figure 20** A Summary Operator*

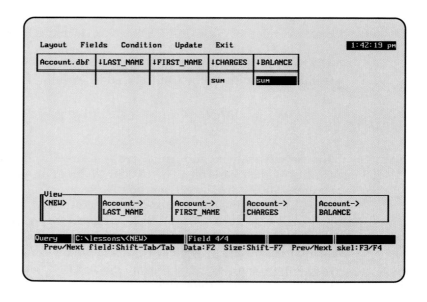

Figure 21 The Summary Values

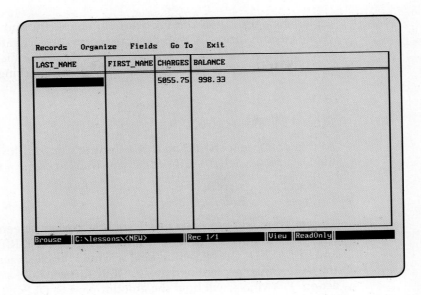

Step 4: Examine the View

Execute the Data command to display the Browse screen to see the view you have created:

Press   **F2**

Figure 21 shows the result. The program shows only the summary values in the appropriate columns. No records are displayed, and all the other fields are blank.

Step 5: Return to the Control Center

You do not need to save this view query, so exit the Browse screen and return to the Control Center:

Press   **Alt-E**
Type   **e**
Type   **n**

Practice   Create a view of ACCOUNT.DBF that computes the average of the CHARGES field and presents the maximum outstanding balance. Display the Browse screen to examine your work. When you are finished, return to the Control Center without saving the view query.

Lesson 8: Designing Custom Forms

You have learned how to display the contents of a data base file or a view on either the Browse screen or the Edit screen. The Browse screen is convenient for looking at a group of records at once. Its format is always a table; each row represents a record, and each column represents a field. The Edit screen is convenient for entering or modifying one record at a time. Unlike the Browse screen table, however, the form on the Edit screen can be redesigned. You can arrange the fields in different positions, draw boxes and lines for emphasis, include explanatory text, omit certain fields for simplicity, and add calculated fields to create custom forms. A well-designed form can facilitate data entry and reduce errors. As an example, let's create a new data base file named CHECKING to maintain Paddle and Portage Canoe Outfitters' checking account.

Step 1: Design the Data Base

At this point, you should be at the Control Center. Move the highlight bar into the Data panel. Tell dBASE IV that you want to create a new data base file:

Highlight   **<create>**
Press   **Enter**

The program will present a new Data Base Design screen. The CHECKING data base file will have six fields: NUMBER, DATE, DESCRIP, PAYMENT, DEPOSIT, and CLEARED. The NUMBER field will hold the check number. DATE will record the date of the payment or deposit. DESCRIP will hold a description of the transaction. PAYMENT will hold the amount paid or DEPOSIT will hold the amount deposited. CLEARED is a Logical field that will indicate whether the check has cleared. Fill in the field names, types, and widths shown in Figure 22. Check your work and correct any errors you make. When your screen matches Figure 22, save the data base design:

Press   **Alt-E**
Type   **s**
Type   **checking**
Press   **Enter**

The program will return to the Control Center.

Figure 22 The Data Base Design for CHECKING.DBF

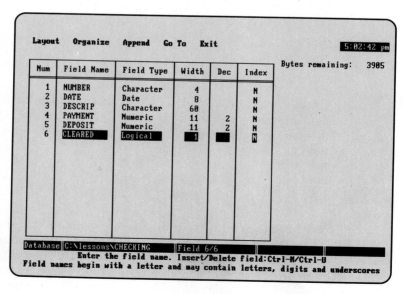

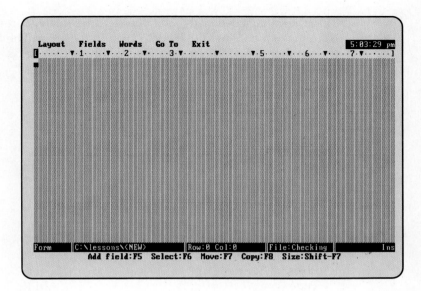

Figure 23 The Form Design Screen

Step 2: Display the Form Design Screen

Before you enter any data for this data base file, you are going to design a custom form. Move the highlight bar to the Forms panel and select the <create> option:

Press	**Right Arrow** (2 times)
Highlight	**<create>**
Press	**Enter**

The Layout menu will be activated automatically. You do not need it right now, so make it disappear:

Press	**Escape**

Your screen will look like Figure 23. The Form Design screen has a menu bar, ruler line, shaded work surface, status bar, and message line. A blinking block cursor is in the upper left corner. Note that the status bar reports the current row and column of the cursor.

Step 3: Lay Out the Names and Fields

You can move the cursor to any position on the screen and type a descriptive name. Then you can activate the Fields menu, select the Add Field option, and select a field from the data base file. Follow these directions to lay out the name and field for NUMBER:

Move	the cursor to row 6, column 10
Type	**Number :**
Press	**Space Bar**
Press	**Alt-F**
Type	**a**
Type	**n**
Press	**Enter**
Press	**Ctrl-End**

The bright bar filled with Xs is the **field template.** It represents the width and contents of a data field to be displayed in the form. The Xs stand for characters; the number of Xs indicates the field width. Follow these directions to lay out the rest of the fields:

Move	the cursor to row 6, column 34
Type	**Date:**
Press	**Space Bar**
Press	**Alt-F**
Type	**a**
Type	**da**
Press	**Enter**
Press	**Ctrl-End**
Move	the cursor to row 6, column 60
Type	**Cleared:**
Press	**Space Bar**
Press	**Alt-F**
Type	**a**
Type	**c**
Press	**Enter**
Press	**Ctrl-End**
Move	the cursor to row 9, column 10
Type	**Payment:**
Press	**Space Bar**
Press	**Alt-F**
Type	**a**
Type	**p**
Press	**Enter**
Press	**Ctrl-End**
Move	the cursor to row 9, column 50
Type	**Deposit:**
Press	**Space Bar**
Press	**Alt-F**
Type	**a**
Type	**dep**
Press	**Enter**
Press	**Ctrl-End**
Move	the cursor to row 12, column 10
Type	**Description of Transaction:**
Move	the cursor to row 13, column 10
Press	**Alt-F**
Type	**a**
Type	**des**
Press	**Enter**
Press	**Ctrl-End**

At this point, your screen should look like Figure 24. In the field templates, 9s represent numeric data, "MM/DD/YY" stands for a date, and "L" refers to a Logical value (True or False).

Figure 24 The Names and
Fields Laid Out

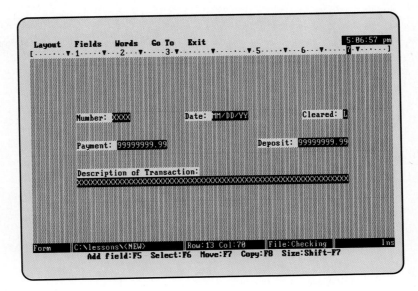

Step 4: Draw a Box

The Box option of the Layout menu lets you draw a box on the form. Boxes are
often used to visually group related information or just to make the form appear
more attractive. Follow these directions to draw a double-line box around the
fields in your form:

Move	the cursor to row 4, column 8
Press	**Alt-L**
Type	**b**
Type	**d**
Press	**Enter**
Move	the cursor to row 15, column 71
Press	**Enter**
Press	**Home**

Your screen should look like Figure 25.

Step 5: Enter a Title

How about a title for the form?

Move	the cursor to row 4, column 14
Type	**Paddle and Portage Canoe Outfitters Checking Account**

Step 6: Save the Form

You are now finished designing the form. Save it in a file named CHECKING
and return to the Control Center:

Press	**Alt-E**
Type	**s**
Type	**checking**
Press	**Enter**

The program will generate the form and create a file named CHECKING.SCR in
the Forms panel of the Control Center.

**Figure 25 A Box Around
the Form**

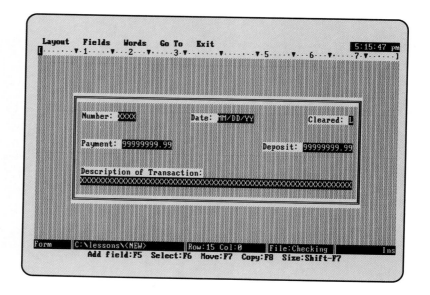

— **Step 7: Use the Form**

To use a form for data entry or modification, first highlight its name in the Forms panel. The CHECKING form should already be highlighted. Execute the Data command to display the Edit screen:

> Press **F2**

The program will display a blank data entry form on the screen. Follow these directions to enter data into the form:

> Type   **001**
> Press   **Enter**
> Type   **010191**
> Type   **f**
> Press   **Enter**
> Type   **25000**
> Press   **Enter**
> Type   **Initial deposit to open account**

Your screen should look like Figure 26. Now return to the Control Center:

> Press   **Alt-E**
> Type   **e**

Practice   1. Display the Edit screen again and add a second record to the CHECKING data base file using the customized form. Make up the data for a payment record.

2. Execute the Design command to display the Form Design screen:

> Press   **Shift-F2**

Move the cursor to the PAYMENT field template. Activate the Fields menu, select Modify Field, and then select Template:

> Press   **Alt-F**
> Type   **m**
> Type   **t**

Figure 26 The Form on the Edit Screen

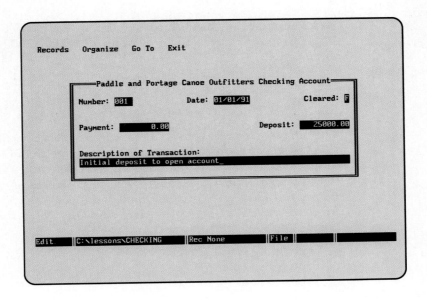

Tell dBASE IV to display the contents of the PAYMENT field as a currency value:

Press **Home**
Press **Ctrl-Y**
Type   **$999,999.99**
Press **Enter**
Press **Ctrl-End**

Repeat the procedure for the DEPOSIT field. Then save the changes, return to the Control Center, execute the Data command to display the Edit screen, and see the result. When you are finished examining your work, return to the Control Center.

Lesson 9: Designing Custom Reports

You can use a report to print data you have stored with dBASE IV. In the previous chapter, you learned how to use the Quick Report command (Shift-F9) to print the contents of a data base file in a table format. Quick Report is easy to use, but it is not very flexible. It does not give you much control over the placement of fields on the page and does not let you add explanatory text. One way to select and arrange the fields in a report is to create a view query and then print a Quick Report from the view. But this still limits you to an inflexible, table-style report. The best way to produce customized output from your data base files is to design reports. If you design your own reports with dBASE IV, you can

- group related data together.
- print fields exactly where you want them.
- control pagination.
- perform calculations and summary statistics on data.
- insert custom headings and other text.
- insert data into text to create form letters.

As an example, let's create a custom report that prints output from both MAIL-ING.DBF and ACCOUNT.DBF by using the WHO_OWES view query you created in Lesson 4.

Step 1: Select the View Query File

Custom reports are generated directly from a data base file or from a view query. If you want a report to present data from more than one file, you must create a view that links the files. In Lesson 4, you created the WHO_OWES view query, which displays the names, addresses, and balances of customers who still owe money to Paddle and Portage Canoe Outfitters. You will create a custom report from this view. First, select the view query file. Move the highlight bar into the Queries panel.

Highlight	**WHO_OWES**
Press	**Enter**
Type	**u**

The program will make WHO_OWES.QBE the current file.

Step 2: Display the Report Design Screen

Now move the highlight bar into the Reports panel.

Press	**Right Arrow** (2 times)
Highlight	**<create>**
Press	**Enter**

The program will present the Report Design screen and automatically activate the Layout menu (see Figure 27).

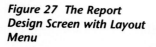

Figure 27 The Report Design Screen with Layout Menu

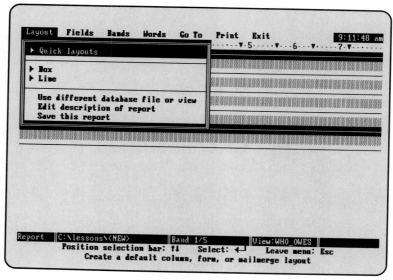

Figure 28 The Quick Layout

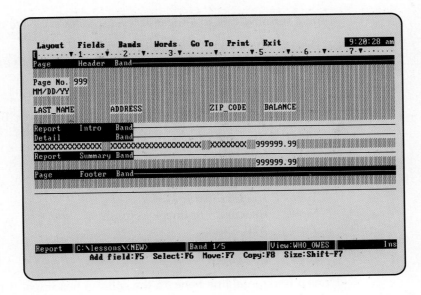

Step 3: Create a Quick Layout

It is often easiest to generate a default report layout, then modify the design to suit your specific needs. Select the Quick Layouts option from the Layout menu, then select the Column Layout option:

    Type   **q**
    Type   **c**

The program will create the report design shown in Figure 28.

Step 4: Examine the Report Design Screen

The work surface of the Report Design screen is divided into report bands. A **report band** is a logical piece of a report design. The Page Header Band contains information printed at the top of every page of the report. In this case, the Page Header Band includes the page number, the date, and a heading for each data column. The Report Intro Band contains text that appears only at the beginning of a report. You might use the Report Intro Band to print a cover letter explaining the report. The Report Intro Band in your report is empty right now. Next is the Detail Band, which presents the actual data from the records in the data base file or view. The Report Summary Band contains information that appears at the end of a report, such as concluding remarks or final totals. In this case, the Report Summary Band contains a calculated field for the total outstanding balances. Finally, the Page Footer Band contains information printed at the bottom of every page. Your Page Footer Band is empty, but it could be used to print a running title or the page number.

Step 5: Modify the Page Header Band

Let's spruce up the report layout. If "Ins" appears in the status bar at the right edge of the screen, turn off insert mode:

    Press   **Down Arrow**
    Press   **Insert**

Type a running title to appear at the top of every page of the report:

Move	the cursor to line 1, column 17
Type	**Paddle and Portage Canoe Outfitters**
Move	the cursor to line 2, column 20
Type	**Outstanding Customer Balances**

Now change the column headings in the Page Header Band as follows.

Move	the cursor to line 4, column 0
Type	**Customer**
Press	**Space Bar**
Move	the cursor to line 4, column 17
Type	**Street Address**
Move	the cursor to line 4, column 39
Type	**ZIP Code**
Move	the cursor to line 4, column 51
Type	**Balance**

Draw a horizontal line beneath the column headings. Follow these directions to activate the Layout menu, select the Line option, select the Single Line option, and specify the endpoints:

Press	**Alt-L**
Type	**L**
Type	**s**
Move	the cursor to line 5, column 0
Press	**Enter**
Move	the cursor to line 5, column 58
Press	**Enter**

Step 6: Modify the Report Summary Band

You do not need a Report Intro Band, and the default Detail Band is fine. Let's draw a line below the last record in the table and type a name for the total outstanding balances.

Press	**Home**
Move	the cursor into the Report Summary Band
Move	the cursor to line 0, column 0
Press	**Insert**
Press	**Enter**
Press	**Insert**
Press	**Up Arrow**
Press	**Alt-L**
Type	**L**
Type	**s**
Press	**Enter**
Move	the cursor to line 0, column 58
Press	**Enter**
Move	the cursor to line 1, column 22
Type	**Total Outstanding Balances**
Press	**Home**

Your screen should look like Figure 29.

Figure 29 The Completed Report Design

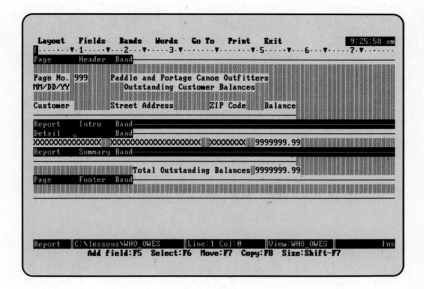

Step 7: Save the Report Design

The report design is complete. Save it so that it can be used again. Activate the Exit menu, select Save Changes and Exit, and name the report file WHO_ OWES:

Press	**Alt-E**
Type	**s**
Type	**who_owes**
Press	**Enter**

The program will return to the Control Center.

Step 8: View the Report on the Screen

Before you print a report, you can view it on your screen. First, highlight the name of the report you want to see in the Reports panel of the Control Center. This is already done. Tell dBASE IV that you want to use the highlighted report file:

Press	**Enter**

The program will present a menu with three options: Print Report, Modify Layout, and Display Data. Select the Print Report option:

Type	**p**

The program will then present the Print menu. Select the View Report On Screen option:

Type	**v**

Your screen will look like Figure 30. Except for the bottom line, the screen shows how the report will look when it is printed. When you are finished examining the screen, return to the Control Center:

Press	**Escape**
Press	**Enter**

Figure 30 The Custom Report Viewed on the Screen

```
Page No.    1     Paddle and Portage Canoe Outfitters
08/18/91              Outstanding Customer Balances

Customer         Street Address        ZIP Code    Balance

Alexander        102 White              21233         60.64
Becker           402 Main               48106         55.13
Calhoon          809 Maple              54880         27.56
Davis            7822 Kostner           60652        220.50
Franklin         2012 Anderson          92314        110.25
Hudson           1007 Barclay           44309         83.24
Irving           1329 Grandview         31728        110.25
Kelley           805 Randolf            12207        192.94
Quinlan          311 Southmoor          33030         55.13
Savage           2209 Philo             84720         27.56
Young            1104 Grand             99502         55.13

                 Total Outstanding Balances          998.33


        Cancel viewing: ESC,   Continue viewing: SPACEBAR
```

Step 9: Prepare the Printer

Make sure the printer is connected to the computer and turned on. Also, make sure that paper is loaded and aligned to the top of a new page. Finally, make sure that the printer's On Line light is lit. (If it isn't, press the On Line button.)

Step 10: Print the Custom Report

To print an existing custom report from the Control Center, move the highlight bar into the Reports panel and highlight the name of the report you want to print. This is already done. Tell dBASE IV that you want to use the highlighted file, select Print Report, and select Begin Printing:

Press	**Enter**
Type	**p**
Type	**b**

The report will be output on your printer.

Practice   Modify the WHO_OWES report design so that the Balance figures and total are presented in a financial format. Follow these directions:

Move	the cursor to the BALANCE field template
Press	**Alt-F**
Type	**m**
Type	**p**
Type	**f**
Press	**Ctrl-End** (2 times)

Repeat this process for the TOTAL field template. When you are finished, activate the Print menu and view the report on the screen. Save the modified report layout and return to the Control Center.

Lesson 10: Creating Mailing Labels

Data base management packages are often used to maintain mailing lists and print mailing labels. Fortunately, dBASE IV makes it easy to create and print mailing labels from the records stored in a data base file. As an example, let's print mailing labels for Paddle and Portage Canoe Outfitters from MAILING.DBF.

Step 1: Select the Mailing List Data Base File

First, select the data base file from which you want to create the mailing labels. Move the highlight bar into the Data panel.

Highlight	**MAILING**
Press	**Enter**
Press	**Enter**

Step 2: Display the Label Design Screen

Now, tell dBASE IV that you want to create a mailing label:

Press	**Right Arrow** (4 times)
Highlight	**<create>**
Press	**Enter**

The program will display the Label Design screen, shown in Figure 31.

Step 3: Select the Label Dimensions

The dBASE IV program is already set up to handle the most popular label sizes and arrangements. The default size is $^{15}/_{16}$ by 3½ inches by 1. The 1 refers to one label across the page. Let's tell dBASE IV to create the same size label but to put

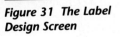

Figure 31 The Label Design Screen

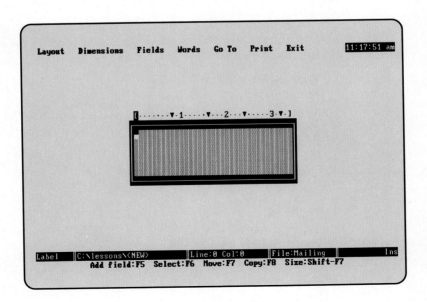

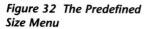

Figure 32 The Predefined Size Menu

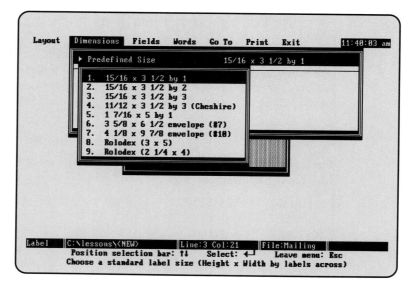

two labels across the page. Activate the Dimensions menu and select the Pre-defined Size option:

Press **Alt-D**
Type   **p**

Figure 32 shows the menu of predefined label sizes that will appear on the screen. The first option is the default size. Select the second option to print two standard-size labels across a page:

Type   **2**

The program will return to the Label Design screen.

Step 4: Add the Fields

The work surface in the center of the screen is where you design the layout of your mailing labels. Follow these directions to place the fields of MAILING.DBF on the label work surface:

Press **Down Arrow**
Press **Alt-F**
Type   **a**
Type   **f**
Press **Enter**
Press **Ctrl-End**

Press **Space Bar**
Press **Alt-F**
Type   **a**
Type   **L**
Press **Enter**
Press **Ctrl-End**

Press **Home**
Press **Down Arrow**

**Figure 33 The Completed
Label Design**

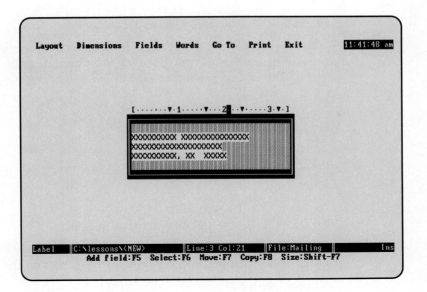

Press	**Alt-F**
Type	**a**
Type	**a**
Press	**Enter**
Press	**Ctrl-End**

Press	**Home**
Press	**Down Arrow**
Press	**Alt-F**
Type	**a**
Type	**c i**
Press	**Enter**
Press	**Ctrl-End**

Type	**,**
Press	**Space Bar**
Press	**Alt-F**
Type	**a**
Type	**s**
Press	**Enter**
Press	**Ctrl-End**

Press	**Space Bar** (2 times)
Press	**Alt-F**
Type	**a**
Type	**z**
Press	**Enter**
Press	**Ctrl-End**

All the necessary fields have been placed on the mailing label. Your screen should
look like Figure 33.

Step 5: Save the Label Design

Paddle and Portage Canoe Outfitters will want to use this mailing label design over and over again, so you should save it in a disk file named MAILING.LBL. Activate the Exit menu and select Save Changes and Exit:

Press **Alt-E**
Type **s**
Type **mailing**
Press **Enter**

The program will generate a file named MAILING.LBL and return to the Control Center.

Step 6: View the Labels on the Screen

The file MAILING.LBL is already selected in the Labels panel of the Control Center. Follow these directions to view the labels on the screen:

Press **Enter**
Type **p**
Type **v**

Your screen should look like Figure 34. View the rest of the labels:

Press **Space Bar**

After each screen, press the Space Bar to continue. When you have seen all of the labels, dBASE IV will return to the Control Center.

Step 7: Prepare the Printer

Make sure the printer is connected to the computer and turned on. Also, make sure that paper is loaded and aligned to the top of a new page. If you were really printing labels, you would insert blank label sheets instead of ordinary paper

Figure 34 The Mailing Labels Viewed on the Screen

```
Mike Skubic              Oscar Griffith
321 Gregory              805 Florida
Champaign, IL  61820     Urbana, IL  61801


George Carver            David Banks
906 Busey                604 Armory
Brainerd, MN  56401      Green Bay, WI  54035


Susan Young              Dan Mitchell
1104 Grand               310 Paddock
Anchorage, AK  99502     Flagstaff, AZ  86001


Henry Hudson             Molly Becker
1007 Barclay             402 Main
Akron, OH  44309         Ann Arbor, MI  48106


         Cancel viewing: ESC,  Continue viewing: SPACEBAR
```

into the printer. Finally, make sure that the printer's On Line light is lit. (If it isn't, press the On Line button.)

Step 8: Print the Labels

To print labels from the Control Center, move the highlight bar into the Labels panel and highlight the name of the label design you want to use. This is already done. Tell dBASE IV that you want to use the highlighted file, select Print Label, and select Begin Printing:

> Press   **Enter**
> Type   **p**
> Type   **b**

The labels will be output on your printer.

Practice   Activate the Label Design screen for MAILING.LBL and change the label dimensions to $^{15}/_{16} \times 3\frac{1}{2} \times 1$. Save the modified label design. View the labels on the screen, then print them. Return to the Control Center.

Lesson 11: Using Applications

The dBASE IV package has a powerful built-in programming language. In the next chapter, you will learn how to use the dBASE language to create programs that can perform several separate tasks with a single command. Large programs created with the dBASE language are sometimes called applications. The Applications panel of the Control Center is a place where you can put dBASE applications and other programs. Then you can conveniently select and run these programs from the Control Center. As an example, let's create a very simple dBASE program and store it in the Applications panel.

Step 1: Select the <create> Option

Unless some programs have already been created and stored in the Applications panel, your Applications panel should be empty. You can create a new application. Move to the Applications panel in the Control Center.

> Highlight   **<create>**
> Press   **Enter**

The program will present a box with two options: dBASE Program and Applications Generator. The first option activates the word-wrap editor, a text editor that you can use to type in a dBASE program. The second option activates the **Applications Generator,** an easy-to-use tool for creating a customized data base system without programming. Select the first option to activate the editor:

> Press   **Enter**

The word-wrap editor will appear on your screen (see Figure 35).

Step 2: Type the dBASE Program

In the word-wrap editor, you can type in a dBASE program. As an example, let's create a simple program that will contain only one command: Browse. The Browse command tells dBASE IV to present the Browse screen and display the contents

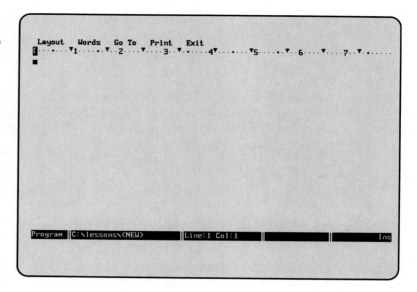

*Figure 35 The Word-Wrap
Editor for Typing a dBASE
Program*

of the current data base file in a table. If no data base file is active, the Browse command will prompt you to enter a file name. Type the Browse command into the word-wrap editor, save the program under the name BROWSE, and return to the Control Center:

Type   **browse**
Press   **Alt-E**
Type   **s**
Type   **browse**
Press   **Enter**

The dBASE IV program will create a file named BROWSE.PRG and return to the Control Center. You should see BROWSE listed in the Applications panel (see Figure 36).

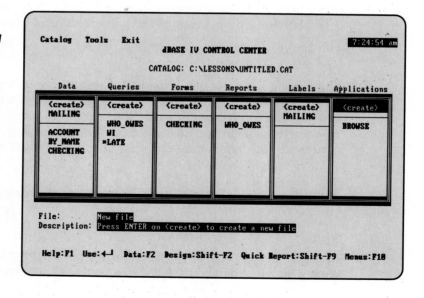

*Figure 36 BROWSE Listed
in the Applications Panel*

Step 3: Run a dBASE Application

To run the program you have created, highlight BROWSE in the Applications panel, press Enter, and select the Run Application option:

Press **Down Arrow**
Press **Enter**
Type **r**
Type **y**

The BROWSE program will be compiled and executed. If no data base file is currently selected, the program will prompt you for a name. If it asks, do this:

Type **mailing**
Press **Enter**

The program will then present the Browse screen, just as if you had pressed F2 to execute the Data command. Obviously, the BROWSE program you have created is very simple and unnecessary, but it illustrates how you can create and run an application from the Control Center. Return to the Control Center:

Press **Alt-E**
Type **e**

Practice Use the word-wrap editor to create an application named EDIT that will contain the single dBASE IV command Edit. Run the application from the Control Center. What does it do? Use the Escape key to return to the Control Center when you are finished examining the screen.

Lesson 12: Using the Catalog Menu

Examine the Control Center screen. By now you have studied and used all of the panels: Data, Queries, Forms, Reports, Labels, and Applications. In this lesson, you will learn more about the Catalog menu. The next lesson will examine the Tools menu. The Exit menu, which you have already used, contains only two options: Exit to Dot Prompt and Quit to DOS. You will learn about the dot prompt in the next chapter. You have already used the Quit to DOS option.

Step 1: Activate the Catalog Menu

Display the Catalog menu on your screen:

Press **Alt-C**

Your screen should look like Figure 37.

Step 2: Examine the Catalog Menu

As you work with dBASE IV, it is likely that you will create many data base files, queries, forms, reports, applications, and other files. Catalogs can help you organize and identify your files. A dBASE IV catalog is simply a list of file names, locations, and descriptions. You decide which files to put in a catalog and which catalog you want to use. Although both dBASE IV catalogs and DOS subdirectories are used to organize files, they are different. A subdirectory contains files on your disk. A catalog merely lists files. When you delete a file from a subdirectory, it

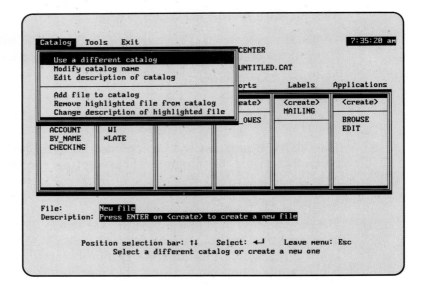

Figure 37 The Catalog Menu

is removed from the disk. When you remove a file from a catalog, its name is removed from the catalog, but the file can still remain on the disk. Catalogs are often used to group all the files needed for a particular job, office, department, or person. You can have as many different catalogs as you want. The purpose of catalogs is to shorten the lists of files that appear in the panels of the Control Center.

Step 3: Select Use a Different Catalog

When you start dBASE IV, the Control Center automatically loads the catalog you used last. If you have not created any catalogs yet, dBASE IV will create the first catalog for you. This initial catalog is named UNTITLED.CAT, and it contains all of the dBASE IV files in your current directory. The first option in the Catalog menu lets you create a new catalog or select an existing catalog.

Type **u**

The program will present a menu with the <create> option and a list of the available catalogs. Select <create> to create a new catalog, or select the name of the existing catalog you want to use. Return to the Catalog menu:

Press **Escape**

Step 4: Select Modify Catalog Name

The second option in the Catalog menu lets you change the name of an existing catalog.

Type **m**

The program will prompt you for a new name for your current catalog, which should be UNTITLED.CAT.

Press **Home**
Press **Ctrl-Y**
Type **lessons**
Press **Enter**

Your catalog will now be called LESSONS.CAT. Activate the Catalog menu again:

Press   **Alt-C**

Step 5: Select Edit Description of Catalog

The third option in the Catalog menu lets you create or change the description of a catalog.

Type   **e**
Type   **Microcomputer Applications Lessons**
Press **Enter**

This catalog description will now appear whenever you choose the Use a Different Catalog option. Activate the Catalog menu again:

Press   **Alt-C**

Step 6: Select Add File to Catalog

The fourth option of the Catalog menu lets you add a file to the current catalog. Each panel of the Control Center can contain up to 200 files.

Type   **a**

The program will present a list of the files in the current subdirectory that are relevant to the current Control Center panel. You simply choose the files you want to include. Return to the Catalog menu:

Press   **Escape**

Step 7: Select Remove Highlighted File From Catalog

The fifth option in the Catalog menu lets you remove the highlighted file from the catalog. It also lets you delete the file from the disk. If no file is highlighted in the current panel, you cannot select this option. As an example, let's remove and delete the EDIT file that you created in the Practice exercise of the previous lesson.

Press   **Escape**
Highlight   **EDIT** (in the Applications panel)
Press   **Alt-C**
Type   **r**
Type   **y**
Type   **y**

EDIT will be removed from the Applications panel and deleted from the disk.

Step 8: Select Change Description of Highlighted File

The last option in the Catalog menu lets you create or change the description of the currently highlighted file. This description will then appear on the Control Center screen below the panels. Follow these directions to create a description for BROWSE in the Applications panel:

Highlight   **BROWSE** (in the Applications panel)
Press   **Alt-C**
Type   **c**
Type   **Sample application to execute Browse command**
Press   **Enter**

The program will return to the Control Center screen. Note the file description that now appears below the panels.

 Practice   Create a file description for each file in all panels of your Control Center screen.

Lesson 13: Using the Tools Menu

The Tools menu of the Control Center provides a number of options that perform useful functions within dBASE IV. Let's briefly examine the options of the Tools menu.

Step 1: Activate the Tools Menu

Display the Tools menu on your screen:

Press   **Alt-T**

Your screen should look like Figure 38.

Step 2: Select Macros

The Macros option of the Tools menu lets you create, modify, and use keyboard macros. A **keyboard macro** records keystrokes that you plan to use over and over again. After you create a macro, you can play back the recorded keystrokes automatically. Macros can save time by reducing a long sequence of repetitive keystrokes to just a few keystrokes.

Type   **m**

The program will display a menu that lets you record, modify, and play back macros. Macros can be a time-saving feature, but we won't discuss them further in this chapter. Return to the Tools menu:

Press   **Escape**

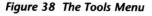

Figure 38 The Tools Menu

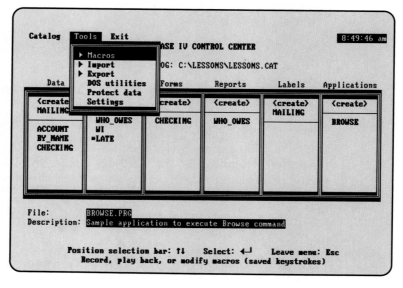

Step 3: Select Import

The Import option of the Tools menu lets you read data created by some programs other than dBASE IV.

Type   **i**

A menu of program names will appear on the screen. These are the programs from which you can import data. For example, you could select Lotus 1-2-3 to create a dBASE IV data base file from a worksheet file with a .WK1 extension. Return to the Tools menu:

Press   **Escape**

Step 4: Select Export

The Export option of the Tools menu lets you create data files that can be read by programs other than dBASE IV.

Type   **e**

A menu of programs and data file formats will appear on the screen. Most data base, spreadsheet, and word processing packages can read files created with a format from this list. Return to the Tools menu:

Press   **Escape**

Step 5: Select DOS Utilities

The DOS utilities option presents a screen that contains its own menu bar and a directory listing.

Type   **d**

Figure 39 shows the result. The directory listing that appears on your screen will depend on the files in your current subdirectory. The menus available on the DOS Utilities screen provide many options for managing disk files. Some of these options duplicate operations that can be performed from DOS, such as deleting, copying, and renaming files. Many of the options available from the DOS Utilities menus, however, go beyond DOS. They are similar to the functions available with a DOS shell. Return to the Tools menu:

Press   **Escape**
Type   **y**
Press   **Alt-T**

Step 6: Select Protect Data

The Protect Data option of the Tools menu lets you assign passwords to your data files.

Type   **p**

This feature can be used to control access to sensitive information. It is most often used on local area networks and on computers used by many different people to prevent unauthorized access to dBASE IV and private data files. You should not use Protect Data unless you are familiar with dBASE IV security measures. Return to the Tools menu:

Press   **Escape**

Figure 39 The DOS Utilities Screen

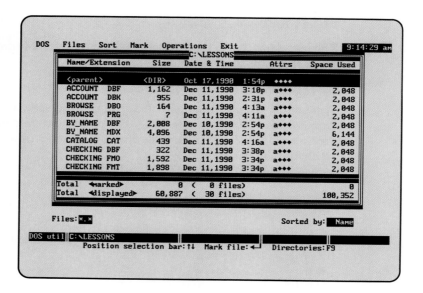

Step 7: Select Settings

The Settings option of the Tools menu lets you customize the way dBASE IV displays and handles data.

> Type   **s**

The Settings screen contains a menu bar with three options: Options, Display, and Exit. The Options menu is automatically invoked when you select the Settings option. It lets you set certain default dBASE IV options. Now examine the Display menu:

> Press   **Right Arrow**

The Display menu lets you change the colors assigned to different parts of dBASE IV if you have a color monitor. Return to the Control Center:

> Press   **Escape**

Practice

1. Activate the Tools menu and select the DOS Utilities option. Use the Down Arrow key to highlight BY_NAME.DBF in the directory listing. Activate the Operations menu and select the Delete option to delete this file. Delete BY_NAME.MDX too. Return to the Control Center.

2. Activate the Control Center's Exit menu and select the Quit to DOS option.

Summary

- *Using memo fields.* A memo field must be specified in the data base design. To enter text in a memo field, move the cursor to that field and press Ctrl-Home.

- *Creating view queries.* Execute the <create> option in the Queries panel and enter filter conditions in the file skeleton.

- *Creating relational data bases.* A relational data base includes two or more files with at least one field in common.

- *Linking files.* You must link files to create a view that displays data from more than one file. The files are placed on the Query Design screen and an example variable is placed in the common field to link the files.

- *Creating update queries.* Activate the Update menu from the Query Design screen and specify the update operation.

- *Using calculated fields.* Calculated fields can be created in views, forms, and reports to present values computed from data fields.

- *Summarizing data.* Summary operators can be used in view queries to compute the sum, average, minimum, maximum, or count of a data field.

- *Designing custom forms.* Execute the <create> option in the Forms panel and lay out the names and fields on the Form Design screen.

- *Designing custom reports.* Execute the <create> option in the Reports panel and complete the desired report bands on the Report Design screen.

- *Creating mailing labels.* Execute the <create> option in the Labels panel and lay out the fields on the Label Design screen.

- *Using applications.* Execute the <create> option in the Applications panel to use the word-wrap editor or Applications Generator to produce a dBASE program.

- *Using the Catalog menu.* Activate the Catalog menu to help you organize and identify your dBASE IV files.

- *Using the Tools menu.* Activate the Tools menu to create keyboard macros, import and export files, use the DOS utilities, protect data, and select default dBASE IV settings.

Key Terms

As an extra review of this chapter, try defining the following terms.

Applications Generator	relational data base
calculated field	relational operator
example variable	report band
field template	Soundex search
file skeleton	summary (aggregate) operator
filter condition	update query
keyboard macro	view
link field	view query
memo marker	view skeleton
query	

Multiple Choice

Choose the best selection to complete each statement.

1. Which type of data base field would you use to hold a half page of text?
   (a) Character
   (b) Logical
   (c) Memo
   (d) Text

2. Which key(s) do you press to activate the word-wrap editor to enter or view the contents of a Memo field?

   (a) Home   (b) Ctrl-Home

   (c) Enter   (d) Ctrl-Enter

3. What type of query would you use to correct a consistent error made throughout an entire data base?

   (a) link query   (b) Soundex query

   (c) update query   (d) view query

4. Which skeleton lists the fields that actually will be displayed by a query?

   (a) calculated field skeleton   (b) file skeleton

   (c) link field skeleton   (d) view skeleton

5. A data base that includes two or more files with at least one field in common is called a

   (a) common data base.   (b) flat-file data base.

   (c) query data base.   (d) relational data base.

6. What is a symbol or word that specifies how two items are to be compared?

   (a) example variable   (b) link field

   (c) logical operator   (d) relational operator

7. Which of the following filter conditions would retrieve all the records that contain the substring "old" anywhere in the specified field?

   (a) $"old"   (b) Like "old*"

   (c) Sounds Like "old"   (d) = "old"

8. Which operation is not available for an update query?

   (a) Alphabetize   (b) Mark

   (c) Replace   (d) Unmark

9. Which type of field is not actually stored in a data base file, but can be created in views, forms, and reports?

   (a) calculated field   (b) character field

   (c) float field   (d) numeric field

10. Which of the following terms is **not** a summary operator available for use in view queries?

    (a) AVG   (b) SQRT

    (c) MAX   (d) SUM

11. Which screen is redesigned when you create a custom form?

    (a) Browse screen   (b) Edit screen

    (c) View screen   (d) Help screen

12. Which symbol represents the contents of a character field in a field template?

    (a) L   (b) MM/DD/YY

    (c) 9   (d) X

13. Custom reports are generated directly from a data base file or from a(n)

    (a) entry form.   (b) mailing label.

    (c) update query.   (d) view query.

14. Which report band specifies the placement of the data fields in a report?

    (a) Report Intro Band   (b) Detail Band

    (c) Report Summary Band   (d) Page Footer Band

15. What is the default predefined size for mailing labels?

    (a) $15/16 \times 3\frac{1}{2} \times 1$ (b) $15/16 \times 3\frac{1}{2} \times 3$

    (c) $3\frac{5}{8} \times 6\frac{1}{2}$ (d) Rolodex (3×5)

16. Which Control Center panel lists dBASE programs created with the word-wrap editor or Applications Generator?

    (a) Applications   (b) Labels

    (c) Reports   (d) Forms

17. Which menu is not available on the Control Center screen?

    (a) Catalog   (b) Tools

    (c) Field   (d) Exit

18. In dBASE IV, a list of file names, locations, and descriptions is called a

    (a) catalog.   (b) menu.

    (c) tool.   (d) subdirectory.

19. Which Tools menu option would you use to record and play back keystroke sequences?

    (a) Macros   (b) DOS Utilities

    (c) Protect Data   (d) Settings

20. Which Tools menu option would you use to see a directory listing and delete a file?

    (a) Macros   (b) DOS Utilities

    (c) Protect Data   (d) Settings

Fill-In

1. The _____ field type allows you to include a block of text in a data base record.

2. A _____ is a set of instructions that lets you retrieve, display, organize, or edit data.

3. A _____ is an arrangement of data on the screen.

4. Query-by-Example or QBE is the approach used by dBASE IV on the _____ Design screen.

5. A _____ condition is an expression that determines which records are selected for a view.

6. A relational data base includes two or more files with at least one _____ in common.

7. A _____ search finds words that sound like the word you specify.

8. Files are _____ by placing the same example variable in the common field.

9. An _____ query allows you to make changes to selected records throughout an entire data base file.

10. A _____ field contains the result of an expression instead of a value entered directly into a data base file.

11. The _____ operator can be used in a view query to add up the values in a column of fields.

12. The Form Design screen can be used to customize the form presented on the _____ screen.

13. A field _____ represents the width and contents of a data field on the Form Design, Report Design, and Label Design screens.

14. The work surface of the Report Design screen is divided into report _____.

15. You can specify the size of a mailing label design by activating the _____ menu.

16. Programs written in the dBASE IV programming language can be created and run from the _____ panel on the Control Center screen.

17. A dBASE IV _____ is a list of file names, locations, and descriptions.

18. The Use a Different Catalog option in the Catalog menu allows you to load an existing catalog or _____ a new catalog.

19. The _____ menu of the Control Center contains options for importing and exporting dBASE IV files.

20. The Protect Data option of the Tools menu lets you assign _____ to your data files.

Short Problems

1. Add the following text to the COMMENTS field of Dan Mitchell's record in the MAILING data base file:

   Dan would like us to supply a full-size axe instead of a small hatchet for chopping firewood.

   Return to the Control Center.

2. Create and perform a view query of ACCOUNT.DBF that will display the FIRST_NAME, LAST_NAME, and CHARGES fields of all customers who have balances equal to zero. Save the view query in a file named PAID and return to the Control Center.

3. Create and perform a view query of MAILING.DBF that will display only the cities, states, and ZIP codes, sorted by city. Examine the Browse screen and then return to the Control Center.

4. Create and perform an update query to change each "WI" to "WS" in the STATE field of MAILING.DBF. Use the following replacement instruction in the STATE field:

   "WI", with "WS"

   Note that the comma is necessary and it must be outside the quotation mark. Examine the modified data base file on the Browse screen. Return to the Query Design screen. Change the "WS" entries back to "WI" entries and perform the update again. Return to the Control Center without saving the update query.

5. Create and perform an update query to mark all MAILING.DBF records with "IL" in the STATE field for deletion. Examine the altered file on the Browse screen. Highlight a record of a customer from Illinois. Note that the record still appears on the Browse screen, but it is marked for deletion as indicated by the "Del" in the status bar. Now modify your update query to unmark all of the records of customers from Illinois. Perform the update. Return to the Control Center without saving the update query.

6. Modify the CHECKING form to automatically enter today's date in the DATE field. Place the cursor on the DATE field, activate the Fields menu, select

Modify Field, select Edit Options, and then select Default Value. Follow these instructions:

Type   **date ( )**
Press **Enter**
Press **Ctrl-End** (2 times)

Now use what you have learned to assign the initial value .F. to the CLEARED field. (A period must be entered before and after the F.) Execute the Data command to display the form, and add a new record to see the results of your modifications. Return to the Control Center.

7. Make up and add at least ten records to the CHECKING data base file.

8. Create a custom report of the CHECKING data base file. Use the Quick Layouts option of the Layout menu. Summary fields that will add up the payments and deposits will be created automatically by dBASE IV. Modify the summary field for PAYMENT to name it PSUM. Modify the summary field for DEPOSIT to name it DSUM. Create a new calculated field in the Report Summary Band named BALANCE. Enter this expression to compute the BALANCE: DSUM − PSUM. Save the report in a file named BALANCE. Print the report or view it on the screen. When you are finished, return to the Control Center.

9. Design a custom data entry form for the MAILING data base file.

10. Activate the DOS Utilities option of the Tools menu. Then execute the Help command to read more about this feature.

Long Problems

1. In Long Problem 1 of the previous chapter, you created a data base file of information about your collection of LP records, cassette tapes, and compact discs. Create a custom data entry form, a useful view query, and a custom report for this data base file.

2. In Long Problem 2 of the previous chapter, you created a data base file containing your personal property inventory. Create a custom data entry form, a useful view query, and a custom report for this data base file.

3. In Long Problem 3 of the previous chapter, you created an "electronic Rolodex" with dBASE IV. Create a custom data entry form, a useful view query, and a custom report for this data base file. In addition, print mailing labels of all your records.

4. In Long Problem 4 of the previous chapter, you created a data base file to keep track of student grades. Create a custom data entry form, a useful view query, and a custom report for this data base file.

5. In Long Problem 5 of the previous chapter, you created a data base file of information about the courses you have taken in your college career. Create a custom data entry form, a useful view query, and a custom report for this data base file.

6. In Long Problem 6 of the previous chapter, you created a data base file to keep track of car expenses. Create a custom data entry form, a useful view query, and a custom report for this data base file.

7. In Long Problem 7 of the previous chapter, you created a data base file containing your academic schedule. Create a custom data entry form, a useful view query, and a custom report for this data base file.

8. In Long Problem 8 of the previous chapter, you created a data base file of information about your books. Create a custom data entry form, a useful view query, and a custom report for this data base file.

9. In Long Problems 9 and 10 of the previous chapter, you created a data base of information about the fifty states. Create a custom data entry form, a useful view query, and a custom report for this data base file.

10. Design a relational data base of your own choosing made up of two separate files linked by a common field. Create custom data entry forms for your files. Enter at least twenty records for each file using the forms you have created. Generate and save a useful view query that links the files and presents information from both. Design and print a custom report based on the view query you have created. Try to use what you have learned about summary and calculated fields.

ADVANCED dBASE IV

In This Chapter

Preview

Chapters 4 and 5 taught you most of what the average user needs to know about dBASE IV. This chapter proceeds to more advanced data base management topics. You may not need all of the commands and features presented in this chapter, but many of them can make your work easier, quicker, and less tedious. Learning more about dBASE IV can help you maintain more complex and powerful data base systems.

After studying this chapter, you will know how to

- access the dot prompt.
- examine a data base file from the dot prompt.
- enter and modify records from the dot prompt.
- delete records from the dot prompt.
- sort and index a file from the dot prompt.
- find data from the dot prompt.
- relate files from the dot prompt.
- use other dBASE IV commands.
- use dBASE IV functions.
- create a dBASE IV program.
- use the Applications Generator.
- use SQL commands.

Getting Started

You've already learned how to start dBASE IV and use its basic features and commands. This chapter assumes you have completed all of the lessons and exercises in Chapters 4 and 5. Furthermore, it assumes that you have a computer with a hard disk and dBASE IV installed on it in a subdirectory named DBASE. A DOS path should be set up so that you can run dBASE IV from within any subdirectory. You should have a subdirectory named LESSONS in which to store your data base files.

Lesson 1: Accessing the Dot Prompt

In the previous two chapters you learned how to use the Control Center, the menu-system interface of dBASE IV. The Control Center is easy to learn and convenient, and it lets you perform most basic data base management tasks. Advanced users, however, sometimes prefer to use the **dot prompt,** the command-line interface of dBASE IV. Instead of choosing options from menus, you can enter commands directly at the dot prompt, named for the dot (.) that appears on the screen. Using dot prompt commands requires more knowledge of dBASE IV, but it is faster, more flexible, and allows access to features not available from the Control Center. Learning dot prompt commands is a prerequisite to dBASE programming, because dBASE programs are made up of commands that are very similar to dot prompt commands. They might seem a little cryptic at first, but once you learn them, dot prompt commands are a quick and efficient way to harness the full power of dBASE IV.

Step 1: Start dBASE IV

If you are not already running dBASE IV, switch to your LESSONS subdirectory and start the program:

Type **cd \lessons**
Press **Enter**
Type **dbase**
Press **Enter** (2 times)

The Control Center will appear on your screen.

Step 2: Exit to the Dot Prompt

The Control Center is automatically activated when you start dBASE IV. Switch to the dot prompt by selecting the Exit to Dot Prompt option from the Exit menu:

Press **Alt-E**
Type **e**

Your screen will look like Figure 1. The dot prompt and a blinking cursor appear at the lower left of the screen, just above the status bar. You enter dBASE commands at the dot prompt, just as you enter DOS commands at the DOS prompt.

Step 3: Enter a Dot Prompt Command

Let's start with a simple example. The dBASE IV command DIR is similar to the DOS command DIR. It displays a list of the data base files in your current directory. To execute a dot prompt command, type it and press the Enter key:

Type **dir**
Press **Enter**

Figure 2 shows the result. After the command is executed, the information scrolls up the screen and a new dot prompt appears.

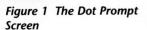

Figure 1 The Dot Prompt Screen

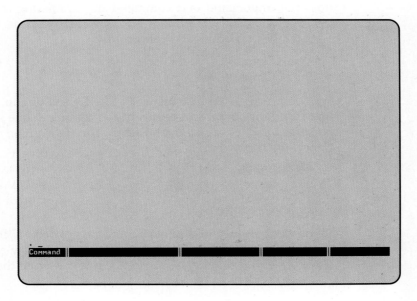

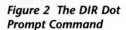

Figure 2 The DIR Dot Prompt Command

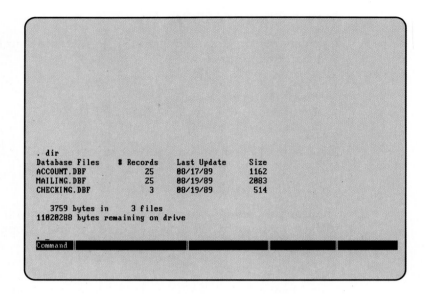

```
. dir
Database Files    # Records    Last Update    Size
ACCOUNT.DBF           25        08/17/89       1162
MAILING.DBF           25        08/19/89       2083
CHECKING.DBF           3        08/19/89        514

    3759 bytes in     3 files
11020288 bytes remaining on drive
.
┌──────────┐
│ Command  │
└──────────┘
```

Note that you may enter dot prompt commands in uppercase or lowercase letters. Only the first four letters of any command are necessary. A command such as DISPLAY, for example, could be executed by entering just "disp." If you make a mistake before you press the Enter key, you can use the Backspace key to erase characters and retype them. You can press the Left Arrow key or the Right Arrow key to move the cursor within the line, press the Insert key to insert characters, press the Delete key to delete characters, or press the Escape key to erase the entire command.

Step 4: Try an Invalid Command

You don't have a menu of options when using the dot prompt. It is possible, therefore, to enter an invalid command. If you enter a command that dBASE IV does not understand or a command that is missing required information, the program will display a prompt box with three choices: Cancel, Edit, and Help. For example, try an invalid command:

Type **xxx**
Press **Enter**

Your screen will look like Figure 3. The Cancel option will clear the command line. The Edit option will return to the command line so you can modify what you typed and try the command again. The Help option invokes the help system. Cancel the command:

Press **Enter**

Step 5: Get Help

If you enter an invalid command, you can get help by choosing the Help option from the prompt box. You can also press the F1 key, just as you do from the Control Center. Another way to get help is to execute the HELP command. Type

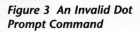

Figure 3 An Invalid Dot Prompt Command

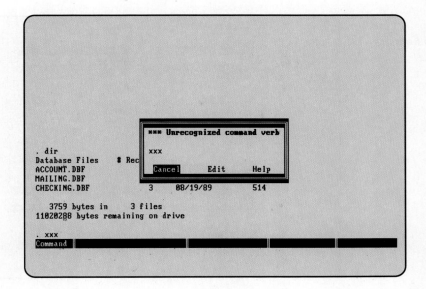

the command you want to learn about after typing "help." For example, to get help about the DIR command:

Type   **help dir**
Press   **Enter**

The help box containing information about the DIR command will appear on your screen (see Figure 4). When you are finished reading the help box, return to the dot prompt:

Press   **Escape**

Step 6: Clear the Screen

When you use the dot prompt, dBASE IV merely scrolls the screen up in response to each command. After several commands, your screen can get cluttered. Fortunately, you can use the CLEAR command to erase the screen.

Type   **clear**
Press   **Enter**

The screen will be erased.

Step 7: Return to the Control Center

Many seasoned dBASE IV users switch back and forth between the Control Center and the dot prompt. You can return to the Control Center from the dot prompt by executing the ASSIST command.

Type   **assist**
Press   **Enter**

The Control Center will appear on your screen. Now go back to the dot prompt:

Press   **Alt-E**
Type   **e**

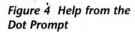

Figure 4 Help from the Dot Prompt

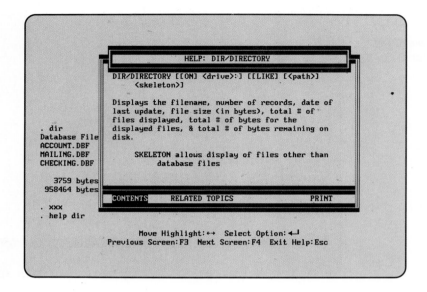

Step 8: Quit from the Dot Prompt

You don't have to return to the Control Center to exit dBASE IV. The QUIT command closes all open files, terminates the dBASE IV session, and returns to DOS.

Type **quit**
Press **Enter**

You should see the DOS prompt on your screen.

Practice

1. Start dBASE IV and activate the dot prompt.
2. Execute the HELP command to read about the QUIT command. Return to the dot prompt.
3. Switch to the Control Center from the dot prompt, then activate the dot prompt again.

Lesson 2: Examining a Data Base File

Every operation that can be performed from the Control Center can also be performed with dot prompt commands. For example, let's use dot prompt commands to open the MAILING data base file and examine its contents.

Step 1: Open a Data Base File

The USE command opens an existing data base file. Once a file is open you can use other dot prompt commands to examine the contents of the file or manipulate its data. Tell dBASE IV that you want to use MAILING.DBF:

Type **use mailing**
Press **Enter**

The program will make MAILING.DBF the current data base file, as revealed in the status bar. The current record is 1 of 25.

*Figure 5 The DISPLAY
STRUCTURE Command*

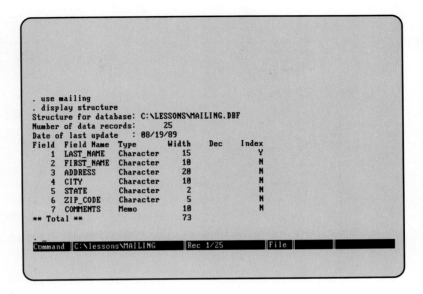

```
. use mailing
. display structure
Structure for database: C:\LESSONS\MAILING.DBF
Number of data records:      25
Date of last update   : 08/19/89
Field  Field Name  Type       Width   Dec   Index
    1  LAST_NAME   Character     15            Y
    2  FIRST_NAME  Character     10            N
    3  ADDRESS     Character     20            N
    4  CITY        Character     10            N
    5  STATE       Character      2            N
    6  ZIP_CODE    Character      5            N
    7  COMMENTS    Memo          10            N
** Total **                     73

.
Command  C:\lessons\MAILING         Rec 1/25          File
```

Step 2: Display the Structure of the File

Suppose you want to see the names, types, and widths of the fields in the current data base file. The DISPLAY STRUCTURE command will present this information on the screen.

> Type **display structure**
> Press **Enter**

Your screen should look like Figure 5.

Step 3: Display All of the Records

You can use a variation of the DISPLAY command to see all the records in a data base presented one screen at a time. Execute this command:

> Type **display all**
> Press **Enter**

Your screen should look like Figure 6. Examine the remaining records:

> Press **Enter** (2 times)

The LIST command is similar to the DISPLAY command, except that it scrolls the screen, if necessary, without pausing. For example, try the LIST ALL command:

> Type **list all**
> Press **Enter**

All the records will be listed on the screen without pauses.

Step 4: Move the Record Pointer

A unique record number is assigned to each record in a data base file. As you work with a file, dBASE IV keeps track of the current record number by means of the **record pointer**. When you open a file, the record pointer is set to the first record. Certain dot prompt commands change the record pointer. Displaying all

Figure 6 The DISPLAY ALL Command

```
Record#  LAST_NAME      FIRST_NAME ADDRESS              CITY        STATE ZIP_CO
DE COMMENTS
      1  Skubic         Mike       321 Gregory          Champaign   IL    61820
MEMO
      2  Griffith       Oscar      805 Florida          Urbana      IL    61801
memo
      3  Carver         George     906 Busey            Brainerd    MN    56401
memo
      4  Banks          David      604 Armory           Green Bay   WI    54035
memo
      5  Young          Susan      1104 Grand           Anchorage   AK    99502
memo
      6  Mitchell       Dan        310 Paddock          Flagstaff   AZ    86001
memo
      7  Hudson         Henry      1007 Barclay         Akron       OH    44309
memo
      8  Becker         Molly      402 Main             Ann Arbor   MI    48106
memo
      9  Franklin       Melissa    2012 Anderson        Big Bear    CA    92314
memo
     10  Savage         Julian     2209 Philo           Cedar City  UT    84720
Press any key to continue...
Command  C:\lessons\MAILING        Rec 1/25°        File
```

the records, for example, moves the record pointer from the first record to the end of the file. Examine the status bar. The EOF/25 means that the record pointer is now at the end of the file, past the last record. The GO command lets you change the record pointer. Move the record pointer to record number 12:

Type **go 12**
Press **Enter**

Move the record pointer to the last record in the file:

Type **go bottom**
Press **Enter**

Now move the record pointer to the first record in the file:

Type **go top**
Press **Enter**

Step 5: Display a Particular Record

You can see the contents of the current record with the DISPLAY command.

Type **display**
Press **Enter**

This command displays all of the fields in the record. You can tell dBASE IV to display only specific fields. Try this command:

Type **display last_name, city**
Press **Enter**

The program will display only the contents of LAST_NAME and CITY in the current record.

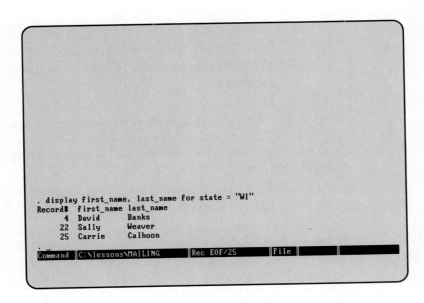

Figure 7 *A Group of Records Displayed*

```
. display first_name, last_name for state = "WI"
Record#  first_name last_name
      4  David      Banks
     22  Sally      Weaver
     25  Carrie     Calhoon
.
Command  C:\lessons\MAILING        Rec EOF/25      File
```

Step 6: Display a Group of Records

The DISPLAY and LIST commands can be followed by the word "FOR" and a condition to present the records that fulfill that condition. For example, suppose you want to see the names of all customers from Wisconsin. Execute this command:

Type   **display first_name, last_name for state = "WI"**
Press **Enter**

Figure 7 shows the result.

Step 7: Use the Logical Operators

More complex searches can be specified by using logical operators. A **logical operator** modifies the TRUE or FALSE result of one or two conditions. Three logical operators are available:

.NOT.	Changes TRUE to FALSE and FALSE to TRUE
.AND.	Produces TRUE only if both conditions are TRUE
.OR.	Produces FALSE only if both conditions are FALSE

Note that the periods before and after the logical operators are necessary for dBASE IV to identify them in expressions. Let's try each of the logical operators. Suppose you want to see the last names of all customers who do *not* live in Wisconsin. Execute this command:

Type   **list last_name for .not. state = "WI"**
Press **Enter**

The program will list only those last names from records in which the contents of the STATE field is not WI.

You can use the .AND. logical operator when you want to fulfill two conditions. Suppose you want to see the records of customers who live in Hometown, Illinois. A large data base might have records from several towns named Hometown in different states. Execute this expression to list only those records of customers from Hometown, Illinois:

Type **list last_name for state = "IL" .and. city = "Hometown"**

Press **Enter**

The program should present the last name Jenkins from record number 24.

The .OR. logical operator is used to fulfill either of two conditions. Suppose you want to see all the last names of customers who live in Illinois or Wisconsin. Execute this command:

Type **list last_name for state = "IL" .or. state ="WI"**

Press **Enter**

You should see the names Skubic, Griffith, Banks, Davis, Weaver, Jenkins, and Calhoon listed on the screen.

Step 8: Copy a List of Records to a Text File

By default, the LIST command presents data base records on the screen. It can also be used to copy data base records to an ordinary text file. This text file then can be read by any text editor or word processing program, or printed from DOS. Suppose you want to create a text file called NAMES.TXT from the MAILING data base. Execute this command:

Type **list first_name, last_name to file names.txt**

Press **Enter**

The names will be listed on your screen and also copied to a text file called NAMES.TXT in your current directory.

Step 9: Print a List of Records

The LIST command can also be used to copy data base records to the printer. Suppose you want to print the list of first names and last names in MAILING.DBF. Make sure your printer is turned on, on line, and loaded with paper. Then execute this command:

Type **list first_name, last_name to printer**

Press **Enter**

The names will be printed just as they appeared on the screen. Using LIST in this manner is a quick and easy way to obtain simple printed output. You can design and produce a custom report from the Control Center if you need a more sophisticated printout.

Step 10: Close a Data Base File

Several methods are available to close a data base file when you are finished working with it. You can execute the USE command without providing a file name:

Type **use**

Press **Enter**

The current data base file, in this case MAILING.DBF, will be closed. Another way to close a file is with the CLOSE command. The CLOSE command may be used when you have more than one file opened at a time. For example, execute this command to close all opened data base files:

Type   **close databases**
Press   **Enter**

Another way to close the current data base file is to open a different data base file. The current data base file will be closed automatically. For example, execute these commands:

Type   **use account**
Press   **Enter**
Type   **use mailing**
Press   **Enter**

The first USE command opens ACCOUNT.DBF. The second USE command closes ACCOUNT.DBF and opens MAILING.DBF.

Practice
1. Open the ACCOUNT data base file.
2. Display the current record.
3. Move the record pointer to record number 10, then display the current record.
4. Display all of the records in the file.
5. List only the LAST_NAME and BALANCE fields of all the records in the file.
6. Close the ACCOUNT data base file.

Lesson 3: Entering and Modifying Records

Entering and modifying records from the dot prompt is similar to entering and modifying records from the Control Center.

Step 1: Open the Data Base File

If the data base file you want to modify is not already open, you must open it. Tell dBASE IV that you want to use the MAILING data base file:

Type   **use mailing**
Press   **Enter**

Step 2: Add a Record

The APPEND command lets you add new records to the end of a new or existing data base file.

Type   **append**
Press   **Enter**

As Figure 8 shows, a blank data entry form will appear on the screen in which you can add a new record to the end of the current data base file. From this point, the procedure is the same as entering a new record from the Control Center. Follow these directions to enter a new record:

Type   **Eaton**
Press   **Enter**

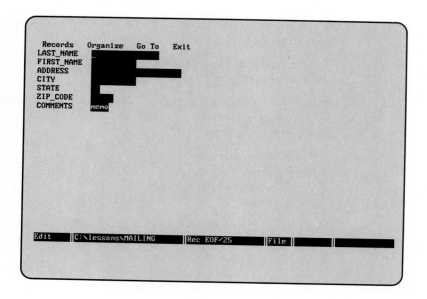

*Figure 8 A Blank Data
Entry Form Presented By
the APPEND Command*

Type	**Candy**
Press	**Enter**
Type	**2314 Sunset**
Press	**Enter**
Type	**Rantoul**
Press	**Enter**
Type	**IL**
Type	**61866**
Press	**Ctrl-Home**
Type	**Candy prefers the nylon Duluth packs.**
Press	**Ctrl-End**

If you have more records to add, you can press Enter, Tab, Down Arrow, or Page Down and answer "Yes" to the prompt to add new records. After you have entered all your new records, save the last record and return to the dot prompt:

Press **Ctrl-End**

Step 3: Edit an Existing Record

Several methods can be used to update and maintain a data base file from the dot prompt. The EDIT command lets you modify one record at a time. It activates the same Edit screen available from the Control Center. For example, execute this command:

Type **edit**
Press **Enter**

The program will display the Edit screen containing the current record, in this case Candy Eaton's record. You can modify the record by editing the contents of any field. Follow these directions to change the address in Candy Eaton's record:

Press **Down Arrow** (2 times)
Type **1458 Clearwater**
Press **Enter**
Type **Gary**
Press **Delete** (3 times)
Press **Enter**
Type **IN**
Type **46401**

If you want to change another record, you can press the Page Up or Page Down key to move within the file and display it on the Edit screen. Or, you can return to the dot prompt, move the record pointer to the record to be changed, and then execute the Edit command again. When you have finished editing a record, press Ctrl-End to save the record and return to the dot prompt.

Press **Ctrl-End**

Step 4: Display the Browse Screen

Another way to view, add, or edit records is to activate the Browse screen from the dot prompt. Execute the BROWSE command and move to the beginning of the file:

Type **browse**
Press **Enter**
Press **Ctrl-PgUp**

The result is the same as if you had activated the Browse screen from the Control Center. Return to the dot prompt without making any changes:

Press **Escape**

Step 5: Update Records

The REPLACE command lets you make a specific change to selected records throughout a data base file. Suppose you wanted to change all the "WI" abbreviations to "WS" in the STATE field. Execute the following command:

Type **replace all state with "WS" for state = "WI"**
Press **Enter**

Observe what you have done:

Type **list for state = "WS"**
Press **Enter**

Figure 9 shows the result. All the records that had "WI" in the STATE field now have "WS" in the STATE field.

Practice
1. Replace each "WS" with "WI" in the STATE field of the records in the MAILING data base file.
2. Activate the Browse screen to check your work. Return to the dot prompt when you are finished.

Figure 9 The REPLACE Command

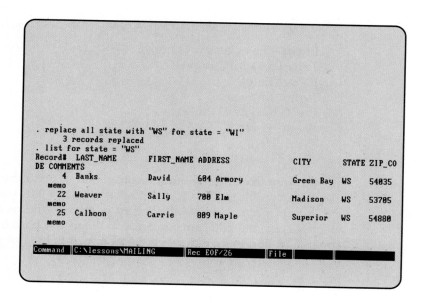

```
. replace all state with "WS" for state = "WI"
    3 records replaced
. list for state = "WS"
Record# LAST_NAME      FIRST_NAME ADDRESS            CITY      STATE ZIP_CO
DE COMMENTS
     4  Banks          David      604 Armory         Green Bay WS    54835
   memo
    22  Weaver         Sally      700 Elm            Madison   WS    53705
   memo
    25  Calhoon        Carrie     809 Maple          Superior  WS    54880
   memo
. _
```
```
Command  C:\lessons\MAILING        Rec EOF/26        File
```

Lesson 4: Deleting Records

Records can be deleted from a data base file when they are no longer needed.
Use the DELETE command from the dot prompt to mark one or more records
for deletion. You can use the RECALL command to unmark records marked for
deletion. The PACK command permanently removes the records marked for
deletion in the current data base file.

Step 1: Locate the Record to be Deleted

Unless otherwise specified, the DELETE command marks the current record for
deletion. Suppose you want to delete Candy Eaton's record. The first step is to
move the record pointer to her record. If you don't remember the exact record
number, you can use the LOCATE command to find it.

Type   **locate for last_name = "Eaton"**
Press **Enter**

The program will report the record number and move the record pointer to that
record.

Step 2: Execute the DELETE Command

After the record to be removed has been located, execute the DELETE command
to mark the record for deletion.

Type   **delete**
Press **Enter**

The program will report that one record has been deleted.
    If you know the record number of the record to be deleted, you can specify
it after the DELETE command and skip Step 1. For example, the following command could also be used to mark Candy Eaton's record for deletion:

delete record 26

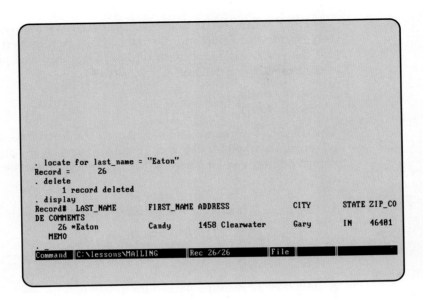

Figure 10 A Record Marked For Deletion

```
. locate for last_name = "Eaton"
Record =       26
. delete
      1 record deleted
. display
Record#  LAST_NAME     FIRST_NAME ADDRESS          CITY       STATE ZIP_CO
DE COMMENTS
     26 *Eaton         Candy      1458 Clearwater   Gary       IN    46401
   MEMO
._
Command  C:\lessons\MAILING        Rec 26/26        File
```

Step 3: Display the Record

The DELETE command does not actually remove a record from the data base file. It only marks the record for deletion. The record pointer remains in the same position. You can confirm the action of the DELETE command by displaying the record marked for deletion.

Type   **display**
Press **Enter**

As Figure 10 shows, Candy Eaton's record is displayed with an asterisk (*) after the record number, which indicates that the record is marked for deletion.

Step 4: Recall a Deleted Record

Suppose you change your mind about deleting Candy Eaton's record. A record marked for deletion can be reinstated in the data base file with the RECALL command. You can recall the current record, a particular record number, a group of records, or every record marked for deletion in the data base file. Recall Candy Eaton's record:

Type   **recall**
Press **Enter**

The program will report that one record has been recalled. To confirm that Candy Eaton's record has been reinstated, execute the DISPLAY command:

Type   **display**
Press **Enter**

The record will be displayed without an asterisk following the record number.

Step 5: Permanently Remove Deleted Records

Suppose you really do want to remove Candy Eaton's record from MAIL-ING.DBF. Mark it again for deletion:

Type   **delete**
Press **Enter**

The PACK command permanently removes all records marked for deletion. After you execute this command, the data cannot be retrieved. Obviously, you should use the PACK command with caution. Go ahead and permanently remove the record marked for deletion:

> Type   **pack**
> Press   **Enter**

The dBASE IV program will reconstruct the MAILING data base file, removing all records marked for deletion. It will also update any associated index files. The record pointer will be placed at the beginning of the file.

> **Practice**

1. Execute the following command to mark the records of customers from Wisconsin for deletion:

   > Type   **delete for state = "WI"**
   > Press   **Enter**

2. Reinstate all records marked for deletion:

   > Type   **recall all**
   > Press   **Enter**

Lesson 5: Sorting and Indexing

Data base files can be sorted and indexed easily from the dot prompt.

Step 1: Sort a Data Base File on One Field

The SORT command creates a new data base file in which the records from the current file are arranged in the specified order. Suppose you want to create a new data base file named BY_NAME.DBF that contains the records of MAILING.DBF arranged alphabetically by last name. Execute this command:

> Type   **sort to by_name on last_name**
> Press   **Enter**

To check your work, open BY_NAME.DBF and list its contents:

> Type   **use by_name**
> Press   **Enter**
> Type   **list**
> Press   **Enter**

The records of BY_NAME.DBF are arranged alphabetically by the contents of the LAST_NAME field.

Step 2: Sort a Data Base File on Several Fields

You can sort a data base file on more than one field. For example, you may want a file arranged by city, last name, then first name. Execute this command:

> Type   **sort to by_city on city, last_name, first_name**
> Press   **Enter**

Now, examine your work:

Type   **use by_city**
Press **Enter**
Type   **list**
Press **Enter**

The records are first arranged by the contents of the CITY field, then by LAST_NAME and FIRST_NAME within each city.

Step 3: Index a File

Indexing also arranges the records of a data base in a specified order. Rather than creating a new data base file, however, indexing creates an index file of field values and record numbers. Indexing is faster and usually takes up less disk space than sorting. In addition, index files are automatically updated whenever you make a change to the original data base file. Indexing is better than sorting if you often want to view your records in a particular order.

Two indexing methods are available in dBASE IV. The first method stores one index per index file, which is identified by the extension NDX. This is the method that was used with dBASE III PLUS and earlier versions of dBASE. You can still use this method of indexing in dBASE IV to remain compatible with earlier versions of the package. A better method of indexing, however, has been introduced with dBASE IV. This new method uses **multiple index files,** each of which can contain up to 47 separate indexes and is identified by the extension MDX. A default multiple index file is always opened with a data base file when you execute the USE command. Each individual index within a multiple index file is identified by its own unique tag. A **tag** is essentially the name of an index within a multiple index file.

In a previous chapter, you indexed the MAILING data base file by LAST_NAME. The multiple index file for MAILING.DBF, which is MAILING.MDX, already contains one index with the tag LAST_NAME. Suppose you want to index MAILING.DBF by STATE as well. Execute these commands:

Type   **use mailing**
Press **Enter**
Type   **index on state tag state**
Press **Enter**

A new index, tagged STATE, will be created and added to the multiple index file MAILING.MDX. The STATE index arranges the records of MAILING.DBF alphabetically by state.

Step 4: Activate an Index Tag

The default multiple index file of a data base file is automatically opened when you execute the USE command to open the data base file. No index tag, however, is automatically activated. Records are initially displayed in record number order, the order in which they were entered. You must use the SET ORDER command to rearrange the records on the basis of a tag in the multiple index file. Suppose you want to see the records of MAILING.DBF listed in STATE order. Execute these commands:

Type   **set order to tag state**
Press **Enter**
Type   **list**
Press **Enter**

**Figure 11 Records
Indexed By STATE**

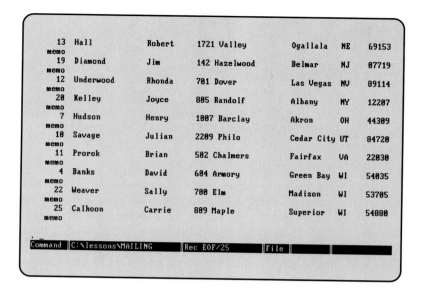

When the screen stops scrolling, it will look like Figure 11. The records are arranged alphabetically by state abbreviation.

Practice

1. Activate the LAST_NAME tag and list the records of MAILING.DBF in alphabetical order by last name:

   Type   **set order to tag last_name**
   Press **Enter**
   Type   **list**
   Press **Enter**

2. You can create an index based on two or more fields. Suppose you want to index a file by state and then by city within each state. Change the existing STATE tag:

   Type   **index on state + city tag state**
   Press **Enter**
   Press **Enter**

   To see the result, execute these commands:

   Type   **set order to tag state**
   Press **Enter**
   Type   **list for state = "IL"**
   Press **Enter**

   Note that the four records from Illinois are now arranged alphabetically by city name.

Lesson 6: Finding Data

Several dot prompt commands are available to help you find specific records within a data base file.

Step 1: Search with the LOCATE Command

The LOCATE command finds records based on the criteria you specify. You have already used this command in Lesson 4 to find Candy Eaton's record. Try it again, but this time use a more specific condition to find Brian Prorok's record:

Type   `locate for last_name = "Prorok" .and. first_name = "Brian"`

Press   **Enter**

Type   `display`

Press   **Enter**

The LOCATE command always begins its search at the top of the file, regardless of the current record pointer position. Note that the LOCATE command does not display the record; it merely advances the record pointer.

Step 2: Search for Several Records with LOCATE

The LOCATE command can be used to find several records that meet specified criteria. Suppose you want to see the records of all customers whose last names begin with the letter *W*. Execute these commands:

Type   `locate for last_name >= "W"`

Press   **Enter**

Type   `display`

Press   **Enter**

To continue searching for other records that begin with *W*, execute the CONTINUE command:

Type   `continue`

Press   **Enter**

Type   `display`

Press   **Enter**

Type   `continue`

Press   **Enter**

Type   `display`

Press   **Enter**

Type   `continue`

Press   **Enter**

When no more records are found, dBASE IV will display the message

`End of LOCATE scope`

Step 3: Use the SEEK Command

If a file is indexed and you want to search for records on the basis of the contents of a tag field, the SEEK and FIND commands are faster than the LOCATE command. Activate the LAST_NAME index tag:

Type   `set order to tag last_name`

Press   **Enter**

Suppose you want to see Dan Mitchell's record. Execute a SEEK command followed by a DISPLAY command:

Type   `seek "Mitchell"`

Press   **Enter**

Type   `display`

Press   **Enter**

The SEEK command advances the record pointer to the record that contains "Mitchell" in the field on which the file has been indexed. SEEK is much faster than LOCATE, especially in large data base files, because it uses an index.

Step 4: Use the FIND Command

The SEEK command can be followed by an expression of the same data type as the index field. The FIND command works even faster than the SEEK command because you can specify a character string not enclosed in quotes. For example, execute this command to see Susan Young's record:

    Type   **find Young**
    Press   **Enter**
    Type   **display**
    Press   **Enter**

Step 5: Set a Filter Condition

Many dBASE IV commands let you specify the word "FOR" followed by a condition that specifies the records you want to manipulate. Essentially, the FOR clause acts as a filter to select only certain records. The SET FILTER command allows you to specify a condition that selects records to be acted on by all subsequent commands. For example, suppose you want to work with only the records of customers from Illinois. Execute the following commands:

    Type   **set filter to state = "IL"**
    Press   **Enter**
    Type   **go top**
    Press   **Enter**

The GO command is necessary because you must move the record pointer after issuing a SET FILTER command for the filter to take effect. Any command you enter now will affect only those records with "IL" in the STATE field. For example, try this command:

    Type   **display all**
    Press   **Enter**

Your screen should look like Figure 12.

Step 6: Set Fields

The SET FILTER command limits the action of subsequent commands to a specified set of records. The SET FIELDS command can be used to limit the action of subsequent commands to a specified set of fields. Suppose you are interested only in the LAST_NAME, FIRST_NAME, and CITY fields. Execute this command to set the fields you want to use:

    Type   **set fields to last_name, first_name, city**
    Press   **Enter**

Now, list all of the records:

    Type   **list**
    Press   **Enter**

Figure 13 shows the result. The SET FILTER command limits the records to only those from Illinois, and the SET FIELDS command limits the fields to LAST_NAME, FIRST_NAME, and CITY.

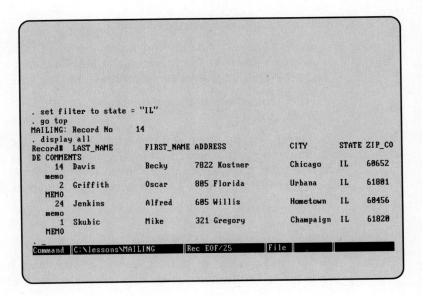

Figure 12 The SET FILTER Command

```
. set filter to state = "IL"
. go top
MAILING: Record No    14
. display all
Record# LAST_NAME        FIRST_NAME ADDRESS              CITY        STATE ZIP_CO
DE COMMENTS
     14 Davis            Becky      7822 Kostner         Chicago     IL    60652
   memo
      2 Griffith         Oscar      805 Florida          Urbana      IL    61801
   MEMO
     24 Jenkins          Alfred     605 Willis           Hometown    IL    60456
   memo
      1 Skubic           Mike       321 Gregory          Champaign   IL    61820
   MEMO

Command  C:\lessons\MAILING        Rec EOF/25        File
```

Step 7: Turn Off Filter and Fields

You can turn off a previous SET FILTER or SET FIELDS command by entering the command again without specifying a condition or list of fields. Execute these commands to include all records and fields in subsequent actions:

Type   **set filter to**
Press   **Enter**
Type   **set fields to**
Press   **Enter**

Execute the LIST command to confirm that all records and fields are now available:

Type   **list**
Press   **Enter**

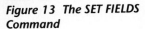

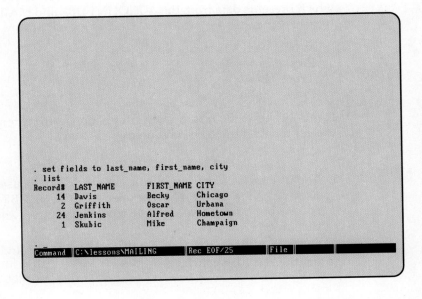

Figure 13 The SET FIELDS Command

```
. set fields to last_name, first_name, city
. list
Record# LAST_NAME        FIRST_NAME CITY
     14 Davis            Becky      Chicago
      2 Griffith         Oscar      Urbana
     24 Jenkins          Alfred     Hometown
      1 Skubic           Mike       Champaign

Command  C:\lessons\MAILING        Rec EOF/25        File
```

Step 8: Create or Modify Query Files

For more advanced data-finding capabilities, you can use view queries, which you learned about in the previous chapter. To create a new query file named EXAMPLE.QBE from the dot prompt, execute the CREATE QUERY command:

Type   **create query example**
Press   **Enter**

The Query Design screen will appear. Here you can specify conditions in the file skeleton and specify fields in the view skeleton just as you did in the previous chapter from the Queries panel of the Control Center. Let's not create a new query file. Exit the Query Design screen and return to the dot prompt:

Press   **Alt-E**
Type   **a**
Type   **y**

You can also modify an existing query file from the dot prompt. Use the DIR command to list the view query files in your current directory:

Type   **dir *.qbe**
Press   **Enter**

Tell dBASE IV that you want to modify the file WHO_OWES.QBE:

Type   **modify query who_owes**
Press   **Enter**

The program will display the Query Design screen containing the view query WHO_OWES. You could now modify the design. Let's leave it alone and return to the dot prompt:

Press   **Alt-E**
Type   **a**

Step 9: Use an Existing Query File

Once a view query has been designed, you can execute the SET VIEW command from the dot prompt to use it. Suppose you want to see the WHO_OWES view, which presents data from the ACCOUNT.DBF and MAILING.DBF files. Execute these commands:

Type   **set view to who_owes**
Press   **Enter**
Type   **list**
Press   **Enter**

Figure 14 shows the result. Only information from customers who have a balance greater than zero will be presented.

Practice

1. The CLEAR ALL or CLOSE ALL command can be used to close all open files. Execute either command, then open ACCOUNT.DBF. Set a filter condition to specify only those records with nonzero balances, and list all the records on the screen.
2. Tell dBASE IV to display only the LAST_NAME and BALANCE fields, and list the records again.

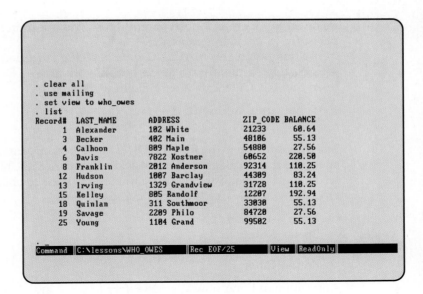

Figure 14 The SET VIEW Command

```
. clear all
. use mailing
. set view to who_owes
. list
Record#  LAST_NAME     ADDRESS            ZIP_CODE BALANCE
      1  Alexander     102 White          21233     60.64
      3  Becker        402 Main           48106     55.13
      4  Calhoon       809 Maple          54880     27.56
      6  Davis         7822 Kostner       60652    220.50
      8  Franklin      2012 Anderson      92314    110.25
     12  Hudson        1007 Barclay       44309     83.24
     13  Irving        1329 Grandview     31728    110.25
     15  Kelley        805 Randolf        12207    192.94
     18  Quinlan       311 Southmoor      33030     55.13
     19  Savage        2209 Philo         84720     27.56
     25  Young         1104 Grand         99502     55.13
.
Command  C:\lessons\WHO_OWES    Rec EOF/25    View  ReadOnly
```

3. Turn off the SET FILTER and SET FIELDS commands, and list the records again. Execute the CLEAR ALL command to close all open files.

Lesson 7: Relating Files

The dBASE IV program is a relational data base manager that can access and share information from several files at once. This ability to **relate** files allows you to create large, efficient, and flexible data base systems. In the previous chapter you learned how to link two files in a view query and display information from both. This lesson explores how you can relate multiple files from the dot prompt.

Step 1: Use Multiple Work Areas

A dBASE IV **work area** is a place in memory that holds an open data base file. Ten work areas are available. They are referred to by the numbers 1 to 10, by the letters A through J, or by the name of the file currently open in the work area. A number, letter, or name that refers to a work area or data base file is called an **alias** in dBASE IV. Open the MAILING data base file:

Type   **use mailing**
Press **Enter**

Unless you specify otherwise, a file opened with the USE command will be placed into work area 1. Only one data base file can be open at a time in any work area. In this case, the first work area can be referred to by any of these aliases: 1, A, or MAILING. The ALIAS function can be used to find out the default alias of the current work area. For example, execute this command:

Type   **? alias()**
Press **Enter**

The program will tell you that MAILING is the alias of the current work area. You will learn more about dBASE IV functions in a subsequent lesson. Basically, a **function** is a predefined expression that returns a value. Functions must be followed by open and close parentheses. The question mark command (?) displays the value of an expression.

At this point, the MAILING data base file is loaded into work area 1. The dBASE IV program always starts out in work area 1. Execute this command to open the ACCOUNT data base file in work area 2:

Type   **use account in 2**
Press   **Enter**

The program opens the file ACCOUNT.DBF in work area 2, but does not actually switch to that work area. Both MAILING and ACCOUNT are now open in different work areas. The SELECT command is used to change to a different work area. For example, try these commands:

Type   **select 2**
Press   **Enter**
Type   **? alias**()
Press   **Enter**

Any command you now execute refers to work area 2. Display the structure of the current file:

Type   **display structure**
Press   **Enter**

Your screen should look like Figure 15. Now change back to the work area that contains the MAILING data base file:

Type   **select mailing**
Press   **Enter**

The program will switch to work area 1, which can also be referred to by its aliases, A and MAILING.

Figure 15 MAILING in Work Area 1 and ACCOUNT in Work Area 2

```
. use mailing
. ? alias()
MAILING
. use account in 2
. select 2
. ? alias()
ACCOUNT
. display structure
Structure for database: C:\LESSONS\ACCOUNT.DBF
Number of data records:      25
Date of last update   : 08/17/89
Field  Field Name  Type       Width    Dec    Index
    1  LAST_NAME   Character     15              N
    2  FIRST_NAME  Character     10              N
    3  CHARGES     Numeric        7      2       N
    4  BALANCE     Numeric        7      2       N
** Total **                      40
.
Command  C:\lessons\ACCOUNT         Rec°1/25        File
```

Step 2: Index the Files

Before you can relate files, the files must have a field in common and they should be indexed on that field. The MAILING data base file is already indexed by LAST_NAME. Follow these directions to index the ACCOUNT file by LAST_NAME and activate the index tags in both files:

Type   `set order to tag last_name`
Press   **Enter**
Type   `select account`
Press   **Enter**
Type   `index on last_name tag last_name`
Press   **Enter**
Type   `set order to tag last_name`
Press   **Enter**
Type   `select mailing`
Press   **Enter**

Step 3: Execute the SET RELATION Command

After you have opened and indexed multiple files, you can execute the SET RELATION command to relate them. Execute this command:

Type   `set relation to last_name into account`
Press   **Enter**

Two files in a relation are often called parent and child files. The **parent file** is the more general file that looks up the information. The **child file** is the more specific file that contains the information. In this case, MAILING.DBF is the parent, and ACCOUNT.DBF is the child. More complex data bases can have multiple child relations, in which a parent file may have active links with several child files. Chains of relations are also possible. For example, a parent file can look up information in a child file, which in turn is a parent file that looks up information in another child file.

Step 4: List Fields from Multiple Files

Now that the two files are related, you can access data from both of them. You must, however, precede field names from the related file with the alias of that file and a pointer symbol ($->$). The pointer symbol is made up of a dash ($-$) and a greater than sign ($>$). Suppose you want to list the last names, cities, and balances of the customers. Execute this command:

Type   `list last_name, city, account->balance`
Press   **Enter**

The dBASE IV program will list the contents of LAST_NAME and CITY from MAILING, along with the matching contents of the BALANCE field from ACCOUNT (see Figure 16).

Step 5: Save the Relation Conditions

You can store the relationship you have established in a special view file with the CREATE VIEW FROM ENVIRONMENT command.

Type   `create view balances from environment`
Press   **Enter**

Figure 16 Fields Listed from MAILING and ACCOUNT

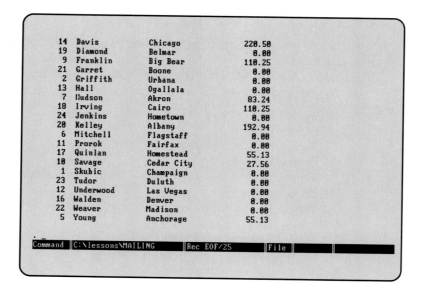

```
    14  Davis       Chicago        220.50
    19  Diamond     Belmar           0.00
     9  Franklin    Big Bear       110.25
    21  Garret      Boone            0.00
     2  Griffith    Urbana           0.00
    13  Hall        Ogallala         0.00
     7  Hudson      Akron           83.24
    18  Irving      Cairo          110.25
    24  Jenkins     Hometown         0.00
    20  Kelley      Albany         192.94
     6  Mitchell    Flagstaff        0.00
    11  Prorok      Fairfax          0.00
    17  Quinlan     Homestead       55.13
    10  Savage      Cedar City      27.56
     1  Skubic      Champaign        0.00
    23  Tudor       Duluth           0.00
    12  Underwood   Las Vegas        0.00
    16  Walden      Denver           0.00
    22  Weaver      Madison          0.00
     5  Young       Anchorage       55.13
```

```
Command  C:\lessons\MAILING        Rec EOF/25         File
```

The program will create a file named BALANCES.VUE that remembers all currently open files, relations, filters, and field lists. To use the view file sometime later, you would execute this command:

    SET VIEW TO BALANCES

Practice

1. List the contents of the LAST_NAME and STATE fields from MAILING, and the CHARGES field from ACCOUNT.

2. Execute the CLEAR ALL command to close all files. Tell dBASE IV that you want to use the BALANCES.VUE view file. Then list the last names, ZIP codes, and balances of all the customers with a balance greater than zero. Note that you must specify the alias ACCOUNT before both instances of the field name BALANCE. When you are finished, execute the CLEAR ALL command to close all files.

Lesson 8: Using Other dBASE IV Commands

The dBASE IV language includes more than 145 different commands, not including the 77 variations of the SET command. The *dBASE IV Language Reference* manual that explains these commands is several hundred pages long. Obviously, we cannot cover every dBASE IV command here. This lesson, however, briefly illustrates a few additional dBASE IV commands. See the Command Summaries appendix at the end of this book for a comprehensive list of dBASE IV commands.

Step 1: Use the ? Command

The ? command displays the value of one or more expressions. It is often used to display the result of a function. You have already seen how ? is used with the ALIAS function. Follow these directions to see other examples of the use of the ? command:

Type   **? date()**
Press   **Enter**

Type   **? time()**
Press   **Enter**

Step 2: Use the ACCEPT Command

The ACCEPT command prompts a user for a keyboard entry and stores the input in a character memory variable. A **memory variable** is a place in RAM that temporarily holds a data value. It is given a name and can contain a value used to perform a calculation, comparison, or other operation. Unlike the data values stored in the record fields of a data base file, the data values stored in memory variables are lost when you quit dBASE IV. The ACCEPT command, which reads a character value and assigns it to a memory variable, is used primarily in dBASE IV programs. Execute the following command to have dBASE IV prompt the user for his or her name and assign this name to a memory variable named M_NAME:

Type   **accept "Enter your name: " to m_name**
Press   **Enter**

The program will prompt you to enter your name. Type your name and press the Enter key. Now, use the ? command to display the value stored in M_NAME:

Type   **? m_name**
Press   **Enter**

Step 3: Use the CREATE Command

The CREATE command is used to design a new data base file from the dot prompt. It activates the Data Base Design screen, in which you enter the field names, types, and widths of your records. Suppose you want to create a new data base file named CUSTOMER. Execute this command:

Type   **create customer**
Press   **Enter**

Follow these directions to specify the fields and save the structure:

Type   **last_name**
Press   **Enter** (2 times)
Type   **15**
Press   **Enter** (2 times)
Type   **first_name**
Press   **Enter**
Type   **10**
Press   **Enter** (2 times)
Type   **address**
Press   **Enter** (2 times)
Type   **20**
Press   **Enter** (2 times)
Type   **city**
Press   **Enter** (2 times)
Type   **10**
Press   **Enter** (2 times)
Type   **state**
Press   **Enter** (2 times)
Type   **2**

Press **Enter** (2 times)
Type **zip**
Press **Enter** (2 times)
Type **5**
Press **Enter**
Press **Alt-E**
Type **s**
Press **Enter**

A new, but still empty data base file named CUSTOMER.DBF will be created.

Step 4: Use the APPEND FROM Command

The APPEND FROM command is used to copy records from an existing file, which does not have to be a dBASE IV file, to the current data base file. It is often used to import data from other programs, such as previous versions of dBASE and Lotus 1-2-3. Let's use the APPEND FROM command to copy the records from MAILING.DBF into the new CUSTOMER file:

Type **append from mailing**
Press **Enter**

The records from MAILING.DBF will be copied to CUSTOMER.DBF. Confirm this by executing the LIST command:

Type **list**
Press **Enter**

Step 5: Use the AVERAGE Command

The AVERAGE command computes the arithmetic mean of the numbers stored in the specified fields and records. Suppose you want to see the average outstanding balance of customers who have a balance greater than zero. Execute these commands:

Type **use account**
Press **Enter**
Type **average balance for balance > 0**
Press **Enter**

The result should be 90.76, as shown in Figure 17.

Step 6: Use the COPY Command

The COPY command creates a new file by duplicating all or part of the current data base file. It is often used to prepare data for use in programs other than dBASE IV. Suppose you want to create a Lotus 1-2-3 spreadsheet file from the current data base file. Execute this command:

Type **copy to account type wks**
Press **Enter**

The program will create a Lotus 1-2-3 file named ACCOUNT.WKS, with records converted to worksheet rows and fields converted to worksheet columns. The field names are written as column headers in the new file.

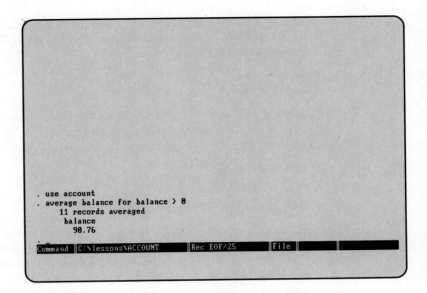

Figure 17   The AVERAGE Command

```
. use account
. average balance for balance > 0
    11 records averaged
    balance
      90.76
.
Command  C:\lessons\ACCOUNT      Rec EOF/25      File
```

Step 7: Use the COUNT Command

The COUNT command adds up the number of records in the current file that match the specified conditions. Suppose you want to know how many customers have balances greater than zero. Execute this command:

Type   **count for balance > 0**
Press   **Enter**

The program should count 11 records.

Step 8: Use the DO Command

The DO command executes a dBASE program. For example, in the previous chapter you created a short dBASE program named BROWSE.PRG that simply executes the BROWSE command. Execute this program from the dot prompt:

Type   **do browse**
Press   **Enter**

The BROWSE.PRG program will be compiled and executed. When it is finished, you should see the Browse screen. Return to the dot prompt:

Press   **Escape**

Step 9: Use the ERASE Command

The ERASE or DELETE FILE command removes a file from the disk. It is similar to the DOS ERASE or DEL command. Suppose you want to delete the file ACCOUNT.WKS. Execute this command:

Type   **erase account.wks**
Press   **Enter**

The file will be deleted from the disk immediately, with no confirmation prompt, so you should use the ERASE command with caution.

dBASE IV commands that accept a file name can usually be entered with a ? in place of the file name to display a menu of file names from which to choose. For example, execute this command:

Type   **erase ?**
Press **Enter**

The program will present a menu of all the files in the current directory (see Figure 18). If you highlight a file name and press the Enter key, that file will be deleted. Return to the dot prompt without erasing another file:

Press **Escape**

Step 10: Use the INSERT Command

The APPEND command adds a new record to the end of the current data base file. The INSERT command adds a new record to the data base file just after the current record. Suppose you want to add a new record with a record number of 10 to the current file. Move the record pointer to record 9 and execute the INSERT command:

Type   **go 9**
Press **Enter**
Type   **insert**
Press **Enter**

A blank data entry form will appear in which you can enter the data for the new record number 10. Let's not change the data base file. Abandon the INSERT command:

Press **Escape**

Step 11: Use the STORE Command

The STORE command creates one or more memory variables and initializes their contents. Suppose you want to create a memory variable named M_TOTAL and initially store the value 0 in it. Execute this command:

Type   **store 0 to m_total**
Press **Enter**

Another way to achieve the same result is to do this:

Type   **m_total = 0**
Press **Enter**

You can see the contents of a memory variable by using the ? command.

Type   **? m_total**
Press **Enter**

Step 12: Use the SUM Command

The SUM command adds up the contents of the specified fields and records. Suppose you want to see the sum of all charges. Execute this command:

Type   **sum charges**
Press **Enter**

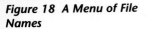

Figure 18 A Menu of File Names

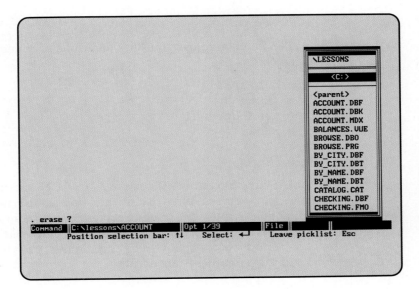

You can use the SUM command to assign a value to a memory variable too. Execute this command to compute the sum and store it in the memory variable M_TOTAL:

Type **sum charges to m_total**
Press **Enter**

Now, display the value of M_TOTAL:

Type **? m_total**
Press **Enter**

Practice

1. Compute the average of the CHARGES field in the ACCOUNT data base file and store the result in a memory variable named M_AVG.
2. Count the number of records in ACCOUNT.DBF with CHARGES greater than $100.

Lesson 9: Using dBASE IV Functions

A **function** is a predefined expression that returns a data value of a specific type. Functions are often used as parts of other expressions to perform calculations and manipulate text strings. Many dBASE IV functions are similar to functions found in spreadsheet packages, such as Lotus 1-2-3, and programming languages, such as BASIC and Pascal. The dBASE IV package has more than 125 built-in functions. Obviously, we cannot cover them all. This lesson presents only a few examples of dBASE IV functions. See the Command Summaries appendix at the end of this book for a more comprehensive list of dBASE IV functions.

Step 1: Use the ALIAS Function

The ALIAS function returns the alias name of a specified work area. Execute the following commands:

Type   **clear all**
Press **Enter**
Type   **use account**
Press **Enter**
Type   **? alias()**
Press **Enter**

The ALIAS function returns the name ACCOUNT and the ? command presents the name on the screen. Note that the function name is followed by parentheses. Some functions require one or more expressions to be supplied within the parentheses. Other functions, such as ALIAS, do not require any expressions. All function names must be followed by parentheses, even if they require no expressions and the parentheses are empty.

Step 2: Use the DATE Function

The DATE function returns the current date. Execute this command:

Type   **? date()**
Press **Enter**

The program will present the current date in the form mm/dd/yy.

Step 3: Use the DISKSPACE Function

The DISKSPACE function returns a number that represents the number of bytes available on the default disk drive. Execute this command:

Type   **? diskspace()**
Press **Enter**

The number returned is the amount of free space on the disk in bytes.

Step 4: Use the EOF Function

The EOF function returns a logical value (.T. for TRUE or .F. for FALSE) if the record pointer is past the last record in the file. Execute these commands:

Type   **go bottom**
Press **Enter**
Type   **? eof()**
Press **Enter**
Type   **skip**
Press **Enter**
Type   **? eof()**
Press **Enter**

The GO BOTTOM command moves the record pointer to the last record in the file, so the result of EOF() is .F. or FALSE. The SKIP command advances the record pointer one position, past the last record in the file. Then the result of EOF() is .T. or TRUE.

Step 5: Use the INT Function

The INT function truncates any numeric expression to create an integer value. For example, execute this command:

Type **i_value = 10 + int(25.45)**
Press **Enter**
Type **? i_value**
Press **Enter**

The first command is an example of using a function in an expression. The 25.45 is truncated to produce 25, which is added to the 10. The result displayed by the ? command is 35.

Step 6: Use the TRIM and LEN Functions

The dBASE IV language includes many functions that work with strings of characters. For example, the TRIM function removes the trailing blanks from a character string, and the LEN function returns the number of characters in a string. These two functions are often used together. Suppose you want to determine the length of the name in the LAST_NAME field of the first record in the current data base file. Execute these commands:

Type **go 1**
Press **Enter**
Type **? len(trim(last_name))**
Press **Enter**
Type **display**
Press **Enter**

The last name in the first record is Alexander, so the value returned by the LEN function is 9.

Step 7: Use the RECCOUNT, RECNO, and RECSIZE Functions

The RECCOUNT function returns the number of records in the current data base file. The RECNO function returns the record number of the current record. The RECSIZE function returns the number of bytes occupied by a record in the current data base file. Try these functions:

Type **? reccount()**
Press **Enter**
Type **? recno()**
Press **Enter**
Type **? recsize()**
Press **Enter**

Step 8: Use the ROUND Function

The ROUND function rounds a number to a specified number of decimal places. For example, try this command:

Type **? round(162.34789,2)**
Press **Enter**

The number after the comma in the parentheses is the number of decimal places, so the result is 162.35. Your screen should look like Figure 19.

Figure 19 dBASE IV
Functions

```
. ? eof()
.T.
. i_value = 10 + int(25.45)
        35
. ? i_value
        35
. go 1
ACCOUNT: Record No      1
. ? len(trim(last_name))
        9
. display
Record# LAST_NAME        FIRST_NAME CHARGES BALANCE
      1 Alexander        Barbara    125.00   60.64
. ? reccount()
        25
. ? recno()
        1
. ? recsize()
        40
. ? round(162.34789,2)
      162.35
. _
```
```
Command  C:\lessons\ACCOUNT      Rec 1/25       File
```

Practice

1. The SQRT function returns the square root of the specified number. Use this function to display the square root of 144.
2. The MEMORY function returns the amount of unused memory in kilobytes (1024-byte units). Use this function to display the amount of RAM you have free.
3. Use the TIME function to display the current time.
4. Use the VERSION function to display the dBASE version you are running.

Lesson 10: Creating a dBASE IV Program

A dBASE IV program is a sequence of commands stored in a text file that can be compiled and executed. It is similar to a DOS batch file or a program in a standard programming language, such as BASIC or Pascal. When you use the dot prompt, you enter a command, and it is executed immediately. When you create a dBASE program, you enter all the commands needed to perform some task into a text file. The commands are not actually executed by dBASE IV until you run the program later. The commands, functions, and expressions of dBASE IV make up a language as sophisticated as a standard programming language such as BASIC or Pascal. Obviously, we cannot cover all aspects of dBASE IV programming here. This lesson, however, will show you how to create a simple dBASE IV program.

Step 1: Design the Program

Suppose you want to create a program that will ask the user for a state abbreviation and then list on the screen the full names and addresses of all customers from that state in the MAILING data base file. The first step would be to design the program by deciding which dBASE IV commands are needed to complete this task. You would probably have to study dBASE commands further to design such a program yourself. In this lesson the program has been designed for you.

Step 2: Activate the Editor

A dBASE IV program can be entered into a text file with the word-wrap editor. Close all files and start up the editor to create a program file named STATE.PRG:

Type `clear all`
Press **Enter**
Type `modify command state`
Press **Enter**

The word-wrap editor screen will appear. Notice that the status bar indicates that you are editing a program named STATE.

Step 3: Enter the Program

Figure 20 shows the completed program. Type your program from the figure. When you are finished, check the program carefully against Figure 20 and correct any mistakes you made.

The program works as follows. The CLEAR command clears the screen. SET TALK OFF suppresses the messages that dBASE IV normally displays at the bottom of the screen. The SET PATH command establishes the internal path to the MAILING data base file. The next command creates a memory variable named M_STATE and stores an empty string in it. The USE command opens MAILING.DBF, and the ORDER clause activates the LAST_NAME index. The ACCEPT command prompts the user for input and stores the entry in the memory variable M_STATE. The UPPER function in the next line converts the entry to uppercase letters. The DO WHILE command repeats the sequence of instructions up to the ENDDO statement as long as the length of the entry in M_STATE is greater than zero. The SCAN command processes the records in the data base file, selecting only those in which the contents of the STATE field is equal to the contents of M_STATE. The ? commands display the contents of the specified fields for each selected record. ENDSCAN indicates the end of the sequence of commands to be performed for each selected record. The second ACCEPT command and

Figure 20 The Completed STATE Program

```
   Layout   Words   Go To   Print   Exit
   [......▼1.■..▼..2.....▼...3..▼....4▼.....▼5....▼.6...▼...7.▼.....
   clear
   set talk off
   set path to \lessons
   M_state = ""
   use mailing order last_name
   accept "Enter two-letter state abbreviation: " to M_state
   M_state = upper(M_state)
   do while len(M_state) > 0
      scan for state = M_state
         ?
         ? first_name, last_name
         ? address
         ? city, state, zip_code
      endscan
      ?
      accept "Enter two-letter state abbreviation: " to M_state
      M_state = upper(M_state)
   enddo
   clear all
   set talk on
   Program  C:\lessons\STATE      Line:20 Col:12              Ins
```

M_STATE assignment statement repeat the request for user input and convert the state abbreviation to uppercase letters. The CLEAR ALL command closes all files, and the SET TALK ON command turns on dBASE IV messages again.

In simpler terms, the program will ask the user for a state abbreviation and then present the names and addresses of all customers from that state. It will repeat this process until the user presses the Enter key without entering a state abbreviation.

Step 4: Exit the Editor and Save the Program

To save your work, activate the Exit menu and select Save Changes and Exit:

Press   **Alt-E**
Type   **s**

The dot prompt will again appear on your screen.

Step 5: Run the Program

Execute the DO command to compile and run your dBASE IV program:

Type   **do state**
Press   **Enter**

Enter a state abbreviation:

Type   **il**
Press   **Enter**

Your screen should look like Figure 21. Note that it does not matter if you use lowercase, uppercase, or a combination of both for the state abbreviation. Enter a different state abbreviation:

Type   **Wi**
Press   **Enter**

Figure 21 Running the STATE Program

```
Enter two-letter state abbreviation: il

Becky     Davis
7822 Kostner
Chicago    IL 60652

Oscar     Griffith
805 Florida
Urbana     IL 61801

Alfred    Jenkins
605 Willis
Hometown   IL 60456

Mike      Skubic
321 Gregory
Champaign  IL 61820

Enter two-letter state abbreviation: _

STATE    C:\lessons\MAILING        Rec 23/25        File
```

You can try as many states as you like. When you are finished, simply press the Enter key without typing a state abbreviation:

Press **Enter**

The STATE program will terminate and return to the dot prompt.

Practice   Execute the STATE program again. Enter an invalid state abbreviation, such as XX. What happens? Try a state for which no records have been entered in MAILING.DBF, such as Massachusetts (MA). Return to the dot prompt when you are finished.

Lesson 11: Using the Applications Generator

The Applications Generator is a sophisticated tool that lets you create custom menu-driven data base systems without programming. Basically, you tell the Applications Generator what you want dBASE IV to do and it automatically creates the dBASE IV program that will perform those tasks. You can then run the new application as is or modify it by adding or changing dBASE commands. The Applications Generator is most often used to set up specialized menus that simplify data base management tasks for a particular individual, department, company, or organization. For example, let's use the Applications Generator to set up a simple mailing list management system for Paddle and Portage Canoe Outfitters.

Step 1: Return to the Control Center

The Applications Generator can be activated from either the dot prompt or the Control Center. Close all files and return to the Control Center:

Type   **clear all**
Press   **Enter**
Type   **assist**
Press   **Enter**

Step 2: Activate the Applications Generator

Move the highlight bar to the Applications panel, select the <create> option, and select the Applications Generator option:

Press   **Right Arrow** (5 times)
Press   **Enter**
Type   **a**

The program will display the Application Definition screen shown in Figure 22.

You can also activate the Applications Generator from the dot prompt by entering the command CREATE APPLICATION followed by the name of the new application file.

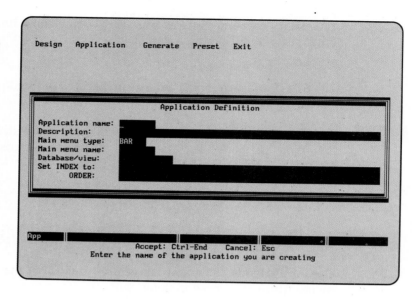

Figure 22 The Application Definition Screen

Step 3: Complete the Applications Definition Screen

Follow these directions to complete the Applications Definition screen:

Type	**mailing**
Press	**Enter**
Type	**Paddle and Portage Mailing List System**
Press	**Enter**
Press	**Space Bar**
Press	**Enter**
Type	**options**
Press	**Enter**
Type	**mailing**
Press	**Enter**
Type	**mailing.mdx**
Press	**Enter**
Type	**last_name**
Press	**Enter**
Press	**Ctrl-End**

The program will present the Applications Generator screen shown in Figure 23.

Step 4: Create a Quick Application

The Applications Generator has many features that let you create specialized menu-driven data base systems. We cannot cover all of its options. We can, however, demonstrate an easy way to create an application that will allow users to perform the most common data base operations. Activate the Application menu and select the Generate Quick Application option:

Press	**Alt-A**
Type	**g**

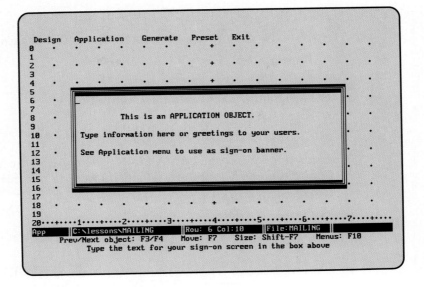

Figure 23 The Applications Generator Screen

The program will display the Quick Application screen, shown in Figure 24. Specify MAILING as the Label Format File, then return to the Applications Generator screen:

Press **Tab** (3 times)
Type **mailing**
Press **Enter**
Press **Ctrl-End**
Type **y**

A few minutes will pass as the Applications Generator creates the dBASE program file. When it is finished, it will ask you to press any key.

Press **Enter**

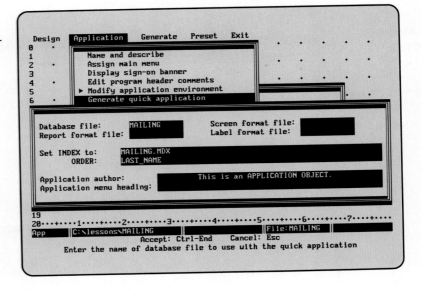

Figure 24 The Quick Application Screen

Step 5: Return to the Control Center

Activate the Exit menu and select the Save All Changes and Exit option:

Press   **Alt-E**
Type   **s**

The program will return to the Control Center.

Step 6: Use the Application

A new application named MAILING will appear in the Applications panel of the Control Center. Tell dBASE IV that you want to run this application:

Highlight   **MAILING**
Press   **Enter**
Type   **r**
Type   **y**

The first time you try to run a new application, dBASE IV will compile it, which can take a few minutes. dBASE IV will then load and run the application. Your screen should look like Figure 25. For a dBASE IV novice, this application is easier to use than the Control Center or the dot prompt for managing the Paddle and Portage Canoe Outfitters mailing list data base. For example, select the Browse Information option:

Type   **b**

The Browse screen will appear. Press Escape or select the Exit opt'on from the Exit menu to return to the MAILING application:

Press   **Escape**

Now try the Mailing Labels option:

Type   **m**

Figure 25 The MAILING Application Menu

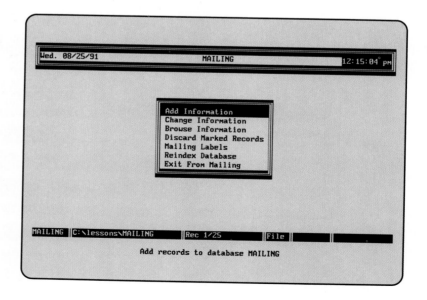

The MAILING application will list the fields and allow you to change the record pointer position. Press the Escape key to generate mailing labels for all the records.

    Press **Escape**

A new menu will pop up that lets you select where to send the labels. Select the Screen option:

    Type **s**

The labels will be "printed" on your screen. You could actually print them on paper by choosing the Printer option instead of the Screen option. Press any key to return to the MAILING application:

    Press **Enter**

Step 7: Return to the Control Center

When you are finished using the MAILING application, return to the Control Center by selecting the Exit From Mailing option:

    Type **e**

Practice

1. Switch to the dot prompt and run the MAILING application. *Hint:* use the DO command followed by the name of the application.
2. Try every option in the MAILING menu except Mailing Labels. Select the last option to return to the dot prompt, and then switch to the Control Center.

Lesson 12: Using SQL Commands

SQL stands for Structured Query Language. It is a standardized language for managing relational data bases, developed from research conducted at IBM in the 1970s. SQL has since been adopted by many companies as the standard language for mainframe and minicomputer data base systems. In the mid- to late 1980s, several publishers of microcomputer data base software also began to support SQL so that their customers could better standardize data base applications across mainframe, minicomputer, and microcomputer systems. The dBASE IV package allows you to use SQL commands instead of or in addition to dBASE commands. Although SQL consists of fewer than thirty commands, it is an advanced topic. We cannot thoroughly cover SQL data base management here. Nevertheless, we can briefly illustrate SQL by using its commands to create a simple data base.

Step 1: Switch to the Dot Prompt

If you are not already at the dot prompt, activate the Exit menu from the Control Center and select Exit to Dot Prompt:

    Press **Alt-E**
    Type **e**

Step 2: Turn On Interactive SQL Mode

Like the dBASE language, SQL can be used interactively from a prompt, or its commands can be entered into a file to be run as a program. The easiest and quickest way to learn SQL is to start by executing commands interactively. You must turn on the SQL mode, however, before you can enter SQL commands in dBASE IV. This is done with the SET SQL ON command.

> Type **set sql on**
> Press **Enter**

The status bar will say SQL at the left side, and the dot prompt will change to the SQL prompt, which looks like this:

> SQL.

Step 3: Create a New Data Base

As an example, let's create a simple data base for Paddle and Portage Canoe Outfitters that keeps track of their canoes. In SQL, the CREATE DATABASE command creates a new data base. Create a new data base named CANOES:

> Type **create database canoes;**
> Press **Enter**

Note that each SQL command must end with a semicolon.

Step 4: Activate a Data Base

You must activate a data base before you can issue any SQL commands to define or access data. The START DATABASE command activates an existing data base.

> Type **start database canoes;**
> Press **Enter**

Step 5: Create a New Table

The **table** is the basic component of an SQL data base. A table consists of rows and columns. A **row** is like a dBASE record and a **column** is like a field. Each intersection of a row and a column contains a data value. Our example data base will have only one table. Each row will refer to an individual canoe. Three columns will store the data values for each canoe: a unique ID number, the date purchased, and the price paid. The CREATE TABLE command is used to define a new table. It lists the table name and each column name and data type. Execute this command:

> Type **create table bought (id char(3), bought date, paid numeric(7,2));**
> Press **Enter**

This SQL command tells the data base manager that the BOUGHT table will have three columns. The ID column will hold character data up to three characters long, the BOUGHT column will hold dates, and the PAID column will hold numeric data up to seven digits long (including the decimal point), with two digits to the right of the decimal point.

Step 6: Insert Data Into the Table

The INSERT INTO command is used to enter each row of data into the table. Execute these commands to insert the data for three canoes:

Type   **insert into bought values ("001", {10/15/89}, 299.95);**
Press   **Enter**
Type   **insert into bought values ("002", {07/02/90}, 315.55);**
Press   **Enter**
Type   **insert into bought values ("003", {04/09/91}, 345.75);**
Press   **Enter**

Step 7: Query the Data Base

The SELECT command is used to retrieve data. The simplest form of the SELECT command displays the specified columns from a single table. For example, execute this command:

Type   **select id, bought, paid from bought;**
Press   **Enter**

Your screen should look like Figure 26.

Step 8: Turn Off SQL Mode

Other SQL commands are available for performing typical data base management chores, such as deleting data, modifying data, modifying tables, relating tables, indexing data, maintaining catalogs, and querying data bases. These topics, however, are beyond the scope of this book. Return to the dBASE IV dot prompt by turning off the SQL mode:

Type   **set sql off**
Press   **Enter**

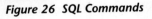

Figure 26 SQL Commands

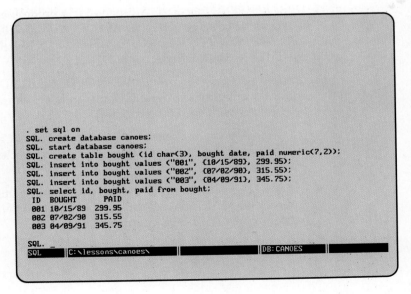

```
. set sql on
SQL. create database canoes;
SQL. start database canoes;
SQL. create table bought (id char(3), bought date, paid numeric(7,2));
SQL. insert into bought values ("001", {10/15/89}, 299.95);
SQL. insert into bought values ("002", {07/02/90}, 315.55);
SQL. insert into bought values ("003", {04/09/91}, 345.75);
SQL. select id, bought, paid from bought;
 ID  BOUGHT      PAID
 001 10/15/89  299.95
 002 07/02/90  315.55
 003 04/09/91  345.75

SQL. _
SQL     C:\lessons\canoes\                          DB:CANOES
```

Practice

Turn on the SQL mode and execute the HELP command. You can learn more about SQL from the Help facility. Select and read each of the SQL Main Topics. Read about some of the SQL commands. When you are finished, return to the SQL prompt and execute the QUIT command to exit dBASE IV and return to DOS.

Summary

- *Accessing the dot prompt.* Select Exit to Dot Prompt from the Exit menu of the Control Center.

- *Examining a data base.* USE opens a file. DISPLAY and LIST reveal the contents of a file. GO moves the record pointer.

- *Entering and modifying records.* APPEND adds new records. EDIT, BROWSE, and REPLACE let you modify records.

- *Deleting records.* DELETE marks records for deletion and RECALL unmarks them. PACK permanently removes deleted records.

- *Sorting and indexing.* SORT sorts a file. INDEX indexes a file. SET ORDER rearranges records by a tag in the multiple index file.

- *Finding data.* LOCATE finds records. SEEK and FIND are faster commands for searching indexed files. SET FILTER and SET FIELDS let you limit the records and fields found by subsequent commands. SET VIEW activates a view query.

- *Relating files.* Ten work areas are provided for different files. SELECT lets you change work areas. SET RELATION relates two files.

- *Using other dBASE IV commands.* Question mark (?), ACCEPT, CREATE, APPEND FROM, AVERAGE, COPY, COUNT, DO, ERASE, INSERT, STORE, and SUM are other commonly used dBASE IV commands.

- *Using dBASE IV functions.* A function is a predefined expression that returns a data value of a specific type. ALIAS, DATE, DISKSPACE, EOF, INT, TRIM, LEN, RECCOUNT, RECNO, RECSIZE, and ROUND are a few commonly used dBASE IV functions.

- *Creating a dBASE IV program.* MODIFY COMMAND activates the word-wrap editor for entering a program. Commands are simply entered into the file to be run later with the DO command.

- *Using the Applications Generator.* From the Control Center, move to the Applications panel, select the <create> option, and select the Applications Generator option.

- *Using SQL commands.* From the dot prompt, execute SET SQL ON. CREATE DATABASE, START DATABASE, CREATE TABLE, INSERT INTO, and SELECT are commonly used SQL commands.

Key Terms

As an extra review of this chapter, try defining the following terms.

alias	parent file
child file	record pointer
column	relate
dot prompt	row
function	table
logical operator	tag
memory variable	work area
multiple index file	

Multiple Choice

Choose the best selection to complete each statement.

1. What is the command-line user interface of dBASE IV?
   - (a) Control Center
   - (b) dot prompt
   - (c) Applications Generator
   - (d) Presentation Manager

2. To execute a dot prompt command, simply type it and press
   - (a) Enter.
   - (b) Ctrl-End.
   - (c) Space Bar.
   - (d) F1.

3. Which command returns to the Control Center from the dot prompt?
   - (a) ASSIST
   - (b) CLEAR
   - (c) CONTROL
   - (d) SQL

4. Which dot prompt command opens an existing data base file?
   - (a) ACCEPT
   - (b) LOAD
   - (c) OPEN
   - (d) USE

5. Which dot prompt command presents all of the records without pausing?
   - (a) COPY ALL
   - (b) DISPLAY ALL
   - (c) LIST ALL
   - (d) SHOW ALL

6. Which dot prompt command moves the record pointer?
   - (a) ASSIST
   - (b) DO
   - (c) GO
   - (d) USE

7. Which of the following operators is not a valid logical operator?
   - (a) .AND.
   - (b) .OR.
   - (c) .NOT.
   - (d) .SUM.

8. Which dot prompt command lets you add new records to the end of a new or existing data base file?
   - (a) ADD
   - (b) APPEND
   - (c) CONTINUE
   - (d) CREATE

9. Which dot prompt command lets you make a specific change to selected records throughout a data base file?
   - (a) BROWSE
   - (b) EDIT
   - (c) LOCATE
   - (d) REPLACE

10. Which dot prompt command permanently removes all records marked for deletion in the current data base file?

(a) ERASE   (b) DELETE

(c) PACK   (d) RECALL

11. Which dot prompt command rearranges records on the basis of a tag in the multiple index file?

(a) ACCEPT   (b) IMPORT FROM

(c) SET ORDER   (d) SORT

12. Which dot prompt command would you use to find a record in a data base file that is not indexed?

(a) FIND   (b) LOCATE

(c) SEEK   (d) SELECT

13. Which dot prompt command lets you specify a condition to select records for all subsequent commands?

(a) LOCATE   (b) SELECT

(c) SET FILTER   (d) SET FIELDS

14. Which dot prompt command lets you change work areas?

(a) CHANGE   (b) EDIT

(c) REPLACE   (d) SELECT

15. Which dot prompt command copies records from an existing file, not necessarily a dBASE IV file, into the current data base file?

(a) ACCEPT   (b) APPEND FROM

(c) COMPILE   (d) CREATE

16. Which dot prompt command executes a dBASE program?

(a) CONTINUE   (b) DO

(c) GO   (d) USE

17. Which function returns a logical value of .T. if the record pointer is past the last record in the file?

(a) BOF   (b) EXP

(c) EOF   (d) LEN

18. Which dot prompt command do you use to create a new program file with the word-wrap editor?

(a) CREATE APPLICATION   (b) DO

(c) MODIFY COMMAND   (d) SELECT

19. Which is a sophisticated tool for creating custom menu-driven data base systems without programming?

(a) Control Center   (b) dot prompt

(c) Applications Generator   (d) Presentation Manager

20. What is the basic component of an SQL data base?

(a) column   (b) file

(c) record   (d) table

Fill-In

1. The _____ dot prompt command closes all open files, terminates the dBASE IV session, and returns to DOS.
2. The DISPLAY _____ command presents the names, types, and widths of the fields in the current data base file.
3. As you work with a file, dBASE IV keeps track of the current record number by means of the record _____.
4. A _____ operator modifies the TRUE or FALSE result of one or two conditions.
5. A record marked for deletion can be reinstated in the data base file by executing the _____ command.
6. The _____ dot prompt command creates a new data base file with records from the current file arranged in the specified order.
7. Sorting is usually slower and takes up more disk space than _____.
8. You must use the SET ORDER command to rearrange records on the basis of a _____ in the multiple index file.
9. If a file is indexed and you want to search for records on the basis of the contents of a tag field, the _____ and _____ commands are faster than the LOCATE command.
10. The FOR clause in many dBASE IV commands acts as a _____ to select only certain records.
11. Once a view query has been designed, you can execute the SET _____ command from the dot prompt to use it.
12. A _____ area is a place in memory that holds an open data base file.
13. Two files in a relation are often called _____ and _____ files.
14. The _____ command displays the value of one or more expressions.
15. The _____ dot prompt command removes a file from the disk.
16. The _____ command adds a new record to the current data base file just after the current record.
17. A memory _____ is a place in RAM that temporarily holds a data value used in a calculation, comparison, or other operation.
18. A _____ is a predefined expression that returns a data value of a specific type.
19. A dBASE IV _____ is a sequence of commands stored in a text file that can be compiled and executed.
20. A standardized language for managing relational data bases, _____ was developed from research conducted at IBM in the 1970s.

Short Problems

1. From your LESSONS subdirectory, start dBASE IV and activate the dot prompt. Display a directory of the available data base files. Open the ACCOUNT data base file. List all of the records in which the BALANCE field is greater than zero.

2. Compute the sum of the CHARGES field and assign it to a memory variable named M_CSUM. Then compute the sum of the BALANCE field and assign it to a memory variable named M_BSUM.

3. Activate the LAST_NAME index tag. Use the FIND command to move the record pointer to Henry Hudson's record and use the DISPLAY command to view it on the screen.

4. Count the number of records in ACCOUNT with a BALANCE greater than $50.

5. The CMONTH function returns the name of the month from a date. Use the CMONTH and DATE functions to display the name of the current month.

6. The RUN dot prompt command executes a DOS command, or any program that can be executed by DOS, from within dBASE IV. Use the RUN command to execute the DOS CHKDSK command without leaving dBASE IV.

7. Execute the DISPLAY STATUS command to see information about your current dBASE IV session.

8. You can activate existing view queries and reports from the dot prompt. Follow these directions:

Type	`set view to ?`
Press	**Enter**
Highlight	**WHO_OWES.QBE**
Press	**Enter**
Type	`report form ?`
Press	**Enter**
Highlight	**WHO_OWES.FRG**
Press	**Enter**

9. Execute the CLEAR ALL command to close all files. Then open the MAILING data base file. Follow these directions to produce mailing labels from the dot prompt:

Type	`label form ?`
Press	**Enter**
Highlight	**MAILING.LBG**
Press	**Enter**

10. Execute the CLEAR ALL command to close all files. Then turn on SQL mode. Execute the SHOW DATABASE command to list available SQL data bases. (Remember to end SQL commands with a semicolon.) Use the START DATABASE command to activate the CANOES data base. Execute the SELECT command to list the ID, BOUGHT, and PAID columns from the BOUGHT table. Then turn off SQL mode.

Long Problems

1. Create a data base to maintain your checking account. Include the following fields: NUMBER, DATE, PAYMENT, DEPOSIT, CLEARED, and DESCRIP. NUMBER and DESCRIP should be Character fields, DATE should be a Date field, PAYMENT and DEPOSIT should be Numeric fields, and CLEARED should be a Logical field. Enter at least ten records. Create a dBASE program that will calculate the current balance by subtracting the sum of the PAYMENT fields from the sum of the DEPOSIT fields.

2. The CLEARED field in your checking account data base is a logical field in which you will enter T for TRUE when you receive the cashed check back from your bank. Create another dBASE program that will reconcile your data base with the monthly statements you receive from your bank. Hint: compute a balance as you did in the first program, but only for those records that have T in the CLEARED field. The resulting balance should then match the balance reported on your monthly bank statement.

3. In Long Problem 3 of the previous two chapters, you created an "electronic Rolodex" with dBASE IV. Use the Applications Generator to create a Quick Application for this data base file.

4. In Long Problem 4 of the previous two chapters, you created a student grades data base. Develop a dBASE program that will automatically generate and update the final letter grade based on a calculation involving the homework grades and test grades.

5. In Long Problem 5 of the previous two chapters, you created a data base of information about the courses you have taken throughout your college career. Create a dBASE program that will compute your grade-point average.

6. In Long Problem 6 of the previous two chapters, you created a data base of car expenses. Develop a dBASE program that will calculate the total car expenses for a year.

7. Switch to the dot prompt. Create a data base file for a video rental store to catalog their selection of movies. Include the following fields: TAPE_NO, TITLE, DATE, and COST. Make up and enter at least ten records. List the records on the screen and to the printer.

8. Use dBASE IV to create a quick reference guide to dBASE IV dot prompt commands and functions. In other words, create a data base with two fields: COMMAND and DESCRIP. Refer to the Command Summaries appendix at the end of this book or the dBASE IV help facility to find out about commands and functions not mentioned in this chapter. Index the data base by the COMMAND field. After your data base is finished, you can quickly get a description of a command or function by searching the COMMAND field.

9. Use the Applications Generator from the dot prompt to create a Quick Application for the ACCOUNT data base file.

10. Create an SQL data base of your own choosing. You might want to reproduce a dBASE IV data base you already have. You may have to use the Help facility within SQL to learn more about SQL to complete your task.

END-OF-SECTION EXERCISES

1. Reproduce this page by creating and printing a data base report of mutual fund information. Use numeric fields for the Total % Gain, Annual Growth Rate, and 5-Year Total % Gain columns. Use a logical field for the Load column.

```
Page No.        1
05/31/90
                        Selected Common Stock Mutual Funds
                        Aggressive Growth and Growth Funds

                                15 Years
```

Name	Total % Gain	Annual Growth Rate	5-Year Total % Gain	Load	Telephone Number
AMCAP Fund	578	13.6	116	.T.	800-421-9900
Acorn Fund	668	14.6	136	.F.	312-621-0630
American Capital Comstock	855	16.2	131	.T.	800-231-3638
Charter Fund	745	15.3	91	.T.	800-231-0803
Columbia Growth Fund	453	12.1	137	.F.	800-547-1037
Evergreen Fund	1244	18.9	138	.F.	800-235-0064
Fidelity Magellan Fund	1722	21.3	271	.T.	800-544-6666
International Investors	1553	20.6	68	.T.	800-221-2220
Janus Fund	751	15.3	128	.F.	800-525-3731
NEL Growth Fund	623	14.1	197	.T.	800-343-7104
New York Venture Fund	656	14.4	171	.T.	800-545-2098
Nicholas Fund	472	12.3	168	.F.	800-227-5987
Over-the-Counter Securities	950	17.0	114	.T.	800-523-2578
Partners Fund	577	13.6	147	.F.	800-367-0770
Putnam Voyager Fund	742	15.3	136	.T.	800-225-1581
Templeton Growth Fund	1335	19.4	133	.T.	800-237-0738
Tudor Fund	602	13.9	155	.F.	800-223-3332
Twentieth Century Growth	1523	20.4	92	.F.	800-345-2021
Twentieth Century Select	1483	20.2	175	.F.	800-345-2021
Weingarten Equity Fund	734	15.2	167	.T.	800-231-0803

2. Reproduce these two pages below by creating and printing a data base report of business expenses. Use a date field for the Date, a numeric field for the Amount, and a logical field for the Owe State Tax column. You do not have to enter the records in any particular order, but you should index them by Category before you create the report. Note that the records are grouped and subtotaled by Category.

```
Page No.       1
05/31/90
                                      Business Expenses


                                          Owe
               Expense                   State
Date           Category        Amount    Tax?   Description


**  Freight
   01/02/91 Freight            20.95  .F.    U.S. Postage and stamps
   02/01/91 Freight            10.50  .F.    Shipping for WordPerfect
                                             Update
   02/06/91 Freight            13.00  .F.    Federal Express
   02/12/91 Freight             6.40  .F.    U.S. Postage
   02/09/91 Freight             3.00  .F.    PC Connection Shipping
   02/19/91 Freight             3.00  .F.    PC Connection Shipping
   02/26/91 Freight             3.00  .F.    PC Connection Shipping
   02/26/91 Freight             3.34  .F.    Jameco Shipping
** Subtotal **
                              63.19


**  Hardware
   02/09/91 Hardware          159.00  .T.    Intel 2400B Classic Modem
   02/26/91 Hardware           52.90  .T.    Modem/Fax Protectors
** Subtotal **
                             211.90


**  Publications
   02/05/91 Publications       12.96  .F.    Computer Graphics book
   02/06/91 Publications       34.97  .F.    MacUser Subscription
** Subtotal **
                              47.93


**  Sales Tax
   02/23/91 Sales Tax         510.00  .F.    On out-of-state purchases
** Subtotal **
                             510.00


**  Services
   02/23/91 Services          325.00  .F.    Tax Return Preparation
** Subtotal **
                             325.00


**  Software
   01/17/91 Software            9.98  .T.    Computer Solutions Software
   02/01/91 Software           85.00  .T.    WordPerfect Update
   02/09/91 Software           39.00  .T.    Microsoft Flight Simulator
   02/09/91 Software           99.00  .T.    Turbo Pascal 5.5
   02/19/91 Software           49.00  .T.    Software Carousel
** Subtotal **
                             281.98


**  Supplies
   02/26/91 Supplies          249.00  .T.    Bernoulli Disks
   03/07/91 Supplies            4.87  .F.    Paper & Disk Labels
   03/07/91 Supplies           55.65  .F.    Copier & Printer Paper
```

```
Page No.      2
05/31/90
                                    Business Expenses


                                    Owe
                 Expense            State
Date             Category           Amount Tax?  Description

** Subtotal **
                                    309.52


**   Travel
  02/06/91 Travel                   345.62 .F.   National Sales Meeting
  02/28/91 Travel                    95.85 .F.   Lodging at national sales
                                                 meeting
** Subtotal **
                                    441.47


**   Utilities
  01/01/91 Utilities                  2.56 .F.   Telephone Calls
  01/13/91 Utilities                  1.50 .F.   CompuServe
  01/31/91 Utilities                  7.83 .F.   Telephone Calls
  02/06/91 Utilities                  1.50 .F.   CompuServe
  02/13/91 Utilities                 25.00 .F.   MCI Mail Annual Fee
  03/05/91 Utilities                 21.33 .F.   Telephone Calls
  03/09/91 Utilities                 42.74 .F.   CompuServe
** Subtotal **
                                    102.46
*** Total ***
                                   2293.45
```

3. Reproduce the following three pages by creating and printing a data base report of customer records. Use a character field for the Customer Code, and index the data base on this field. Use numeric fields for the Credit Limit and Balance. Do not include an available field in the data base itself; instead, create a calculated field in the report by subtracting the Balance from the Credit Limit. Use data fields for the Last Sale and Last Payment entries. Finally, remember to include the report title and to separate records by dashed lines as shown.

```
Page No.   1
06/15/91

Customer File

---------------------------------------------------------------------
Customer Code: C0001
Company Name:  NCR Corporation              Contact:  Gilbert P. Williamson
Address:       1700 S. Patterson Blvd.        Phone:  (513) 445-5000
City:          Dayton
State/ZIP:     OH   45749

Credit Limit:      $25000.00              Last Sale:  04/05/91
Balance:            $5000.00           Last Payment:  04/01/91
Available:         $20000.00
---------------------------------------------------------------------
Customer Code: C0002
Company Name:  U.S. Robotics, Inc.          Contact:  Casey Cowell
Address:       8100 N. McCormick Blvd.        Phone:  (708) 982-5001
City:          Skokie
State/ZIP:     IL   60079

Credit Limit:      $15000.00              Last Sale:  02/14/91
Balance:            $2500.00           Last Payment:  01/01/91
Available:         $12500.00
---------------------------------------------------------------------
Customer Code: C0003
Company Name:  Spectrum Holobyte            Contact:  Phillip G. Adam
Address:       2061 Challenger Drive          Phone:  (415) 522-3584
City:          Alameda
State/ZIP:     CA   94501

Credit Limit:      $15000.00              Last Sale:  05/14/91
Balance:            $1200.00           Last Payment:  03/15/91
Available:         $13800.00
---------------------------------------------------------------------
Customer Code: C0004
Company Name:  Atari Corporation            Contact:  Jack Tramiel
Address:       1196 Borregas Avenue           Phone:  (408) 745-2000
City:          Sunnyvale
State/ZIP:     CA   94086

Credit Limit:      $25000.00              Last Sale:  02/04/91
Balance:            $3200.00           Last Payment:  01/15/91
Available:         $21800.00
---------------------------------------------------------------------
Customer Code: C0005
Company Name:  Microsoft Corporation        Contact:  William H. Gates III
Address:       16011 NE 36th Way              Phone:  (206) 882-8080
City:          Redmond
State/ZIP:     WA   98073

Credit Limit:     $100000.00              Last Sale:  05/02/91
Balance:           $15000.00           Last Payment:  04/15/91
Available:         $85000.00
```

```
Page No.    2
06/15/91
--------------------------------------------------------------------
Customer Code: C0006
Company Name:  TRW Inc.
Address:       1900 Richmond Road      Contact:   Joseph T. Gorman
City:          Cleveland               Phone:     (216) 291-7000
State/ZIP:     OH   44124

Credit Limit:   $25000.00              Last Sale:    03/18/91
Balance:         $1250.00              Last Payment: 01/15/91
Available:      $23750.00
--------------------------------------------------------------------
Customer Code: C0007
Company Name:  T/Maker Company
Address:       1390 Villa St.          Contact:   Heidi Roizen
City:          Mountain View           Phone:     (415) 962-0195
State/ZIP:     CA   94041

Credit Limit:   $15000.00              Last Sale:    12/10/90
Balance:            $0.00              Last Payment: 01/10/91
Available:      $15000.00
--------------------------------------------------------------------
Customer Code: C0008
Company Name:  Silicon Beach Software
Address:       Box 261430              Contact:   Kaiulani Schuler
City:          San Diego               Phone:     (619) 695-6956
State/ZIP:     CA   92126

Credit Limit:   $20000.00              Last Sale:    04/12/91
Balance:         $2200.00              Last Payment: 03/15/91
Available:      $17800.00
--------------------------------------------------------------------
Customer Code: C0009
Company Name:  NeXT Inc.
Address:       3475 Deer Creek Road    Contact:   Steven P. Jobs
City:          Palo Alto               Phone:     (415) 424-0200
State/ZIP:     CA   94304

Credit Limit:   $25000.00              Last Sale:    02/14/91
Balance:         $1250.00              Last Payment: 01/15/91
Available:      $23750.00
--------------------------------------------------------------------
Customer Code: C0010
Company Name:  Iomega Corporation
Address:       1821 West 4000 South    Contact:   David J. Dunn
City:          Roy                     Phone:     (206) 821-2140
State/ZIP:     UT   84067

Credit Limit:   $15000.00              Last Sale:    02/21/91
Balance:         $1250.00              Last Payment: 01/15/91
Available:      $13750.00
```

```
Page No.   3
06/15/91
-----------------------------------------------------------------------
Customer Code: C0011
Company Name:  Digital Research Inc.     Contact:   Gary Kildall
Address:       60 Garden Court             Phone:   (408) 649-3896
City:          Monterey
State/ZIP:     CA   93940

Credit Limit:     $25000.00             Last Sale:  01/12/91
Balance:              $0.00          Last Payment:  02/15/91
Available:        $25000.00

      -----------------------------------------------------------------
Customer Code: C0012
Company Name:  Chips & Technologies     Contact:   Keith R. Lobo
Address:       3050 Zanker Road           Phone:   (408) 434-0600
City:          San Jose
State/ZIP:     CA   95135

Credit Limit:     $25000.00             Last Sale:  04/11/91
Balance:           $2500.00          Last Payment:  04/01/91
Available:        $22500.00
      -----------------------------------------------------------------
Customer Code: C0013
Company Name:  Borland International     Contact:   Philippe Kahn
Address:       4585 Scotts Valley Drive    Phone:   (408) 438-8400
City:          Scotts Valley
State/ZIP:     CA   95066

Credit Limit:     $25000.00             Last Sale:  01/22/91
Balance:              $0.00          Last Payment:  12/15/90
Available:        $25000.00

      -----------------------------------------------------------------
Customer Code: C0014
Company Name:  Cray Research            Contact:   John F. Carlson
Address:       608 Second Avenue South    Phone:   (612) 333-5889
City:          Minneapolis
State/ZIP:     MN   55402

Credit Limit:     $50000.00             Last Sale:  05/02/91
Balance:           $1500.00          Last Payment:  04/15/91
Available:        $48500.00

      -----------------------------------------------------------------
Customer Code: C0015
Company Name:  Intel Corporation        Contact:   Andrew S. Grove
Address:       3065 Bowers Avenue         Phone:   (408) 765-8080
City:          Santa Clara
State/ZIP:     CA   95051

Credit Limit:     $50000.00             Last Sale:  03/11/91
Balance:              $0.00          Last Payment:  04/15/91
Available:        $50000.00
```

APPENDIX A

SELECTING A SYSTEM

More and more people are buying microcomputers for business and home use. Most companies already have at least one microcomputer, and they are continually acquiring more. Schools at all levels have been purchasing microcomputers for both students and faculty. It's been estimated that at least 20% of all U.S. households will ultimately have some type of microcomputer. Just as most of you will eventually purchase stereo systems, video systems, other high-tech home appliances, and automobiles, it's likely that in the near future you may be investing in a computer system, too. Perhaps you won't be buying a computer for your home, but you might still be involved in the process of selecting a system for your school or work. This appendix offers some guidelines that can help both individuals and organizations in their process of computerization.

Computers are complicated equipment. Although their prices have been steadily dropping, computers still represent a substantial investment for most people. With so many different computer models and an overwhelming array of software packages on the market, unless you're wealthy or are already a computer expert, purchasing a system is no trivial task. The choices you make can have profound effects on the quantity and quality of work you will accomplish with your computer. To make good choices, you need to have a plan.

Selecting a computer system is somewhat like selecting a stereo system or automobile. If you buy on irrational impulses, you risk regretting your decision for years to come. If, on the other hand, you follow a well-thought-out, step-by-step selection process, chances are good that you'll end up with an economical labor-saving system. One such approach involves six basic steps:

1. Learn about computers.
2. Define your needs.
3. Select the software.
4. Select the hardware.
5. Purchase the system.
6. Install the system.

Step 1: Learn About Computers

You need not be a computer scientist to effectively select and use computers. Some basic knowledge, however, can help a great deal. The first step in selecting a system is to become familiar with the capabilities and limitations of computers. In other words, you need to know what computers can and cannot do for you. The chapters in this book are designed to provide you with an understanding of the capabilities and limitations of microcomputers.

Of course, this book can by no means cover all relevant microcomputer topics. Although learning more is not absolutely required, the more you do know the better prepared you'll be to take advantage of what computers have to offer. Fortunately, there are many opportunities for you to learn more about computers. Some of the possibilities include books, periodicals, organizations, shows, courses, conferences, and workshops.

Books

An astonishing number of computer books are available in local bookstores, libraries, and computer stores. Some are quite technical, but many others have been written especially for novices. Some of the most common books you'll find are "How to" books that cover specific computer models or software packages. Others teach programming in certain languages or deal with the philosophical and sociological aspects of using computers. You can even buy books that discuss how to select a computer system.

Periodicals

In 1975, only two magazines were devoted solely to microcomputers. Today, hundreds of microcomputer newspapers, newsletters, and magazines are available. Although books can cover topics in great detail, they're usually somewhat out of date by the time they actually hit the shelves. Newspapers, newsletters, and magazines reveal what's happening in the marketplace *now*. They frequently contain reviews and in-depth evaluations of hardware and software products. Periodicals also contain informative articles and columns that answer questions and provide tips from other computer users. They are crammed with ads from manufacturers, retailers, and mail-order outfits. Many owners have at least one subscription to a microcomputer periodical. Some of the more popular publications include *A+*, *BYTE*, *Infoworld*, *Macworld*, and *PC Magazine*.

In addition to traditional periodicals printed on paper, *disk magazines* have been gaining popularity recently. These publications are issued on floppy disks and are aimed at users of particular computer models. They uniquely provide subscribers with tested programs for business, education, entertainment, and home use.

Organizations

Computer users, it seems, are a very sociable lot. At regular intervals, thousands of folks gather in societies, clubs, and user groups to share computer experiences, help solve each others' problems, and trade software. Although most people don't join such organizations until after they purchase a computer system, joining before buying can be advantageous. Many user groups are centered around a particular computer model or type of popular software. Group members can usually offer advice on where to get the best deals. Joining a computer organization may even qualify you for certain group discounts off the retail prices of selected hardware and software products. Once you have your system, a computer organization can put you in contact with people who have the same hardware and software. These colleagues can be an invaluable source of information because it's likely that they've already solved problems you might be having as a beginning user.

Computer organizations offer fellowship, support, general information, and answers to those tricky questions not answered in any manuals. Many groups have been established since the advent of microcomputers in the mid-1970s. For example, more than 850 groups in the United States serve Apple computer users. Some groups have remained local, small, and dedicated to one particular type of computer, like the Champaign-Urbana, Illinois Apple II Users Group with its 40 or so members. Other groups have grown immense and wield a good deal of influence over the microcomputer industry. The Boston Computer Society, for instance, was founded in 1977 by Jonathan Rotenberg when he was thirteen years old. Today, with about 24,000 members, it's perhaps the nation's largest microcomputer users group. The Boston Computer Society has its own magazine, *Computer Update*, sponsors around 100 monthly events, and has approximately 40 special-interest subgroups, each of which publishes its own newsletter.

Shows

Every year, computer shows are held in various cities across the United States. These events may be sponsored by individual entrepreneurs, manufacturers, retail stores, magazine publishers, or other associations that deal with computers. Although many shows specifically target manufacturers and retailers, others are open to the general computer-buying public. They are typically held in large exhibit halls, with booth space rented to hardware manufacturers, software manufacturers, dealers, distributors, retailers, computer clubs, publishers, and any other organizations that want to sell or advertise products. Admission is often charged. Besides exhibiting new products and services, many shows also offer short talks, seminars, and classes for attendees, frequently given by well-known computer personalities. These shows may last several days and attract thousands of people who come from all over the country.

Computer shows can offer the following opportunities:

- *See new products*. Manufacturers often introduce products at computer shows, so it may be an early chance to see what's new in the market. Furthermore, most shows exhibit a wider variety of products than you can usually find in the typical computer store. It's easy to collect all kinds of brochures, product descriptions, advertisements, and other handouts.
- *Try out products*. Many computer show exhibits are specifically designed to let you "test drive" hardware and software products. This may be your only chance to get hands-on experience with an item before you actually buy it.
- *Buy products*. Frequently, computer shows allow exhibitors to sell their products directly to consumers. At some shows, you can buy anything from a single diskette to an entire microcomputer system. Prices are generally less than retail and it's possible to get some good bargains at computer shows, especially as closing time nears.
- *Learn more*. As we mentioned before, many computer shows sponsor lectures and seminars. Subjects may include very specific topics, such as how to use a particular feature of a software package, or more general matters, such as the role of microcomputers in our society.

- *Meet people.* Computer shows offer excellent opportunities to come into contact with other people who have similar interests. You may meet just one person at a booth looking for the same product, or you may discover an entire users group that you want to join. The people you meet can offer advice, answer questions, and share some of their computer experiences with you.
- *Talk to manufacturers.* Since many hardware and software manufacturers send representatives to computer shows, you may get an opportunity to ask questions, get more information, or even complain about a particular product.

Courses

For people who seek a more structured approach to learning about computers, a wide variety of formal courses is offered to both students and the general public. Traditional educational institutions, like high schools, community colleges, and universities, hold classes aimed primarily at those seeking diplomas. Many community colleges and university continuing education and extension services also offer computer courses for non-degree students. Classes range from simple, non-technical introductions for novices to in-depth studies for those pursuing computer careers. Alternative learning centers, such as those affiliated with local churches, libraries, and park districts, often conduct classes taught by computer experts in their spare time. Although such courses may be less academic than those run by traditional educational institutions, they may be more accessible to the general public. Computer stores often teach courses about particular hardware and software products, but these courses may be limited to customers. Several proprietary (for-profit) schools also offer computer-related coursework. Many accredited home study schools as well as colleges and universities have correspondence courses that teach computer subjects by mail. Finally, some private individuals offer computer courses too. Before you enroll in any course, however, be sure to investigate it thoroughly to determine just what is being offered and how much it will cost.

Conferences and Workshops

Many organizations offer conferences and workshops covering particular computer topics. Some of these events are expensive, intensive training sessions aimed specifically at computer professionals. Others are less technical and attract novice computer users. They typically last from several hours to several days, and are held in various cities across the country.

Step 2: Define Your Needs

Once you have a general picture of what microcomputers can do, you can begin to examine how you might use one. It's important to carefully consider exactly what you want to do with a computer before you purchase anything. Of course, you probably can't anticipate every possible use you'll find for your computer once you get it, but you should have some clearly stated, specific reasons for investing in a system. A good approach is to make a list. Write down, in order of importance, all of the uses you expect to have for a computer. At this stage, try not to think too much about costs, but keep your ideas realistic. As a sample, your list might look something like this:

1. *Word Processing*. For term papers, reports, class notes, and letters.
2. *Record Keeping*. For addresses, phone numbers, personal property inventory, bank account numbers, credit cards, and tax-deductible expenses.
3. *Calculating*. For bills, budgets, and income taxes.
4. *Education*. For math review, foreign language study, college entrance test review, and learning about computer programming.
5. *Entertainment*. For fun with computer games and simulations.

This list is probably fairly typical of the uses a student or other individual might have for a computer at home or school. A business, however, might have a more specific list of computer needs, especially if it is computerizing for the first time, or perhaps considering replacing an existing system. A small business, for example, might have the following uses for a microcomputer system:

1. *General Ledger*. To keep track of financial records and produce reports, such as balance sheets and profit and loss statements, that summarize the financial status of the firm.
2. *Accounts Receivable*. To keep track of the money owed to the company and when payments are due.
3. *Accounts Payable*. To keep track of money the company owes to its suppliers.
4. *Payroll*. To calculate each employee's gross pay, withhold taxes, subtract deductions, print paychecks, and maintain necessary payroll records.
5. *Inventory*. To monitor the goods on hand and make sure enough are in stock for production and customer requests.
6. *Mailing List*. To prepare direct mailing of ads and notices.
7. *Word Processing*. To create letters, reports, newsletters, and memos.
8. *Personnel Files*. To hold information for insurance, retirement, and governmental regulations.

Step 3: Select the Software

Now comes perhaps the most difficult step in acquiring a computer system: selecting the software. First of all, from the user's standpoint, software is much more important than hardware. Software is what makes the computer accomplish useful work. Without programs, computer hardware is utterly worthless. It's likely that you'll pay much more for all the software you'll eventually buy than the hardware. If you have a stereo system, this probably doesn't surprise you, since most people have more money invested in records, tapes, or compact discs than they originally paid for the stereo components. Shopping for software is also more difficult than shopping for hardware, because there is so much more software on the market than hardware. Some software companies sell only by mail, so it may be difficult to obtain information about their programs. A thorough evaluation of software requires using it in your own particular situation for a substantial amount of time. This may be difficult, if not impossible, to do by running a program at a single sitting in your local computer store. Finally, because software usually has a smaller profit margin than hardware, computer salespeople may not be as enthusiastic or helpful about selling a program as they would an entire computer system.

All those difficulties aside, it really is possible, even for novices, to make good software selections. First, go back to your list of computer uses. For each item, come up with at least three different software packages. Here you'll need some of those learning resources we talked about previously. Perhaps the best source of possible selections may be people you know from school, work, clubs, user groups, or computer shows. See if you can arrange to try a potential software selection for an extended period of time. Perhaps a friend or relative has a computer and software you can use. If your school has a computer lab, you may be able to use it at times when classes aren't in session. Many school labs have software you can check out and run on a computer at your own pace.

Probably the best source of information comparing various software packages are computer magazines. Most have reviews of new software products; some even devote entire issues to comparing all the major competitors in a particular application. The publications extensively test each package by using it for a pre-determined set of activities, and then quantitatively rate how each one does. Often, the reviewers will conclude with one or more "editor's choices," and give their reasons for selecting these packages as the best of the lot. Scanning the magazine stands and going through back issues in the library are excellent ways to find out more about specific application packages.

As you begin to compile your list of potential software selections, make your own evaluations and rank the packages, if possible. As you talk to people and read product reviews, note the following characteristics of good software:

- *Competent.* Capable of performing an important job well.
- *Easy to Learn.* Can be mastered with moderate effort in a reasonable amount of time.
- *Easy to Use.* Intrudes as little as possible between the user and getting the job done.
- *Tolerant.* Gently and sensibly handles errors made by the user.
- *Layered.* Simple and self-evident on the outside for beginners, and progressively more complex and powerful as internal features are mastered.
- *Flexible.* Can be adapted to handle variations in its basic task.
- *Compatible.* Works well with other software by using standard conventions and being able to share files.
- *Well-Documented.* Comes with clearly written, correct instruction and reference manuals designed with both novices and experts in mind.
- *Supported.* Backed by its manufacturer, which conscientiously fixes errors, provides updated versions, and answers users' questions.
- *Reasonably-Priced.* Provides value comparable to its cost.

Once you complete this process, you'll have a list of computer uses ordered according to your priorities, within which will be sublists of potential software packages ranked by preference. You're not ready to buy anything yet, and you haven't singled out the exact packages you'll eventually get, but you have a pretty good idea of the field of contenders.

Step 4: Select the Hardware

By seriously considering software first, the selection of hardware is much easier. The idea is to choose hardware that can run the software packages you've selected. This helps you put together a system that really matches your needs.

Computer

Some of the software packages you've selected have versions that run on different computers, but many will only work on a single machine. This is where you begin to determine the most important hardware decision facing you: which computer to get. Although there are hundreds of different companies making microcomputers, the great majority of machines fit into one of just a few categories. Today, these categories are IBM and IBM-compatible computers, Apple Macintoshes, Apple II computers, and all others. This is not to belittle all those "other" computers. There are quite a few great machines with large numbers of devoted users. However, there's no doubt that the microcomputers in the first three categories far outnumber all the rest, especially in businesses, offices, and schools.

IBM and IBM-Compatible Computers　　IBM is the recognized leader in the microcomputer industry. They sell more microcomputers than any other single manufacturer. People who prefer other computers may not concede that IBM sells the "best" computers, but the fact remains that they sell the most. Although IBM no longer manufactures members of its original Personal Computer line (PC Jrs, PCs, PC Portables, XTs, and ATs), millions of these machines remain in use and some dealers are still selling new ones. The current IBM Personal System/2 line of computers improves on the previous models while still being able to run all the old software. IBM computers tend to be solidly-built, reliable machines that have been traditionally popular in the business world. Even though IBM computers might be a bit more expensive than comparable machines from other manufacturers, they have been getting more price-competitive lately. It's been said that "no manager ever got fired for buying IBM."

A true **IBM-compatible** computer is one that can run all the software and accept all the expansion boards and peripheral units that IBM microcomputers can use. Because IBM chose standard parts, published detailed design descriptions in technical references, and used an operating system designed and also sold by Microsoft, it was relatively easy for other manufacturers to produce compatible computers. Although there may still be some exceptions, most IBM-compatibles produced today do a very good job of mimicking the way IBM computers work. Many such "clones" offer more advanced features at a significantly lower price than IBM computers. Some IBM-compatible manufacturers, such as COMPAQ, have become highly-respected microcomputer industry leaders in their own right. Many well-established computer and electronic companies, like Tandy and Zenith, have expanded their lines to include IBM-compatible machines. In addition, quite a few mail-order firms, such as Dell Computer Corporation and Northgate Computer Systems, sell IBM-compatibles that they construct themselves from standard components. In fact, many more IBM-compatibles are sold today than IBM microcomputers.

Although IBMs and IBM-compatibles have their critics, selecting such computers has many advantages. American businesses have over $80 billion invested in IBM and IBM-compatible computers. This includes over 72 million software and hardware products, and hundreds of millions of hours of training. Books, magazines, and user groups devoted solely to IBM-compatible computers abound. Chances are good that you can find experts nearby to help you if you have problems. Most IBM and IBM-compatible systems can be easily expanded if you need to add more capabilities later.

Apple Macintosh Computers   In the early days of IBM microcomputers, many people considered them to be powerful and expandable, but not particularly easy to set up and use. Apple, building on their great success with the Apple II line, decided to address these concerns and build a computer "for the rest of us." In 1984, Apple introduced the Macintosh. Easy to learn and fun to use, the Macintosh has changed the way people perceive computers. Today's models preserve the philosophy of simplicity, yet have become more powerful and expandable. The Macintosh is becoming increasingly popular in businesses, especially for word processing, graphics, and desktop publishing applications. Many individuals and schools are also purchasing Macintoshes in ever greater numbers. Hundreds of software packages and a variety of optional peripherals are now available for this machine.

Apple II Computers   The original Apple II computer was introduced in 1977. Since then, several million of the Apple II family (including the Apple II +, Apple IIe, Apple III, Apple IIc, and Apple IIGS) have been sold. These computers have done very well in elementary and secondary schools. The Apple II's share of sales in this market is currently around 50%, although some schools are turning more toward Macintoshes and low-cost IBM-compatibles. Apple II computers have also been quite popular as home computers and were common in businesses before the introduction of the IBM Personal Computers. At least 10,000 software packages run on Apple II computers and a wide variety of expansion devices and peripherals are available. Although this family of computers is not as powerful and fast as Macintoshes and IBM-compatibles, they are still viable machines with a large number of devoted users.

Memory

In the early days of microcomputers, RAM was expensive and most machines could have no more than 64K. This situation has changed dramatically. Many microcomputers now have the potential to use up to 4 gigabytes of RAM, and memory chips are less expensive. For many people, the memory that comes with the computer will be sufficient for most of their needs. For example, most IBM microcomputers now come with at least 640K standard and all Macintoshes come with at least one megabyte installed. On other machines, you'll have to make sure you get enough memory to run the application packages you've selected. Since most software manufacturers state how much memory is required for their programs, figuring out how much memory to buy should be fairly simple. If you can, try to choose a computer system that can accept more RAM than you may initially need. Then if you later purchase software that requires more memory, you can add more RAM to upgrade your system.

Disk Drives

When it comes to secondary storage, you have several choices to make. The first one is whether you need the high capacity and rapid data access of a hard disk. This depends on the types of applications you'll run and the quantity of data you'll be working with. Some application packages require a hard disk. Others don't actually require one, but would work much better and faster with a hard disk. If the application programs you run and the data files you'll work with won't each fit on a single floppy disk, you probably need a hard disk. If you're not sure if you want to invest the extra few hundred dollars in a hard disk, make sure that you get a computer system that can accommodate a hard disk if you decide to add one later.

The other most common secondary storage decisions involve what kind and how many floppy drives to get. The 5¼-inch diskette drives are still more common, less expensive, and use less expensive floppies than 3½-inch drives. However, many computers, like the Macintosh and IBM Personal System/2 computers, come with only 3½-inch disk drives standard. Most software is now distributed on either type of disk. Each type of floppy drive has its advantages, but your major concern should be whether you can trade diskettes with colleagues, co-workers, and friends. It's best to get the same type of diskette drives as people with whom you'll be frequently exchanging programs and data. If you do get a hard disk, one floppy drive will probably be sufficient. However, if you often need to copy entire diskettes, it might be worth investing in two drives. In systems without hard disks, having two floppy drives is the most practical arrangement.

Display

With some computers, you have no choice as to what kind of display to get. The Apple Macintosh Plus and Macintosh SE, for example, come with a built-in 9-inch monochrome graphics display. On most computers, however, you have a choice among several alternatives. Older and less-expensive computers give you a choice among monochrome text, monochrome graphics, and color graphics monitors. Many newer microcomputers, like the IBM Personal System/2 series, support only graphics monitors, but you do have a choice between monochrome and color. To complicate matters more, many computers can accept several different display adapters, each of which may support several video modes.

To resolve your display dilemma, first look at your software selections. If you want to run software that uses graphics, you'll need a graphics display. On the other hand, if you're *positive* that you'll only be working with text, you may want to opt for a less expensive monochrome text monitor. Although in most cases color is not absolutely necessary, many people find that color monitors are more pleasant to work with, despite the added expense. If you are planning to use software that manipulates detailed graphics, you'll need a high-resolution display. As with most hardware selections, try to choose a system that can be upgraded later, if possible. Your needs may expand and prices may fall to a point where you would like to invest in a more sophisticated display. It's much easier and less expensive to replace a display adapter and monitor than an entire computer system.

Printer

Literally hundreds of microcomputer printers are on the market. Before you choose a particular model, you must first decide on what type of printer you need. Most microcomputer users have 9-pin dot-matrix printers. These printers can do graphics and can print fairly rapidly in draft mode, yet also have a more attractive, but much slower, near-letter-quality mode. If you will be printing letters on bond or letterhead paper, be sure to look for models that can easily accept single sheets as well as the fan-fold, pin-feed computer paper most dot-matrix printers use. For true letter quality, you might want to get a daisy-wheel printer. These printers produce text that looks just like that from typewriters, but they are quite slow. Applications that produce very high-quality text and graphics may require a 24-pin dot-matrix printer or perhaps even an expensive laser printer. Before you make your final decision on any printer, be sure to see samples of the text and graphics it can produce. Also consider the cost of supplies like paper, ribbons, toner cartridges (for laser printers) and additional typefaces.

Other Peripherals

A wide range of optional peripheral devices can be connected to a microcomputer. In your selection of a system, you should try to choose initially only those devices that will be absolutely necessary. You can always add more peripherals later, provided that you've chosen a system that can be expanded. If you'll be accessing remote computers, you'll need to select a modem. Many graphics applications require the use of a mouse. Some computer games use joysticks or trackballs. Examine your software selections carefully to make sure that you understand exactly what hardware devices are necessary.

Specifications and Benchmarks

In the preceding sections, we've briefly described the hardware you need to select. But, how do you pick the exact models to buy? Just as in making software selections, one method is to look carefully at what people around you have purchased. Some experts have even suggested that you get a system exactly like another one you have access to, perhaps at school, work, or a friend's. This way, you can become familiar with the components before you buy, and after you get your system, you have access to an exact duplicate in case your system isn't working. Although it definitely helps to have access to a similar system, if you only buy what someone else has, you're depending a great deal on their judgment, which may or may not be better than your own.

Another method of selecting hardware is to read reviews published in computer and consumer magazines. Just like software reviews, hardware reviews compare and evaluate actual products. For computers, hardware reviews can provide in-depth information about how they are constructed and how they work. For devices like displays, printers, and modems, reviews can compare models quantitatively and tabulate their features. Be forewarned, however, that these reviews are often saturated with specifications and benchmarks.

Specifications are a detailed list of the exact components, options, and capabilities of a particular hardware device. Microcomputer specifications typically list the manufacturer, exact size, microprocessor, coprocessors, system clock speed, amount of standard RAM, total possible RAM, amount of ROM, disk drives and capacities, number and type of expansion slots, number and type of interfaces, retail list price, and many other details. Sometimes, specifications include measures of performance. For example, many printer specifications include the number of characters printed per second. Although specifications can be one way to compare different devices, they may be misleading. Performance measurements are often made under ideal conditions. So, a printer advertised at 200 characters per second, may not actually be that fast when printing a document from your word processor, especially if it contains underlining, boldface, and italics.

A **benchmark** is an objective, reproducible measure of hardware or software performance, typically the amount of time it takes to run a standard program or process a particular set of data. Just like specifications, benchmarks are one way to compare hardware, but they can also be misleading. For example, a common benchmark for computer performance is one cycle of a calculation known as the *Sieve of Eratosthenes*. This is a method of finding prime numbers (numbers only evenly divisible by themselves and 1) that has been adapted to computers. Although benchmarks such as these may be useful for measuring the time required for certain very specific kinds of computer operations, they provide little or no information about ease of use, reliability, maintainability, the amount of manufacturer support for a product, or other equally important attributes. Sometimes, magazines like *BYTE* and *PC Magazine* develop their own benchmarks for reviewing products. Although these benchmarks are designed to measure performance under typical conditions, they may still not reflect how fast your software will run on your machine. Benchmark results, like specifications, should be taken with a grain of salt.

Step 5: Purchase the System

After selecting your hardware, you may have to go back and modify your list of software packages so that you have ones that will all run on the machine you've chosen. Before you even think of buying anything, you should have a fairly complete list of the exact software and hardware products you'll need. Since most product reviews and ads contain prices, you should also have a good notion of how much all this will cost. This is the time to look at your budget and make some realistic choices. You may not be able to afford all the software packages and optional peripherals you want to get. Fortunately, some of these purchases can be postponed. If you've listed your selections by priority, you can initially buy only those most essential items.

When to Buy

For many people, the most disconcerting circumstances of microcomputer shopping are the rate at which technology advances and how quickly prices can drop. Computer newspapers and magazines are filled with rumors, educated guesses, and pre-release previews about new products and upgrades to existing ones. Most manufacturers, it would seem, are constantly on the verge of releasing a computer, peripheral, or software package that will render every preceding product hopelessly obsolete. Even worse, what you pay $4,000 for this year may cost less than $1,000 two years from now. This perpetual anticipation can immobilize some potential computer shoppers.

Unfortunately, you must simply accept the facts that whichever hardware and software you choose, prices will drop and new versions will be released. There may be some prudence in waiting one or two months if a product is about to be released that will truly meet your needs. However, production often lags behind the demand for new products and it's sometimes best not to be one of the first owners of a brand-new piece of hardware or software. New technology, such as automobiles, stereos, hardware, and software, frequently has unsuspected flaws. It's nearly impossible to detect all of the potential problems in a complex product that's being rushed out of the factory into a highly competitive marketplace. Although it's tempting to be one of the first to get the latest hardware or software, you may wind up as a guinea pig whose complaints contribute to the design of Version 2.0.

In most cases, the time to buy is *now*. If you truly need a computer, you probably can't afford to wait months for the release and delivery of a brand-new product. A great deal of hardware and software is currently available that will provide years of valuable service, even if new versions are released after your purchase. Assuming you've done your homework and selected a system that fulfills your requirements, it shouldn't matter that less expensive, more powerful alternatives will eventually be released. Even if your computing needs grow, you can most likely expand your current system later. Someday, you may even want to select a completely new system, but in the meantime you will have a computer that can help you now.

Where to Buy

Nowadays, computer hardware and software can be purchased from a variety of sources. The outlet you select often depends upon such factors as how much you know about computers, how much money you want to save, how soon you need a system, whether you're buying a well-established brand name product, and whether you're buying hardware or software. You can purchase a computer system from computer stores, department stores, school stores, manufacturers, mail-order firms, and used equipment dealers.

Computer Stores   Local retail outlets that specialize in computers, such as Computerland and Radio Shack Computer Centers, are the traditional source of hardware and software products for many shoppers, especially novices. Salespeople are usually knowledgeable and can help a great deal in putting together a system that meets your needs. Most computer stores can also service your hardware should it need repair after the purchase. Many items are in stock or can be ordered and obtained in a few days. Unfortunately, many computer stores sell only a few brands. Although the brands tend to be from a select group of well-established manufacturers, your choices may be somewhat limited at a computer store. Items are usually sold at retail list prices, but there may be occasional sales or discounts given to certain groups of people. It may cost a bit more to buy a computer or peripheral device at a computer store, but dealers are nearby, accessible, and stand behind the hardware they sell.

Despite the additional cost, it often makes sense to buy hardware from a computer store. There is less advantage, however, to buying brand name software from a computer store. Software doesn't break down in the sense that hardware does, so a computer store technician can't repair a program. For most software packages, any problems or questions you have must usually be taken directly to the manufacturer. Although computer store salespeople may be able to answer some of your software questions, they simply can't be experts on every program they sell. In many cases, brand name software can be purchased for less from other sources.

Department Stores   Sometimes, retail department stores like Sears, Target, and Service Merchandise sell computers and software. List prices are usually discounted and you can get items immediately if they are in stock. Unfortunately, department store salespeople may not be very knowledgeable about computers. Furthermore, each store typically only carries a single computer brand. In most cases, service after the sale may only be obtained from the original manufacturer. However, if you're fairly knowledgeable about computers and a local department store has exactly what you want, you may be able to get a good bargain.

School Stores   If you're a student, faculty, or staff member of a college or university and in the market for a computer system, you may be in luck. Many schools have special deals with computer hardware and software manufacturers enabling them to offer products to qualified buyers at substantial savings. Hardware and software may be sold through a university bookstore, student union, educational consortium, or local computer center at discounts of up to 50% for students, faculty, and staff. Computer manufacturers like Apple, IBM, Hewlett-Packard, and Zenith often make deals with schools to sell their equipment at very low prices. In many cases, sales agents are knowledgeable and schools may also have their own service centers.

Manufacturers   Sometimes, there's no dealer in the area that sells the computer you want. Or, you may qualify for a volume discount by wanting to purchase a number of systems all at once. In such situations it may be advantageous to go directly to the manufacturer of a particular hardware or software product. Unless you're purchasing in volume, you'll probably pay the list price and it may take several days or weeks for the item to be shipped to you. However, at least you know that you're going directly to the source and eliminating the middleman. Some large manufacturers, like IBM, may even have a local office through which you can purchase products and get equipment serviced after the sale.

Mail-Order Firms   In the past, computer mail-order firms have had a somewhat less than prestigious reputation. With very few exceptions, that reputation is no longer justified. In fact, the seventh largest domestic microcomputer manufacturer, Dell Computer Corporation, is strictly a mail-order firm. This particular company even offers an optional next-day, on-site service contract for most major metropolitan areas and unlimited access to technicians over toll-free phone lines. Although most mail-order firms may not be this accommodating, a great many individuals, schools, and businesses buy computer hardware and software through the mail. Mail-order buying can save you money, and, in this day of overnight package delivery, can also be very convenient.

Still, the rule is "let the buyer beware" when it comes to mail-order purchasing. Ordering hardware over the phone can be daunting to computer novices. Many mail-order firms put together their own computers from standard components. These computers can be fantastic machines, but unless you know exactly what you're doing, it's probably best to stick to established brand names. Although, as we said, some mail-order firms offer repair service, most of them don't. Many advertise technical support over the phone, but it can sometimes be difficult to get through and have your questions answered politely, quickly, and accurately. Make sure that any mail-order firm you do choose has been in business for awhile.

Buying brand name software through the mail, however, offers several advantages. Discounts are usually substantial and the package you get in the mail is identical to what you would get from your local computer store or directly from the manufacturer. Large mail-order firms may have many items in stock and can often deliver them the next day via an overnight carrier for a modest extra charge.

Used Equipment Dealers   A recent market study showed that most people buying new computers have owned at least one computer before. What's happening to all those computers that are being replaced? Some are winding up at used computer dealers. As the microcomputer industry ages, more and more used computer stores are opening. Sometimes you can find real bargains at such stores but, like buying a used car, purchasing a pre-owned computer or hardware component can be somewhat risky. Many of the machines in used computer stores are obsolete. They may still be quite useful, but it might be difficult to get parts, service, and software for computers no longer in production. If, on the other hand, a used computer is being sold because its owner simply upgraded to a more powerful system, there may be no reason not to buy it as long as it's been thoroughly tested and guaranteed by the dealer.

Step 6: Install the System

You've chosen and purchased your software and hardware. The system was delivered today and now it's at home still in the boxes. What do you do? Well, first open all the boxes and get out the instructions. Make sure all the components, cables, disks, and other items are there. Follow the directions and set up the machine. Some computers come with tutorial programs you can run to teach you the basics of using the hardware and running the operating system. Besides being entertaining, these tutorials are usually quite informative and well worth the time. Once you feel comfortable with the fundamentals, you can follow the instructions to install your software on your computer. Don't be surprised if you have problems or if things don't work exactly as the tutorials and manuals indicate. Reread the instructions and try again. If you're still having problems, call your dealer or the manufacturer's customer service department. If you still can't get your system running, you may have an honest-to-goodness defect and will have to return your system.

Once you do get your system up and running, try out all of the hardware and software components as soon as possible. Read your warranties and mail in the cards that register you with the manufacturers as a new owner. Not only will this validate your warranties, it will also put you on mailing lists so that you can get information about new versions and upgrades. At this time you might be thinking about insurance and service contracts. If your computer system represents a substantial investment to you, and you come to need it on a daily basis, you'll want make sure that it's insured and that you can get it repaired if it breaks down.

Finally, consider the surroundings in which you set up your system. A sturdy, roomy table or desktop and a well-designed, comfortable chair are musts if you expect to use your computer system for hours at a time. Keep your system clean and free from dust, spills, food crumbs, and other foreign materials. Try to keep any cooling vents unobstructed so that your system won't overheat. Unplug your hardware when not in use and try not to run it during electrical storms. Computer equipment, like other electronic devices, can be easily damaged or even destroyed by electrical surges caused by lightning or other power line disturbances. It might be prudent to plug all of your equipment into a **surge protector**. This is a relatively inexpensive device with a main switch, several electrical sockets, and circuitry to rapidly cut off power when a voltage surge occurs. Careful installation of your computer system can help ensure its reliability and usefulness for years to come.

SOFTWARE INSTALLATION

Most operating systems and application packages must be **installed** on your computer before you can use them. This typically involves running a special installation or setup program included with the software. Installation programs often create a new subdirectory on your hard disk, copy the files from the floppy disks included with the package to that subdirectory, and let you specify what kind of hardware you have. At most school microcomputer labs, this has already been done for you by the attendants. If you own a computer, however, you will probably have to install any new software you purchase yourself. The documentation that comes with the software should explain, step-by-step, how to run the installation program and answer any questions that may be asked about your hardware and software. Let's briefly go over the steps necessary to install the software discussed in this book: PC-DOS and MS-DOS Version 3.30, IBM DOS 4.00, MS-DOS 4.01, WordPerfect Version 5.1., Lotus 1-2-3 Release 2.01, Lotus 1-2-3 Release 2.2, Lotus 1-2-3 Release 3.1, and dBASE IV Version 1.1.

PC-DOS and MS-DOS Version 3.30

MS-DOS 3.30 and PC-DOS 3.30 are very similar. The MS-DOS package comes with two manuals entitled *MS-DOS User's Guide* and *MS-DOS User's Reference*. The first one contains the instructions for installing the system. The package can be purchased on either 3½-inch, 720K floppy disks, or 5¼-inch, 360K floppy disks. The 5¼-inch package comes with two disks, one labeled *Startup* and the other *Operating*.

Although the DOS 3.30 *Startup* diskette can be copied to another diskette to routinely boot up the computer from drive A, many people install the operating system on their hard disk C, if they have one. To install DOS 3.30 on a hard disk, follow these steps:

1. Insert the DOS 3.30 Startup disk into drive A.
2. Turn on the computer. If it is already on, press **Ctrl-Alt-Del** to reboot.

A15

3. If the hard disk is not formatted (e.g., if you have a brand new computer), enter **format c: /s**. WARNING: Do not use this command if your hard disk is already formatted, or you will lose all files stored on it.

4. If the hard disk is already formatted with a previous version of DOS, enter **sys c:** instead of using the FORMAT command.

5. Enter **copy command.com c:** to copy the command processor to the hard disk.

6. If a subdirectory named DOS already exists on the hard disk, enter **del c:\dos*.*** to delete its contents. If such a subdirectory does not exist, enter **md c:\dos** to create it.

7. Enter **copy *.* c:\dos** to copy all the files from the Startup diskette to the DOS subdirectory on the hard disk.

8. Take the Startup diskette out of drive A, replace it with the Operating diskette, press **F3**, and press **Enter** to repeat the previous command and copy all of the files from the Operating diskette to the DOS subdirectory on the hard disk.

9. Remove the diskette from drive A, store all your original DOS diskettes in a safe place, and press **Ctrl-Alt-Del** to reboot your computer from the hard disk with DOS 3.30.

10. Enter **path c:\;c:\dos;** to set up the search paths for the root directory and the DOS subdirectory. You can add other search paths on the end of this command if you like. Ideally, this path command should be put in your AUTOEXEC.BAT file.

IBM DOS Version 4.00

The IBM DOS 4.00 package comes with two short manuals entitled *Getting Started with Disk Operating System Version 4.00* and *Using Disk Operating System Version 4.00*. The first one contains the instructions for installing the system. The package can be purchased on either 3½-inch, 720K floppy disks or 5¼-inch, 360K floppy disks. You should get the package with disks that match your floppy drive A. The 3½-inch package comes with two disks, one labeled *Install* and the other *Operating*. The 5¼-inch package comes with five disks labeled *Install, Select, Operating 1, Operating 2,* and *Operating 3*.

Although DOS 4.00 can be installed on floppy disks to boot up the computer from drive A, most people install the operating system on their hard disk C, if they have one. To install DOS 4.00 on a hard disk, follow these steps:

1. Insert the DOS 4.00 Install disk into drive A.

2. Turn on the computer. If it is already on, press **Ctrl-Alt-Del** to reboot.

3. After the copyright screen appears, press **Enter** and follow the instructions given by the installation program, which is called Select.

4. When you are finished with the installation program, remove the DOS floppy disk from drive A, store all your DOS disks in a safe place, and press **Ctrl-Alt-Del** to reboot your computer from the hard disk with DOS 4.00.

MS-DOS Version 4.01

The MS-DOS 4.01 package comes with three manuals entitled *MS-DOS User's Guide, MS-DOS User's Reference*, and *MS-DOS Shell User's Guide*. The first one contains the instructions for installing the system. The package can be purchased on either 3½-inch, 720K floppy disks or 5¼-inch, 360K floppy disks. You should get the package with disks that match your floppy drive A. The 3½-inch package comes with two disks, one labeled *Install* and the other *Operating*. The 5¼-inch package comes with six disks labeled *Install, Select, Operating 1, Operating 2, Operating 3*, and *Shell*.

Although MS-DOS 4.01 can be installed on floppy disks to boot up the computer from drive A, most people install the operating system on their hard disk C, if they have one. To install MS-DOS 4.01 on a hard disk, follow these steps:

1. Insert the MS-DOS 4.01 Install disk into drive A.
2. Turn on the computer. If it is already on, press **Ctrl-Alt-Del** to reboot.
3. After the copyright screen appears, press **Enter** and follow the instructions given by the installation program, which is called Select.
4. When you are finished with the installation program, remove the DOS floppy disk from drive A, store all your DOS disks in a safe place, and press **Ctrl-Alt-Del** to reboot your computer from the hard disk with MS-DOS 4.01.

WordPerfect Version 5.1

When you purchase WordPerfect Version 5.1, you get a softcover book entitled *WordPerfect Workbook*, a three-ring reference manual, and two plastic keyboard templates. The 5¼-inch package contains eleven floppy disks:

- *Install/Learn/Utilities 1* and 2. These disks hold the WordPerfect installation program, the files for the *WordPerfect Workbook* tutorial, and utility programs.
- *Program 1* and 2. These disks hold the actual WordPerfect program.
- *Spell/Thesaurus 1* and 2. These disks hold the spelling checker dictionary and the thesaurus.
- *PTR Program/Graphics 1* and 2. These disks hold the PTR program, which lets you change the files that control your printer, and clip art images.
- *Printer 1* through *Printer 3*. These disks contain printer drivers, the files needed to use WordPerfect with many different kinds of printers.

The files on the WordPerfect diskettes are stored in a compressed format. You must run the Install program to create a working copy of WordPerfect. For example, to install WordPerfect on a hard disk, follow these steps:

1. Turn on your computer and boot up DOS.
2. Insert the Install/Learn/Utilities 1 diskette into drive A.
3. Type **a**: and press **Enter** to switch to drive A.
4. Type **install** and press **Enter**.
5. Press any key to continue and then select Basic Installation.
6. Follow the directions and answer the questions presented by the Install program.
7. Remove the diskette from drive A and store all the original WordPerfect diskettes in a safe place.

8. Press **Ctrl-Alt-Del** to reboot your computer from the hard disk.

9. Now you have to run WordPerfect to select your printer driver. Type **wp** and press **Enter** to start WordPerfect.

10. Hold down the **Shift** key and press the **F7** function key to activate the Print menu.

11. Type **s** to choose the Select Printer option.

12. Type **2** to select the Additional Printers option.

13. Press **Up Arrow** or **Down Arrow** to highlight the name of your printer or of a model that works similarly.

14. After you have highlighted your printer, type **1** to choose the Select option and then press **Enter**.

15. Keep pressing the **F7** key until you return to the editing screen. Now you can continue using WordPerfect or press **F7** again to return to DOS.

Lotus 1-2-3 Release 2.01

When you purchase Lotus 1-2-3 Release 2.01, you get three softcover manuals entitled *Getting Started, Tutorial,* and *Reference.* Also included are various keyboard guides and a quick reference card. The 5¼-inch package contains six floppy disks:

- *System Disk.* This disk holds the actual 1-2-3 program, along with a program called Lotus that lets you switch between 1-2-3 and the other programs included with it.
- *PrintGraph.* This disk holds a separate program called PrintGraph that allows you to print your 1-2-3 graphs. Depending on your printer's ability, this program lets you control colors, fonts, and the layout of your graphs.
- *Utility Disk.* This disk contains the Install program that lets you set up 1-2-3 to use a printer and display graphs, and the Translate program that lets you transfer data between 1-2-3 and other application packages.
- *Install Library Disk.* This disk contains files used by the Install program to set up 1-2-3 to run with various monitors and printers.
- *A View of 1-2-3.* This disk holds View, an onscreen tutorial program to help you learn about 1-2-3.
- *Backup System Disk.* This is simply a backup copy of the System Disk, in case you damage or lose the original.

To install Lotus 1-2-3 on a hard disk, follow these steps:

1. Turn on your computer.

2. Type **md \123** and press **Enter** to create a new subdirectory named 123 on your hard disk.

3. Type **cd \123** and press **Enter** to switch to the subdirectory you've just created.

4. Insert the System Disk into drive A.

5. Type **copy a:*.*** and press **Enter.**

6. After the contents of the floppy disk have been copied into the 123 subdirectory, remove the disk from drive A.

7. Repeat Steps 4 through 6 for all the remaining floppy disks included with the package, except the Backup System Disk.

8. Type **install** and press **Enter.**

9. Press **Enter** after reading the introductory screen.

10. The Install program displays the Main menu on the screen. Press **Enter** to select the First-Time Installation option from the menu and follow the directions to answer questions about your monitor and printer.

11. When you finish the First-Time Installation, select the Exit Install option.

12. Put your original Lotus 1-2-3 floppy disks away in a safe place.

Lotus 1-2-3 Release 2.2

When you purchase Lotus 1-2-3 Release 2.2, you get two softcover manuals entitled *Reference* and *Setting Up 1-2-3, Tutorial, Quick Start, and Sample Applications*. Also included are various keyboard templates and two booklets: *Upgrader's Handbook* and *Quick Reference*. The 5¼-inch package contains twelve floppy disks:

- *System Disk.* This disk holds the actual 1-2-3 program, along with a program called Lotus that lets you switch between 1-2-3 and the other programs included with it.
- *Help Disk.* This disk holds the on-line help facility, which lets you get information about a topic while you are using 1-2-3.
- *PrintGraph Disk.* This disk holds a separate program called PrintGraph that allows you to print your 1-2-3 graphs. Depending on your printer's ability, this program lets you control colors, fonts, and the layout of your graphs.
- *Install Disk.* This disk holds the Install program that lets you set up 1-2-3 to use a printer and display graphs.
- *Install Library Disk.* This disk contains files used by the Install program to set up 1-2-3 to run with various monitors and printers.
- *Translate Disk.* This disk holds the Translate program that lets you transfer data between 1-2-3 and other application packages.
- *Sample Files Disk.* This disk holds worksheet files that you use while following instructions in the Tutorial, Quick Start, and Sample Applications sections of the manual.
- *Always Setup Disk.* This disk holds the Allways spreadsheet publishing add-in program, which lets you format worksheets and graphs.
- *Allways Disk 1* through *Allways Disk 4.* These disks contain font files and device driver files for Allways.

To install Lotus 1-2-3 Release 2.2 on a hard disk, follow these steps:

1. Turn on your computer.

2. Insert the System Disk in drive A and close the door.

3. Type **a:** and press **Enter** to switch to the disk in drive A.

4. Type **init** and press **Enter** to start the Initialization program.

5. Follow the directions to complete the Initialization program, recording your name and company's name on the System Disk.

6. Type **c:** and press **Enter** to switch back to the hard disk.

7. Type **md \123** and press **Enter** to create a new subdirectory named 123 on your hard disk.

8. Type **cd \123** and press **Enter** to switch to the subdirectory you've just created.

9. Make sure the System Disk is in drive A.

10. Type **copy a: *. *** and press **Enter.**
11. After the contents of the floppy disk have been copied into the 123 subdirectory, remove the disk from drive A.
12. Repeat Steps 9 through 11 for the remaining floppy disks included with the package, except the Allways disks.
13. Type **install** and press **Enter.**
14. Press **Enter** after reading the introductory screen.
15. The Install program displays the Main menu on the screen. Press **Enter** to select the First-Time Installation option from the menu and follow the directions to answer questions about your monitor and printer.
16. When you finish the First-Time Installation, select the Exit Install option.
17. Put your original Lotus 1-2-3 floppy disks away in a safe place.

Lotus 1-2-3 Release 3.1

Lotus 1-2-3 Release 3.1 can run only on IBM-compatible computers that have an 80286, 80386, or 80486 microprocessor, a hard disk drive, and at least one megabyte of memory. When you purchase Lotus 1-2-3 Release 3.1, you get a three-ring manual entitled *Reference* and five booklets: *Setting Up, Tutorial, Upgrader's Handbook, Wysiwyg Publishing and Presentation,* and *Quick Reference.* Also included are various keyboard templates.

To install Lotus 1-2-3 Release 3.1, follow these steps:

1. Turn on your computer.
2. Insert Disk 1 (the Install Disk) in drive A and close the door.
3. Type **a:** and press **Enter** to switch to the disk in drive A.
4. Type **install** and press **Enter** to start the Install program.
5. Follow the directions to complete the Install program.
6. Put your original Lotus 1-2-3 floppy disks away in a safe place.

dBASE IV Version 1.1

The dBASE IV program can be installed only on computers that have a hard disk drive. When you purchase dBASE IV, you get several booklets and manuals: *Getting Started with dBASE IV, dBASE IV Change Summary, Introduction to the Dot Prompt, Network Installation, Learning dBASE IV, Using the Menu System, Using the dBASE IV Applications Generator, Language Reference, Quick Reference,* and *Advanced Topics.* Also included are various keyboard templates. The 5¼-inch package contains ten floppy disks:

- *Install Disk.* This disk holds the program that lets you install dBASE IV on your computer.
- *System Disk #1* through *System Disk #7.* These disks contain the actual dBASE IV program.
- *Sample Programs Disk.* This disk holds files that are used as examples in the manuals.
- *Tutorial Disk.* This disk contains the on-line tutorial program, which teaches the basics of using dBASE IV.

To install dBASE IV, follow these steps:

1. Turn on your computer.
2. Insert the Installation Disk in drive A and close the door.
3. Type **a:** and press **Enter** to switch to the disk in drive A.
4. Type **install** and press **Enter** to start the Installation program.
5. Follow the directions to complete the Installation program.
6. Put your original dBASE IV floppy disks away in a safe place.

COMMAND
SUMMARIES

■ MS-DOS Version 4.01

DOS Keys

Keypress	Description
Ctrl-Alt-Del	Reboots DOS.
Ctrl-Break	Cancels a command.
Ctrl-PrtSc	Echoes to the printer.
Enter	Processes a command.
Esc	Cancels the current line.
Pause	Pauses screen scrolling (Enhanced keyboards).
Ctrl-Num Lock	Pauses screen scrolling (PC and AT keyboards).
Print Screen	Prints the contents of the screen (Enhanced keyboards).
Shift-PrtSc	Prints the contents of the screen (PC and AT keyboards).
F1	Retypes one character from the previous command.
F2	Retypes previous command up to the specified character.
F3	Retypes all of the previous command.
F4	Deletes previous command up to the specified character.
F5	Saves current command as if it were the previous command.
F6	Inserts an end-of-file code (Ctrl-Z).
Del	Skips over a character from the previous command.
Ins	Switches insert/overwrite mode in the command line.
>	Redirects output.
>>	Redirects and appends output.
<	Redirects input.
|	Pipes output.

DOS Commands

These conventions are used in the list of DOS commands that follows.

Command Format Conventions	
[ ]	optional command switch or parameter, such as [/a]
or	either/or choice, such as DEL **or** ERASE
...	optional repetition of the previous item as necessary
italics	name or value you must enter, such as the following:
drive:	disk drive name, such as A: or B:
path	directory name, such as \WP\LETTERS\WORK
filename	file name, including extension, such as JIM.DOC
pathname	path plus a *filename*, such as \WP\LETTERS\WORK\JIM.DOC
(Internal)	indicates an internal (resident) DOS command.
(External)	indicates an external (transient) DOS command.
(No Network)	indicates a command that does not work over a network.

You can specify a drive and/or path before any external command in the table below.

DOS Command	Formats and Description
APPEND	APPEND [/x] [/e] [;] **or** APPEND [*drive:*]*path*[;[*drive:*][*path*]...] **or** APPEND [*path*] [/x:[off **or** on]] [/path:[off **or** on]] Specifies the paths to be searched for files with extensions other than BAT, COM, and EXE. (External) /x Searches for BAT, COM, and EXE files, too. /e Stores appended paths in the DOS environment. /path If on, searches for files in the appended paths even if the files have drive or path prefixes.
ASSIGN	ASSIGN [*x* [=] *y*] ... Reassigns a disk drive letter to another drive. (External)
ATTRIB	ATTRIB [+r **or** -r] [+a **or** -a] [*drive:*]*pathname* [/s] Changes a file's read-only or archive attribute. (External) +r Turns on read-only attribute. -r Turns off read-only attribute. +a Turns on archive attribute. -a Turns off archive attribute. /s Processes files in subdirectories.
BACKUP	BACKUP [*drive1:*][*path*][*filename*] [*drive2:*] [/s] [/m] [/a] [/f:*size*] [/d:*date*] [/t:*time*] [/L:[[*drive:*][*path*]*filename*]] Backs up one or more files from one disk to another. (External)

DOS Command	Formats and Description
BACKUP *(continued)*	/s Backs up subdirectories. /m Backs up only changed files. /a Adds files without erasing backup disks. /f: Formats target disks if necessary; *size* indicates type of disk (160K, 180K, 320K, 360K, 720K, 1.2M, or 1.44M) /d: Backs up only those files modified on or after *date*. /t: Backs up only those files modified on or after *time*. /L: Makes a backup log entry in the specified file.
BREAK	BREAK [off **or** on] Turns Ctrl-Break off or on for certain operations. (Internal)
CD or CHDIR	CD **or** CHDIR [*path*] Switches between subdirectories or displays the current directory. (Internal)
CHCP	CHCP [*nnn*] Displays or changes the current code page, where *nnn* is the code page. (Internal)
CHKDSK	CHKDSK [*drive:*][*pathname*] [/f] [/v] Displays a disk and memory status report and checks for errors. (External) (No Network) /f Fixes lost cluster chains on the disk. /v Displays the name of every file on the disk.
CLS	CLS Clears the screen. (Internal)
COMMAND	COMMAND [*drive:*][*path*] [*device*] [/e:*nnnnn*] [/p] [/c *string*] Starts a new command processor. (External) /e: Specifies the environment size, where *nnnnn* is the size in bytes. /p Keeps the secondary command processor in memory. /c Performs the commands specified in *string* and then returns to the primary command processor.
COMP	COMP [*drive:*][*pathname1*] [*drive:*][*pathname2*] Compares the contents of two sets of files. (External)
COPY	COPY [*drive:*]*pathname1* [*drive:*][*pathname2*] [/v] [/a] [/b] **or** COPY [*drive:*]*pathname1* [/v] [/a] [/b] [*drive:*][*pathname2*] **or** COPY *pathname1* + *pathname2* ... *pathnameN* Duplicates one or more files. Also appends files. (Internal)

DOS Command	Formats and Description
COPY *(continued)*	/v Turns on the verify switch. /a Copies ASCII files. /b Copies binary files.
CTTY	CTTY *device* Changes the console (terminal) to another device. (Internal)
DATE	DATE [*mm-dd-yy*] Displays or sets the date. (Internal)
DEL or ERASE	DEL **or** ERASE [*drive:*] *pathname* [/p] Removes one or more files from a disk. (Internal) /p Prompts user before each deletion.
DIR	DIR [*drive:*][*pathname*] [/p] [/w] Lists the files on a disk or in a subdirectory. (Internal) /p Pauses after each screen. /w Displays a wide listing.
DISKCOMP	DISKCOMP [*drive1:*] [*drive2*] [/1] [/8] Compares two diskettes. (External) (No Network) /1 Compares just the first sides. /8 Compares just the first 8 sectors of each track.
DISKCOPY	DISKCOPY [*drive1:*] [*drive2:*] [/1] Duplicates an entire floppy disk. (External) (No Network) /1 Copies only one side.
DOSSHELL	DOSSHELL Starts the DOS Shell. (Batch File)
EXE2BIN	EXE2BIN [*drive:*]*pathname1* [*drive:*]*pathname2* Converts EXE files to BIN or COM files. (External)
EXIT	EXIT Exits the COMMAND.COM program. Also, returns to the DOS Shell from the DOS prompt. (Internal)
FASTOPEN	FASTOPEN [*drive:*[= *n*][…]] /x **or** FASTOPEN [*drive:*[= (*n,m*)][…]] /x **or** FASTOPEN [*drive:*[= ([*n*],*m*)][…]] /x Speeds up disk access by storing directory and file names and locations in a memory cache. (External) (No Network) *n* The number of files FASTOPEN will work with (10–999). *m* The number of file extent entries (1–999). /x Puts the cache in expanded memory.
FDISK	FDISK Partitions a hard disk. (External) (No Network)
FIND	FIND [/v] [/c] [/n] "*string*" [[*drive:*][*pathname*] …] Searches for a text string in one or more files. (External)

DOS Command	Formats and Description
FIND *(continued)*	/v Displays all lines *not* containing the string. /c Displays only the number of lines that contain the string. /n Precedes each line with its line number in the file.
FORMAT	FORMAT *drive:* [/1] [/4] [/8] [/n:*sectors*] [/t:*tracks*] [/v[:*label*]] [/s] **or** FORMAT *drive:* [/1] [/b] [/n:*sectors*] [/t:*tracks*] **or** FORMAT *drive:* [/v[:*label*]] [/f:*size*] [/s] Prepares a disk for use. (External) (No Network) /1 Formats only one side. /4 Formats a 360K disk in a 1.2M drive. /8 Formats 8 sectors per track. /n: Specifies the number of sectors. /t: Specifies the number of tracks. /v: Specifies the disk name (volume label). /b Leaves room for the DOS hidden system files. /s Creates a bootup disk. /f: Specifies the disk size (160K, 180K, 320K, 360K, 720K, 1.2M, 1.44M)
GRAFTABL	GRAFTABL [*xxx*] **or** /status **or** [?] Enhances the display of graphics characters on a Color Graphics Adapter. (External) *xxx* The code page id number. /status Displays the active character set. ? Displays instructions for using GRAFTABL.
GRAPHICS	GRAPHICS *type* [*profile*] [/r] [/b] [/lcd] [/printbox:*id*] Allows printing of graphics screens. (External) /r Prints black on the screen as black on the page. /b Prints the background in color. /lcd Uses aspect ratio of LCD screens. /printbox Selects the printbox size.
JOIN	JOIN [*drive: drive:path*] **or** *drive:* /d Treats a disk drive as if it were a subdirectory. (External) (No Network) /d Unjoins a previous JOIN.
KEYB	KEYB [*xx*[,[*yyy*],[[*drive:*][*path*]*filename*]]] [/ID:*nnn*] Loads a keyboard-translation table for a country, where *xx* is a two-letter country code and *yyy* is the code page that defines the character set. (External) /ID: Specifies the keyboard in use to be *nnn*.
LABEL	LABEL [*drive:*][*label*] Creates or changes a disk's name (volume label). (External) (No Network)

DOS Command	Formats and Description
MD or MKDIR	MD **or** MKDIR [*drive:*]*path* Creates a new subdirectory. (Internal)
MEM	MEM [/program **or** /debug] Displays a memory report. (External) /program Displays programs in memory. /debug Displays technical information.
MODE	MODE [*device*] [/status] **or** MODE LPT*n*[:][*c*][,[*l*][,r]] **or** MODE LPT*n* [cols = *c*] [lines = *l*] [retry = r] **or** MODE COM*m*[:]*b*,[,*p*[,*d*[,*s*[,r]]]] **or** MODE COM*m* baud = *b* [data = *d*] [stop = *s*] [parity = *p*] [retry = r] **or** MODE *display, n* **or** MODE [*display*], *shift* **or** MODE CON[:] [cols = *m*] [lines = *n*] **or** MODE CON[:] rate = *r* delay = *d* **or** MODE *device* codepage prepare = ((*yyy*)[*drive:*][*path*]*filename*) **or** MODE *device* codepage select = *yyy* **or** MODE *device* codepage refresh **or** MODE *device* codepage [/status] **or** MODE LPT*n*[:] = COM*m*[:] Establishes settings for various input/output devices. See the *MS-DOS User's Reference* for detailed information. (External)
MORE	MORE < *source* **or** *source*	MORE Accepts input and presents it one screen at a time as output. (External)
NLSFUNC	NLSFUNC [[*drive:*][*path*]*filename*] Specifies country-specific language and code page. (External)
PATH	PATH [*drive:*[*path*][;[*drive:*][*path*]...] **or** PATH [;] Tells DOS where to search for BAT, COM, and EXE files, or displays the current path. (Internal)
PRINT	PRINT [/d:*device*] [/b:*size*] [/u:*value1*] [/m:*value2*] [/s:*timeslice*] [/q:*qsize*] [/t] [*drive:*][*pathname*] [/c] [/p] Prints a text file. (External) /d: Specifies the device name. /b: Specifies the size of the internal buffer in bytes. /u: Specifies the number of clock ticks PRINT will wait for a printer. /m: Specifies the number of clock ticks PRINT can take to print a character. /s: Specifies the timeslice for background printing.

DOS Command	Formats and Description

PRINT *(continued)*

/q:	Specifies the number of files allowed in the print queue.
/t	Deletes all files in the print queue.
/c	Removes the preceding file and all following files from the print queue.
/p	Adds the preceding file and all following files to the print queue.

PROMPT

PROMPT [[*text*][$*character*]...]
Changes the format of the DOS prompt. (Internal) The *character* may be one of the following:

q	The = character.
$	The $ character.
t	The current time.
d	The current date.
p	The current directory.
v	The DOS version number.
n	The default drive.
g	The > character.
l	The < character.
b	The | character.
—	The Enter key.
e	The Escape key.
h	The Backspace key.

RD or RMDIR

RD **or** RMDIR [*drive:*]*path*
Removes an empty subdirectory. (Internal)

RECOVER

RECOVER [*drive:*][*path*]*filename* **or**
RECOVER *drive*
Reconstructs damaged files or disks. (External) (No Network)

RENAME or REN

RENAME **or** REN [*drive:*][*path*]*filename1 filename2*
Changes the name of one or more files. (Internal)

REPLACE

REPLACE [*drive:*]*pathname1* [*drive:*][*pathname2*] [/a] [/p] [/r] [/s] [/w] [/u]
Updates a set of files. (External)

/a	Adds new files to the target instead of replacing existing ones.
/p	Prompts user before replacing each file.
/r	Replaces read-only files.
/s	Searches all subdirectories.
/u	Replaces only older files.
/w	Prompts user before beginning.

RESTORE

RESTORE *drive1*: [*drive2:*][*pathname*] [/s] [/p] [/b:*date*] [/a:*date*] [/e:*time*] [/L:*time*] [/m] [/n]
Restores files backed up with the BACKUP command. (External)

/s	Restores subdirectories.
/p	Prompts the user before restoring read-only files or files that have been changed.

DOS Command	Formats and Description
RESTORE *(continued)*	/b: Restores only files modified on or before *date*.
	/a: Restores only files modified on or after *date*.
	/e: Restores only files modified at or earlier than *time*.
	/L: Restores only files modified at or later than *time*.
	/m Restores only files modified since the last backup.
	/n Restores only files that no longer exist on the target disk.
SELECT	SELECT menu Installs DOS. SELECT is usually executed by inserting the MS-DOS Install diskette in drive A and pressing Ctrl-Alt-Del. (External)
SET	SET [*string* = [*string*]] Displays or changes the contents of the DOS environment. (Internal)
SHARE	SHARE [/f:*space*] [/L:*locks*] Permits file sharing and locking on network systems. (External) /f: Specifies the storage space used to record file sharing information. /L: Specifies the number of locks to allow.
SORT	[*source*] | SORT [/r] [/ + *n*] **or** SORT [/r] [/ + *n*] *source* Accepts input, arranges it in order, and writes it out. (External) /r Reverses the sort (Z–A, 9–0). / + *n* Sorts the file according to the character in column *n*.
SUBST	SUBST [*drive*: *drive*:*path*] **or** SUBST *drive:* /d Treats a subdirectory as if it were a disk drive. (External) (No Network) /d Cancels a previous substitution.
SYS	SYS *drive*: Installs hidden system files on a properly formatted disk. (External) (No Network)
TIME	TIME [*hour:minute*[:*second*][*.centisecond*]]] Displays or sets the time of day. (Internal)
TREE	TREE [*pathname*:] [/f] [/a] Displays the directory structure of a disk. (External) /f Displays the names of the files in each directory. /a Uses only characters that can be output on any display or printer.

DOS Command	Formats and Description
TYPE	TYPE [*drive:*]*filename* Displays a text file on the screen. (Internal)
VER	VER Displays the DOS version number. (Internal)
VERIFY	VERIFY [off **or** on] Turns verification off or on when copying files. (Internal)
VOL	VOL [*drive:*] Displays the disk name (volume label). (Internal)
XCOPY	XCOPY [*drive:*]*pathname* [*drive:*][*pathname*] [/a] [/d:*date*] [/e] [/m] [/p] [/s] [/v] [/w] **or** XCOPY *drive:*[*pathname*] [*drive:*][*pathname*] [/a] [/d:*date*] [/e] [/m] [/p] [/s] [/v] [/w] Duplicates files faster and more flexibly than COPY. (External)

/a	Copies files that have their archive bit set.
/d:	Copies files modified on or after *date*.
/e	Copies subdirectories, even if they are empty.
/m	Same as /a, but turns off archive bit.
/p	Prompts user before copying each file.
/s	Copies subdirectories, unless they are empty.
/v	Turns on the verify switch.
/w	Waits before copying files.

Batch File Command	Formats and Description
CALL	CALL [*drive:*][*path*]*batchfile* [*argument*] Invokes *batchfile* from within the current batch file. The *argument* is the command in the current batch file that will be run following *batchfile*. (Internal)
ECHO	ECHO [off **or** on **or** *message*] Turns screen messages off or on, or displays *message*. (Internal)
FOR	FOR %%c in *set* do *command* **or** FOR %c in *set* do *command* Sets up a repeating loop in a batch file to perform a command for a set of files. The character *c* represents a variable name, the *set* is a set of files, and the *command* is a DOS command or program. (Internal)
GOTO	GOTO [:]*label* Transfers execution in a batch file to the line after *label*. (Internal)

Batch File Command	Formats and Description
IF	IF [not] errorlevel *number command* **or** IF [not] *string1* = = *string2 command* **or** IF [not] exist *filename command* Executes a command based on the result of a condition. (Internal)
PAUSE	PAUSE [*message*] Temporarily suspends the execution of a batch file until the user presses a key. (Internal)
REM	REM [*comment*] Identifies a batch file comment or remark. (Internal)
SHIFT	SHIFT Sets up more than nine batch file parameters. (Internal)

CONFIG.SYS Command	Formats and Description
BREAK	BREAK = [off **or** on] Turns Ctrl-Break off or on for certain operations.
BUFFERS	BUFFERS = *n*[,*m*] [/x] Sets the number of disk buffers. *n* The number of disk buffers (1–99). *m* The maximum number of sectors that can be read or written in one input/output operation (1–8). /x Sets the maximum number of disk buffers to 10,000 or the largest number of buffers that will fit in memory, whichever is less.
COUNTRY	COUNTRY = *xxx*[,[*yyy*]][,[*drive*:]*filename*]] Changes country-specific information. *xxx* The country code. *yyy* The code page for the country. *filename* The file containing country information.
DEVICE	DEVICE = [*drive*:][*path*]*filename* [*argument*] Installs a device driver.
DRIVEPARM	DRIVEPARM = /d:*number* [/c] [/f:*factor*] [/h:*heads*] [/i] [/n] [/s:*sectors*] [/t:*tracks*] Defines parameters for block devices such as disk and tape drives. /d: Specifies the physical drive number (0–255). /c Indicates that the drive can sense if its door has been opened. /f: Specifies the device type or form factor (0–7).

CONFIG.SYS Command	Formats and Description	
DRIVEPARM *(continued)*	/h:	Specifies the maximum head number (1–99).
	/i	Specifies an electrically-compatible 3½-inch disk drive.
	/n	Specifies a nonremovable block device.
	/s:	Specifies the number of sectors per track (1–99).
	/t:	Specifies the number of tracks per side (1–999).
FCBS	FCBS = *x,y* Allows access to file control blocks.	
	x	The number of files that can be open at one time.
	y	The number of files that DOS cannot close automatically.
FILES	FILES = *x* Specifies the maximum number of open files (*x*).	
INSTALL	INSTALL = [*drive:*][*path*]*filename* [*parameters*] Installs RAM-resident features. The *filename* must be FASTOPEN.EXE, KEY.EXE, NLSFUNC.EXE, or SHARE.EXE.	
LASTDRIVE	LASTDRIVE = *x* Specifies the last accessible drive, where *x* is the drive letter (A–Z).	
REM	REM *comment* Allows a comment or remark to be entered in the CONFIG.SYS file.	
SHELL	SHELL = [*drive:*][*path*]*filename* [*parameters*] Begins execution of the top-level command processor.	
STACKS	STACKS = *n,s* Supports the dynamic use of data stacks.	
	n	The number of stacks (0–64).
	s	The size of each stack (0–512).

WordPerfect Version 5.1

Cursor Movement Commands

Up one line	Up Arrow
Down one line	Down Arrow
Left one character	Left Arrow
Right one character	Right Arrow
Left one word	Ctrl-Left Arrow
Right one word	Ctrl-Right Arrow
Next tab stop	Tab
End of line	End
Up one screen	Grey − (NumPad)
Down one screen	Grey + (NumPad)
Up one page	Page Up
Down one page	Page Down
Right edge of screen	Home, Right Arrow
Left edge of screen	Home, Left Arrow
Beginning of Line (Before Text)	Home, Home, Left Arrow
Beginning of Line (Before Codes)	Home, Home, Home, Left Arrow
Beginning of document	Home, Home, Up Arrow
End of document	Home, Home, Down Arrow
Go to specified page	Ctrl-Home

Insert and Delete Commands

Switch insert/typeover mode	Insert
Insert hard return	Enter
Insert page break	Ctrl-Enter
Insert hard space	Home, Space Bar
Delete character or block	Delete
Delete character left of cursor	Backspace
Delete word at cursor	Ctrl-Backspace
Delete word left	Home, Backspace
Delete word right	Home, Delete
Delete to end of line	Ctrl-End
Delete to end of page	Ctrl-PgDn

Function Key Commands

Cancel last command	F1
Temporarily return to DOS	Ctrl-F1
Invoke Setup Menu	Shift-F1
Invoke thesaurus	Alt-F1
Search forward for text	F2
Invoke spelling checker	Ctrl-F2
Search backward for text	Shift-F2
Global search and replace	Alt-F2
Invoke Help facility	F3
Split screen into windows	Ctrl-F3
Switch to other window	Shift-F3
Reveal hidden formatting codes	Alt-F3
Indent paragraph	F4

Move, copy, or delete text	Ctrl-F4
Center paragraph	Shift-F4
Turn on block marking	Alt-F4
Invoke List Files menu	F5
Save or load ASCII text file	Ctrl-F5
Invoke Date/Outline menu	Shift-F5
Invoke Mark Text menu	Alt-F5
Boldface text	F6
Align text to tab stop	Ctrl-F6
Center text	Shift-F6
Align text flush right	Alt-F6
Exit menu, document, or program	F7
Create footnotes	Ctrl-F7
Invoke Print menu	Shift-F7
Create columns, tables, or use math	Alt-F7
Underline text	F8
Invoke Font menu	Ctrl-F8
Invoke Format menu	Shift-F8
Invoke Style menu	Alt-F8
Insert end-of-field merge code	F9
Invoke Merge/Sort menu	Ctrl-F9
Invoke Merge Codes menu	Shift-F9
Invoke Graphics menu	Alt-F9
Save current document	F10
Define new keyboard macro	Ctrl-F10
Retrieve existing document	Shift-F10
Invoke macro	Alt-F10
Reveal hidden formatting codes	F11
Turn on block marking	F12

Pull-Down Menus

Hold down the Alternate key and press the equal sign (Alt-=) to activate the menu bar. Highlight the menu or option you want and press Enter, or type the mnemonic letter shown on your screen in bright white or red. The following list gives the WordPerfect 5.1 pull-down menus and options. Mnemonic letters are shown in boldface.

    File
        Retrieve
        Save
        Text **I**n
            DOS Text (CR/LF to **H**Rt)
            DOS Text (CR/LF to **S**Rt)
            Spreadsheet
        Text **O**ut
            DOS **T**ext
            Generic
            WP5.0
            WP4.2
        Password
            Add/Change
            Remove

List Files
Summary
Print
Setup
    Mouse
    Display
    Environment
    Initial Settings
    Keyboard Layout
    Location of Files
Go to DOS
Exit
Edit
    Move (Cut)
    Copy
    Paste
    Append
        To File
        To Clipboard
    Delete
    Undelete
    Block
    Select
        Sentence
        Paragraph
        Page
        Tabular Column
        Rectangle
    Comment
        Create
        Edit
        Convert to Text
    Convert Case
        To Upper
        To Lower
    Protect Block
    Switch Document
    Window
    Reveal Codes
Search
    Forward
    Backward
    Next
    Previous
    Replace
    Extended
        Forward
        Backward
        Next
        Previous
        Replace
    Go to

Layout
   Line
   Page
   Document
   Other
   Columns
      On
      Off
      Define
   Tables
      Create
      Edit
   Math
      On
      Off
      Define
      Calculate
   Footnote
      Create
      Edit
      New Number
      Options
   Endnote
      Create
      Edit
      New Number
      Options
      Placement
   Justify
      Left
      Center
      Right
      Full
   Align
      Indent ->
      Indent -><-
      Margin Rel <-
      Center
      Flush Right
      Tab Align
      Hard Page
   Styles
Mark
   Index
   Table of Contents
   List
   Cross-Reference
      Reference
      Target
      Both
   Table of Authorities
      Mark Short
      Mark Full
      Edit Full

Define
  Index
  Table of Contents
  List
  Table of **A**uthorities
Generate
Master Documents
  Expand
  Condense
Subdocument
Document Compare
  Add Markings
  Remove Markings
Tools
  Spell
  Thesaurus
  Macro
    Define
    Execute
  Date Text
  Date Code
  Date Format
  Outline
    On
    Off
    Move Family
    Copy Family
    Delete Family
  Paragraph Number
  Define
  Merge Codes
    Field
    End Record
    Input
    Page Off
    Next Record
    More
  Merge
  Sort
  Line Draw
Font
  Base Font
  Normal
  Appearance
    Bold
    Underline
    Double Underline
    Italics
    Outline
    Shadow
    Small **C**ap
    Redline
    Strikeout

Superscript
Subscript
Fine
Small
Large
Very Large
Extra Large
Print Color
Characters
Graphics
  Figure
    Create
    Edit
    New Number
    Options
  Table Box
    Create
    Edit
    New Number
    Options
  Text Box
    Create
    Edit
    New Number
    Options
  User Box
    Create
    Edit
    New Number
    Options
  Equation
    Create
    Edit
    New Number
    Options
  Line
    Create Horizontal
    Create Vertical
    Edit Horizontal
    Edit Vertical
Help
  Help
  Index
  Template

Alphabetical List of Features

In the table below, the Keypresses column lists the keys to press and characters to type to invoke the feature. For example, to invoke the Advance feature (to advance the printer), press **Shift-F8**, type **4**, then type **1**.

Feature	Keypresses
Absolute Tab Settings	Shift-F8, 1, 8, t, 1
Acceleration Factor (Mouse)	Shift-F1, 1, 5
Add Password	Ctrl-F5, 2
Additional Printers	Shift-F7, s, 2
Advance (To Position, Line, etc.)	Shift-F8, 4, 1
Advanced Macro Commands (Macro Editor)	Ctrl-PgUp
Advanced Merge Codes	Shift-F9, 6
Align/Decimal Character	Shift-F8, 4, 3
Align Text on Tabs	Ctrl-F6
Alphabetize Text	Ctrl-F9, 2
Alt/Ctrl Key Mapping	Shift-F1, 5
Appearance of Printed Text	Ctrl-F8
Append Text to a File (Block On)	Ctrl-F4, 1-3, 4
Append to Clipboard (Block On)	Ctrl-F1, 3
ASCII Text File	Ctrl-F5, 1
Assign Keys	Shift-F1, 5
Assign Variable	Ctrl-PgUp
Attributes, Printed	Ctrl-F8
Attributes, Screen	Shift-F1, 2, 1
Authorities, Table of (Define)	Alt-F5, 5, 4
Authorities, Table of (Edit Full Form)	Alt-F5, 5, 5
Authorities, Table of (Mark)	Alt-F5, 4
Automatically Format and Rewrite	Shift-F1, 2, 6, 1
Auxiliary Files Location	Shift-F1, 6
Backspace (Erase)	Backspace
Backup Directory Location	Shift-F1, 6
Backup Files, Automatic	Shift-F1, 3, 1, 1
Backup Options	Shift-F1, 3, 1
Backward Search	Shift-F2
Base Font	Ctrl-F8, 4
Base Font (Document)	Shift-F8, 3, 3
Base Font (Printer)	Shift-F7, s, 3, 5
Baseline Placement for Typesetters	Shift-F8, 4, 6, 5
Beep Options	Shift-F1, 3, 2
Binding Offset	Shift-F7, b
Binding Offset (Default)	Shift-F1, 4, 8, 1
Black and White, View Document In	Shift-F1, 2, 5, 1
Block	Alt-F4
Block, (Assign Variable w/Block On)	Ctrl-PgUp
Block, Append (Block On)	Ctrl-F4, 1, 4
Block, Center (Block On)	Shift-F6
Block, Comment (Block On)	Ctrl-F5
Block Copy (Block On)	Ctrl-F4, 1, 2
Block Copy (Block On)	Ctrl-Ins
Block, Delete (Block On)	Del
Block, Move (Block On)	Ctrl-F4, 1, 1
Block Move (Block On)	Ctrl-Del
Block, Print (Block On)	Shift-F7

Feature	Keypresses
Block Protect (Block On)	Shift-F8
Bold	F6
Bold (Print Attribute)	Ctrl-F8, 2, 1
Border Options (Table and Graphic Box)	Shift-F8, 4, 8
Bottom Margin	Shift-F8, 2, 5
Box (Fig, Table, Text, User, Equation)	Alt-F9, 1-4 or 6
Cancel	F1
Cancel Hyphenation Code	Home, /
Cancel Print Job(s)	Shift-F7, 4, 1
Capitalize Block (Block On)	Shift-F3, 1
Cartridges and Fonts	Shift-F7, s, 3, 4
Case Conversion (Block On)	Shift-F3
Center Block (Block On)	Shift-F6
Center Justification	Shift-F8, 1, 3, 2
Center Page (Top to Bottom)	Shift-F8, 2, 1
Center Tab Setting	Shift-F8, 1, 8, c
Center Text	Shift-F6
Centered Text With Dot Leaders	Shift-F6, Shift-F6
Centimeters, Units of Measure	Shift-F1, 3, 8
Change Comment to Text	Ctrl-F5, 4, 3
Change Default Directory	F5, =, Dir name, Enter
Change Font	Ctrl-F8
Change Supplementary Dictionary	Ctrl-F2, 4
Change Text to Comment (Block On)	Shift-F5
Character Sets	Ctrl-v or Ctrl-2
Character Spacing	Shift-F8, 4, 6, 3
Clear Screen	F7, n or y, n
Clipboard	Ctrl-F1, 2-4
Codes, Default	Shift-F1, 4, 5
Codes, Merge	Shift-F9
Codes, Reveal	Alt-F3
Color Print	Ctrl-F8, 5
Colors/Fonts/Attributes	Shift-F1, 2, 1
Columns	Alt-F7, 1
Columns, Define	Alt-F7, 1, 3
Columns, Move Through	Ctrl-Home, Arrow key
Columns, Side-by-side Display	Shift-F1, 2, 6, 7
Commands, Programming (Macro Editor)	Ctrl-PgUp
Comment in Document	Ctrl-F5, 4
Comment to Text	Ctrl-F5, 4, 3
Comments Display	Shift-F1, 2, 6, 2
Compare Screen and Disk Documents	Alt-F5, 6, 2
Compose	Ctrl-v or Ctrl-2
Concordance	Alt-F5, 5, 3
Condense Master Document	Alt-F5, 6, 4
Conditional End of Page	Shift-F8, 4, 2
Control Characters	Shift-F9

Feature	Keypresses
Control Printer	Shift-F7, 4
Convert Documents (5.1 to 5.0 or 4.2)	Ctrl-F5, 3, 2 or 3
Convert Old Merge Codes	Ctrl-F9, 3
Copy Block (Block On)	Ctrl-F4, 1, 2
Copy Block (Block On)	Ctrl-Ins
Copy File(s)	F5, Enter, 8
Copy, Keyboard	Shift-F1, 5, 5
Copy Text (Block On or Off)	Ctrl-F4, 1-3, 2
Count Words	Ctrl-F2, 6
Create Spreadsheet Link	Ctrl-F5, 5, 2
Cross Reference	Alt-F5, 1
Ctrl/Alt Key Mapping	Shift-F1, 5
Cursor Movement	Arrow keys
Cursor Movement, Specialized	Grey + or − (NumPad)
Cursor Movement, Specialized	PgUp or PgDn
Cursor Movement, Specialized	Ctrl-Home or Esc
Cursor Speed	Shift-F1, 3, 3
Cut text (Block On or Off)	Ctrl-F4, 1-3, 3
Date Format	Shift-F5, 3
Date Format (Default)	Shift-F1, 4, 2
Date of File Creation	Shift-F8, 3, 5, 1
Date/Time	Shift-F5
Decimal/Align Character	Shift-F8, 4, 3
Decimal Tab Setting	Shift-F8, 1, 8, d
Default Codes	Shift-F1, 4, 5
Default Directory	F5
Default Settings	Shift-F1
Define Macros	Ctrl-F10
Define Paragraph/Outline Numbering	Shift-F5, 6
Define Printer	Shift-F7, s
Define Text (Highlight)	Alt-F4
Define ToC, Lists, ToA, Index	Alt-F5, 5
Delete	Backspace or Delete
Delete Block (Block On)	Backspace or Delete
Delete File	F5, Enter, 2
Delete Text (Block On or Off)	Ctrl-F4, 1-3, 3
Delete to End of Page	Ctrl-PgDn
Delete to End of Line	Ctrl-End
Delete to Word Boundary	Ctrl, Del or Bksp
Delete Word	Ctrl-Backspace
Diacriticals/Digraphs	Ctrl-v or Ctrl-2
Dictionary	Ctrl-F2
Directories	F5, Enter
Display	Shift-F1, 2
Display Attributes	Shift-F1, 2, 1
Display Disk Space	F5, Enter
Display Document Comments	Shift-F1, 2, 6, 2
Display Filenames, Short/Long	F5, Enter, 5

Feature	Keypresses
Display Pitch	Shift-F8, 3, 1
Display Setup	Shift-F1, 2
Document Backup	Shift-F1, 3, 1
Document Comment	Ctrl-F5, 4
Document Compare	Alt-F5, 6, 2
Document Format	Shift-F8
Document Management/Summary	Shift-F1, 3, 4
Document Preview	Shift-F7, 6
Document, Retrieve	Shift-F10
Document Summary, Create/Edit	Shift-F8, 3
Document Summary, Create on Save/Exit	Shift-F1, 3, 4, 1
Documents Directory	Shift-F1, 6, 7
DOS Command	Ctrl-F1, 5
DOS Text File	Ctrl-F5, 1
Dot Leader Tab	Shift-F8, 1, 8
Double Underline	Ctrl-F8, 2, 3
Download Fonts to Printer	Shift-F7, 7
Downloadable Fonts	Shift-F7, s, 3, 4
Downloadable Fonts Path	Shift-F7, s, 3, 6
Draw Lines	Ctrl-F3, 2
Dual Document Editing	Shift-F3
Edit Find Conditions	F5, Enter, 9, 5
Edit Screen Options	Shift-F1, 2, 6
Edit Spreadsheet Link	Ctrl-F5, 5, 3
Encrypt a Document	Ctrl-F5, 2
End of Field	F9
End of Line, Delete to	Ctrl-End
End of Line (Move to)	End
End of Page, Delete to	Ctrl-PgDn
End of Record	Shift-F9, 2
Endnote	Ctrl-F7, 2
Endnote Placement	Ctrl-F7, 3
Endnotes, Generate	Alt-F5, 6, 5
Enhanced Keyboard Definition	Shift-F1, 5
Enter Inserts Paragraph Number	Shift-F5, 6, 7
Environment	Shift-F1, 3
Equation Editor	Alt-F9, 6, 1, 9
Equation Options	Shift-F1, 4, 3
Execute Macro	Alt-F10
Exit WordPerfect	F7, n or y, y
Expand Master Document	Alt-F5, 6, 3
Extended Characters	Ctrl-v or Ctrl-2
Extended Replace	Home, Alt-F2
Extended Search	Home, F2
Extra Large Print	Ctrl-F8, 1, 7
Fast Save (Unformatted)	Shift-F1, 3, 5
Fast Text Display	Shift-F1, 2, 1, 2
Field	Shift-F9, 1
Figure Box	Alt-F9, 1

Feature	Keypresses
File, DOS text	Ctrl-F5, 1
File Management	F5, Enter
File, Mark	F5, Enter, *
File Search	F5, Enter, 9
Filename on Status Line	Shift-F1, 2, 6, 3
Files, Backup	Shift-F1, 3, 1
Files Location, Auxiliary	Shift-F1, 6
Find	F5, Enter, 9
Find Filename	F5, Enter, 9, 1
Fine Print	Ctrl-F8, 1, 3
Flush Right	Alt-F6
Flushed Right Text With Dot Leaders	Alt-F6, Alt-F6
Font Appearance	Ctrl-F8, 2
Font Attributes	Ctrl-F8, (1, 2 or 5)
Font, Base	Ctrl-F8, 4
Font Color	Ctrl-F8, 5
Font, Initial (Document)	Shift-F8, 3, 3
Font, Initial (Printer)	Shift-F7, s, 3, 5
Font Size	Ctrl-F8, 1
Fonts Directory	Shift-F7, s, 3, 6
Fonts, Download to Printer	Shift-F7, 7
Fonts, Downloadable	Shift-F7, s, 3, 4
Footers	Shift-F8, 2, 4
Footnote	Ctrl-F7, 1
Force Odd/Even Page	Shift-F8, 2, 2
Forced Insert	Home, Home, Ins
Forced Typeover	Home, Ins
Foreign Characters	Ctrl-v or Ctrl-2
Foreign Languages (International)	Shift-F8, 4, 4
Format Line/Page/Document/Other	Shift-F8
Format Screen	Ctrl-F3, 3
Format Screen, Automatically	Setup, 2, 6, 1
Forms, Define	Shift-F8, 2, 7
Forward Search	F2
Full Justification	Shift-F8, 1, 3, 4
Generate Tables, Indexes, etc.	Alt-F5, 6, 5
Generic Word Processor Format	Ctrl-F5, 3, 1
Global Search and Replace	Home, Alt-F2
Go To	Ctrl-Home
Go to DOS/Shell	Ctrl-F1, 1
Graphics	Alt-F9
Graphics Box Options	Alt-F9, 1-4 or 6, 4
Graphics Files Directory	Shift-F1, 6, 6
Graphics Quality	Shift-F7, g
Graphics Quality (Default)	Shift-F1, 4, 8, 3
Graphics Screen Type	Shift-F1, 2, 2
H-Zone	Shift-F8, 1, 2
Hanging Indent	F4, Shift-Tab
Hard Hyphen	Home, -
Hard Page Break	Ctrl-Enter

Feature	Keypresses
Hard Return Display Character	Shift-F1, 2, 6, 4
Hard Space	Home, Space
Hard Tab	Home, Tab
Headers	Shift-F8, 2, 3
Help	F3
Help, Printer	Shift-F7, s, 6
Hidden Codes	Alt-F3
Hide Document Comments	Shift-F1, 2, 6, 2
Hyphen Character	-
Hyphen, Hard	Home, -
Hyphen, Soft	Ctrl, -
Hyphenation	Shift-F8, 1, 1
Hyphenation Dictionaries	Shift-F1, 3, 6
Hyphenation Files	Shift-F1, 6, 3
Hyphenation Prompt	Shift-F1, 3, 7
Hyphenation Rules	Shift-F1, 3, 6
Hyphenation Zone	Shift-F8, 1, 2
Import Spreadsheet	Ctrl-F5, 5, 1
Inches (Units of Measure)	Shift-F1, 3, 8
Indent Left and Right	Shift-F4
Indent Left Only	F4
Index (Define or Generate)	Alt-F5, 5 or 6
Index, Mark Text for (Block on)	Alt-F5, 3
Initial Base Font, Printer	Shift-F7, s, 3, 5
Initial Base Font, Document	Shift-F8, 3, 3
Initial Codes, Default	Shift-F1, 4, 5
Initial Codes, Document	Shift-F8, 3, 2
Initial Settings, Default	Shift-F1, 4
Initialize Printer	Shift-F7, 7
Input (Merge)	Shift-F9, 3
Insert any Character	Ctrl-v or Ctrl-2
Insert, Forced	Home, Home, Ins
Insert Page Number	Shift-F8, 2, 6, 3
Insert/Replace Mode	Insert
Insert Subdocument	Alt-F5, 2
International Characters	Ctrl-v or Ctrl-2
Interrupt Print Job	Shift-F7, 4, 5
Invisible Soft Return	Home, Enter
Italics Print	Ctrl-F8, 2, 4
Item Down	Alt-Down Arrow
Item Left	Alt-Left Arrow
Item Right	Alt-Right Arrow
Item Up	Alt-Up Arrow
Justification	Shift-F8, 1, 3
Justification Limits	Shift-F8, 4, 6, 4
Keep Lines Together	Shift-F8, 4, 2
Kerning	Shift-F8, 4, 6, 1
Keyboard Definitions/Layout	Shift-F1, 5
Keyboard/Macro Files	Shift-F1, 6, 2
Keyboard Map	Shift-F1, 5, 8

Feature	Keypresses
Labels	Shift-F8, 2, 7, 5, 8
Landscape Fonts	Shift-F7, s, 3, 4
Landscape Forms	Shift-F8, 2, 7
Landscape Paper Size/Type	Shift-F8, 2, 7
Languages	Shift-F8, 4, 4
Large Print	Ctrl-F8, 1, 5
Leaders (Centered Text)	Shift-F6, Shift-F6
Leaders (Flushed Right Text)	Alt-F6, Alt-F6
Leading	Shift-F8, 4, 6, 6
Left and Right Margins	Shift-F8, 1, 7
Left Justification	Shift-F8, 1, 3, 1
Left Margin Release	Shift-Tab
Left Tab Setting	Shift-F8, 1, 8, l
Letter/Word Spacing	Shift-F8, 4, 6, 3
Line (Border) Appearance	Shift-F8, 4, 8
Line Draw	Ctrl-F3, 2
Line Format	Shift-F8, 1
Line, Graphics	Alt-F9, 5
Line Height	Shift-F8, 1, 4
Line Numbering	Shift-F8, 1, 5
Line Spacing	Shift-F8, 1, 6
Link Options	Ctrl-F5, 5, 4
Link, Update	Ctrl-F5, 5, 4, 3
Links, Spreadsheet	Ctrl-F5, 5, 2-4
List Files	F5, Enter
List Printer Files	Shift-F7, s, 2, 4
Lists, Mark Text for (Block On)	Alt-F5, 2
Lists (Define or Generate)	Alt-F5, 5 or 6
Location of Backup Files	Shift-F1, 6, 1
Location of Files	Shift-F1, 6
Location of Forms	Shift-F8, 2, 7
Location of Hyphenation Files	Shift-F1, 6, 3
Location of Keyboard/Macro Files	Shift-F1, 6, 2
Location of Main Dictionary	Shift-F1, 6, 3
Location of Spell Files	Shift-F1, 6, 3
Location of Thesaurus Files	Shift-F1, 6, 3
Locked Document	Ctrl-F5, 2
Long Document Name	Shift-F1, 3, 4, 3
Long Form, Table of Auth (Block On)	Alt-F5, 4
Long/Short Filename Display	F5, Enter, 5
Look at a File	F5, Enter, 6
Lower/Upper Case (Block On)	Shift-F3
Macro Editor	Ctrl-F10
Macro Commands	Ctrl-PgUp
Macro Commands, Help On	Ctrl-F10
Macros, Define	Ctrl-F10
Macros, Execute	Alt-F10
Macros, Keyboard Definition	Shift-F1, 5
Mail Merge	Ctrl-F9, 1

Feature	Keypresses
Main Dictionary Location	Shift-F1, 6, 3
Manual Hyphenation	Shift-F8, 1, 1
Map, Keyboard	Shift-F1, 5, 8
Map Special Characters	Shift-F1, 5
Margin Release	Shift-Tab
Margins, Left and Right	Shift-F8, 1, 7
Margins, Top and Bottom	Shift-F8, 2, 5
Mark Text For Index (Block On)	Alt-F5, 3
Mark Text For List (Block On)	Alt-F5, 2
Mark Text For ToA (Block On)	Alt-F5, 4
Mark Text For ToC (Block On)	Alt-F5, 1
Master Document	Alt-F5, 2
Math	Alt-F7, 3
Menu Bar	Alt-=
Menu Bar Letter Display	Shift-F1, 2, 4, 5
Menu Bar Separator Line	Shift-F1, 2, 4, 7
Menu Bar Text	Shift-F1, 2, 4, 6
Menu Letter Display	Shift-F1, 2, 4, 1
Menu Options	Shift-F1, 2, 4
Merge	Ctrl-F9, 1
Merge Codes	Shift-F9
Merge Codes (Convert Old Codes)	Ctrl-F9, 3
Merge Codes Display	Shift-F1, 2, 6, 5
Merge Options	Shift-F1, 4, 1
Mnemonics	Shift-F1, 2, 4
More Merge Codes	Shift-F9, 6
Mouse	Shift-F1, 1
Move Block (Block On)	Ctrl-Del
Move Down One Paragraph	Ctrl-Down Arrow
Move Down One Item (Columns & Tables)	Alt-Down Arrow
Move Left One Item (Columns & Tables)	Alt-Left Arrow
Move One Word Right	Ctrl-Right Arrow
Move One Word Left	Ctrl-Left Arrow
Move/Rename File	F5, Enter, 3
Move Right One Item (Columns & Tables)	Alt-Right Arrow
Move Text (Block On or Off)	Ctrl-F4, 1-3, 1
Move Up One Item (Columns & Tables)	Alt-Up Arrow
Move Up One Paragraph	Ctrl-Up Arrow
Multiple Copies Generated By	Shift-F7, u
Multiple Copies Generated By (Default)	Shift-F1, 4, 8, 2
n= (Default)	Shift-F1, 4, 6
n= (Set Temporarily)	Esc, #, Enter
New Page	Ctrl-Enter
New Page Number	Shift-F8, 2, 6, 1
New Supplementary Dictionary	Ctrl-F2, 4

Feature	Keypresses
Newspaper Columns	Alt-F7, 1, 3, 1
Next Document	F5, Enter, 6, 1
Normal Font	Ctrl-F8, 3
Number Lines	Shift-F8, 1, 5
Number of Copies (Default)	Setup, 4, 8, 2
Number of Copies	Shift-F7, n
Number Pages	Shift-F8, 2, 6, 4
Odd/Even Page, Force	Shift-F8, 2, 2
Offsets, Page	Shift-F8, 2, 7, 5, 9
Orientation, Fonts	Shift-F8, 2, 7
Orientation, Forms	Shift-F8, 2, 7
Orientation, Paper Size/Type	Shift-F8, 2, 7
Original Document Backup	Shift-F1, 3, 1, 2
Original Keyboard	Shift-F1, 5, 6
Original Keyboard (Temporary)	Ctrl-6
Orphan/Widow	Shift-F8, 1, 9
Other Format	Shift-F8, 4
Outline	Shift-F5, 4
Outline Style Name	Shift-F5, 6, 9
Overstrike	Shift-F8, 4, 5
Page Break, Hard	Ctrl-Enter
Page Down	PgDn
Page Format	Shift-F8, 2
Page Format, Suppress	Shift-F8, 2, 8
Page Length	Shift-F8, 2, 7
Page Number, Go To	Ctrl-Home, page #
Page Number in Text	Ctrl-b
Page Number in Text	Shift-F8, 2, 6, 3
Page Number, New	Shift-F8, 2, 6, 1
Page Number Style	Shift-F8, 2, 6, 2
Page Numbering	Shift-F8, 2, 6, 4
Page Offsets	Shift-F8, 2, 7, 5, 9
Page Up	PgUp
Page View	Shift-F7, 6
Paper Location	Shift-F8, 2, 7
Paper Size/Type	Shift-F8, 2, 7
Paper Trays	Shift-F7, s, 3, 3
Paragraph Down	Ctrl-Down Arrow
Paragraph Numbering	Shift-F5, 5
Paragraph Numbering, Auto	Shift-F5, 5
Paragraph Up	Ctrl-Up Arrow
Parallel Columns	Alt-F7, 1, 3, 1
Password	Ctrl-F5, 2
Path for Downloadable Fonts	Shift-F7, s, 3, 6
Path for Printer Command Files	Shift-F7, s, 3, 6
Percent of Optimal Spacing	Shift-F8, 4, 6, 3
Pitch, Display	Shift-F8, 3, 1
Port, Mouse	Shift-F1, 1, 2
Port, Printer	Shift-F7, s, 3, 2
Portrait Fonts	Shift-F8, 2, 7

Feature	Keypresses
Portrait Forms	Shift-F8, 2, 7
Portrait Paper Size\Type	Shift-F8, 2, 7
Preview	Shift-F7, 6
Previous Document	F5, Enter, 6, 2
Primary File, Merge	Ctrl-F9, 1
Primary Leading	Shift-F8, 4, 6, 6
Print	Shift-F7
Print (Cancel, Rush, Display, Stop)	Shift-F7, 4, 1-3 or 5
Print Block (Block On)	Shift-F7
Print Color	Ctrl-F8, 5
Print Document on Disk	Shift-F7, 3
Print From Disk	Shift-F7, 3
Print From Disk	F5, Enter, 4
Print Full Document	Shift-F7, 1
Print List Files	F5, Enter, Shift-F7
Print Multiple Pages	Shift-F7, 5
Print Options (Default)	Shift-F1, 4, 8
Print Options (Document)	Shift-F7
Print Page	Shift-F7, 2
Print Preview	Shift-F7, 6
Print Quality, Graphics	Shift-F7, g
Print Quality, Graphics (Default)	Shift-F1, 4, 8, 3
Print Quality, Text (Default)	Shift-F1, 4, 8, 4
Print Quality, Text	Shift-F7, t
Printed Attributes	Ctrl-F8
Printer Command	Shift-F8, 4, 6, 2
Printer Command Files Path	Shift-F7, s, 3, 6
Printer Control	Shift-F7, 4
Printer Edit	Shift-F7, s, 3
Printer Files Location	Shift-F1, 6, 4
Printer Fonts (Location)	Shift-F7, s, 3, 6
Printer Functions	Shift-F8, 4, 6
Printer, Initialize	Shift-F7, 7
Printer Name	Shift-F7, s, 3, 1
Printer Port	Shift-F7, s, 3, 2
Printer, Select	Shift-F7, s
Program Macros (Macro Editor)	Ctrl-PgUp
Program Macros, Help on	Ctrl-F10
Prompt For Hyphenation	Shift-F1, 3, 7
Prompt for Document Summary	Shift-F1, 3, 4, 1
Protect a Document	Ctrl-F5, 2
Protect Block (Block On)	Shift-F8
PRS file, Edit	Shift-F7, s, 3
PRS files, View	Shift-F7, s, 2, 4
Pull Down Letter Display	Shift-F1, 2, 4, 2
Pull Down Text	Shift-F1, 2, 4, 3
Quality of Text and Graphics	Shift-F7, t or g
Quality of Text and Graphics (Default)	Setup, 4, 8, 3 or 4
Quit WordPerfect	F7, y or n, y

Feature	Keypresses
Reassign Keys	Shift-F1, 5
Recover Text	F1, 1
Rectangle, Move/Copy (Block On)	Ctrl-F4, 3
Redline Method	Shift-F8, 3, 4
Redline Method (Default)	Shift-F1, 4, 8, 5
Redline Print	Ctrl-F8, 2, 8
Redline, Remove	Alt-F5, 6, 1
Reference, Cross	Alt-F5, 1
References, Generate	Alt-F5, 6, 5
Reformat Screen	Ctrl-F3, 3
Relative Tab Settings	Shift-F8, 1, 8, t, 2
Remove Password	Ctrl-F5, 2, 2
Remove Redline and Strikeout	Alt-F5, 6, 1
Rename/Move File	F5, Enter, 3
Repeat Value (Default)	Shift-F1, 4, 6
Repetition Number (n)	Esc
Replace	Alt-F2
Replace, Extended	Home, Alt-F2
Report Printer Status	Shift-F7, 4
Restore Deleted Text	F1, 1
Retrieve a File	F5, Enter, 1
Retrieve a File	Shift-F10
Retrieve Clipboard	Ctrl-F1, 4
Retrieve Column	Ctrl-F4, 4, 2
Retrieve Document	F5, Enter, 1
Retrieve Document	Shift-F10
Retrieve DOS Text File	Ctrl-F5, 1, 2 or 3
Retrieve Text (Move Key)	Ctrl-F4, 4, 1-3
Reveal Codes	Alt-F3
Reveal Codes Window Size	Ctrl-F3, 1
Reveal Codes Window Size (Default)	Shift-F1, 2, 6, 6
Reverse Search	Shift-F2
Rewrite Screen	Ctrl-F3, 3
Right Justification	Shift-F8, 1, 3, 3
Right Margin	Shift-F8, 1, 7
Right Tab Setting	Shift-F8, 1, 8, r
Ruler	Ctrl-F3, 1, 23
Save, Clipboard	Ctrl-F1, 2
Save, Fast (Unformatted)	Shift-F1, 3, 5
Save Text	F10
Screen	Ctrl-F3
Screen Display	Shift-F1, 2
Screen Down	Grey + (NumPad)
Screen Rewrite	Ctrl-F3, 3
Screen Setup	Shift-F1, 2, 6
Screen Split	Ctrl-F3, 1
Screen Up	Grey − (NumPad)
Scrolling Speed	Shift-F1, 3, 3
Search	F2
Search and Replace	Alt-F2

Feature	Keypresses
Search for File(s)	F5, Enter, 9, 1
Secondary File, Merge	Ctrl-F9, 1
Secondary Leading	Shift-F8, 4, 6, 6
See Codes	Alt-F3
Select Printer	Shift-F7, s
Send Printer a "GO"	Shift-F7, 4, 4
Set Pitch (Letter/Word Spacing)	Shift-F8, 4, 6, 3
Set Tabs	Shift-F8, 1, 8
Settings, Initial (Default)	Shift-F1, 4
Setup	Shift-F1
Shadow Print	Ctrl-F8, 2, 6
Sheet Feeder	Shift-F7, s, 3, 3
Sheet Feeder Help	Shift-F7, s, 6, Shift-F3
Shell, Go To	Ctrl-F1, 1
Short Form	Alt-F5, 4
Short Form, Table of Authorities	Alt-F5, 4
Short/Long Filename Display	F5, Enter, 5
Side-by-side Columns Display	Shift-F1, 2, 6, 7
Size Attribute Ratios	Shift-F1, 4, 8, 6
Size of Print (Attributes)	Ctrl-F8, 1
Small Capitalized Print	Ctrl-F8, 2, 7
Small Print	Ctrl-F8, 1, 4
Soft Hyphen	Ctrl, -
Sort	Ctrl-F9, 2
Space, Hard	Home, Space
Spacing Justification Limits	Shift-F8, 4, 6, 4
Spacing Lines	Shift-F8, 1, 6
Spell	Ctrl-F2
Speller Files Location	Shift-F1, 6, 3
Split Screen	Ctrl-F3, 1
Spreadsheet	Ctrl-F5, 5
Spreadsheet, Import	Ctrl-F5, 5, 1
Spreadsheet, Link	Ctrl-F5, 5, 2-4
Status Line Display	Shift-F1, 2, 6, 3
Stop Printer	Shift-F7, 4, 5
Strikeout	Ctrl-F8, 2, 9
Style	Alt-F8
Style Files Directory	Shift-F1, 6, 5
Style Library File Location	Shift-F1, 6, 5
Style Library Filename	Shift-F1, 6, 5
Style, Outline	Shift-F5, 6, 9
Style, Outline	Alt-F8
Subdocument	Alt-F5, 2
Subject Search Text	Shift-F1, 3, 4, 2
Subscript Print	Ctrl-F8, 1, 2
Summary, Document	Shift-F8, 3, 5
Summary Prompt	Shift-F1, 3, 4, 1
Superscript Print	Ctrl-F8, 1, 1
Supplementary Dictionary, Location	Shift-F1, 6, 3
Suppress Page Format	Shift-F8, 2, 8

Feature	Keypresses
Swappable Fonts & Cartridges	Shift-F7, s, 3, 4
Switch Documents	Shift-F3
Tab	Tab
Tab Align	Ctrl-F6
Tab, Hard	Home, Tab
Tab Ruler	Ctrl-F3, 1, 23
Tab Set	Shift-F8, 1, 8
Tab Type	Shift-F8, 1, 8, t
Table	Alt-F7, 2
Table Box	Alt-F9, 2
Table of Authorities (Default)	Shift-F1, 4, 7
Table of Authorities, Mark (Block On)	Alt-F5, 4
Table of Authorities (Define or Generate)	Alt-F5, 5 or 6
Table of Contents, Mark (Block On)	Alt-F5, 1
Table of Contents (Define or Generate)	Alt-F5, 5 or 6
Target	Alt-F5, 1, 2
Text Box	Alt-F9, 3
Text Columns	Alt-F7, 1
Text In/Out	Ctrl-F5
Text Quality	Shift-F7, t
Text Quality (Default)	Shift-F1, 4, 8, 4
Text Screen Type	Shift-F1, 2, 3
Text to Comment (Block On)	Ctrl-F5
Thesaurus Files	Alt-F1
Thesaurus Files	Shift-F1, 6, 3
Thousands' Separator	Shift-F8, 4, 3
Time/Date	Shift-F5
Timed Document Backup	Shift-F1, 3, 1, 1
Top and Bottom Margin	Shift-F8, 2, 5
Type, Mouse	Shift-F1, 1, 1
Typeover, Forced	Home, Insert
Typeover Mode	Insert
Undelete	F1, 1
Underline Spaces and Tabs	Shift-F8, 4, 7
Underline Text	F8
Underline Text	Ctrl-F8, 2, 2
Units of Measure	Shift-F1, 3, 8
Unlock a Document	Ctrl-F5, 2
Update Spreadsheet Link	Ctrl-F5, 5, 4, 3
Update Printer Driver	Shift-F7, s, 7
Update References	Alt-F5, 6, 5
Upper/Lower Case (Block On)	Shift-F3
User-defined Box	Alt-F9, 4
Variable	Ctrl-PgUp
Very Large Print	Ctrl-F8, 1, 6
View Codes	Alt-F3
View Document	Shift-F7, 6

Feature	Keypresses
View-Document Options	Shift-F1, 2, 5
Widow/Orphan Protection	Shift-F8, 1, 9
Window	Ctrl-F3, 1
Word Count	Ctrl-F2, 6
Word Left, Cursor Movement	Ctrl-Left Arrow
Word/Letter Spacing	Shift-F8, 4, 6, 3
Word Look Up	Ctrl-F2, 5
Word Right, Cursor Movement	Ctrl-Right Arrow
Word Spacing Justification Limits	Shift-F8, 4, 6, 4
Word Spell	Ctrl-F2, 1
WP 4.2 format, Save As	Ctrl-F5, 3, 3
WP 5.0 format, Save As	Ctrl-F5, 3, 2

Lotus 1-2-3 Release 2.2

Lotus 1-2-3 Keys

Keypress	Description
/	Activates the Main menu.
Enter	Completes an entry.
Backspace	Erases preceding character.
Delete	Deletes character at cursor.
Insert	Switches INSERT/OVERWRITE mode.
Escape	Exits a menu; erases entry in control panel.
Home	Moves to cell A1.
Left Arrow	Moves left one cell.
Right Arrow	Moves right one cell.
Up Arrow	Moves up one cell.
Down Arrow	Moves down one cell.
Ctrl-Left Arrow	(BIG LEFT) Moves left one screen.
Shift-Tab	Moves left one screen.
Ctrl-Right Arrow	(BIG RIGHT) Moves right one screen.
Tab	Moves right one screen.
Page Up	Moves up one screen.
Page Down	Moves down one screen.
End, Right Arrow	Moves right to intersection of a blank and a nonblank cell.
End, Left Arrow	Moves left to intersection of a blank and a nonblank cell.
End, Up Arrow	Moves up to intersection of a blank and a nonblank cell.
End, Down Arrow	Moves down to intersection of a blank and a nonblank cell.
F1	(HELP) Activates the help facility.
Alt-F1	(COMPOSE) Creates international and graphics characters.
F2	(EDIT) Changes to EDIT mode.
Alt-F2	(STEP) Turns on STEP mode, which executes macros one step at a time for debugging.
F3	(NAME) Displays a menu of range names.
Alt-F3	(RUN) Displays a menu to select the name of the macro to run.
F4	(ABS) Changes the type of cell addressing.
Alt-F4	(UNDO) Cancels the previous change.
F5	(GOTO) Moves to a particular cell address.
Alt-F5	(LEARN) Turns macro learn feature on and off.
F6	(WINDOW) Switches to other split-screen window.
F7	(QUERY) Repeats most recent Data Query command.
F8	(TABLE) Repeats most recent Data Table command.
F9	(CALC) Recalculates all worksheet formulas.
F10	(GRAPH) Displays the most recently specified graph.

Lotus 1-2-3 Release 2.2 Menu Commands
(Levels 1 and 2)

Command	Description
/WG	Worksheet Global Specifies the default settings applied to all cells for items such as numeric format, label alignment, column width, recalculation method, cell protection, and the display of zero values.
/WI	Worksheet Insert Adds blank rows or columns to an existing worksheet.
/WD	Worksheet Delete Removes rows or columns from an existing worksheet.
/WC	Worksheet Column Specifies settings for column width and column hiding.
/WE	Worksheet Erase Completely erases the entire worksheet.
/WT	Worksheet Titles Freezes rows and/or columns so they can always be seen.
/WW	Worksheet Window Allows use of two horizontal or vertical windows.
/WS	Worksheet Status Displays information about memory, global settings, and hardware.
/WP	Worksheet Page Inserts a printer page break into the worksheet.
/WL	Worksheet Learn Specifies the learn range where macro instructions will be stored in LEARN mode.
/RF	Range Format Sets the numeric format for a range of cells.
/RL	Range Label Aligns existing labels in a range of cells.
/RE	Range Erase Removes the contents of a range of cells.
/RN	Range Name Creates or deletes cell range names.
/RJ	Range Justify Rearranges words in a column to fit within a specified width.
/RP	Range Protect Prevents changes and deletions to a range of cells.

Command	Description
/RU	Range Unprotect Allows changes and deletions to a range of cells.
/RI	Range Input Restricts cell pointer movement to unprotected cells.
/RV	Range Value Converts formulas to their computed values in a range of cells.
/RT	Range Transpose Reorders a range of cells, switching rows and columns.
/RS	Range Search Locates strings in labels and/or formulas within a specified range.
/C	Copy Creates a copy of existing cell contents.
/M	Move Moves a range of cells to another place in the worksheet.
/FR	File Retrieve Loads a worksheet from a disk into memory.
/FS	File Save Copies a worksheet from memory to a disk file.
/FC	File Combine Copies, adds, or subtracts values from one worksheet to another.
/FX	File Xtract Extracts and saves part of one worksheet in another file.
/FE	File Erase Removes one or more files from a disk.
/FL	File List Displays the names of files on a disk.
/FI	File Import Imports data from a text file into the worksheet.
/FD	File Directory Changes the current disk drive directory.
/FA	File Admin Recalculates linked formulas, shares files on a network, or creates a table of information about the files on a disk.
/PP	Print Printer Sends a worksheet directly to the printer.
/PF	Print File Sends a worksheet to a file to be printed later.

Command	Description
/GT	Graph Type Specifies the type of graph to be created.
/GX	Graph X Specifies the range of cells for the X-axis labels.
/GA	Graph A Specifies the first range of cells to be used as data for the graph.
/GB–/GF	Graph B–Graph F Specify additional data ranges.
/GR	Graph Reset Cancels graph settings.
/GV	Graph View Displays the current graph on the screen.
/GS	Graph Save Stores the current graph in a disk file so it can be printed later.
/GO	Graph Options Specifies various options for enhancing a graph's appearance.
/GN	Graph Name Creates, uses, deletes, or resets a graph name.
/GG	Graph Group Specifies all graph data ranges at once, when the X and A through F data ranges are in consecutive columns or rows of a range.
/GQ	Graph Quit Exits from the Graph submenu.
/DF	Data Fill Enters a sequence of numbers into a range of cells.
/DT	Data Table Tabulates the effects of changing values in formulas.
/DS	Data Sort Rearranges rows of cells in a specified order.
/DQ	Data Query Searches for, copies, extracts, or removes specified rows of cells.
/DD	Data Distribution Creates a frequency distribution of the values in a range of cells.
/DM	Data Matrix Multiplies and inverts matrices of cells.
/DR	Data Regression Fits a line to a set of data points.

Command	Description
/DP	Data Parse Breaks up long labels into individual cell entries.
/S	System Allows the use of DOS commands while working with 1-2-3.
/AA	Add-In Attach Loads an add-in program, such as Allways, into memory.
/AD	Add-In Detach Removes an attached add-in program from memory, freeing the memory it occupied.
/AI	Add-In Invoke Activates an attached add-in program.
/AC	Add-In Clear Removes all attached add-in programs from memory, freeing the memory they occupied.
/AQ	/Add-In Quit Returns to READY mode from the Add-In menu.
/Q	Quit Ends 1-2-3 and returns to DOS.

Lotus 1-2-3 Functions

Function	Format and Description
@@	@@(*location*) Returns the contents of the cell at *location*.
@ABS	@ABS(*x*) Calculates the absolute value of *x*.
@ACOS	@ACOS(*x*) Calculates the arc cosine of *x*.
@ASIN	@ASIN(*x*) Calculates the arc sine of *x*.
@ATAN	@ATAN(*x*) Calculates the arc tangent of *x*.
@ATAN2	@ATAN2(*x,y*) Calculates the four-quadrant arc tangent of *y/x*.
@AVG	@AVG(*list*) Averages the values in *list*.
@CELL	@CELL(*attribute,range*) Returns information about an *attribute* for the first cell in *range*.

Function	Format and Description
@CELLPOINTER	@CELLPOINTER(*attribute*) Returns information about an *attribute* for the current cell.
@CHAR	@CHAR(*x*) Returns the character that corresponds to Lotus International Character Set code *x*.
@CHOOSE	@CHOOSE(*offset,list*) Returns value or string in *list* specified by *offset*.
@CLEAN	@CLEAN(*string*) Removes control characters from *string*.
@CODE	@CODE(*string*) Returns the Lotus International Character Set code for the first character in *string*.
@COLS	@COLS(*range*) Counts columns in *range*.
@COS	@COS(*x*) Calculates the cosine of *x*.
@COUNT	@COUNT(*list*) Counts the nonblank cells in *list*.
@CTERM	@CTERM(*interest,future-value,present-value*) Calculates the number of compounding periods for an investment *present-value* to grow to a *future-value*, given a fixed periodic *interest* rate.
@DATE	@DATE(*year,month,day*) Calculates the date number for *year, month,* and *day.*
@DATEVALUE	@DATEVALUE(*string*) Calculates the date number for a *string* that looks like a date.
@DAVG	@DAVG(*input,field,criteria*) Averages value in a *field* of a data base (*input* range) that meet criteria in *criteria* range.
@DAY	@DAY(*date-number*) Calculates the day of the month in *date-number*.
@DCOUNT	@DCOUNT(*input,field,criteria*) Counts nonblank cells in a *field* of a data base (*input* range) that meet the criteria in *criteria* range.
@DDB	@DDB(*cost,salvage,life,period*) Calculates depreciation allowance of an asset using the double-declining balance method.
@DMAX	@DMAX(*input,field,criteria*) Finds the largest value in a *field* of a data base (*input* range) that meets the criteria in *criteria* range.

Function	Format and Description
@DMIN	@DMIN(*input,field,criteria*) Finds the smallest value in a *field* of a data base (*input* range) that meets the criteria in *criteria* range.
@DSTD	@DSTD(*input,field,criteria*) Calculates the population standard deviation of values in a *field* of a data base (*input* range) that meet the criteria in *criteria* range.
@DSUM	@DSUM(*input,field,criteria*) Sums values in a *field* of a data base (*input* range) that meet the criteria in *criteria* range.
@DVAR	@DVAR(*input,field,criteria*) Calculates the population variance of values in a *field* of a data base (*input* range) that meet the criteria in *criteria* range.
@ERR	@ERR Returns the error value.
@EXACT	@EXACT(*string1,string2*) Returns 1 (true) if *string1* and *string2* are the same; returns 0 (false) otherwise.
@EXP	@EXP(*x*) Calculates the value of *e* (2.718282) raised to the power *x*.
@FALSE	@FALSE Returns the logical value 0 (false).
@FIND	@FIND(*search-string,string,start-number*) Returns the number of the first occurrence of *search-string* in *string*, beginning with *start-number*.
@FV	@FV(*payments,interest,term*) Calculates the future value of a series of equal *payments*, given a periodic *interest* rate and number of payment periods (*term*).
@HLOOKUP	@HLOOKUP(*x,range,row-offset*) Returns the contents of the cell in *row-offset* of the horizontal lookup table (*range*).
@HOUR	@HOUR(*time-number*) Calculates the hour (0–23) in *time-number*.
@IF	@IF(*condition,x,y*) Evaluates *condition* and returns *x* if *condition* is 1 (true), *y* if *condition* is 0 (false).
@INDEX	@INDEX(*range,column-offset,row-offset*) Returns the value in the cell located at *column-offset* and *row-offset* in *range*.
@INT	@INT(*x*) Returns the integer portion of *x*, without rounding.

Function	Format and Description
@IRR	@IRR(*guess,range*) Calculates the internal rate of return for a series of cash flows in *range*, based on the percentage *guess*.
@ISAAF	@ISAAF(*name*) Returns 1 (true) if *name* is a defined add-in @function; otherwise it returns 0 (false).
@ISAPP	@ISAPP(*name*) Returns 1 (true) if *name* is an attached add-in @function; otherwise it returns 0 (false).
@ISERR	@ISERR(*x*) Returns 1 (true) if *x* is the value ERR; otherwise it returns 0 (false).
@ISNA	@ISNA(*x*) Returns 1 (true) if *x* is the value NA; otherwise it returns 0 (false).
@ISNUMBER	@ISNUMBER(*x*) Returns 1 (true) if *x* is a value or a blank cell; otherwise it returns 0 (false).
@ISSTRING	@ISSTRING(*x*) Returns 1 (true) if *x* is a string; otherwise it returns 0 (false).
@LEFT	@LEFT(*string,n*) Returns the first *n* characters in *string*.
@LENGTH	@LENGTH(*string*) Counts the characters in *string*.
@LN	@LN(*x*) Calculates the natural logarithm (base *e*) of *x*.
@LOG	@LOG(*x*) Calculates the common logarithm (base 10) of *x*.
@LOWER	@LOWER(*string*) Converts all letters in string to lowercase.
@MAX	@MAX(*list*) Returns the largest value in *list*.
@MID	@MID(*string,start-number,n*) Returns *n* characters from *string*, beginning with the *start-number* position.
@MIN	@MIN(*list*) Returns the smallest value in *list*.
@MINUTE	@MINUTE(*time-number*) Calculates the minute (0–59) in *time-number*.
@MOD	@MOD(*x,y*) Returns the remainder (modulus) of *x/y*.

Function	Format and Description
@MONTH	@MONTH(*date-number*) Calculates the month (1–12) in *date-number*.
@N	@N(*range*) Returns the entry in the first cell of *range* as a value.
@NA	@NA Returns the value of NA (Not Available).
@NOW	@NOW Calculates the date and time numbers that correspond to the current date and time.
@NPV	@NPV(*interest*,*range*) Calculates the net present value of a series of future cash flows (*range*), discounted at a fixed, periodic *interest* rate.
@PI	@PI Returns the value of π (pi), calculated at 3.1415926536.
@PMT	@PMT(*principal*,*interest*,*term*) Calculates the payment needed to pay off a loan (*principal*), given the *interest* rate and number of payment periods (*term*).
@PROPER	@PROPER(*string*) Capitalizes the first letter of each word in *string*.
@PV	@PV(*payments*,*interest*,*term*) Calculates the present value of a series of equal *payments*, discounted at a periodic *interest* rate and given a number of payment periods (*term*).
@RAND	@RAND Generates a random number between 0 and 1.
@RATE	@RATE(*future-value*,*present-value*,*term*) Calculates the periodic interest rate necessary for the investment *present-value* to grow to *future-value*, given the number of compounding periods (*term*).
@REPEAT	@REPEAT(*string*,*n*) Repeats *string* *n* times.
@REPLACE	@REPLACE(*string1*,*start-number*,*n*,*string2*) Replaces *n* characters in *string1* beginning at *start-number* from *string2*.
@RIGHT	@RIGHT(*string*,*n*) Returns the last *n* characters from *string*.
@ROUND	@ROUND(*x*,*n*) Rounds the value *x* to *n* decimal places.
@ROWS	@ROWS(*range*) Counts the number of rows in *range*.

Function	Format and Description
@S	@S(*range*) Returns the entry in the first cell of *range* as a label.
@SECOND	@SECOND(*time-number*) Calculates the seconds (0–59) in *time-number*.
@SIN	@SIN(*x*) Calculates the sine of *x*.
@SLN	@SLN(*cost,salvage,life*) Calculates the straight-line depreciation allowance of an asset for one period.
@SQRT	@SQRT(*x*) Calculates the square root of *x*.
@STD	@STD(*list*) Calculates the population standard deviation of the values in *list*.
@STRING	@STRING(*x,n*) Converts the value *x* to a string with *n* decimal places.
@SUM	@SUM(*list*) Calculates the sum of the values in *list*.
@SYD	@SYD(*cost,salvage,life,period*) Calculates the sum-of-the-years'-digits depreciation allowance of an asset for a specified *period*.
@TAN	@TAN(*x*) Calculates the tangent of *x*.
@TERM	@TERM(*payments,interest,future-value*) Calculates the number of payment periods in the term of an investment necessary to accumulate *future-value*, given *payments* of equal value, when the investment earns a periodic *interest* rate.
@TIME	@TIME(*hour,minute,second*) Calculates the time number for *hour, minute,* and *second*.
@TIMEVALUE	@TIMEVALUE(*string*) Calculates the time number for a *string* that looks like a time.
@TRIM	@TRIM(*string*) Removes the leading, trailing, and consecutive spaces in *string*.
@TRUE	@TRUE Returns the logical value 1 (true).
@UPPER	@UPPER(*string*) Converts all letters in *string* to uppercase.
@VALUE	@VALUE(*string*) Converts the number entered as *string* to its numeric value.

Function	Format and Description
@VAR	@VAR(*list*) Calculates the population variance of the values in *list*.
@VLOOKUP	@VLOOKUP(*x,range,column-offset*) Returns the contents of the cell in *column-offset* of the vertical lookup table *range*.
@YEAR	@YEAR(*date-number*) Calculates the year, an integer from 0 (1900) to 199 (2099), in *date-number*.

dBASE IV Version 1.1

dBASE IV Keys

Keypress	Description
Right Arrow	Move right one position.
Left Arrow	Move left one position.
Down Arrow	Move down one row.
Up Arrow	Move up one row.
Page Down	Move down one screen.
Page Up	Move up one screen.
End	Move to end of field or record.
Home	Move to beginning of field or record.
Backspace	Delete previous character.
Tab	Move to next field.
Shift-Tab	Move to previous field.
Enter	Move to next field.
Escape	Abandon changes and exit.
Delete	Delete selected item.
Insert	Toggle insert/overwrite mode.
Ctrl-Right Arrow	Move to beginning of next word or field.
Ctrl-Left Arrow	Move to beginning of previous word or field.
Ctrl-PgDn	Move to last record.
Ctrl-PgUp	Move to first record.
Ctrl-Home	Move into memo field.
Ctrl-End	Save changes and exit.
Ctrl-Enter	Save changes and remain.
F1	(HELP) Invoke help facility.
Shift-F1	(PICK) Display list of items to choose from.
F2	(DATA) Switch to Browse or Edit screen.
Shift-F2	(DESIGN) Display the design screens.
F3	(PREV) Move to previous field, object, or page.
Shift-F3	(FIND PREV) Locate previous occurrence of search string.
F4	(NEXT) Move to next field, object, or page.
Shift-F4	(FIND NEXT) Locate next occurrence of search string.
F5	(FIELD) Add field to layout or skeleton.
Shift-F5	(FIND) Find specified search string.
F6	(SELECT) Select contiguous text and fields.
Shift-F6	(REPLACE) Replace search string with another string.
F7	(MOVE) Move selected text and fields.
Shift-F7	(SIZE) Change size of design elements and column widths.
F8	(COPY) Copy selected text and fields.
Shift-F8	(DITTO) Copy data from corresponding field of previous record into current field.
F9	(ZOOM) Enlarge or shrink memo fields, condition boxes, data fill-ins, and file skeletons.
Shift-F9	(QUICKRPT) Print a Quick Report.
F10	(MENUS) Access menus for current screen.
Shift-F10	(MACRO) Access macros prompt box.

Control Center Menus

Catalog	Use a different catalog
	Modify catalog name
	Edit description of catalog
	Add file to catalog
	Remove highlighted file from catalog
	Change description of highlighted file
Tools	Macros
	Import
	Export
	DOS utilities
	Protect data
	Settings
Exit	Exit to dot prompt
	Quit to DOS

Browse Screen Menus

Records	Undo change to record
	Add new records
	Mark record for deletion/Clear deletion mark
	Record blank
	Lock record
	Follow record to new position
Organize	Create new index
	Modify existing index
	Order records by index
	Activate .NDX index file
	Include .NDX index file
	Remove unwanted index tag
	Sort database on field list
	Unmark all records
	Erase marked records
Fields	Lock fields on left
	Blank field
	Freeze field
	Size field
Go To	Top record
	Last record
	Record number
	Skip
	Index key search
	Forward search
	Backward search
	Match capitalization
Exit	Exit
	Transfer to Query Design
	Return to (object) Design

Edit Screen Menus

Records
Undo change to record
Add new records
Mark record for deletion/Clear deletion mark
Blank record
Lock record
Follow record to new position

Organize
Create new index
Modify existing index
Order records by index
Activate .NDX index file
Include .NDX index file
Remove unwanted index tag
Sort database on field list
Unmark all records
Erase marked records

Go To
Top record
Last record
Record number
Skip
Index key search
Forward search
Backward search
Match capitalization

Exit
Exit
Transfer to Query Design
Return to (object) Design

Data Panel Menus

Layout
Print database structure
Edit database description
Save this database file structure

Organize
Create new index
Modify existing index
Order records by index
Activate .NDX index file
Include .NDX index file
Remove unwanted index tag
Sort database on field list
Unmark all records
Erase marked records

Append
Enter records from keyboard
Append records from dBASE file
Copy records from non-dBASE file

Go To
Top field
Last field
Field number

Exit
Save changes and exit
Abandon changes and exit

Queries Panel Menus

Layout   Add file to query
Remove file from query
Create link by pointing
Write view as database file
Edit description of query
Save this query

Fields   Add field to view
Remove field from view
Edit field name
Create calculated field
Sort on this field
Include indexes

Condition   Add condition box
Delete condition box
Show condition box

Update   Perform the update
Specify update operation

Exit   Save changes and exit
Abandon changes and exit
Return to (module)

Forms Panel Menus

Layout   Quick layout
Box
Line
Use different database file or view
Edit description of form
Save this form

Fields   Add field
Remove field
Modify field
Insert memory variable

Words   Style
Display
Position
Modify ruler
Hide ruler
Enable automatic indent
Add line
Remove line
Insert page break
Write/read text file

Go To   Go to line number
Forward search
Backward search
Replace
Match capitalization

Exit   Save changes and exit
                    Abandon changes and exit

Reports Panel Menus

Layout   Quick layouts
                    Box
                    Line
                    Use different database file or view
                    Edit description of report
                    Save this report

Fields   Add field
                    Remove field
                    Modify field
                    Change hidden field

Bands   Add a group band
                    Remove group
                    Modify group
                    Group intro on each page
                    Open all bands
                    Begin band on new page
                    Word wrap band
                    Text pitch for band
                    Quality print for band
                    Spacing of lines for band
                    Page headings in report intro

Words   Style
                    Display
                    Position
                    Modify ruler
                    Hide ruler
                    Enable automatic indent
                    Add line
                    Remove line
                    Insert page break
                    Write/read text file

Go To   Go to line number
                    Forward search
                    Backward search
                    Replace
                    Match capitalization

Print   Begin printing
                    Eject page now
                    View report on screen
                    Use print form
                    Save settings to print form
                    Destination
                    Control of printer
                    Output options
                    Page dimensions

Exit   Save changes and exit
                    Abandon changes and exit

Labels Panel Menus

Layout   Use different database file or view
                    Edit description of label design
                    Save this label design

Dimensions   Predefined size
                    Width of label
                    Height of label
                    Indentation
                    Lines between labels
                    Spaces between label columns
                    Columns of labels

Fields   Add field
                    Remove field
                    Modify field

Words   Style
                    Display
                    Position
                    Modify ruler
                    Hide ruler
                    Enable automatic indent
                    Add line
                    Remove line
                    Insert page break
                    Write/read text file

Go To   Go to line number
                    Forward search
                    Backward search
                    Replace
                    Match capitalization

Print   Begin printing
                    Eject page now
                    Generate sample labels
                    View labels on screen
                    Use print form
                    Save settings to print form
                    Destination
                    Control of printer
                    Output options
                    Page dimensions

Exit   Save changes and exit
                    Abandon changes and exit

Applications Panel Menus

Layout   Modify a different program
                    Edit description of program
                    Save this program

Words	Style
	Display
	Position
	Modify ruler
	Hide ruler
	Enable automatic indent
	Add line
	Remove line
	Insert page break
	Write/read text file
Go To	Go to line number
	Forward search
	Backward search
	Replace
	Match capitalization
Print	Begin printing
	Eject page now
	Line numbers
	Use print form
	Save settings to print form
	Destination
	Control of printer
	Output options
	Page dimensions
Exit	Save changes and exit
	Abandon changes and exit
	Run program
	Debug program

Selected Dot Prompt Commands

See the *dBASE IV Language Reference* manual from Ashton-Tate for a complete listing of all dBASE IV dot prompt commands.

Command	Formats and Description
? or ??	? **or** ?? *expression* Displays the value of an expression.
@	@ *row,col* [SAY *expression*] [GET *variable*] Displays an expression or accepts information at the given screen row and column.
ACCEPT	ACCEPT [*prompt*] TO *variable* Prompts the user for keyboard entry.
APPEND	APPEND [BLANK] Adds a new record to the end of the active data base file.

Command	Formats and Description
APPEND FROM	APPEND FROM *filename* [FOR *condition*] Copies records from *filename* and adds them to the end of the active data base file.
ASSIST	ASSIST Activates the dBASE IV Control Center.
AVERAGE	AVERAGE *field* [*scope*] [FOR *condition*] [WHILE *condition*] Computes the arithmetic mean of a numeric field.
BROWSE	BROWSE [*record-number*] [FIELDS *field-list*] [*scope*] [FOR *condition*] [WHILE *condition*] Activates the Browse screen.
CANCEL	CANCEL Stops the execution of a command file and returns to the dot prompt.
CLEAR	CLEAR [ALL **or** FIELDS **or** GETS **or** MEMORY **or** MENUS **or** POPUPS **or** TYPEAHEAD **or** WINDOWS] Erases the screen and positions the cursor in the lower left corner. Can also close data base files; release memory variables, field lists, windows, popups, and menus; and empty the type-ahead buffer.
CLOSE	CLOSE [ALL **or** ALTERNATE **or** DATABASES **or** FORMAT **or** INDEX **or** PROCEDURE] Closes files.
CONTINUE	CONTINUE Searches for the next record in the active data base file that meets the condition specified by the most recent LOCATE command.
COPY FILE	COPY FILE *filename* TO *filename* Duplicates any file.
COPY MEMO	COPY MEMO *memo-field-name* TO *filename* [ADDITIVE] Copies the information from a single memo field to another file.
COPY STRUCTURE TO	COPY STRUCTURE TO *filename* [FIELDS *field-list*] Copies the structure of the active data base file to a new file, but does not copy any records.
COPY TO	COPY TO *filename* [FIELDS *field-list*] [*scope*] [FOR *condition*] [WHILE *condition*] Duplicates all or part of an active data base file, creating a new file.
COPY TO	COPY TO *filename* STRUCTURE EXTENDED Creates a new data base file whose records have the structure of the current file.

Command	Formats and Description
COUNT	COUNT [TO *variable*] [*scope*] [FOR *condition*] [WHILE *condition*] Counts the number of records in the active data base file that meet the specified conditions.
CREATE	CREATE *filename* Activates the data base design screen.
CREATE LABEL	CREATE LABEL **or** QUERY **or** VIEW **or** REPORT **or** SCREEN *filename* Activates the label, query, report, or forms design screen.
DELETE	DELETE [*scope*] [FOR *condition*] [WHILE *condition*] Marks records in the active data base file for deletion.
DIR	DIR [*drive*:][*filename*] Displays a directory of data base files or other files if an extension is specified.
DISPLAY	DISPLAY **or** LIST [*scope*] [*field-list*] [FOR *condition*] [WHILE *condition*] Displays one or more records from the active data base file.
DISPLAY HISTORY	DISPLAY **or** LIST HISTORY Displays a list of commands that have been executed and are stored in the history buffer.
DISPLAY MEMORY	DISPLAY **or** LIST MEMORY Displays all active memory variables.
DISPLAY STATUS	DISPLAY **or** LIST STATUS Displays information about the current dBASE IV session.
DISPLAY STRUCTURE	DISPLAY **or** LIST STRUCTURE Displays the data base structure.
DO	DO *program-filename* [WITH *parameter-list*] Starts execution of a dBASE IV command file.
EDIT	EDIT **or** CHANGE [*record-number*] [FIELDS *field-list*] [*scope*] [FOR *condition*] [WHILE *condition*] Activates the Edit screen.
FIND	FIND "*string*" Searches an indexed data base file for the first record with an index key that matches *string*.
GO	GO **or** GOTO [BOTTOM **or** TOP] [[RECORD] *record-number*] [IN *alias*] Positions the record pointer to the specified record in the active data base file.
HELP	HELP [*dBASE-IV-keyword*] Activates the help facility.

Command	Formats and Description
IMPORT FROM	IMPORT FROM *filename* [TYPE] PFS **or** DBASEII **or** FW2 **or** RPD **or** WK1 Creates a dBASE IV data base file from a PFS:FILE form, dBASE II file, Framework II file, RapidFile file, or a Lotus 1-2-3 worksheet.
INPUT	INPUT [*prompt*] TO *variable* Prompts the user for input from the keyboard.
INSERT	INSERT [BLANK] [BEFORE] Inserts a new record after the current record, or before if BEFORE is specified.
JOIN	JOIN WITH *alias* TO *filename* FOR *condition* [FIELDS *field-list*] Creates a new data base file by merging specified records and fields from two open data base files.
LABEL FORM	LABEL FORM *label-filename* [*scope*] [FOR *condition*] [WHILE *condition*] [SAMPLE] [TO PRINTER] [TO FILE *filename*] Use specified label format file to display, print, or write labels to a disk file.
LOCATE	LOCATE [FOR] *condition* [*scope*] [WHILE *condition*] Searches the active data base file for a record that matches the specified condition.
MODIFY COMMAND	MODIFY COMMAND **or** FILE *filename* Starts the word-wrap editor for creating and editing dBASE program and format files.
PACK	PACK Permanently removes records marked for deletion from the active data base file.
QUIT	QUIT Closes all open files, terminates the dBASE IV session, and returns to DOS.
RECALL	RECALL [*scope*] [FOR *condition*] [WHILE *condition*] Reinstates records that are marked for deletion in the active data base file.
REINDEX	REINDEX Rebuilds all active index files in the current work area.
RELEASE	RELEASE [*variable-list*] [ALL] Removes all or specified memory variables.
RENAME	RENAME *old-filename* TO *new-filename* Changes the name of a file.
REPLACE	REPLACE [*scope*] [FOR *condition*] [WHILE *condition*] *field* WITH *expression* ... Replaces the contents of specified fields with new values.

Command	Formats and Description
REPORT FORM	REPORT FORM *filename* [*scope*] [FOR *condition*] [WHILE *condition*] [TO PRINTER **or** TO FILE *filename*] Prints a report from the active data base file.
RUN	RUN **or** ! *DOS-command* Executes the specified DOS command or program from within dBASE IV.
SEEK	SEEK *expression* Searches for the first record in an indexed data base file with a key that matches *expression*.
SELECT	SELECT *work-area-name* **or** *alias* Chooses a work area in which to open a data base file.
SET	SET Displays a menu for setting most parameters of dBASE IV.
SKIP	SKIP [*expression*] [IN *alias*] Moves the record pointer forward or backward in a data base file.
SORT TO	SORT TO *filename* ON *field1* [/A] [/C] [/D] ... [ASCENDING **or** DESCENDING] [*scope*] [FOR *condition*] [WHILE *condition*] Creates a new data base file in which the records of the active data base file are sorted in the specified order.
SUM	SUM *field* [*scope*] [FOR *condition*] [WHILE *condition*] Computes the sum of a numeric field.
USE	USE [*database-filename*] [IN *work-area*] Opens an existing data base file.
ZAP	ZAP Removes all records from the active data base file.

Selected dBASE IV Functions

See the *dBASE IV Language Reference* manual from Ashton-Tate for a complete listing of all dBASE IV functions.

Function	Format and Description
ALIAS	ALIAS([*work-area-number*]) Returns alias name of a work area.
ASC	ASC(*string*) Returns the decimal ASCII code of the first character of *string*.

Function	Format and Description
BOF	BOF([*alias*]) Indicates the beginning of the file.
CDOW	CDOW(*date*) Returns the day of the week from *date*.
CEILING	CEILING(*x*) Calculates the smallest integer greater than or equal to *x*.
CHR	CHR(*x*) Converts ASCII code *x* to a character.
CMONTH	CMONTH(*date*) Returns the name of the month from *date*.
COL	COL() Returns the current column position of the cursor on the screen.
CTOD	CTOD(*string*) **or** {*string*} Converts *string* to a date type variable.
DATE	DATE() Returns the current date as a character string in the format mm/dd/yy.
DAY	DAY(*date*) Returns the day-of-the-month number from *date*.
DBF	DBF([*alias*]) Returns the name of the data base file in use in the currently selected work area.
DELETED	DELETED([*alias*]) Returns logical true (.T.) if the current record in the specified work area is marked for deletion; otherwise, returns false (.F.).
DISKSPACE	DISKSPACE() Returns the number of bytes available on the default drive.
DTOC	DTOC(*date*) Converts *date* to a character string.
EOF	EOF([*alias*]) Returns true (.T.) if the end of the file has been reached; otherwise, returns false (.F.).
FIELD	FIELD(*field-number* [, *alias*]) Returns the field name of *field-number* from the file structure of the data base file.
FILE	FILE(*filename*) Returns true (.T.) if *filename* exists on the selected disk; otherwise, returns false (.F.).

Function	Format and Description
FLOOR	FLOOR(*x*) Returns the largest integer less than or equal to *x*.
FOUND	FOUND([*alias*]) Returns true (.T.) if the previous FIND, LOCATE, SEEK, or CONTINUE command was successful; otherwise, returns false (.F.).
INKEY	INKEY([*n*]) Returns an integer representing the most recent key pressed by the user.
INT	INT(*x*) Truncates *x* to an integer.
LEN	LEN(*string* **or** *memo-field*) Returns the number of characters in *string* or *memo-field*.
LIKE	LIKE(*pattern, string*) Returns true (.T.) if *string* matches *pattern*; otherwise, returns false (.F.).
LUPDATE	LUPDATE([*alias*]) Returns the date of the last update to the specified data base file.
MEMLINES	MEMLINES(*memo-field*) Returns the number of lines contained in *memo-field*.
MEMORY	MEMORY([0]) Returns the number of kilobytes of RAM currently unused.
MLINE	MLINE(*memo-field, line-number*) Extracts a line from *memo-field*.
MONTH	MONTH(*date*) Returns the month number from *date*.
PCOL	PCOL() Returns the current column position on the printer.
PRINTSTATUS	PRINTSTATUS() Returns true (.T.) if the printer is ready to accept output; otherwise, returns false (.F.).
PROW	PROW() Returns the current row on the printer.
RECCOUNT	RECCOUNT([*alias*]) Returns the number of records in the specified data base file.
RECNO	RECNO([*alias*]) Returns the current record number of the specified data base file.

Function	Format and Description
RECSIZE	RECSIZE([*alias*]) Returns the size of a record in the specified data base file.
ROUND	ROUND(*x, decimal-places*) Rounds *x* to the specified number of *decimal-places*.
ROW	ROW() Returns the row number of the current cursor position on the screen.
SEEK	SEEK(*expression* [,*alias*]) Evaluates *expression* and attempts to find it in the master index of the data base file. Returns true (.T.) if the index key is found; otherwise, returns false (.F.).
SELECT	SELECT() Returns the number of the highest unused work area.
SOUNDEX	SOUNDEX(*string*) Returns a four-character code representing the phonetic or sound-alike match to *string* when the exact spelling is not known.
SQRT	SQRT(*x*) Returns the square root of *x*.
STR	STR(*x* [,*length*] [,*decimal-places*]) Converts the number *x* to a character string.
TIME	TIME() Returns the current time as a character string in the format hh:mm:ss.
TRIM	TRIM(*string*) **or** RTRIM(*string*) Removes all trailing blanks from *string*.
VERSION	VERSION() Returns the dBASE IV version number in use.
YEAR	YEAR(*date*) Returns the year number from *date*.

COMMAND
STRUCTURE
OUTLINES

WordPerfect 5.1

File Edit Search Layout Mark Tools Font Graphics Help

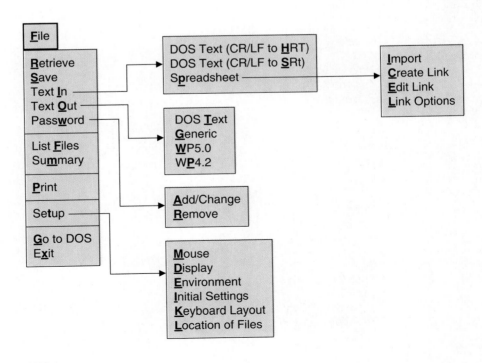

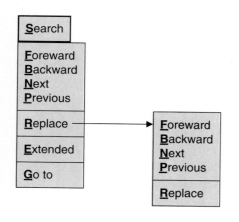

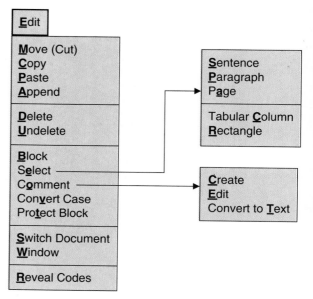

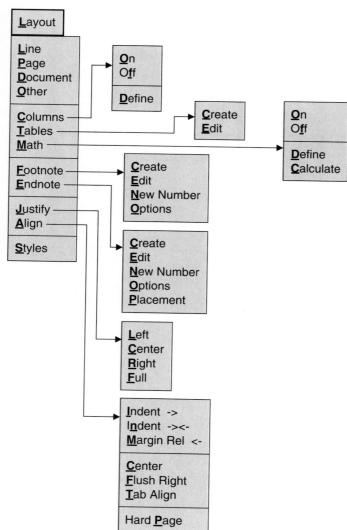

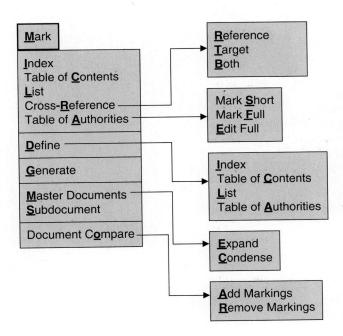

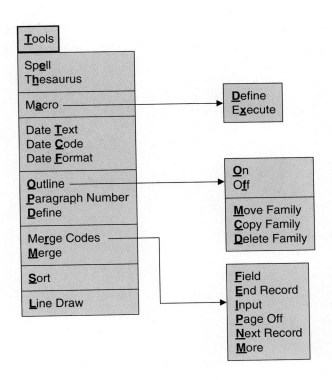

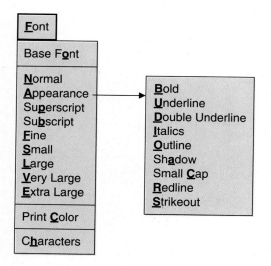

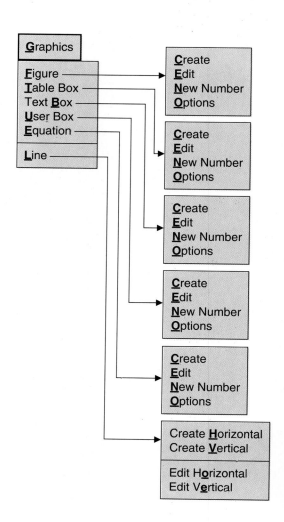

Help

Help
Index
Template

Lotus 1-2-3 Release 2.2

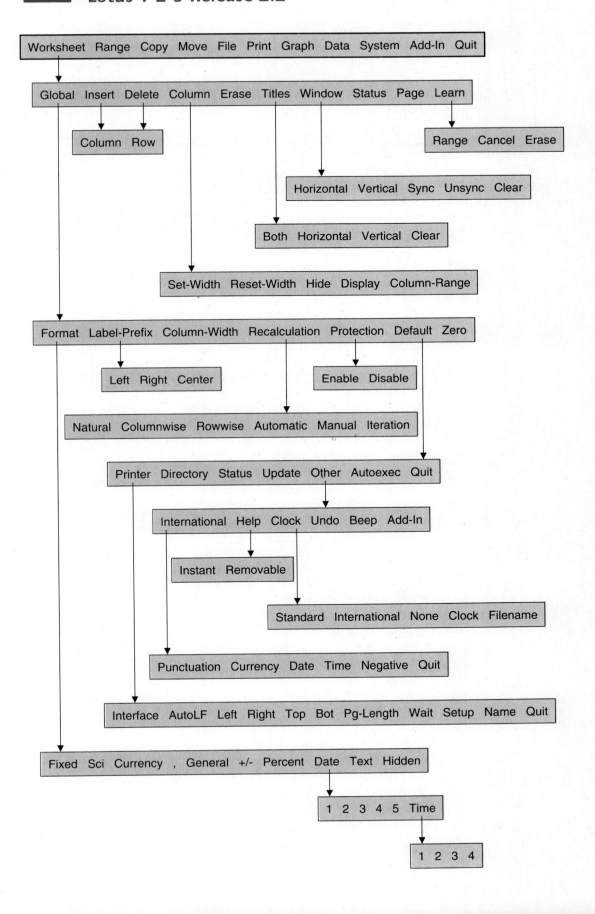

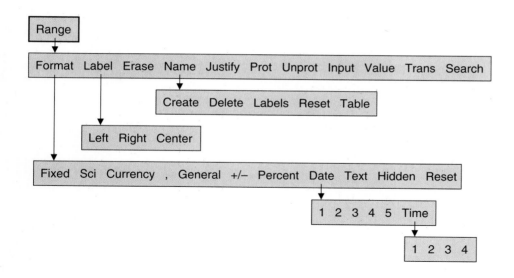

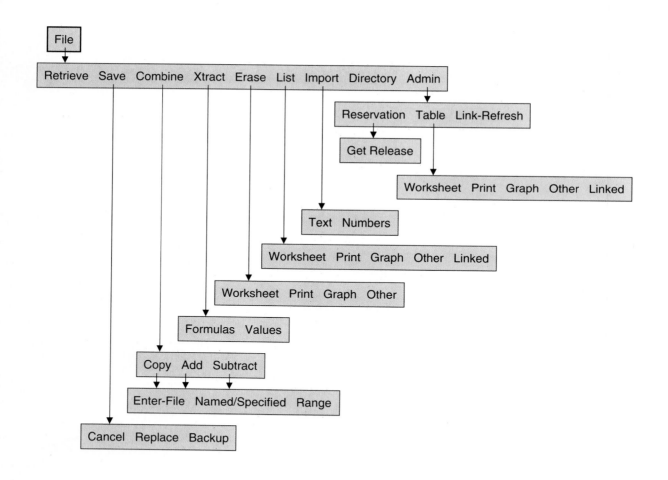

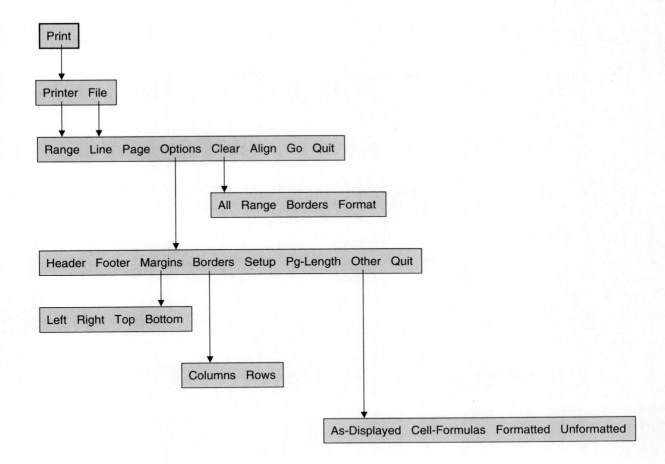

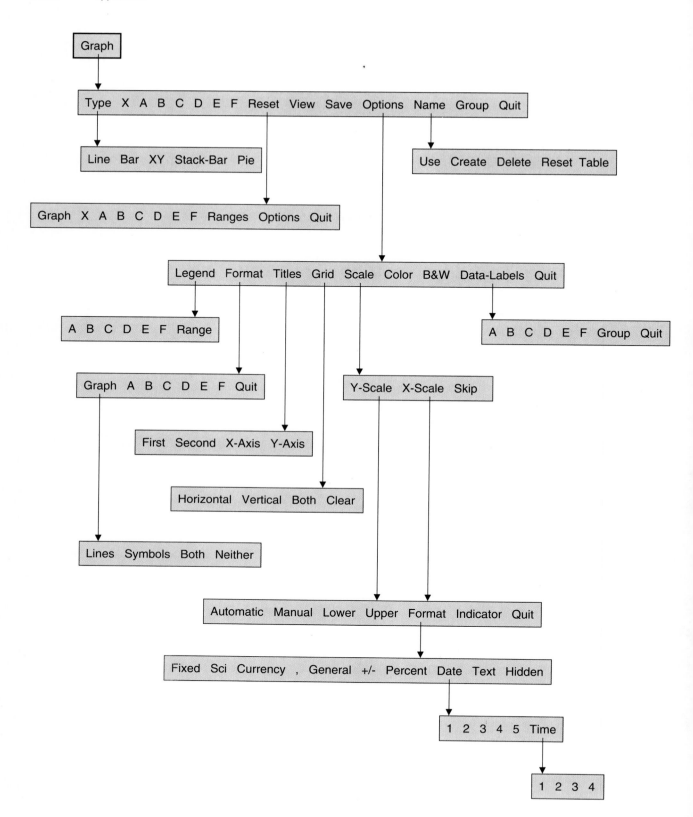

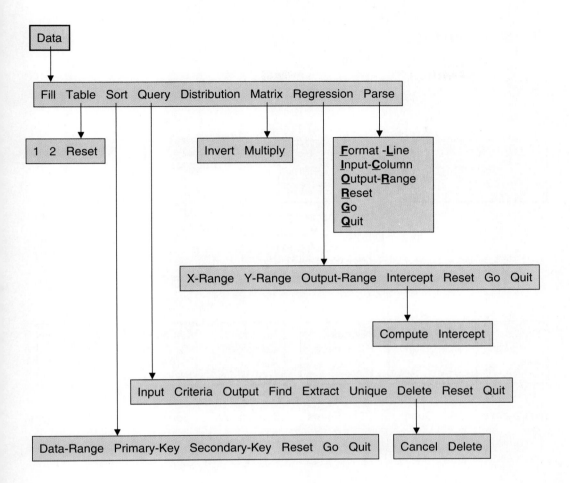

Data

Fill Table Sort Query Distribution Matrix Regression Parse

1 2 Reset

Invert Multiply

Format -**L**ine
Input-**C**olumn
Output-**R**ange
Reset
Go
Quit

X-Range Y-Range Output-Range Intercept Reset Go Quit

Compute Intercept

Input Criteria Output Find Extract Unique Delete Reset Quit

Data-Range Primary-Key Secondary-Key Reset Go Quit

Cancel Delete

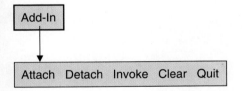

Add-In

Attach Detach Invoke Clear Quit

dBASE IV Version 1.1

The Control Center

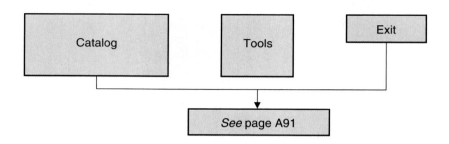

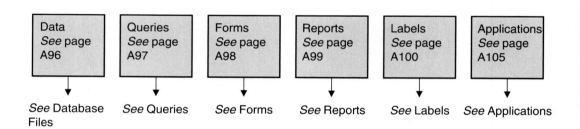

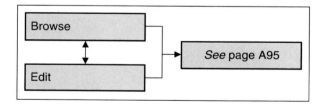

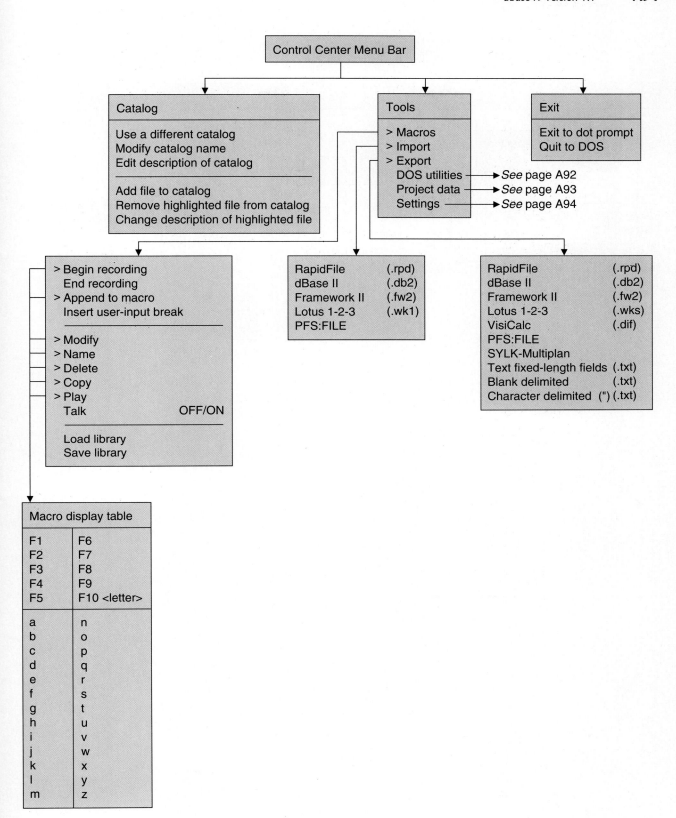

Control Center Menu Bar

Catalog

Use a different catalog
Modify catalog name
Edit description of catalog
___
Add file to catalog
Remove highlighted file from catalog
Change description of highlighted file

Tools

> Macros
> Import
> Export
  DOS utilities ────▶ *See* page A92
  Project data ────▶ *See* page A93
  Settings ────▶ *See* page A94

Exit

Exit to dot prompt
Quit to DOS

> Begin recording
  End recording
> Append to macro
  Insert user-input break
___
> Modify
> Name
> Delete
> Copy
> Play
  Talk   OFF/ON
___
Load library
Save library

RapidFile	(.rpd)
dBase II	(.db2)
Framework II	(.fw2)
Lotus 1-2-3	(.wk1)
PFS:FILE	

RapidFile	(.rpd)
dBase II	(.db2)
Framework II	(.fw2)
Lotus 1-2-3	(.wks)
VisiCalc	(.dif)
PFS:FILE	
SYLK-Multiplan	
Text fixed-length fields	(.txt)
Blank delimited	(.txt)
Character delimited (")	(.txt)

Macro display table

F1	F6
F2	F7
F3	F8
F4	F9
F5	F10 <letter>
a	n
b	o
c	p
d	q
e	r
f	s
g	t
h	u
i	v
j	w
k	x
l	y
m	z

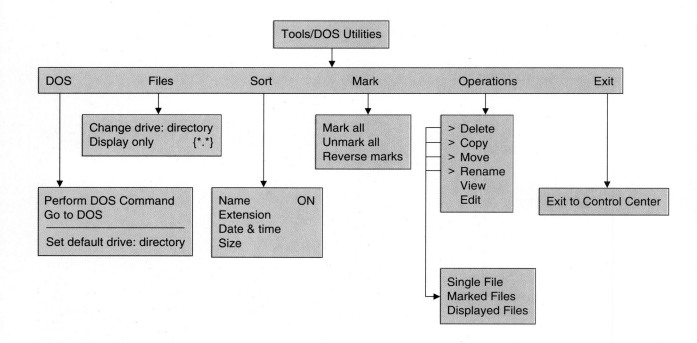

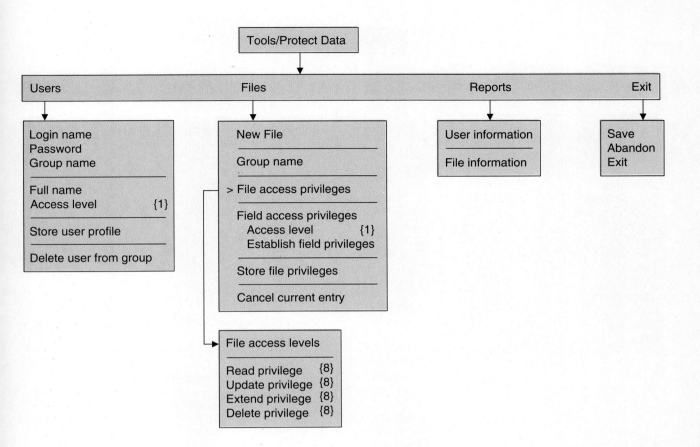

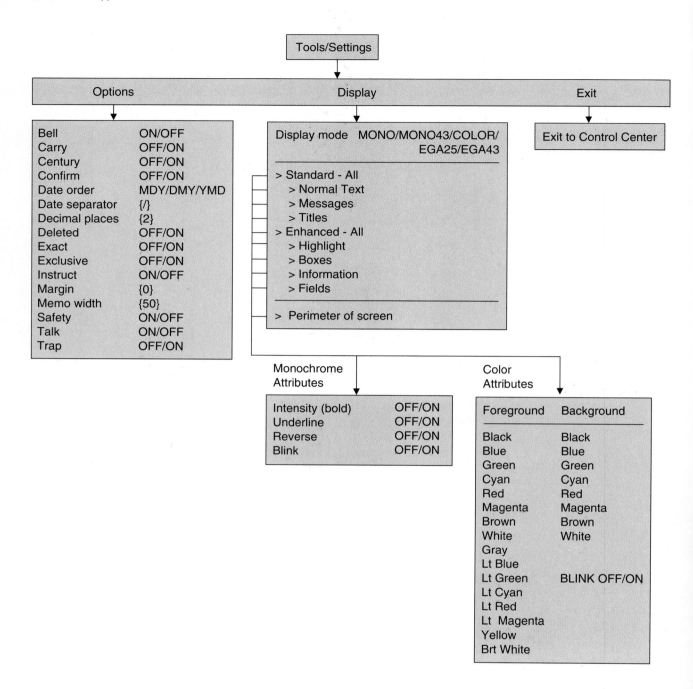

Tools/Settings

Options | Display | Exit

Bell	ON/OFF
Carry	OFF/ON
Century	OFF/ON
Confirm	OFF/ON
Date order	MDY/DMY/YMD
Date separator	{/}
Decimal places	{2}
Deleted	OFF/ON
Exact	OFF/ON
Exclusive	OFF/ON
Instruct	ON/OFF
Margin	{0}
Memo width	{50}
Safety	ON/OFF
Talk	ON/OFF
Trap	OFF/ON

Display mode   MONO/MONO43/COLOR/
EGA25/EGA43

> Standard - All
   > Normal Text
   > Messages
   > Titles
> Enhanced - All
   > Highlight
   > Boxes
   > Information
   > Fields

> Perimeter of screen

Exit to Control Center

Monochrome
Attributes

Intensity (bold)	OFF/ON
Underline	OFF/ON
Reverse	OFF/ON
Blink	OFF/ON

Color
Attributes

Foreground	Background
Black	Black
Blue	Blue
Green	Green
Cyan	Cyan
Red	Red
Magenta	Magenta
Brown	Brown
White	White
Gray	
Lt Blue	
Lt Green	BLINK OFF/ON
Lt Cyan	
Lt Red	
Lt Magenta	
Yellow	
Brt White	

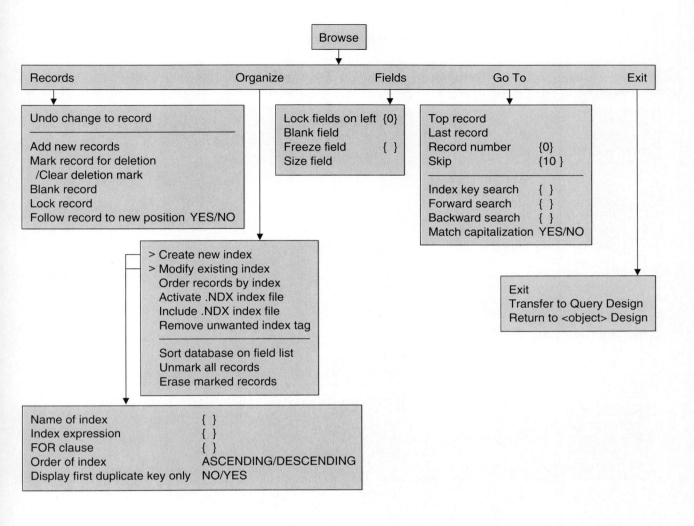

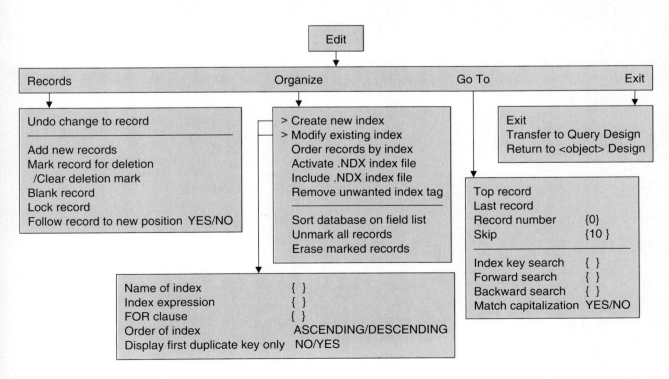

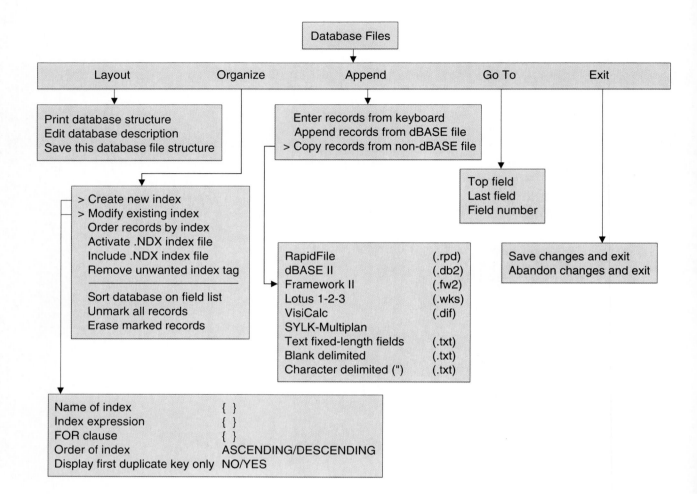

Database Files

| Layout | Organize | Append | Go To | Exit |

Layout
Print database structure
Edit database description
Save this database file structure

Append
Enter records from keyboard
Append records from dBASE file
> Copy records from non-dBASE file

Organize
> Create new index
> Modify existing index
  Order records by index
  Activate .NDX index file
  Include .NDX index file
  Remove unwanted index tag
  ────────────────
  Sort database on field list
  Unmark all records
  Erase marked records

Go To
Top field
Last field
Field number

Exit
Save changes and exit
Abandon changes and exit

RapidFile	(.rpd)
dBASE II	(.db2)
Framework II	(.fw2)
Lotus 1-2-3	(.wks)
VisiCalc	(.dif)
SYLK-Multiplan	
Text fixed-length fields	(.txt)
Blank delimited	(.txt)
Character delimited (")	(.txt)

Name of index	{ }
Index expression	{ }
FOR clause	{ }
Order of index	ASCENDING/DESCENDING
Display first duplicate key only	NO/YES

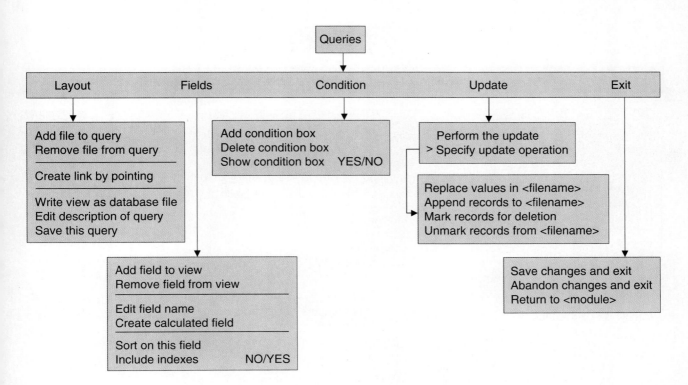

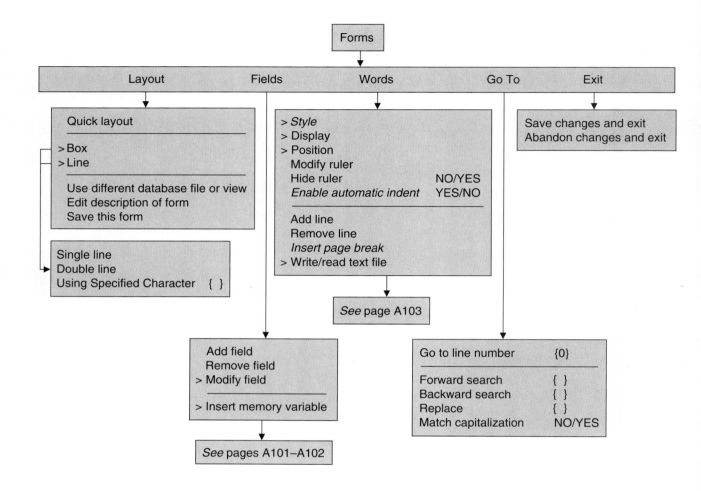

Forms

Layout   Fields   Words   Go To   Exit

Layout

Quick layout
_____

> Box
> Line
_____

Use different database file or view
Edit description of form
Save this form

Single line
Double line
Using Specified Character   { }

Words

> *Style*
> Display
> Position
Modify ruler
Hide ruler   NO/YES
Enable automatic indent   YES/NO
_____

Add line
Remove line
Insert page break
> Write/read text file

See page A103

Exit

Save changes and exit
Abandon changes and exit

Fields

Add field
Remove field
> Modify field
_____

> Insert memory variable

See pages A101–A102

Go To

Go to line number   {0}
_____

Forward search   { }
Backward search   { }
Replace   { }
Match capitalization   NO/YES

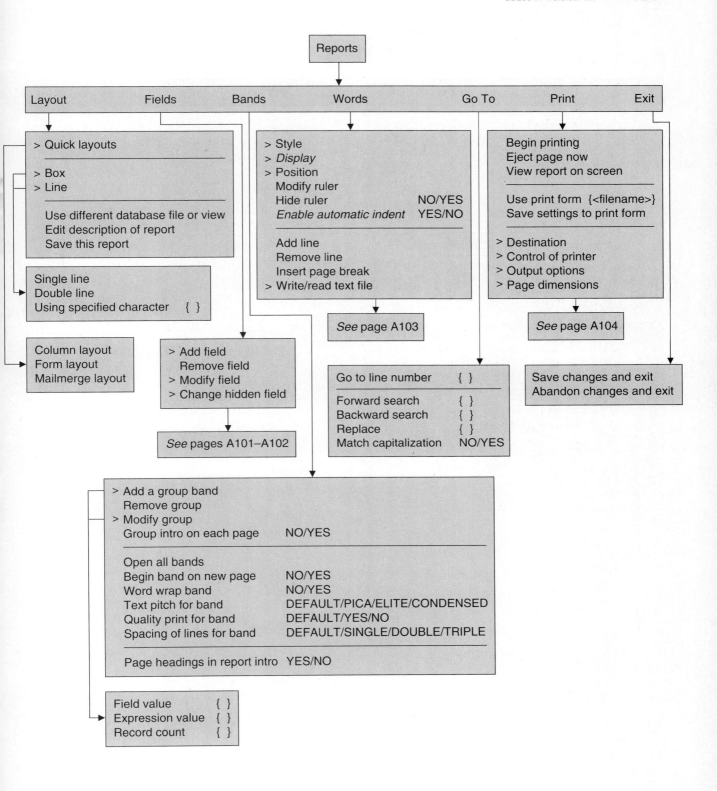

Reports

Layout   Fields   Bands   Words   Go To   Print   Exit

> Quick layouts
―――――――――
> Box
> Line
―――――――――
  Use different database file or view
  Edit description of report
  Save this report

Single line
Double line
Using specified character   { }

Column layout
Form layout
Mailmerge layout

> Add field
  Remove field
> Modify field
> Change hidden field

See pages A101–A102

> Style
> *Display*
> Position
  Modify ruler
  Hide ruler   NO/YES
  Enable automatic indent   YES/NO
―――――――――
  Add line
  Remove line
  Insert page break
> Write/read text file

See page A103

Go to line number   { }
―――――――――
Forward search   { }
Backward search   { }
Replace   { }
Match capitalization   NO/YES

Begin printing
Eject page now
View report on screen

Use print form   {<filename>}
Save settings to print form
―――――――――
> Destination
> Control of printer
> Output options
> Page dimensions

See page A104

Save changes and exit
Abandon changes and exit

> Add a group band
  Remove group
> Modify group
  Group intro on each page   NO/YES
―――――――――
  Open all bands
  Begin band on new page   NO/YES
  Word wrap band   NO/YES
  Text pitch for band   DEFAULT/PICA/ELITE/CONDENSED
  Quality print for band   DEFAULT/YES/NO
  Spacing of lines for band   DEFAULT/SINGLE/DOUBLE/TRIPLE
―――――――――
  Page headings in report intro   YES/NO

Field value   { }
Expression value   { }
Record count   { }

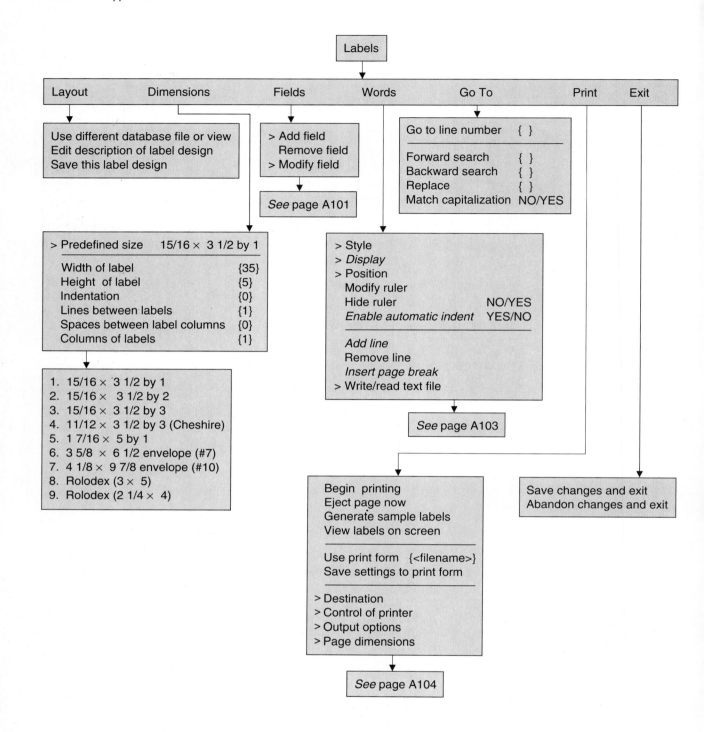

Labels

Layout   Dimensions   Fields   Words   Go To   Print   Exit

Use different database file or view
Edit description of label design
Save this label design

> Add field
Remove field
> Modify field

See page A101

Go to line number   { }

Forward search   { }
Backward search   { }
Replace   { }
Match capitalization   NO/YES

> Predefined size   15/16 × 3 1/2 by 1

Width of label   {35}
Height of label   {5}
Indentation   {0}
Lines between labels   {1}
Spaces between label columns   {0}
Columns of labels   {1}

> Style
> *Display*
> Position
Modify ruler
Hide ruler   NO/YES
Enable automatic indent   YES/NO

Add line
Remove line
Insert page break
> Write/read text file

See page A103

1. 15/16 × 3 1/2 by 1
2. 15/16 × 3 1/2 by 2
3. 15/16 × 3 1/2 by 3
4. 11/12 × 3 1/2 by 3 (Cheshire)
5. 1 7/16 × 5 by 1
6. 3 5/8 × 6 1/2 envelope (#7)
7. 4 1/8 × 9 7/8 envelope (#10)
8. Rolodex (3 × 5)
9. Rolodex (2 1/4 × 4)

Begin printing
Eject page now
Generate sample labels
View labels on screen

Use print form   {<filename>}
Save settings to print form

> Destination
> Control of printer
> Output options
> Page dimensions

Save changes and exit
Abandon changes and exit

See page A104

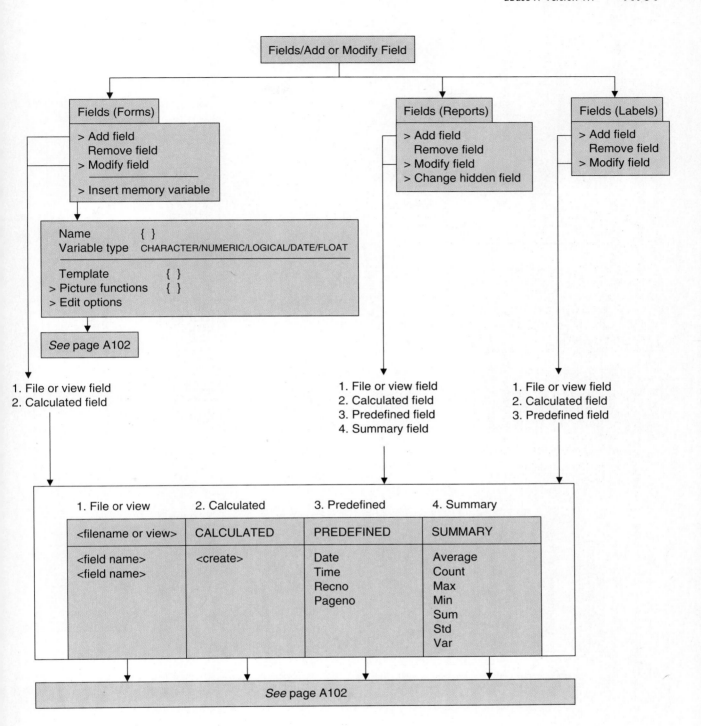

Fields/Add or Modify Field

Fields (Forms)
> Add field
  Remove field
> Modify field
────────────────
> Insert memory variable

Name   { }
Variable type   CHARACTER/NUMERIC/LOGICAL/DATE/FLOAT
────────────────
Template   { }
> Picture functions   { }
> Edit options

See page A102

Fields (Reports)
> Add field
  Remove field
> Modify field
> Change hidden field

Fields (Labels)
> Add field
  Remove field
> Modify field

1. File or view field
2. Calculated field

1. File or view field
2. Calculated field
3. Predefined field
4. Summary field

1. File or view field
2. Calculated field
3. Predefined field

1. File or view	2. Calculated	3. Predefined	4. Summary
<filename or view>	CALCULATED	PREDEFINED	SUMMARY
<field name>	<create>	Date	Average
<field name>		Time	Count
		Recno	Max
		Pageno	Min
			Sum
			Std
			Var

See page A102

Fields/Add or Modify Field, continued

1. File or View field

Field name:
Type:
Length:
Decimals:

Template　　　　　　　{}
> Picture functions　　{}
> Edit options
Display as　　　MARKER/WINDOW
> Border lines
Suppress repeated values　NO/YES

2. Calculated field

Name　　　　　　　{}
Description　　　　　{}
Expression　　　　　{}

Template　　　　　　{}
> Picture functions　{}
Suppress repeated
　　values　　　　　NO/YES
Hidden　　　　　　　NO/YES

3. Predefined field

Name　　DATE/TIME/
　　　　　RECNO/PAGENO

Template　　　　　　{}
> Picture functions　{}
Suppress repeated
　　values　　　　　NO/YES

4. Summary field

Name　　　　　　　{}
Description　　　　{}
Operation
Field to summarize on
Reset every　< REPORT >

Template　　　　　{}
> Picture functions　{}
Suppress repeated
　　values
Hidden

Editing allowed　　　　　YES/NO
Permit edit if　　　　　　{}
Message　　　　　　　　{}
Carry forward　　　　　　NO/YES
Default value　　　　　　{}
Smallest allowed value　{}
Largest allowed value　{}
Accept value when　　{}
Unaccepted message　{}

Only numeric and character data types have picture
functions. The type of functions are different.

Picture functions (numeric field)

Positive credits followed by CR　C OFF/ON
Negative debits followed by DB　X OFF/ON
Use ( ) around negative numbers　(OFF/ON
Show leading zeros　　　　　　　L OFF/ON
Blanks for zero values　　　　　Z OFF/ON
Financial format　　　　　　　　$ OFF/ON
Exponential format　　　　　　　^ OFF/ON

Trim　　　　　　　　T OFF/ON
Left align　　　　　　B OFF/ON
Center align　　　　　I OFF/ON
Horizontal stretch　　H OFF/ON
Vertical stretch　　　V OFF/ON

Picture functions (character field)

Alphabetic characters only　A OFF/ON
Upper-case conversion　　　! OFF/ON
Literals not part of data　　R OFF/ON
Scroll within display width　S OFF/ON
Multiple choice　　　　　　M OFF/ON

Trim　　　　　　　　T OFF/ON
Right align　　　　　J OFF/ON
Center align　　　　I OFF/ON
Horizontal stretch　H OFF/ON
Vertical stretch　　V OFF/ON
Wrap-semicolons　　: OFF/ON

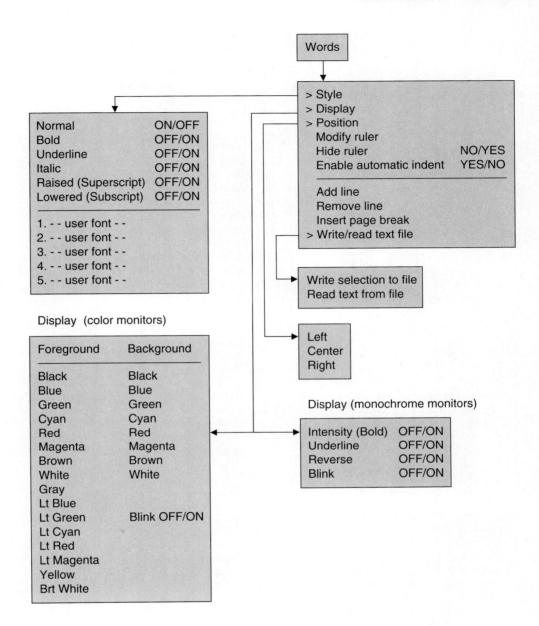

Words

> Style
> Display
> Position
Modify ruler
Hide ruler   NO/YES
Enable automatic indent   YES/NO

Add line
Remove line
Insert page break
> Write/read text file

Normal	ON/OFF
Bold	OFF/ON
Underline	OFF/ON
Italic	OFF/ON
Raised (Superscript)	OFF/ON
Lowered (Subscript)	OFF/ON

1. - - user font - -
2. - - user font - -
3. - - user font - -
4. - - user font - -
5. - - user font - -

Write selection to file
Read text from file

Left
Center
Right

Display (color monitors)

Foreground	Background
Black	Black
Blue	Blue
Green	Green
Cyan	Cyan
Red	Red
Magenta	Magenta
Brown	Brown
White	White
Gray	
Lt Blue	
Lt Green	Blink OFF/ON
Lt Cyan	
Lt Red	
Lt Magenta	
Yellow	
Brt White	

Display (monochrome monitors)

Intensity (Bold)	OFF/ON
Underline	OFF/ON
Reverse	OFF/ON
Blink	OFF/ON

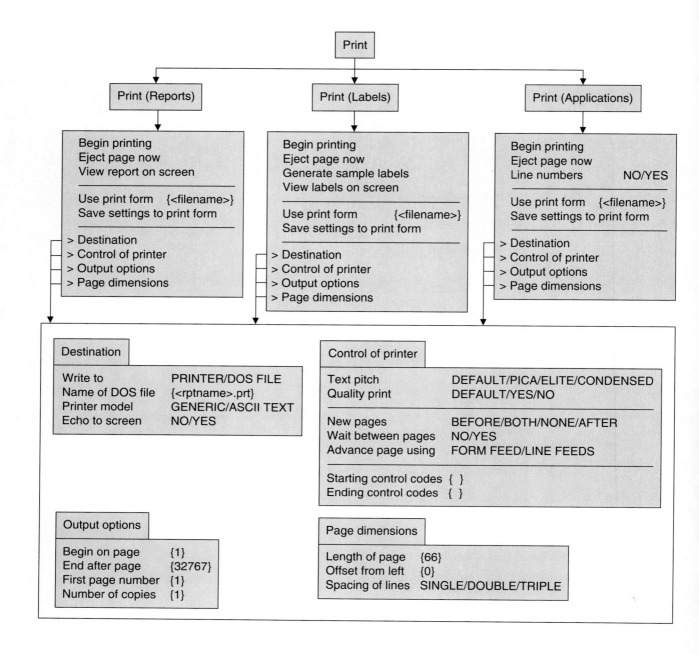

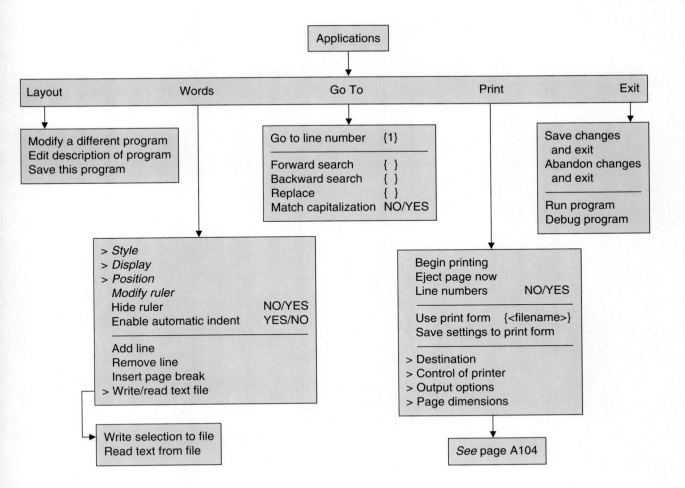

Applications

Layout | Words | Go To | Print | Exit

Layout:
Modify a different program
Edit description of program
Save this program

Go To:
Go to line number   {1}

Forward search   { }
Backward search   { }
Replace   { }
Match capitalization NO/YES

Exit:
Save changes
 and exit
Abandon changes
 and exit

Run program
Debug program

Words:
> *Style*
> *Display*
> *Position*
  Modify ruler
  Hide ruler   NO/YES
  Enable automatic indent YES/NO

  Add line
  Remove line
  Insert page break
> Write/read text file

Write selection to file
Read text from file

Print:
Begin printing
Eject page now
Line numbers   NO/YES

Use print form   {<filename>}
Save settings to print form

> Destination
> Control of printer
> Output options
> Page dimensions

See page A104

GLOSSARY

absolute reference a cell address that does not change when it is moved or copied

access arm a mechanical extension in a disk drive that moves the read-write head toward or away from the center of the disk

account a file containing financial information

accounting package software that manages an organization's finances

accounts payable the accounting subsystem that records the purchases of goods and services from each vendor

accounts receivable the accounting subsystem that records all sales of goods and services

action line in dBASE III PLUS, the line above the status bar that shows the command generated by the current Assistant operation

active cell see *current cell*

Ada a powerful, comprehensive high-level programming language applicable to a wide range of problems

adapter see *expansion board*

address a unique identifying number for a storage location in memory

address file see *secondary merge file*

aggregate operator see *summary operator*

alias in dBASE, a number, letter, or name that refers to a work area or data base file

allocation unit in DOS, a group of contiguous sectors, also known as a cluster

alphanumeric characters letters, numbers, and punctuation marks

alternate operating environment see *windowing environment*

American Standard Code for Information Interchange (ASCII) the code used by most microcomputers for representing text in binary form

application see *application software*

application generator see *fourth generation language*

application package see *application software*

application software a program or set of programs that applies the computer to useful tasks like helping you write letters, figure taxes, maintain mailing lists, and draw charts

Applications Generator in dBASE, an easy-to-use tool for creating a customized data base system without programming

archive attribute the file attribute that indicates if a file has been changed since it was last saved with the DOS BACKUP command

artificial intelligence (AI) a field of study combining aspects of computer science, mathematics, philosophy, psychology, and linguistics whose main goal is to mimic human learning and decision making

ascending order the arrangement of numbers from smallest to largest, and of text alphabetically from A to Z

ASCII file see *text file*

assembler a program that translates assembly language instructions into the binary numbers of machine language

assembly language a programming language that substitutes meaningful abbreviations for the numerically coded instructions of a machine language

Autokey macro A VP-Planner Plus macro created by recording keystrokes

automated vision a type of software that allows computers to distinguish and interpret images from optical sensors

automatic hyphenation a word processing feature that uses a set of built-in rules to split words at the ends of lines when necessary without confirmation from the user

automatic recalculation the ability of a spreadsheet program to immediately update the entire worksheet whenever the contents of a cell are changed

background in OS/2, where an application that does not have control of the physical console is running

backup an extra copy of vital programs or data; to make such a copy

balance sheet a report that summarizes the assets, liabilities, and capital of a business

bar graph a chart in which numeric values are represented by evenly spaced, thick vertical lines

BASIC (Beginners' All-purpose Symbolic Instruction Code) a simple, interactive programming language originally designed to teach students about computer programming

Basic Input/Output System (BIOS) on some computers, the hardware interface that controls physical components such as disk drives, monitor, keyboard, and printer

batch file a text file that lists operating system commands to be performed automatically when the name of the batch file is entered

batch processing using batch files to reduce several frequently used operating system commands to just one command to save time and effort

batch processing commands a special set of internal DOS commands, such as CALL and ECHO, that add power and flexibility to batch files

benchmark an objective, reproducible measure of hardware or software performance

Bernoulli box see *Bernoulli disk drive*

Bernoulli disk drive a secondary storage device that combines the advantages of both floppy and hard disk drives

billing the accounting subsystem that prepares and records invoices

binary file a file that contains programs or data that are not encoded as ASCII characters

binary point the period that separates the whole part from the fractional part of a mixed binary number

bit the basic unit of data processing; a single binary digit, 0 or 1, off or on

bit-mapped see *pixel-based*

bits per second (bps) unit of modem transmission speed

block a contiguous section of text—can consist of a single character up to an entire document

booting up initially loading and executing the operating system

border palette a menu of line thicknesses used to draw lines and outline shapes

branching altering the order in which batch file commands are executed using IF and GOTO commands

briefcase computer see *laptop computer*

browse to casually scan the records of a data base

bug an error or problem in a computer program

built-in dictionary an automatic proofreading feature that looks for spelling errors

bus a set of wires and connectors that link the CPU to memory and other computer components

bus network a topology in which each workstation is connected to a single cable running past all the workstations

byte a contiguous group of eight bits; the amount of memory it takes to store a single character or a numeric quantity from 0 to 255

C a concise, yet powerful programming language frequently used for the development of system software and application packages

cache an intermediary storage place

calculated field a field that contains the result of an expression instead of a value entered directly in a data base file

capture to gather incoming data from a host computer and save it in a disk file

carrier sense multiple access (CSMA) a protocol that requires each network workstation to listen before sending messages or data

catalog in dBASE, a list of files

cathode ray tube (CRT) a display that uses an electronic gun to paint images on a phosphor-coated glass screen

cell the box at the intersection of a row and a column in a worksheet

cell address a designation that specifies a cell's exact location within a worksheet

cell pointer the highlighted cell that marks the current location in a worksheet

cell reference see *cell address*

central processing unit (CPU) the part of a computer that performs calculations, logic, and control operations

chaining executing a batch file as the last command in another batch file

chamfer a CAD feature that joins two lines with another straight line

character formatting specifying the way individual letters or words are presented

charting program a program that produces graphs, plots, and charts from data entered directly or imported from a spreadsheet or data base file

chassis a metal and plastic frame that houses all of the internal components of a computer

child file the more specific file in a relation that contains the information to be looked up by the parent file

chip see *integrated circuit chip*

circular reference the result of a formula in a cell being either directly or indirectly dependent on the value in that very same cell

clicking moving the mouse pointer on top of an item to be selected and briefly pressing and releasing the mouse button

clipboard a temporary storage area for copying data

clone a computer that works just like, or very similar to, another computer

coaxial cable a center conductor surrounded by a shield or wire braid, used for cable television and local area networks

COBOL a high-level programming language introduced in 1960 especially for business data processing

code in WordPerfect, a hidden formatting indicator generated when you press a key such as Enter or Tab, or execute a command that changes a document's appearance, such as Center or Bold

code page a conversion table that tells DOS how to translate data stored as numeric values into letters, numbers, punctuation, and other symbols to be displayed or printed

color graphics monitor a monitor that can display both text and graphics in more than one color

column a field in an SQL table

column-wise recalculation the order of worksheet recalculation that begins with cell A1 and proceeds down column A, goes on to cell B1 and proceeds down column B, and so on

combining see *merging*

command a directive that is issued to a program

command-line interface (CLI) a user interface, such as DOS without the DOS Shell, that presents a prompt and accepts commands instead of using menus, icons, and windows

comment out temporarily shut off a command in a program or batch file by inserting a comment in front of it on the same line

communications package software that lets a computer transfer messages, programs, and data to other computers

communications parameters the settings that specify the technical details of how a computer will communicate with another computer

communications server a network workstation that lets users communicate with computers outside the network via serial ports and a high-speed modem

compact disc read-only memory (CD-ROM) an optical disk drive that allows access to previously recorded data, but not storage of any new data

compiler a program that translates high-level language instructions into machine language

complex instruction set computer (CISC) a microprocessor, such as the Intel 80486 or Motorola 68040, that incorporates many relatively slow instructions especially designed for high-level languages

computer an electronic device that performs calculations and processes data into information

computer-aided design (CAD) a type of software package for drafting complex plans, blueprints, models, schematics, and other detailed drawings of parts, mechanisms, and buildings

computer-aided engineering (CAE) a system that allows engineers to simulate and test their designs on a computer before they are built

computer-aided manufacturing (CAM) a system in which a computer controls the machines that make or assemble products

computer-assisted instruction (CAI) a system that uses computers to teach students at their own pace

computer graphics the presentation of images such as figures, charts, graphs, maps, diagrams, and other pictures on a display screen

computer-managed instruction (CMI) a system that uses computers to help with school administrative tasks

computer matching a technique that involves comparing records in various data bases to identify individuals who meet overlapping sets of criteria

computer virus a hidden program that secretly copies itself from disk to disk and across networks, often causing mischief or outright destruction of data

computerized axial tomography (CAT or CT) a computer-controlled, three-dimensional X-ray machine

context-sensitive the ability of a help facility to display information specifically relevant to the current activity

Control Center the menu system of dBASE IV

control panel the space on the screen that displays cell information, menus, messages, and the operating mode

coprocessor integrated circuit chip designed to perform a specialized task for the main microprocessor

copy-and-paste a word processing operation in which a section of text is reproduced in another location

copy-protection a way to prepare diskettes so that it is difficult or impossible to copy them with ordinary operating system commands

CP/M a single-user, single-tasking generic microcomputer operating system sold by Digital Research

criteria requirements that a record must fulfill to be retrieved by a search or query

Critical Path Method (CPM) a scheduling method that focuses on the sequence of critical activities that must be performed to complete a project

crosshair two lines that intersect on the screen to indicate the current cursor position

current cell the cell marked by the cell pointer, where you can enter data or initiate commands

cursor a small, blinking underscore or box that marks the position where characters will appear on the screen when typed

cut-and-paste a word processing operation in which a section of text is moved from one location to another

daisy-wheel printer a printer with solid, raised characters embossed on the ends of little arms arranged like the spokes of a wheel, for producing slow, but letter-quality output

data numbers, text, pictures, and sounds that are to be processed into information; in a spreadsheet program, data can be numbers, labels, or formulas

data base an organized collection of one or more files of related data

data base management package software that lets you organize large quantities of information, such as mailing lists and inventories

data bus the pathway connecting the microprocessor to memory

data encryption a security method that encodes information so that it can be read and changed only by authorized users who know the password

data entry form a listing of each field in a record, accompanied by an empty box for each field's contents

debug to remove the errors from a computer program

debugger a program that helps to detect errors in software under development

decision support system (DSS) a computer system that helps managers make decisions by applying statistical models and mathematical simulation

dedicated server a network workstation reserved solely as a file, printer, or communications server

dedicated word processor a microcomputer system expressly designed and solely used to prepare, store, and print documents

de facto standard   a standard that emerges from many manufacturers voluntarily making products that will work together

default   predefined settings for certain features (margins, line spacing, column widths, etc.) that a software package uses automatically if the user does not explicitly establish settings

default drive   the disk drive where DOS will look for programs and data files unless otherwise specified

delete   to remove, erase, or destroy one or more pieces of information

delimiter   a space, comma, semicolon, equal sign, or tab

descending order   the arrangement of numbers from largest to smallest, and of text alphabetically from Z to A

desk accessory   a utility program that provides commonly used desk functions such as a calculator, calendar, or address book

desktop computer   the most common type of microcomputer, small enough to fit on top of a table or desk

desktop organizer   see *desk accessory*

desktop publishing   using a computer and laser printer to produce near-typeset-quality documents

desktop publishing package   software that combines the results of word processing and graphics to produce near-typeset-quality documents

device controller   a set of chips or a circuit board that operates a piece of computer equipment such as a disk drive, display, keyboard, mouse, or printer

device driver   a file that contains the programming code needed to attach and use a special device, such as a nonstandard disk drive, memory board, mouse, monitor, or printer

digitizer   see *graphics tablet*

direct access medium   storage medium, such as magnetic disk, that allows data items to be retrieved in any order

direct-connect modem   see *external modem*

directory   a list of the files stored on a disk; another term for subdirectory

disk   a medium used by computers to store information, consisting of one or more flat surfaces on which bits are recorded magnetically or optically

disk backup utility   a program that facilitates making backup copies of a hard disk on floppy disks

disk buffer   an area of memory DOS uses to temporarily hold data being read from or written to a disk

disk caching utility   a program that reserves part of memory as an intermediary storage place to speed up the retrieval of frequently used software and data

disk copying utility   a program that specializes in duplicating files and disks, especially those that are copy protected

disk drive   a computer system component that reads and writes programs and data on disks

diskette   see *floppy disk*

Disk Operating System (DOS)   see *PC-DOS*

disk optimizing utility   a program that makes secondary storage devices operate more efficiently

display   output screen on which the computer presents text and graphic images

display adapter   a circuit board or set of chips that controls a monitor

display-only field   see *read-only field*

document   the paper output of a word processor

documentation   the user manual or technical information about a computer or software package

document file   a collection of text created by a word processing program in such a way that the text includes embedded formatting codes

DOS   a generic name for PC-DOS and MS-DOS

DOS Compatibility Box   see *DOS Session*

DOS environment   a special area of memory, like a scratch pad for DOS, that some programs use to hold variables, values, and text

DOS prompt   a symbol that identifies the current default drive and indicates that DOS is waiting for a command

DOS Session   the special environment in OS/2 that can run a single DOS application at a time

DOS shell   a menu-driven addition to DOS that helps manage disk files and directories

DOS Shell   the DOS shell developed by IBM and Microsoft and included with DOS versions 4.0 and newer

dot-matrix printer   a common type of printer that constructs character images by repeatedly striking pins against the ribbon and paper

dot pitch   the distance between the illuminated centers of any two adjacent dots on a display screen

dot prompt   the dBASE command-line interface

dot prompt command   a dBASE command entered in response to the dot prompt and not selected from a menu

double clicking   pressing and releasing a mouse button twice in rapid succession

downloading   transferring a file from a host computer to your computer

draft mode   the fastest print mode in which low-quality characters are formed by a single pass of the printhead

dragging   holding down the mouse button while moving the mouse—used to pull down menus, outline parts of a picture, move selections, and stretch objects

drive specifier   a disk drive letter immediately followed by a colon

edit   to make changes in a file

electronic mail (E-mail)   a way to send and receive messages with a computer

electronic typewriter   an electric typewriter with a built-in microprocessor

Encapsulated PostScript (EPS) file   a graphics file containing gray-shade information that can be imported and printed by page layout programs that use the PostScript language

encryption   a method of protecting sensitive data by scrambling it so that it cannot be read without the proper key

end user   see *user*

endnote a numbered comment or explanation similar to a footnote, except that it appears at the end of the document instead of at the bottom of each page

erasable optical disk drive a disk drive that uses optical disks that can be written to and read from any number of times

ergonomics the science of designing objects so that they can be most easily, effectively, comfortably, and safely used by people

example variable in dBASE IV, a place holder for the value of a field entered in the link field to link two data base files

expansion board a circuit board that plugs into an expansion slot

expansion card see *expansion board*

expansion slot an internal connector that allows you to plug an additional circuit board into the motherboard; an extension of the bus

expert an experienced computer user

expert system a computer program that contains both a collection of facts and a list of rules for making inferences about those facts

expert system shell microcomputer software that contains an inference engine and lets nonprogrammers set up expert systems by supplying (1) their own facts to create knowledge bases and (2) rules to create rule bases

exponent in scientific notation, the number indicating the power of ten to be multiplied by the mantissa

exporting writing data in a format that can be accepted by a different program

extension the second part of a DOS file's name

external command a DOS command that is kept in disk storage and temporarily loaded into memory only when needed or specifically requested

external modem a modem built into its own separate housing

fiber-optic cable glass filaments that transmit data in the form of extremely rapid pulses of light generated by lasers, used for high-speed local area networks

field a group of related characters in a data base record; a single data item, such as a number, character, word, or phrase

field template in dBASE, a representation of the width and contents of a data field to be displayed in a form

file a collection of information kept in secondary storage and loaded into primary memory when needed by a program; in a data base, a group of related records

file attribute a characteristic of a file, such as read-only or archive

file compression utility a program that squeezes files into less disk space by eliminating waste and redundant data

file control block (FCB) a data structure used by early versions of DOS to manage open files

file conversion utility a program that modifies files from one application so that they can be used by another application

file locking allowing only one person or program to use the same file at the same time on a network

filename the primary part of a DOS file's name

file recovery utility a program that can reinstate accidentally erased files, restore reformatted hard disks, or perform other useful file operations

file server a network workstation used to store shared program and data files on a large-capacity, high-speed hard disk

file sharing allowing two or more people or programs to use the same file at the same time on a network

file skeleton a graphic representation of a data base file

file specification the combination of a disk drive specifier, a filename, and an extension

file transfer utility a program that can move data among different types of computers

fillet a CAD feature that joins two lines to create a rounded corner

film recorder a graphics output device that turns screen images into 35-mm slides

filter a DOS command (FIND, MORE, or SORT) that normally reads input from the keyboard, changes it in some way, and then displays it as output on the screen

filter condition in dBASE, an expression that determines which records are to be selected for a view

Finder a part of the Apple Macintosh operating system that allows users to run application programs, set up disks, and organize, copy, and delete files

firmware low-level, system software stored in ROM chips, such as the BIOS

first line indent a format in which only the first line of the paragraph is moved in from the left margin

fixed currency format a worksheet format in which two places are to the right of the decimal point, thousands are separated by commas, and each number is preceded by a dollar sign

fixed disk drive see *hard disk drive*

fixed-point number a number whose decimal or binary point is in a fixed place in relation to the digits

flat-file data base manager a program that works with one file of structured data at a time

floating-point number a number in which the position of the decimal or binary point can vary

floor model a powerful, expensive microcomputer with a system unit larger than that of the typical desktop computer and designed to accommodate more add-in hardware components

floppy disk an inexpensive, flexible magnetic medium for storing computer programs and data that can be removed from the disk drive when not in use

floppy disk drive a disk drive that accepts floppy disks

font a set of letters, numbers, punctuation marks, and other symbols with a consistent appearance

footer   one or more lines of text printed at the bottom of every page

footnote   a numbered comment or explanation at the bottom of a page

foreground   in OS/2, where the application that has control of the physical console is running

form   a screen or printout that shows the fields of an individual record

formatting   initializing a disk so that files can be stored on it

formula   an expression that instructs a spreadsheet program to perform calculations or other manipulations on numbers, labels, or the contents of cells

FORTRAN   one of the first high-level programming languages, designed to fulfill the computational needs of scientists, engineers, and mathematicians

fourth generation language (4GL)   the most abstract type of programming language, designed to make it as easy as possible for users to tell a computer what to do

free-form data base manager   a program designed to handle narrative text and irregular pieces of data, such as paragraphs, pages, articles, notes, discussions, and instructions

full-duplex   a communications mode in which the characters sent to the host computer are echoed back to the terminal's screen

function   a ready-made procedure that performs tedious, complex, or often-used computations or other manipulations

function keys   on an IBM-compatible computer, the keys on the left side or top of the keyboard labeled F1 through F10 or F12, used to perform common operations

game adapter   a circuit board or set of chips that allows the use of joysticks or trackballs

Gantt chart   a horizontal bar graph that shows the major tasks of a project, when each task must be performed, and how long each task will take to perform

general ledger   the main listing of the accounts of a business

generic operating system   an operating system that can be adapted to almost any type of computer

gigabyte (G)   1,073,741,824 bytes

global   pertaining to or acting upon an entire document, spreadsheet, or data base file

global delete   the ability to remove all those records that meet certain criteria

global filename character   the * (which matches any group of characters) or the ? (which matches any single character) used in a DOS file specification to indicate names with one or more characters in common

global modify   the ability to change all those records that meet certain criteria

global search and replace   changing a word or phrase automatically throughout an entire document

graphical user interface (GUI)   a sophisticated, easy-to-use system that includes pull-down menus, icons, windows, and a simulated desktop

graphics   any kind of graphs, plots, drawings, and other images not restricted to text characters

graphics adapter   a display adapter that can produce graphics

graphics-based windowing environment   a windowing environment that can work with programs that display pictures and characters of all different sizes, styles, and fonts

graphics package   software that can produce graphs, plots, drawings, pictures, or charts

graphics tablet   a flat surface on which the user draws with a stylus, pen, or some other pointing device

greeking   representing text too small to be distinguished by tiny characters or shaded bars to show its position on a page

grid   criss-crossed lines used to keep objects lined up with each other on the screen; a visual aid for placing objects in a drawing

hacker   a hardware designer or programmer with an obsession for computing

half-duplex   a communications mode in which the characters sent to the host computer are not echoed back to the terminal's screen

hand-held computer   the smallest type of microcomputer, smaller than a paperback book and weighing less than a pound

handle   a little black square on the boundary of a selected object, used to drag or resize the object

hanging indent   a format in which all lines of a paragraph except for the first are moved in from the left margin

hard disk   a circular platter of rigid aluminum or glass covered with a thin magnetic coating for storing computer programs and data

hard disk drive   a disk drive that contains one or more hard disks

hard hyphen   a hyphen created by pressing the - key

hard page break   in WordPerfect, a division between two pages that is manually generated by pressing Ctrl-Enter

hard return   in WordPerfect, a new line or paragraph begun by pressing the Enter key

hard space   in WordPerfect, a blank created by pressing the Space Bar

hardware   the physical components of a computer system

Hayes-compatible modem   a modem that operates like a Hayes Smartmodem

head crash   the result of a disk drive's read-write head colliding with a minute obstruction or hitting the surface of a disk

header   one or more lines of text printed at the top of every page

headword   in WordPerfect, a word that can be looked up in the thesaurus

hexadecimal system   base 16 number system

hidden column   a worksheet column that exists and contains data, but is not displayed or printed

hidden file   a special file used by DOS or some other program that does not appear in the disk directory

hierarchical   a method of organizing files into rank-ordered groups

high-level language   an abstract programming language that facilitates the expression of complex data processing operations

host computer   the computer being called by another computer

hypermedia   the nonsequential organization and presentation of information, including graphics, audio, and video

hypertext   the nonsequential organization and presentation of information with a computer

hyphenation   the division of certain words at the ends of lines to improve the appearance of text

IBM-compatible   a microcomputer that works just like, or in some ways better than, an IBM microcomputer, and can run the same software

icon   a small pictorial symbol that represents a file, a file folder, an action to be performed, or a program to be run

importing   reading and, if necessary, translating data originally created with some other program

income statement   a report that summarizes the revenues and expenses of a business for a given period of time

incremental backup   a backup procedure that copies only those files that have been changed since the last backup

indenting   moving text away from the margin toward the center of the page

index file   a file that contains record numbers listed in a particular order

indexing   a way to reorder the records of a data base without actually duplicating the data in a new file or rearranging the actual records in the original file

information   a more organized and useful form of input data

ink-jet printer   a printer with a mechanism for squirting tiny droplets of ink to form text and graphics on paper

input   any data or information entered into a computer

insertion point   another term for *cursor*; where text is inserted with a word processing package

insert mode   a typing mode in which all characters typed at the current cursor location push aside existing text to the right

installed   when a software package is copied to a hard or floppy disk and set up to be run

instruction set   a limited collection of low-level tasks a computer can do with a single instruction

integrated circuit chip   a thin slice of semiconductor material, such as pure silicon crystal, impregnated with carefully selected impurities, commonly used in computers and many other electronic devices

integrated software   a software package that includes word processing, spreadsheet, data base, graphics, and communications capabilities

intelligent recalculation   see *smart recalculation*

interface   a connection between a computer's CPU and an external device operated under its control

internal command   an essential or frequently used DOS command that is kept in memory

internal modem   a modem built onto an expansion board or directly onto the motherboard

interpreter   a program that translates and runs one high-level language instruction at a time as it is entered into a computer

interrupt   a signal that suspends the current program to tell the CPU that some critical event has occurred

inventory control   the accounting subsystem that tracks products and materials on hand

invoice   a bill sent to a customer

iteration   a way to obtain an approximate result to an indirect circular reference in a worksheet by recomputing the formulas a number of times

journal   a chronological listing of transactions

joystick   a vertical lever that can be tilted in any direction to control a cursor or steer a simulated vehicle

justified   a type of text alignment in which text is flush to both the left and right margins

key   a field used to sort or index the records of a data base

keyboard   the primary input device with which you enter data and tell a computer what to do

keyboard macro   see *macro*

keyboard template   a plastic or cardboard guide that fits over or near the function keys on the keyboard listing the most common keyboard commands

kilobyte (K)   1,024 bytes

knowledge-based system   see *expert system*

label   in a DOS batch file, a place for a GOTO command to branch to; in a spreadsheet program, any kind of text, such as a heading, title, name, address, or note in a worksheet cell

label macro   a macro created by entering the labels that represent the keystrokes to be performed when the macro is run

label prefix character   a special character (', ^, ", \) that tells the program that the following item is a label and not a number or formula, and indicates how to align labels within cells or if a character is to be repeated within a cell

laptop computer   a full-fledged microcomputer squeezed into a 4- to 15-pound housing smaller than most briefcases

laser printer   a high-quality printer that uses tightly focused beams of light to transfer images to paper

layer a CAD feature like a transparent overlay sheet that can be created separately and superimposed on top of other layers

learn feature in Lotus 1-2-3, a way to create a macro by recording keystrokes

learn mode an easy-to-use method of defining a macro by recording keystrokes

learn range in Lotus 1-2-3, the single-column range of cells where keystrokes will be recorded for a macro definition

left indent a format in which all lines of a paragraph are moved in from the left margin

letter-quality like the output of a good electric typewriter

light pen a rod used to point at or draw on a computer display screen

line editor a simple program that can only work with a single line of text at a time

line graph a plot that represents each data value by a point at an appropriate distance above the horizontal axis and connects the points by line segments

line height in WordPerfect, the distance between lines of printed text

link field a common field that connects two data base files

linker a program that combines the output files of programming language translators into a single executable program file

liquid crystal display (LCD) a flat-panel screen that presents black characters against a grey background, commonly used in watches, clocks, calculators, and hand-held and laptop microcomputers

load to copy a program or data file from disk into memory

local area network (LAN) several microcomputers connected together within the same building, or nearby buildings, to share hardware, software, and data

locked cell see *protected cell*

logged the current disk drive or directory

logical formula in a worksheet, a formula that compares values and produces a result of 1 for true or 0 for false

logical operator in dBASE, an operator (.AND., .OR., or .NOT.) that modifies the true or false result of one or two conditions

log-in to enter the assigned group name, user name, and password to gain access to a system

Lotus Access System a program called Lotus that lets you start 1-2-3 or any of the other programs that come with the Lotus 1-2-3 package

machine language the only programming language that can be directly used by a computer, consisting of binary numbers that represent CPU instructions, memory addresses, and data

machine learning a method by which computers can program themselves, through trial and error, to accomplish a particular task

macro a sequence of keystrokes that can be recorded, stored, and replayed

magnetic disk a semipermanent storage medium that can be erased and written over and over again

magnetic resonance imaging (MRI) a medical scanning method that produces high-quality cross-sectional pictures of the body without X-rays or other radiation

magnetic tape a long strip of thin plastic covered with a magnetic coating

magnetic tape drive a secondary storage device that uses magnetic tape to hold programs and data

mail-merge a word processing or data base feature that lets you combine a master document with a data file of names and addresses to create personalized form letters

mainframe a big, powerful, fast, expensive computer

management information system (MIS) a computer system that provides managers with the information they need to do their jobs more effectively

mantissa in scientific notation, the decimal part of the number that is to be multiplied by the power of ten indicated by the exponent

manual hyphenation a hyphenation method that requires you to confirm the splitting of each word as you scroll through the document

manual recalculation a feature that causes the formulas in a worksheet to be recalculated only when explicitly directed to do so

many-to-many link a type of link that connects multiple records to other multiple records in data base files

master document a document containing text and special commands to be mail-merged with a data file

master index file the index file that specifies the order in which all records will be displayed unless otherwise specified

megabyte (M) 1,048,576 bytes

megahertz (MHz) a unit of frequency equal to one million cycles per second

memo marker in dBASE IV, an indicator that appears in a record to show if the associated memo field contains any text

memory a computer's internal storage for temporarily holding programs and data

memory-resident a type of program that allows a user to temporarily suspend an activity and switch to another one under a single-tasking operating system such as DOS

memory variable in dBASE, a place in RAM that temporarily holds a data value

menu a list showing options available in a program

menu bar a list of the names of pull-down menus across the top of the screen

menu pointer the highlighted block that shows the command that will be invoked if you press the Enter key

merging combining two worksheets into one

message line in dBASE, a line near the bottom of the screen that displays messages

Micro Channel Architecture the high-performance bus (underlying circuit) design of IBM's Personal System/2 Models 50 through 80 microcomputers

microcomputer a small computer that uses a single microprocessor chip as its central processing unit

microcomputer standard a generally accepted set of rules by which hardware and software operate

microprocessor a central processing unit made up of a single integrated circuit chip

million instructions per second (MIPS) a unit of computer performance that represents the execution of computer instructions

minicomputer a medium-sized computer that simultaneously serves several users or controls complex equipment

minimal recalculation a spreadsheet program feature that increases speed by recalculating only those cells that have changed, and the cells that depend on them, since the worksheet was last recalculated

mixed reference a cell address that is half-relative and half-absolute, in which either a row or column is absolute, but not both

mnemonic an easy-to-remember abbreviation for a computer operation, such as ADD

mode indicator the highlighted block in the upper right corner of the control panel that describes the current operating mode, such as READY or MENU

modem a device that allows a computer to transmit and receive programs and data over ordinary phone lines

modem cable a cable that connects an external modem to a serial interface socket at the back of a computer

modular phone jack a socket that accepts the little plastic plug on the end of a telephone cord

monitor a computer display screen (see *display*)

monochrome graphics monitor a single-color screen that can display both text and graphics

monochrome text monitor a single-color screen that displays sharply-defined characters, but no graphics

motherboard the main circuit board of a computer

mouse an input device consisting of a small box with one or more buttons that is slid across the tabletop to manipulate objects on the screen, draw, and select menu options

MS-DOS see *PC-DOS*

multidimensional spreadsheet a spreadsheet program that allows every cell in a worksheet to be connected to corresponding cells in other worksheets

MultiFinder an addition to the Apple Macintosh operating system that allows some multitasking capabilities and lets users run application programs, set up disks, and organize, copy, and delete files

multifunction board an expansion board that includes several add-on options, such as memory, a real-time clock, a game adapter, a display adapter, and serial and parallel interfaces

multiple index file in dBASE IV, a file with an extension of MDX that can contain up to 47 separate indexes of a data base file

multiprocessing the ability to run several programs simultaneously by using more than one processing unit

multiscan monitor a monitor that can change its resolution to match a number of different display adapters

multitasking the ability to run more than one program concurrently

natural language processing getting computers to understand portions of ordinary human languages such as English

natural recalculation the order of worksheet recalculation that updates a cell only after evaluating any cells on which it depends

navigation line in dBASE, a line near the bottom of the screen that lists some of the available keystrokes

near letter-quality (NLQ) a dot-matrix print mode that produces attractive output by having the printhead make two or more passes over each character

nesting in DOS, using the CALL command to invoke one batch file from within another batch file without ending the first batch file

NETBIOS (Network Basic Input/Output System) low-level programs that send and receive data to and from the network adapter

network computers connected to share hardware, software, and data

network adapter a sophisticated expansion board that connects a microcomputer to a local area network

network interface the adapter and connector that link a workstation to a network

network media the cables that connect network workstations

network server a network workstation that handles special chores

network software a set of programs, mostly on the file server, that moves data and messages between the workstations and servers, and controls the sharing of files and hardware devices

network workstation an ordinary microcomputer used to run software, transfer files, and send messages on a network

neural network a type of computer or a software simulation loosely modeled after the interconnection of neurons, or nerve cells, in the human brain

newspaper-style columns text that continues from the bottom of one column on the left to the top of the next column to the right on the same page

nonprocedural language see *fourth generation language*

novice a beginning computer user

null-modem cable a cable for directly connecting the serial ports of two computers

number a numeric quantity, such as 100, 52.34, or 0.05

numeric formula in a worksheet, a mathematical expression that calculates using numeric values and produces a numeric result

numeric keypad on an IBM-compatible computer, the area on the right side of the keyboard arranged like the number keys on a calculator

object code software that has been translated into machine language

object-oriented a package that lets you create and manipulate images made up of only discrete geometric objects such as lines, curves, rectangles, ovals, irregular outlines, polygons, and text

octal system base 8 number system

one-to-many link a type of link that connects a single record in one file to multiple records in one or more other files

one-to-one link a type of link that connects a single record in one file to a single record in another file

on-line connected to and controlled by the computer

on-line help information about how a program works that you can display on the screen, without your having to look it up in a printed reference manual

on-line information service a service that allows computers equipped with a modem to retrieve vast quantities of information and communicate with other users

on-line reference a program such as a spelling checker, thesaurus, or user manual that you can use while running another program

open style in WordPerfect, a style that has just a beginning code, often used to set formats for an entire document

operand a number on which an operation is to be performed

operating system a set of programs that controls a computer's hardware and manages the use of software

operation code (opcode) the part of a machine language instruction that indicates which operation is to be performed

operator a symbol that represents an action to be performed in a formula, such as + or *

optical disk drive a secondary storage device that uses a laser to read or write data on a plastic disk

optimal recalculation see *minimal recalculation*

orphan the first line of a paragraph that appears at the bottom of a page

OS/2 a single-user, multitasking operating system, developed by IBM and Microsoft, for IBM and IBM-compatible microcomputers that use the Intel 80286, 80386, and 80486 microprocessors

output any information produced by the computer; the computer's responses to your input

overwrite mode a typing mode in which characters typed at the current cursor location replace existing characters

packet-switching network see *public data network*

page break a division between two pages

page description language a specialized computer programming language for defining the size, format, and position of text and graphic elements on a printed page

page formatting specifying the general organization of an entire page of text

page layout software a package for arranging text and graphics on pages before they are printed

painting program a pixel-based program for producing pictures on a computer screen

paired style in WordPerfect, a style that has a beginning and ending code

palette the total number of colors to choose from in a particular video mode

pan a CAD feature that lets you move the viewing window up, down, left, or right

paragraph formatting specifying the appearance of individual blocks of text

parallel columns text that continues in the same column on the next page

parallel interface a connection that transmits data, an entire byte at a time, between a computer and an external device, such as a printer

parallel port see *parallel interface*

parameter an entry that designates possible alternate actions

parent file the more general file in a relation that looks up the information in the child file

parity a method of error checking used to help ensure that all of the data bits of a character were received correctly after a transmission

partition a separate section of a hard disk that may contain its own operating system

Pascal a general-purpose, high-level language originally designed to teach students the principles of good programming

patent an exclusive right to produce or sell an invention for a given time

path a drive specifier followed by a list of subdirectory names, separated by backslashes, that describes the route to a particular subdirectory

pattern palette a menu of patterns that can be used with drawing tools to create objects and to fill in enclosed areas on the screen

payroll the accounting subsystem that maintains personnel information, generates paychecks, computes tax withholdings, and creates summary reports of employee earnings

PC-DOS a single-user, single-tasking operating system developed by Microsoft for IBM microcomputers

pel see *pixel*

personal computer see *microcomputer*

physical console the display and keyboard

pie chart a graph that represents values as wedges of a circle, used to show the parts of a whole

piping a DOS feature, symbolized by the | (vertical bar), that takes the output of one command, which would normally go to the display screen, and feeds it as input to another command

pixel picture element; a tiny dot on a computer display

pixel-based a package that has control over every dot on the screen

plotter an output device that uses one or more pens to draw on paper

point a typographical measure equal to about 1/72-inch

pointer movement keys keys that you press to move the cell pointer

polling a protocol in which a controlling workstation sends messages to other workstations on the network, asking each one in turn if it has any messages or data to transmit

pop-up menu a list of options that appears on the screen only when a user issues a special command

pop-up utility see *desk accessory*

portable computer a microcomputer about the size of a small suitcase, designed to be moved, but not used, in transit

positron emission tomography (PET) a medical scanning technique that produces images by detecting positively charged particles emitted from radioactive substances injected into the bloodstream

PostScript a page description language for high-resolution printers and typesetters

power supply a refined source of electrical power for a computer that contains a transformer to lower and regulate the voltage level

power user see *expert*

Presentation Manager the graphical user interface of OS/2

primary file in WordPerfect, the text of a form letter containing special mail-merge codes

primary key the field on which records are sorted first

primary storage a computer's internal memory

print buffering see *print spooling*

printer a device for producing permanent copies of computer output on paper

printer setup string a group of special control codes directing the printer to turn on such options as compressed print

print queue a list of files to be printed in the background

print server a network workstation used to control a printer shared by other workstations on a network

print spooler a utility program that reduces or eliminates waiting for a printer to produce documents

print spooling the ability to print one document while working on another

procedure file see *batch file*

ProDOS a single-user, single-tasking proprietary operating system for the Apple II family of microcomputers

program a sequence of step-by-step instructions that tell a computer what to do

Program Evaluation and Review Technique (PERT) a scheduling method for tasks whose completion times are difficult to estimate

programmable data base manager a relational or flat-file data base manager that includes its own programming language or works with a standard programming language such as BASIC, C, COBOL, FORTRAN, or Pascal

programmer a person who creates computer programs

programming language a set of symbols and rules that direct the operations of a computer

project management software a package that helps to formally plan and control complex undertakings

prompt a symbol or statement that indicates the computer is waiting for a response from the user

proportional spacing allotting different amounts of space for different characters

proprietary hardware or software, with tightly controlled patents or copyrights, that cannot be legally duplicated without being licensed by the originator

proprietary operating system an operating system designed specifically for a single model or line of computers

protected cell a cell that cannot be altered, deleted, or moved unless its protection is first turned off

protocol a set of rules that govern how computers communicate

public data network a way to call a distant communications service from a local telephone number

pull-down menu a list of options that appears when the list's title or symbol is selected from the top of the screen

query a search for records that meet one or more specific criteria; in dBASE, a set of instructions to retrieve, display, organize, or edit data

Query-by-Example (QBE) a highly interactive query language that makes it easy for a user to extract information from a data base

query file in dBASE III PLUS, a special type of file that filters a data base to display or print only those records that meet specific criteria

query language a specialized set of commands for rearranging or extracting data from data bases

QuickDraw laser printer a laser printer designed especially for Apple Macintosh computers as a lower-cost alternative to PostScript printers

RAM cache a part of memory specially reserved for data that must be frequently retrieved

RAM disk an area of memory that is set up to simulate a disk drive

RAM resident see *memory resident*

random access memory (RAM) storage in which all addresses are equally accessible; the portion of a computer's primary storage used to hold programs and data temporarily

range a block of adjacent cells in a worksheet, indicated by the address of the upper left cell, two periods, and the address of the lower right cell

read-only attribute the file attribute that determines if a file can be written, modified, or deleted

read-only field a data base field whose contents can be viewed but not altered

read-only memory (ROM) permanent primary storage that is encoded with programs and data at the factory, retains its contents when the power is turned off, and can be read and used but never erased, changed, or augmented

read-write head   a tiny electromagnet on a disk drive's access arm that can create or erase minuscule magnetic spots on the disk directly below

real number   see *floating-point number*

real-time clock   a built-in clock that keeps the date and time-of-day for a computer

record   an array of related fields that contains all the data about a particular person or object

record buffer   in Lotus 1-2-3 Release 3.0, a 512-byte area of memory that stores the most recent keystrokes

record feature   in Lotus 1-2-3 Release 3.0, a way to create a macro by copying keystrokes saved in the record buffer

record locking   preventing the deletion or modification of an individual record currently being used by another person on the same network

record number   a unique number assigned to each record in a data base file

record pointer   in dBASE, an invisible pointer that keeps track of the current record

redirection   changing the normal source or destination of information processed by a DOS command by using the >, <, or >> symbols

redirector   a layer of software that acts as a traffic controller for the data and messages transmitted over a network

reduced instruction set computer (RISC)   a microprocessor that has a relatively small number of simple instructions that all execute very quickly

reformatting   erasing and reinitializing a previously formatted disk

register   a storage compartment inside the CPU for temporarily holding numbers that are currently being manipulated

relate   to link two or more data base files

relational data base   a data base that includes two or more files with at least one field in common

relational data base manager   a program that allows you to create, maintain, reorganize, and print structured data from more than one file at a time

relational operator   a symbol or word that specifies how items are to be compared

relative reference   a cell address that pertains to a cell's position relative to the current cell, and changes when the cell is moved or copied

replace   a word processing feature used to automatically substitute one word or phrase for another throughout a document

replaceable parameter   a special code inserted into a batch file that allows the user to pass information to the batch file while it is running

report   a printed listing of the contents of a data base

report band   in dBASE IV, a logical piece of a report design

resident routine   see *internal command*

resolution   the sharpness of a display screen

ring network   a topology in which each workstation is connected to a single cable that runs past all of the workstations, with the two ends of the central cable hooked together

robot   a computer-controlled machine that performs mechanical tasks

root directory   the main directory on every DOS disk

row   a record in an SQL table

row-wise recalculation   the order of worksheet recalculation that begins with cell A1 and proceeds across row 1, then row 2, and so on

ruler guide   in a page layout program, a dotted line that helps keep text and graphics aligned

ruler line   a line that shows the positions of the margins and tab stops

rules   dividing lines placed to separate columns and offset blocks of text

running head   the same title printed on every page

sans serif   a kind of plain typeface without serifs

scanner   an input device that can read text and/or graphics from paper and enter it directly into the computer

scatterplot   see *XY graph*

scroll bar   an on-screen tool used to allow movement within a document, usually found in word processing packages with graphics interfaces

scrolling   the upward movement of text on a display screen

search   a word processing feature used to locate a name or topic within a document

secondary key   the field on which records are sorted second, after the primary key

secondary merge file   in WordPerfect, the data file that contains the names and addresses for a mail-merge

secondary storage   storage that supplements primary storage by providing a place to keep programs and data when they are not needed

sector   a division of a disk track

semiconductor   a substance that conducts electricity poorly at low temperatures, but well at high temperatures, and is used to make integrated circuit chips

sequential access medium   storage medium, such as magnetic tape, on which data items can be retrieved only in the order in which they were recorded

serial interface   a connection that transmits bytes of data, one bit at a time, between a computer and an external device, such as a modem

serial port   see *serial interface*

serif   a kind of typeface that has lines crossing and finishing off the main strokes of the characters

service program   low-level program in the BIOS or DOS that can be invoked by other software to perform hardware-related tasks

shared word processor   a word processing system on a large, multiuser computer

single-tasking   the simplest type of operating system that accommodates a single user and runs a single program at a time

site license   permission to make copies of software for internal use at a reduced fee for each copy

slide show program a program that allows you to present a sequence of pictures on a computer screen, either automatically timed or directly controlled

Small Computer System Interface (SCSI) a connection that provides high-speed access to peripheral devices such as hard disks

smart recalculation the ability of a spreadsheet program to automatically update only those cells, if any, that are affected when a new entry is made

snaking columns see *newspaper-style columns*

snap a CAD feature that automatically aligns objects to the nearest grid lines

soft hyphen a hyphen generated by the auto-hyphenation feature

soft page break a division between two pages automatically generated by the word processing software

soft return a new line begun by the word wrap feature

soft space an extra blank generated by a word processing program to justify text

software a program or set of programs that tells a computer system what to do

software licensing a legal agreement in which a program is not actually sold, but licensed to a user with limits on what can be done with the program

software piracy the practice of illegally copying software

sorting arranging items in some particular order

Soundex search a search technique that finds words that sound like the specified word

source a disk or file to be copied

source code software in an assembly language or a high-level language before it is translated into machine language

specifications a detailed list of the exact components, options, and capabilities of a particular hardware device

speech synthesizer an output device that either mimics human speech or constructs it out of prerecorded sounds

spelling checker see *built-in dictionary*

spooling multitasking technique that prints files in the background while the computer is used for other work

spreadsheet see *worksheet*

spreadsheet package software that helps you manipulate tables of numbers

stack a data structure used by the CPU, operating system, or application program as a temporary storage area

stacked bar graph a variation of the basic bar graph that shows components and total amounts for each category by dividing each bar into sections

stackware information systems created with the Hypertalk language of Apple's Hypercard program

star network a topology in which an individual cable is run from a central server to each workstation

startup directory the disk drive and directory automatically used to store and retrieve worksheet files unless otherwise specified

static menu a list of options that usually remains on the screen in a fixed position

status bar in dBASE, a line near the bottom of the screen that displays information about the operation you have chosen

status line in WordPerfect, the line at the bottom of the screen that displays messages and warnings

stop bits bits that mark the end of an individual data character transmission

string combination operator the & (ampersand), which joins two labels

Structured Query Language (SQL) a standardized language for extracting information from a relational data base

style in WordPerfect, a collection of formatting codes and possibly text that can be created, saved, and inserted into documents to automate formatting and provide a consistent appearance to documents

style sheet a collection of formatting instructions that can be saved in a file and applied to different documents

subdirectory a group of files on a disk organized under a single name

submenu a menu that is activated by selecting an option from a higher-level menu

summary operator in dBASE IV, an operator for performing operations in view queries such as SUM, AVERAGE, and COUNT

supercomputer an extremely fast mainframe

supermicro see *workstation*

supermini a powerful minicomputer with capabilities similar to those of some mainframes

surge protector a device that rapidly cuts off the electricity when a voltage surge occurs

switching drives telling DOS to use a different disk drive as the default

symbolic addressing the assignment of meaningful names, such as TOTAL, to computer memory locations

system board see *motherboard*

system call see *service program*

system clock a crystal, oscillating several million times per second, that synchronizes the internal operations of the microprocessor and other computer components

system prompt see *DOS prompt*

system software the software that handles the many details of managing a computer system

system unit in many microcomputers, the box that houses the central processing unit, control circuitry, expansion boards, memory, and disk drives

table a screen that displays a record in each row and a field in each column; the basic component of an SQL data base

tag in dBASE IV, the name of an index in a multiple index file

target a disk or file copy to be created

telecommute to work at home using a microcomputer or a terminal connected to a computer at the office

teleconference an electronic forum that allows computer users who share special interests to communicate and hold on-line meetings

template   a general-purpose, ready-made worksheet in which the user fills in the blanks or changes selected entries

terminal   a computer input/output station consisting of a keyboard and a display

terminal emulation   a communications software feature that lets you use a microcomputer as a computer terminal

text area   in WordPerfect, the area on the screen where you enter text and edit a document

text-based windowing environment   a windowing environment that uses only the standard character set built into the computer and that cannot work with graphics programs

text file   a file, also known as an ASCII file, that contains only ordinary letters, numbers, and punctuation marks

time-sharing   an operating system that rapidly switches among several users at fixed intervals of time

token-passing   a protocol that uses a control signal called a token that determines which workstation is allowed to transmit messages or data

tool palette   a menu of icons for drawing, adding text, moving about, and selecting parts of a picture created with a painting or drawing program

topology   the way hardware components are arranged in a network

touch screen   an input device built into or over a display screen that uses infrared light beams or an electrically conductive surface to identify the position of a finger as it points to the screen

track   a ring on a disk where data can be stored

trackball   a box that contains a protruding ball that can be freely rotated in any direction and is often used as an alternative to a mouse

trademark   a legal protection for creative expression, usually limited to a word, phrase, or graphic symbol representing a company or product

transient routine   see *external command*

Transputer   a special microprocessor that can be connected with other Transputers to construct a fast, powerful multiprocessing computer

twisted-pair wire   two wires that have been partially wrapped around each other, used for ordinary telephone lines and inexpensive local area networks

typeface   see *font*

ultrasound scanner   a medical imaging device that uses very high-frequency sound waves

undo   a feature that lets you cancel your most recently performed operation

UNIX   a multiuser, multitasking generic operating system originally developed at AT&T's Bell Laboratories

update query   in dBASE IV, a query used to add, modify, or delete data in a data base file

uploading   transferring a file from your computer to a host computer

upwardly compatible   the ability of a new software product to handle every official command that worked with previous versions of it

user   a person who runs software on a computer to accomplish some task

user friendly   easy-to-learn; can be used by people who don't have a lot of computer experience

user interface   how a user directs the actions of software and how the software responds to these requests

utility   a small, specific program that adds handy features to a particular operating system or application package

value-added network   see *public data network*

very high level language   see *fourth generation language*

video mode   a combination of screen resolution and number of colors that can be used at one time

view   in dBASE, an arrangement of data on the screen

view file   in dBASE III PLUS, a file that displays data from two or more data base files

view query   in dBASE IV, a set of instructions that displays selected data on the screen

view skeleton   in dBASE IV, a graphic representation of the fields that will be displayed by the view query

virtual console   a simulated display and keyboard used by programs that run in the background under OS/2

voice recognition system   an input device that can recognize a finite number of isolated sounds, words, and phrases

volume label   in DOS, the name of a disk

widow   the last line of a paragraph that appears at the top of a page

wildcard character   in WordPerfect and dBASE, the * (which represents any group of characters) or the ? (which represents any single character) used in search and replace operations

what-you-see-is-what-you-get (WYSIWYG)   a feature in which a document is printed on paper exactly as it appears on the screen

window   a boxed-in area on the screen that shows the activity of a particular software program

windowing environment   system software that lets you divide your screen into a number of different boxes and run a separate program in each one

word processing   a common computer application that allows you to produce documents, such as letters and reports, with a computer

word processing package   a software package used to create, enter, edit, format, store, and print documents

word wrap   a word processing feature that automatically begins new lines when necessary without the user having to press the Enter key (carriage return)

work area   in dBASE, a place in memory that holds an open data base file

worksheet   a table of columns and rows of numbers, text labels, and formulas used in a spreadsheet package for the manipulation of numerical, financial, and accounting data

workstation   a small, yet powerful computer generally used by only one person at a time, traditionally used by scientists and engineers for drafting, design, and map-making

write once, read many (times) (WORM)   an optical disk drive that allows users to record data once, and then only read it thereafter

write-protection   a diskette feature that can be used to prevent the contents from being erased or altered

write-protect notch   a small rectangle cut out of one side of a 5¼-inch diskette that can be covered with a gummed tab to write-protect the disk

write-protect switch   a tab on a 3½-inch diskette that can be slid to open a little hole in the disk's plastic case, thereby write-protecting the disk

XY graph   a plot that shows the relationship between two or more variables

INDEX

Word processor, capabilities of, WP2
Words, deleting, WP20, WP75
Word wrap, WP13–14

Work area, dB127–128
Worksheet, L7
Write-protection, DOS37
Write-protect notch, DOS37–38

Write-protect switch, DOS38
WYSIWYG (What-You-See-Is-What-You-Get), WP33

XY graph, L75–79

MS-DOS® 4.01

F1	Retype one character from previous command
F2	Retype previous command up to specified character
F3	Retype all of previous command
F4	Delete previous command up to specified character
F5	Save current command as previous command
F6	Insert End-of-file code Ctrl-Z
F7	
F8	
F9	
F10	

Ctrl-Alt-Del	Reboot
Ctrl-Break	Cancel
Ctrl-Print Screen	Echo
Print Screen	Print
Enter	Process cmd.
Esc	Cancel line
Del	Skip char.
Ins	Toggle insert

D.C. Heath

Cut here

WordPerfect® 5.1
for IBM Personal Computers

Key	*Ctrl*	*Alt*	*Shift*	
F1	Shell	Thesaurus	Setup	Cancel
F2	Spell	Replace	▼Search	▲Search
F3	Screen	Reveal Codes	Switch	Help
F4	Move	Block	▲Indent▼	▲Indent
F5	Text In/Out	Mark Text	Date/Outline	List
F6	Tab Align	Flush Right	Center	Bold
F7	Footnote	Columns/Table	Print	Exit
F8	Font	Style	Format	Underline
F9	Merge/Sort	Graphics	Merge Codes	End Field
F10	Macro Define	Macro	Retrieve	Save

Delete to End of Ln/Pg	End/Pg Dn
Delete Word	Backspace
Go To	Home
	Enter
Hard Page	Tab
▼Margin Release	-/+ (num)
Screen Up/Down	=
Pull-Down Menus	←-/→
Word Left/Right	←/→

© WordPerfect Corp. 1988
D.C. Heath

Cut here

Lotus 1-2-3® R. 2.2

Key	*Alt*	
F1	COMPOSE	HELP
F2	STEP	EDIT
F3	RUN	NAME
F4	UNDO	ABS
F5	LEARN	GOTO
F6		WINDOW
F7	APP1	QUERY
F8	APP2	TABLE
F9	APP3	CALC
F10	APP4	GRAPH

/	Main menu
Enter	Process entry
Esc	Exit menu
Home	Go to A1
Ctrl←	Left screen
Ctrl→	Right screen

D.C. Heath

Cut here

dBASE IV® 1.1

Key	*Shift*	
F1	PICK	HELP
F2	DESIGN	DATA
F3	FIND PREV	PREV
F4	FIND NEXT	NEXT
F5	FIND	FIELD
F6	REPLACE	SELECT
F7	SIZE	MOVE
F8	DITTO	COPY
F9	QUICKRPT	ZOOM
F10	MACRO	MENUS

Enter	Next field
Tab	Next field
Shift-Tab	Previous field
Esc	Abandon
Ctrl-End	Save & exit
Ctrl-Enter	Save & remain
Ctrl-PgUp	First record
Ctrl-PgDn	Last record

D.C. Heath

MS-DOS® 4.01

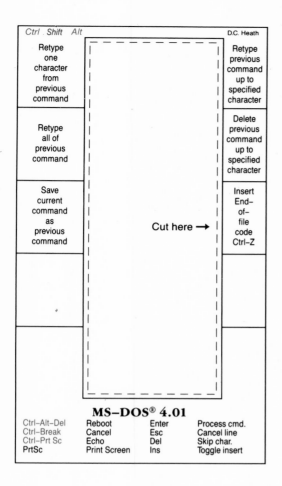

Ctrl Shift Alt   D.C. Heath

Left (Ctrl / Shift / Alt)	Right (Ctrl / Shift / Alt)
Retype one character from previous command	Retype previous command up to specified character
Retype all of previous command	Delete previous command up to specified character
Save current command as previous command	Insert End-of-file code Ctrl-Z

Cut here →

Ctrl-Alt-Del	Reboot	Enter	Process cmd.
Ctrl-Break	Cancel	Esc	Cancel line
Ctrl-Prt Sc	Echo	Del	Skip char.
PrtSc	Print Screen	Ins	Toggle insert

WordPerfect® 5.1 for IBM Personal Computers

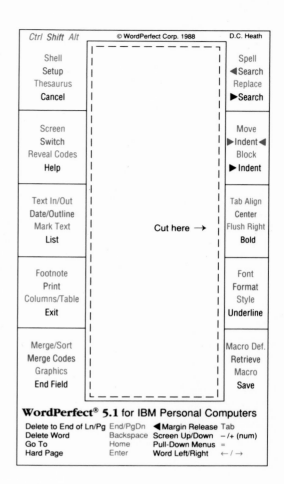

Ctrl Shift Alt   © WordPerfect Corp. 1988   D.C. Heath

Shell / Setup / Thesaurus / Cancel	Spell / ◄Search / Replace / ►Search
Screen / Switch / Reveal Codes / Help	Move / ►Indent / Block / ►Indent
Text In/Out / Date/Outline / Mark Text / List	Tab Align / Center / Flush Right / Bold
Footnote / Print / Columns/Table / Exit	Font / Format / Style / Underline
Merge/Sort / Merge Codes / Graphics / End Field	Macro Def. / Retrieve / Macro / Save

Cut here →

Delete to End of Ln/Pg	End/PgDn	◄Margin Release	Tab
Delete Word	Backspace	Screen Up/Down	– /+ (num)
Go To	Home	Pull-Down Menus	=
Hard Page	Enter	Word Left/Right	← / →

Lotus 1–2–3® R. 2.2

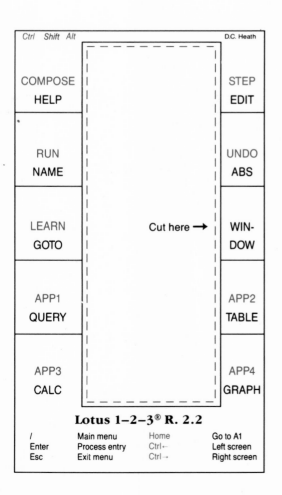

Ctrl Shift Alt   D.C. Heath

COMPOSE / HELP	STEP / EDIT
RUN / NAME	UNDO / ABS
LEARN / GOTO	WIN-DOW
APP1 / QUERY	APP2 / TABLE
APP3 / CALC	APP4 / GRAPH

Cut here →

/	Main menu	Home	Go to A1
Enter	Process entry	Ctrl←	Left screen
Esc	Exit menu	Ctrl→	Right screen

dBASE IV® 1.1

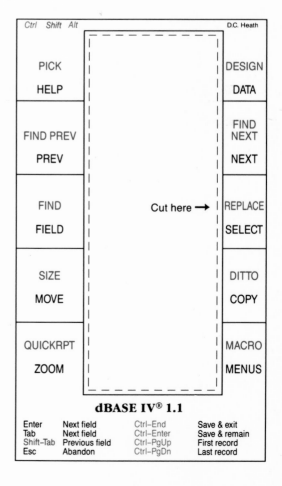

Ctrl Shift Alt   D.C. Heath

PICK / HELP	DESIGN / DATA
FIND PREV / PREV	FIND NEXT / NEXT
FIND / FIELD	REPLACE / SELECT
SIZE / MOVE	DITTO / COPY
QUICKRPT / ZOOM	MACRO / MENUS

Cut here →

Enter	Next field	Ctrl-End	Save & exit
Tab	Next field	Ctrl-Enter	Save & remain
Shift-Tab	Previous field	Ctrl-PgUp	First record
Esc	Abandon	Ctrl-PgDn	Last record